# Selected Papers from the American Anthropologist

# Selected Papers
# from the
# American Anthropologist
# 1946 – 1970

edited by ROBERT F. MURPHY

*Published by the*

AMERICAN ANTHROPOLOGICAL ASSOCIATION
1703 New Hampshire Avenue, NW
Washington, DC 20009

# Contents

# CONTENTS

# Introduction:
## A Quarter Century of American Anthropology

The Executive Board of the American Anthropological Association paid me the honor in 1974 of inviting me to edit a selection of articles from the *American Anthropologist* for the period of 1946 to 1970, in celebration of the 75th anniversary of the journal. George Stocking of the University of Chicago was asked at the same time to edit an anthology of the years 1921 to 1945, both volumes to be published with a reissue of Dr. Frederica de Laguna's earlier collection of essays from the first years of the journal. Our mandate was to choose articles that reflect the highest qualitative standards of the *American Anthropologist* and the discipline it serves and, at the same time, represent trends and interests within anthropology at various phases of its history.

The constraint upon length dictated by the economics of publishing have made for an extraordinarily high degree of selectivity, and less than two percent of the articles published during the period were chosen. Every effort was made to include selections from the major anthropological persuasions, but this was not always possible, often owing to the fact that my criteria of excellence and representativeness were in conflict. In this enterprise, I have tried to maintain a stance of neutrality, sometimes in the face of my own predelictions, and I have avoided overrepresentation in the volume of my closest personal and theoretical affinities.

A measure of evenhandedness was also maintained through the simple expedient of not consulting with others regarding my choices in cultural anthropology, though I profited from the kind advice of Ralph Holloway in physical anthropology, Harvey Pitkin in linguistics, and Richard Keatinge in archaeology. This social anthropological exclusiveness is in keeping with the first principle of etic anthropology, which is: "Objectivity begins at home." The only exception to the rule has been an exchange of views and procedures with George Stocking, the editor of the 1921-45 volume. Our correspondence had less to do with the choices themselves, however, than with deciding upon matters of length, format, and criteria. I would like to take this opportunity to gratefully acknowledge his help and cooperation. Morton Fried was also kind enough to read this essay and to suggest certain changes, all of which were made.

The *American Anthropologist* was published as a quarterly journal from its inception through 1952; after that year, each annual volume was issued in six separate numbers. The 25-year period, then, encompasses 136 different issues of the journal. By my count, some 1,006 articles were published during this time, not including brief communications, letters to the editor, book reviews, and obituaries. This remarkable outpouring of anthropological erudition required that only articles be reviewed for inclusion, though there were some true gems published as brief communications. In all candor, I found it impossible to reread all 1,006 essays with care, and a first winnowing was done by scanning the contents of each issue and selecting those articles having the greatest intrinsic merit. These articles were then read and culled again for theoretical and substantive importance, and the final selection took into account the problem of representativeness of authors, disciplinary subfields, and theoretical perspectives. Finally, the limits posed by economy upon the length of the volumes forced both Stocking and me to adopt a rule of thumb excluding articles of over 30 pages.

The reader will immediately note that most of the selections fall within the general area of cultural-social anthropology. Of the 22 essays, there are two in archaeology, two in physical anthropology, and one in linguistics. This disparity is less a function of my interests than of the publishing patterns characteristic of the four fields of anthropology. Despite the fact that cultural anthropologists form a majority of the profession, there was no American journal exclusively devoted to that branch until the appearance of *Ethnology* in 1962. Like the *American Anthropologist*, the *Southwestern Journal of Anthropology* accepted articles from all four fields of anthropology, as did the major foreign journals. In contrast, each of the three smaller subfields had its own publications: *American Antiquity* for archaeology, physical anthropology's *American Journal of Physical Anthropology* and *Human Biology*, and the *International Journal of Linguistics* and *Language* for anthropological and other linguists. There were also smaller journals specializing in these fields both in this country and abroad. The editors of the *American Anthropologist*, however, always attempted to observe the catholicity of the discipline, and each volume usually contained a sample from around the profession. Of the 1,006 articles published from 1946 to 1970, 805 were in cultural anthropology, 86 in archaeology, 68 in physical anthropology, and 47 in linguistics. The selections in this volume are in the same rough proportion.

My review of articles in archaeology, physical anthropology and linguistics reveals a pattern that must be discussed, however contrary it may be to our goal of synthesis. This is, baldly, that the best writings in the three minor fields are usually sent to specialized journals and not to the *American Anthropologist*. The reasons for this are clear. One makes his way in the discipline, and in our institutions, as a specialist, and the archaeologist wishing to reach a broad audience of his peers will send an essay to *American Antiquity*, where it will receive maximum archaeological readership and discussion. Similarly, a linguist presenting what he considers to be a broadly significant paper will publish it in a journal that will be read by non-anthropological linguists, just as the physical anthropologist will choose the *American Journal of Physical Anthropology* or *Human Biology* as the vehicle to reach not only his subdisciplinary colleagues but also those in medicine, anatomy, zoology, and so forth, who regularly read those journals. The result of this is that only a limited number of essays having broad theoretical significance in a subfield, or in anthropology at large, reach the pages of the *American Anthropologist*. That I could find only one in this category in linguistics should not, then, be taken as a reflection upon that profession but as an indication that their best work is sent elsewhere.

A reading of the journal leads to another conclusion that contradicts anthropology's self-image. This is that, for all our vaunted "holism," there were very few articles in this entire quarter-century period that reached beyond their subfield, except, perhaps, by the readers' own processes of extrapolation. Certain of the essays chosen do have such a function, especially the two archaeological selections written by Julian Steward and by Philip Philips and Gordon Willey. Given the two problems posed by the inadequacy of publishing outlets in the field of cultural anthropology and the lack of synthesizing articles that span parochial frontiers, one can only applaud the Association's decision to found the *American Ethnologist* and to continue the *American Anthropologist* as a vehicle for broadly conceived essays.

In addition to quality, theoretical significance, and representativeness, I sought also to include essays by the leading anthropologists of the time, a consideration that was easier to observe for the early part of my period than for recent years. Most of the names listed in the table of contents are familiar to all anthropologists, but there are also certain significant omissions. No author was chosen twice, and Stocking and I agreed to minimize overlap in our selections; the only authors appearing in both volumes are Fred Eggan, Julian Steward, Carl Voegelin, and Leslie White, all major figures in the history of our discipline and authors of essays which, for each period, could not be overlooked.

That some eminent anthropologists, both living and dead, were omitted from my list is a result, in some cases, of their not having published much in the *American Anthropologist* during the period in question. Certain others published only a limited amount in the journal, none of which contributions were appropriate for inclusion. Some of the selection problems may be illustrated by concrete examples. Claude Lévi-Strauss wrote one article for the *American Anthropologist* during the period which, under the title "Language and the Analysis of Social Laws" (Lévi-Strauss 1951), attempted to find an isomorphism between kinship structures and linguistic structures. The effort was doomed to failure, for it was based upon continent-wide generalizations regarding both languages and kinship systems, yielding results of the most impressionistic sort. Neither Lévi-Strauss nor his students ever attempted to follow up the hypothesis, and I saw no reason to revive it in these pages. And although Lévi-Strauss's admirers are inclined to consider much more important his paper "Reciprocity and Hierarchy" (Lévi-Strauss 1944), it unfortunately appeared too early to be included in this volume. Radcliffe-Brown presented a somewhat different problem. He published a number of items during the early part of our period, but these were either brief communications or articles written in direct response to another article in the journal. It is obvious that one-half of an argument between two scholars cannot be published, and I did not find any of the debates of sufficient lasting interest to merit publication of both sides. Again, any sense of constraint that so noted an anthropologist as Radcliffe-Brown must be included at all costs was eased by the fact that Stocking has selected his 1935 article on California kinship systems (Radcliffe-Brown 1935). The supplementary functions of the two volumes for each other was reciprocal, for Stocking was able to find but one appropriate article by Julian Steward during the period 1921-45 and was gratified by my selection of "Cultural Causality and Law" (Steward 1948). Steward is an interesting example, for in all his long and remarkably productive career, he published very few articles in the *American Anthropologist*. Excluding letters, reviews, obituaries, and comments appended to papers written by others, he wrote only seven articles for the journal, most of which were short ethnographic or archaeological notes. The essay included in this volume was indeed the only one in which he attempted to draw broad conclusions or addressed a wide audience.

Steward's case was not unusual, for there is a tendency with growing professional prestige for most of a scholar's later publications to be by invitation, and edited volumes preempt a good deal of the production of mature anthropologists. This is to be deplored, in one sense, for the journal of our Association is subscribed to and read by almost the entire profession, whereas the books on special subjects are directed toward more limited audiences. One could accept this state of affairs more cheerfully if the edited volumes were of greater significance, but most are eminently forgettable, however much interest they may draw immediately after publication. With regard to age of the authors chosen for this volume, most are indeed elder statesmen in the profession, and a few are no longer with us. Lest it be thought that the volume reflects the gerontocratic bent of the discipline, however, it should be stressed that most of the writers were either young or in their middle years at the time of publication. That is, in turn, a function of the fact that most scholars—though not all— say what they are going to say by the age of 50, after which they usually become rather repetitive. Such a progression in the life cycle is in keeping with Murphy's Law of Academic Careers, which states that there are two stages to the scholar's life—during the first he is anxious as to whether he will be discovered; in the second he is worried about whether he will be found out.

## AN ANTHROPOLOGICAL QUARTER-CENTURY: 1946-70

The place of our selections within the discipline may best be seen against the background of anthropology during the 25 years from 1946 to 1970. The years of World War II were a fallow period in most scholarly disciplines, and anthropology was especially affected by the virtual discontinuation of overseas research, except for strategic and military purposes. The universities had been stripped of male students at both the graduate and undergraduate levels, and most younger professional anthropologists were either members of the military or assigned to government agencies directly connected with the war effort. It may be apposite for younger members of the American Anthropological Association to learn that there was no debate among anthropologists, nor were there significant reservations, about the role of the profession in the conduct of the war. Anthropologists served in the Office of Strategic Services, Naval Intelligence, the War Resources Board, and numerous other organizations, and their participation was considered to be appropriate and professionally beneficial. Such positive sanction was in marked and dramatic contrast to the bitter division that occurred within the Association during World War I and, to a far greater extent, the Vietnam War. World War II, of course, was strongly and unequivocally supported by the entire population, including intellectuals, as opposed to the Vietnam War, but it is well to remember that the pattern of professional involvement was established during the former conflict.

The end of the war brought the anthropologists back to the campuses but with empty notebooks, and the *American Anthropologist* reflected this lack of a research backlog for the first few years of our period. The hiatus continued for two years or so after the war, for it took time to readapt foundations and public agencies to peacetime research and to regroup the personnel of the profession before sending them off again. Research began early in the Trust Territory of the Pacific under the sponsorship of the naval administrators of the region, but the full reestablishment of field investigations waited until about 1948.

The immediate post-war period continued the research interlude, but it was a time of intense educational activity, foreshadowing the enormous growth of the discipline for the next quarter century. Anthropology was among the smallest of the scholarly disciplines at the time, and the full fellow roster of the American Anthropological Association in 1947 was only 408, as compared to the 1976 figure of 2,526. The war contributed to the expansion of the discipline in many ways. First, several million young Americans had been exposed to overseas experience and had been scattered throughout the world, often in the remote outlying districts so favored by anthropologists. It was an unusual kind of experience, to be sure, but it broke the insularity of the American population and served as a forerunner to the extension of American influence throughout the world. Minimally, it awakened us to cultural diversity, and, maximally, it excited a desire to understand this array of cultures. Another effect of the war came about through a large package of veteran's benefits which included comprehensive educational subsidies. Public Law 346 provided full tuition, books and supplies, and a living stipend to all veterans of military service for a period of up to the time they spent in the military plus a year. For many, it subsidized a complete college education and all or part of graduate school. The veterans returned to the campuses in the millions, and they entered anthropology in unprecedented numbers. Even those who did not take advantage of the educational part of the "GI Bill of Rights" contributed by applying the housing benefits to the purchase of small houses, where they raised rather large families; the children from this "baby-boom" completed the process by inundating the universities in the 1960s, anthropology's greatest period of expansion.

The GI Bill of Rights changed the profile as well as the numbers of the anthropological profession. In common with the rest of the academic disciplines, anthropology had been largely a white, middle class domain. The expenses of schooling effectively screened out lower class and lower middle class students who, if they made it as far as post-graduate education, were better advised to seek the superior economic rewards of medicine and other professions. As for persons of minority background, there were no professionally established black anthropologists at all until after the war, and even so eminent a scholar as Edward Sapir experienced Ivy League anti-Semitism in the immediate pre-war period. Public Law 346 changed the recruitment situation completely, although discriminatory patterns of employment were to persist for a longer period. For the first time, the young, bright and indigent could not only afford to go to graduate school but, given the economic incentives, they could hardly afford not to. A small number of black students enrolled in our graduate departments of anthropology along with a much larger number of members of other minorities. That students of the lower class were now entering the scholarly disciplines did not have as much effect as might be anticipated, however, for their conditions of employment soon made them members of the same middle class that had previously rejected them.

Ironically, the same movement that brought large numbers of young men of diverse backgrounds into anthropology also saw a decline of female participation in the discipline relative to the feminist ferment of the 1920s. In keeping with the ethos of the time, women redirected their interests to family and children or, in a more negative sense, found themselves squeezed out of graduate schools and jobs by the returning veterans. It was not until the late 1960s that women would return with renewed vitality into academic life. This decline of female involvement is manifest in the authorship of *American Anthropologist* articles. I did a count of sex of all authors of articles during the 1946-70 period. The total number of authors was 1,219—a number greater than the total number of articles, due to co-authorships—of whom 1,060 were men and 158 women. For the entire period, then, 13% of the authors were female. The male-female ratio of authorship was further broken down by five-year periods, yielding the following percentages of women authors: 1966-70—12%; 1961-65—13%; 1956-60—10%, 1951-55—13%; 1946-50—22%. By themselves, these figures might be straws in the wind, but they follow the pattern already documented by careful studies of women in the academic professions.

Nourished by growing graduate and undergraduate enrollments, anthropology departments slowly increased in size and number during the early part of our period, but the expansion was miniscule compared to what happened in the 1960s. Looking back at my own personal experience in the profession, I was trained in the Columbia department in the late 1940s and early 1950s with a group of graduate students numbering close to 150 being taught by a faculty of ten; this made it one of the largest in the United States. When I went to the University of Illinois in 1953, there were only three anthropologists in a Department of Sociology and Anthropology which offered no advanced degrees in our subject. In 1955, I joined the University of California at Berkeley, where I became the ninth person in the department; by 1960 it had doubled in size. The change was of the same order nationwide.

The immediate post-war years from 1946 to 1950 saw a considerable change in the areal and theoretical interests of anthropology. The bulk of our research had previously been in the study of the American Indian, which served more than any other influence to produce the rather flat, descriptive tone of our writings. It was the reservation situation, the culling of memory culture unvitalized by extant patterns of activity, that led to Americanist nominalism, and not the anti-evolutionism of Boas. By the end of the 1930s, however, American anthropologists were becoming interested in culture change and "acculturation" studies, and they were already venturing into other areas. Melville Herskovits began his African studies during this decade, and Ruth Bunzel and Robert Redfield were working in Guatemala and Mexico as early as the 1920s. This is also the time that saw Margaret Mead undertake her pioneering researches in the Pacific, which serve as well as a landmark of the development of "culture and personality" studies in the 1930s.

The basis for change and diversification of interest was laid down during the pre-war years, but the post-war period brought it to fruition. American anthropologists, financed by an influx of new funds that were clearly responsive to the country's expanded overseas interests, broke out of their traditional insularity and embarked on research on a global scale. In the beginning their efforts were hesitant and often blocked by scholarly hegemonies. If one wanted to do African research, he had to work under the auspices of one of the British universities or through Northwestern, and Columbia's control of South American fieldwork dated back to the group sent there by Ruth Benedict in the late 1930s. By the mid-1950s, these barriers had broken down, departments were expanding, and the major universities sponsored research on almost every continent. The turn to foreign research, backed by the Social Science Research Council, the Ford Foundation, and the newly established anthropological units of the National Science Foundation and the National Institute of Mental Health, was so complete that by the late 1950s universities were experiencing difficulty in locating younger North Americanists.

The post-war group was not just studying in different places, for they were branching out into types of societies that were not within the traditional purview of anthropology. The study of peasants and complex societies began in the 1920s and 1930s with research among the Indian populations of highland Middle and South America. What had been a marginal interest during that period had now become a major preoccupation, and I would estimate that by the 1950s most anthropologists were no longer working with primitive peoples. Younger scholars such as Morton Fried and G. William Skinner, trained in the Chinese language and in general Sinology, undertook the study of Chinese communities, John Embree initiated his Japanese research, and such well known students of the American Indian as Morris Opler and David Mandelbaum redirected their energies to India. Julian Steward initiated a program of Latin American studies through the Smithsonian Institution's Institute of Social Anthropology during World War II, and in 1948 launched a Columbia University research program that attempted a comprehensive understanding of the island of Puerto Rico (Steward et al. 1956).

The spate of research in communities and districts of complex societies set anthropologists adrift on uncharted seas, and they were soon forced to sit back and conceptualize the units they were dealing with and try to place these units in larger structures. Steward's monograph *Area Research: Theory and Practice* (Steward 1950) presented a framework for the study of national, or horizontal, institutions, and local, or vertical, ones. The book also elaborated for the first time Steward's theory of levels of sociocultural integration, an idea that was seen to have wide evolutionary significance but which was devised as a means of studying acculturation. Robert Redfield had earlier drawn on Weberian theory to develop a polar typology of folk and urban society, with peasants occupying an intermediate position on the continuum (Redfield 1940). Three of the articles in this volume emerged directly from the community study method. Eric Wolf's "Types of Latin American Peasantry" (1955; see below pp. 188-207) was one of the first, and surely one of the more influential of papers essaying a typology of communities (cf. Wagley and Harris 1955). In this paper, Wolf juxtaposes a closed or corporate type of community to an open type and relates the differences to modes of land tenure. George Foster's "Peasant Society and the Image of Limited Good" (1965; see below pp. 382-404) was one among a number of attempts to find a consistent definition of the characteristics of peasant populations. Foster outlines one element of what he considers peasant world view and relates it to the economic processes inherent to peasant society. Conrad Arensberg's paper "The Community as Object and as Sample" (1961; see below pp. 295-318) tries to place the locality within the context of larger social systems and considers the always vexatious problems of community boundaries and representativeness. The major significance of Arensberg's article is a methodological one, for the change in scale of the research subject wrenched anthropology out of its age of innocence and ended forever (or at least until the rise of cognitive studies) ethnographies written from the head of one old informant sitting in the anthropologist's hotel room. Although quantification, sampling, and so forth, are used even in the study of primitive villages today, the more sophisticated techniques of our sociological colleagues first entered the profession through the study of peasant communities. And as early as 1950, Ralph Beals in his presidential address to the American Anthropological Association (Beals 1951) warned his colleagues in the budding field of urban anthropology that they were reinventing survey research and statistics without bothering to inquire into sociological methods first.

American anthropology's expansion in scope and numbers had ramifications that extended deep into the realm of theory. By the end of World War II, we had already come far from the period of Boas, Wissler, and the other dominant figures of early 20th century anthropology. There was a pervasive interest in culture change that had transformed the research being done among the American Indians and was a dominant theme in the community study approach as well. The study of social and cultural change is probably the most consistent thread binding our twenty-five year period, a fact that owes less to theoretical consistency than to the simple premise that change and transformation were inescapable parts of most research situations. Interest in the phenomenon was not so much a theoretical concern as the very ethnography itself.

Studies of change were gaining greatly in sophistication, as compared to the first formulations of "acculturation" studies (cf. Redfield, Linton, and Herskovits 1936), and they were increasingly focused on specific problem areas. One of the better examples of the new kind of study was a comparative analysis entitled "Navaho and Zuni Veterans: A Study of Contrasting Modes of Culture Change" by John Adair and Evon Vogt (1949; see below pp. 83-97). This well known paper reported a radically different response of the Navaho and Zuni to their returning war veterans: the Navaho regarded the demobilized soldiers as positive influences toward culture change, while the Zuni looked upon their veterans as potential threats to the tranquility of the community and the integrity of traditional values. The authors related these differential attitudes to the histories of the two societies, the physical layout of their communities and to the values of each group. The latter emphasis was in keeping with the major orientation of the Harvard group, especially of those associated with the Department of Social Relations, to the key function of value orientations as guarantors of cultural integration and as selective elements in culture change.

The two other preoccupations of the discipline at the end of the war were a continuing interest in personality and culture studies and a newly reawakened fascination with theories of cultural evolution. I will turn to personality studies first, because the development of a psychological anthropology was aborted during our period, an unraveling that I consider one of the more unfortunate episodes in the history of anthropology. This field, begun by Freud and continued by psychoanalysts such as Kardiner and Fromm and such anthropologists as Mead, Benedict, Hallowell, and Henry, attempted to relate the symbolic aspects of culture to intra-psychic process through the study of the basic institutions of family and socialization. The psychological orientation of the field was Freudian, which can be explained by the dominance of this theoretical persuasion during the 1920s and 1930s and also by the manifest applicability of its theory of symbolism to cultural materials. Personality and culture studies went into sharp decline by the early 1950s, a function of diversification of psychoanalytic theory and the rise of neo- (and anti-) Freudian schools on the psychological side. Within anthropology, psychological anthropology experienced heavy criticism from both the cultural evolutionists and the structural-functionalists. The latter two groups, so frequently at odds with each other, managed to agree that culture and personality studies were a form of "reductionism" in that they sought to explain cultural facts by psychological ones, a stand that was usually sanctified by reference to a much overworked passage of Emile Durkheim's *Rules of Sociological Method* (1964:104). Reductionism, of course, really means explaining the particular and the variable by invocation of a general principle and by no means were all of the personality and culture specialists guilty of this sin. A much better example of reductionism would be Radcliffe-Brown's use of the principle of the unity of the sibling group to explain the terminological merging of father and father's brother in some kinship systems.

The attack upon personality and culture studies was highly successful, but it had some help from within the ranks of the psychologically oriented. One of the great weaknesses of the group was its espousal of the notion of "modal personality," an assumption of a degree of personality homogeneity in primitive societies that was mercilessly lampooned by C. W. M. Hart in a lovely essay entitled "The Sons of Turimpi" (Hart 1954). The apotheosis of modal personality, the idea of national character, probably did as much damage to psychological anthropology as did all the writings of Leslie White, its most trenchant opponent. Personality and culture studies did not end completely, and the interest has been continued by a growing band of anthropologists who are pronouncedly less optimistic and self-confident than their predecessors. Freud, however, did give us the only cross-culturally applicable theory of symbolism that is available in anthropology, and the approach remains useful and productive in the interpretation of mythology and the more symbolically stylized aspects of culture that we were wont to refer to as "projective." After all, what else are you going to say about the New Guinea group in which young male initiates practice fellatio on their mother's brothers?

It is in the firm belief that we will have to return to the depth psychologies if we are going to escape from an anthropology that has become sterile of lust and will that I have selected what I believe to be the best representative of the genre to appear in the *American Anthropologist*: "Earth-Diver: Creation of the Mythopoeic Male" by Alan Dundes (1962; see below pp. 349-368). This is a classically Freudian piece, both in conception and execution, in which Dundes relates the very widespread myth of the animal or bird who retrieves the earth from the primeval flood to the womb-envying urges of males and the fantasy of anal birth. One can easily see the structural dimensions of the myth as well, but structuralism deals with relationships between symbols rather than with the content of the symbols themselves, and it should be clear that the two approaches are complementary. In passing, it must be remarked that scholarship suffers from a propensity to say "if this, then *not* that," which leads to all or nothing theorization and ideological imperialism. As in the earth-diver myth, there is no reason why two approaches may not be thoroughly compatible with each other, representing merely two questions that one asks of the same material.

The revival of evolutionism in the early part of our period was largely the work of two men, Leslie White and Julian Steward. Leslie White was one of the more interesting figures in recent anthropology. Scrappy, pugnacious, unflinching in the defense of his ideas, he remained marginal to the mainstream of anthropology by choice. His closest ties were to his students, not his peers, and he had little to do with the anthropological establishment. Starting with a series of papers written during the early 1940s, he championed the discredited theories of Lewis Henry Morgan in a campaign that was dignified by its lack of political and professional wisdom. He argued for Morgan's ideas and for philosophical materialism at a time when Senator Joseph McCarthy, Congressman Richard Nixon and a host of other political troglodytes and opportunists were combing the campuses and the media for signs of subversion, and he took on an entire profession, most of which had not read Morgan but were sure he was wrong. White's evolutionism was not simply Morgan warmed over, but a systematic theory that related the progression of culture to technology and man's control over forms of energy. It suffered from being disembodied in time and space, an essential ahistoricism, but this was a function of its universal generality. Although White's most important paper on evolution, "Energy and the Evolution of Culture" (1943), falls outside the span of years covered by this volume, I have chosen to include his paper, "The Definition and Prohibition of Incest" (1948; see below pp. 36-55). The essay has an evolutionary theme insofar as White saw the incest taboo and marriage as an essential means for the establishment of larger social units through marital alliance. He goes beyond this idea, however, to present what he called a "culturalogical" interpretation of the taboo, which can be translated here as one that does not rely upon biological and psychological explanations. White always found satisfaction in finding old precedents for his ideas, and he attributed the genesis of the theory to St. Augustine's admonition that people must either marry out or die out. In a sense, White's views on incest are a continuation of his anti-Freudianism but, while writing this preface, I met a psychoanalyst who had done his undergraduate work at Michigan and told me that he was directly motivated into his calling by attending White's course on the mind of primitive man. It was White's fervor and dedication that had inspired my acquaintance, and not what he said about the mind. This is what attracted us all to the man.

White's theories had a certain following but, except for a common theme of materialism, they seldom influenced empirical research, including White's own fieldwork among the Rio Grande pueblos. The reasons for this lay in the very general and global nature of his notions on evolution and the difficulty of translating them into the analysis of ethnographic data. Julian Steward's evolutionism, however, was more a methodology than a schema of cultural development, and his influence was, therefore, more lasting. Multilinear evolutionism—a term coined by Robert Lowie to describe the *kulturkreiselehre* (1948:33-35)—was predicated on the naturalistic maxim that what has happened once in a universe governed by law can happen again—and given the same conditions probably will. The natural conditions for recurrence, and cultural regularity, lay in the domain of the cultural ecological equation in Steward's view. This, in turn, is the premise that the relationship between society and environment is a function of tools and techniques brought to bear upon resources through the process of work, which is a creative part of any social system. Following this logic, the regular reappearance of any constellation of basic social characteristics indicates a similar causal process at work and suggests that common ecological features underlie all cases. Translated into working terms, the strategy of multilinear evolution is to look for similarities between cultures and, through analysis, ascertain whether they reveal common ecological solutions. And if history is available for the societies in question, then the next step is to determine whether in fact, the historical sequence admits of similarities, or convergences, as well.

Steward's paper "Cultural Causality and Law: A Trial Formulation of the Development of Early Civilizations" (1949; see below pp. 56-82) must stand as one of the great essays in the long publishing history of the *American Anthropologist*. In this article, Steward tests the 'hydraulic society' theory of Karl Wittfogel, using both comparative and historical analysis of the growth of civilization in Egypt, northern Peru, Mesopotamia, northern China and Meso-America. The central determinant in all five cases was found to be irrigation agriculture, which was based upon, and in turn made possible, the control of large populations in the construction and maintenance of public works. Steward and his students applied the method in a number of subsequent empirical studies, but today it no longer stands out as a distinct procedure and is understood to be a general part of any anthropological approach that is both comparative and ecological.

The most enduring part of Steward's legacy to anthropology is the theory of cultural ecology, which stimulated much of the development of modern ecological anthropology and is a part also of a tradition of materially oriented analyses in anthropology. Leslie White, of course, was also important in the growth of what has been called "cultural materialism," but the main impetus undoubtedly belongs to Julian Steward, although he would have shunned the label. Steward's influence extended beyond the students he trained at Illinois and Columbia, for he was widely read in this country and abroad. One of the best examples of the cultural ecological approach to appear in the journal during the quarter century was by a Norwegian anthropologist who had never studied with Steward: Fredrik Barth's paper 'Ecologic Relationships of Ethnic Groups in Swat, North Pakistan" (1956). The article is also significant in supplying a key to the "mosaic" phenomenon that Kroeber and others had noted among pastoral nomads, and it stands as a model for later studies of herding societies.

Cultural ecology and personality and culture may be regarded as two typically American approaches in anthropology, but this was mainly a result of their virtual restriction to this country and not to their universality within it. Freudian psychology never achieved the currency in France or England that it enjoyed in the United States, and anthropologists in both countries took Durkheim's strictures on the limits of the profession quite literally. As for ecological studies, the British were too preoccupied with the study of jural norms to worry much about activity imposed by force of circumstance, and any French inclinations toward materialism were instantly swallowed by an ubiquitous academic Marxism. Moreover, in the tight little scholarly worlds of each country, there was only so much room for deviation from established theory, and I have a strong suspicion that American heterodoxies were no more welcome than Coca Cola and Yank neologisms. Whatever the causes, there never has been much of an export market for American anthropological theory.

The tariff barriers on the exchange of ideas were, however, unidirectional, for American anthropologists have been remarkably on the *qui vive* for new continental theory (and loan words). This is nowhere more evident in the history of the discipline than during the 1950s, when a British-derived sociologically oriented anthropology—structural-functionalism—became the primary direction of younger American anthropologists. There are many reasons for this other than simple diffusion of ideas, and it would be useful to briefly consider the history of the phenomenon. American anthropologists have, paradoxically, had closer associations with the discipline of sociology than have their British colleagues. It must be remembered that social anthropology preempted the field of social inquiry in Britain until the growth, largely in the red brick universities of the post-war period, of departments of sociology. Quite to the contrary, sociology had an earlier and stronger development in this country than anthropology, and most anthropologists until the 1950s and after found themselves in joint departments of sociology and anthropology. Moreover, they were usually very much in the minority and under the chairmanship of sociologists, who tolerated them as one would a troublesome, but exotically interesting, pet. A certain amount of mutual influence inevitably resulted from the close association of the disciplines, bringing immediately to mind the Weberian slant picked up by Ralph Linton in the joint department at Wisconsin and by Robert Redfield through his collegial and affinal ties at Chicago. What is more notable, however, is the relative *lack* of influence of sociological method and theory upon anthropology during the decades in which they roomed together, for our rejection of most sociological theory was notable. One may conjecture that physical closeness bred intellectual distance, for the isolated little pockets of anthropologists had to struggle to maintain their identities and separateness. To have embraced Durkheim, Weber, Cooley, George Herbert Mead,

Pareto, and Simmel would have constituted the erosion of a boundary and the concession of an important bargaining chip in intra-departmental politics. We did read the great social theorists, to be sure, for their relevance to anthropology was manifest, but we read them defensively.

A shift of interest to the classics of social theory began with the separation of departments, but, and more important, it developed as our research moved into new areas. Structural-functionalism, or Durkheimian sociology, is based on a model of society in which norms guide actions which then feed back to reinforce the system of norms. However handy this may be as a starting point for the analysis of functioning social systems, it was less than useful when studying the shattered remnants of American Indian society. But as a new generation of researchers went off to study societies in which social life, though changed, still maintained a certain autonomy and vitality of its own, the fiction of a system that seeks to perpetuate itself became of heuristic value. Many American anthropologists undertook study in areas that had already been investigated by British scholars, as in Africa and Melanesia. There they found not only empirical situations that loaned themselves to functional analysis, but a background of literature done in the metier. If theories had not impelled people to read Fortes on the Tallensi and Evans-Pritchard on the Nuer, then the very fact that they were going to Africa for research certainly would. And all the problems dealt with by the British Africanists, especially descent and monarchy—two very English preoccupations—were waiting for the Americans as well.

During the 1950s and as late as the mid-1960s, many Americans went to Oxford and Cambridge for graduate work, either for advanced training in Africa studies or as regular graduate students and degree candidates. A number of professional anthropologists went to the British universities as exchange scholars or simply to write while on sabbatical leave. Many came back from their year abroad with a new orientation towards structural-functional analysis, and a slight accent. In a reverse flow, many British anthropologists accepted visiting professorships and permanent posts in the United States, where superior salaries prevailed and vacancies abounded. The height of the anthropological entente between the British and American scholars was marked by a conference sponsored by the Association of Social Anthropologists of the Commonwealth and held at Cambridge in June 1963. From this meeting of some dozen American anthropologists and twice that number of their British counterparts came the series of books published as Association of Social Anthropology monographs, under the editorship of Michael Banton. The participants in the meeting felt themselves to be taking part in a climactic event that marked a new beginning. Nobody was able to predict at the time that the conference marked an end, an end of the close community of interest that had grown up among the "social anthropologists" on both sides of the ocean and the end of the primacy of structural-functionalism. Americans still go to Britain, of course, but often on their way to Paris. And the British scholars, in turn, have found that employment in the United States is quite as difficult to find as in Great Britain.

During the first half of our quarter century period, structural-functionalism became strongly rooted in American universities, independently of the exchange of personnel with Great Britain. The earlier peregrinations of A. R. Radcliffe-Brown had brought him to the University of Chicago from 1931 to 1937, during which time he trained Fred Eggan, Sol Tax, and others, who built the Chicago department during the post-war era. Radcliffe-Brown's students continued the tradition of their teacher, and their students, in turn, became more orthodox in their functionalism than even the grandfather. Another center of sociologically oriented anthropology was Harvard University. The establishment there of the Department of Social Relations, chaired by Talcott Parsons and including representatives from sociology, anthropology, social psychology, and political science, brought together a number of disciplines within the broad confines of a general social theory. The "general theory of action" represented Parsons' own synthesis of Weber and Durkheim, with an additional mix of Pareto, Mannheim, and Freud. It became a dominant persuasion in sociology, and filtered into anthropology through Parsons' students, including David M. Schneider, Clifford Geertz, John Roberts, and others. The Parsonian syntax caused many anthropologists to bridle at his sociology, but it is a far more sophisticated brand of functionalism than that of Radcliffe-Brown. The major problems of the school, however, were not with Radcliffe-Brown or Parsons in particular, but with functionalism in general. And it failed not because it was proven wrong but because it had exhausted its possibilities.

The *American Anthropologist* carried a large number of articles in the structural-functional vein during the decade of 1953 to 1963—indeed, it still does, but their numbers and interest are no longer dominant. One of the most important was "The Structure of Unilineal Descent Groups" by Meyer Fortes, an essay that summarized two decades of British research on African descent systems (1953; see below pp. 110-134). The paper presented Fortes's views on "complementary filiation," a concept that was later to become a pivotal issue in the debate with French structuralism and which can still evoke a lively argument. Fortes' article is still considered required reading by every graduate student of anthropology, and is reprinted here as a classic in the discipline. Fred Eggan's article "Social Anthropology and the Method of Controlled Comparison" (1954; see below pp. 154-174) is in the tradition of social anthropology, but it has a uniquely American dimension in that it proposes a comparative method that seeks to find resemblances and divergences between societies that are historically, or genetically, linked. As such, one of its principal purposes is the discovery of regular processes of change, a procedure that Eggan had already tested in his studies of American Indian kinship.

The best exemplar of the Parsonian approach in anthropology to appear in the *American Anthropologist* was Clifford Geertz's "Ritual and Social Change: A Javanese Example" (1957; see below pp. 249-271). Aside from his substantive conclusions, the essay is particularly valuable as an illustration of the differences between the social system and the cultural system in Parsonian usage and the utility of distinguishing between the two. Geertz went beyond Parsons in applying the theory to the analysis of social change, an area in which most social scientists recognize weakness in the Parsonian system. Very much in the sociological tradition, because it was written by a sociologist, is another of our selections "The Nature of Deference and Demeanor" by Erving Goffman (1956; see below pp. 208-237). This is the only essay in the volume written by a non-anthropologist, but I selected it because Goffman's approach and intellectual affinities are essentially anthropological, to the extent that he attends every meeting of the American Anthropological Association. The paper is most important in that it encapsulates the essence of Goffman's interaction theory and remains thoroughly consistent with his present writings. Moreover, the essay is written with a simple, yet elegant, prose style, and is structurally splendid, one of the finest examples I have read of the scholarly form. Finally, I call the reader's attention to S. F. Nadel's paper "Witchcraft in Four African Societies: An Essay in Comparison"

(1952; see below pp. 98-109) as an example of the one leading scholar of the British school who was trying in a systematic way to introduce a psychological dimension into studies of social structure. Significantly, Nadel's sociological orientation was toward German sociology and not the French; his antecedents belonged to Weber rather than Durkheim.

Two articles in the area of social structure, included in this volume, are marginal to the structural-functional tradition and represent rather different directions. The first is an historically important essay by Ward Goodenough under the title "A Problem in Malayo-Polynesian Social Organization" (1955; see below pp. 175-187). Goodenough's point of departure is George P. Murdock's reconstruction of proto-Malayo Polynesian social organization, which was postulated to have been based on bilocality, the bilateral kindred and the absence of unilineal descent. Goodenough argues that the widespread Polynesian pattern in which individual land rights were derived from kin group membership precludes the kindred as a proto-unit because its ego-centered nature prevents it from becoming an effective holder of a corporate estate. He points instead to a land-oriented kin group, which had not been adequately delineated in the literature and which he refers to as a "non-unilinear descent group." The paper was important beyond the field of Oceanian studies, for it did much to clarify bilaterality and its relation to unilineality. Moreover, Goodenough stressed the significance of the relationship between descent group and land by delineating a type of social unit in which property and residence transcend regular rules of kinship in ascribing status. The primacy of property over kinship and of situation over norm was a key feature of other, later studies of descent, including the work of Morton Fried (1957), Mervyn Meggitt (1965), and Peter Worsley (1956).

An article by Sally Falk Moore, "Descent and Symbolic Filiation" (1964; see below pp. 369-381), attacks a problem in social structure using the perspectives of symbolic studies and French structuralism. Moore takes the apparent anomaly of myths of the origins of exogamic social groups from the incestuous union of brother and sister or, less frequently, parent and child, and relates them to the belief that descent flows through lineages as a mystical stream. Brother and sister in actual fact are taboo to each other, but may have a symbolic connection with each other's fertility. On one level, then, the myth is a reversal of the real world, but on another level it presents an underlying theme of the lineage as a symbolically autocthonous unit. "Kind reproduces kind in the animal and human kingdoms," writes Moore of totemism (1964:1319). This statement is a corrective of Lévi-Strauss's *Le Totemisme Aujourd'hui*, but the latter book clearly inspired the article.

As in evolution, successive forms co-exist and overlap in intellectual history. In just this way, the anthropological currents that would eventually displace structural-functionalism arose during a time when that school was dominant; in turn, functional thought outlived its own 'demise' and continues to be active, though not salient, to the present day. This is not the place for an autopsy of structural-functionalism, and I will only mention a few of the factors that are commonly believed to have bred disillusionment. The first was already suggested; this is that we had gone as far with functionalism as we could go. It was essentially a rather simple approach, based on a set of assumptions which, while never true, were at least useful for a time. Functionalism posited an "as if" world in which social norms and social action were isomorphic and directly complementary to one another. It assumed further that social systems were bounded, if not in fact then in theory, and that these boundaries were conditions by which systems maintained themselves. The very problem of system maintenance was based on the working proposition that a society in a slice of time could be extrapolated out to historical societies. In this way, the coherence of the parts of a system were taken to be the result of a strain toward coherence over time. This is at best a dangerous assumption, but if it turns out that this equilibrium is in good part a function of the anthropolgist's mind, or his theories, then it leads to solipsism. Edmund Leach in *Political Systems of Highland Burma* (1954) leveled this critique at his colleagues with devastating effect, though, in balance, Leach's treatment of his empirical data were much in keeping with traditional social anthropology. Positivism is a hard habit to break, deriving as it does from our penchant for reducing the world to little nuggets of reality.

Classic functionalism was a valuable heuristic device in the days when anthropologists were conducting their studies in small homogeneous societies in New Guinea or in outlying bush villages in Africa, but its utility waned as the postwar world intruded into even the remotest parts of the earth, destroying forever whatever tissues bound these primitive worlds together. At the same time, anthropological interests were changing, and we were shifting our locales of study to cities and towns, to market places and mining camps, and to the newly emergent nations of the post-colonial world. This teeming hodge-podge of humanity seemed to defy all efforts to reduce it to bounded systems, with uniform value-imbeddedness and internal equilibrating mechanisms. Max Gluckman attempted in an *American Anthropologist* article titled "The Utility of the Equilibrium Model in the Study of Social Change" (1968) to salvage the method, but even he was forced to admit that when rapid change takes place our descriptions become little more than historical narrative. Gluckman's colleagues at Manchester, who had long worked in the central African areas most violently affected by the modern world, developed a series of strategies such as "event analysis" and "network theory" to study these untidy situations. These methods took hold in the United States as well, and the grant applications of American graduate students make monotonous reference to the new technique of network analysis, which they apparently believe was born in the Copper Belt in the 1960s. The method actually saw the first light of day in the Westinghouse Company's Hawthorne Plant in the 1930s and was described by Eliot Chapple and Conrad Arensberg in 1940 (Chapple and Arensberg 1940), but as was noted earlier, we are prone to importing ideas.

With the failure of the functionalist consensus in anthropology, a number of scholars turned from the analysis of social interaction to the study of culture as a domain of symbol and meaning. The new approaches—variously called "cognitive anthropology," "the new ethnography," "componential analysis," "ethnoscience," and the like—had in common a preoccupation with the old problems of classification and the relations between language, culture, and thought. They took as their subject the means by which people of different cultures characteristically perceive and categorize the social and natural worlds, and the rules by which they assign meanings to certain symbols. The methods borrowed heavily from linguistics, especially semantics, for the symbols analyzed were generally words and one of the primary aims of the enterprise was to discover those meanings which were correct for certain words while incorrect for all others. These rules of classification, it was posited, are rules by which people apprehend reality, determine cultural correctness of interpretation of social situations, and, ultimately, are rules by which people act.

The apical ancestor of the new ethnographers was A. L. Kroeber, a truly *cultural* anthropologist, and the author of the seminal article "Classificatory Systems of Relationship" (1909). In this essay, Kroeber elaborated a series of principles by which kinship categories are terminologically merged or distinguished to produce a cognitive map of kinship that can be described by a limited number of abstract rules. The paper was generally looked upon as having chief significance for the debate as to the primacy of cultural or psychological determinants of kin terms, an issue that was as arid as it was confusing, and was read as a curio in the history of anthropology. The essentials of Kroeber's method were revived and modified, however, by Floyd Lounsbury and his students at Yale; the first results of their work were published in the linguistics journal *Language* in 1956 (Lounsbury 1956; Goodenough 1956). The Lounsbury approach, called "componential analysis," was intended to supplant the usual procedure of defining a kin term by listing all the genealogical positions to which it applies. Componential analysis went beyond this to elucidate the criteria that the speakers themselves used in conceptualizing kinship. The methodology was summarized and described by Anthony Wallace and John Atkins in their paper "The Meaning of Kinship Terms," which is reprinted in this volume (Wallace and Atkins 1960; see below pp. 272-294).

The method of componential analysis was clearly adaptable to domains of meaning other than kinship. Harold Conklin's paper on Hanunóo color categories (1955) actually preceded the publications on kinship, and the same author's doctoral dissertation was on the ethnobotany of that group (Conklin 1954). Formal analysis of the same kind was extended to the spheres of folk science, ritual and disease; a paper presenting a componential analysis of Tzeltal Maya terms for firewood (Metzger and Williams 1966) was viewed by many anthropologists as the ultimate application of the method. One of the areas most seriously studied by the school was ecology, although, as Charles Frake's paper "Cultural Ecology and Ethnography" clearly indicates, it is a far different cultural ecology than that pioneered by Steward (Frake 1962; see below pp. 319-325).

The expansion of cognitive and formal approaches into areas other than kinship provoked strong rebuttal from several anthropologists, for nobody seemed to be particularly troubled by the method until it showed imperial symptoms. Robbins Burling asked whether componential analysis was "God's truth" or "hocus-pocus," and clearly opted for the latter answer (Burling 1964). Marvin Harris took vigorous issue with the ambitious claims that, even if ethnoscience did not tell you how the natives think, it will at least tell you how they are supposed to act (Harris 1968:568-604). Denying that a behavioral code can be found anywhere but in behavior, Harris dismissed the entire method as "cultural idealism." One of the sharpest attacks on the new ethnography came from Gerald Berreman, in his paper "Anemic and Emetic Analyses in Social Anthropology," a title that suggests the tenor of the article (Berreman 1966; see below pp. 405-413). Berreman wrote that in their concern for methodological purity, the group was forced to study the trivial—an accusation that is often leveled at mathematical sociologists as well—and he deplored the subservience of anthropological procedures to linguistic method.

The latter is an interesting point, for social anthropologists occasionally apply the insights of other fields to their own data with very mixed results. Prime examples of this, in addition to the near reduction of ethnography to semantics, are the excesses of national character study and the new biological sociology. There seems almost to be a law by which synthesizers carry their enthusiasms into ethereal realms, leaving more cautious souls to come along later and pick up from the method whatever is useful, putting it together with what had been neglected by the overly eager pioneers. In the case of the new ethnography, reconstructive theory would call for establishing relationships between the domain of cognition and the world of sensate activity.

An even more powerful attack on traditional social anthropology was launched from France. Although "structuralism" bears certain resemblances to componential analysis in that both are formal procedures having affinities to linguistics, the theory forged by Lévi-Strauss was at once less linguistic in its methods and more sweeping in its rejection of social science positivism. Structuralism, of course, can be dated as far back as Claude Lévi-Strauss's writings on South American ethnography in the early 1940s, though its true beginnings must be found in the publication of *Les Formes Élémentaires de la Parenté* in 1949. It had limited influence, however, outside of France until the appearance of translations of most of his work in the 1960s. In England, Edmund Leach and Rodney Needham publicized, and criticized, the work of the French anthropologist, and in the United States George Homans' and David Schneider's *Marriage, Authority, and Final Causes* (1955) provided a critique that did much to impel others to turn to the original. Nonetheless, interest in the movement was slow to develop in this country, and I believe that my seminar on structuralism in 1961 at Berkeley—a course which was dubbed "The French Disease" by irreverent students—was the first offered in the United States.

The two main reasons for the slowness with which structuralism diffused to these shores can probably be found in the regnant functionalism of the period and the unwillingness of most of us to cope with Lévi-Strauss's elegant but difficult French. The latter difficulty was removed with the translation into English of *Tristes Tropiques* (1961), *Structural Anthropology* (1963), *Totemism* (1963), *The Savage Mind* (1968), *The Raw and the Cooked* (1969), and, finally, *The Elementary Structures of Kinship* (1969). As for functionalism, it was exactly during the period in which most of Lévi-Strauss's work was appearing in English that interest in the school waned. The conversion of David Schneider, one of the leading structural-functionalists, and of Marshall Sahlins, a pillar of cultural materialism, to French structuralism marked the dimensions of the theoretical migration that ensued.

What has been the attraction of structuralism in a discipline that was founded in naturalism and empiricism? I suspect that the intriguing character of Lévi-Strauss's dialectics have had much to do with the surge of interest in this country, for he was read at a juncture in our intellectual history that was highlighted by a growing distrust of positivism and disbelief in the "objectivity" of social science. The profession found itself in a theoretical dead end, and structuralism promised an alternative to an empiricism that did not go much beyond appearances and had never resolved the dilemma posed by the fact that the observer and what is observed are inseparable. Moreover, there was a certain consistency between the traditional interests of American anthropology and those of the French school, for both dealt with culture as a set of symbols that is *sui generis* and not merely an epiphenomenon or refraction of activity. There is continuity in this respect between the work of Lévi-Strauss, the products of componential analysis and the earlier writings of Kroeber and his teacher Boas. Lévi-Strauss himself recognized these affinities, which should not be occasion for surprise in view of the fact that he really learned his anthropology in the Brazilian forest and New York City.

17

The awakening of deep American interest in structuralism came too close to the end of our period to have had an extensive impact upon the *American Anthropologist*. Except for the Moore article and kindred pieces addressing structuralist issues (cf. Murphy and Kasdan 1959; Murphy 1967; Scholte 1966), there are surprisingly few essays done in the structuralist vein in the journal. This has, of course, changed since 1970, and the full influence of structuralism on American anthropology will have to await a centennial volume, if the world lasts that long.

My discussion of the history of anthropology during this period has neglected the three smaller subfields for the simple reason that their histories are not well reflected in the *American Anthropologist*. Although it is satisfying to reprint the excellent summarization of taxonomy and conceptual units in archaeology by Phillips and Willey (1953; see below pp. 135-153), there was a sad dearth in the pages of the journal of all the developments of the past 25 years that have brought about a "new archaeology." As for linguistics, the pages of the journal during our period do not reveal the dimensions of the revolution created by Chomsky's generative grammar; and in lexico-statistics, there is little in the *American Anthropologist* on the method itself and but a few articles giving results. The one article chosen, "The Scope of Linguistics" by Carl Voegelin and Zelig Harris (1947; see below pp. 23-25), does not tell us of these new directions but is a summary of the state of the science at the beginning of our period. The enormous expansion of the fossil record over the past quarter century is relatively undocumented in the journal, although C. Loring Brace's vigorous defense of our Neanderthal ancestry (Brace 1962; see below pp. 326-338) is a valuable exception. Also of importance is Ashley Montagu's scathing attack on racial studies and on the concept of "race" itself (Montagu 1962; see below pp. 339-348). In an age that demanded social relevance of anthropology, he wrote:

> It may be difficult for those who believe in what I. A. Richards has called "The Divine Right of Words" to accept the suggestion that a word such as "race," which has exercised so evil a tyranny over the minds of men, should be permanently dethroned from the vocabulary, but that constitutes all the more reason for trying, remembering that the meaning of a word is the action it produces [Montagu 1962:927].

The theoretical flux within the discipline during our period was matched by profound institutional change. We entered the epoch a small and exotic branch of study with a membership that could be numbered in the hundreds and with but a dozen or so graduate schools granting advanced degrees. The great expansion of the late 1950s and the entire decade of the 1960s saw our ranks grow to the thousands, with several thousand more graduate students scattered through scores of graduate departments. During the height of academic growth, new Ph.D.s and promising candidates were beleaguered with attractive job offers, and research funds were more plentiful than applicants. By the time our period ended, however, the first effects of economic depression and inflation were joining with a cresting of the college population to flatten out the boom. Six years later, at the time of this writing, the prospects for all academia appear bleak, and the profession is searching anxiously for other outlets than teaching for its talents and energies.

The mood and climate of the campuses changed as much as did their finances. We began the period with the entry of millions of World War II veterans into our colleges and universities, but only a decade later, the younger siblings of the war group were referred to as the "silent generation." American campuses were as unpolitical as our professional association, and many people believed this to represent the shape of the future. The atmosphere changed in the early 1960s with the idealistic involvement of young people in the civil rights movement, the Peace Corps and other activities. That all was not well on the campuses, however, was indicated by the Berkeley uprising of 1964, a protest whose target was bureaucracy itself. By the late 1960s, the Vietnam War had soured the tone and quality of American political life, and caused anthropologists to question their own involvement in policies that were neither of their making nor their choice. The American Anthropological Association became a forum of political debate for the first time since World War I, and our survival of the acerbic exchanges of the late 1960s and early 1970s is a testament to the organizational entrenchment of the scholarly disciplines.

The political turmoil of the time had an interesting side-effect in the resurgence of Marxian thought in anthropology, which became interwoven with both the dialectical method underlying structuralism and the materialism of the "techno-environmental determinists." We are at an interesting juncture in the discipline of anthropology, for the present period has strong parallels to the historical situation that prevailed at the founding of the American Anthropological Association. Both times found the theoretical orientations of the profession in total disarray, a previous consensus as to aims and methods having foundered, and both times were characterized by a groping out in all directions for a new epistemology and a new common purpose. The very growth of anthropology has made for ever greater specialization and diversification of research, and this process has joined with external political crisis to make this the most unsettled period in the history of the discipline. There has been a burgeoning of schools of thought that are all with us today—structural-functionalism, structuralism, Marxism in several different varieties, personality and culture, cultural ecology and just plain ecology, cognitive anthropologies, neo-evolutionisms, cultural materialism, and so forth—and none is dominant. Indeed, this may just be the future condition of anthropology: a pluralistic discipline that loosely shelters a plethora of interests and which lacks a center.

There are, however, certain quite general enduring qualities that distinguish anthropology. However much specialization may have sapped the overall integrity of the four fields of the discipline, it still forms the only scholarly community that unites the cultural, biological, historic and linguistic aspects of human life. Very few of us stray outside our specialties, but most of us read the work of our colleagues in other subfields and are conditioned, albeit subtly, by their perspectives. The other distinctive characteristic of the discipline is the common enterprise of fieldwork, which joins all the varieties of cultural anthropologists with their colleagues in archaeology, linguistics, and physical anthropology. This, after all, is the praxis of anthropology, and it is in this bedrock kind of activity that our sense of the profession is formed. And if there is one aspect of fieldwork that separates it from all other forms of scholarly research, it is that we become immersed in our work in a total sense; we *live* anthropology in a direct and literal way.

One might be tempted to be pessimistic about the future of anthropology, for the doomsayers are certainly today's prophets. Let me end, instead, with a note on our lasting strength. This lies not in anthropology as science but in anthropology as a humanistic study. We set our task over a hundred years ago to chronicle and preserve the many and wonderful expressions of humanity, and we have largely succeeded in this formidable venture. Finally, in an age of growing secularization and disenchantment of life, we have become the residual heirs of the myth-makers' task, which is nothing less than to explain Man to Mankind.

# REFERENCES CITED

Adair, John, and Evon Vogt
  1949 Navaho and Zuni Veterans: A Study of Contrasting Modes of Culture Change. American Anthropologist 51:547-561.
Arensberg, Conrad
  1961 The Community as Object and as Sample. American Anthropologist 63:241-264.
Beals, Ralph
  1951 Urbanism, Urbanization and Acculturation. American Anthropologist 53:1-10.
Barth, Fredrik
  1956 Ecologic Relationships of Ethnic Groups in Swat, North Pakistan. American Anthropologist 58:1079-1089.
Berreman, Gerald D.
  1966 Anemic and Emetic Analyses in Social Anthropology. American Anthropologist 68:346-354.
Brace, C. Loring
  1962 Refocusing on the Neanderthal Problem. American Anthropologist 64:729-741.
Burling, Robbins
  1964 Cognition and Componential Analysis: God's Truth or Hocus-Pocus. American Anthropologist 66:20-28.
Chapple, Eliot D., and Conrad M. Arensberg
  1940 Measuring Human Relations: An Introduction to the Study of the Interaction of Individuals. Genetic Psychology Monographs 22.
Conklin, Harold C.
  1954 The Relation of Hanunóo Culture to the Plant World. Unpublished Ph.D. dissertation, Yale Universtiy.
  1955 Hanunóo Color Categories. Southwestern Journal of Anthropology 11:339-344.
Dundes, Alan
  1962 Earth-Diver: Creation of the Mythopoeic Male. American Anthropologist 64:1032-1051.
Durkheim, Emile
  1964 The Rules of Sociological Method. New York: The Free Press.
Eggan, Fred
  1954 Social Anthropology and the Method of Controlled Comparison. American Anthropologist 56:743-763.
Fortes, Meyer
  1953 The Structure of Unilineal Descent Groups. American Anthropologist 55:17-41
Foster, George M.
  1965 Peasant Society and the Image of Limited Good. American Anthropologist 67:293-315.
Frake, Charles O.
  1962 Cultural Ecology and Ethnography, American Anthropologist 64:53-59.
Fried, Morton
  1957 The Classification of Corporate Unilineal Descent Groups. Journal of the Royal Anthropological Institute 87:1-29.
Geertz, Clifford
  1957 Ritual and Social Change: A Javanese Example. American Anthropologist 59:32-54
Gluckman, Max
  1968 The Utility of the Equilibrium Model in the Study of Social Change. American Anthropologist 70:219-237.
Goffman, Erving
  1956 The Nature of Deference and Demeanor. American Anthropologist 58:473-502.

Goodenough, Ward H.
  1955  A Problem in Malayo-Polynesian Social Organization. American Anthropologist 57:71-83.
  1956  Componential Analysis and the Study of Meaning. Language 32:195-216.
Harris, Marvin
  1968  The Rise of Anthropological Theory. New York: Crowell.
Hart, C. W. M.
  1954  The Sons of Turimpi. American Anthropologist 56:242-261.
Homans, George, and David M. Schneider
  1955  Marriage, Authority and Final Causes. Glencoe, IL: The Free Press
Kroeber, A. L.
  1909  Classificatory Systems of Relationship. Journal of the Royal Anthropological Institute 39:77-84.
Leach, Edmund
  1954  Political Systems of Highland Burma. Boston: Beacon Press.
Lévi-Strauss, Claude
  1944  Reciprocity and Hierarchy. American Anthropologist 46:266-268.
  1951  Language and the Analysis of Social Laws. American Anthropologist 53:155-163.
  1961  Tristes Tropiques. New York: Criterion.
  1963  Structural Anthropology. New York: Basic Books.
  1963  Totemism. Boston: Beacon Press.
  1968  The Savage Mind. Chicago: University of Chicago Press.
  1969  The Raw and the Cooked. John Weightman, trans. New York: Harper and Row.
  1969  The Elementary Structures of Kinship. J. Bell and J. von Sturmer, trans. R. Needham, ed. Boston: Beacon Press.
Lounsbury, F. G.
  1956  A Semantic Analysis of the Pawnee Kinship Usage. Language 32:158-194.
Lowie, Robert H.
  1948  Social Organization. New York: Rinehart.
Meggitt, Mervyn J.
  1965  The Lineage System of the Mae-Enga of New Guinea. Edinburgh: Oliver and Boyd.
Metzger, Duane, and Gerald Williams
  1966  Some Procedures and Results in the Study of Native Categories: Tzeltal Firewood. American Anthropologist 68:389-407.
Montagu, Ashley
  1962  The Concept of Race. American Anthropologist 64:919-928.
Moore, Sally Falk
  1964  Descent and Symbolic Filiation. American Anthropologist 66:1308-1320.
Murphy, Robert F.
  1967  Tuareg Kinship. American Anthropologist 69:163-171.
Murphy, Robert F., and Leonard Kasdan
  1959  The Structure of Parallel Cousin Marriage. American Anthropologist 61:17-29.
Nadel, S. F.
  1952  Witchcraft in Four African Societies: An Essay in Comparison. American Anthropologist 54:18-29.
Phillips, Philip, and Gordon R. Willey
  1953  Method and Theory in American Archeology: An Operational Basis for Culture-Historical Integration. American Anthropologist 55:615-633.
Radcliffe-Brown, A. R.
  1935  Kinship Terminologies in California. American Anthropologist 37:30-35.
Redfield, Robert
  1940  The Folk Culture of Yucatan. Chicago: University of Chicago Press.
Redfield, Robert, Ralph Linton, and Melville Herskovits
  1936  Memorandum on the Study of Acculturation. American Anthropologist 38:149-152.

21

Scholte, Bob
    1966  Epistemic Paradigms: Some Problems in Cross-Cultural Research on Social Anthropological History and Theory. American Anthropologist 68:1192-1201.
Steward, Julian H.
    1949  Cultural Causality and Law: A Trial Formulation of the Development of Early Civilizations. American Anthropologist 51:1-27.
    1950  Area Research: Theory and Practice. New York: Social Science Research Council, 63.
Steward, Julian H., et al.
    1956  The People of Puerto Rico. Urbana: University of Illinois Press.
Voegelin, C. F., and Z. S. Harris
    1947  The Scope of Linguistics. American Anthropologist 49:588-600.
Wagley, Charles, and Marvin Harris
    1955  A Typology of Latin American Culture. American Anthropologist 57:428-451.
Wallace, Anthony F. C., and John Atkins
    1960  The Meaning of Kinship Terms. American Anthropologist 62:58-80.
White, Leslie A.
    1943  Energy and the Evolution of Culture. American Anthropologist 45:335-356.
    1948  The Definition and Prohibition of Incest. American Anthropologist 50:416-435.
Wolf, Eric
    1955  Types of Latin American Peasantry: A Preliminary Discussion. American Anthropologist 57:452-471.
Worsley, Peter M.
    1956  The Kinship System of the Tallensi: A Reevaluation. Journal of the Royal Anthropological Institute 86:37-77.

# THE SCOPE OF LINGUISTICS

*By* C. F. VOEGELIN *and* Z. S. HARRIS

MAJOR subdivisions of this paper are concerned with: (1) the place of linguistics in cultural anthropology; (2) trends in linguistics. Neither parts are to be taken in an excluding sense. Besides cultural anthropology under 1, we include also reference to archaeology; besides trends under 2, we include reference to continuities, as the undiminished flow of work based on the comparative method in Indo-European.

Discussion in this paper is placed under italicized statements of a general nature. These general points or general assertions were first assembled by the writers and then discussed between them; rather to their surprise, some points which appeared promising for discussion proved quite sterile when discussion was actually attempted. This is reflected in our paper by the brevity of some of the discussion paragraphs which do no more than list or outline agenda. Other discussion paragraphs are a summary of the more fruitful considerations that preceded this writing.

## 1. LINGUISTICS AND CULTURAL ANTHROPOLOGY

*The data of linguistics and of cultural anthropology are largely the same.*

Human behavior, as well as (or rather, which includes) behavior between humans, is never purely verbal; nor, in the general case, is it non-verbal. Linguists characteristically study only that part of a situation which we here call verbal. Cultural anthropologists often segregate the non-verbal from the verbal, relegating the latter to special chapters or volumes (such as folklore), as contrasted with chapters devoted to various aspects of material culture, such as house types; one might infer from some ethnographies that houses are built in sullen silence.

There are exceptions: these we call ethno-linguistic because they attempt to integrate the verbal and non-verbal aspects of behavior, whether in a single historical problem or in a single synchronic situation. We are more indebted to ethnographers than to linguists for contributions which have been made thus far to ethno-linguistics. The main contributions have been historical.

For native America, Sapir summarized the work of a generation of scholars in his "Time Perspective,"[1] in general showing interrelations of languages, cultures, and populations. For reliability in relative chronology, Sapir rates inferences based on linguistic data second only to those based on archaeological data (though admitting that reliability is enhanced when linguistic and archaeological work are correlated). In dealing with the less remote history of Indians of California, Kroeber[2] controls both cultural and linguistic data.

Much good interpretation has been made in reconstructing early aboriginal

---

[1] Sapir, 1916.    [2] Kroeber, 1925.

history in the New World; nevertheless, the more successful use of historical ethno-linguistics has been in the Old World. Migrations have been traced by means of place names, as for the Phoenicians in the Mediterranean Basin.

Analysis of proper names has been used as evidence for the ethnic composition of populations, as, for example, the evidence for Syria and Palestine in the El-Amarna tablets written in the middle of the second millennium B.C. Thousands of names occur in these tablets; many are Semitic names of various branches, some are Hittite, some are Hurrian. The information thus derived concerning the distribution and relative numbers of Semites, Hittites, Hurrians, and others is in part corroborated by archaeological and other historical data. The most famous use of historical ethno-linguistics is in the investigation of the last common home of the Indo-Europeans, and in the use of cognate terms from the various Indo-European branches to give information on the culture then obtaining.

The linguistic parts of such historical reconstructions call for great exactness. And if either sobriety in cultural interpretation, or sophistication in comparative linguistics is lacking, the results are inevitably absurd, as for example, in the Japhetic theory of the Marr Institute.

Compared to the very specific historical work of which examples are given above, the work in non-historical, that is to say, synchronic ethno-linguistics has so far been either particularistic or programmatic. Thus, particular parts of full-length ethnographies actually integrate the non-verbal and verbal aspects of culture, namely the parts devoted to ceremonies and to some aspects of social organization, such as kinship systems; the Dakota materials prepared by Ella Deloria (now in manuscript in the Boas Collection of the American Philosophical Society) go beyond these particular parts of the culture and attempt to give, for all parts of the culture treated, commentary from persons in the culture, and in a situational context.

Malinowski, in his last monographic work,[3] exhibits a programmatic interest in ethno-linguistics which is on the whole good and in part brilliant; he also makes a futile attempt to integrate non-verbal and verbal aspects of Trobriand Island culture: futile, perhaps, because the integration is attempted without knowledge of Trobriand linguistic structure.[4]

---

[3] Malinowski, 1935.

[4] For the sake of brevity and comparability with our recent paper in the Southwestern Journal of Anthropology (Vol. 1, pp. 455–465, 1945), we paraphrase closely Malinowski's methodological points from his "Coral Gardens and Their Magic" (New York, 1935); our paraphrase of Malinowski is in italics, with parenthetic page references to volume two of "Coral Gardens"; our comment is in roman.

*Language must be linked up with all other aspects of human culture (vii).* To make the correlation between L and X, Y, Z, requires structural statements of L and of X, Y, Z, as well as a technique of correlation.

*The drift of most modern missionary writings on linguistics is towards the method of cultural*

*The techniques of linguistics and of cultural anthropology are in general different.*

Linguistic techniques enable a worker to state the parts of the whole (for any one language), and to give the distribution of the parts within the whole. This provides criteria of relevance: it is possible to distinguish sharply between

---

*interpretation of language which is also adopted in "Coral Gardens and Their Magic" (ix). The missionary, the administrator, the trader and even the traveller needs to translate the white man's point of view to the native, while the anthropologist needs to translate the native point of view to the white man (x).* It is assumed by Malinowski that this problem of translation may be met by extensive commentary which combines both linguistic information and cultural information.

*The only correct presentation of linguistic material is in combination with ethnographic description: such a presentation follows the technique of the field-worker, seeing and hearing at the same time and recording in full without trying to be concise; material illuminated from two sides will stand out, so to speak, stereoscopically (3).* Since ethnographic material is allowed separate presentation by Malinowski, it would seem somewhat partisan of him to insist on a dependent status for linguistic material; but the fact remains that activities observed in the field are often ethno-linguistic situations, and that the final presentation of life as it is lived loses color because scholars select data according to their specialization, reporting either the ethnographic or the linguistic, but not both.

*Language is the ethnographer's most important tool: through his practical handling of native grammar and vocabulary he can ask clear questions and receive relevant answers (4).* This is a practical question rather than an ethno linguistic question.

*The methodological classification of utterances is three-fold: statement in answer to a direct question (definition texts); volunteered statement; traditional sayings (magical formulae, gardening cries and ditties) (5).* The first class of utterance constituting definition texts comprises three-fourths of all texts listed by Malinowski; most of his materials are therefore scarcely ethno-linguistic because in the definition text the Trobriand Islander does not exhibit verbal behavior in correlation with a non-verbal expression of culture. Instead, he uses his own language to explain to someone outside of his culture, namely Malinowski, how or why that culture is as it is. This would be taken for granted by anyone living inside the culture,—that is to say, the definition text must be a Trobriand Island innovation occasioned by the arrival and demands of Malinowski. The second class of utterance, volunteered statement, is usually but not always marked as belonging to this class. The third class of utterance, traditional sayings, would usually be classified as folklore. And folklore may enter into an ethno-linguistic situation only when the things said are correlated with non-verbal cultural behavior. In so far as Malinowski has found and noted such correlations, he has succeeded in presenting ethno-linguistic situations. In folklore, then, a rather conventional field in anthropology, Malinowski is most fertile.

*Language is more than a means to an end: it stands in a definite relation to the life of the people who speak it; thus, when a magician declares, "I cut thee—my garden site; I make thy belly blossom with my charmed axe . . . " he is definitely commenting on his actions (6).* Malinowski is not content with a simple analysis into two factors, verbal and non-verbal behavior; he warns against the danger of imagining "that language is a process running parallel and exactly corresponding to mental process" (7), and in order to avoid "the danger" he sets up a third factor, "the mental reality of man."

*Language is an adjunct to bodily activities, an indispensable ingredient of all concerted human action (7); it does not always serve to communicate, but is always part of concerted activity (8).* To exemplify this distinction Malinowski cites an ethno-linguistic situation in which some old men go off to survey an area for agricultural purposes; in this, Malinowski equates technical terminology with gestures and other kinds of non-verbal behavior such as blazing trees and cutting saplings.

25

what is and what is not linguistic. Such criteria are lacking in ethnographies where culture traits are none too clearly distinguished from culture complexes and where a given segment of behavior may be regarded by one worker as an expression of culture, by another as an expression of personality; another segment of behavior, thought to be entirely physiological (as morning sickness in

---

But communication is not lacking here; rather everything said is in the context of the survey, so that if the words were recorded alone, out of their context, they would appear as gibberish.

*Speech interwoven with manual behavior is primarily used for the achievement of a practical result; secondarily, it also fulfills an educational purpose in that the older and better-informed men hand on the results of their past experiences to the younger ones (8).* The diagnostic feature of an ethno-linguistic situation is for Malinowski some teleology, some purpose, some function. Whether a boundary is surveyed, a garden area cleared, a fence or arbor constructed, such work for one objective "would be impossible without speech." This is based on the practice of one culture; we have observed members of another culture, the Ojibwa north of the Great Lakes, perform parallel tasks silently. A group of people can work together without chattering.

*Multiplicity of meanings will be found a characteristic of most native words, but in no case is there any confusion in the mind of the speaker as to which of several distinct realities he wishes to indicate by the use of one homonym or another (20).* Where most of us find some ambiguity in language, Malinowski reads the mind of the speaker and avoids confusion. When *pwaypwaya* is used in the sense of *earth* it is regarded as homonymous with *pwaypwaya* used in the sense of *land*. Since all words have some range of meaning, each word represents a group of homonyms, and in this sense is untranslatable by a single equivalent. The translation of untranslatable words, that is, of all words, is accomplished partly by mentalistic mind reading, partly by knowing the context.

*In Trobriand, we can divide words into parts of speech: noun, verb, pronoun, adjective, preposition, adverb, and conjunction stand out as clearly as in English by the simple device of translating a word by an English noun when the root is nominal and by a verb when it is an action word, and similarly with adverbs, adjectives and so on (30, 31).* This device is indeed simple but it begs the question. Having learned to recognize a part of speech by its formal features and its distribution, it is possible to return to a generalization of meaning of a class of words sharing the same features and distribution. By beginning with meaning Malinowski arrives at the curious conclusion that the parts of speech of Trobriand are precisely the same as those of English. We conclude, on the other hand, that Malinowski has failed to make a linguistic analysis of Trobriand.

*In all communities, certain words are accepted as potentially creative acts: you utter a vow or you forge a signature and you may find yourself bound for life to a monastery, a woman or a prison; in each case words are equally powerful causes of action (53).* For the Trobriand Islanders, contracts are not only verbal but are effected by non-verbal ritual, as the giving and accepting of certain objects of value. Gifts are neither given nor received without "the phraseology of gifts" (54). By virtue of describing both the act of giving and the phraseology of gifts, Malinowski's treatment begins to be ethno-linguistic. From the phraseology of gifts to the phraseology of ritual is but a short step for Malinowski; yet there is a difference not to be overlooked. In contractual relationships two or more individuals are involved; in religion on the Trobriand Islands as elsewhere, the person or power addressed is apt not to be present, so that all technical descriptions of the phraseology of ritual, including Malinowski's, resolve themselves essentially into narrative texts.

*If we wanted to emphasize the opposition between words when they are "idle" and words when they are a matter of life and death, we could take any situation where words mean life or death to a human being; an imperative, a noun, an adjective, even an adverb, screamed from a distance in the dark might reorientate completely the movements of the rescuers or those in danger.* The crux of the problem is how to analyze such life and death situations. We may say: (1) our hero called for help;

pregnancy), may later be shown to be stimulated by cultural expectation. Accordingly, neither the historian treating of past cultures, nor the anthropologist dealing with present cultures is ever half as comfortable as is the linguist in excluding any datum as irrelevant.

The elements in linguistics may be stated exhaustively: given an utterance from a language, it is possible to identify that utterance completely in terms of its constituent phonemes and morphemes. Compare with this a segment of behavior from a given culture, as for example leaching acorns among the Tübatulabal. It is easier to ask than to answer what questions about this process shall be included in our field investigation, what questions shall be excluded: shall we give the age and sex of the person engaged in leaching; shall we note the time of day when leaching takes place; shall we clock the operation and come to a statistical average for the time involved in leaching; or shall we merely (or, and also) record what ideal or proper time is said by informants to be required to leach a certain quantity of acorns?

Now compare with these random, somewhat arbitrary questions, the kind of questions which specialists in material culture actually ask about acorn leaching in California, and note that such specialists show considerable agreement in asking such questions (although the questions do not pretend to arrive at an exhaustive statement of the process): whether the acorns are leached with hot or cold water, how many times water is applied to the acorns, whether in a sand basin or in a dirt basin, whether the water is dripped through pine sprigs or through other material, and so on.

Professional questions such as these are based on an awareness of comparative, that is, more or less neighboring cultures; without this awareness, the initial quest for culture elements remains either arbitrary or without boundary; the ethnographer asks whether the Tübatulabal drip water through pine sprigs because other tribes in California use this material (or some other) for the same purpose.

The elements in anthropology (culture traits) are obtained by a sophisticated awareness of their comparative implications; and it does not matter in

---

or (2) we may quote the hero's very words; and (3) we may cite not only the precise words used but also observe, with pedantic delight, that our hero employed "even an adverb." The problem is at bottom one of correlation: if non-verbal behavior is different (or the same) in emotional crises, is the linguistic structure in the accompanying utterance affected?

*To divide anthropology, as one of the leaders of our science has done recently, into three disciplines, one of which is concerned with the human frame, the other with culture, the third with language—shows that the relation between language and culture has been insufficiently appreciated* (vii). Everyone who has succeeded in making a competent linguistic statement, including Franz Boas, has treated linguistics as a separate discipline, with techniques of its own. The relationship between a language, once analyzed, and a culture, once described, may be appreciated (or neglected) thereafter.

basic definition whether these traits are obtained in original field-work, as by Kroeber and his colleagues at California, or from the published literature, as by Murdock and his colleagues at Yale. But it does seem to matter, in the sense of affecting the basic definition, when one or another school of anthropology is either unaware of or uninterested in comparative implications; as a structural linguist sticks to one language in a given study, so a functional anthropologist, for example, sticks to one culture, and with a parallel objective, because he too attempts to give the distribution or, as he calls it, the function of each trait in that culture. But he cannot treat the distribution (or function) of culture traits until he has a method for obtaining culture traits in the first instance, and he cannot find boundaries between culture traits and culture complexes unaided by comparative considerations.

Cultural anthropology is dependent upon comparative considerations for finding its elements; linguistics is not. Linguistic analysis provides an exhaustive list of its elements (thus, there are between a dozen and a score or two of phonemes for any given language); cultural analysis does not.

Having found all the elements in the structure he is studying, the linguist explains them (i.e., makes statements about sets of phonemes and sets of morphemes) by giving their distribution relative to each other within the utterances of a single language. The ethnologist looks for his elements or groups of elements (without sharp distinction between one trait and a complex of traits) with a knowledge of parallel occurrences among neighboring cultures, and having thus found his culture traits the ethnologist may (or may not) relate them in an internal economy within the single culture he is primarily investigating.

*Use of native language in the study of culture constitutes an associated observation rather than a tool of ethnology.*

A few years ago some half dozen ethnologists published papers in the American Anthropologist[5] on the value of linguistics as a tool in ethnology. Stated quantitatively: given a field-trip of a limited period of time, as the tool-use of language is increased, the time available for non-verbal investigation is lessened; what is an efficient proportion of time for each? One can have no quarrel with the tool-use of language, whatever preference is expressed in time devoted to gaining some sort of communicating command of the language. When so used, this kind of knowledge of the language may make it easier to get ethnographic data, but it probably does not add anything to the ethnography which would not be equally available under conditions which permitted the ethnologist to work with completely bilingual informants.

For additional insights into the culture, tool-use of language is, strictly

---

[5] Elkin, 1941; Henry, 1940; Lowie, 1940; Mead, 1939.

speaking, irrelevant; for insights beyond what a bilingual informant is able to convey, the ethnologist needs (1) to recognize the linguistic structure of utterances which are part of ethno-linguistic situations; (2) to make detailed observations on how the linguistic utterance relates to the rest of the cultural situation. If an ethnologist were observing features connected with hospitality among a tribe which spoke a language like German, with a distinction between formal *Sie* and informal *du* for "You", he would have to learn that the imperative *Pass auf* ("Look out!") is structurally equivalent to *du* in other utterances, (1). He might correlate the use of utterances characterized by *du* structures with certain kinship relationships, and *Sie* structures with formal guest relationships; then if a guest who was in the formal category used the *du* structure rather than the presumably appropriate *Sie* structure, the ethnographer would be immediately prepared to observe how the host reacted to such behavior contrary to cultural expectation, (2).

*Problems which linguistics has in common with other fields are only partly shared by cultural anthropology.*

Throughout the formulation of linguistic structure there are problems of a mathematical or logical nature; in determining the physical bases of phonemes and the manner in which phonemes are produced by speakers, linguists turn to physics and physiology. Problems of the type here mentioned do not occur in cultural anthropology which has, however, other points of contact with these fields, as in the study of diet (physiology).

There remain a number of fields in which linguistics and cultural anthropology share many contacts, but with different emphasis or degrees of interest: semantics, theory of signs, philosophy; psychology, psychiatry, psychoanalysis; oral literature, written literature. Stylistic studies are often recommended but rarely attempted. There are also fields in which cultural anthropology has wide contact and linguistics restricted contact, such as geography.

## 2. TRENDS IN LINGUISTICS

*A central interest in modern linguistics is the synchronic description of one language at a time.*

In descriptive linguistics, a form is regarded as explained when its place is found in the total structure of a single language. In historical linguistics, a form is regarded as explained when the forms from which it developed are reconstructed, or found in early records. During the nineteenth century, formulations of the Indo-European comparative method were brought to full expression.

In contrast to this developmental work on comparative formulations in the nineteenth century, much of the work of the present century has been devoted to formulating descriptive statements about diverse languages (without respect to the historical importance of the speakers of such languages, or to whether written records were or were not available). This interest, in its characteristically comprehensive expression, was very demanding, the more so because the languages of the world are very numerous and very diversified. It turned out that it was not often profitable in following the dominating descriptive interest also to explain or state linguistic forms in one of these languages relative to earlier forms, or to forms in some other language. This is all that is generally meant by the statement that linguistic interest has shifted from historical to descriptive work.

*The fact that linguistics permits exact statements has led to experimentation in compact and highly organized descriptions.*
The older grammars showed some interrelations among the materials treated, usually in the form of paradigms; otherwise the materials were presented with something of an archival organization (with all materials on the nouns in one chapter, materials on the adjectives in another),—perhaps convenient but not compact. Such organizations often followed categories of meanings which reflected some kind of translation from Latin or other western grammatical tradition. These grammars were often neither exact nor consistent. For unwritten languages, a given word or morpheme (if not normalized) would be recorded in several different ways. The first great advance in the direction of exactness and consistency came with phonemic writing.
The old grammars listed facts about a language and (often sporadically) the attendant conditions. Recent grammars tend to set up the elements of a language in such a way that the attendant conditions are included in the definition of the elements. The old grammars listed exceptions to their rules. Recent grammars tend to state asymmetrical features in the same fashion as symmetrical features of the language being described; then no methodological distinction results between rules (symmetries) and exceptions (asymmetries).

*Applied linguistics is used in education and in social control.*
We use the term "applied linguistics" for the entry of research linguists into the field of practical teaching, dictionary work, code work, devising of alphabets, and administrative problems concerned with subject populations. The part that descriptive linguists play in such work is very small, but it has already had some effect in the fields here mentioned.
In language teaching in particular the chief effects include: (1) the use of a phonemic orthography or at least some sophistication in phonemics; (2) in grammatical presentation, the use of formal criteria as distinguished from meaning considerations; (3) partial use of the linguistic structure of a given language, namely, the isolation of small areas in the morphology and the arrangement of these, with illustrative models, for learning the language.

*Structural comparability of languages may be stated independently of their genetic relationships.*

By the side of the major comparative and historical work of nineteenth and twentieth century linguistics, it is possible to distinguish a few approaches to the problem of linguistic types, including an approach which is just beginning to be formulated: (1) grammatical features of Indo-European served as a basis of reference; (2) exotic features of aboriginal languages were noted and these raised the problem of linguistic diversity; (3) grammars were compared more or less implicitly by juxtaposing brief summaries of related or unrelated languages between the covers of one book; (4) early attempts at generalizing were based on arbitrarily selected key characteristics; premature classifications served to stimulate a controversy on genetic relationship versus borrowing which led away from the problem of linguistic types; (5) structural comparability may lead to a solution of the problem of linguistic types. The discussion paragraphs that follow are numbered to correspond with these various approaches.

(1) From the first explorations in comparative work, similarities and differences among genetically related languages could hardly escape attention. Linguists recognized not only cognate words, but also parallel constructions and paradigms. Features which were recurrent among Indo-European languages focussed attention in two essentially different ways: if any language not belonging to the Indo-European family showed some features characteristic of Indo-European, these received central attention; if a language belonging to the Indo-European family failed to have one of the features otherwise recurrent in the family, that was emphasized.

(2) As more languages became known, features were noted even though they might not occur in Indo-European. Thus, for Melanesian languages, the luxuriance in the expression of number was frequently cited: speakers distinguish between *I* (singular), *we two including you* (dual inclusive), *we two including him but not you* (dual exclusive), *we three* (trialis), and *we all* (plural). For Bantu languages of Africa it was discovered that there were often several classes of nouns which marked such notions as person class, wooden-object class, and so on. For American Indian languages, which gave the greatest impetus to the recognition of linguistic diversity, investigators found such unexpected forms as those marking fourth person (the less important or conspicuous of two third persons; in *the man and his wife*, for example, *the man* is marked as a third person, *his wife* as a fourth person), and such noun classes as animate and inanimate, or long object versus round object. Sometimes such features were presented as though they had replaced somewhat similar features in Indo-European or Semitic; instead of sex gender, Algonquian marks animate-inanimate gender, and so on.

(3) It is clear that those who presented such features as these were inter-

ested in comparing grammars. Their method of presentation was to juxtapose summaries of the languages treated, brief paraphrases of the full-length grammars, with special attention given to particular word classes, such as personal pronouns. Juxtaposed summaries of grammars were made both for unrelated languages (as in Finck's[6] famous book on language types), and for the branches of a single language family (as Bergsträsser's[7] work on Semitic).

(4) The early attempts to generalize these comparisons were satisfied by selec ing, rather casually, key characteristi s in respect to which various languages differed or were similar. Languages like Turkish were called agglutinative, Latin and the like were called inflectional, Chinese (and sometimes English) was called isolating, and most native American languages polysynthetic. In some cases languages which showed similarity of this order were grouped together with the implication that a genetic relationship existed which was capable of later demonstration; opponents of this implication suggested an alternative explanation which is often discussed as part of the larger subject of areal linguistics. Besides the implication of genetic relationship (that is, historical connection) among languages of the same generalized type (as proposed by Sapir for native America), there were also theories which stated that one type developed from the other by an evolutionary process or progress (more especially for Old World languages).

(5) The current view on this matter is that implications of any sort, whether of a genetic or diffusional character, will necessarily be delayed until the structure of each language is stated in a way to admit of controlled rather than casual comparability. Having first stated comparable structures, it may then be possible to discover language types so that any particular language can be associated with one type or another.

*Historical and comparative techniques are insufficiently applied to aboriginal languages.*

When nothing more than fragmentary word lists were available for aboriginal languages, it was customary to make preliminary estimates of genetic relationship based on some regularity of sound correspondences, but usually not on reconstructions of the parent languages for each family. Such reconstructions are still largely lacking. Workers in aboriginal languages have not contributed greatly to what is, nevertheless, the great triumph of linguists, namely, the comparative method.

This method deals with the reconstruction of linguistic forms no longer spoken as the parents of later cognate forms used (for the most part) in genetically related languages. Much of Proto-Indo-European was reconstructed in this way; Old French reconstructions were so exact that in some cases they

---

[6] Finck, 1923.  [7] Bergsträsser, 1928.

yielded forms which were lacking in Latin but which were subsequently found in late Latin manuscripts. Among American Indian languages the most important example of the application of the comparative method is the reconstruction of Central Algonquian, chiefly by Bloomfield.

By the side of the comparative method there are other techniques for historical attestation and inference, resting largely on the evidence of written records. Such techniques make it possible to say, for example, that certain German loanwords in Lithuanian were borrowed at an earlier period than certain others. (German words which shared the effects of certain historically known Lithuanian changes must have been borrowed by Lithuanians before those changes occurred; and German loanwords which would have been subject to these changes but did not show them must have entered Lithuanian after the changes had ceased.) Such techniques can be in part applied even when written records are lacking. Thus, Algonquian students first reconstruct a parent language, PA, and then find that certain daughter languages share certain phonemes: (1) PA $\theta$, $l$, $n$ are kept distinct in Cree; (2) PA $\theta$ and $l$ coincide as $l$, but $l$ is kept distinct from $n$ in Shawnee, Miami-Peoria, Delaware, Penobscot and other eastern Algonquian languages; PA $\theta$ and $l$ and $n$ coincide as $n$ in the remaining Central Algonquian languages. In respect to the three phonemes here noted for the parent language, Cree is most archaic; Cree did not join in an innovation affecting some Central and some Eastern languages which must have been contiguous at the time of this innovation; only a few Central languages followed the final innovation.

Increased experience with linguistic structure, which characterizes twentieth century linguistics, has led investigators in both Europe and America to think about the use of the comparative method and historical analysis on whole genetically related language structures rather than merely on groups of cognate words. For American Indian languages, where historical research has been meager though successful, the controlled reconstruction of both groups of words and language structure will no doubt yield much information.

*Dialect geography and diffusional areal studies offer a new approach to historical problems in anthropology.*

Dialect geography is a specialized branch of linguistics, growing by the side of historical linguistics (which employs the comparative method), and descriptive linguistics. Most dialect geography surveys have mapped distributions of isolated grammatical features, pronunciation of particular vowels (and consonants), and the use of different words for the same item in material culture; loanwords are sometimes separately mapped. The primary interest in dialect geography is the study of linguistic diffusion among people who speak a single language (in the sense that the speech of neighbors is mutually intelligible).

In maps which show the distribution of, say, the various pronunciations of the word for "make" in German, forms with $x$ (*maxen* = machen) are found south of an east-west axis; north of this axis, forms with $k$ (*maken* = machen) are found. The east-west line separating the two areas is called the $x$-$k$ isogloss.

Besides isoglosses that divide the whole area in which a language is spoken into roughly two parts, as in the example above, there are cases in which a particular word or pronunciation occurs in one or more restricted, separated regions within the whole area. The lines enclosing such sub-areas or insular regions are also called isoglosses.

As multiple features are mapped, some will share the identical distribution of others or overlap in some regions of the whole area. When, as frequently happens, the isoglosses for different features do run parallel to each other or enclose roughly the same insular areas, we speak of bundles of isoglosses.

A bundle of isoglosses, reflecting parallel distribution of several linguistic features, may extend halfway across the area in which a given language is spoken, and then fan out at that part of the area in which the overlapping distribution of features is interrupted by eccentric or other kinds of independent distributions which cannot be represented by major bundles of isoglosses. Major as well as minor isoglosses may cross each other.

Statements on areal interpretation are elaborate or simple, depending on whether the isoglosses show an elaborate distribution in bundles with fanwise dispersal and crisscrossing of individual isoglosses, or a simple distribution of bundles of isoglosses which remain neatly together as bundles over or within the entire area. The total result of formulations by means of isoglosses leads to a somewhat different kind of mapping than that made for culture areas in anthropology, but the diffusional interpretation of both is much the same.

The historical interpretations made on the basis of the major European and American dialect geographies have been corroborated by external data on movements of population, lines of trade, and changes of political boundaries. In places where there are few external data of this nature available, and where archaeological horizons do not integrate with the culture of the people being studied linguistically, dialect geography may provide the only source of historical interpretation.

INDIANA UNIVERSITY
UNIVERSITY OF PENNSYLVANIA

## BIBLIOGRAPHY

BERGSTRÄSSER, GOTTHELF
    1928  *Einführung in die semitischen sprachen*. Munich.
ELKIN, A. P.
    1941  Native Languages and the Field Worker in Australia. *American Anthropologist*, Vol. 43, pp. 89–94.

FINCK, FRANZ NIKOLAUS
1923   Die haupttypen der sprachbaus. Leipzig.
HENRY, JULES
1940   A Method for Learning to Talk Primitive Languages. American Anthropologist, Vol.
42, pp. 635–641.
KROEBER, A. L.
1925   Handbook of the Indians of California. Bulletin 78, Bureau of American Ethnology.
Washington.
LOWIE, ROBERT H.
1940   Native Languages as Ethnographic Tools. American Anthropologist, Vol. 42, pp. 81–89.
MALINOWSKI, BRONISLAW
1935   Coral Gardens and Their Magic. New York.
MEAD, MARGARET
1939   Native Languages as Field-work Tools. American Anthropologist, Vol. 41, pp. 189–
205.
SAPIR, EDWARD
1916   Time Perspective in Aboriginal American Culture; A Study in Method. Memoir 90,
Anthropological Series No. 13, Canada Department of Mines, Geological Survey. Ottawa.
VOEGELIN, C. F., and Z. S. HARRIS
1945   Linguistics in Ethnology. Southwestern Journal of Anthropology, Vol. 1, pp. 455–465

# THE DEFINITION AND PROHIBITION OF INCEST

*By* LESLIE A. WHITE

"Again and again in the world's history, savage tribes must have
had plainly before their minds the simple practical alternative between marrying-out and being killed out."—E. B. Tylor*

T HE subject of incest has a strange fascination for man. He was preoccupied with it long before he developed the art of writing. We find incestuous episodes in the mythologies of countless peoples. And in advanced
cultures, from Sophocles to Eugene O'Neill, incest has been one of the most
popular of all literary themes. Men seem never to tire of it but continue to
find it ever fresh and absorbing. Incest must indeed be reckoned as one of
man's major interests in life.

Yet, despite this intense and perennial concern, it is a fact that incest is
but little understood even today. Men of science have been obliged all too
often to admit that they are baffled and to declare that it is too mysterious,
too obscure, to yield to rational interpretation, at least for the present.

One of the more common explanations of the universal prohibition of incest
is that it is instinctive. Thus Robert H. Lowie, a distinguished anthropologist,
once accepted "Hobhouse's view that the sentiment is instinctive."[1] To "explain" an element of behavior by saying that it is "instinctive" contributes
little to our understanding of it as a rule. Sometimes it merely conceals our
ignorance with a verbal curtain of pseudo-knowledge. To say that prohibitions
against incest are "instinctive" is of course to declare that there is a natural,
inborn and innate feeling of revulsion toward unions with close relatives. But
if this were the case, why should societies enact strict laws to prevent them?
Why should they legislate against something that everyone already wishes
passionately to avoid? Do not, as a matter of fact, the stringent and worldwide
prohibitions indicate a universal and powerful desire for sexual unions with
one's relatives?[2] There are further objections to the instinct theory. Some
societies regard marriage with a first cousin as incestuous while others do not.
Are we to assume that the instinct varies from tribe to tribe? Certainly when
we consider our own legal definitions of incest, which vary from state to state,
to claim that a biological instinct can recognize state boundary lines is somewhat grotesque. In some societies it is incestuous to marry a parallel cousin
(a child of your father's brother or of your mother's sister) but it is permissible,
and may even be mandatory, to marry a cross cousin (a child of your father's
sister or of your mother's brother). We cannot see how "instinct" can account
for this, either; in fact, we cannot see how instinct can distinguish a cross

---

* Tylor, 1888, p. 267.     [1] Lowie, 1920, p. 15.

[2] "Freud has shown all but conclusively that incestuous tendencies represent one of the most
deeply rooted impulses of the individual." (Goldenweiser, 1937, p. 303, fn. 11.)

416

cousin from a parallel cousin. It is usually incestuous to marry a clansman even though no genealogical connection whatever can be discovered with him, whereas marriage with a close relative in *another* clan may be permissible. Plainly, the instinct theory does not help us at all, and it is not easy to find a scientist to defend it today.[3]

Another theory, championed generations ago by Lewis H. Morgan and others, and not without defenders today, is that incest was defined and prohibited because inbreeding causes biological degeneration.[4] This theory is so plausible as to seem self-evident, but it is wrong for all that. In the first place, inbreeding as such does not cause degeneration; the testimony of biologists is conclusive on this point. To be sure, inbreeding intensifies the inheritance of traits, good or bad. If the offspring of a union of brother and sister are inferior it is because the parents were of inferior stock, not because they were brother and sister. But superior traits as well as inferior ones can be intensified by inbreeding, and plant and animal breeders frequently resort to this device to improve their strains. If the children of brother-sister or father-daughter unions in our own society are frequently feeble-minded or otherwise inferior it is because feeble-minded individuals are more likely to break the powerful incest tabu than are normal men and women and hence more likely to beget degenerate offspring. But in societies where brother-sister marriages are permitted or required, at least within the ruling family, as in ancient Egypt, aboriginal Hawaii and Incaic Peru, we may find excellence. Cleopatra was the offspring of brother-sister marriages continued through several generations and she was "not only handsome, vigorous, intellectual, but also prolific . . . as perfect a specimen of the human race as could be found in any age or class of society."[5]

But there is still another objection to the degeneration theory as a means of accounting for the origin of prohibitions against incest. A number of competent ethnographers have claimed that certain tribes are quite ignorant of the nature of the biological process of reproduction, specifically, that they are unaware of the relationship between sexual intercourse and pregnancy. Or, they may believe that coitus is prerequisite to pregnancy but not the cause of it.[6] B. Malinowski, for example, claims that the Trobriand Islanders denied that copulation has anything to do with pregnancy, not only among human beings but among the lower animals as well.[7] This thesis of ignorance of the facts of

---

[3] In 1932, Professor Lowie abandoned the instinct theory of incest prohibitions. But he comes no closer to an explanation than to observe that "the aversion to incest is, therefore, best regarded as a primeval cultural adaptation" (Lowie, 1933, p. 67). In one of his recent works (Lowie, 1940, p. 232), he again discusses incest but goes no further than to suggest that "the horror of incest is not inborn, though it is doubtless a very ancient cultural feature."

[4] *See* Morgan, 1877, pp. 69, 378, 424.     [5] Mahaffy, 1915, p. 1.

[6] *See* Montagu, 1937, both for a discussion of this subject and for bibliographic references to other articles.     [7] *See* Malinowski, 1929b, especially pp. 153 ff., 3, 171.

life among primitive peoples has been challenged by other ethnologists, and I am not prepared to adjudicate the dispute. But it may be pointed out that such ignorance should not be very surprising. Once a fact becomes well known there is a tendency to regard it as self-evident. But the relationship between coitus and pregnancy, a condition that would not be discovered until weeks or even a few months later, is anything but obvious. Furthermore, pregnancy does not always follow intercourse. And knowing primitive man's penchant for explaining so many things, the phenomena of life and death especially, in terms of supernatural forces or agents, we should not be surprised to find some tribes even today who do not understand the physiology of paternity.

At any rate, there must have been a time at which such understanding was not possessed by any members of the human race. We have no reason to believe that apes have *any* appreciation of these facts, and it must have taken man a long time to acquire it. There are reasons, however, as we shall show later on, for believing that incest tabus appeared in the very earliest stage of human social evolution, in all probability prior to an understanding of paternity. The reason for the prohibition of inbreeding could not therefore have been a desire to prevent deterioration of stock if the connection between copulation and the birth of children was not understood.

This thesis receives additional support from a consideration of the kinship systems of many primitive peoples. In these systems a person calls many of his collateral relatives "brother" and "sister," namely, his parallel cousins of several degrees for example, and the children of his mother's and father's parallel cousins, also of several degrees. Marriage between individuals who call each other "brother" and "sister" is strictly prohibited by the incest tabu, even though they be cousins of the third or fourth degree. But marriage with a *first cross cousin* may be permitted and often is required. Now these people may not understand the biology of conception and pregnancy, but they know which woman bore each child. Thus we see that the marriage rules disregard the degree of biological relationship so far as preventing inbreeding is concerned; they may prohibit marriage with a fourth parallel cousin who is called "brother" or "sister," but permit or require marriage with a first cross cousin who is called "cousin." Obviously, the kinship terms express sociological rather than biological relationships. Obvious also is the fact that the incest tabus follow the pattern of social ties rather than those of blood.

But suppose that inbreeding did produce inferior offspring, are we to suppose that ignorant, magic-ridden savages could have established this correlation without rather refined statistical techniques? How could they have isolated the factor of inbreeding from numerous others such as genetics, nutrition, illnesses of mother and infant, etc., without some sort of medical criteria and measurements—even though crude—and without even the rudiments of statistics?

Finally, if we should grant that inbreeding does produce degeneracy, and that primitive peoples were able to recognize this fact, why did they prohibit marriage with a parallel cousin while allowing or even requiring union with a cross cousin? Both are equally close biologically. Or, why was marriage with a clansman prohibited even though the blood tie was so remote that it could not be established genealogically with the data available to memory, while marriage with a non-clansman was permitted even though he was a close blood relative? Obviously the degeneracy theory is as weak as the instinct hypothesis, although it may be more engaging intellectually.

Sigmund Freud's theory is ingenious and appealing—in a dramatic sort of way at least. Proceeding from Darwin's conjectures concerning the primal social state of man, based upon what was then known about anthropoid apes, and utilizing W. Robertson Smith's studies of totemism and sacrifice, Freud developed the following thesis: in the earliest stage of human society, people lived in small groups each of which was dominated by a powerful male, the Father. This individual monopolized all females in the group, daughters as well as mothers. As the young males grew up and became sexually mature, the Father drove them away to keep them from sharing his females with him.

"One day," says Freud, "the expelled brothers joined forces, slew and ate the father, and thus put an end to the father horde. Together they dared and accomplished what would have remained impossible for them singly."[8] But they did not divide their Father's women among themselves as they had planned. Now that he was dead their hatred and aggressiveness disappeared, and their love and respect for him came to the fore. As a consequence, they determined to give him in death the submission and obedience they had refused in life. They made therefore a solemn pact to touch none of their Father's women and to seek mates elsewhere. This pledge was passed on from one generation to the next:[9] you must have nothing to do with the women of your father's household, i.e., of your own group, but must seek other mates. In this way the incest tabu and the institution of exogamy came into being.

This part of *Totem and Taboo* is great drama and not without value as an interpretation of powerful psychological forces, just as *Hamlet* is great drama in the same sense. But as ethnology, Freud's theory would still be inadequate even if this much were verifiable. It does not even attempt to account for the many and varied forms of incest prohibition.

It is not our purpose here to survey and criticize all of the many theories

---

[8] Freud, 1931, p. 247.

[9] In another work (1938, p. 617, fn. 1), Freud suggests, if he does not say so outright, that the incest tabu became incorporated into the germ plasm and was consequently transmitted by means of biological heredity: "The incest barrier probably belongs to the historical acquisitions of humanity and, like other moral taboos, it must be fixed in many individuals through organic heredity."

that have been advanced in the past to account for the definition and prohibition of incest. We may however briefly notice two others before we leave the subject, namely, those of E. Westermarck and Emile Durkheim.

Westermarck's thesis that "the fundamental cause of the exogamous prohibitions seems to be the remarkable absence of erotic feelings between persons living very closely together from childhood, leading to a positive feeling of aversion when the act is thought of,"[10] is not in accord with the facts in the first place and would still be inadequate if it were. Propinquity does not annihilate sexual desire, and if it did there would be no need for stringent prohibitions. Secondly, incest tabus are frequently in force between persons not living in close association.

Durkheim attempts to explain the prohibition of incest as a part of his general theory of totemism. The savage knew intuitively, Durkheim reasoned, that blood is a vital fluid or principle. To shed the blood of one's own totemic group would be a great sin or crime. Since blood would be shed in the initial act of intercourse, a man must eschew all women of his own totem. Thus the tabu against incest and rules of exogamy came into being.[11] This theory is wholly inadequate ethnologically. Tabus against incest are much more widespread than totemism; the former are virtually universal, the latter is far from being so. And the theory does not even attempt to explain the many diverse forms of the definition and prohibition of incest.

In view of repeated attempts and as many failures to account for the origin of definitions of incest and of rules regulating its prohibition, is it any wonder that many scholars, surveying decades of fruitless theories, have become discouraged and have come to feel that the problem is still too difficult to yield to scientific interpretation?

In the same work in which he presented his theory, but some pages earlier, Freud said: "Still, in the end, one is compelled to subscribe to Frazer's resigned statement, namely, that we do not know the origin of incest dread and do not even know how to guess at it."[12]

Ralph Linton treats of the subject as follows:[13]

The causes which underlie such limitations on marriage, technically known as incest regulations, are very imperfectly understood. Since these regulations are of universal occurrence, it seems safe to assume that their causes are everywhere present, but biological factors can be ruled out at once. Close inbreeding is not necessarily injurious . . . Neither are purely social explanations of incest regulations altogether satisfactory, since the forms which these regulations assume are extremely varied . . . It seems possible that there are certain psychological factors involved, but these can hardly be strong

---

[10] Westermarck, 1921, Table of Contents for Ch. 20.          [11] Durkheim, 1898, pp. 50 ff.

[12] Freud, 1931, p. 217. Frazer's statement was: "Thus the ultimate origin of exogamy and with it the law of incest—since exogamy was devised to prevent incest—remains a problem nearly as dark as ever." (*Totemism and Exogamy*, Vol. I, p. 165.)

[13] Linton, 1936, pp. 125–126.

enough or constant enough to account for the institutionalization of incest regulations . . . They have probably originated from a combination of all these factors . . .

In other words, *somewhere* in the man-culture situation lie the causes of incest regulations, but where they are and why and how they are exercised are matters too obscure for description or explanation.

The late Alexander Goldenweiser, a prominent disciple of Franz Boas, never discovered the secret of the prohibition of incest. In *Early Civilization* he spoke of certain tabus that "are everywhere reinforced by the so-called 'horror of incest,' an emotional reaction of somewhat mysterious origin."[14] Fifteen years later, in *Anthropology*, his last major work, he could go no further than to repeat these identical words.[15]

The sociologists have little to offer. Kimball Young, for example, disavows instinct as the source of incest prohibitions, but he advances no further explanation than to assert that "the taboo is a rather constant and expected result arising from the very nature of the social interaction between parents and children and among the children themselves"[16]—which is virtually equivalent to no explanation at all.

The late Clark Wissler, one of the foremost anthropologists of our day, observes:[17]

. . . so far as we can see, the only facts sufficiently well established to serve as a starting point are that anti-incest responses of some kind are universal among mankind. As to why these are universal, we are no nearer a solution than before.

These are discouraging words indeed. "Anti-incest responses" help us no more than "an instinctive horror" of incest. But in the phrase "we are no nearer a solution [now] than before," we may find a clue to a way out of the dilemma. Perhaps these theorists have been on the wrong track. Science has found itself on the wrong track countless times during its relatively brief career so far. So many, in fact, that many of the important achievements of science consist, not in the discovery of some new fact or principle, but in erecting signs which read "Blind alley. Do not enter!" Phrenology was one of these blind alleys. But until it has been explored, how can one know whether a passage is a blind alley or a corridor leading to a new world? Once it has been found to be a blind alley, however, other scientists need not and should not waste their time exploring it again. Perhaps we are confronted by blind alleys in the various theories of incest and exogamy that we have just surveyed. Wissler's admission that "we are no nearer a solution [now] than before" would lead us to think so.

Fortunately we are not in the situation of a mariner who has lost his bearings and who must try to recover his true course. We do not need to seek a

---

[14] Goldenweiser, 1922, p. 242.     [15] *Idem.*, 1937, p. 303.
[16] Young, 1942, p. 406.     [17] Wissler, 1929, p. 145.

new path in the hope of finding an adequate solution of the problem of incest. The solution has already been found, and that long ago.

Confusion in this field of ethnological theory has been due to circumstances such as we have just described. Theorists who have sought biological or psychological explanations of incest tabus have been on the wrong track; they have only led us into blind alleys. Those who have sought a *culturological* explanation have succeeded fully and well.[18] The culturological point of view is younger and less widely known than the psychological or even the sociological. Although it was set forth simply and adequately by the great English anthropologist, E. B. Tylor, as early as 1871, in the first chapter of *Primitive Culture*—which was significantly enough entitled "The Science of Culture"— it has not become widely known or appreciated among social scientists, even among cultural anthropologists. There are some who recognize in the new science of culture only a mystical, fatalistic metaphysic that should be shunned like the Devil.[19] So habituated to psychological interpretations are many students of human behavior that they are unable to rise to the level of culturological interpretation. Thus, Goldenweiser looked to psychology for ethnological salvation:[20] "It seems hardly fair to doubt that psychoanalysis will ultimately furnish a satisfactory psychological interpretation of this 'horror of incest'." Professor William F. Ogburn observes that:

> Incest taboos and marriage regulations may be quite fully described historically and culturally, yet there is something decidedly strange about incest and about marriage prohibitions. One's curiosity is not satisfied by the cultural facts.[21]

And even men like Lowie and Wissler, who have done excellent work along culturological lines in other areas, have relapsed to the psychological level when confronted with the problem of incest. Thus Lowie once declared that "it is not the function of the ethnologist but of the biologist and psychologist to explain why man has so deep-rooted a horror of incest."[22] And Wissler is inclined to turn over all problems of cultural origins to the psychologist, leaving to the anthropologist the study of traits after they have been launched upon their cultural careers.[23]

The science of culture has, as we have already indicated, long ago given us

---

[18] Cf. White, 1947b.          [19] Cf. White, 1947a, especially pp. 189–205.

[20] Goldenweiser, 1922, p. 242; and 1937, p. 303.

[21] Ogburn, 1922, p. 175. What Professor Ogburn means apparently is that culturology cannot tell us *all* that we want to know about incest. This is true; psychology must be enlisted in the inquiry also. But one must insist upon a sharp and clear distinction between the psychological problem and the culturological problem. Psychology cannot account for the *origin* or the *form* of the prohibitions; only culturology can do this. But for an understanding of the way the human primate organism behaves—thinks, feels, and acts—within, or with reference to, one of these cultural forms, we must go to psychology. *See* White, 1947b, especially the closing pages.

[22] Lowie, 1920, p. 15.          [23] Wissler, 1927.

an adequate explanation of incest prohibitions. We find it set forth simply and succinctly in an essay by E. B. Tylor published in 1888: "On a Method of Investigating the Development of Institutions, Applied to the Laws of Marriage and Descent:"[24]

Exogamy, enabling a growing tribe to keep itself compact by constant unions between its spreading clans, enables it to overmatch any number of small intermarrying groups, isolated and helpless. Again and again in the world's history, savage tribes must have had plainly before their minds the simple practical alternative between marrying-out and being killed out. (p. 267)

The origin of incest tabus greatly antedates clan organization, but a sure clue to an understanding of incest prohibitions and exogamy is given by Tylor nevertheless: primitive people were confronted with a choice between "marrying-out and being killed out." The argument may be set forth as follows:

Man, like all other animal species, is engaged in a struggle for existence. Cooperation, mutual aid, may become valuable means of carrying on this struggle at many points. A number of individuals working together can do many things more efficiently and effectively than the same individuals working singly. And a cooperative group can do certain things that lone individuals cannot do at all. Mutual aid makes life more secure for both individual and group. One might expect, therefore, that in the struggle for security and survival every effort would be made to foster cooperation and to secure its benefits.

Among the lower primates there is little cooperation. To be sure, in very simple operations one ape may coordinate his efforts with those of another. But their cooperation is limited and rudimentary because the means of communication are crude and limited; cooperation requires communication. Monkeys and apes can communicate with one another by means of signs—vocal utterances or gestures—but the range of ideas that can be communicated in this way is very narrow indeed. Only articulate speech can make extensive and versatile exchange of ideas possible, and this is lacking among anthropoids. Such a simple form of cooperation as "you go around the house that way while I go around the other way, meeting you on the far side," is beyond the reach of the great apes. With the advent of articulate speech, however, the possibilities of communication became virtually unlimited. We can readily see its significance for social organization in general and for incest and exogamy in particular.

One might get the impression from some psychologists, the Freudians especially, perhaps, that the incestuous wish is itself instinctive, that somehow a person "just naturally" focuses his sexual desires upon a *relative* rather than upon a *non*-relative, and, among relatives, upon the closer rather than the

[24] Tylor, 1888.

remoter degrees of consanguinity. This view is quite as unwarranted as the theory of an "instinctive horror" of incest; an inclination toward sexual union with close relatives is no more instinctive than the social regulations devised to prevent it. A child has sexual hunger as well as food hunger. And he fixes his sex hunger upon certain individuals as he does his food hunger upon certain edible substances. He finds sexual satisfaction in persons close to him because they *are* close to him, not because they are his relatives. To be sure, they may be close to him because they are his relatives, but that is another matter. As a consequence of proximity and satisfaction the child fixates his sexual desires upon his immediate associates, his parents and his siblings, just as he fixates his food hungers upon familiar foods that have given satisfaction. He thus comes to have definite orientations and firm attachments in the realm of sex as in the field of nutrition. There is thus no mystery about incestuous desire; it is merely the formation and fixation of definite channels of experience and satisfaction.

We find therefore, even in sub-human primate families, a strong inclination toward inbreeding; one strives to obtain sexual satisfaction from a close associate. This tendency is carried over into human society. But here it is incompatible with the cooperative way of life that articulate speech makes possible. In the basic activities of subsistence, and defense against enemies, cooperation becomes important because life is made more secure thereby. Other factors being constant, the tribe that exploits most fully the possibilities of mutual aid will have the best chance to survive. In times of crisis, cooperation may become a matter of life or death. In providing food and maintaining an effective defense against foreign foes, cooperation becomes all-important.

But would primordial man be obliged to construct a cooperative organization for subsistence and defense from the very beginning, or could he build upon a foundation already in existence? In the evolutionary process, whether it be social or biological, we almost always find the new growing out of, or based upon, the old. And such was the case here; the new cooperative organization for food and defense was built upon a structure already present: the family. After all, virtually everyone belonged to one family or another, and the identification of the cooperative group with the sex-based family would mean that the benefits of mutual aid would be shared by all. When, therefore, certain species of anthropoids acquired articulate speech and became human beings, a new element, an *economic* factor, was introduced into an institution which had up to now rested solely upon sexual attraction between male and female. We are, of course, using the term *economic* in a rather broad sense here to include safety as well as subsistence. The human primate family had now become a corporation with nutritive and protective functions as well as sexual and incidentally reproductive functions. And life was made more secure as.a consequence.

But a regime of cooperation confined to the members of a family would be correspondingly limited in its benefits. If cooperation is advantageous *within* family groups, why not between families as well? The problem was now to extend the scope of mutual aid.

In the primate order, as we have seen, the social relationships between mates, parents and children, and among siblings antedates articulate speech and cooperation. They are strong as well as primary. And, just as the earliest cooperative group was built upon these social ties, so would a subsequent extension of mutual aid have to reckon with them. At this point we run squarely against the tendency to mate with an intimate associate. Cooperation *between* families cannot be established if parent marries child; and brother, sister. A way must be found to overcome this centripetal tendency with a centrifugal force. This way was found in the definition and prohibition of incest. If persons were forbidden to marry their parents or siblings they would be compelled to marry into some other family group—or remain celibate, which is contrary to the nature of primates. The leap was taken; a way was found to unite families with one another, and social evolution as a *human* affair was launched upon its career. It would be difficult to exaggerate the significance of this step. Unless some way had been found to establish strong and enduring social ties between families, social evolution could have gone no further on the human level than among the anthropoids.

With the definition and prohibition of incest, *families* became units in the cooperative process as well as individuals. Marriages came to be contracts first between families, later between even larger groups. The individual lost much of his initiative in courtship and choice of mates, for it was now a group affair. Among many primitive peoples a youth may not even be acquainted with his bride before marriage; in some cases he may not even have seen her. Children may be betrothed in childhood or infancy—or even before they are born. To be sure, there are tribes where one can become acquainted or even intimate with his spouse before marriage, but the group character of the contract is there nevertheless. And in our own society today a marriage is still an alliance between families to a very considerable extent. Many a man has expostulated, "But I am marrying *her*, not her family!" only to discover his lack of realism later.

The widespread institutions of levirate and sororate are explainable by this theory also. In the levirate a man marries the wife or wives of his deceased brother. When a man customarily marries the unwed sister of his deceased wife the practice is called sororate. In both cases the group character of marriage is manifest. Each group of consanguinei supplies a member of the other group with a spouse. If the spouse dies, the relatives of the deceased must supply another to take his or her place. The alliance between families is important and must be continued; even death cannot part them.

The equally widespread institutions of bride-price and dowry likewise find their significance in the prohibition of incest to establish cooperation between family groups. The incest tabu necessitates marriage *between* family groups. But it cannot guarantee a continuation of the mutual aid arrangement thus established. This is where bride-price and dowry come in: they are devices for making permanent the marriage tie that the prohibition of incest has established. When a family or a group of relatives has received articles of value as bride-price or dowry, they distribute them as a rule among their various members. Should the marriage tie be broken or dissolved, they may have to return the wealth received at the time of the marriage. This is almost certain to be the case if it can be shown that the spouse whose relatives were the recipients of the bride-price or dowry was at fault. It very often happens that the relatives are reluctant to return the wealth if indeed they still have it. If it has already been consumed they will have to dig into their own pockets. It may already be earmarked for the marriage of one of their own group. In any event, the return of dowry or bride-price would be an inconvenience or a deprivation. Consequently they are likely to take a keen interest in the marriage and to try to prevent their own relative from doing anything to disrupt it.

According to our theory the prohibition of incest has at bottom an economic motivation—not that primitive peoples were *aware* of this motive, however, for they were not. Rules of exogamy originated as crystallizations of processes of a *social system* rather than as products of individual psyches. Inbreeding was prohibited and marriage between groups was made compulsory in order to obtain the maximum benefits of cooperation. If this theory be sound, we should find marriage and the family in primitive society wearing a definite economic aspect. This is, in fact, precisely what we do find. Let us turn for summary statements to two leading authorities in social anthropology. Robert H. Lowie writes as follows:[25]

Marriage, as we cannot too often or too vehemently insist, is only to a limited extent based on sexual considerations. The primary motive, so far as the individual mates are concerned, is precisely the founding of a self-sufficient economic aggregate. A Kai [of New Guinea] does not marry because of desires he can readily gratify outside of wedlock without assuming any responsibilities; he marries because he needs a woman to make pots and to cook his meals, to manufacture nets and weed his plantations, in return for which he provides the household with game and fish and builds the dwelling.

And A. R. Radcliffe-Brown makes similar observations concerning the aborigines of Australia:[26]

The important function of the family is that it provides for the feeding and bringing up of the children. It is based on the cooperation of man and wife, the former providing the flesh food and the latter the vegetable food, so that quite apart from the question of

---

[25] Lowie, 1920, pp. 65–66.      [26] Radcliffe-Brown, 1930, p. 435.

children a man without a wife is in an unsatisfactory position since he has no one to supply him regularly with vegetable food, to provide his firewood and so on. This economic aspect of the family is a most important one . . . I believe that in the minds of the natives themselves this aspect of marriage, i.e., its relation to subsistence, is of greatly more importance than the fact that man and wife are sexual partners.

Turning to the colonial period in America we find the economic character of the family equally pronounced. According to William F. Ogburn:[27]

In colonial times in America the family was a very important economic organization. Not infrequently it produced substantially all that it consumed, with the exception of such things as metal tools, utensils, salt and certain luxuries. The home was, in short, a factory. Civilization was based on a domestic system of production of which the family was the center.

The economic power of the family produced certain corresponding social conditions. In marrying, a man sought not only a mate and companion but a business partner. Husband and wife each had specialized skills and contributed definite services to the partnership. Children were regarded, as the laws of the time showed, not only as objects of affection but as productive agents. The age of marriage, the birth rate and the attitude toward divorce were all affected by the fact that the home was an economic institution. Divorce or separation not only broke a personal relationship but a business one as well.

And in our own society today, the economic basis of marriage and the family is made clear by suits for breach of promise and alienation of affections in which the law takes a very materialistic, even monetary, view of love and romance.[28] Suits for non-support, alimony, property settlements upon divorce, the financial obligations between parents and children, and so on, exhibit further the economic function of the family. Marriage for many women today means a greater economic return for unskilled labor than could be obtained in any other occupation.

It is interesting to note, in this connection, that Freud who, according to

---

[27] Ogburn, 1933, pp. 661–662.

We recall, also, Benjamin Franklin's account of his proposal to marry a girl providing her parents would give him "as much money with their daughter as would pay off my remaining debt for the printing-house." He even suggested that they "mortgage their house in the loan-office" if they did not have the cash on hand. The parents, however, thought the printing business a poor risk and declined to give both money and girl. "Therefore," says Franklin, "I was forbidden the house, and the daughter shut up." (Franklin, 1940, p. 78.)

[28] One court ruling observes that "the gist of the action for alienation of affections is the loss of consortium. 'This is a property right growing out of the marriage relation' . . . " (Supreme Court of Connecticut, Case of Maggay *vs.* Nikitko, 1933), quoted in Turano, 1934b, p. 295.

Another legal statement says that "the law generally takes the rather worldly view that marriage is a 'valuable' consideration; a thing not only possessing value, but one the value of which may be estimated in money, and therefore, in a sense, marriage engagements are regarded as business transactions, entered into with a view, in part, at least, to pecuniary advantage." (Ruling Case Law, Vol. 4, p. 143, quoted in Turano, 1934a, p. 40.)

popular belief, "attributes everything to sex," nevertheless declares that "the motivating force of human society is fundamentally economic."[29]

The notion that marriage is an institution brought into being to provide individuals with a means of satisfying their sex hunger is naive and anthropocentric. Marriage *does* provide an avenue of sexual exercise and satisfaction, to be sure. But it was not sexual desire that produced the institution. Rather it was the exigencies of a social system that was striving to make full use of its resources for cooperative endeavor. Marriage, as an institution, finds its explanation in terms of socio-cultural process rather than individual psychology. In primitive society there was frequently ample means of sexual exercise outside of wedlock. And in our own society the great extent of prostitution, the high incidence of venereal disease as an index of promiscuity, as well as other evidence,[30] show that the exercise of sexual functions is not confined to one's own spouse by any means. As a matter of fact, marriage very often restricts the scope of one's sexual activity. Indeed, monogamy ideally considered is the next thing to celibacy.

Nor is love the basis of marriage and the family, however fondly this notion may be cherished. No culture could afford to use such a fickle and ephemeral sentiment as love as the basis of an important institution. Love is here today but it may be gone tomorrow. But economic needs are with us always. Absence of love is not sufficient grounds for divorce. Indeed, one may despise and loathe, hate and fear one's mate and still be unable to obtain a divorce. At least one state in the Union will grant no divorce at all. And certain religious faiths take the same position. Marriage and the family are society's first and fundamental way of making provision for the economic needs of the individual. And it was the definition and prohibition of incest that initiated this whole course of social development.

But to return to the definitions and prohibitions themselves. These vary, as we saw at the outset, from culture to culture. The variations are to be explained in terms of the specific circumstances under which cooperation is to take place. One set of circumstances will require one definition of incest and one form of marriage; another set will require different customs. The habitat and the technological adjustment to it, the mode of subsistence, circumstances of defense and offense, division of labor between the sexes, and degree of cultural development, are factors which condition the definition of incest and the formulation of rules to prohibit it. No people known to modern science customarily permits marriage between parent and child. Brother-sister

---

[29] Freud, 1920, p. 269.

[30] " . . . virginity at marriage will be close to the vanishing point for males born after 1930, and for females born after 1940 . . . intercourse with future spouse before marriage will become universal by 1950 or 1955." (Lewis M. Terman, *Psychologic Factors in Marital Happiness*, p. 323 [New York, 1938]), as quoted in Hohman and Schaffner, 1947, p. 502.

marriage has been restricted to the ruling families of a few advanced cultures, such as those of ancient Egypt, Hawaii, and the Inca of Peru. But this is not "royal incest," as Reo Fortune calls it,[31] or "sanctioned incest" to use Kimball Young's phrase.[32] Incest is by definition something criminal and prohibited. These marriages between siblings of royal families were not only not prohibited; they were required. They are examples of endogamy, as the prohibition of brother-sister marriages are examples of exogamy. Solidarity is a source of strength and effective action in society, as cooperation is a way of achieving security. And endogamy promotes solidarity as exogamy fosters size and strength of mutual aid groups.

In view of the fact that a sure clue to the reason for the origin of prohibitions of incest was set forth by Tylor as early as 1888, it is rather remarkable that we should find anthropologists and sociologists today who juggle with "anti-incest responses" and who look to psychoanalysis for ultimate understanding. As a matter of fact, we find the reasons for exogamy set forth by Saint Augustine in *The City of God* (Bk. XV), more than 1400 years before Tylor:

> For it is very reasonable and just that men, among whom concord is honorable and useful, should be bound together by various relationships, and that one man should not himself sustain many relationships, but that the various relationships should be distributed among several, and should thus serve to bind together the greatest number in the same social interests. 'Father' and 'father-in-law' are the names of two relationships. When, therefore, a man has one person for his father, another for his father-in-law, friendship extends itself to a larger number.

He comments upon the fact that Adam was both father and father-in-law to his sons and daughters:

> So too Eve his wife was both mother and mother-in-law to her children . . . while had there been two women, one the mother, the other the mother-in-law, the family affection would have had a wider field. Then the sister herself by becoming a wife sustained in her single person two relationships which, had they been distributed among individuals, one being sister, and another being wife, the family tie would have embraced a greater number of persons.

Saint Augustine does not, in these passages at least, make explicit the advantages in security of life which would accrue to the group as a consequence of exogamy. But he makes it quite clear that community of social interest and "greater numbers of persons" in the group are the reasons for the prohibition of incest.

---

[31] Fortune, 1932, p. 622. R. H. Lowie also speaks of brother-sister marriage in Hawaii and Peru as "incest" (Lowie, 1940, p. 233). J. S. Slotkin, too, in a recent article (Slotkin, 1947, p. 613) appears to identify incest with certain specific forms of inbreeding rather than with a kind of union that is defined and prohibited as a crime.

[32] Young, 1942, p. 406.

If an understanding of incest and exogamy is as old in social philosophy as Saint Augustine and as early in anthropological science as Tylor, why is it that the subject is still so obscure and so little understood among scholars today? We have already suggested the answer: a preference for psychological rather than culturological explanations. Anthropomorphism is an inveterate habit in human thought. To explain institutions in terms of psychology—of wish, desire, aversion, imagination, fear, etc.—has long been popular. Explanations of human behavior in terms of psychological determinants preceded therefore explanations in terms of cultural determinants. But culturological problems cannot be solved by psychology. Preoccupation with psychological explanations has not only kept many scholars from finding the answer; it has prevented them from recognizing the solution when it has been reached by the science of culture. The sociological explanation, such as Kimball Young's "social interaction," is no better. As a scientific explanation it is not only inadequate; it is empty and meaningless. The sociologist's fixation upon "social interaction" keeps him, too, from appreciating a scientific interpretation of culture as a distinct class of phenomena.[33] Even men who have made notable contributions to culturology, such as Kroeber, Lowie, and Wissler, have failed to see the significance of Tylor's early discussion of exogamy. The following incident is remarkable and revealing. A. L. Kroeber and T. T. Waterman reprinted Tylor's essay, "On the Method of Investigating the Development of Institutions," in their *Source Book in Anthropology*[34] in 1920. But in a subsequent edition,[35] they cut the article down to conserve space, and omitted this highly significant passage!

Important contributions to science are sometimes made "before their time," that is, before the general level of scientific advance has reached a point where widespread appreciation becomes possible. There was really very little that was novel in the work of Darwin; most if not all of the ideas and facts had been presented before. But the broad front of the cultural process of biologic thought had not advanced sufficiently prior to 1859 to make a general acceptance of this point of view possible. So it is with the problem of incest. An adequate explanation has been extant for decades. But, because the problem is a culturological one, and because the science of culture is still so young and so few scholars even today are able to grasp and appreciate its nature and scope, an understanding of incest and its prohibitions is still very limited. As culturology develops and matures, however, this understanding as well as that of a host of other suprapsychological problems will become commonplace.

We do not wish to minimize the extent of this understanding today. Despite the ignorance and confusion of many scholars, there is a considerable number who do understand incest tabus. Thus Reo Fortune states that:[36]

[33] Cf. White, 1947a, pp. 186 ff.	[34] Kroeber and Waterman, 1920, 1924.
[35] *Ibid.*, 1931.	[36] Fortune, 1932, p. 620.

A separation of affinal relationship from consanguineous relationship assures a wider recognition of social obligation, . . . Any incestuous alliance between two persons within a single consanguineous group is in so far a withdrawal of their consanguineous group from the alliance and so endangers the group's survival.

Malinowski, too, has illuminated the problem of incest tabus. Instead of emphasizing, however, the positive values that would accrue from alliances formed as a consequence of compulsory exogamy, he dwells upon the disruption and discord that the unrestricted exercise of sexual appetites would introduce into a small group of relatives or close associates. He writes:[37]

The sexual impulse is in general a very upsetting and socially disruptive force, [it] cannot enter into a previously existing sentiment without producing a revolutionary change in it. Sexual interest is therefore incompatible with any family relationship, whether parental or between brothers and sisters . . . If erotic passion were allowed to invade the precincts of the home it would not merely establish jealousies and competitive elements and disorganize the family but it would also subvert the most fundamental bonds of kinship on which the further development of all social relations is based . . . A society which allowed incest could not develop a stable family; it would therefore be deprived of the strongest foundations for kinship, and this in a primitive community would mean absence of social order.

B. Z. Seligman expresses somewhat similar views—as well as others that are less discerning.[38] A good statement on the nature and genesis of incest tabus is tucked away in a footnote in a recent monograph by John Gillin.[38a] William I. Thomas sees clearly the reasons for prohibitions of incest: "The horror of incest is thus plainly of social derivation."[39]

And Freud, apart from his drama of patricide, comes close to an understanding of incest tabus and exogamy. He says:

The incest prohibition, had . . . a strong practical foundation. Sexual need does not unite men; it separates them . . . Thus there was nothing left for the brothers [after they had killed their father], if they wanted to live together, but to erect the incest prohibition.[40]

In another work he observes that:[41]

The observance of this [incest] barrier is above all a demand of cultural society, which must guard against the absorption by the family of those interests which it needs for the production of higher social units. Society, therefore, uses all means to loosen those family ties in every individual . . .

The cultural function, if not the genesis, of incest tabus and of rules of exogamy seems to be very clearly seen and appreciated here. It is interesting to note, too, that Freud holds substantially the same view of the relationship

---

[37] Malinowski, 1930, p. 630. *See also, idem*, 1929a, Vol. 13, p. 407.

[38] Seligman, 1929, pp. 243–244, 247, 268–269.          [38a] Gillin, 1936, p. 93.

[39] Thomas, 1937, p. 197.          [40] Freud, 1931, pp. 250–251.          [41] *Idem.*, 1938, pp. 616–617.

between restrictions upon sexual gratification and social evolution that has been set forth earlier in this essay. One of the principal themes of *Civilization and Its Discontents*[42] is "the extent to which civilization is built up on renunciation of instinctual gratifications. . . . This 'cultural privation' dominates the whole field of social relations between human beings" (p. 63). He sees that "the first result of culture was that a larger number of human beings could live together in common" (p. 68); that "one of culture's principal endeavors is to cement men and women together in larger units" (p. 72). Thus, although he proceeds from different premises, Freud comes to essentially the same conclusions as ours.

There is, then, considerable understanding of incest and exogamy extant in the literature today. Yet, in a comparatively recent review of the whole problem a prominent anthropologist, John M. Cooper, has concluded that "the desire to multiply the social bonds [has] in all probability not been [an] important factor" in the origin of incest prohibitions.[43] How far he is from an understanding of the problem is indicated by the two "chief factors" which he cites: "(a) sex callousness, resulting from early and intimate association . . . ; (b) the distinctly social purpose of preserving standards of sex decency within the family and kinship circle." The first factor is contrary to fact; intimacy fosters incest rather than callousness. The second explains nothing at all: what are standards of sex decency, why do they vary from tribe to tribe, and why is it necessary to preserve them?

The culturological theory of incest receives support from a comparison of primitive cultures with our own. The crime of incest is punished with greater severity in primitive societies than in our own, as Reo Fortune[44] has observed. Among the former the penalty of death is quite common; in our society punishment seldom exceeds ten years imprisonment and is often much less. The reason for this difference is not far to seek. In primitive societies, personal and kinship ties between individuals and families were more important than they are in highly developed cultures. The small mutual-aid group was a tremendously important social unit in the struggle for security. The very survival of the group depended to a considerable extent upon alliances formed by exogamy. In advanced cultures the situation is different. Society is no longer based upon kinship ties, but upon property relationships and territorial distinctions. The political state has replaced the tribe and clan. Occupational groups and economic organization also become important bases of social life. The importance of exogamy is thus much diminished and the penalties for incest become less severe. It is not to be expected, however, that restrictions

---

[42] *Idem.*, 1930.      [43] Cooper, 1932, p. 20.

[44] Fortune, 1932, p. 620. Freud also remarks that "This dread of incest . . . seems to be even more active and stronger among primitive races living today than among the civilized." (Freud, 1931, p. 217)

upon inbreeding will ever be removed entirely. Kinship is still an important, though relatively less important, feature of our social organization and will probably remain so indefinitely. Rules of exogamy and endogamy will therefore continue to be needed to regulate and order this aspect of our social life.

In the various interpretations, both sound and unsound, of the definition and prohibition of incest we have a neat example of a contrast between psychological explanations on the one hand and culturological explanations on the other. The problem simply does not yield to psychological solution. On the contrary, the evidence, both clinical and ethnographic, indicates that the desire to form sexual unions with an intimate associate is both powerful and widespread. Indeed, Freud opines that "the prohibition against incestuous object-choice [was] perhaps the most maiming wound ever inflicted . . . on the erotic life of man."[45] Psychology discloses an "incestuous wish" therefore, not a motive for its prevention. The problem yields very readily, however, to culturological interpretation. Man, as an animal species, lives in groups as well as individually. Relationships between individuals in the human species are determined by the *culture* of the group—that is, by the ideas, sentiments, tools, techniques, and behavior patterns, that are dependent upon the use of symbols[46] and which are handed down from one generation to another by means of this same faculty. These culture traits constitute a continuum, a stream of interacting elements. In this interacting process, new combinations and syntheses are formed, some traits become obsolete and drop out of the stream, some new ones enter it. The stream of culture thus flows, changes, grows and develops in accordance with laws of its own. Human behavior is but the reactions of the organism man to this stream of culture. Human behavior—in the mass, or of a typical member of a group—is therefore culturally determined. A people has an aversion to drinking cow's milk, avoids mothers-in-law, believes that exercise promotes health, practices divination or vaccination, eats roasted worms or grasshoppers, etc., because their culture contains trait-stimuli that evoke such responses. These traits cannot be accounted for psychologically.

And so it is with the definition and prohibition of incest. From psychology we learn that the human animal tends to unite sexually with someone close to him. The institution of exogamy is not only *not* explained by citing this tendency; it is contrary to it. But when we turn to the cultures that determine the relations between members of a group and regulate their social intercourse we readily find the reason for the definition of incest and the origin of exogamy. The struggle for existence is as vigorous in the human species as elsewhere. Life is made more secure, for group as well as individual, by cooperation. Articulate speech makes cooperation possible, extensive, and varied in human society. Incest was defined and exogamous rules were formulated in order to

---

[45] Freud, 1930, p. 74.     [46] Cf. White, 1940.

make cooperation compulsory and extensive, to the end that life be made more secure. These institutions were created by *social* systems, not by *neuro-sensory-muscular-glandular* systems. They were syntheses of culture elements formed within the interactive stream of culture traits. Variations of definition and prohibition of incest are due to the great variety of situations. In one situation, in one organization of culture traits—technological, social, philosophic, etc.—we will find one type of definition of incest and one set of rules of exogamy; in a different situation we find another definition and other rules. Incest and exogamy are thus defined in terms of the mode of life of a people—by the mode of subsistence, the means and circumstances of offense and defense, the means of communication and transportation, customs of residence, knowledge, techniques of thought, etc. And the mode of life, in all its aspects, technological sociological, and philosophical, is culturally determined.

UNIVERSITY OF MICHIGAN
ANN ARBOR, MICHIGAN

## BIBLIOGRAPHY

COOPER, J. M.
1932 Incest Prohibitions in Primitive Culture. *Primitive Man*, 5: 1–20.

DURKHEIM, E.
1898 La prohibition de l'incest et ses origines. *L'Anée Sociologique*, 1: 1–70. Paris.

FORTUNE, R.
1932 Incest. *Encyclopedia of the Social Sciences*, Vol. VII. New York.

FRANKLIN, B.
1940 *Autobiography*. Pocket Books, Inc., New York.

FREUD, S.
1920 *General Introduction to Psychoanalysis*. New York.
1930 *Civilization and its Discontents*. New York.
1931 *Totem and Taboo*. The New Republic edition, New York.
1938 Contributions to the Theory of Sex, in: *The Basic Writings of Sigmund Freud*, Modern Library edition. New York.

GILLIN, J.
1936 The Barama River Caribs of British Guiana. *Papers, Peabody Museum*, Vol. XIV, No. 2. Cambridge, Mass.

GOLDENWEISER, A.
1922 *Early Civilization*. New York.
1937 *Anthropology*. New York.

HOHMAN, L. B. and B. SCHAFFNER
1947 The Sex Life of Unmarried Men. *American Journal of Sociology*, 52: 501–507.

KROEBER, A. L., and T. T. WATERMAN
1920, 1924 *Source Book in Anthropology*. Berkeley; New York (1931).

LINTON, R.
1936 *The Study of Man*. New York.

LOWIE, R. H.
1920 *Primitive Society*. New York.
1933 The Family as a Social Unit. *Papers, Michigan Academy of Science, Arts and Letters*, 18: 53–69.

1940    *An Introduction to Cultural Anthropology* (2nd ed.). New York.

MAHAFFY, J. P.

1915    Cleopatra VI. *Journ. Egypt. Archeol.*, Vol. 2.

MALINOWSKI, B.

1929a    Kinship. *Encyclopaedia Britannica*, 14th ed.

1929b    *The Sexual Life of Savages*. London.

1930    Culture. *Encyclopedia of the Social Sciences*, Vol. IV.

MONTAGU, M. F. ASHLEY

1937    Physiological Paternity in Australia. *American Anthropologist*, n.s., 39: 175–183.

MORGAN, L. H.

1877    *Ancient Society*. New York.

OGBURN, W. F.

1922    *Social Change*. New York.

1933    The Family and its Functions, in: *Recent Social Trends in the United States* (one-volume edition). New York.

RADCLIFFE-BROWN, A. R.

1930    The Social Organization of Australian Tribes. *Oceania*, Vol. 1.

SELIGMAN, B. Z.

1929    Incest and Descent: Their Influence on Social Organization. *Journ. Royal Anthropological Institute*, Vol. 59.

SLOTKIN, J. S.

1947    On a Possible Lack of Incest Regulations in Old Iran. *American Anthropologist*, n.s., 49: 612–617.

THOMAS, W. I.

1937    *Primitive Behavior*. New York.

TURANO, A. M.

1934a    Breach of Promise: Still a Racket. *American Mercury*, Vol. 32.

1934b    The Racket of Stolen Love. *American Mercury*, Vol. 33.

TYLOR, E. B.

1888    On a Method of Investigating the Development of Institutions; Applied to Laws of Marriage and Descent. *Journal of the Anthropological Institute*, 18: 245–269.

WESTERMARCK, E.

1921    *The History of Human Marriage*. 3 vols. London.

WHITE, L. A.

1940    The Symbol: the Origin and Basis of Human Behavior. *Philosophy of Science*, 7: 451–463.

1947a    The Expansion of the Scope of Science. *Journal of the Washington Academy of Sciences*, 37: 181–210.

1947b    Culturological vs. Psychological Interpretations of Human Behavior. *American Sociological Review*, 12: 686–698.

WISSLER, C.

1927    Recent Developments in Anthropology, in: *Recent Developments in the Social Sciences*, E. C. Hayes, ed. Philadelphia.

1929    *An Introduction to Social Anthropology*. New York.

YOUNG, K.

1942    *Sociology, a Study of Society and Culture*. New York.

# AMERICAN ANTHROPOLOGIST

| Vol. 51 | JANUARY-MARCH, 1949 | No. 1 |

## CULTURAL CAUSALITY AND LAW: A TRIAL FORMULATION OF THE DEVELOPMENT OF EARLY CIVILIZATIONS

*By* JULIAN H. STEWARD

### I. METHODOLOGICAL ASSUMPTIONS

IT IS about three-quarters of a century since the early anthropologists and sociologists attempted to formulate cultural regularities in generalized or scientific terms. The specific evolutionary formulations of such writers as Morgan[1] and Tylor[2] and the functional or sociological formulations of Durkheim and others were largely repudiated by the 20th century anthropologists, especially by those of the so-called "Boas" school, whose field work tested and cast doubt on their validity. Today, despite an enormous and ever-increasing stock-pile of cultural data, little effort has been made to devise new formulations or even to develop a methodology for doing so, except as White and Childe have kept alive the tradition of Morgan, as Radcliffe-Brown and Redfield have continued in the spirit of Durkheim, and as Malinowski has attempted to reconcile diverse schools of anthropology through a "scientific theory of culture."

Reaction to evolutionism and scientific functionalism has very nearly amounted to a denial that regularities exist; that is, to a claim that history never repeats itself. While it is theoretically admitted that cause and effect operate in cultural phenomena, it is considered somewhat rash to mention causality, let alone "law," in specific cases. Attention is centered on cultural differences, particulars, and peculiarities, and culture is often treated as if it developed quixotically, without determinable causes, or else appeared full-blown.

It is unfortunate that the two approaches are so widely thought of as theoretically irreconcilable rather than as expressions of different purposes or interests. The 19th century writers had the perfectly legitimate purpose of making scientific generalizations from what they considered recurrent cultural patterns, sequences, and processes in different cultures, while the more recent school has the equally legitimate purpose of examining the distinctive or non-recurrent features of cultures. As all cultures, though unique in many respects,

---

[1] Morgan, 1877.    [2] Tylor, 1865, 1871.

1

nonetheless share certain traits and patterns with other cultures, an interest in either or both is entirely defensible. In fact, the analyses of cultural particulars provide the data necessary for any generalizations. If the 19th century formulations were wrong, it was not because their purpose was inadmissible or their objective impossible, but because the data were inadequate and insufficient, the methodology weak, and the application of the schemes too broad.

In spite of a half century of skepticism concerning the possibility of formulating cultural regularities, the conviction is widely held that the discovery of cultural laws is an ultimate goal of anthropology, to be attained when fact-collecting and detailed analyses of particular cultures and sequences are sufficiently advanced. White[3] has already offered some general formulations concerning the relationship of energy to cultural development, and he has argued for the importance of formulations of all kinds. Even some members of the so-called "Boas" school expressly advocate a search for regularities. Lowie, for example, remarks that cultural phenomena "do point toward certain regularities, and these it is certainly our duty to ascertain as rigorously as possible."[4] Lesser cites several trial formulations of regularities, which have been made by various persons, including Boas, and calls for more explicit statement of the regularities which, in the course of his work and thinking, every social scientist assumes to exist.[5] The author has attempted to formulate regularities pertaining to the occurrence of patrilineal bands among hunting and gathering tribes[6] and has suggested others that may occur in the origin and development of clans.[7] In reality, hundreds of formulations appear in the literature—for example, correlations of kinship terminologies with forms of social organization—and the possibility of recognizing the general in the particular is implicit in the very terminology of anthropology. The routine use of such concepts, or typological categories, as "clans," "castes," "classes," "priests," "shamans," "men's tribal societies," "cities," and the like, are tacit recognition that these and scores of other features are common to a large number of cultures, despite the peculiarities of their local patterning.

The present need is not to achieve a world scheme of culture development or a set of universally valid laws, though no doubt many such laws can even now be postulated, but to establish a genuine interest in the scientific objective and a clear conceptualization of what is meant by regularities. It does not matter whether the formulations are sequential (diachronic) or functional (synchronic), on a large scale or a small scale. It is more important that comparative cultural studies should interest themselves in recurrent phenomena as well as in unique phenomena, and that anthropology explicitly recognize that a legitimate and ultimate objective is to see through the differences of

---

[3] White, 1943.        [4] Lowie, 1936, pp. 3, 7.        [5] Lesser, 1930.
[6] Steward, 1936.        [7] *Idem.*, 1937.

cultures to the similarities, to ascertain processes that are duplicated independently in cultural sequences, and to recognize cause and effect in both temporal and functional relationships. Such scientific endeavor need not be ridden by the requirement that cultural laws or regularities be formulated in terms comparable to those of the biological or physical sciences, that they be absolutes and universals, or that they provide ultimate explanations. Any formulations of cultural data are valid provided the procedure is empirical, hypotheses arising from interpretations of fact and being revised as new facts become available.

Three requirements for formulating cultural regularities may be stated in a rough and preliminary way as follows:

(1) *There must be a typology of cultures, patterns, and institutions.* Types represent abstractions, which disregard peculiarities while isolating and comparing similarities. To use Tylor's classic example, the mother-in-law tabu and matrilocal residence, though in each case unique in their local setting, are recurrent types, the cause and effect relationships of which may be compared and formulated. Anthropological terminology demonstrates that hundreds of types of culture elements, patterns, and total configurations are recognized, despite the peculiarities attaching to each in its local occurrence.

(2) *Causal interrelationship of types must be established in sequential or synchronic terms, or both.* Any reconstruction of the history of a particular culture implies, though it may not explicitly state, that certain causes produced certain effects. Insights into causes are deeper when the interrelationships of historical phenomena are analyzed functionally. Functional analysis of archeological data has not been lacking, though archeology has used an atomistic and taxonomic approach[8] far more than has conventional history. Gordon Childe[9] is exceptional in his effort to treat archeological materials functionally. Wittfogel[10] has been outstanding in his use of historical data to make functional-historical analyses of the socio-economic structure of early civilizations.

Where historical data are not available, only the synchronic approach to cause and effect is possible. Radcliffe-Brown, Redfield, and Malinowski, despite important differences in their thinking, are distinctive for their functional analyses.

(3) *The formulation of the independent recurrence of synchronic and/or sequential interrelationships of cultural phenomena is a scientific statement of cause and effect, regularities, or laws.* The particularists, though conceding that such formulations are theoretically possible and even desirable, are inclined to hold that in practice it is virtually impossible to isolate identifiable cause-and-effect relationships that operate in independent cases. Similarities between cultures are interpreted as the result of a single origin and diffusion, provided

---

[8] *See* Steward and Setzler, 1938.        [9] Childe, 1934, 1946.
[10] Wittfogel, 1935, 1938, 1939–1940.

the obstacles to diffusion do not seem too great. If the obstacles are very great, differences are emphasized. Thus, most American anthropologists explain similarities between the early civilizations of the New World as a case of single origin and diffusion, but, impressed by the obstacles to trans-oceanic culture contacts, they stress the dissimilarities between the civilizations of the Old and New Worlds. Some writers, however, like Elliot-Smith, Perry, and Gladwin[11] recognize the similarities between the two hemispheres and, unimpressed by barriers to diffusion, use the similarities as proof of a single world origin.

The use of diffusion to avoid coming to grips with problems of cause and effect not only fails to provide a consistent approach to culture history, but it gives an explanation of cultural origins that really explains nothing. Diffusion becomes a mechanical and unintelligible, though universal, cause, and it is employed, as if in contrast to other kinds of causes, to account for about ninety per cent of the world's culture. One may fairly ask whether, each time a society accepts diffused culture, it is not an independent recurrence of cause and effect. Malinowski[12] states: "Diffusion . . . is not an act, but a process closely akin in its working to the evolutionary process. For evolution deals above all with the influence of any type of 'origins'; and origins do not differ fundamentally whether they occur by invention or by diffusion."[13] For example, the civilizations of the Andes and Mexico were based on dense, sedentary populations, which in turn were supported by intensive irrigation farming. In both cases, the early societies were integrated by a theocratic hierarchy, which controlled communal endeavor and enlisted labor for the construction of religious centers. It is not sufficient to say that the agricultural, social, and religious institutions merely diffused as a unit, for that would be merely stating distributions in historical terms but failing to explain process. Incipient farming appeared first, and it diffused before the other complexes developed. The latter have a functional dependence on intensive farming. They could not have been accepted anywhere until it developed, and in the course of its development similar patterns would undoubtedly have emerged, whether or not they were diffused. The increasing population and the growing need for political integration very probably would have created small states in each area, and these states would almost certainly have been strongly theocratic, because the supernatural aspects of farming—for example, fertility concepts, the need to reckon seasons and to forecast the rise and fall of rivers, and the like—would have placed power in the hands of religious leaders. Diffusion may have hastened the development of theocratic states, but in each case the new developments were within determinable limits, and independently involved the same functional or cause-and-effect relationships.

It is true, of course, that many peculiar features common to New World

---

[11] Gladwin, 1947.      [12] Malinowski, 1944, pp. 214–215.
[13] *See also* Wittfogel, 1939–1940, pp. 175–176.

civilizations do not represent a logical outgrowth of basic patterns and that they can be disposed of with the superficial explanation that they diffused. Thus, the wide distribution of such concepts as the plumed serpent or the jaguar god, or of such constructions as terraced pyramids, may be explained in this manner, though deeper analysis might reveal the reasons for their wide acceptance. In general, it is the rather arbitrary, specific, or stylized features, that is, those features which have the least functional dependence on the basic patterns, that provide the greatest evidence of diffusion. These, in other words, are the particulars, which distinguish tribes or areas and which obscure regularities.

Another means of denying the possibility of isolating cultural regularities is to stress that the complexity or multiplicity of the antecedents or functional correlates of any institution makes it virtually impossible to isolate the true causes of the institution; convergent evolution rather than parallel evolution is generally used to explain similarities that seem not to be the result of diffusion. The answer to this is simply that in dealing with cultural phenomena, as in dealing with all the complex phenomena of nature, regularities can be found only by looking for them, and they will be valid only if a rigorous methodology underlies the framing of hypotheses.

It is not necessary that any formulation of cultural regularities provide an ultimate explanation of culture change. In the physical and biological sciences, formulations are merely approximations of observed regularities, and they are valid as working hypotheses despite their failure to deal with ultimate realities. So long as a cultural law formulates recurrences of similar interrelationships of phenomena, it expresses cause and effect in the same way that the law of gravity formulates but does not ultimately explain the attraction between masses of matter. Moreover, like the law of gravity, which has been greatly modified by the theory of relativity, any formulation of cultural data may be useful as a working hypothesis, even though further research requires that it be qualified or reformulated.

Cultural regularities may be formulated on different levels, each in its own terms. At present, the greatest possibilities lie in the purely cultural or superorganic level, for anthropology's traditional primary concern with culture has provided far more data of this kind. Moreover, the greater part of culture history is susceptible to treatment only in superorganic terms. Both sequential or diachronic formulations and synchronic formulations are superorganic, and they may be functional to the extent that the data permit. Redfield's tentative formulation[14] that urban culture contrasts with folk culture in being more individualized, secularized, heterogeneous, and disorganized is synchronic, superorganic, and functional. Morgan's evolutionary schemes[15]

---

[14] Redfield, 1941.     [15] Morgan, 1877.

and White's formulation concerning the relationship of energy to cultural development[16] are sequential and somewhat functional. Neither type, however, is wholly one or the other. A time-dimension is implied in Redfield's formulation, and synchronic, functional relationships are implied in White's.

Superorganic formulations do not, of course, provide the deeper explanations of culture change that may come from a psychological level or a biological level. Research on these latter levels may profitably run concurrently with the other, but for the present their formulations will be more applicable to synchronic, functional studies than to sequential ones. Thus, to advocate search for regularities in cultural terms is not at all in conflict with those who state that "culture does not exist apart from the individual, its human carrier." To hope for basic and ultimate explanations of behavior that will interrelate cultural, psychological, neurological, physiological, and even physical phenomena is not to deny the desirability of doing what now seems possible and, in view of anthropology's traditional and primary concern with culture, of doing first things first.

The present statement of scientific purpose and methodology rests on a conception of culture that needs clarification. *If the more important institutions of culture can be isolated from their unique setting so as to be typed, classified, and related to recurring antecedents or functional correlates, it follows that it is possible to consider the institutions in question as the basic or constant ones, whereas the features that lend uniqueness are the secondary or variable ones.* For example, the American high civilizations had agriculture, social classes, and a priest-temple-idol cult. As types, these institutions are abstractions of what was actually present in each area, and they do not take into account the particular crops grown, the precise patterning of the social classes, or the conceptualization of deities, details of ritual, and other religious features of each culture center. The latter are secondary and variable so far as the institutions in question are concerned. In a more comprehensive analysis, however, they would serve to distinguish subtypes, which would require more specific formulations.

This conception of culture is in conflict with an extreme organic view, which regards culture as a closed system in which all parts are of equal importance and are equally fixed. It holds that some features of culture are more basic and more fixed than others and that the problem is to ascertain those which are primary and basic and to explain their origin and development. It assumes that, although the secondary features must be consistent and functionally integrated with the primary ones, it is these that are more susceptible to fortuitous influences from inside or outside the culture, that change most

---

[16] White, 1943.

readily, and that acquire such a variety of aspects that they give the impression that history never repeats itself.[17]

For the present, it is not necessary to state criteria for ascertaining the primary features. In general, they are the ones which individual scientists are most interested in studying and which the anthropological record shows to have recurred again and again in independent situations. A procedure which attempts to give equal weight to all features of culture amounts to a negation of typing and of making formulations, for it must include all the unique features, which obscure similarities between cultures.

## II. ERAS IN THE DEVELOPMENT OF EARLY CIVILIZATIONS

The present section deals with the development of early agricultural civilizations in Northern Peru (the sequences are longest and best known in this part of Peru, thanks to the Viru Valley project of the Institute of Andean Research), Mesoamerica (Mexico and the Maya area), Mesopotamia, Egypt, and China. These areas were chosen because they were the cradles of civilization and because their exploitation by a pre-metal technology seems to have entailed similar solutions to similar problems and consequently to have caused similar developmental sequences. The environments are arid or semiarid, which, contrary to a common belief, did not impose great difficulties and thereby stimulate cultural development. Instead, they facilitated culture growth because they were easily tilled by digging-stick and irrigation farming. The tropical rain forests, the northern hardwood forests, and the sodded plains areas, on the other hand, were exploited only with the greatest difficulty by people who lacked iron tools.

The procedure to be followed is first to establish a tentative developmental typology or sequence in which the smaller periods are grouped into major eras, which have similar diagnostic features in each area. This requires considerable revision of current terminology, for no two authors use quite the same criteria for major stages of development. Americanists, who have discussed some of these problems together, are now using such terms as Formative, Developmental, Classical, Florescent, and Empire and Conquest, and they are attempting to reach an understanding about the cultural typology implied by these terms. Old World writers still cling largely to such entrenched terms as Mesolithic, Neolithic, Chalcolithic, Ceramolithic, Bronze, and Dynastic, thereby emphasizing technological features of minor developmental significance. Gordon Childe's use of Neolithic Barbarism, Higher Barbarism of the Copper Age, Urban Revolution, and Early Bronze Age, which incorporate some terms from L. H. Morgan, indicates that his thinking is somewhat closer

---

[17] This proposition has been developed in detail in Steward, 1940: pp. 479–498; 1938: pp. 1–3, 230–262.

## CHART I. ARCHEOLOGICAL AND HISTORICAL PERIODS GROUPED IN MAJOR ERAS

| ERAS | MESOPOTAMIA, SYRIA, ASSYRIA | EGYPT | CHINA | MESOAMERICA | | N. PERU |
|---|---|---|---|---|---|---|
| | | | | MEXICO | MAYA AREA | |
| Industrial Revolution | Euro-American 19th and 20th century economic and political empires | | | | | |
| Iron Age Culture | Influences from Greece, Rome; later from north and central Europe Spanish Conquest in New World destroys native empires | | | | | |
| Cyclical Conquests | Kassites Hammurabi Dyn. Accad | Hyksos New Empire | Ming Sui, Tang Ch'in, Han | | | Inca |
| Dark Ages | Invasions | First Inter-mediate | Warring states | | | Local states |
| Initial Conquest | Royal tombs Ur Early Dyn. Sumer | Pyramid Age Early Dynastic Semainian Gerzian | Chou | Aztec Toltec | Mexican Absorp-tion | Tiahuanaco |
| Regional Florescence | Jedmet Nasr Warkan-Tepe-Gawra Obeidian | | Shang "Hsia" | Teoti-huacan | Initial Series or Classical | Mochica Gallinazo |
| Formative | Halafian Samarran Hassunan Mersian | Amratian Badarian Merimdean Fayumian | Yang Shao Pre-Yang Shao | Archaic or Middle Periods Zacatenco | Formative or Old Em-pire Mamom | Salinar Chavín-Cupisnique |
| Incipient Agriculture | Tahunian Natufian | Tasian | Plain Pottery? | ? | ? | Cerro Prieto |
| Hunting and Gathering | Paleolithic and Mesolithic | | | Pre-Agriculture | | |

to that of the Americanists, but his terminology and his period markers still fail to be very comparable to those of the latter.

The second step in the following procedure (Section III) is to suggest cause-and-effect relationships between the cultural phenomena of the succes-

## CHART II. ABSOLUTE CHRONOLOGY OF THE MAJOR ERAS

| | MESOPO-TAMIA | EGYPT | INDIA | CHINA | N. ANDES | MESO-AMERICA |
|---|---|---|---|---|---|---|
| 2000 | | | | | Spanish Conquest | |
| | | | | Cyclical Conquests | Cyclical Conquests | Cyclical Conquests |
| 1000 | | | | | Regional Florescence | Regional Florescence |
| A.D. B.C. | Cyclical Conquests | Cyclical Conquests | Cyclical Conquests | | Formative | Formative |
| | | | | Dark Ages | | |
| 1000 | | | | Initial Conquests | Incipient Agriculture | Incipient Agriculture? |
| | | Dark Ages | Dark Ages | Regional Florescence | | Hunting and Gathering |
| 2000 | Dark Ages | Initial Conquests | Initial Conquests | | Hunting and Gathering | |
| | Initial Conquests | | | Formative | | |
| 3000 | Regional Florescence | Regional Florescence | Regional Florescence | Incipient Agriculture | | |
| 4000 | | Formative | Formative | | | |
| | Formative | | | | | |
| 5000 | | | | | | |
| | Incipient Agriculture | Incipient Agriculture | Incipient Agriculture | Hunting and Gathering | | |
| 6000 | | | | | | |
| 7000 | | Hunting and Gathering | Hunting and Gathering | | | |
| 8000 | Hunting and Gathering | | | | | |
| 9000 | | | | | | |

sive eras and to formulate as basic regularities those relationships which are common to all areas. These formulations are offered primarily as an illustration of the generalizing approach to cultural data. Tentative and preliminary, they will be revised again and again as long as research continues and as long as scholars probe for a deeper understanding of the basic processes of cultural development. Even if these formulations were entirely scrapped, they would have served their purpose if they stimulated students of culture development to interest themselves in the same problems, to use comparable methods, and to present their findings in comparable terms—in short, to talk one another's language.[18]

Chart I groups the periods of each center into eras that have the same general features. Periods in the same relative position, consequently, were similar but were not contemporaneous. Chart II places the eras of each center on an absolute time-scale, which is fairly precise for the periods of written history but much less accurate for the early periods. The margin of error in dating these early periods does not, however, greatly affect the functional analysis of cultural development.

### Pre-agricultural Era

This era includes all the Old World paleolithic and mesolithic periods, which lacked farming, and the New World pre-agricultural periods. To judge by the simple remains of these periods as well as by the recent hunting-and-gathering cultures, the technologies were devoted principally to satisfying biological needs for food, clothing, and shelter. Pottery, basketry, loom-weaving, metallurgy, permanent houses, and boat and animal transportation were probably absent until they were borrowed to a limited degree from higher centers. Social patterns were based on kinship, age, and sex, but they varied greatly as they became adapted to local conditions. Warfare was restricted to blood feuds, revenge for witchcraft, and perhaps in some areas retaliation against trespass.

### Incipient agriculture

This era cannot be dated exactly, and it is known through very few finds. It must have been very long, passing through several stages, which began when the first cultivation of plant domesticates supplemented hunting and gathering, and ended when plant and animal breeding was able to support permanent communities. To judge by what are the earliest-known evidences of domestication in Mesopotamia and Peru, technologies made little advance over those of the previous era until settled village life was fully achieved.

---

[18] Cultural historical data are from the following sources, unless otherwise cited. Northern Peru: Bennett, 1946; Kroeber, 1940, 1944; Strong, 1947; Willey, 1948. Mesoamerica: Armillas, 1948; Kidder, Jennings, and Shook, 1946; Morley, 1946; Thompson, 1943, 1945; Vaillant, 1944. Mesopotamia and Egypt: Childe, 1934, 1946; Albright, 1946. China: Bishop, 1942; Creel, 1937a, 1937b; Wittfogel, 1935, 1938, 1939–40, 1946.

*Peru:* Cerro Prieto.

Culture: farming based on beans; twined weaving; ceramics absent; semi-subterranean houses.

*Mesoamerica:* As the earliest-known agricultural periods of Mesoamerica appear to have had technologies and temple mounds, which elsewhere characterized the Formative Era, it is generally believed (Morley[19] excepted) that the cultures of these periods were introduced full-blown from elsewhere. Theoretically, however, it would seem that remains of simpler agricultural peoples should antedate the fairly developed theocratic communities in Mesoamerica.

*Mesopotamia:* Natufian, Tahunian.

Culture: probably domesticated millet or wheat and perhaps domesticated animals. Pottery and polished stone lacking.

*Egypt:* Tasian.

Culture: possibly domesticated plants. Pottery present.

*China:* Period of Plain Pottery. This period is considered to be the first phase of neolithic China, though the presence of domesticated plants or animals is doubtful.

## Formative Era of basic technologies and folk culture

The Formative Era is so named because the principal technologies—basketry, pottery, weaving, metallurgy, and construction—appeared and the patterns of community culture took form at this time. It was an era of population growth, area expansion of cultures and peoples, comparative peace, and wide diffusion of culture between centers of civilization.

The principal domesticated plants were brought under intensive cultivation, and irrigation was begun on a community scale. In the Old World, the more important domesticated animals, except the horse, were present from early in the Era. In the New World, the absence of suitable wild species for domestication limited such animals to the dog, and, in the Andes, to the llama and alpaca.

Food production was on a subsistence basis, except as a share was provided for the ruling class. Increasingly efficient farming released considerable labor for the satisfaction of socially derived needs; that is, craft production of finer goods and construction of religious edifices for the theocracy made rapid progress during each period.

The sociopolitical unit seems to have been the small local community. The clustering of rooms in house units suggests that lineages or kin-groups were the basis of society. One to several such units were associated with a ceremonial center, which served as the nucleus and integrating factor of a dispersed community. Control of irrigation, which was on a local scale, was one of the more important practical functions of the religious leaders. Warfare was probably limited to raids and contributed little either to social structure or to expansion of the state.

---

[19] Morley, 1944.

*Peru:* Chavín-Cupisnique, Salinar.

Technologies: domesticated maize, manioc, beans, gourds, peanuts; small-scale irrigation; llamas. Pottery; metallurgy in gold, copper (?); loom-weaving in cotton; twined baskets; surface adobe houses; balsa (reed bundle) boats.

Social: dispersed communities, evidently centering in religious mounds and temples. Feline, condor, and serpent deities. Theocratic control of society; rulers accorded status burial.

*Mesoamerica:* Armillas'[20] and Kidder's[21] Formative; in Mexico, Vaillant's Middle Periods[22]; in Yucatan, Thompson's Formative[23] and Morley's Pre-Maya.[24] These include Zacatenco and Ticomán in highland Mexico, Lower Tres Zapotes on the east coast, Mamom and Chicanel in lowland Guatemala, Miraflores in highland Guatemala, and Playa de los Muertos in Honduras.

Technologies: probably domesticated maize, manioc, and other plants; local irrigation. Pottery; loom-weaving, probably in cotton; basketry (?); no metallurgy. Wattle-and-daub houses in Guatemala.

Social: Small, scattered settlements. Female figurines suggest a fertility cult. Temple mounds; funerary architecture; and beginnings of intellectual development, as evidenced by calendrical stelae of the Maya area, which appeared at the end of the era.

*Mesopotamia:* Childe's[25] Higher Barbarism of the Copper Age and beginnings of his Urban Revolution; beginnings of Albright's[26] Chalcolithic. In Mesopotamia: Sialk I, Mersian, Hassunan, Samarran, and Halafian.

Technologies: domesticated plants, probably wheat, barley, millet, and others; cattle, sheep, goats, pigs; some irrigation. Pottery; loom-weaving, probably in flax; basketry; metallurgy in gold and copper; possibly the wheel; rectangular, adobe houses.

Social: villages have local shrines. Religion involves female and animal figurines; male and female gods are represented.

*Egypt:* Faiyumian, Merimdean, Badarian, Amratian.

Technologies: wheat, barley; cattle, pigs, sheep, goats. Pottery; metallurgy in gold and copper; loom-weaving in linen; coiled basketry. Semi-subterranean, circular houses. Balsa (papyrus bundle) boats.

Social: clans or kin groups (?); captive slaves (?); female and animal figurines in religion; dog-sacrifice in burials.

*China:* Neolithic (Pre-Yang Shao, Yang Shao).

Technologies: millet, sorghum (?), rice, wheat; pigs; probably well-and-ditch irrigation. Pottery; loom-weaving in hemp (?); basketry; metallurgy in copper.

Social: small, semi-permanent settlements of circular pit-houses, possibly based on matrilineal lineages. Religion evidenced by pottery phalli; possibly human sacrifice and cannibalism.

## Era of Regional Development and Florescence

This era was marked by the emergence and florescence of regionally distinctive cultures. No new basic technologies were invented, but irrigation

---

[20] Armillas, 1948.   [21] Kidder, 1946.   [22] Vaillant, 1944.   [23] Thompson, 1943, 1945.
[24] Morley, 1946.   [25] Childe, 1946.   [26] Albright, 1946.

works were enlarged, thus releasing a larger portion of the population to develop arts and crafts and to further intellectual interests. Multi-community states arose.

States were still strongly theocratic, but inter-state competition and state expansion seem to have entailed some militarism. A class-structured society, which was foreshadowed in the previous era, now became fully established. The ruling class appears to have been predominantly theocratic, but it was likely that some status was accorded successful warriors. The priesthood now had sufficient leisure to develop astronomy, mathematics, and writing (these were little developed in Peru). The largest religious edifices were built, and the finest art and manufactures of any era were produced toward the end of this era, each region producing distinctive styles. These products were made by special artisans and were dedicated principally to the upper classes and to the temples. Trade attained important proportions, and improved transportational devices were introduced.

*Peru:* Willey's[27] Regional Classical; Strong's[28] Late Formative and Florescent; Bennett's[29] late Early Periods. Gallinazo and Mochica (Nazca in south Peru).

Technologies: maize, manioc, potatoes, sweet potatoes, calabashes, pumpkins, peanuts; llamas, alpacas. Inter-valley irrigation.

Social: large communities; population maximum; largest mounds, temples; fanged deity, and gods of agriculture, fishing, celestial phenomena, and places. Ruler was warrior-god. Hilltop forts were built. Regional states (entire valley or several valleys?). War captives, human sacrifice, human trophies. Status burial for the upper class.

Roads; probably llama-packing; ocean-going balsa boats with sails (?); trade.

Ideographic writing on beans (?); quipus. Finest art of all eras.

*Mesoamerica:* Armillas'[30] Florescent; Kidder's[31] Classical; Thompson's[32] Initial Series; Morley's[33] Old Empire. These include: Middle and Upper Tres Zapotes on the east coast; Teotihuacan and Monte Alban II and III in Mexico; Esperanza in highland Guatemala; and Tsakol and Tepeu in lowland Guatemala.

Technology: local irrigation, chinampas, and terracing in agriculture.

Social: dispersed settlements; local theocratic states that controlled all settlements of a valley or other natural regions. Population maximum (?).[34] Largest mounds and temples. Priestly hierarchy. Gods of rain, water, jaguar, serpent, quetzal. Child sacrifice (?); possibly ancestor worship (as evidenced by figurine portraits in Mexico, status burial in Guatemala). Militarism evidently restricted to raids, with some captive-taking.

Roads and causeways; widespread trade; (toy wheel).

Phonetic writing, mathematics, astronomy. Finest art of all eras.

*Mesopotamia:* Latter part of Albright's[35] Chalcolithic; Childe's[36] Urban Revolution and Early Bronze Age. These include: Obeidian (Al'Ubaid), Warkan–Tepe Gawra, and Jedmet Nasr.

---

[27] Willey, 1948.    [28] Strong, 1947.    [29] Bennett, 1946.    [30] Armillas, 1948.
[31] Kidder, 1946.    [32] Thompson, 1943, 1945.    [33] Morley, 1947.
[34] Cook, 1947.    [35] Albright, 1946.    [36] Childe, 1946.

Technologies: wheat, barley, millet, date palm, figs, grapes, sesame, onions, garlic, lettuce, melons, chick peas, horse beans; drained fields, large-scale irrigation. Wheel-made ceramics.

Social: urbanization began. Multi-community states, which were essentially theo-cratic, though rulers had also war power. Large palace-temples. Gods of agriculture. Some pressures or infiltration by foot-nomads.

Horse (?), chariot and four-wheeled wagon; balsa (reed bundle) boats; widespread trade.

Phonetic writing, mathematical systems, astronomy.

*Egypt:* Gerzian.

Technologies: farming as in Formative Era, though probably increased irrigation. Rectangular, above-ground, adobe houses.

Social: Tendency to urbanization; multi-community states, each with an associated animal god and under the rule of heads of principal lineages (?). Some warfare imple-ments expansion of state. Status burial shows a cult of the dead.

Sailing vessels; ass; considerable trade.

Beginnings of writing; calendrical and numerical systems.

Possibly the Semainian period and the beginnings of the Early Dynastic periods should be included in the Era of Regional Florescence in Egypt, for the temple cult appeared, class differentiation became definite, and phonetic writing, a calendrical sys-tem, and mathematics were developed. These features, however, continued to develop with little interruption into the era of Conquest and Empire.

*China:* "Hsia" (Black Pottery period) and Shang Dynasty.

Technologies: wheat, millet, rice, pig, cattle, sheep, in north; buffalo and chicken in south. Beginnings of public works in form of dikes; otherwise, local well-and-ditch irrigation were practiced. Bronze manufactures. Horse and chariot. Weaving in silk.

Social: local state, Wittfogel's "feudal" type, under which serfs cultivated the local ruler's land. Divine monarch; status burial in deep grave. Use of oracle bones to fore-cast rain and for other divination; dragon deity; human and animal sacrifice. Warfare arising from conflict over grazing lands[37] and from pressure of herding nomads.

Picture and ideographic writing. Finest esthetic expressions, especially in bronzes.

## Cyclical Conquests

The diagnostic features of this era are the emergence of large-scale mili-tarism, the extension of political and economic domination over large areas or empires, a strong tendency toward urbanization, and the construction of fortifications. In the social structure, priest-warriors constituted the ruling groups, usually under a divine monarch, whose importance is revealed in elab-orate status burial. Social classes now tended to become frozen into hereditary classes, in contrast to society of the previous era, which probably permitted individuals some upward mobility through personal achievements. Gods of war became prominent in the pantheon of deities.

There were no important technological changes. Bronze appeared in Peru,

---

[37] Creel, 1937b, p. 184.

Mesopotamia, and Egypt, and was used for weapons and ornaments, but it contributed little to the production of food or other goods. Iron, though not an iron-age culture, appeared in China. The principal change in manufactures was a strong trend toward standardization and mass production, with a concomitant sacrifice of esthetic freedom and variety. Large-scale trade within the empires, and even beyond, brought the beginnings of a special commercial class, but coinage and an efficient monetary system were not yet developed.

*Peru:* Willey's Expansion and Conquest; Strong's Fusion and Imperial periods; Bennett's Tiahuanaco, Late Periods, and Inca.

Technologies: as before, except that bronze was used for ornaments, weapons, and a few tools. By the Inca period, there was standardized, mass production.

Social: planned urban centers were constructed, and they drew off much population from the local communities. Under the Inca, social classes were finally frozen in a caste system, headed by the divine royal family. A priesthood and bureaucracy ruled the state, and placed levies on the commoners, but the local folk culture persisted. An ancestor cult occurred along with agricultural, place, and animal gods. The state was enlarged by wars of conquest, which perhaps started in the previous era and originated from population pressures. Populations were moved from place to place by imperial command.

*Mesoamerica:* Armillas' Militaristic Period (in Mexico, Toltec, Aztec, Monte Albán V, Tzintzuntzan Tarascan; and, in Yucatan, Mexican Absorption). Thompson's Mexican Period and Morley's New Empire in Yucatan. Kidder's Amatle and Pamplona in highland Guatemala.

Technologies: as before, except that metallurgy in copper and gold appeared, being used mainly for ornaments. There was extensive trade, and money, in the form of cacao beans, was used during the Aztec period.

Social: The population was increasingly concentrated in defensible sites, and special forts were constructed. Larger and larger areas were drawn into empires, and wealth was concentrated through tribute in the hands of the ruling classes. The king-priest had great military power. There were military classes, warrior societies, and slaves. Great population movements are evident in the inroads of Chichimecs into the Valley of Mexico, the Nahuatl migrations to Central America, and the Mexican invasion of Yucatan. Warfare was intensified, gods of war entered the pantheon, and human sacrifice became a major feature of religion.

*Mesopotamia:* Early Dynastic Sumerians to Dynasty of Accad.

Technologies: bronze was used for weapons, ornaments, and a few tools. There was standardized mass production, especially of goods used by commoners, and widespread trade, mainly for luxury items.

Social: Urban communities attained great size and served as military, political, religious, and commercial centers. The king combined religious and military leadership and controlled multicommunity states. Statuses were strongly differentiated: the king, representing the god (sometimes a war god), was supreme; priests and nobles tended to have hereditary status; farmers, artisans, and wage-earners were either attached to the temple or else worked on privately-owned lands; captives became slaves. Soldiers sometimes gained status. Gods included agricultural and local deities; the cult of the dead attained some importance, as shown in status burials.

*Egypt:* Early Dynasties, I–IV.

Technologies: Bronze was used for weapons and ornaments, and there was evidence of mass production and extensive trade.

Social: Planned cities were built. The god-king became the military and political head of large states, which were expanded through warfare, and he eclipsed the power of the priesthood. Social structure became rigid, hereditary nobles controlling great wealth. Warfare, probably originating in population pressures and dislocations throughout the Near East, was waged to create empires and to ward off invasions.

Theology was based on a pantheon of general gods, such as the Sun, on local animal gods, and on a cult of the dead. The last, combined somewhat with the first two, became predominant, as evidenced by the divine power of the king and by his status burial in pyramids.

*China:* Chou through Ming Dynasties. The culture center shifts south from the Yellow River to the Yangtze River,[38] while conquests, starting with the Chou Dynasty, culminate in Wittfogel's type of oriental absolute state[39] by the T'ang Dynasty.

Technologies: irrigation and water works develop under state control and become large scale under the Warring States; plow and fertilizer. Iron, glass, and other technologies diffuse from the west.

Social: the Chou Dynasty initiates the era of conquests. A divine ruler and bureaucracy control a state which is stratified into hereditary nobles with military and economic power, merchants, serfs, and some slaves. Cities develop as administrative, religious, and commercial centers.

## III. TRIAL FORMULATION OF DEVELOPMENTAL REGULARITIES OF EARLY CIVILIZATIONS

At the present time the difficulties in making any formulation of the development of early civilizations in the five principal centers of the world are obviously very great. Data on early periods are incomplete, not only because research has been limited but also because it has been directed toward special and restricted problems. Archeology has, until recently, paid comparatively little attention to settlement patterns, demographic trends, and sociological implications of its materials. Historians on the whole are more interested in the fate of particular societies than in culture and its development, and anthropologists have made comparatively little use of the data of written history. These difficulties mean primarily that any present formulation must be highly tentative.

The successive eras in each of the five principal centers of early civilizations appear to have had similar diagnostic features which, arranged chronologically, might be considered as a superficial formulation of regularities. Such a formulation, however, would fail to provide a satisfactory and generally valid functional explanation of cause-and-effect relationships between phenomena.

---

[38] Chi, 1936.     [39] Wittfogel, 1935.

To provide deeper explanations, it is necessary to make cause-and-effect relationships as explicit as possible and to test the explanations offered for the
sequence in each center by the data of other centers. This purpose is consistent with the comparative approach of anthropology, and it is far more important to achieve a common sense of problem than to construct enduring formulations.

The formulation here offered excludes all areas except the arid and semi-
arid centers of ancient civilizations. In the irrigation areas, environment, production, and social patterns had similar functional and developmental interrelationships. The productivity of farming was limited only by the amount
of water that could be used in irrigation. Metal tools and animal-drawn
ploughs, though essential to maximum efficiency of farming in forest or grassland areas, could not increase the yield of irrigation areas beyond the limits
imposed by water supply.

Early civilizations occurred also in such tropical rain-forest areas as southern Asia and Yucatan. Yucatan appears to fit the formulation made for the
more arid areas to the extent that its sequences were very similar to those of
Mesoamerica generally. Farming in Yucatan, however, required slash-and-
burn rather than irrigation techniques, and the rural population must have
been very scattered. It is possible, therefore, that the Maya were able to
develop a high civilization only because they enjoyed an unusually long period
of peace; for their settlement pattern would seem to have been too vulnerable
to warfare. Yucatan, consequently, should perhaps be excluded from the
present formulation. In southeastern Asia, the environment is extremely
humid, presenting the difficulties of rain forests and also requiring large
drainage projects. And in both areas, the civilizations appear to have been
later than and in part derived from those of the irrigation areas.

The Era of Incipient Agriculture in the irrigation centers is very little
known, but evidence from Peru, Mesopotamia, and Egypt suggests that it
lasted a very long time. Farming was at first supplementary to hunting and
gathering, and the social groups were consequently small and probably semi-
nomadic. Technologies differed little from those of the earlier hunting and
gathering periods. By the end of this era, farming supported permanent communities, and new technologies began to appear.

A local community, or "folk," culture[40] took form during the next era. The
principal crops and animals were brought under domestication, but irrigation
was undertaken only on a small, local scale. In subsequent eras, agricultural
production increased as irrigation works were developed, the only limit being
available land and water, especially the latter. The animal-drawn plough,
which appeared in the Old World much later, during the Era of Cyclical Con-

---

[40] This may be considered to have had the general characteristics of Redfield's "Folk Society"
(1947).

quests, and which was unknown in prehistoric America, no doubt released a certain portion of the population from farm work, but neither it nor iron tools, which appeared still later, could increase production beyond the limits of water supply. Population consequently increased as irrigation works were developed to their maximum. For this reason, the Old World possession of draught animals and the plough does not affect the present formulation.

During the Formative Era, all centers of civilization developed ceramics, loom-weaving, basketry, metallurgy (except Mesoamerica), and the construction of houses and religious edifices. These technologies soon came to be used for two kinds of goods: first, objects that served the simple, domestic—that is, essentially biological—needs of the common folk; second, highly elaborate, stylized goods that served the socially derived needs as well as the more basic needs of the theocratic class. In simple form, some of these technologies spread beyond the areas of irrigation.

Subsequent to the Formative Era, no very important technological advances were made until the Iron Age. Metallurgy ran through similar sequences everywhere (except in Mesoamerica), starting with work in copper and gold and finally achieving bronze. Copper and tin were so rare that the use of bronze was largely limited to ornaments and weapons, while tools of stone, bone, wood, and shell were used for daily chores. Improvement in the other technologies consisted of embellishments and refinements that enhanced their esthetic qualities and produced varied products; but there were no important new inventions.

Transportation improved in successive eras. Domesticated animals were first probably used for packing in all centers except in Mesoamerica, which lacked species suitable for domestication. Wheeled vehicles appeared in the Old World during the Era of Regional Florescence. The wheel was evidently used on toys during the same era in Mesoamerica,[41] but its failure to be used in transportation perhaps may be explained by the absence of draught animals. The importance of transportation increased as states grew larger and as trade expanded. Although draught animals and wheels, which were used on war chariots before they were used on carts and wagons, gave the Old World some technical advantage, every New World center developed roads, boats, and canals to a degree of efficiency which enabled them to achieve states as large as those of the Old World.

The general sequence of social, religious, and military patterns ran a similar course in each center of civilization, and a generally valid formulation is possible. Certain problems which cannot yet be answered will be stated subsequently.

In the Era of Incipient Agriculture it is reasonable to suppose that socio-

---

[41] Ekholm, 1946.

political groups were as varied in nature as they are today among the hunting and gathering peoples of arid areas.

At the beginning of the Formative Era, the sociopolitical unit was a small house cluster, which probably consisted of a kin group or lineage. As population increased, new clusters evidently budded off and established themselves in unsettled lands. In the course of time, as flood plains became densely settled and as need arose to divert water through canals to drier land, collaboration on irrigation projects under some coordinating authority became necessary. That the need was met by the rise to power of a theocratic class is shown by the appearance toward the end of the Formative Era of evidence of religious domination of society, for example, ceremonial centers, such as mounds and temples, and a large number of religious objects. Farming required careful reckoning of the seasons, considerable ritual, and worship of agricultural gods, tasks which necessitated a special priesthood. During the Formative Era, a small number of house clusters were dispersed around a ceremonial center and were ruled by a priesthood. The priesthood provided centralized control of irrigation and new patterns of group religion. Society became differentiated into theocratic and common classes.

In the Formative Era, state warfare was probably of minor importance. There is little archeological evidence of militarism, and it is likely that warfare was limited to raids. As long as there was ample land for the expanding population, competition for terrain cannot have been important. Because pastoral nomads during this era were unmounted and probably had not become very numerous, they cannot have been a great threat. In the Near East, they probably had asses, cattle, sheep and goats, but did not ride horses and camels until the Iron age,[42] and horse riding did not appear in China until the Era of Dark Ages or Warring States.

The precise patterning, content, and history of religion, which supplied the socially integrating factor, varied with each center of civilization. In some centers, such as Egypt, China, Peru, and Guatemala, elaborate burials for certain individuals suggest a cult of the dead or ancestor worship, which elevated these persons to the status of god-priests while living and to the status of gods after death. Other kinds of gods are represented by animal, place, and fertility deities. In some instances, the priesthood may have developed from an earlier class of shamans.

The particular religious patterns of each center arose from complex factors of local development and diffusion, and they gave local distinctiveness to the cultures. In terms of the present formulation, however, these differences are secondary in importance to the fact that in all cases a national religion and a priestly class developed because increasing populations, larger irrigation works,

---

[42] Albright, 1946, pp. 120–123.

and greater need for social coordination called upon religion to supply the integrating factor. The very great importance of religion at the end of the Formative Era is proved by the effort devoted to the construction of temple mounds, temples, palaces, and tombs, and to the special production of religious ornaments, sculpture, and various material appurtenances of the priesthood and temples. It was the priesthood which, devoting full time to religious matters, now laid the foundations of astronomy, writing, and mathematics in all centers.

The Era of Regional Florescence fulfilled the potentialities of the Formative Era. Communities were welded into small states, which, however, continued to be essentially theocratic, for archeological remains of this era are predominantly of a religious nature. The largest mounds, temples, and tombs (mortuary pyramids and burial mounds) of any eras were constructed. Intellectual trends were fulfilled in the development of phonetic writing, numerical systems, and accurate calendars. Even Peru, which never achieved developed writing, may have used an ideographic system at this time.[43] Ceramics, metallurgy, weaving, work in precious stones, and sculpture attained their highest peak of esthetic expression and their most distinctive local stylization.

The relation of militarism to the enlargement of irrigation works and the expansion of states during the Era of Regional Florescence is not clear. Population, irrigation works, and states all increased in size until the end of the era. In Mesoamerica, it is generally believed[44] that the states were peaceful and theocratic, and Cook[45] believes that population reached its maximum at this time, decreasing in the subsequent era. In this case, a priesthood without the backing of armed force was able to create multi-community states, though the extent of irrigation works at this time is not well known. In other areas, it appears that some militarism was present in the Era of Regional Florescence, and that without warfare the rulers could not have increased the size of states and thereby of irrigation works. In northern Peru, warfare was definitely present in the Era of Regional Florescence, and in China, warfare, arising from conflicts over grazing lands[46] enabled local rulers to extend their authority over subject states,[47] perhaps facilitating the enlargement of irrigation works. Irrigation, however, did not attain maximum size in China until true empires appeared in the following era of Cyclical Conquests.[48] Thus, in China the population maximum came only when militarism achieved empire-wide irrigation projects. In Mesopotamia and Egypt, warfare also appeared during the Era of Regional Florescence, and it was no doubt instrumental in enlarging states, but true kingdoms or empires did not appear until the following era. The re-

---

[43] Larco Hoyle, 1946, p. 175.
[44] Armillas, 1948; Kidder *et al.*, 1946; Thompson, 1943, 1945; Morley, 1946.
[45] Cook, 1947.        [46] Creel, 1937, p. 184.        [47] Bishop, 1942, p. 20.
[48] Chi, 1936; Wittfogel, 1938, 1939–1940.

lation of irrigation and population to warfare and state size in Egypt are not clear, but if Childe[49] is correct in believing that warfare resulted from competition for lands as well as from the pressures of nomads, it would seem that population limits may have been reached.

This seeming contradiction cannot be resolved at present, but it may be suspected either that Mesoamerica had unusually powerful priests or else that the population maximum was not really reached until after the Era of Regional Florescence, when militarism increased the size of states and consequently of irrigation works. In all centers, a temporary decrease of population probably followed the initiation of large-scale warfare.

Social structure seems to have been very similar in all centers of civilization. The local community retained its folk culture, that is, its social structure, local shrines, agricultural practices, and the like, and its members constituted the commoners. Rulers were predominantly priests, though they began to acquire some military functions. It is possible that war achievements gave status to special individuals and that war captives formed a slave class, but as the existence of true economic slavery in native America is in doubt, the social role of captives and the problem of the origin and nature of slavery are open problems which are excluded from consideration here.

The Era of Cyclical Conquests was one of comparatively few culture changes, except those produced by warfare. It initiated a succession of empires and then local states or dark ages that alternated in a fairly stereotyped pattern until the Iron Age and Industrial Era brought cultural influences from other areas. In each center, large scale warfare, which probably originated from internal population pressures, from competition for resources, and from the pressures of outside nomads, was an instrument in creating true empires and starting dynasties. As the empires grew, irrigation works were increased to the limits of water supply and population also increased. After reaching a peak, marked by a temporary florescence of culture, population pressure and abuse of the common people brought rebellion, which destroyed the empires and returned society to local states and a period of dark ages. Irrigation works were neglected and population decreased. New conquests initiated another cycle.

The cyclical phenomena are strikingly illustrated in China[50] where, during 1500 years of the Era of Cyclical Conquests, each of the four major peaks of empires and dynasties coincided with a population peak.[51] These were separated by periods of internal strife and local autonomy. The series of empires in the Near East, which began in Mesopotamia with the early Dynasty of Sumer and in Egypt with the Dynastic period, ran through cycles generally comparable with those of China and lasted until the northern Mediterranean

---

[49] Childe, 1946.      [50] Wittfogel, 1938, 1946.      [51] Ta Chen, 1946, pp. 4–6.

states of the Iron Age brought portions of the Near East under periodic conquests. In Peru, the widespread Tiahuanaco culture and the later Inca Empire probably represent two cycles of empire growth, while in Mexico, the first cycle, that of the Aztec conquests, had not run its course when the Spaniards conquered America.

In the Era of Conquest, militarism produced several important social changes. Towns, which previously had been ceremonial, administrative, and trading centers, now became large walled cities, and special forts were built to afford refuge to the dispersed farm settlements. A true military class appeared in the social hierarchy, and warrior-priests ruled the states and empires. War gods became prominent in the pantheons of state deities.

In this era, all aspects of culture were increasingly regimented at the expense of creative effort. There were sharpened differences in social classes, such as nobles, priests, warriors, commoners, slaves, and stronger differentiation of occupational groups. Laws were codified, learning was systematized (astronomy, theology, mathematics, medicine, writing), art became standardized, and goods were mass-produced by specialists.

Specialized production of commodities and wide-spread trade laid a basis for commercialism, but a free commercial class, factory production, and wage labor could not emerge until economy achieved a strong monetary basis, private property, and specialized cash crops, and until trade was disengaged from the system of state tribute and freed from state control. Though foreshadowed everywhere, this did not occur in the Near East until the Iron Age. In China, the development of private property in land and a system of money and taxation was not sufficient to free economy from the control of powerful states, which existed by virtue of grain taxes which their water works made possible.[52] In the New World, this era was not reached until the Spanish Conquest.

The developments of the Iron Age and the Industrial Era are beyond the scope of the present inquiry. Iron appeared in China in the Era of Cyclical Conquests, but it did not revolutionize the patterns of basic production and social structure as it did in the forested areas of the northern Mediterranean.

### IV. SUMMARY AND CONCLUSIONS

The above analysis may be briefly summarized.

In arid and semi-arid regions, agriculture may be carried on by means of flood-plain and irrigation farming, which does not require metal tools. As irrigation works are developed, population will increase until the limits of water are reached. Political controls become necessary to manage irrigation and other communal projects. As early societies were strongly religious, individuals with supernatural powers—lineage heads, shamans, or special priests—formed a

---

[52] Wittfogel, 1935, 1939–1940.

theocratic ruling class, which governed first multi-house-cluster communities and later multi-community states.

The increasing productivity of farming released considerable labor from subsistence activities, and new technologies were developed—basketry, loom-weaving, pottery, metallurgy, domestic and religious construction, and transportational facilities. Products made for home use were simple and utilitarian; those made for the theocratic class and for religious purposes became increasingly rich and varied, and they required an increasing proportion of total productive efforts.

When the limits of agricultural productivity under a given system of irrigation were reached, population pressures developed and interstate competition for land and for produce of all kinds began. The resulting warfare led to the creation of empires, warrior classes, and military leaders. It also led to enlargement of irrigation works and to a further increase of population. But the powerful military empires regimented all aspects of culture, and few new inventions were made. Consequently, each culture entered an era of rising and falling empires, each empire achieving a peak of irrigation, population, and political organization and a temporary florescence, but giving way to a subsequent period of dark ages.

The Iron Age gave the Old World a revolutionary technology, but, as iron tools cannot increase water supply, the irrigation areas were little affected, except as they fell under the empires of the north Mediterranean. Iron Age cultures developed in the forested areas of Europe, which had been exploited only with difficulty under the old technology. The New World never reached an Iron Age in precolumbian times. Instead, the Spanish Conquest brought it an Iron Age culture from the Old World, and native culture development was abruptly ended just after it had entered the Era of Cyclical Conquests.

The above formulation is rough, cursory, and tentative. It applies only to the early centers of world civilization. The eras are not "stages," which in a world evolutionary scheme would apply equally to desert, arctic, grassland, and woodland areas. In these other kinds of areas, the functional interrelationship of subsistence patterns, population, settlements, social structure, cooperative work, warfare, and religion had distinctive forms and requires special formulations.

The principal grounds for questioning the present formulation will, I suspect, be that diffusion between the centers of civilization in each hemisphere can be demonstrated. The relative chronology of the eras (Chart II) fits a diffusionist explanation perfectly. The essential question, however, is just what diffusion amounts to as an explanation. There is no doubt about the spread of domesticated plants and animals and little doubt about the diffusion of many technologies, art styles, and details of both material and non-material culture. Proof of diffusion, however, lies in the unique qualities of secondary features, not in the basic types of social, economic, and religious patterns. The latter could be attributed to diffusion only by postulating mass migration or far-flung conquests.

If people borrow domesticated plants and agricultural patterns, it is evident that population will increase in favorable areas. How shall dense, stable populations organize their sociopolitical relations? Obviously, they will not remain inchoate mobs until diffused patterns have taught them how to live together. (And even diffused patterns had to originate somewhere for good and sufficient reasons.) In densely settled areas, internal needs will produce an orderly interrelationship of environment, subsistence patterns, social groupings, occupational specialization, and over-all political, religious, and perhaps military integrating factors. These interrelated institutions do not have unlimited variability, for they must be adapted to the requirements of subsistence patterns established in particular environments; they involve a cultural ecology. Traits whose uniqueness is proof of their diffusion are acceptable if they are congruent with the basic socio-economic institutions. They give uniqueness and local color, and they may help crystallize local patterns in distinctive ways, but they cannot per se produce the underlying conditions of or the need for greater social and political organization. It is therefore possible to concede wide diffusion of particulars within the hemispheres and even between the hemispheres without having to rely upon diffusion as the principal explanation of cultural development.

We have attempted here to present a conception of culture and a methodology for formulating the regularities of cultural data which are consistent with scientific purpose. The data are those painstakingly gathered and arranged spacially and temporally by culture history. Thorough attention to cultural differences and particulars is necessary if typology is to be adequate and valid, but historical reconstructions need not be the sole objective of anthropology. Strong observed that "The time is coming when the rich ethnological and archeological record of the New World can be compared in full detail and time perspective with similar records from Europe, Egypt, Mesopotamia, India, China, and Siberia. When such comparative data are in hand the generalizations that will emerge may well revolutionize our concept of culture history and culture process over the millennia."[53] Any generalizations or formulations must be subject to frequent revision by new data, for, as Kroeber remarks,[54] "Detailed case-by-case analyses are . . . called for if interpretations are not to become vitiated over generalizations which more and more approach formulas." At the same time, it is obvious that the minutiae of culture history will never be completely known and that there is no need to defer formulations until all archeologists have laid down their shovels and all

---

[53] Strong, 1943, p. 34.        [54] Kroeber, 1940, p. 477.

ethnologists have put away their notebooks. Unless anthropology is to interest itself mainly in the unique, exotic, and non-recurrrent particulars, it is necessary that formulations be attempted no matter how tentative they may be. It is formulations that will enable us to state new kinds of problems and to direct attention to new kinds of data which have been slighted in the past. Fact-collecting of itself is insufficient scientific procedure; facts exist only as they are related to theories, and theories are not destroyed by facts—they are replaced by new theories which better explain the facts. Therefore, criticisms of this paper which concern facts alone and which fail to offer better formulations are of no interest.

COLUMBIA UNIVERSITY
NEW YORK CITY, N.Y.

## BIBLIOGRAPHY

ALBRIGHT, WILLIAM FOXWELL
   1946   *From the Stone Age to Christianity.* Baltimore.
ANDERSSON, J. G.
   1934   *Children of the Yellow Earth.* London.
ARMILLAS, PEDRO
   1948   A Sequence of Cultural Development in Mesoamerica. In: *A Reappraisal of Peruvian Archaeology*, Soc. Amer. Arch., Mem. 4.
BENNETT, WENDELL C.
   1946   *The Andean Highlands: An Introduction.* Handbook of South American Indians (J. H. Steward, Editor). Bur. Amer. Ethnol. Bull. 143, Vol. 2, pp. 1–60.
BISHOP, C. W.
   1942   *Origin of the Far Eastern Civilizations.* Smithsonian Institution War Background Studies, No. 1.
CHI, CH'AO-TING
   1936   *Key Economic Areas in Chinese History.* London.
CHILDE, V. GORDON
   1934   *New Light on the Most Ancient East.* New York.
   1946   *What Happened in History.* New York (Pelican Books).
COOK, S. F.
   1947   The Interrelation of Population, Food Supply, and Building in Pre-Conquest Central Mexico. *Amer. Antiquity*, Vol. 13, pp. 45–52.
CREEL, H. G.
   1937a   *The Birth of China.* New York.
   1937b   *Studies in Early Chinese Culture.* Baltimore.
EKHOLM, GORDON F.
   1946   Wheeled Toys in Mexico. *Amer. Antiquity*, Vol. 11, pp. 222–227.
ELLIOTT-SMITH, G.
   1929   *Human History.* New York
GLADWIN, HAROLD S.
   1947   *Men Out of Asia.* New York.
KIDDER, ALFRED V.
   1945   Excavations at Kaminaljuyú, Guatemala. *Amer. Antiquity*, Vol. 11, pp. 65–75.

KIDDER, ALFRED V., JESSE D. JENNINGS and EDWIN M. SHOOK
    1946  *Excavations at Kaminaljuyú.* Carnegie Institution of Washington, Publ. No. 561.
KROEBER, A. L.
    1940  The Present Status of Americanistic Problems. In: *The Maya and Their Neighbors*, pp. 460–487. New York.
    1944  *Peruvian Archaeology in 1942.* Viking Fund Publ. Anthrop., No. 4.
LARCO HOYLE, RAFAEL
    1946  A Culture Sequence for the North Coast of Peru. Handbook of South American Indians (J. H. Steward, Editor). Bur. Amer. Ethnol. Bull. 143, Vol. 2, pp. 149–173.
LESSER, ALEXANDER
    1939  Research Procedure and Laws of Culture. *Philosophy of Science*, Vol. 6, pp. 345–355.
LOWIE, ROBERT H.
    1925  *Primitive Society.* New York.
    1936  Cultural Anthropology: A Science. *Amer. Journ. Soc.*, Vol. 42, pp. 301–320.
MALINOWSKI, BRONISLAW
    1944  *A Scientific Theory of Culture.* Univ. North Carolina Press.
MORGAN, LEWIS H.
    1910  *Ancient Society.* Chicago.
MORLEY, SYLVANUS G.
    1946  *The Ancient Maya.* Stanford Univ. Press.
PERRY, W. J.
    1926  *Children of the Sun.* London
REDFIELD, ROBERT
    1941  *The Folk Culture of Yucatan.* Univ. Chicago Press.
    1947  The Folk Culture. *Journ. Amer. Soc.*, Vol. 52, pp. 293–308.
STEWARD, JULIAN H.
    1936  The Economic and Social Basis of Primitive Bands. In: *Essays in Honor of A. L. Kroeber.* Berkeley, California.
    1937  Ecological Aspects of Southwestern Society. *Anthropos*, Vol. 32, pp. 87–104.
    1938  *Basin-Plateau Aboriginal Socio-political Groups.* Bur. Amer. Ethnol. Bull. 120.
    1940  Native Cultures of the Intermontane (Great Basin) Area. *Essays in Historical Anthropology of North America.* Smithsonian Miscl. Coll., Vol. 100, pp. 445–498.
    1947  American Culture History in the Light of South America. *Southwest Journ. Anthrop.*, Vol. 3, pp. 85–107.
    1948  A Functional-Developmental Classification of the American High Cultures. In: *A Reappraisal of Peruvian Archaeology*, Soc. Amer. Arch. Mem. 4.
STEWARD, JULIAN H., and FRANK M. SETZLER
    1938  Function and Configuration in Archaeology. *Amer. Antiquity*, Vol. 4, pp. 4–10.
STRONG, WM. DUNCAN
    1936  Anthropological Theory and Archaeological Fact. *Essays in Honor of A. L. Kroeber*, pp. 359–370. Berkeley.
    1943  *Cross Sections of New World Prehistory.* Smithsonian Misc. Coll., Vol. 104, No. 2.
    1947  Finding the Tomb of a Warrior-God. *National Geographic Magazine*, April, pp. 453–482.
THOMPSON, J. ERIC
    1943  A Trial Survey of the Southern Maya Area. *Amer. Antiquity*, Vol. 9, pp. 106–134.
    1945  A Survey of the Northern Maya Area. *Ibid.*, Vol. 11, pp. 2–24.
TA CHEN
    1946  *Population in Modern China.* Univ. Chicago Press.

VAILLANT, GEORGE C.

  1944   *The Aztecs of Mexico*. New York.

WENLEY, A. G., and JOHN A. POPE

  1944   *China*. Smithsonian Institution War Background Studies, No. 20.

WHITE, LESLIE A.

  1943   Energy and the Evolution of Culture. *Amer. Anthropologist*, Vol. 45, pp. 335–356.

  1945   Diffusion vs. Evolution: an Anti-Evolutionist Fallacy. *Ibid.*, Vol. 47, pp 339–356.

  1947   Evolutionary Stages, Progress, and the Evaluation of Cultures. *Southwest Journ. Anthrop.*, Vol. 3, pp. 165–192.

  1947   The Expansion of the Scope of Science. *Journ. Washington Acad. Sci.*, Vol. 37, pp. 181–210.

WILLEY, GORDON R.

  1948   New World Cultures. Byron Cummings Anniv. Volume.

WITTFOGEL, KARL A.

  1935   The Foundations and Stages of Chinese Economic History. *Zeitschrift für Sozialforschung*, Vol. 4, pp. 26–60. Paris.

  1938   Die Theorie der Orientalischen Gesellschaft. *Ibid.*, Vol. 7, Nos. 1–2. Paris.

  1939–1940   *The Society of Prehistoric China*. Studies in Philosophy and Social Science. Institute of Soc. Research, Vol. 8 (1939), pp. 138–186, New York, 1940.

  1946   General Introduction (to *History of Chinese Society. Liao*, by Karl A. Wittfogel and Fêng Chia-Shêng). Amer. Philos. Soc., Trans., Vol. 36, pp. 1–35.

# AMERICAN ANTHROPOLOGIST

VOL. 51          OCTOBER-DECEMBER, 1949          NO. 4, PART 1

## NAVAHO AND ZUNI VETERANS: A STUDY OF CONTRASTING MODES OF CULTURE CHANGE

*By* JOHN ADAIR *and* EVON VOGT

IN A recent field study of Navaho and Zuni veterans of World War II, the writers discovered a number of significant contrasts in the attitudes of the two tribes toward the war situation and its aftermath.[1] Although we both went into the field to analyze acculturation with reference to the returning veterans, Adair (at Zuni) found himself studying a "nativistic reaction" rather than a change in the direction of white patterns of culture. The problem became even more challenging when we discovered that although the veterans from the two tribes experienced the same range and kinds of culture contact while they were in the armed forces, there were important differences in the meaning of this contact and in the ways in which the Navaho and Zuni communities responded to the returning veterans at the end of the war. The Navaho veterans have tended to be regarded as potential forces for constructive change even by the most conservative Navaho leaders; the Zuni veterans have tended to be regarded as forces for destructive change and have been forced to accept the traditional Zuni values or to leave the pueblo.

Our objective in this paper is to describe some of the varying modes of responses of the Zuni and Navaho to the war situation, especially with reference to the departure and return of the veterans; to suggest how these responses are related to the historical development of the two tribes and to contrasting patterns of Zuni and Navaho culture at the present time; and to delineate some of the mechanisms of cultural dynamics revealed by a comparative analysis of the two cases.

### THE ZUNI VETERANS

Between February, 1941, and March, 1946, a total of 213 Zuni men left their pueblo for war service. This number represents approximately 10 per cent

[1] This paper is based on field research carried on by Adair at Zuni from June, 1947, to January 1948, and by Vogt in the Ramah Navaho area from June, 1947 to March, 1948. Our data come from life histories of thirteen Navaho veterans and six Zuni veterans, from extensive interviews with older Navaho and Zuni leaders, and from daily observations made during the course of the field work. We are both indebted to the Social Science Research Council for the financial support of this research. The paper has benefited from the criticism and suggestions of David Aberle, Fred Eggan, Allan Holmberg, Clyde Kluckhohn, Alexander and Dorothea Leighton, and Morris Opler.

547

of the total population of the village which was 2,205 in 1941.[2] An even larger number of men would have been drafted if the governor of the pueblo, his civil council, and the council of high priests had not ordered the tribal secretary to write a letter to the Selective Service Board in Gallup, New Mexico, requesting the deferment of men who were in religious offices of both short and lifetime tenure.[3] Subsequently the United Pueblo Agency office in Albuquerque supported the Zuni in their request and a classification of 4-D, used to designate clergy-in-training, was given to these religious leaders. An advisory board for registrants consisting of two Indian Service officials and one trader was set up in the village. The council of priests then made immediate appeal for deferment to them, and they passed on recommendations to the local draft board.

The Zuni capitalized on this situation and an ever-increasing number of deferments were requested by the heads of the various priesthoods. As a result, government policy was modified and the Zuni were asked to defer only priests who were serving for life, and only older men or young boys not subject to the draft were to be selected for roles in the important annual ceremony, Shalako. The Zuni reacted to this by selecting even more draft age men for these positions than before.

Nor did the matter end when the men were drafted. Zuni soldiers requested furloughs from training camps to be present at Shalako and other rituals. After the cessation of hostilities the council of priests, leaders of certain curing societies, and family heads urged Zuni soldiers to obtain furloughs and come back to the pueblo for religious functions.[4]

The result of all this was an increase in religious activity during the war years and later, and a wider participation in ritual than before the war. As one informant put it in speaking of a young member of the *koyemshi*, "He wanted to get some ceremonial position to keep from being drafted, and they put him with the *koyemshi*. Now he is in that job for life." Certain ceremonies that have not been performed in years were revived.[5]

Prior to leaving the village the draftees were given a brief blessing ceremony known as *eulak$^y$a* at which the members of the priestly council said prayers to protect them. This ceremony was not given at the outset when the first men

---

[2] Official census, U.S.I.S. files, Zuni-Sub Agency, Black Rock, N. Mex.

[3] The importance of this request is indicated by the fact that the high priests thumb-printed the letter. In terms of ideal patterns the priests do not enter into transactions with government officials. "Civil law and relations with aliens, especially the United States Government, are delegated to the secular officers appointed by the council" (Bunzel, 1932, p. 478).

[4] The Zuni families from which the priests are selected probably made a greater effort to keep their boys from going to war, as well as attempts to get them back to the village sooner, than those families which were less important in the religious hierarchy.

[5] One of these is the scalp dance, performed in 1945 when a bow-priest was installed, prior to that in 1937, and before that in 1921. Another is *owinahaiye*, which according to Parsons was last given in 1910. (*See* Parsons, 1939, p. 881.)

were drafted, but after a lapse of time when pressure was brought to bear on the one surviving bow-priest, the traditional war leader. In all probability this ceremony had not been given in many years, as there had been no need for it with the abeyance of war practices.

Four out of five men, questioned in regard to traditional religious observance when they were away from Zuni, said that they carried sacred prayer meal with them. In at least two instances their families sent on additional quantities of the meal, or supplied their sons with it if they had failed to take it with them when they left the pueblo. The meal was used in various ways. One informant reported that he used it weekly, and another buried it at the suggestion of his mother who wrote to him: "Sprinkle a little every morning, or if you miss, then in the evening, and that meal will last six months. If you are ashamed to do that, then dig a hole and say the prayers there."

Several of the same informants carried amulets consisting of arrow-heads, bits of fox-tail grass and other objects with protective power. All five of these men said their prayers in the Zuni language under the tension of combat even if they did not have prayer meal with them.

Prayers were said by the priests in the village for the protection of those away from the village. A member of one of the minor rain priesthoods said:

> The priests even though they didn't go off to war spent a good deal of their time praying for the successful return of the men, as well as for rain. That is why so few of the Zuni men were killed.

Communication with the pueblo by mail served not only the individual religious needs of the Zuni serviceman but also as a channel for pueblo news and gossip. One informant reported that he asked a close friend to write him if his wife paid attention to other men while he was away. Many divorces resulted from such news carried by mail.[6] News of a political fight in the village which resulted in the impeachment of the Zuni governor reached Zuni men stationed on many battle fronts.[7]

The return to the pueblo was also attended by ceremonial behavior, but of a very attenuated form as compared to the Navaho. A cleansing rite, *hanasema isuʔwaha* (bad luck get rid of it), was performed for all but a few of the veterans before they returned to the pueblo. This ceremony, presumably part of the older war procedure, took place either at the Reservation border or at the edge of the Zuni river about a mile from the village. Cedar bark was waved over the head of the returning soldier, a ritual means of purification used in war and curing rites.[8] The ceremony was conducted by a male member of one of the

---

[6] In several instances the parents of the soldiers reported the philandering of the wives in order to have allotment checks transferred to their names.

[7] This letter-writing engaged in by all of the Zuni men away from the village is, of course, an indication of the fact that the level of literacy is high among those under thirty-five years of age.

[8] Bunzel, 1932, p. 506.

curing societies, preferably a member of either the mother's or the father's clan, and frequently a member of either the ant society or the clown society, *Newekwe*. Traditionally both of these societies had war functions.[9] One veteran was met in Gallup by his mother who refused to touch her son, even in greeting, until he had undergone this rite. This ceremony was the only ritually prescribed technique by which the returning veterans were purified upon their return home.[10]

The months following the discharge of the Zuni servicemen was a period of marked dysphoria in the village. The anxieties of the veterans were manifest in a great increase in drunkenness and restless behavior. Trips to town were more frequent. Many of the veterans would not work on their family farms, at sheep camp, or at their trade as silversmiths. The older generation was greatly concerned over the peculiar behavior of these men. Some of the veterans were probably suffering from combat fatigue, at least in a mild form. One such veteran called out in his sleep and developed stomach cramps. At his parents' request a curer was called in who sucked out an object which they thought had been shot into the body by a witch. The veteran was as convinced of this fact as were his parents.

During this period of tension and anxiety the curers were summoned to attend many of the veterans and there has been a resulting increase in the numbers of men awaiting initiation into the curing societies. By 1948 there was a change in the overt behavior of the Zuni veterans. Drinking had fallen off, an increasing number of the men had returned to their work in the fields and homes; many men who had been without wives when they returned from the outside were now married. Social reintegration was taking place.

Some of the processes whereby the Zuni veterans were reintegrated into the social framework were gossip, rumor and ridicule. An older veteran who belongs to one of the most acculturated families wanted to establish a branch of the American Legion in Zuni. It was not long before gossip to the effect that he was going to use the money collected in dues for his own ends grew into a rumor campaign. After a few meetings, indifferently attended, the project was dropped. Terminal leave pay which could be collected upon application to the War Department was rumored by some of the elders to be a method of getting Zuni men into debt to the government, and would have to be paid off by more military service. One of the veterans was seen in the village dressed in a double breasted suit. Members of the community ridiculed him and accused him of "trying to be a big shot, trying to act like a white man."

The most dreaded of all rumors is to be labeled as a witch. Peculiar be-

---

[9] For ant society war functions *see* Parsons, 1939, p. 192; for *Newekwe* war functions *see* Parsons, 1939, p. 227.

[10] Since leaving the pueblo Adair has heard that the veterans were all assembled in the plaza and ritually whipped, another Pueblo method of exorcising evil. This report needs further checking.

havior and aggressive action which makes the individual stand out from the community may elicit this rumor. In Zuni belief conspicuous conduct is also to be avoided because it attracts the attention of witches and their malevolent action. Witches are believed to be jealous of those with wealth. An informant said that he had considered opening a store in the village but had not done so because he was afraid of those "jealous people."[11]

An important aspect of the postwar period at Zuni has been a drift of the younger men from the pueblo—twenty-three of their number were living on the outside in the summer of 1947. There are good indications that a selective process is at play now as in the past. Those who leave the village and live on the outside are the ones who are the least willing to conform with the sentiments of the group and who are made to feel uncomfortable by the gossip occasioned by their deviant behavior. To get along in Zuni society at least outward conformance is necessary. The result is that many of the most "progressive" members of the pueblo leave the village and are thus lost as agents of acculturation.

## THE NAVAHO VETERANS

This description of Navaho attitudes toward the war situation and the veterans is focused primarily on the Ramah Navaho who occupy an area just to the east of the Zuni reservation. The Ramah Navaho now number approximately 600, and there are thirteen veterans in this Navaho group.

The attitude of the Navaho toward the war situation contrasted sharply with that of the Zuni. Although one could not describe the attitude as one of complete enthusiasm and whole-hearted co-operation, there was not the disinterest in and the reluctance to go to war that was so characteristic of the Zuni. Even before the United States actively entered the war, observers in Navaho country reported that there was great interest on the part of the Navahos in the events in Europe and Asia which led up to our participation in the war. Navahos who lived many miles from the railroad, read no newspapers, and spoke no English would constantly ask: "What is happening in the war?" "Who is winning, the Germans or the English?"[12]

After the American declaration of war, there were almost 800 Navaho enlistments among the total of approximately 3,600 Navahos who served in the armed forces.[13] Furthermore, there were (as far as we know) no formal efforts

---

[11] An analysis of the functioning of witchcraft in Zuni society is reserved for fuller treatment in a later paper. Suffice it to say that during this period of tension, witchcraft accusations and beliefs were more frequent than twenty years ago. Ruth Benedict reported to Adair (December, 1947) that when she and Ruth Bunzel were at Zuni in the 1920's these witch fears were not evident. Treatment of the bewitched by the curers served to alleviate anxieties of the veterans during the postwar period and their action played an important part in the reintegrative process.

[12] Leighton and Kluckhohn, 1947, p. 103.

[13] This number of Navaho servicemen represents 6 percent of the total population of approxi-

on the part of Navaho headmen, or other officials, to secure exemptions for their young men. To the contrary, formal speeches were made by the delegates to the Tribal Council stating that "we are glad all our boys are going to the army and doing what they are told to do." After the war, speeches were again made in the Tribal Council to the effect that "we are glad all the boys went to the army and didn't come home until they turned them loose. Maybe if our boys hadn't gone and we lost the war, this country would be ruined now."

The departure of the Navaho servicemen from their native communities was usually ritualized by the performance of Blessing Way[14] for the individual serviceman. This particular ceremonial was selected because it is the one frequently given ceremonial which does not have as its primary putative purpose the curing of illness, but is intended rather to invoke positive blessings, and thus to avert potential misfortune for the individual.[15] Blessing Way was also one of the traditional ritual Ways used in Navaho warfare.[16]

The pattern which was considered most desirable, if arrangements could be made in time, was the performance of Blessing Way in the interval between formal induction into service and basic training. But this was only done in four cases with the Ramah Navaho veterans. The alternative and more frequent practice was the performance of the ceremonial during the first furlough after basic training (six cases among the Ramah Navaho). In two cases the ceremonial was given at both times. In one case the ceremonial was performed in absentia for the serviceman while he was in Europe. And in three cases Blessing Way was not given at all until the servicemen returned at the end of the war. But there were no cases in which Blessing Way was not performed at all.

The purpose of Blessing Way for the departing servicemen was typically expressed by the veterans as follows: "My people told me: 'you are going far away from us. We want to give you Blessing Way so that you will feel fine when you're away and nothing will happen to you.' "

During their service experience the Navaho soldiers showed less disposition to carry over their religious patterns into the war situation. In this respect they

mately 60,000. At first sight, these figures might seem to indicate that the Navahos were *less* eager to go to war than the Zunis. This apparent contradiction results from the high number of Navaho rejects (from illiteracy and bad health) as compared to the low number of Zuni rejects. According to Navaho Service records at Window Rock, there were only 2,500 inductees out of 4,000 examined by Selective Service Boards from 1943 to 1945. Accurate records were not kept previous to 1943. The even lower percentage of inductees in the Ramah area (approximately 2 percent) is due to the greater percentage of illiteracy in this area as compared to many other Navaho districts.

[14] The translations of the names of ceremonials are those given in Wyman and Kluckhohn, 1938.

[15] Wyman and Kluckhohn, 1938, p. 18. For a description of the Blessing Way ceremonial, *see* Kluckhohn and Leighton, 1947, pp. 149–150, and Haile, 1935, p. 506.

[16] *Cf.* Hill, 1936, p. 6.

were under less pressure from their kinsmen at home than was was the case with the Zuni. Less than one-half of the Ramah Navaho veterans carried corn pollen with them, and only two veterans used the pollen in reciting Navaho prayers away from home. A typical response on the part of those who did carry pollen was: "I never did think about using it."

Our data also indicate that Navaho servicemen had much less frequent communication with home than did the Zuni during the war. To some extent this was, of course, due to the fact that most members of Navaho families could not write but had to enlist the aid of an educated kinsman or a white friend to write for them. Even among the Navaho veterans themselves there were many who could not speak English, much less write letters home.[17] But over and above these facts there appeared to be a formal effort on the part of Zuni families to keep the communication lines open which was lacking among the Navaho.

The return of the Navaho veterans at the end of the war was ritualized in at least three ways. Again, the most common practice was the performance of Blessing Way for the individual servicemen, usually within a few weeks after their return (seven cases among the Ramah Navaho). For those veterans who came into contact with dead German or Japanese soldiers, Enemy Way, the traditional ceremonial for dispelling the harmful effects of alien ghosts, was also quite frequently performed.[18] In two cases among the Ramah Navaho this ceremonial was given even though the veterans had neither dreamed of nor had otherwise been "bothered" by the enemy ghosts. In the words of one of the veterans:

The ceremony was arranged by my grandfather. He said we needed it because we seen lots of dead Germans. Not only see them, but step on them and smell some dead German bodies. He was afraid that later on we might go loco if we don't have this ceremony.

In other cases the ceremonial was not performed unless the veteran was troubled by dreams of the ghosts, or by illnesses which were attributed to this infection by alien ghosts. This exposure to alien ghosts involved not only the Germans and Japanese but also contact with white Americans. One veteran who had never been in combat zones was given Enemy Way simply because he had been in contact with a dead white soldier in a training camp. To date three of the Ramah Navaho veterans have had Enemy Way; the families of two other veterans are planning to have the ceremonial for them in the near future.[19]

---

[17] We have one case in our field notes of a veteran who spoke no English, had never been to school, and yet served three years in the army.

[18] Hill discusses the traditional use of Enemy Way for returned warriors. *Cf.* Hill, 1936, pp. 16–17. For a technical description of the Enemy Way ceremonial, *see* Haile, 1938.

[19] The data we have from other areas of the Reservation, principally from Shiprock, Ft.

A third practice which was much less common than the performance of Blessing Way and Enemy Way was the taking of sweat baths by the veterans with older male relatives. These were usually taken within a day or so after the return of the veteran and at the suggestion of the older men.[20] This ritual sweat bathing appeared in only two cases in the Ramah Navaho.

Although there were these formalized ritual observances when the Navaho veterans returned from the war, it is significant that the function of the ritual was not phrased primarily in terms of making "good" Navahos of them again, or of reintegrating them into the community. Instead the emphasis was always more upon helping the individual veterans and averting potential misfortune for them as well as welcoming them back to the community in these public ritual occasions. By way of contrast the Zuni ceremonies were secret and in no sense a "welcome home."

Similarly, in the realm of social and political organization there has been a notable lack of formal resistance to white cultural patterns which the veterans learned in service and have sought to introduce into traditional Navaho culture. The words of the most conservative Navaho leader in the Ramah group are instructive on this point: "The way I feel about these soldier boys is that most of them can already speak English and write. It looks like they should go on with the white people and learn more and more and then lead their people."

This is not to say that *no* reabsorption of the veterans into traditional Navaho culture is taking place. The significant point is rather that the strong pressures for conformity which are so characteristic of Zuni are relatively absent among the Ramah Navaho. There has been no resistance, for example, to the Veterans Administration agricultural training program, and almost all of the Ramah veterans are now participating in this program with the approval of the older Navaho leaders. There has been no "drifting out" under pressure from the elders in the community. Even a great deal of disbelief in the ceremonials is tolerated without resulting in formal ostracism. Gossip, ridicule, and witchcraft accusations are all features of current Navaho social controls, but so far as we could discover they have not been directed specifically against the cultural innovations being promoted by the veterans.[21]

## HISTORICAL COMPARISONS

The problem thus arises: why have the Zuni responded with a "nativistic

---

Defiance, and Chaco Canyon, suggest that the use of Blessing Way and Enemy Way for veterans was general practice among Navaho groups.

[20] Hill points out that the taking of sweat baths for purification after a warrior had killed a man is part of the traditional warfare pattern. *Cf.* Hill, 1936, p. 17.

[21] The focus of this paper is upon the response of the Ramah Navaho "community" to the returning veterans. A detailed description and analysis of the cultural innovations being promoted by the veterans is reserved for a later paper.

reaction," going to great great lengths to reabsorb their veterans into the traditional social and cultural forms, while the neighboring Ramah Navaho have tended to regard their veterans as potential forces for change in the direction of white patterns of culture? We now turn to an analysis of this problem in terms of the differing historical developments and the differing sociocultural systems that are now current in these two tribes.

## ZUNI

The Zuni have lived for several hundred years within the area now encompassed by their Reservation. As long ago as 1539 when Fray Marcos de Niza reached the pueblo of Hawikuh (about eighteen miles from the present village of Zuni) the Zuni were already living in well constructed multi-storied pueblos. During the 16th and 17th centuries Zuni was on the periphery of the pueblo area lying to the east which was exploited by the Spanish colonials. Contacts were sporadic rather than constant as they were in the Rio Grande valley. Although a Franciscan mission was established in 1629, it was abandoned several times, and was not re-established at its modern site in the village until 1920. Neither the Catholic nor the Christian Reformed church, which was established in the 1890's, has had any marked success if the criterion is one of number of converts.

While the Zuni have resisted the religion of the conquering majority group and have successfully retained their complex and tightly-knit socioreligious organization, they have selectively borrowed traits of our material culture during this long period of contact. In the last thirty years the village has changed from a compact terraced pueblo to a modern village which has stone houses that rival those built in many parts of contemporary rural New Mexico.

A preponderance of the male population under 40 (and the greater number of women under 30) can read and write English, and as a group speak much better English than a comparable group of the most acculturated Navaho. Yet if a Zuni is observed talking too much English with anyone, outsider or fellow Zuni, he is ridiculed for being *memi·ashe·?a*—the Zuni term for those who follow white ways.

The process is one of antagonistic acculturation as formulated by Devereux and Loeb:

> The adoption of new means without a corresponding adoption of the relevant goals is a common process in socio-cultural change. The new means are adopted in order to support existing goals, sometimes even for the specific purpose of resisting the compulsory adoption of the goals of the lending group.[22]

It is significant to note that in the last twenty years the Zuni governors through whom the priests and villagers channel their business with the Indian Service

---

[22] Devereux and Loeb, 1943, p. 140.

and other Government agencies have been well versed in the English language and have demonstrated their ability to hold their own with the white men economically. Recent governors have all been successful stockmen prior to their term in office, but the religious leaders and others in the community have effectively used this ability of the governor to get on in the white man's world to their own ends, witness the governor's letter requesting draft deferment for those in religious office.

As the village has become more modern in its technology, antagonism to white culture has become increasingly apparent, especially to those values which threaten Zuni religion. Consequently, the people have become more secretive in their determination to hold to the Zuni way of life. This reaction of retreat into religion with accompaning secrecy is enforced by two corollaries which might be called cultural "themes": to share religious knowledge is to dissipate ritual efficacy, and to increase secrecy is to insure power. An informant in speaking of the time when the ethnographer Frank Hamilton Cushing was initiated into the sacrosanct bow-priesthood sixty years ago said, "Our priests are no longer soft the way they used to be."

The veterans returning to a pueblo antagonistic to white ways were suspected of favoring the ways of those among whom they had been living. They were thought of as the exponents of the very way of life the Zuni rejected, and their lack of status was in part due to this fact.[23]

## Navaho

There is now a large body of linguistic, archeological and ethnographic data from which it is possible to describe at least the major trends of Navaho history.[24] It is generally agreed that the Navahos are a branch of the Southern Athabascan tribes who migrated into the Southwest from the north sometime within the last millennium. At the time of their arrival in the Southwest the available evidence suggests that the Navahos possessed a hunting and gathering culture with a simple social and religious system. Their history in the Southwest has been characterized by rapid change. The economy has shifted from hunting and gathering to the present system that includes herding, farming, weaving, silversmithing, and wage work for white enterprises; the social system is now organized on the basis of extended families, matrilineal clans, and local groups; the religious system now includes a large number of complex ceremonials. Throughout this process of change the Navahos have shown an as-

---

[23] One of the older veterans had been asked by one of the Indian Service officials to take part in the testing of the New Mexico voting laws which said that "Indians not-taxed" could not vote. He was called before the villagers in a public meeting, was severely reprimanded and forced to withdraw from the case.

[24] Kluckhohn and Leighton give a brief, but judicious, summary of the historical picture to date. *Cf.* Kluckhohn and Leighton, 1936, pp. 3–12.

tonishing capacity to borrow elements of Pueblo, Spanish, and white American culture and fit them into the pre-existent patterns. The record is definitely one of a strongly "borrowing" group in all categories of culture except language.

The historical record of the Navahos in the Southwest is also one of great mobility as compared to the Zuni and other Pueblo societies. After the introduction of the horse the mobility of the Navahos was enormously increased. Although they never became "nomads"—their movements were confined, for the most part, to well-defined areas during given periods of their history— they did come into frequent raiding and trading contacts with peoples all over the Southwest. Over longer periods of history there have been many changes in area of settlement. From the earliest region of settlement in north central New Mexico there were shifts to the west and south. Then in the early 1860's most of the tribe was placed in captivity at Ft. Sumner in eastern New Mexico. In 1868 they were released and permitted to resettle in northwestern New Mexico and northeastern Arizona where a Reservation was formally established.

Although the Navahos hunted and cultivated a few fields in the Ramah country prior to 1868, permanent Navaho settlement did not take place until after the Ft. Sumner episode when a few related families drifted into the Ramah area instead of settling on the Reservation. Here they came into contact with the neighboring Zuni. In 1872 Spanish-American ranchers began to push across the mountains from their settlements to the east and establish ranches in the Ramah region. The first few years of contact with the Spanish-Americans were marked by sporadic warfare, but through the years the Navahos have developed more friendly contacts with them. Today many Navahos maintain reciprocal guest-friendship connections with Spanish-American families.

In 1882 the Mormons established a farming village in the area and "persuaded" the Navahos to give up some of their best land. Since that time the Navahos have been subjected to continuing economic and missionary pressure from the Mormons. Between 1925 and 1935 two additional farming communities were established in the same region by Anglo-American families from Texas. Both the Mormons and the Texans own trading posts in the area and employ Navahos on their farms during the harvest season.

Thus during the 80 years that the Navahos have lived in the Ramah region they have been in a constant process of adjustment to these diverse cultural groups: Zuni, Spanish-American, Mormon, and Texan. This historical picture contrasts with that of the Zuni who have lived in the same area for several hundred years and have been subjected to less effective pressure from the other groups.

Even in this brief characterization of Navaho history in the Southwest, and of Ramah Navaho history in the Ramah-Zuni area, we see how the new elements of culture impinging upon the Navahos via the veterans of World War

II constitute only another phase of a long record of cultural change and development. We might say that the stage had been set by historical experience for adaptation rather than resistance to new patterns learned by the veterans during their war experience.

### COMPARISONS AND CONTRASTS IN THE PRESENT SOCIOCULTURAL SYSTEMS

Turning now to the present scene, we raise the question as to what features of the Navaho and Zuni sociocultural systems as we observe them today help us to account for the "receptiveness" of the Navaho as compared to the "resistance" of the Zuni to their veterans as cultural innovators.

The widely scattered Navaho settlement pattern with the frequent shifting of residence, which is largely a function of the Navaho technological adaptation to a meager resource base, results in a loosely-organized, informal sociopolitical system. The importance of these features of Navaho life was strongly evident in the case of the veterans. Most veterans returned from the war to take up residence in separate extended families and local groups which were far removed geographically from other localized social units. The adjustments of the veterans took place, for the most part, within each of these separate local units. Indeed, the veterans might not even see one another for weeks at a time, except for chance encounters at the larger ceremonials, or more recently at the meetings of the Veterans Administration training classes.

The Navaho elders also seldom meet in large groups which would provide occasions for a discussion of the veterans, except for infrequent chapter meetings. In short, the basic economic and social conditions of Navaho life limit the possibilities of widespread, formal resistance to such a matter as the new cultural elements being promoted by the veterans.

Zuni social organization, on the other hand, is tightly knit. "The foundation of Zuni society is the family. . . . Life centers around the house,"[25] Kroeber wrote thirty years ago, and this is true now as then. But the household is enmeshed in a complicated web of social units—the matrilineal lineage group through which religious prerogatives are inherited, the clan, the kiva, and the curing society all of which cross-cut one another in membership and function. The veterans returned to the pueblo and took up residence not in family units isolated one from another, as was the case with the Navaho, but in groups which were close physically as well as sociometrically. As a result, social control through gossip, rumor, ridicule and witchcraft was most effective. The behavior of the veterans was readily observable to the village as a whole. Their actions were discussed in the kiva and curing society houses. These well-defined groups were capable of exerting pressure on the individual veteran and his family in such a way as to bring about effective conformance.

---

[25] Kroeber, 1917, p. 47.

The informal and flexible nature of Navaho sociopolitical organization has another important implication for our problem. Inasmuch as political and ceremonial positions are not filled by men from particular kinship units (as at Zuni), the Navaho system was not threatened by the loss of young men during the war, nor by loss of young men through disbelief and nonparticipation after the war. In other words, the Navaho system of social selection for functionally differentiated positions in the social system is so flexible and informal that the system itself was not threatened in the war situation. The Zuni system, on the other hand, is much more rigid. Ritual knowledge is handed down in prescribed lineages within the clans. Loss of particular priests means loss of religious control.

A second significant contrast which affects the current attitudes toward the veterans is to be found in the traditional Navaho and Zuni patterns of warfare. Although the Navaho never developed warfare of the extent found on the Plains, it was nevertheless an important feature of Navaho life, especially after the introduction of the horse. The Zuni participated in war only when attacked, and whereas the success of Zuni war parties was believed to depend largely upon the prayers of the priests who stayed at home, the success of Navaho war and raiding parties depended more upon the individual warriors and ceremonial practitioners who went along.[26] It followed that the individual Zuni warriors enjoyed little prestige, but that the Navaho warriors obtained a good deal of prestige from their raiding exploits, especially insofar as they added horses, food, and other economic goods to the tribe. Furthermore, Navaho warfare persisted until the 1860's, while the Zuni have done little fighting in the last 150 years. Even today the traditional Enemy Way continues to be one of the most popular Navaho ceremonials, and it is the only ceremonial in which whites are rigidly excluded from the strictly ritual parts.

There is considerable evidence from interviews with older Navahos that the Navaho veterans tended to be regarded as returning warriors in the traditional sense, and that this is one factor in their being placed in socially valued roles in Navaho society. They were not just school-boys coming home with white ideas; they were returning warriors with prestige. The Zuni, on the other hand, did not look upon this war as any concern of theirs. They were concerned only with the safe return of their veterans which they believed depended upon the prayers of their priests.

A third contrast of some significance is the Navaho disposition to be intensely curious about the outside world as compared to the Zuni disposition to be utterly uninterested in outside affairs. This is culturally patterned and probably derives from the long Navaho experience of travel and mobility as contrasted with the long Zuni experience of immobility. Until quite recently

---

[26] *Cf.* Hill, 1936, pp. 6–13.

there were Zunis who had not traveled as far as Ojo Caliente, one of the Zuni farming villages only 15 miles from the central pueblo. It is of significance here that Zuni is regarded as "the middle place" and that a shrine on the outskirts of the village is believed to be the "center of the universe." The Navaho veterans have spent many hours passing along information about the outside world to their kinsmen at home; the Zuni were less interested in the experiences of their veterans.

Finally, we should like to point out that these contrasts are also manifested at the level of "themes"[27] or "configurations"[28] in the two cultures. These "themes" can be regarded as governing values of the social-structural features we have been describing. Thus, Kluckhohn has described Navaho social relations as being premised upon a "familistic individualism" which permits a relatively large area of freedom for the expression of individuality in Navaho society.[29] By contrast, Benedict describes Zuni culture as one with strong communal orientations which demand a high degree of social and cultural conformity on the part of the individual.[30] This is in line with the actual operation of the two social systems in the case of the veterans. The Navaho permit innovations on the part of the veterans; the Zuni do not.

In conclusion we submit that the contrasting modes of change that have taken place in the two societies, "acculturative" on the one hand and "nativistic" on the other, provide an instance of Keesing's "factor of adaptability."[31] We have contrasted the "adaptable" Navaho with the "rigid" Zuni and have pointed up the social and cultural processes which produce and maintain these two types of sociocultural systems.

CORNELL UNIVERSITY
ITHACA, NEW YORK

HARVARD UNIVERSITY
CAMBRIDGE, MASSACHUSETTS

---

[27] Opler, 1945, p. 198.     [28] Kluckhohn, 1943, p. 221.
[29] Kluckhohn, 1949, p. 367.     [30] Benedict, 1934.
[31] "Broadly speaking, systems of life may vary in the degree to which they are what might be called adaptable or rigid, this affecting the response of the people trained in them to a contact situation. . . . A group with a long history of contact and cultural modification, for example, is likely to prove more adaptable, other things being equal, when exposed to a new experience of acculturation than one long isolated, or 'set' in some very specialized physical environment. Again where a culture allows great scope for 'individualism,' as with the dream revelations of some American Indian tribes, or the flexible social system of the Isneg people in the northern Philippines, innovation may be tolerated in many phases of culture from which it would be rigidly excluded in societies which stress formal organization and ritualism, and which have fixed statuses and vested interests that may be threatened by such innovation." (Keesing, 1939, p. 62).

BIBLIOGRAPHY

BENEDICT, RUTH, 1934, *Patterns of Culture.* Houghton Mifflin, New York.

BUNZEL, RUTH, L., 1932, *Introduction to Zuni Ceremonialism.* 47th Annual Report, Bureau of American Ethnology, Washington, D. C.

DEVEREUX, GEORGE and LOEB, E. M., 1943, Antagonistic Acculturation. *American Sociological Review,* Vol. 8, pp. 133–148.

HAILE, BERARD, 1938, *Origin Legend of the Navaho Enemy Way.* Yale University Publications in Anthropology, No. 17, New Haven.

HILL, W. W., 1936, *Navaho Warfare.* Yale University Publications in Anthropology, No. 5, New Haven.

KEESING, FELIX, M., 1939, Some Notes on Acculturation Study. *Proceedings of the Sixth Pacific Science Congress,* Vol. IV, Berkeley.

KLUCKHOHN, CLYDE, 1943, Covert Culture and Administrative Problems. *American Anthropologist,* Vol. 45, pp. 213–227.

———, 1949, The Philosophy of the Navaho Indians. In: *Ideological Differences and World Order,* edited by F. S. C. Northrup, pp. 356–385.

KLUCKHOHN, CLYDE and LEIGHTON, DOROTHEA, 1946, *The Navaho.* Harvard University Press, Cambridge.

KROEBER, A. L., 1917, *Zuni Kin and Clan.* Anthropological Papers, American Museum of Natural History, No. 18, Part 2, New York.

LEIGHTON, DOROTHEA and KLUCKHOHN, CLYDE, 1947, *Children of the People.* Harvard University Press, Cambridge.

OPLER, MORRIS E., 1945, Themes as Dynamic Forces in Culture. *American Journal of Sociology,* Vol. 51, pp. 198–206.

PARSONS, ELSIE CLEWS, 1939, *Pueblo Indian Religion.* University of Chicago Press, Chicago.

WYMAN, LELAND C., and KLUCKHOHN, CLYDE, 1938. *Navaho Classification of Their Song Ceremonials.* Memoir 50, American Anthropological Association.

# Witchcraft in Four African Societies: An Essay in Comparison

## By S. F. NADEL

IN THIS paper[1] it is proposed to present a small-scale model of a comparative analysis, more precisely, of an analysis of "concomitant variations" (to borrow Durkheim's term), such as any enquiry concerned with the explanation of social facts must employ. The facts in question are particular variants of the belief in witchcraft. Indirectly, the study will also refer to a much discussed hypothesis, the assumption that infantile experiences represent a paramount determinant of culture.

The comparison concerns two pairs of societies—the Nupe and Gwari in Northern Nigeria, and the Korongo and Mesakin tribes in the Nuba Mountains of the Central Sudan. Each pair shows wide cultural similarities combined with a few marked divergences, one of these being the diversity in witchcraft beliefs. This discussion will proceed on two assumptions: (1) that any one relevant cultural divergence entails further, concomitant, divergences in the respective cultures; and (2) that witchcraft beliefs are causally related to frustrations, anxieties or other mental stresses precisely as psychopathological symptoms are related to mental disturbances of this nature.

### WITCHCRAFT IN NUPE AND GWARI

The two societies are neighbors in an identical environment and also maintain frequent contacts. They speak closely related languages and have an identical kinship system, based on patrilineal succession, patrilocal residence, and localized extended families. Political organization and the regulation of male adolescence are closely similar in both tribes; so is their economy, though marketing and trade are on a much larger scale in Nupe. The religion of Nupe and Gwari is again closely similar (ignoring here the more recent spread of Islam), and the conceptions of life and death, of a body possessed of a double soul ("shadow-" and "life-soul"), or of the reincarnation of ancestral souls, are identical even as regards nomenclature.

Both groups, too, firmly believe in witchcraft; several grave incidents showing the strength of the beliefs occurred even during the period of field work among the two tribes. Both conceive of witchcraft as unequivocally evil, as destroying life, mainly through mysterious wasting diseases, and as implying the power of witches to "eat" the "life-soul" of their victims. Witches are active at night and cannot be seen or discovered by ordinary

---

[1] In slightly abridged form and under the title "A Comparative Study of Witchcraft," the paper was presented at the Berkeley meeting of the A.A.A. For a fuller account of some of the ethnographical material see the writer, 1942, esp. Chap. IX; 1935, and 1946.

18

means. Everything connected with witchcraft takes place in a fantasy realm which is, almost *ex hypothesi*, intangible and beyond empirical verification. This is shown most clearly in the tenet that it is only the "shadow-souls" of witches which roam about and attack victims, while their bodies remain asleep at home, thus deceiving any ordinary attempts at proving, or disproving, these mystic activities.

The two beliefs, however, differ radically in the ascription of sex to the witch. In Nupe witches are always women (called *găci*, from *egá*, "witchcraft"). They are thought to be organized in a society closely modelled on similar human associations and headed by the woman who is also, in real life, the titled official head of the women traders. It may be noted that this is the only instance of the fantasy world of witchcraft projecting into and becoming tangible in concrete, everyday life. The woman said to preside over the association of witches occupies an exceptional position also in another sense; for she is the only "good" female witch, sometimes a "reformed" witch, and hence a person willing and able to control the sinister activities of her companions.

The men fit into this pattern in an ambiguous way. Certain individuals are said to possess a power similar to witchcraft, which enables them to see and deal with witches. This power is known by a different name (*'eshe'*) and is essentially good; so that the men possessed of it can control and combat the women witches. At the same time the female witches need the co-operation of the men, for only when the female and male powers are joined does female witchcraft become fully effective, that is, deadly. Here again, the men are said to use their power not to assist, but to restrain the female witches, by withholding the required aid. The ambiguity referred to, then, lies in this: men are necessary for the fullest effect of witchcraft; but as a class, they also stand aloof and are not themselves evil; rather do they attempt to block evil witchcraft. Even so, the fatal effects of female witchcraft are admitted to occur; in which case one argues that a few evil individuals among the men (whom no one can name) have betrayed their own sex and become the helpers of a woman witch. The general picture is that of a sharp sex-antagonism, which assigns the evil intentions to the female, and to the male, a benevolent and ideally decisive—if somewhat utopian—role.

Characteristically, the men are never blamed or accused of witchcraft, and the main collective weapon against witchcraft lies in the activities of a male secret society which, by threats and torture, "cleanses" villages of witchcraft. The same idea that the men alone have the secret power of defeating female witchcraft is expressed in the legends on the origins of witchcraft and anti-witchcraft. The case studies collected add a further twist to this sex-antagonism; for in the majority of cases the alleged witch is a woman, usually an older and domineering female, who would attack a younger man who somehow fell under her dominance; which situation is again pictured in the legends. The men, therefore, though on the utopian or fantasy plane the masters of female witchcraft, are, on the plane of "real" incidents and fears, its main victims.

One case history and one legend may be quoted. The former concerns a young man from a village on the river Niger who one night suddenly disappeared. A body which the police had good reason to believe was his was later fished out of the river; but the people refused to accept this "natural" explanation, maintaining that the young man had been spirited away by a witch. Suspicion at once fell on an elderly wealthy woman whose house the young man had frequently been visiting; he had, in fact, been something like a protegé of that woman or, in Nupe parlance, her *egi kata*—"son of the house" —which term is applied to any individual who seeks the patronage of some influential older person and becomes dependent upon his patron's advice and material help.

The legend tells of a young king "in ancient times," whose mother was an overbearing old woman, constantly interfering with her son's plans and actions. At last the son decided to rid himself of her influence. He consulted a (male) diviner, who told him the secret of a certain cloth mask, which would drop on his mother and remove her from the earth. Thus, it is said, originated the Nupe anti-witchcraft cult *ndakó gboyá*, which is today vested in the male secret society mentioned before and employs the cloth masks as its main paraphernalia.

As regards the Gwari beliefs, a brief outline will suffice. They involve no sex antagonism or sex polarity. Witches and their victims are indiscriminately male and female. Witchcraft is discovered by ordinary divination, practiced by both men and women, and anti-witchcraft measures consist in the main in an annual "cleansing" ritual which embraces the whole community, again irrespective of sex.

So much for the general picture of the two cultures and their divergent conceptions of witchcraft. Turning now to the search for "concomitant" divergences, and taking our lead from psychoanalysis, we might start with infantile experiences and the techniques of child-rearing. Here we meet with one relevant difference only, concerning children of two and over. Until a newborn child has reached the age of two or three the parents in both tribes refrain from cohabitation. Afterwards, when cohabitation is resumed, the Nupe wife visits the husband's hut, the children staying in her sleeping quarters, while in Gwari the husband visits the wife, so that cohabitation takes place in the presence of the young children. The people have no doubt that the children do in fact witness the sexual act. Assuming, with Freudian psychology, that this fact entails deeply unsettling psychological effects, it should foster the oedipus trauma and definite tensions between child (perhaps more specifically son) and father.[2] Assuming further that these tensions, normally repressed or blocked in overt behavior, might find an outlet in the fantasy of witchcraft beliefs, we should expect these to reveal some bias towards sex-antagonism and towards identifying the evil witches either with males (the hated father image) or perhaps, by a more devious transference, with females (the mother avenging herself on all males). In fact, neither assumption is borne out by the evidence, the sex antagonism occurring in the tribe where the traumatic experience is absent.

Certain other cultural divergences, however, concerning adult life, seem to be congruent with the diversity in witchcraft beliefs. They revolve upon marriage, which, generally speaking, is without serious complications and relatively tension-free in Gwari, but full of stress and mutual hostility in Nupe. Two facts may be mentioned. (1) The economic position of the Nupe wives, many of whom are successful itinerant traders, is generally much better than that of their peasant husbands. Thus husbands are often heavily in debt to their wives, and the latter assume many of the financial responsibilities which should rightly belong to the men as fathers and family heads, such as finding bride-price for sons, paying for the children's education, bearing the expenses of family feasts, and the like. This reversal of the institutionalized roles is openly resented by the men, who are, however, helpless and unable to redress the situation. (2) As has been said, many married women become itinerant traders. According to the tenets of Nupe morality, this occupation should be reserved for childless women, in whose case one also excuses the moral laxity which, in that society, goes together with this livelihood. But in fact mothers too become itinerant traders, leaving their children once they are four or five years old; more importantly, women also refuse to have children, practicing abortion and using alleged contraceptives, in order to be free to choose this occupation. Again, the men are helpless; they can only brand this voluntary sterility as the gravest possible form of immorality.

In practice, then, the men must submit to the domineering and independent leanings of the women; they resent their own helplessness, and definitely blame the "immorality" of the womenfolk. The wish to see the situation reversed is expressed in nostalgic talk about "the good old days" when all this was unheard of (and which are disproved by all genealogies and concrete records of the past). Equally, it can be argued, the hostility between men and women *plus* this wish-fulfilment are projected into the witchcraft beliefs with their ambivalent expression of sex-antagonism, in which men are the "real" victims but the "utopian" masters of the evil women. A final item of evidence, mentioned before, lies in the identification of the head of the witches

---

[2] Gwari informants in fact claimed that a marked hostility between father and son was a common feature of their family life. The writer's material on the Gwari, however, is not sufficiently full to permit any more definite statement.

with the official head of the women traders. It relates the "projection" in a direct and overt manner to the conscious hostility and the concrete situations evoking it. The psychological "symptom," we might say, and the anxieties and stresses which are its cause are connected by a clear thread of meaning.

## WITCHCRAFT IN KORONGO AND MESAKIN

These two tribes are once more neighbors in the same environment; though speaking different languages they know one another and are often bilingual. They share the same economy, political organization, and religious beliefs and practices. Both reckon descent in the mother's line and have the same kinship system and domestic arrangements; more particularly, in both groups children of six or seven are free to leave their father's house, where they were born, for that of their mother's-brother to grow up under his tutelage. A detailed census showed that in each tribe this change of residence and affiliation occurred in about half of all cases. In all other respects, too, child-rearing is identical in the two societies.

So is the regulation of male adolescence, with one exception to be discussed later. It may be pointed out here that male adolescence and, indeed, the whole life-cycle of the men, revolve upon a highly formalized division into age classes, each of which is characterized by the right to engage in particular sporting contests, which are exhibitions of virility as well. These sports are light wrestling, wrestling of a more strenuous kind, and fighting with spears. In the first, lowest, age class, before puberty, no sports are practiced. The severe variety of wrestling marks the peak of physical vigor, attained towards the end of adolescence; while spear-fighting, which implies more skill than bodily strength, is considered appropriate to an age of already declining physical vigor. After the spear-fighting stage, the tests or exhibitions of virility cease altogether, the men having become "too old." At the same time the men give up sleeping in the cattle camps out in the bush, which more arduous mode of life is once more regarded as appropriate for youths only. This decline in physical vigor at the end of adolescence is attributed to the cumulative effects of sexual activity, especially to the sex life involved in marriage and procreation. In both groups, finally, the first sporting contest after puberty is celebrated with much ceremony and is made the occasion for an important gift on the part of the boy's mother's-brother. This consists of an animal taken from the mother's-brother's herd, the same herd which the sister's son is in due course bound to inherit. The gift therefore represents something like an "anticipated inheritance," and is in fact known by the term "inheritance," a point which is of crucial importance for the understanding of the witchcraft beliefs.

To turn now to the contrast between the two groups. The Korongo have no witchcraft beliefs at all; the Mesakin are literally obsessed by fears of witchcraft (known as *torogo*) and witchcraft accusations, entailing violent quarrels, assaults, and blood revenge, are frequent. Witchcraft itself is a mysterious, malignant and often deadly power, emanating directly from evil wishes, though it is subject to two significant restrictions. Mesakin witchcraft is believed to operate only between maternal kin, especially between a mother's-brother and sister's son, the older relative assailing the younger. Mesakin witchcraft further operates only if there is a reason, some legitimate cause for resentment or anger; and the latter is almost invariably a quarrel over the 'anticipated inheritance' mentioned before. As has been said, both tribes acknowledge this particular duty of the mother's-brother. But in Korongo it is never refused. The gift can be postponed, but is also sometimes made twice, and rarely raises any serious difficulty. In Mesakin the exact opposite is true. The gift is always refused to begin with, and has often to be taken by force, a procedure which is fully sanctioned by public opinion. The gift cannot be postponed, nor is it ever repeated. Quarrels over it between the youth and his mother's-brother are the rule; and if by any chance the former falls ill, dies, or suffers some other misfortune, the older man is invariably suspected of having employed witchcraft.

Practices of child-rearing, being identical in the two tribes, offer no clue either to the sharply divergent attitude towards the anticipated inheritance or to the witchcraft beliefs which, in one of the two groups, come into play in this connection. The clue seems to lie, rather, in certain cultural differences shaping the adult attitudes towards life and, more especially, towards the fate of growing old.

To begin with, the two tribes deal differently with pre-marital sex relations. Both groups, as will be remembered, firmly believe that regular sexual intercourse is physically weakening for the male, yet also glorify physical vigor and manliness. In both groups, for example a "born" coward or weakling is called by the name normally given to the male homosexuals (who invariably turn transvestite), is treated with the same contempt, and is often forced to join their ranks. In both groups, too, the men hate growing old, which means, above all, withdrawing from the "manly" pursuits and admitting their physical debility; thus the "old men" will always try to join the sports for which they are supposed to be no longer fit, even at the risk of being ridiculed, or sneak out for a night in the cattle camps to join the company of the younger men. Yet while among the Korongo pre-marital and highly promiscuous sex relations are fully accepted and openly engaged in, among the Mesakin they are carefully concealed; indeed, the Mesakin insisted that formerly pre-marital chastity was rigidly observed. In other words, the Korongo accept the "dissipation" of strength through sexual intercourse as something one can do nothing about; the Mesakin at least believe that it should be restricted and postponed, and face the failure of the ideal with all the symptoms of a feeling of guilt.[3]

Furthermore, the two tribes schematize their age classes differently, thus establishing a different correspondence between "social age," as indicated in the age class, and physical age.[4] The Korongo have six age classes, as against three among the Mesakin, so that in the former tribe the various phases of individual life are much more faithfully represented; also, the rights and responsibilities changing with age are more evenly spaced. Above all, the pursuits typical of youth, tribal sports and life in the cattle camps, are discarded gradually, allowance being made for transitional stages. Thus the severe wrestling, indicative of the peak of physical vigor, is assigned to the third age class, of as yet unmarried youths, but lasts into the next grade, when marriage, at the age of 20–22, and regular sexual relations are expected to show their weakening effect. At this stage spear-fighting is the appropriate sport, again lasting into the next higher grade. This, the fifth grade, starts with parenthood and the assumption of the responsibilities of a family head; but the final farewell to sports and life in the cattle camps does not take place until a few years afterwards, at the age of 28–30. The Korongo also specifically name their sixth and last grade the age class of "old men," the criterion now being the visible physical decline of the really old. In short, the Korongo accept a gradual process of growing old, the social "old age" being only one of many steps and congruent with physical age.

The Mesakin, on the other hand, distinguish explicitly only between boys before puberty, youths (unmarried and married) before parenthood, and "men," without further separation of the really old. Wrestling, spear-fighting, and life in the cattle camps all cease together, at the end of the second grade, that is, at the age of about 22–24. The Mesakin, therefore, introduce the indices of social "old age" early in life, and expect men to renounce the cherished privileges of youth abruptly and on purely conventional grounds, which take little account of physical age.

Let us now return to the demand for the anticipated inheritance which figures so prominently in Mesakin witchcraft beliefs. In both tribes the mother's-brother must see in this insistent demand a reminder that he has definitely grown old; not only has he by then probably begotten children (which fact would merely announce his declining youth), but he has now a ward sufficiently old to claim his "inheritance," that is, a gift explicitly an-

---

[3] There is an interesting trace of this also among the Korongo; for here the fiancée of a young man will refuse to have pre-marital relations with him (and with him only), thus avoiding responsibility for the dissipation of strength of her beloved (Nadel, 1946, p. 289).

[4] See chart 1.

### 1. Korongo and Mesakin Age Classifications and Activities

| Approx. Age | Korongo | | | Mesakin | | |
|---|---|---|---|---|---|---|
| | Age Class | Activities | General Circumstances | Age Class | Activities | General Circumstances |
| Up to 12–13 | 1. belad | None | Pre-puberty | 1. ŋate | None | Pre-puberty |
| 13–16 | 2. dere | Light wrestling | Post-puberty; first sex-relations | | | |
| 17–20 | 3. adere | Severe wrestling; live in cattle camps | Unmarried; pre-marital sex relations | 2. kaduma | Light wrestling; severe wrestling; spear-fighting; live in cattle camps | Post-puberty; pre-marital sex relations; later marriage |
| 21–25 | 4. adumok | Severe wrestling; later spear-fighting; live in cattle camps part of the time | Married | | | |
| 26–50 | 5. asnda-gan | Spear-fighting; visits to cattle camps; both end after 3–4 years | Fathers, family heads. | 3. mede | None | Fathers, family heads; including physically old men |
| 50– | 6. tgif | None | Physically old men | | | |

ticipating the donor's impending death. Now, among the Korongo the older man is prepared for the gradual decline of age and accepts its onset, which coincides with sex life, with good grace or at least without struggle; furthermore, since among the Korongo the anticipated inheritance can be postponed, the mother's-brother may by then be an older or old man also in the physical sense. Among the Mesakin, who know no such gradual transition to old age and idealize pre-marital chastity (which would postpone its onset), the "reminder" must find the donor mentally unprepared; and since the gift cannot be postponed it will often be demanded of men still physically young. Hence the violent resentment on the part of the mother's-brother when the demand is made and his invariable first refusal.

The resentment and refusal merely express the older man's envy of youth and virility, the loss of which is brought home to him by the very request for the anticipated inheritance. Clearly, every man in the tribe has gone through this phase or knows about it in the case of others; everybody also knows that the mother's-brother's refusal is bound to be abortive in the end, that he can be forced to yield the gift, and that tribal morality is against him. It is suggested that the belief in the mother's-brother's power to use witchcraft against his would-be heirs arises from this knowledge. The hostility which, one knows, the older man feels but should not feel, and which he has no means of realizing finally and successfully, is accepted as operating in the sphere of secret as well as anti-social aims, that is, in the sphere of witchcraft. Differently expressed, every man projects his own frustrations of this nature into the allegations that others are guilty of witchcraft. In punishing them, the accuser vicariously wipes out his own guilt, unadmitted or admitted.

The picture just drawn is to some extent over-simplified. For the Mesakin believe that witchcraft may also be practiced by a sister's son against his mother's-brother or by full brothers against one another. Here, too, there must be a legitimate motive, which lies again in a grievance over inheritance; but this may be ordinary as well as "anticipated" inheritance. Nor need the alleged witch attack only the kinsman by whom he feels he has been injured; he may equally attack a close relative (patrilineal or matrilineal) of that kinsman or any one of the latter's matrilineal kin, thus venting his anger almost at random. These facts, however, seem significant: the belief in the powers of witchcraft of a sister's-son over his mother's-brother is pure "theory," for which the people themselves can cite no concrete cases; in all the remaining instances, too, including that of brothers bewitching one another, it is invariably the older man who is accused; and finally, even where witchcraft is believed to strike at random, both victim and assailant are always males.[5] If, then, the accusations of witchcraft are not invariably directed against a mother's-brother resentful of his kinship obligations, they are always directed against a person likely to feel the resentment and anxieties that go with mature age; and though the motives imputed to the witch are less single-minded than the previous discussion would suggest, and the occasions thought to provoke them less conspicuously "reminders" of the loss of virility, the witchcraft accusations remain a projection of the hostility of the old towards the young and of the frustrations springing from such envy of youth. This is perhaps

---

[5] Only in one case, said to have occurred "a long time ago," a woman was accused of having bewitched her brother's young son. But the people considered this a most unusual case, which they themselves were at a loss to explain. Nor were they certain of the circumstances.

borne out most strikingly by the following, admittedly atypical, instance. In one of the witchcraft cases recorded the alleged witch was a transvestite homosexual who had no livestock property, so that the question of inheritance did not arise; he was said to have bewitched his sister's young boy for no reason other than "envy of a true male."

## CONCLUSIONS

Before attempting to summarize our findings, some general remarks may be interjected. The correlations suggested in the preceding discussion, between witchcraft beliefs and particular features of the cultures in which they appear (or fail to appear), are not the only ones that can be discovered, even in the few societies here considered. These other correlations have been neglected mainly because they seem to be of lesser relevance; more precisely, they appear to belong only to the background of facilitating or impeding conditions, and not to the core of basic causes and determinants. Two examples may be given.

The Korongo, who have no witchcraft, possess a full and explicit mythology concerned with explaining all the things in the world—the creation of man and animals, the origin of death and disease, the invention of fire, and so forth. The witchcraft-ridden Mesakin, on the other hand, have nothing of the kind. Now it may be argued that an explicit explanatory mythology presents a picture of the universe less obscure and puzzling than does a religion backed by no such intellectual efforts; their absence, therefore, may be taken to foster anxieties and a sense of insecurity, and hence, indirectly, to predispose people toward also accepting the mysterious and malevolent powers of witches. Yet it seems clear that this factor can only have contributory significance since too many instances could be quoted of cultures combining an explicit mythology with belief in witchcraft.

The second example refers to the dualistic nature of the Nupe witchcraft beliefs, which occur in a culture and idea system generally characterized by a marked bias for dichotomous conceptions. Among the Gwari, where the witchcraft beliefs ignore the polarity of the sexes, the idea system is similarly devoid of any dualistic trend. Witchcraft beliefs, then, and that wider orientation hang together logically. Here we are once more dealing merely with predispositions of a general kind—with ways of thinking about the universe and of ordering its phenomena. Nor, in fact, does this last correlation exhibit any causal nexus, however indirect or contributory, but only a general "fit," a logical consistency, linking witchcraft beliefs with a general mode of thought.

Even so, an exhaustive analysis must obviously include these, and further, additional factors also. More generally speaking, in any inquiry like ours, based upon "concomitant variations," we must be prepared to reckon with several concomitants and multiple forms of interdependence, rather than with simple one-to-one correlations. That only studies of this far-reaching order can do justice to the complexity of social situations, need hardly be defended. As regards the present inquiry, this ideal degree of completeness was beyond its scope. Perhaps, too, such completeness will often remain an ideal, unattainable in the present stage of our science.[6]

To turn to the conclusions proper: (1) The witchcraft beliefs here examined are causally as well as conspicuously related to specific anxieties and stresses arising in social life. The word "conspicuously" is relevant because the witchcraft beliefs also indicate the precise nature of the social causes of which they are the symptoms—marriage-relations in Nupe, and the relationship between mother's-brother and sister's son in Mesakin.

(2) The anxieties and stresses need not arise from infantile experiences alone; rather, the present evidence tends to show that adult experiences, too, may be responsible for their emergence, and hence for the emergence also of the particular cultural features indicative of the anxieties and stresses.

(3) The witchcraft beliefs of the Nupe and Mesakin seem to represent two basic potentialities or types. In Nupe, the witch is identified with the person openly and successfully setting aside the social values and thus denying the state of society desired and thought "good"; attacks against witches are thus attacks upon the successful enemies of the ideal society. In Mesakin, the witch is identified with the person who cannot live up to the social values yet cannot openly rebel against them; the attacks upon witches are attacks upon the victims of the ideal society. In the first case one punishes the human agents responsible for the frustrations suffered by the believers in the ideal; in the second, one punishes and tries to obliterate the very fact that submission to the social ideal can give rise to frustration. In both types, then, the imputation of witchcraft serves to uphold the desired, if utopian, state of society by identifying the witch with the transgressor—whether in successful action or in unadmitted, suppressed desire. Gwari witchcraft, so far as the somewhat incomplete data go, seems to stand halfway between these extremes. We may note in passing that if the Mesakin belief in witchcraft wielded by aggrieved brothers and sister's-sons were more than "theory," this would illustrate a third type of witchcraft in which the witch is identified with the victim of the "transgressor" and the act of witchcraft with punitive action—though of a disproportionate and unlawful kind.

(4) It is sometimes said that witchcraft beliefs "canalize" hostility or "deflect" hostile impulses into socially relatively harmless channels, that is, help society to function. Our evidence does not quite bear out this assumption. The witchcraft fears and accusations only accentuate concrete hostilities and

---

[6] The methodological issues touched upon above have been treated more fully in Nadel, 1951, pp. 234 and 258 ff.

in fact give them free rein. The concrete hostilities *are* "canalized," in the sense that they are directed against a few scapegoats rather than against more numerous victims. But every witchcraft accusation or punishment of witches adds to the stresses of the society, through causing a serious disturbance of social life, entailing blood revenge, and the like. The accusations of witchcraft *do* deflect tensions and aggressive impulses; these are deflected, as it were, from the maladjusted institutions which cause them—marriage and the economic system in Nupe, kinship relations and the regulation of adolescence in Mesakin—so that these institutions can continue to operate. But they remain maladjusted and their continued operation only creates further tensions. Each persecution of witches no doubt relieves the tensions and stresses in a cathartic manner; but the relief is itself creative of new difficulties; equally, it is short-lived, for witchcraft cases go on happening all the time.

In brief, the witchcraft beliefs enable a society to go on functioning in a given manner, fraught with conflicts and contradictions which the society is helpless to resolve; the witchcraft beliefs thus absolve the society from a task apparently too difficult for it, namely, some radical readjustment. But from the observer's point of view it is doubtful if this is more than a poor and ineffectual palliative or can be called a solution "less harmful" than open hostility or even the break-up of the existing institutions and relationships.

AUSTRALIAN NATIONAL UNIVERSITY
CANBERRA, AUSTRALIA

## BIBLIOGRAPHY

NADEL, S. F., 1935, Nupe Witchcraft and Anti-Witchcraft, *Africa*, Vol. VIII.
————, 1942, *A Black Byzantium*, London.
————, 1946, *The Nuba*, London.
————, 1951, *The Foundations of Social Anthropology*, Free Press, Glencoe, Illinois.

# The Structure of Unilineal Descent Groups[1]

### By MEYER FORTES

AS IS well known, Africa has loomed large in British field research in the past twenty-five years. It is, indeed, largely due to the impact of ethnographic data from Africa that British anthropologists are now giving so much attention to social organization, in the widest sense of that term. In this paper what I shall try to do is to sum up some positive contributions that seem to me to have come out of the study of African social organization. I want to add this. British anthropologists are well aware that their range of interests seems narrow in comparison with the wide and adventurous sweep of American anthropology. This has been due to no small extent to lack of numbers and there are signs that a change is on the way with the increase in the number of professional anthropologists since the end of the war. At the same time, I believe that the loss in diversity is amply balanced by the gains we have derived from concentration on a limited set of problems.[2]

Social anthropology has undoubtedly made great progress in the past twenty years. I would give pride of place to the accumulation of ethnographic data obtained by trained observers. It means, curiously enough, that there is going to be more scope than ever for the "armchair" scholar in framing and testing hypotheses with the help of reliable and detailed information. For Africa the advance from the stage of primitive anecdotage to that of scientific description has been almost spectacular; and most of it has taken place since 1930, as can be judged by comparing what we know today with the state of African ethnography as described by Dr. Edwin Smith in 1935. Mainly through Malinowski's influence we now have a respectable series of descriptive monographs on specific institutional complexes in particular African societies. Studies like Evans-Pritchard's on Zande witchcraft (1937), Schapera's on Tswana law (1937) and Richards' on Bemba economy (1939), to cite only three outstanding prewar examples, typify the advance made since 1930. They are significant not only for their wealth of carefully documented detail but also for the evidence they give of the validity of the thesis, now so commonplace, that the customs and institutions of a people can only be properly understood in relation to one another and to the "culture as a whole." They show also what a powerful method of ethnographic discovery intensive fieldwork on "functionalist" lines can be.

The field-work of the past two decades has brought into clearer focus the characteristics of African socieites which distinguish them from the classical simple societies of, say, Australia, Melanesia or North America; and the mark of this is easily seen in the thought and interests of Africanists. One of these is the relatively great size, in terms both of territorial spread and of numbers, of many ethnographic units in Africa as compared with the classical

17

simple societies. There are few truly isolated societies in Africa. Communication takes place over wide geographical regions; and movements of groups over long stretches of time, exactly like those that are known from our own history, have spread languages, beliefs, customs, craft and food producing techniques, and the network of trade and government, over large areas with big populations. A tribe of ten thousand Tswana, two hundred thousand Bemba or half a million Ashanti cannot run their social life on exactly the same pattern as an Australian horde, which is, after all, basically a domestic group. In Africa one comes up against economics where in Australia or parts of North America one meets only housekeeping; one is confronted with government where in societies of smaller scale one meets social control; with organized warfare, with complex legal institutions, with elaborate forms of public worship and systems of belief comparable to the philosophical and theological systems of literate civilizations. Even before its subjugation by Europe, Africa boasted big and wealthy towns. Certainly there was knowledge of all this before professional anthropologists began to work in Africa. But it was patchy and on the whole superficial. In particular, it lacked the explicit conceptualization and integral presentation that mark the kind of monograph I have mentioned. That a belief in witchcraft occurred in many African cultures was known long ago. But the precise nature of the belief, and how it was related to the notion of causation, the rules of moral conduct, the practice of divination and the art of healing to form with them a coherent ideology for daily living, was not understood till Evans-Pritchard's book appeared. It was known, from the works of nineteenth century travellers and administrators, that many African societies had forms of government similar to what political philosophers call the State. But there was little or no accurate information about the constitutional laws, the structure of administration, the machinery of justice, the sanctions of rank, the getting and spending of public revenues, and so forth, in any African state before Rattray's important studies in Ashanti in the twenties (Rattray, 1929 and later). Rattray's description of African state structure has now been superseded. We have a pretty good idea of how a monarchy was kept in power not only by ritual constraints and prerogatives, as in the case of the Divine Kingship of the Shilluk (see Evans-Pritchard, 1948) but also by means of shrewd secular sanctions and institutions such as the control of public revenues and armed forces in Dahomey, described by Herskovits (1938); or the manipulation of a rank and class based administration as in Nupe (Nadel, 1942); or by means of both ritual and secular institutions as has been so vividly described for the Swazi by Dr. Hilda Kuper (1947).

Of course, African customs and institutions often have significant resemblances to those of the simpler peoples of other continents. Indeed it is just these resemblances that make the distinctive features of African ethnology stand out in proper theoretical perspective. Take the customs of avoidance between affines or between successive generations, known from many parts of the world. We are apt to think of them, even with reference to such characteristically African cultures as those of the Southern Bantu (cf. Hunter, 1936) as expressing specific interpersonal relationships. It is the more striking to find among the Nyakyusa (Wilson, 1951) that the whole scheme of local organization in age villages turns on such avoidances. Moreover we can, in this case, see sharply and writ large, how the avoidance between father-in-law and daughter-in-law is an aspect of the tension between successive generations in a patrilineal kinship system.

Implicit and sometimes explicit comparison of African cultures with those of other areas is important in the recent history of field research in Africa. Seligman's pioneering researches in the Sudan were done against the background of his experiences in New Guinea and among the Veddas (cf. C. G. and B. Z. Seligman, 1932). More important, though, is the fact that the main theoretical influence behind the field work of British anthropologists in Africa in the middle twenties and the thirties was that of Malinowski. Now Malinowski's "functional" theory is ordered to the concept of *culture*, essentially in a sense derived from Tylor and Frazer, and his empirical model was always the Trobrianders. It has taken twenty years for the Trobrianders to be placed in a proper comparative perspective in British social anthropology.

It is not, I think, a gross distortion to say that Malinowski thought of culture fundamentally in terms of a utilitarian philosophy. The individual using his culture to satisfy universal needs by attaining culturally defined ends is central to his ethnographic work. It is in the real events of social life, in situations of work, ceremony, dance, dispute, that he saw the interconnection of all aspects of culture. And this approach, crystallized in his formula for the institution—the group, the universal need, the material basis, the legal or mythical charter—has proved to be of the greatest value for the empirical task of field observation. Methodologically, it might be described as a form of clinical study. The net of enquiry is spread to bring in everything that actually happens in the context of observation. The assumption is that everything in a people's culture is meaningful, functional, in the here-and-now of its social existence. This is the cardinal precept for the anthropological study of a living culture. It is the basis of the rigorous observation and comprehensive binding together of detail that marks good ethnographic field work of today. However we may now regard Malinowski's theories we cannot deny him credit for showing us how intensive field work can and must be done. That is, I believe, one of the major contributions made by social anthropology to the social sciences, though it can probably only be satisfactorily used in homogeneous and relatively stable societies or sections of societies.

What I am concerned with in these remarks is the local history of British social anthropology. We all know that Malinowski's functionalism was part of a wider movement; but this is not my subject. The point I am leading up to is this. Malinowski had no sense for social organization, though paradoxically enough his most valuable specific hypotheses fall within the frame of reference of social organization. This applies, for instance to his restatement of the Durkheimian hypothesis of the function of myth as the "charter" of an institution, to his remarkable analysis of the configuration of social relations in the matrilineal family, and to his development of the concept of reciprocity. But he had no real understanding of kinship or political organization. Thus he never overlooked an opportunity of pouring scorn on what he called "kinship algebra," as I can vouch for from personal experience. This prejudice prevented him from completing his often promised book on kinship. It is beautifully documented in the *Sexual Life of Savages* (p. 447). Kinship is to him primarily a tissue of culturally conditioned emotional attitudes. So he is puzzled by the extension of the term for "father" to the father's sister's son; and being quite unable to think in what we should now call structural terms, he commits the appalling methodological solecism of attributing it to an anomaly of language. Malinowski was reacting against the preoccupation with terminologies and with conjectural reconstructions of extinct marriage rules which was so widespread in the early years of this century. It is a measure of the progress made since 1929 that no one today coming across so obvious a case of a Choctaw type lineage terminology would make Malinowski's blunder.

Malinowski's bias is the more instructive because of the debt we owe to his genius. It is reflected in the field work directly inspired by him. We see this in what I regard as the most outstanding contribution to African ethnography we have as yet had, Evans-Pritchard's Zande book (1937). It is notable that he refers only incidentally and casually to the way witchcraft and oracles are tied up with Zande political organization. Firth's study of Tikopia kinship (1937) is an exception for its grasp of the theory of social organization; but he still held the view that social organization is an aspect of culture of the same modality as the others usually enumerated by Malinowski. I mention these two books because they mark important steps in the advance of both ethnography and theory; and I am not suggesting that they follow a wrong track. What I want to stress is that they follow the track which leads to "culture" as the global concept subsuming everything that goes on in social life. A serious limitation to this point of view is that it is bound to treat everything in social life as of equal weight, all aspects as of equal significance. There is no way of establishing an order of priority where all institutions are interdependent, except by criteria that cannot be used in a synchronic study; and synchronic study is the *sine qua non* of functional research. There is, for instance, the criterion of viability over a stretch of time which enables us to say that parliamentary government is a more vital institution in the British Commonwealth than slavery because it has outlived the latter; or that, for the same reason, matrilineal kinship is more significant among the coastal Akan of the Gold Coast than the worship of their pagan gods. Such a criterion, for what it is worth, is not applicable in the absence of historical documents. It is arguable, of course, that this is a false problem, that in fact all the customs and institutions of a society at a given time *are* of equal weight. But it is not scientifically satisfying to accept this assumption without more ado. If our colleagues in human biology had been content with such an assumption in the nature-nurture problem they would have given up their studies of twins and so left the science of human heredity lacking in some of its most critical data. For human society and culture the problem has hitherto been posed and dogmatically answered by the various brands of determinists. Or at the other extreme it has been implied and subtly evaded by the hypostatization of patterns, geniuses and styles. But the problem remains wide open and Malinowski, in common with all who think in terms of a global concept of culture, had no answer to it.

Social anthropology has made some advance on this position since the thirties. Most social anthropologists would now agree that we cannot, for analytical purposes, deal exhaustively with our ethnographic observations in a single frame of reference. We can regard these observations as facts of custom—as standardized ways of doing, knowing, thinking, and feeling—universally obligatory and valued in a given group of people at a given time. But we can also regard them as facts of social organization or social structure. We then seek to relate them to one another by a scheme of conceptual operations different from that of the previous frame of reference. We see custom as symbolizing or expressing social relations—that is, the ties and cleavages by which persons and groups are bound to one another or divided from one another in the activities of social life. In this sense social structure is not an aspect of culture but the entire culture of a given people handled in a special frame of theory. Lastly, we can consider ethnographic facts in terms of a socio-psychological or bio-psychological frame of reference, seeking relevant connections between them as they come into action in the whole or a part of an individual life process, or more widely, as they represent general human aptitudes and dispositions. And no doubt as our subject develops other special techniques and procedures will emerge for handling the data. No one denies the close connection between the different conceptual frames I have mentioned. By distinguishing them we recognize that different modes of abstraction calling for somewhat different emphases in field enquiry are open to us. What I am saying is commonplace today. It was not so in the middle thirties and this was a source of theoretical weakness as Bateson pointed out (1937).

British anthropologists owe their realization of this methodological distinction both to ethnographic discoveries of recent years and to the catalytic influence exercised on their thought by Radcliffe-Brown since his return to England from Chicago in 1937. But the distinction had of course long been implicit in the work of earlier ethnologists. We need only think of the contrast between Lewis Morgan, whose idiom of thought was in terms of a social system, and Tylor, who thought in terms of custom and often had recourse to psychological hypotheses. Rivers (1914) whose own work and influence in England contributed significantly to the development of the idea of social structure, saw this. So did Lowie whose *Primitive Society* (1921) is, I suppose, the first attempt at a systematic analysis of what we should now call the principles of social structure in primitive society. What he brought out was the very obvious but fundamental fact that closely similar, if not identical, forms of social relationship occur in widely separate societies and are expressed in varied custom.

By social organization or social structure, terms which they used interchangeably, Rivers and Lowie meant primarily the kinship, political and legal institutions of primitive peoples. And these, in fact, are the institutions with which British anthropologists are mainly concerned when they write about social structure. The advantage of this term, as opposed to the more usual term "social organization" is that it draws attention to the interconnection and interdependence, within a single system of all the different classes of social relations found within a given society. This leads to questions being asked about the nature of these interconnections and the forces behind the system as a whole.

What I want to stress is that the spur to the current interest in structural studies in Britain comes in equal measure from field experience, especially in Africa, and theory. Anybody who has tried to understand African religious beliefs and practices in the field knows, for example, that one cannot get far without a very thorough knowledge of the kinship and political organization. These studies have thus given new content to the familiar postulate that a living culture is an integrated unity of some sort. We can see more clearly than twenty years ago that this is due not to metaphysical qualities mysteriously diffused through it but to the function of customs and institutions in expressing, marking and maintaining social relations between persons and groups. It is this which underlies the consistencies between the customs and institutions of a people that are commonly emphasized. A unit must, by definition, have a boundary. A culture, certainly in most of Africa, and I venture to believe in many other areas too (as indeed Wissler long ago stressed), has no clear-cut boundaries. But a group of people bound together within a single social structure have a boundary, though not necessarily one that coincides with a physical boundary or is impenetrable. I would suggest that a culture is a unity in so far as it is tied to a bounded social structure. In this sense I would agree that the social structure is the foundation of the whole social life of any *continuing* society. Here again Rivers showed great insight when he stated (1911) that the social structure is the feature of a people's social life which is most resistant to change. It is certainly a striking fact that the family and kinship institutions of a continuing society in Africa display remarkable persistence in the face of big changes in everyday habits, in ritual customs and belief, and even in major economic and social goals. The Tswana (cf. Schapera, 1940 and 1950) are a good instance. But we must be careful. There is also plenty of evidence from emigrant groups, such as Chinese, East Indians and particularly the Negro populations of the New World (cf. Hersko-vits, 1948, p. 542 ff.) of the retention of religious and aesthetic customs in the face of radical changes in structural arrangements. This is a warning against thinking of culture and social structure as mutually exclusive. The social structure of a group does not exist without the customary norms and activities which work through it. We might safely conclude that where structure persists there must be some persistence of corresponding custom and where custom survives there must be some structural basis for this. But I think it would be agreed that though the customs of any continuing and stable society tend to be consistent because they are tied to a coherent social structure, yet there are important factors of autonomy in custom. This has often been pointed out ever since the facts of diffusion became known. The part played by dispositional and psychogenetic factors in the content and action of custom is now being clarified. A house is not reducible to its foundations and custom is not reducible simply to a manifestation of social structure.

The recent trend in British social anthropology springs, as I have said, primarily from field experience. Evans-Pritchard's description of Nuer lineage organization (1933–35), Firth's account of Tikopia kinship (1937) and Forde's analysis of clan and kin relations among the Yakö (1938–39) are the important ethnographic landmarks. A prominent feature in all three is the attention given to the part played by descent rules and institutions in social organization, and the recognition that they belong as much to the sphere of political organization as to that of kinship. Following this lead, other students have been making intensive studies of the role of descent principles in African societies where unilineal descent groups often constitute the genealogical basis of social relations. Good ethnography is both a continuous test of existing hypotheses and continuously creative of theory and technique; and this is happening so rapidly just at present that one can hardly keep pace with it. The younger research workers to whose unpublished material I shall be referring are developing structural analysis into a very effective technique and applying it not only in Africa but also in India, New Guinea and Indonesia.

Seen against the background I have sketched, there is no doubt that big gains have been made in the study of social structure since the nineteen-twenties. This is well illustrated in recent investigations of unilineal descent groups, both in Africa and elsewhere (cf. Eggan, 1950; Gough, 1950) but I will deal mainly with the African data. We are now in a position to formulate a number of connected generalizations about the structure of the unilineal descent group, and its place in the total social system which could not have been stated twenty years ago. It is moreover important to note that they seem to hold for both patrilineal and matrilineal groups. Some of the conditions governing the emergence of such descent groups have recently been discussed by Forde (1947). He makes the interesting suggestion that poverty of habitat and of productive technology tend to inhibit the development of unilineal descent groups by limiting the scale and stability of settlement. Taking this in association with Lowie's hypothesis of 1921 (Lowie, 1921, p. 149) that the establishment of the principle of unilateral descent is mainly due to the transmission of property rights and the mode of residence after marriage, we have two sides of an hypothesis that deserves much further testing. The ground has been well cleared for this by Murdock (1949). For it does seem that unilineal descent groups are not of significance among peoples who live in small groups, depend on a rudimentary technology, and have little durable property. On the other hand, there is evidence that they break down when a modern economic framework with occupational differentiation linked to a wide range of specialized skills, to productive capital and to monetary media of exchange is introduced (Spoehr, 1947; Eggan, 1950; Gough, 1950). Where these groups are most in evidence is in the middle range of relatively homogeneous, pre-capitalistic economies in which there is some degree of technological sophistication and value is attached to rights in durable property. They may be pastoral economies like the Nuer (Evans-Pritchard, 1940) and the Beduin (Peters, 1951), or agricultural economies like those of the Yakö (Forde, 1938, 1950), the Tallensi (Fortes, 1945, 1949) and the Gusii (Mayer, 1949)— or if we look outside Africa, the Tikopia (Firth, 1937) and the Hopi (Eggan, 1950) and many other peoples. The Nayar of South India, classically a test case of kinship theories, are of particular interest in this connection, as a recent intensive field study by Dr. E. J. Miller and Dr. E. K. Gough shows. Though the total economy of South India was even formerly a very complex one, the Nayar themselves traditionally formed a caste of very limited occupational range. It is only during the past hundred years or so that they have gradually entered other occupations than soldiering and passive landlordism. And with this change has come the breakdown previously mentioned in their rigid matrilineal lineage organization. This does not imply that unilineal descent groups are either historically or functionally the product of economic and property institutions alone. Other factors are undoubtedly involved. There is the example of the Hausa of Northern Nigeria, for instance, who have a rural economy of the same type as that of the Tallensi, though technically more elaborate, and well developed property concepts; but they have no unilineal descent groups. The socially significant genealogical grouping among them is of the cognatic type based on the equal recognition of kin ties on both sides, as among the Lozi and other Central African tribes (Dry, 1950; Colson and Gluckman, 1951). Nor can the Hausa arrangement be ascribed to the local influence of Islam since the Cyrenaican Beduin have sharply defined patrilineal lineages (Peters, 1951).

I have lingered a little on this problem to bring home a point which I have already referred to. It is the problem of assigning an order of relative weight to the various factors involved in culture and in social organization, or alternatively of devising methods for describing and analyzing a configuration of factors so as to show precisely how they interact with one another. Much as we have learned from intensive field work in relation to this task, we shall learn even more, I believe, from such studies of local variations within a uniform culture region as Radcliffe-Brown's (1930), Schapera's (in Radcliffe-Brown and Forde, 1950) and Eggan's (1950).

The most important feature of unilineal descent groups in Africa brought into focus by recent field research is their corporate organization. When we speak of these groups as corporate units we do so in the sense given to the term "corporation" long ago by Maine in his classical analysis of testamentary succession in early law (Maine, 1866). We are reminded also of Max Weber's sociological analysis of the corporate group as a general type of social formation (Weber, 1947), for in many important particulars these African descent groups conform to Weber's definition. British anthropologists now regularly use the term *lineage* for these descent groups. This helps both to stress the significance of descent in their structure and to distinguish them from wider often dispersed divisions of society ordered to the notion of common—but not demonstrable and often mythological—ancestry for which we find it useful to reserve the label *clan*.

The guiding ideas in the analysis of African lineage organization have come mainly from Radcliffe-Brown's formulation of the structural principles found in all kinship systems (cf. Radcliffe-Brown, 1950). I am sure I am not alone in regarding these as among the most important generalizations as yet reached in the study of social structure. Lineage organization shows very clearly how these principles work together in mutual dependence, so that varying weight of one or the other in relation to variations in the wider context of social structure gives rise to variant arrangements on the basis of the same broad ground-plan.

A lineage is a corporate group from the outside, that is in relation to other defined groups and associations. It might be described as a single legal personality—"one person" as the Ashanti put it (Fortes, 1950). Thus the way a lineage system works depends on the kind of legal institutions found in the society; and this, we know, is a function of its political organization. Much fruitful work has resulted from following up this line of thought. As far as Africa is concerned there is increasing evidence to suggest that lineage organization is most developed in what Evans-Pritchard and I (1940), taking a hint from Durkheim, called segmentary societies. This has been found to hold for the Tiv of Nigeria (P. J. Bohannan, 1951), for the Gusii (Mayer, 1949) and other East and South African peoples, and for the Cyrenaican Beduin (Peters, 1951), in addition to the peoples discussed in *African Political Systems*. In societies of this type the lineage is not only a corporate unit in the legal or jural sense but is also the primary political association. Thus the individual has no legal or political status except as a member of a lineage; or to put it in another way, all legal and political relations in the society take place in the context of the lineage system.

But lineage grouping is not restricted to segmentary societies. It is the basis of local organization and of political institutions also in societies like the Ashanti (Fortes, 1950; Busia, 1951) and the Yoruba (Forde, 1951) which have national government centered in kingship, administrative machinery and courts of law. But the primary emphasis, in these societies, is on the legal aspect of the lineage. The political structure of these societies was always unstable and this was due in considerable degree to internal rivalries arising out of the divisions between lineages; that is perhaps why they remained federal in constitution. In Ashanti, for instance, this is epitomized in the fact that citizenship is, in the first place, local not national, is determined by lineage membership by birth and is mediated through the lineage organization. The more centralized the political system the greater the tendency seems to be for the corporate strength of descent groups to be reduced or for such corporate groups to be nonexistent. Legal and political status are conferred by allegiance to the State not by descent, though rank and property may still be vested in descent lines. The Nupe (Nadel, 1942), the Zulu (Gluckman in Fortes and Evans-Pritchard, 1940), the Hausa (Dry, 1950), and other state organizations exemplify this in different ways. There is, in these societies, a clearer structural differentiation between the field of domestic relations based on kinship and descent and the field of political relations, than in segmentary societies.

However, where the lineage is found as a corporate group all the members of a lineage are to outsiders jurally equal and represent the lineage when they exercise legal and political rights and duties in relation to society at large. This is what underlies so-called collective responsibility in blood vengeance and self-help as among the Nuer (Evans-Pritchard, 1940) and the Beduin (Peters, 1951).

Maine's aphorism that corporations never die draws attention to an important characteristic of the lineage, its continuity, or rather its presumed perpetuity in time. Where the lineage concept is highly developed, the lineage is thought to exist as a perpetual corporation as long as any of its members survive. This means, of course, not merely perpetual physical existence ensured by the replacement of departed members. It means perpetual structural existence, in a stable and homogeneous society; that is, the perpetual exercise of defined rights, duties, office and social tasks vested in the lineage as a corporate unit. The point is obvious but needs recalling as it throws light on a widespread custom. We often find, in Africa and elsewhere, that a person or descent group is attached to a patrilineal lineage through a female member of the lineage. Then if there is a danger that rights and offices vested in the lineage may lapse through the extinction of the true line of descent, the attached line may by some jural fiction be permitted to assume them. Or again, rather than let property or office go to another lineage by default of proper succession within the owning lineage, a slave may be allowed to succeed. In short, the aim is to preserve the existing scheme of social relations as far as possible. As I shall mention presently, this idea is developed most explicitly among some Central African peoples.

But what marks a lineage out and maintains its identity in the face of the continuous replacement by death and birth of its members is the fact that it emerges most precisely in a complementary relationship with or in opposition to like units. This was first precisely shown for the Nuer by Evans-Pritchard and I was able to confirm the analysis among the Tallensi (Fortes, 1949). It is characteristic of all segmentary societies in Africa so far described, almost by definition. A recent and most interesting case is that of the Tiv of Northern Nigeria (P. J. Bohannan, 1951). This people were, until the arrival of the British, extending their territory rapidly by moving forward *en masse* as their land became exhausted. Among them the maximal lineages are identified by their relative *positions* in the total deployment of all the lineages and they maintain these positions by pushing against one another as they all move slowly forward.

The presumed perpetuity of the lineage is what lineage genealogies conceptualize. If there is one thing all recent investigations are agreed upon it is that lineage genealogies are not historically accurate. But they can be understood if they are seen to be the conceptualization of the existing lineage structure viewed as continuing through time and therefore projected backward as pseudo-history. The most striking proof of this comes from Cyrenaica. The Beduin there have tribal genealogies going back no more than the fourteen generations or thereabouts which we so commonly find among African Negro peoples; but as Peters points out, historical records show that they have lived in Cyrenaica apparently in much the same way as now for a much longer time than the four to five hundred years implied in their genealogies. Dr. P. J. and Dr. L. Bohannan have actually observed the Tiv at public moots rearranging their lineage genealogies to bring them into line with changes in the existing pattern of legal and political relations within and between lineages. A genealogy is, in fact, what Malinowski called a legal charter and not an historical record.

A society made up of corporate lineages is in danger of splitting into rival lineage factions. How is this counteracted in the interests of wider political unity? One way is to extend the lineage framework to the widest range within which sanctions exist for preventing conflicts and disputes from ending in feud or warfare. The political unit is thought of then as the most inclusive, or maximal, lineage to which a person can belong, and it may be conceptualized as embracing the whole tribal unit. This happens among the Gusii (Mayer, 1949) as well as among the Nuer, the Tiv and the Beduin; but with the last three the tribe is not the widest field within which sanctions against feud and war prevail. A major lineage segment of the tribe is the *de facto* political unit by this definition.

Another way, widespread in West Africa but often associated with the previously mentioned structural arrangement, is for the common interest of the political community to be asserted periodically, as against the private interests of the component lineages, through religious institutions and sanctions. I found this to be the case among the Tallensi (Fortes, 1940) and the same principle applies to the Yakö (Forde, 1950 (b)) and the Ibo (Forde and Jones, 1950). I believe it will be shown to hold for many peoples of the Western Sudan among whom ancestor worship and the veneration of the earth are the basis of religious custom. The politically integrative functions of ritual institutions have been described for many parts of the world. What recent African ethnography adds is detailed descriptive data from which further insight into the symbolism used and into the reasons why political authority tends to be invested with ritual meaning and expression can be gained. A notable instance is Dr. Kuper's (1947) account of the Swazi kingship.

As the Swazi data indicate, ritual institutions are also used to support political authority and to affirm the highest common interests in African societies with more complex political structures than those of segmentary societies. This has long been known, ever since the Divine Kingship of the Shilluk (cf. Evans-Pritchard, 1948) brought inspiration to Sir James Frazer. But these ritual institutions do not free the individual to have friendly and co-operative relations with other individuals irrespective of allegiance to corporate groups. If such relations were impossible in a society it could hardly avoid splitting into antagonistic fractions in spite of public ritual sanctions, or else it would be in a chronic state of factional conflict under the surface. It is not surprising therefore to find that great value is attached to widely spreading bonds of personal kinship, as among the Tallensi (Fortes, 1949). The recent field studies I have quoted all confirm the tremendous importance of the web of kinship as a counterweight to the tendency of unilineal descent grouping to harden social barriers. Or to put it slightly differently, it seems that where the unilineal descent group is rigorously structured within the total social system there we are likely to find kinship used to define and sanction a personal field of social relations for each individual. I will come back to this point in a moment. A further point to which I will refer again is this. We are learning from considerations such as those I have just mentioned, to think of social structure in terms of levels of organization in the manner first explicitly followed in the presentation of field data by Warner (1937). We can investigate the total social structure of a given community at the level of local organization, at that of kinship, at the level of corporate group structure and government, and at that of ritual institutions. We see these levels are related to different collective interests, which are perhaps connected in some sort of hierarchy. And one of the problems of analysis and exposition is to perceive and state the fact that all levels of structure are simultaneously involved in every social relationship and activity. This restatement of what is commonly meant by the concept of integration has the advantage of suggesting how the different modes of social relationship distinguished in any society are interlocked with one another. It helps to make clear also how certain basic principles of social organization can be generalized throughout the whole structure of a primitive society, as for instance the segmentary principle among the Nuer and the Tallensi.

This way of thinking about the problem of social integration has been useful in recent studies of African political organization. Study of the unilineal descent group as a part of a total social system means in fact studying its functions in the widest framework of social structure, that of the political organization. A common and perhaps general feature of political organization in Africa is that it is built up in a series of layers, so to speak, so arranged that the principle of checks and balances is necessarily mobilized in political activities. The idea is used in a variety of ways but what it comes to in general is that the members of the society are distributed in different, nonidentical schemes of allegiance and mutual dependence in relation to administrative, juridical and ritual institutions. It would take too long to enumerate all the peoples for whom we now have sufficient data to show this in detail. But the Lozi of Northern Rhodesia (Gluckman, 1951) are of such particular theoretical interest in this connection that a word must be said about them. The corporate descent group is not found among them. Instead their political organization is based on what Maine called the corporation sole. This is a title carrying political office backed by ritual sanctions and symbols to which subjects, lands, jurisdiction, and representative status, belong. But every adult is bound to a number of titles for different legal and social purposes in such a way that what is one allegiance group with respect to one title is split up with reference to other titles. Thus the only all-inclusive allegiance is that of all the nation to the kingship, which is identified with the State and the country as a whole. A social structure of such a kind, knit together moreover by a widely ramifying network of bilateral kinship ties between persons, is well fortified against internal disruption. It should be added that the notion of the "corporation sole" is found among many Central African peoples. It appears, in fact, to be a jural institution of the same generality in any of these societies as corporate groups are in others, since it is significant at all levels of social structure. A good example is the Bemba (cf. Richards, 1936, 1940b) among whom it is seen in the custom of "positional inheritance" of status, rank, political office and ritual duty, as I will explain later.

What is the main methodological contribution of these studies? In my view it is the approach from the angle of political organization to what are traditionally thought of as kinship groups and institutions that has been specially fruitful. By regarding lineages and statuses from the point of view of the total social system and not from that of an hypothetical EGO we realize that consanguinity and affinity, real or putative, are not sufficient in themselves to bring about these structural arrangements. We see that descent is fundamentally a jural concept as Radcliffe-Brown argued in one of his most important papers (1935); we see its significance, as the connecting link between the external, that is political and legal, aspect of what we have called unilineal descent groups, and the internal or domestic aspect. It is in the latter context that kinship carries maximum weight, first, as the source of title to membership of the groups or to specific jural status, with all that this means in rights over and toward persons and property, and second as the basis of the social relations among the persons who are identified with one another in the corporate group. In theory, membership of a corporate legal or political group need not stem from kinship, as Weber has made clear. In primitive society, however, if it is not based on kinship it seems generally to presume some formal procedure of incorporation with ritual initiation. So-called secret societies in West Africa seem to be corporate organizations of this nature. Why descent rather than locality or some other principle forms the basis of these corporate groups is a question that needs more study. It will be remembered that Radcliffe-Brown (1935) related succession rules to the need for unequivocal discrimination of rights *in rem* and *in personam*. Perhaps it is most closely connected with the fact that rights over the reproductive powers of women are easily regulated by a descent group system. But I believe that something deeper than this is involved; for in a homogeneous society there is nothing which could so precisely and incontrovertibly fix one's place in society as one's parentage.

Looking at it from without, we ignore the internal structure of the unilineal group. But African lineages are not monolithic units; and knowledge of their internal differentiation has been much advanced by the researches I have mentioned. The dynamic character of lineage structure can be seen most easily in the balance that is reached between its external relations and its internal structure. Ideally, in most lineage-based societies the lineage tends to be thought of as a perpetual unit, expanding like a balloon but never growing new parts. In fact, of course, as Forde (1938) and Evans-Pritchard (1940) have so clearly shown, fission and accretion are processes inherent in lineage structure. However, it is a common experience to find an informant who refuses to admit that his lineage or even his branch of a greater lineage did not at one time exist. Myth and legend, believed, naturally, to be true history, are quickly cited to prove the contrary. But investigation shows that the stretch of time, or rather of duration, with which perpetuity is equated varies according to the count of generations needed to conceptualize the internal structure of the lineage and link it on to an absolute, usually mythological origin for the whole social system in a first founder.

This is connected with the fact that an African lineage is never, according to our present knowledge, internally undifferentiated. It is always segmented and is in process of continuous further segmentation at any given time. Among some of the peoples I have mentioned (e.g. the Tallensi and probably the Ibo) the internal segmentation of a lineage is quite rigorous and the process of further segmentation has an almost mechanical precision. The general rule is that every segment is, in form, a replica of every other segment and of the whole lineage. But the segments are, as a rule, hierarchically organized by fixed steps of greater and greater inclusiveness, each step being defined by genealogical reference. It is perhaps hardly necessary to mention again that when we talk of lineage structure we are really concerned, from a particular analytical angle, with the organization of jural, economic, and ritual activities. The point here is that lineage segmentation corresponds to gradation in the institutional norms and activities in which the total lineage organization is actualized. So we find that the greater the time depth that is attributed to the lineage system as a whole, the more elaborate is its internal segmentation. As I have already mentioned, lineage systems in Africa, when most elaborate, seem to have a maximal time depth of around fourteen putative generations. More common though is a count of five or six generations of named ancestors between living adults and a quasi-mythological founder. We can as yet only guess at the conditions that lie behind these limits of genealogical depth in lineage structure. The facts themselves are nevertheless of great comparative interest. As I have previously remarked, these genealogies obviously do not represent a true record of all the ancestors of a group. To explain this by the limitations and fallibility of oral tradition is merely to evade the problem. In structural terms the answer seems to lie in the spread or span (Fortes, 1945) of internal segmentation of the lineage, and this apparently has inherent limits. As I interpret the evidence we have, these limits are set by the condition of stability in the social structure which it is one of the chief functions of lineage systems to maintain. The segmentary spread found in a given lineage system is that which makes for maximum stability; and in a stable social system it is kept at a particular spread by continual internal adjustments which are conceptualized by clipping, patching and telescoping genealogies to fit. Just what the optimum spread of lineage segmentation in a particular society tends to be depends presumably on extra-lineage factors of political and economic organization of the kind referred to by Forde (1947).

It is when we consider the lineage from within that kinship becomes decisive. For lineage segmentation follows a model laid down in the parental family. It is indeed generally thought of as the perpetuation, through the rule of the jural unity of the descent line and of the sibling group (cf. Radcliffe-Brown, 1951), of the social relations that constitute the parental family. So we find a lineage segment conceptualized as a sibling group in symmetrical relationship with segments of a like order. It will be a paternal sibling group where descent is patrilineal and a maternal one where it is matrilineal. Progressive orders of inclusiveness are formulated as a succession of generations; and the actual process of segmentation is seen as the equivalent of the division between siblings in the parental family. With this goes the use of kinship terminology and the application of kinship norms in the regulation of intra-lineage affairs.

As a corporate group, a lineage exhibits a structure of authority, and it is obvious from what I have said why this is aligned with the generation ladder. We find, as a general rule, that not only the lineage but also every segment of it has a head, by succession or election, who manages its affairs with the advice of his co-members. He may not have legal sanctions by means of which to enforce his authority in internal affairs; but he holds his position by consent of all his fellow members, and he is backed by moral sanctions commonly couched in religious concepts. He is the trustee for the whole group of the property and other productive resources vested in it. He has a decisive jural role also in the disposal of rights over the fertility of the women in the group. He is likely to be the representative of the whole group in political and legal relations with other groups, with political authorities, and in communal ritual. The effect may be to make him put the interests of his lineage above those of the community if there is conflict with the latter. This is quite clearly recognized by some peoples. Among the Ashanti for instance, every chiefship is vested in a matrilineal lineage. But once a chief has been installed his constitutional position is defined as holding an office that belongs to the whole community not to any one lineage. The man is, ideally, so merged in the office that he virtually ceases to be a member of his lineage, which always has an independent head for its corporate affairs (cf. Busia, 1950).

Thus lineage segmentation as a process in time links the lineage with the parental family; for it is through the family that the lineage (and therefore the society) is replenished by successive generations; and it is on the basis of the ties and cleavages between husband and wife, between polygynous wives, between siblings, and between generations that growth and segmentation take place in the lineage. Study of this process has added much to our understanding of well known aspects of family and kinship structure.

I suppose that we all now take it for granted that filiation—by contrast with descent—is universally bilateral. But we have also been taught, perhaps most graphically by Malinowski, that this does not imply equality of social weighting for the two sides of kin connection. Correctly stated, the rule should read that filiation is always complementary, unless the husband in a matrilineal society (like the Nayar) or the wife in a patrilineal society, as perhaps in ancient Rome, is given no parental status or is legally severed from his or her kin. The latter is the usual situation of a slave spouse in Africa.

Complementary filiation appears to be the principal mechanism by which segmentation in the lineage is brought about. This is very clear in patrilineal descent groups, and has been found to hold for societies as far apart as the Tallensi in West Africa and the Gusii in East Africa. What is a single lineage in relation to a male founder is divided into segments of a lower order by reference to their respective female founders on the model of the division of a polygynous family into separate matricentral "houses." In matrilineal lineage systems, however, the position is different. Segmentation does not follow the lines of different paternal origin, for obvious reasons; it follows the lines of differentiation between sisters. There is a connection between this and the weakness in law and in sentiment of the marriage tie in matrilineal societies, though it is usual for political and legal power to be vested in men as Kroeber (1938) and others have remarked. More study of this problem is needed.

Since the bilateral family is the focal element in the web of kinship, complementary filiation provides the essential link between a sibling group and the kin of the parent who does not determine descent. So a sibling group is not merely differentiated within a lineage but is further distinguished by reference to its kin ties outside the corporate unit. This structural device allows of degrees of individuation depending on the extent to which filiation on the noncorporate side is elaborated. The Tiv, for example, recognize five degrees of matrilateral filiation by which a sibling group is linked with lineages other than its own. These and other ties of a similar nature arising out of marriage exchanges result in a complex scheme of individuation for distinguishing both sibling groups and persons within a single lineage (L. Bohannan, 1951). This, of course, is not unique and has long been recognized, as everyone familiar with Australian kinship systems knows. Its more general significance can be brought out however by an example. A Tiv may claim to be living with a particular group of relatives for purely personal reasons of convenience or affection. Investigation shows that he has in fact made a choice of where to live within a strictly limited range of nonlineage kin. What purports to be a voluntary act freely motivated in fact presupposes a structural scheme of individuation. This is one of the instances which show how it is possible and feasible to move from the structural frame of reference to another, here that of the social psychologist, without confusing data and aims.

Most far-reaching in its effects on lineage structure is the use of the rule of complementary filiation to build double unilineal systems and some striking instances of this are found in Africa. One of the most developed systems of this type is that of the Yakö; and Forde's excellent analysis of how this works (Forde, 1950) shows that it is much more than a device for classifying kin. It is a principle of social organization that enters into all social relations and is expressed in all important institutions. There is the division of property, for instance, into the kind that is tied to the patrilineal lineage and the kind that passes to matrilineal kin. The division is between fixed and, in theory, perpetual productive resources, in this case farm land, with which goes residence rights, on the one hand, and on the other, movable and consumable property like livestock and cash. There is a similar polarity in religious cult and in the political office and authority linked with cult, the legally somewhat weaker matrilineal line being ritually somewhat stronger than the patrilineal line. This balance between ritual and secular control is extended to the fertility of the women. An analogous double descent system has been described for some Nuba Hill tribes by Nadel (1950) and its occurrence among the Herero is now classical in ethnology. The arrangement works the other way round, too, in Africa, as among the Ashanti, though in their case the balance is far more heavily weighted on the side of the matrilineal lineage than on that of the jurally inferior and noncorporate paternal line.

These and other instances lead to the generalization that complementary filiation is not merely a constant element in the pattern of family relationships but comes into action at all levels of social structure in African societies. It appears that there is a tendency for interests, rights and loyalties to be divided on broadly complementary lines, into those that have the sanction of law or other public institutions for the enforcement of good conduct, and those that rely on religion, morality, conscience and sentiment for due observance. Where corporate descent groups exist the former seem to be generally tied to the descent group, the latter to the complementary line of filiation.

If we ask where this principle of social structure springs from we must look to the tensions inherent in the structure of the parental family. These tensions are the result of the direction given to individual lives by the total social structure but they also provide the models for the working of that structure. We now have plenty of evidence to show how the tensions that seem normally to arise between spouses, between successive generations and between siblings find expression in custom and belief. In a homogeneous society they are apt to be generalized over wide areas of the social structure. They then evoke controls like the Nyakyusa separation of successive generations of males in age villages that are built into the total social structure by the device of handing over political power to each successive generation as it reaches maturity (Wilson, 1951). Or this problem may be dealt with on the level of ritual and moral symbolism by separating parent and first born child of the same sex by taboos that eliminate open rivalry, as among the Tallensi, the Nuer, the Hausa and other peoples.

Thus by viewing the descent group as a continuing process through time we see how it binds the parental family, its growing point, by a series of steps into the widest framework of social structure. This enables us to visualize a social system as an integrated unity at a given time and over a stretch of time in relation to the process of social reproduction and in a more rigorous way than does a global concept of culture.

I do want to make clear, though, that we do not think of a lineage as being just a collection of people held together by the accident of birth. A descent group is an arrangement of persons that serves the attainment of legitimate social and personal ends. These include the gaining of a livelihood, the setting up of a family and the preservation of health and well-being as among the most important. I have several times remarked on the connection generally found between lineage structure and the ownership of the most valued productive property of the society, whether it be land or cattle or even the monopoly of a craft like blacksmithing. It is of great interest, for instance, to find Dr. Richards attributing the absence of a lineage organization among the Bemba to their lack of heritable right in land or livestock (Richards, 1950). A similar connection is found between lineage organization and the control over reproductive resources and relations as is evident from the common occurrence of exogamy as a criterion of lineage differentiation. And since citizenship is derived from lineage membership and legal status depends on it, political and religious office of necessity vests in lineages. We must expect to find and we do find that the most important religious and magical concepts and institutions of a lineage based society are tied into the lineage structure serving both as the necessary symbolical representation of the social system and as its regulating values. This is a complicated subject about which much more needs to be known. Cults of gods and of ancestors, beliefs of a totemic nature, and purely magical customs and practices, some or all are associated with lineage organization among the peoples previously quoted. What appears to happen is that every significant structural differentiation has its specific ritual symbolism, so that one can, as it were, read off from the scheme of ritual differentiation the pattern of structural differentiation and the configuration of norms of conduct that goes with it. There is, to put it simply, a segmentation of ritual allegiance corresponding to the segmentation of genealogical grouping. Locality, filiation, descent, individuation, are thus symbolized.

Reference to locality reminds us of Kroeber's careful argument of 1938 in favor of the priority of the local relationships of residence over those of descent in determining the line that is legally superior. A lineage cannot easily act as a corporate group if its members can never get together for the conduct of their affairs. It is not surprising therefore to find that the lineage in African societies is generally locally anchored; but it is not necessarily territorially compact or exclusive. A compact nucleus may be enough to act as the local center for a group that is widely dispersed. I think it would be agreed that lineage and locality are independently variable and how they interact depends on other factors in the social structure. As I interpret the evidence, local ties are of secondary significance, *pace* Kroeber, for local ties do not appear to give rise to structural bonds in and of themselves. There must be common political or kinship or economic or ritual interests for structural bonds to emerge. Again spatial dispersion does not immediately put an end to lineage ties or to the ramifying kin ties found in cognatic systems like that of the Lozi. For legal status, property, office and cult act centripetally to hold dispersed lineages together and to bind scattered kindred. This is important in the dynamic pattern of lineage organization for it contains within itself the springs of disintegration, at the corporate level in the rule of segmentation, at the individual level in the rule of complementary filiation.

As I have suggested before, it seems that corporate descent groups can exist only in more or less homogeneous societies. Just what we mean by a homogeneous society is still rather vague though we all use the term lavishly. The working definition I make use of is that a homogeneous society is ideally one in which any person in the sense given to this term by Radcliffe-Brown in his recent (1950) essay, can be substituted for any other person of the same category without bringing about changes in the social structure. This implies that any two persons of the same category have the same body of customary usages and beliefs. I relate this tentative definition to the rule of sibling equivalence, so that I would say that, considered with respect to their achievable life histories, in a homogeneous society all men are brothers and all women sisters.

Societies based on unilineal descent groups are not the best in which to see what the notion of social substitutability means. For that it is better to consider societies in which descent still takes primacy over all other criteria of association and classification of persons in the regulation of social life but does not serve as the constitutive principle of corporate group organization.

Central Africa provides some admirable instances (cf. Richards, 1950; Colson and Gluckman, 1951). Among the Bemba, the Tonga, the Lozi and many of their neighbors, as I have already remarked, the social structure must be thought of as a system of interconnected politico-legal statuses symbolized and sanctioned by ritual and not as a collection of people organized in self-perpetuating descent units. The stability of the society over time is preserved by perpetuating the status system. Thus when a person dies his status is kept alive by being taken up by an heir; and this heir is selected on the basis of descent rules. At any given time an individual may be the holder of a cluster of statuses; but these may be distributed among several persons on his death in a manner analogous to the widespread African custom by which a man's inherited estate goes to his lineage heir and his self-acquired property to his personal heir. Ideally, therefore, the network of statuses remains stable and perpetual though their holders come and go. Ritual symbols define and sanction the key positions in the system. What it represents, in fact, is the generalization throughout a whole society of the notion of the corporation sole as tied to descent but not to a corporate group. Descent and filiation have the function of selecting individuals for social positions and roles—in other words, for the exercise of particular rights and obligations—just as in cross cousin marriage they serve to select ego's spouse.

The concept of the "person" as an assemblage of statuses has been the starting point of some interesting enquiries. A generalization of long standing is that a married person always has two mutually antagonistic kinship statuses, that of spouse and parent in one family context and that of child and sibling in another (cf. Warner, 1937). This is very conspicuous in an exogamous lineage system; and the tensions resulting from this condition, connected as they are with the rule of complementary filiation, have wide consequences. A common rule of social structure reflected in avoidance customs is that these two statuses must not be confounded. Furthermore, each status can be regarded as a compound of separable rights and obligations. Thus a problem that has to be solved in every matrilineal society is how to reconcile the rights over a woman's procreative powers (rights *in genetricem* as Laura Bohannan has called them in her paper of 1949) which remain vested in her brother or her lineage, with those over her domestic and sexual services (rights *in uxorem,* cf. L. Bohannan, *loc. cit.*) which pass to her husband. Among the Yao of Nyassaland, as Dr. Clyde Mitchell has shown (1950), this problem underlies the process of lineage segmentation. Brothers struggle against one another (or sisters' sons against mothers' brothers) for the control of their sisters' procreative powers and this leads to fission in the minimal lineage. It is of great significance that such a split is commonly precipitated by accusations of withcraft against the brother from whose control the sisters are withdrawn. By contrast, where rights over a woman's child-bearing powers are held by her

husband's patrilineal lineage the conflicts related to this critical interest
occur between the wives of a lineage segment; and among the Zulu and Xhosa
speaking tribes of South Africa these lead to witchcraft accusations between
co-wives (cf. Hunter, 1936). As Laura Bohannan's paper shows, many widespread customs and institutions connected with marriage and parenthood,
such as the levirate and the sororate, wife-taking by women, exchange marriage as practiced by the Tiv, and ghost marriage as found among the Nuer
(Evans-Pritchard, 1951) have structural significance not hitherto appreciated
if they are regarded from the point of view I have indicated.

But one thing must be emphasized. This method of analysis does not explain why in one society certain kinds of interpersonal conflict are socially
projected in witchcraft beliefs whereas in another they may be projected in
terms of a belief in punitive spirits. It makes clear why a funeral ceremony is
necessary and why it is organized in a particular way in the interest of maintaining a stable and coherent social system. It does not explain why the
ritual performed in the funeral ceremonies of one people uses materials, ideas
and dramatizations of a different kind from those used by another people. In
short, it brings us nearer than we were thirty years ago to understanding the
machinery by which norms are made effective, not only in a particular primitive society but in a type of primitive society. It does not explain how the
norms come to be what they in fact are in a particular society.

In this connection, however, it is worth drawing attention to certain
norms that have long been recognized to have a critical value in social organization. Marriage regulations, incest prohibitions and the laws of homicide and
warfare are the most important. Analysis of lineage structure has revealed an
aspect of these norms which is of great theoretical interest. It is now fairly
evident that these are not absolute rules of conduct which men are apt to
break through an outburst of unruly instinct or rebellious self-assertion, as
has commonly been thought. They are *relatively* obligatory in accordance with
the structural relations of the parties. The Beduin of Cyrenaica regard homicide within the minimal agnatic lineage, even under extreme provocation, as
a grave sin, whereas slaying a member of a different tribal segment is an admirable deed of valor. The Tallensi consider sex relations with a near sister
of the same lineage as incest but tacitly ignore the act if the parties are very
distant lineage kin. Among the Tiv, the Nuer, the Gusii and other tribes the
lineage range within which the rule of exogamy holds is variable and can be
changed by a ceremony that makes formally prohibited marriages legitimate
and so brings marriage prohibitions into line with changes in the segmentary
structure of the lineage. In this way previously exogamous units are split into
intermarrying units. In all the societies mentioned, and others as well, an act
of self-help that leads to negotiations if the parties belong to closely related

lineages might lead to war if they are members of independent—though not necessarily geographically far apart—lineages. Such observations are indications of the flexibility of primitive social structures. They give a clue to the way in which internal adjustments are made from time to time in those structures, either in response to changing pressures from without or through the momentum of their own development. They suggest how such societies can remain stable in the long run without being rigid. But this verges on speculation.

The contributions to African ethnography mentioned in this paper are only a small and arbitrary selection from a truly vast amount of new work that is now going on in several countries. My aim has been to suggest how this work links up with a theoretical approach that is much in evidence among British social anthropologists. It is perhaps needless to add that this approach is also being actively applied by American, French, Belgian and Dutch anthropologists concerned with the problems of social organization. What I wish to convey by the example of current studies of unilineal descent group structure is that we have, in my belief, got to a point where a number of connected generalizations of wide validity can be made about this type of social group. This is an advance I associate with the structural frame of reference. I wish to suggest that this frame of reference gives us procedures of investigation and analysis by which a social system can be apprehended as a unity made of parts and processes that are linked to one another by a limited number of principles of wide validity in homogeneous and relatively stable societies. It has enabled us to set up hypotheses about the nature of these principles that have the merit of being related directly to the ethnographic material now so abundantly at hand and of being susceptible of testing by further field observation. It cannot be denied, I think, that we have here a number of positive contributions of real importance to social science.

UNIVERSITY OF CAMBRIDGE
    CAMBRIDGE, ENGLAND

## NOTES

[1] *Editorial note:* This paper was presented by Professor Fortes at the Symposium on the "Positive Contributions of Social Anthropology," held at the 50th annual meetings of the American Anthropological Association in Chicago, November 15-17, 1951. Professor Fortes' participation in the symposium was made possible by the generosity of the Wenner-Gren Foundation for Anthropological Research, Inc.

[2] This was written before I saw the discussion between Dr. Murdock and Professor Firth on the limitations of British social anthropology in the October–December 1951 number (Vol. 53, No. 4, Pt. 1) of the *American Anthropologist.*

[3] In the bibliography that follows, references marked by an asterisk are cited by permission of the author.

BIBLIOGRAPHY

BATESON, G., 1937, *Naven.*

BOHANNAN, LAURA, 1949, Dahomean Marriage: a revaluation. *Africa,* 19. 4.

————, 1951, *A Comparative Study of Social Differentiation in Primitive Society.* (D.Phil. thesis, University of Oxford.)*

BOHANNAN, P. J., 1951, *Political and Economic Aspects of Land Tenure and Settlement Patterns among the Tiv of Central Nigeria.* (D.Phil. thesis, University of Oxford.)*

BUSIA, K. A., 1951, *The Position of the Chief in the Modern Political System of Ashanti.*

DRY, P. D. L., 1950, *The Social Structure of a Hausa Village.* (B.Sc. thesis, University of Oxford.)*

EGGAN, F., 1937, Cheyenne and Arapaho Kinship Systems, in *Social Organisation of North American Tribes.*

————, 1950, *Social Organization of the Western Pueblos.*

EVANS-PRITCHARD, E. E., 1933–35, The Nuer: tribe and clan. *Sudan Notes and Records,* Volume XVI, Part 1, Volume XVII, Part 1, Volume XVIII, Part 1.

————, 1937, *Witchcraft, Oracles and Magic among the Azande.*

————, 1940 (a), *The Nuer.*

————, 1940 (b), The Political System of the Nuer, in *African Political Systems.*

————, 1948, *The Divine Kingship of the Shilluk of the Nilotic Sudan.* Frazer Lecture.

————, 1951, *Kinship and Marriage among the Nuer.*

FIRTH, R., 1936, *We, the Tikopia.*

FORDE, C. DARYLL, 1938, Fission and Accretion in the Patrilineal Clans of a Semi-Bantu Community. *Journal of the Royal Anthropological Institute,* Volume 68.

————, 1939, Kinship in Umor: Double Unilateral Organization in a Semi-Bantu Society, *American Anthropol.* Volume 41.

————, 1947, The Anthropological Approach in Social Science, in *The Advancement of Science,* Volume IV.

————, 1950(a), Double Descent among the Yakö, in Radcliffe-Brown and Forde, 1950.

————, 1950 (b), "Ward Organisation among the Yakö" *Africa,* 20. 4.

————, 1951, The Yoruba Speaking Peoples of South-Western Nigeria. *Ethnographic Survey of Africa.* Pt. IV.

FORDE, C. DARYLL and G. I. JONES, 1950, The Ibo and Ibibio-Speaking Peoples of South Eastern Nigeria, *Ethnographic Survey of Africa, Western Africa, Part III.*

FORTES, M., 1945, *The Dynamics of Clanship among the Tallensi.*

————, 1949, *The Web of Kinship among the Tallensi.*

————, 1949, Time and Social Structure: an Ashanti Case Study, in *Social Structure: studies presented to A. R. Radcliffe-Brown,* Ed. by M. Fortes.

————, 1950, Kinship and Marriage among the Ashanti, in Radcliffe-Brown and Forde, 1950.

FORTES, M., and E. E. EVANS-PRITCHARD 1940, (edit.) *African Political Systems.*

GLUCKMAN, M., 1950, Kinship and Marriage among the Lozi of Northern Rhodesia and the Zulu of Natal, in Radcliffe-Brown and Forde, 1950.

————, 1951, The Lozi of Barotseland in North Western Rhodesia, in *Seven Tribes of British Central Africa,* edited by E. Colson and M. Gluckman.

HERSKOVITS,M. J., 1938, *Dahomey.*

————, 1948, *Man and His Works.*

HUNTER, MONICA, 1936, *Reaction to Conquest.*

GOUGH, E. K., 1950, *Kinship among the Nayar of the Malabar Coast of India.* (D. Phil. thesis, University of Cambridge.)*

KUPER, HILDA, 1947, *An African Aristocracy.*

————, 1950, Kinship among the Swazi, in Radcliffe-Brown and Forde, 1950.

KROEBER, A. L., 1938, Basic and Secondary Patterns of Social Structure. *Journal of the Royal Anthropological Institute*, Volume 68.

LOWIE, R., 1921, *Primitive Society*.

MALINOWSKI, B., 1929, *The Sexual Life of Savages*.

MAINE, SIR HENRY, 1866, *Ancient Law*.

MAYER, P., 1949, The Lineage Principle in Gusii Society. *International African Institute, Memorandum XXIV*.

MITCHELL, J. CLYDE, 1950, *Social Organisation of the Yao of Southern Nyasaland*. (D.Phil. thesis, University of Oxford.)*

———, 1951, The Yao of Southern Nyasaland, in *Seven Tribes of British Central Africa*, edited by E. Colson and M. Gluckman.

MURDOCK, G. P., 1949, *Social Structure*.

NADEL, S. F., 1942, *A Black Byzantium*.

———, 1950, Dual Descent in the Nuba Hills, in Radcliffe-Brown and Forde, 1950.

PETERS, E. L., 1951, *The Sociology of the Beduin of Cyrenaica*. (D.Phil. thesis, University of Oxford.)*

RADCLIFFE-BROWN, A. R., 1930–31, "Social Organisation of Australian Tribes," *Oceania*, 1.

———, 1935, Patrilineal and Matrilineal Succession. *Iowa Law Review*, Vol. XX. 2.

———, 1950, Introduction to *African Systems of Kinship and Marriage*.

RADCLIFFE-BROWN, A. R., and C. DARYLL FORDE (edit.), 1950, *African Systems of Kinship and Marriage*.

RATTRAY, R. S., 1929, *Ashanti Law and Constitution*.

RICHARDS, A. I., 1936, Mother Right in Central Africa, in *Essays presented to C. G. Seligman*.

———, 1939, *Land, Labour and Diet in Northern Rhodesia*.

———, 1940 (a), Bemba Marriage and Modern Economic Conditions, *Rhodes-Livingstone Institute Papers No. 3*.

———, 1940 (b), The Political System of the Bemba, in *African Political Systems*.

———, 1950, Some Types of Family Structure among the Central Bantu, in Radcliffe-Brown and Forde, 1950.

RIVERS, W. H. R., 1911, Presidential address, *British Association for the Advancement of Science*, Section H.

———, 1914, *Kinship and Social Organisation*.

SCHAPERA, I., 1940, *Married Life in an African Tribe*.

———, 1950, Kinship and Marriage among the Tswana, in Radcliffe-Brown and Forde, 1950.

SELIGMAN, C. G. and B. Z. SELIGMAN, 1932, *Pagan Tribes of the Nilotic Sudan*.

SMITH, E. W., 1935, Africa: what do we know of it? *Journal of the Royal Anthropological Institute*, Volume 65.

SPOEHR, A., 1947, Changing Kinship Systems. *Anthropological Series, Chicago Natural History Museum*, Vol. 33, No. 4.

———, 1950, Observations on the Study of Kinship. *American Anthropologist*, Vol. 52.

WARNER, W. L., 1937, *A Black Civilization*.

WEBER, MAX, 1947, *The Theory of Social and Economic Organisation*, translated by A. R. Hudson and Talcott Parsons.

WILSON, MONICA, 1950, Nyakyusa Kinship, in Radcliffe-Brown and Forde, 1950.

———, 1951 (a), Nyakyusa Age Villages, *Journal of the Royal Anthropological Institute*, Vol. 79.

———, 1951 (b), *Good Company: A Study of Nyakyusa Age Villages*.

# AMERICAN ANTHROPOLOGIST

| Vol. 55 | DECEMBER | No. 5, Part 1 |

## METHOD AND THEORY IN AMERICAN ARCHEOLOGY: AN OPERATIONAL BASIS FOR CULTURE-HISTORICAL INTEGRATION

### By PHILIP PHILLIPS and GORDON R. WILLEY

#### INTRODUCTION

IN REVIEWING past and current trends of American archeological thinking, it seems possible, without violent oversimplification, to discern three general and more or less sequent points of view. The older antiquarianism of the nineteenth century gave place to the "scientific" archeology of the twentieth, and this in turn is undergoing profound modification, the end of which is not in sight. The motivations of antiquarianism were almost as numerous and diverse as the antiquarians and their private interests, whereas the prevalent point of view of the "scientific" era was order and system. The archeologist not only concerned himself with phenomena, but sought their meaning in patterned relationships. Such patterns were pursued through descriptive taxonomy or taxonomy combined with temporal and spatial distribution studies. For the most part the outlook was that, with sound field work, careful analysis, and classification, the archeologist discharged his duties to science and society. The over-all problem, so far as it was envisaged at all, was seen as the bit-by-bit discovery of a pre-existing order in the culture-historical universe, the outlines of which would miraculously emerge when sufficient pieces were ready to be fitted together. Thank Heaven, archeology was not a "theoretical" science but something "you could get your teeth into." As time wore on, however, and the archeologist got his teeth into mountainous accumulations of facts, the expected miracle failed to take place. Something was apparently wrong with the "jigsaw" hypothesis. It became apparent that such order as could be discerned was not altogether inherent in the data but was in large part the product of the means employed to organize the data. In short, the means, if not becoming the ends, had assumed a determinative importance in relation to them. It became, then, necessary to examine those means and the conceptual bases that underlay them. That is the stage we are in at present and in the following pages we propose to examine the main lines of theory that have so far emerged in the Americas and to make certain suggestions about future possibilities.

## THE NATURE OF ARCHEOLOGICAL UNIT CONCEPTS

The ultimate objective of archeology is the creation of an image of life within the limits of the residue that is available from the past. The procedural objectives toward such a goal may be dichotomized into reconstructions of space-time relationships, on the one hand, and contextual relationships on the other.[1] Operationally, neither is attainable without the other. The reconstruction of meaningful human history needs both structure and content. Cultural forms may be plotted to demonstrate geographical contiguity and contemporaneity, but when we move to establish an historical relationship between forms so placed we immediately invoke processes like diffusion, trade, or migration and in so doing shift the problem from the bare frame of space and time into the realm of context and function. Conversely, processes such as diffusion have no specific historical applicability without control of the spatial and temporal factors. Taylor (1948) is undoubtedly correct in stating that American archeologists have placed heavy emphasis upon skeletal chronicle at the expense of the recovery of context, but a review of the more recent literature indicates a drift in the opposite direction. Although there is little agreement upon what kind of problem should be pursued (and this lack of agreement is a healthy sign), there is every reason to believe that American archeology will be increasingly concerned with cultural and natural contexts and functional interpretation. Without slighting Taylor's contribution, we submit that this is an area of agreement for American archeologists: history—and prehistory—is both the space-time scale and the content and processes which it measures.

A method basic to archeology—as to all science—is taxonomy, in the general sense of typology and classification. Some recent disputes reveal the fact that fundamental differences in attitude toward the concept of type still obtain in American archeology. Opposition is between those who believe that types are "designed" and those who think of them as "discovered." According to the first view types are segments of the cultural continuum—a segmentation made or imposed by the classifier. The second maintains that types reflect—or should reflect—a cultural segmentation that is inherent in the data, that "designed" or empirical types, while admirably suited to space-time measuring, only accidentally correspond to types or models which were in the mind of the artisan who made the artifacts. Our attitude is that these opposing views are not hopelessly antagonistic. We maintain that all types possess some degree of correspondence to cultural "reality" and that increase of such correspondence must be the constant aim of typology.[2] Types which had cultural significance to the makers, if such can be "discovered," would not only have greater historical value, but would in addition be better adapted to problems of functional understanding. Their determination will involve considerably more testing than the first sort, but statistical analysis along these lines holds promise (Spaulding 1953).

Taxonomy applies to "cultures," as well as artifacts. Inverted commas are appropriate when the archeologist speaks of "culture," for reasons of which he is only too painfully aware. He doesn't need to be reminded what a small segment of the total cultural content is represented by his pitiful pots and stones. Nevertheless he can not, and should not, dispense with the term. Those poor stones and pots are meaningful only in terms of culture. They are indeed the raw materials of his craft, but culture—or the reconstruction of culture—is the finished product. But, because that product is never finished and never can be, the word has a special interim meaning for the archeologist. Childe (1950: 2) has defined an *archeological culture* as "an assemblage of artifacts that recur repeatedly associated together in dwellings of the same kind and with burials of the same rite. The arbitrary peculiarities of implements, weapons, ornaments, houses, burial rites and ritual objects are assumed to be the concrete expressions of the common social traditions that bind together a people." If this sounds as though he were describing a discrete unit, *a* culture, we have only to recall the essential conditions of its existence. Before it in time was another "culture" separated from it by a transition which is usually difficult if not impossible to fix, after it another; beside it in geographical space, contemporary "cultures" with frontiers quite as difficult to draw. It is in effect merely a chunk torn loose from the cultural matrix. It cannot be said to have existed as an entity until the archeologist named and defined it. Putting the case in terms of current jargon, an archeological culture is an arbitrary division of the space-time-cultural continuum[3] defined by reference to its imperishable content and whatever of "common social tradition" can be inferred therefrom.

The same problem confronts us here as in the matter of artifact typology. An archeological "culture" conceived of as a sliced-out section of the space-time-cultural continuum corresponds to the observed facts of cultural continuity and cultural interrelationships; but, as with the empirical "designed" artifact types, it may or may not parallel the reality of a past social unit as this might have been conceived by the peoples who composed it. Archeo-sociological correlations may eventually be possible but it is our opinion that the archeologist is on a firmer footing at present with the conception of an archeological culture as an arbitrarily defined unit or segment of the total continuum.

If this view be accepted, it follows that a fundamental unvarying characteristic of all archeological concepts, whether in the domain of artifact typology or cultural taxonomy, is the fact that they are the resultant combination of three unlike basic properties: space, time, and form. It is impossible to imagine an artifact type or a cultural "unit" that is not defined with reference to specific forms and does not also have distribution in space and duration in time. However, though invariably present, these three diverse properties may and do vary enormously in proportion one to the other. Probably a large share of our classificatory difficulties and the ensuing arguments could be avoided by the recognition of that simple fact. It becomes essential, therefore, in the definition and use of archeological concepts of whatever nature to understand precisely what quantities of space, time, and formal content are involved in the mixture.

Thus far, we have argued that the unifying themes of spatial-temporal ordering, contextual reconstruction, and taxonomic identification afford a common ground for archeological research. In so doing we have been talking in general terms, skirting many of the questions as to how these objectives may be drawn together into a comprehensive methodology. To construct such a methodological apparatus we must strive for maximum coverage and utility and, at the same time, minimum complexity of machinery. An operational system is needed that will be sufficiently broad and flexible to incorporate past research in all fields of American archeology and to facilitate its integration on the basic levels of historical synthesis. It must, similarly, provide for current and future investigations. Its theoretical bases must be clearly stated and understood. Above all, it must serve as the foundation for further theoretical formulations in the fields of culture continuity and change as these processes are observed and plotted from the data of prehistory. Such a system should in no way inhibit the development of multiple, successive, and radically differing trial hypotheses but should be the common starting point of more searching exploration.

## NOMENCLATURE

In the search for practicable units of study archeologists in the Americas have invented a large number of taxonomic concepts and designated them by an even larger number of names. The initial task, then, is to reduce a diversity of existing terminology to some degree of order and it seems both necessary and practicable to do this by means of a scheme, which is in no sense another taxonomic system for doing archeology, but merely a standard nomenclature by means of which existing systems and their working parts can be roughly equated. Fortunately, as already pointed out, all such concepts, whatever the actual intentions of their originators, have three elements in common: formal content, and space and time dimensions. For intelligibility we need to know not only what forms, but what order of space and time, are involved. Taxonomic concepts can, therefore, be roughly classified by reference to the amounts of space and time they take up. If this be granted it seems a practical approach to bring one of these two variables under control before considering it in combination with the other. The spatial factor is clearly the easier to deal with, so we may start by setting forth a series of geographical categories that we have found useful in characterizing space-time-culture formulations.

### Spatial Divisions

*Locality:*—The smallest unit of area ordinarily dealt with in archeology, varying in size from a single site to a district of uncertain size, generally speaking not larger than might be occupied by a single community or "local group." It is hardly necessary to add that such limits as are implied in this qualification have the variability found in the size of local groups from one sort of society to another. In strictly archeological terms the locality is a space not large enough to preclude complete cultural homogeneity at any given time.

*Region:*—A considerably larger unit of area usually determined by archeologico-historical accident. Quite often it is simply the result of concentrated research by an individual or group. Rightly or wrongly such a region comes to be thought of as having problems of its own that set it apart from other regions. Regional terms are those most often found in the titles of archeological papers of wider scope than excavation reports. Through constant reiteration they become fixed in the literature and achieve a kind of independent existence. Regions are not altogether without reference to the facts of geography, however. In stressing the accidental factor in their formulation, we must not overlook the tendency for environmental considerations to assert themselves. In portions of the New World where physical conditions of sharp diversity obtain, archeological regions are very apt to coincide with minor physiographic subdivisions. Of the various units of area defined here, the region certainly offers the most practicable field for the study of culture-environmental correlations.

In socio-political terms—and here we must tread warily—the region is roughly equivalent to the space that might be occupied by a social unit larger than the community, to which we may with extreme trepidation apply the term "tribe" or "society." This rough equation is based on what we know of American tribal distributions in historic times and must be accorded the same flexibility that we see in the size of those distributions. The same caution is required in attempting to qualify the definition of region in archeological terms. Generally speaking it is a space in which at a given time a high degree of cultural homogeneity may be expected.

*Area:*—A unit very considerably larger than the region corresponding roughly to the culture area of the ethnographer. Archeological areas, like regions, have come into existence by common consent, but they also have physiographic implications of a fairly definite nature. In the formulation of areas the element of historical accident is reduced by the fact that so many more individuals and institutions are involved in their investigation. That the Southwest has maintained its identity as an area through a half-century of intensive investigation is almost certainly due to culture-environmental determinants beyond the control of the investigators.

It is hardly necessary to add that, though the area as defined here may have considerable physiographic reality, its limits are not so easy to draw on a map as those of the smaller regions. The problem is familiar in all culture area studies.

### FORMAL OR CONTENT UNITS

*Component.*—This useful term which has achieved currency in eastern North American archeology has been defined as the manifestation of a given *focus* (here called *phase*, see below) at a specific site (McKern 1939: 308).

Strictly speaking the component is not a taxonomic unit. In theory the basic unit (McKern's *focus*, our *phase*) comprises a number of components. It is a working assumption that no culture worthy of the name will fail to manifest itself in more than one component. In practice, of course, it often happens that a phase is initially defined on the strength of one component, i.e., a site or a level within a site—but the expectation is implicit that other components will be found and the original definition modified accordingly. It will be noted presently, however, in connection with the sociological implications of the phase, that it is theoretically and actually possible for a phase to consist of only one component and in such cases the latter word, with its suggestion of incompleteness, would not apply.

*Phase.*—The *phase* is the basic space-time-culture concept in all that follows. It is, in our opinion, the practicable and intelligible unit of archeological study. Choice of the term accords with prevailing usage in a preponderance of New World areas, including the Southwest, sections of South America, and Middle America. Kidder (Kidder, Jennings, and Shook 1946: 9) has defined it as:

> A cultural complex possessing traits sufficiently characteristic to distinguish it for purposes of preliminary archaeological classification, from earlier and later manifestations of the cultural development of which it formed a part, and from other contemporaneous complexes.

Like him we prefer phase to the approximately equivalent "focus" commonly used in eastern North America, because of its stronger temporal implication.[4] The emphasis cannot be placed entirely on time, however. Modifying Kidder's definition, we would prefer to describe the concept in the following terms: A space-time-culture unit possessing traits sufficiently characteristic to distinguish it from all other units similarly conceived, whether of the same or other cultural traditions, geographically limited to a *locality* or *region* and chronologically limited to a relatively brief span of time. It must be acknowledged that this gives a specious impression of uniformity. It would be fine if phases could be standardized as to the amount of time and space they occupy. One thinks with nostalgia of the former neat 200-year phases of the Hohokam. Unfortunately there are so many variable conditions entering into the formulation that it is neither possible nor desirable to define its scope except within rather broad limits. A phase may be anything from a thin level in a site reflecting no more than a brief encampment, to a protracted occupation represented in a large number of sites distributed over a *region* of very elastic proportions.

It will be noted that Kidder's definition of phase lays more emphasis on cultural continuity than ours does, since it implies necessary relations to what goes before and what comes after. We have freed it from this requirement in order to provide for the many instances in which we simply do not know what goes before or comes after, or those less frequent occasions when a new phase appears as an intrusion without apparent relation to the precedent continuity. In any case, whether as an instance of continuity or discontinuity the phase most often appears as one member of a series which will be referred to hereinafter as a *local* or *regional sequence*. These terms will be defined presently, but let us first examine some further implications of the archeological phase.

We have already alluded briefly to the impossibility of close delimitation of phase in respect to the dimensions of time and space. It may help clarify the problem to consider it in relation to various levels of cultural development. We propose to submit in the near future a developmental sequence for the New World with six general stages, Early Lithic, Archaic, Preformative, Formative, Classic and Postclassic. It is not necessary to anticipate the definitions of these stages to point out here that the space and time dimensions of phase are not going to be the same in all six stages. For example, in the Archaic, in which a semisedentary catching and gathering economy is assumed, phases can be expected to occupy wider spaces than in the sedentary Formative. There is no regular reduction from stage to stage, however; in the Classic and Postclassic stages the space dimensions may also be larger than in the Formative, but for a different reason, this time because the socio-political groups are larger. Time dimensions, on the other hand, may actually exhibit a regular diminution from stage to stage, if the common assumption is correct that the rate of cultural change accelerates with increased advancement and complexity. It does not seem necessary to elaborate on this point here or to attempt any further refinements of definition. It is enough if we have made it clear that the concept of phase has no appropriate scale independent of the cultural situation with which it happens to be involved. This is not as great a deficiency as it might appear. Looked at *internally* so to speak, the phase may have very considerable and highly variable space and time dimensions; looked at from the standpoint of the total range of New World prehistory they are very small quantities indeed, and it is from this point of view that they assume a rough sort of *relative* equivalence that enables us to use the concept of phase as an operational tool regardless of the developmental stage involved.

In considering the phase concept from another point of view, we must recall that the archeologist is constantly admonished by his cultural anthropological brethren to remember that his ridiculous stones and pots are products of social behavior, with the result that he is ever guiltily conscious of his inability, except on the very lowest levels, to relate his formulations to sociological units. The sociological equivalent of the component is the "community," as defined by Murdock (1949: 79) and others, "the maximal group of persons who normally reside together in a face-to-face association." Murdock's three types of community: band, neighborhood, and village, manifest themselves archeologically in the component, and it is even possible as a rule to tell which type is represented. So far, so good. The equivalent of phase, then, ought to be "society," and in a good many cases it probably is. The fact that in practice phases often consist of a single component need not disturb us; on the lower levels of cultural development the society likewise frequently consists of only one community. At the other end of the developmental scale, however, society becomes a larger concept, spatially at least, than phase. For the purpose of this discussion, however, let us think of society in the terms most often implied in the older ethnographic studies, i.e., a relatively small aggregate comprising a number of closely integrated communities. How does this correspond to the concept of phase? Logically the correspondence is perfect. The society consists of a number of communities; the phase consists of a number of components; component equals community; therefore phase equals society. Q.E.D. Unfortunately in practice it doesn't work. We have no means of knowing whether the components we group together into a phase are the same communities an ethnographer (supposing such a person happened to be on hand when these components were living communities) would group into a society. We cannot be sure that the individual members of these communities would recognize themselves as belonging to the same "people." They might not even speak the same language. Ethnography offers abundant examples of different societies sharing a material culture that would be impossible to differentiate archeologically. Probably it would be only slightly more difficult to find examples in which the culture of individual communities within a society diverged sufficiently to cause them to be classified archeologically in separate phases. A frontier garrison community specialized for defense might be a case in point.

More vexing perhaps are questions having to do with the relative stability of material and social culture through time, a dimension happily ignored by the ethnographer. Within the time span of a phase, determined by material traits which can, under certain circumstances, be remarkably stable, it is conceivable that sociological changes might be sufficient to enable our hypothetical ethnographer to speak of several societies. Conversely, under special conditions even a primitive population may exhibit revolutionary changes in material culture without losing its identity as a society. We have abundant examples of this in recent history.

In sum, it looks as though the present chances were against the phase having any sociological meaning whatever, but that is not to say that it cannot have. Our attitude here is the same as that already expressed in relation to the problem of typology. As archeology develops to a point where it can afford the luxury of Taylor's "conjunctive" or contextual approach, it will become increasingly possible to define archeological culture in terms that reflect sociological realities. The phase might then become in effect an "extinct society" and the archeologist could legitimately experience the emotional satisfaction he now purloins by the simple substitution of the word "people" for "culture."

This is a possibility, but it is not really the point of the present discussion. We do not maintain that any specific archeological phase corresponds to a former society. We simply call attention to the fact that there is a certain conceptual agreement between phase and society. Both are the intelligible units of their respective fields of study. They have a similar *role* and a similar *scale*—subject to the important difference that in phase the temporal dimension is explicit whereas in society it is implicit—and in this crucial matter of scale both exhibit the same relativism with respect to the level of cultural stage. Our contention is, therefore, that this congruence, which can as yet be demonstrated only on the theoretical level, offers the best hope of incorporating archeology into general anthropological science. Even if this hope be illusory, it may be still maintained that the phase is the best available instrument for the integration of culture-historical data at the present stage of archeological development.

## TEMPORAL SERIES

*Local Sequence.*—In its purest form a local sequence is a series of components found in vertical stratigraphic relationship in a single site. It may, however, also be a composite series made by combining shorter stratigraphic "runs" from several sites within a locality, or it may be derived from seriating components without benefit of stratigraphy at all. However derived, the important feature of the local sequence is that it is local. The spatial dimension, not larger than the locality, is small enough to permit the assumption that cultural differences between components reflect differences in time.

We have already referred to the fact that members of a local sequence, though technically regarded as components, are often referred to as phases on the ground that they are local manifestations of the larger units; also that it is theoretically possible for the phase to be represented by a single component only, in which case the "higher" designation is appropriate. The local sequence, therefore, may be defined as a chronological series of *components or phases* within a locality as defined above.

*Regional Sequence.*—A regional sequence is not the same thing as a local sequence with merely a larger spatial dimension. The difference can best be approached from the operational standpoint. In the normal course of extension of archeological information, components, phases, and local sequences multiply and questions of relationships come to the fore. Ideally, the archeologists of a region come together in harmonious session where a careful matching of local sequences produces a new sequence of larger scope. Actually this happy event occurs but rarely. What more often happens is that phases and local sequences gain in scope by a sort of osmosis. They flow outward so to speak, not seldom propelled by their inventors, uniting to themselves their weaker correlates over a widening circle. The process is necessarily accompanied by a progressive generalization of definitions until their original usefulness is impaired.

Nevertheless we will assume that local sequences remain local and that regional sequences are the result of correlating them—not combining them, be it noted; this is not a taxonomic operation, because in the process the original formulations are retailored to fit the wider spatial and (perhaps) deeper temporal requirements. The phase now appears in its widest extension and at its furthest remove from the original data, for it is our contention (to be discussed further along) that the concept of phase cannot be safely extended beyond the limits of a region.

With these operational differences in mind we may define the regional sequence as a chronological series of phases within a space defined here as a region.

At this point it may be well to emphasize the artificiality of the relationship between phase and region in a regional sequence. We have said that the maximum practicable spatial dimension of a phase is comparable to that of a region, but no actual geographical coextension is implied. Such a one-to-one relationship may occur fortuitously because it oftens happens that a region comes into existence on the heels of a phase, so to speak, but there is no reason whatever to expect that earlier or later phases in the sequence will also coincide with that region.

*Period and Area Chronology.*—We now move onto a "higher" plane of abstraction where definitions become more difficult to frame. An area chronology may be described as a series of cultural formulations—here called periods—conceived on the scale of an *area* as defined in this study. Logically, *period* is simply phase with amplified space and time dimensions. Operationally this is not the case. Progress from region to area involves a greater leap into the abstract than from locality to region. A shift to the word *chronology* is made because sequence no longer seems applicable. The regional sequence, notwithstanding differences in operational procedure, is not radically different conceptually from the local sequence. It still maintains some contact with the primary stratigraphic data. With the area chronology, however, the spatial dimension has become so large that the interpretation of cultural similarities as evidence of contemporaneity becomes a theoretical question; the ever-present possibility of cultural "lag" comes into play. It would seem reasonable that the time dimension subsumed in the concept *period* would also be larger, that is to say the period would be of considerably longer duration than the phase. The fact is, however, that most area chronologies operate on approximately the same temporal scale as the local and regional sequences from which they took their original departure. For some mysterious reason they usually wind up with exactly the same number of subdivisions. This has a very important bearing on general archeological theory, for obviously it can only be justified on the assumption that cultural changes do take place synchronously over wide geographical spaces. Now whether this proposition is the cause or the result of area chronologies is one of those impossible chicken-egg questions, but there is no question that it has become one of the basic assumptions of American archeology. It might be termed the microcosmic theory since it sees reflected in the locality or region the pattern of culture-history of the area. To examine this theory critically would take us too far afield. It was necessary to allude to it only to show that the concepts of period and area chronology are different in kind, not merely in scale, from those already dealt with, in that they involve an assumption that it was not necessary to make in proceeding from the local to the regional level.

It may also be pointed out that area chronologies almost invariably tend to take on the characteristics of a developmental sequence, in which case it is more appropriate to refer to *stages* rather than *periods*. More often in such cases, however, the two terms are used interchangeably as though they meant exactly the same thing. Fortunately, deliverance from this kind of ambiguity will come, as it has for the later periods in the Southwest, when current techniques of absolute dating have reached a point of sufficient dependability. Then we shall be able to place a given unit within a temporal framework, on the one hand, and a developmental sequence, on the other, without confusing the two operations.

The above remarks are an evaluation unfavorable to area chronologies in general. They have undoubtedly served a useful purpose in focusing attention on larger issues, but have done equal disservice in fomenting endless controversies over fictitious problems. We submit that, when it comes to dealing with major spatial and temporal distributions on levels so far removed from the concrete data, it is preferable to employ formulations of a more fluid nature, those which carry the least implications of precision in respect to the dimensions of space and time. Such are the terms remaining to be defined. Before proceeding to do so, it may be well to pause long enough to explain again what we are doing, or rather what we are not doing. This is not a description of a taxonomic method either actual or contemplated. A regional sequence may be the result of correlating local sequences, but it is not the result of combining them. That would be taxonomy. The area chronology has even less formal relationship to the regional sequence. In sum, we are simply recognizing the fact that certain cultural and chronological formulations differ from others of larger spatial and temporal dimensions, because the operations involved are different, and we find it useful to distinguish them by the nomenclature suggested here.

## INTEGRATIVE DEVICES

*Horizon.*—The horizon style concept, first introduced into Andean archeology by Max Uhle (1913) and formulated by Kroeber (1944), has amply proved its utility in that area. It represents an idea different in kind from those already considered here, in that the usual ingredients of space and time are mixed in very unequal proportions. A horizon style, as the name implies, occupies a great deal of space but very little time. It may be briefly described as a spatial continuum represented by the wide distribution of a recognizable art style.[5] On the assumption of "historical uniqueness of stylistic pattern" coupled with the theory that styles normally change with some rapidity, the time dimension is reduced to a point where the horizon style becomes useful in equating in time phases of culture widely separated in space. As one of the present authors (Willey 1945: 55) has already observed: "The horizon styles are the horizontal stringers by which the upright columns of specialized regional development are tied together in the time chart."

Unfortunately this excellent synchronic device has a limited application since it presupposes a level of esthetic sophistication that many New World cultures failed to reach. In some cases it has been possible to regard certain highly specialized and widely traded artifacts as horizon "markers," but they must be used with considerable caution on account of the possibility that such highly prized objects may be preserved for long periods as heirlooms or "antiques."

*Tradition.*—This is another methodological tool that seems to have originated in South American archeology, but has recently found favor in other areas of the New World. A familiar, not to say indispensable, word in any historical context, it has of late acquired a special archeological meaning, or rather a number of meanings, for it is still in an incipient stage of formulation and doesn't mean quite the same thing to all who use it. Owing to the fact that this concept is designated by a term that has always been used in archeology, it is difficult to say just when it began to be a definite methodological tool. In the Andean area it came about in connection with the very different idea of horizon style, and was first applied to pottery only. Once it became apparent that the utility of the horizon style depended upon the combination of wide space and short time dimensions, it was equally clear that some other formulation was required to express a somewhat different kind of ceramic unity in which these proportions were reversed. This gave rise to the term *pottery tradition*, certainly not a verbal innovation, but perhaps the first time the idea of tradition entered into a definite space-time formulation.

The relationship of the two concepts, horizon style and pottery tradition, is so important that one of us may be permitted to repeat himself, as follows:

These speculations concerning the relationships of the later White-on-red styles to the earlier component styles of the White-on-red horizon lead us to wonder if there are not other widely inclusive historical units of an order different from that of the horizon style. It appears certain that the Peruvian Andes and coast were a unified culture area in that the important cultural developments were essentially local and basically inter-related for at least a thousand years. This fundamental cultural unity justifies seeing ceramic developments in terms of long-time traditions as well as coeval phenomena. The concept of a pottery tradition, as used here, includes broad descriptive categories of ceramic decoration which undoubtedly have value in expressing historical relationships when the relationships are confined to the geographical boundaries of Peruvian-Andean cultures. The pottery tradition lacks the specific quality of the localized pottery style, and it differs from the horizon style in that it is not an integration of artistic elements which has been widely diffused at a given time period. A pottery tradition comprises a line, or a number of lines, of pottery development through time within the confines of a certain technique or decorative constant. In successive time periods through which the history of ceramic development can be traced, certain styles arose within the tradition. Transmission of some of these styles during particular periods resulted in the formation of a horizon style; other styles in the continuum of the tradition remained strictly localized. The distinctions between a horizon style and a pottery tradition . . . are opposable concepts in archaeological reconstruction [Willey 1945: 53].

Shortly after this first limited injection of tradition into Peruvian studies,

Wendell C. Bennett (1948: 1) enlarged the concept very considerably under the name "area co-tradition." This formulation, as Bennett clearly saw, is nothing more than the familiar culture area concept with the addition of time depth,[6] "the over-all unit of cultural history of an area within which the component cultures have been inter-related over a period of time." The emphasis, implied in the "co-" is on the *linkage* of "whole cultures," each with its own history and persistent traditions, and on the *area* in which this linkage takes place. Thus the co-tradition is an enlargement over the simple tradition in terms of content, since it is no longer confined to a single technological or cultural development, but becomes a broad coalescent cultural continuum. At the same time it introduces a restriction in that stable geographical boundaries are implied.

About the same time that the Peruvianists were beginning to talk about pottery traditions, John McGregor[7] introduced the term into the Southwest with somewhat different connotations. He defined tradition very broadly as "more or less deeply rooted human characteristics—persistent attitudes or ways of doing things—which are passed on from one generation to another," thus emphasizing the non-material and configurational aspects of culture. He maintained that characteristic attitudes can be inferred from material traits and that the determination of traditions (as defined by him) is not only possible but essential in making broad cultural comparisons.

This is an enlargement of the concept of tradition in another direction— it is not a co-tradition or anything like it. McGregor's traditions are actually technologically oriented; house types, pottery, ground stone, etc.; he merely advocates that they be formulated in terms of the preference and attitudes they reflect. There is nothing revolutionary about this surely, but it is a point of view that cannot be too often stated.

The first significant use of the tradition concept in eastern North America was by John M. Goggin. His definition is more like McGregor's, at least on the philosophical side:

> My concept of Florida cultural traditions is similar in theory but more inclusive in content than a ceramic tradition. A cultural tradition is a distinctive way of life, reflected in various aspects of culture; perhaps extending through some period of time and exhibiting normal internal cultural changes, but nevertheless throughout this period showing a basic consistent unity. In the whole history of a tradition certain persistent themes dominate the life of the people. These give distinctiveness to the configuration. [Goggin 1949: 17.]

Goggin recognizes ten cultural traditions in Florida, allowing to them a great deal of latitude in space and time dimensions. It seems to us that here Goggin has discovered the outstanding merit of the tradition as an archeological tool, namely its flexibility. He has treated it as a space-time-culture formulation in which the three components can be mingled in almost any proportion required by the data. In the case of the time component he has overdone it perhaps. Surely inherent in the idea of tradition is persistence through time. Actually what happens in Florida is that certain traditions make a brief appearance, his "Florida Mississippian" for example. Such a configuration has a long history of development elsewhere before its brief appearance in Florida.

Goggin, rather more than others, has emphasized the importance of environmental factors in the shaping and conserving of cultural traditions. Here again he has put his finger on another virtue of the concept. It offers to the reconstructed environmentalists, in which category we are not ashamed to declare ourselves, the most effective means for giving expression to culture-environmental correlations.

We are at last in a position to essay some sort of definition. All aspects—technological, configurational, environmental—must find a place and there must be, above all, freedom from set limitations of space, time and content. A tradition, then, is a major large-scale space-time-cultural continuity, defined with reference to persistent configurations in single technologies or total (archeological) culture, occupying a relatively long interval of time and a quantitatively variable but environmentally significant space.

*Climax.*—There remains but to mention briefly this useful but largely neglected concept (see Kroeber 1939). It may be defined, in the terms used here, as the phase or phases of maximum cultural intensity of a cultural tradition. This is necessarily a value judgment, but only in relation to the tradition involved. So far as possible the emphasis should be placed on population density and like factors rather than exquisite developments in esthetics. The latter may conceivably take place in periods of low cultural intensity. Theoretically, there ought to be a climax development in every tradition, but it cannot always be identified archeologically. Another way to describe it would be the phase or phases when-where the tradition comes closest to realization of its full potential development within the limits imposed by history and environment.

## CULTURE-HISTORICAL INTEGRATION

In the preceding sections we have outlined a terminology for reducing existing classificatory concepts to a set of common denominators. In doing so we have perhaps revealed a personal bias for or against some of these concepts and it now becomes our task to show whither these predilections are tending. What has been offered so far is in no sense a system but it will not have escaped the reader that a system lurks within.

In briefest possible terms, we submit that archeology can be historically integrated by means of a very simple apparatus consisting of the two static formal concepts *component* and *phase* and the two fluid historical concepts *tradition* and *horizon style*. The essence of this departure is, we think, recognition of the fact that taxonomy cannot be profitably carried beyond the order of phase as defined herein. The phase itself is admittedly an abstraction corresponding only roughly to *society*, but it is only one remove from the primary data and the gap between it and the ethnographic "reality" can theoretically be closed. Beyond phase we take off into the ether. "Higher" taxonomic concepts—really higher, in the sense of further from the ground—are subject to variables of space and time such as to render, in the time-honored phrase, any resemblance to actual societies living or dead purely coincidental.

We are accordingly taking the obvious and straightforward course of pursuing cultural configurations of greater magnitude than phase by means of concepts that make no pretense to sociological or any other kind of reality. Tools like tradition and horizon style have come into existence precisely in response to an awareness that the main currents of culture flow through space and time without regard for social and political boundaries. It seems to us that these main currents, essential to an understanding of prehistory on an areal or continental scale, cannot be apprehended by combining with ant-like industry smaller archeological units into larger ones. It may be seen that we are at once for and against taxonomy. We believe strongly in the sound-ness of phase as a taxonomic unit. It has the importance of *species* to the biologist, or *society* to the cultural anthropologist. What happens in the higher taxonomy is that once a group or series of phases becomes an "aspect," "branch," or what you will, it seems to be taken for granted that something more significant has been created and the phases tend to drop out of sight.[8] We propose to keep them in sight. They may and should be constantly subject to modification and redefinition, always with a view to closer approximation to the theoretically possible ethnographic "reality," but they must remain to the end the basic formulations of the data.

There will be too many phases for comfort, of course. How many species are recognized in the insect world? How many societies in the ethnographic world? It has been frequently pointed out that archeology is to cultural anthropology what paleontology is to biology. It was necessary for paleon-tology to reveal the processes of organic evolution because they take time. Cultural processes are much more rapid, but they also take time and cannot therefore be fully understood without the aid of archeology. So we are con-cerned with process as well as history. This may seem far removed from the glorification of the phase, but it appears to the writers that you cannot hope to shed light on processes by means of abstractions that have no theoretically possible counterparts in cultural and social "reality." We believe that all taxonomic concepts above the rank of phase as defined herein are subject to that disqualification. On the other hand, it is not necessary to know all there is to know about all recognizable phases of New World archeology or even a major division thereof. As in all science, fortunately for its practitioners, processes are revealed by partial selected data. This disposes of the objection of too many phases. Are we trying to understand the processes of culture change or merely to simplify its manifold effects?

The apparatus that we are attempting to describe may be crudely dia-grammed as on the following page.

This diagram is intended to show that there are actually two "systems" in-volved, one formal and the other historical, or spatial-temporal. The relation-ships in the system *component-phase* are formal, even structural in a social

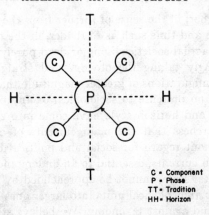

sense. They are located in space and time but are not dependent on these properties for their meaning. Operationally, components are combined into phases because analysis reveals cultural uniformity amounting to practical identity. We usually know, to be sure, that they are closely associated geographically and we assume contemporaneity but neither of these considerations is necessary for the recognition of the relationship. This is because the space and time dimensions that inhere in all archeological concepts are here, on this low level of classification, reduced to negligibility. For all practical purposes the space occupied by a phase may be regarded as a point; the time, an instant. The phase, in other words, is a formal abstraction that can be manipulated independently of space and time.

Up to this point most archeologists would probably "go along" though many, depending upon the areas in which they have worked, would prefer to use other terms in place of phase. Where our point of view differs is in the conviction that phase, as defined in these pages, is the largest unit of archeological culture that can be so manipulated. When formal abstractions are expanded to embrace a wider range of forms they cease to be merely formal and become spatial and/or temporal as well. Actually, by some seemingly paradoxical process, they lose rather than gain in formal content—the familiar phenomenon of shorter trait lists for higher taxonomic divisions. Why is this? Because forms are also fluid, changing constantly through space and time, and you cannot expand an archeological concept without expanding one or both, usually both, of these dimensions. The result is that the change in forms *within* the concept are such that it can no longer be apprehended on a strictly formal basis. Space and time have become dominant in a system that is theoretically supposed to be a formal one operating independently of space and time. It should surprise no one when such a system fails to work.

These remarks apply specifically to the Gladwin (1934), Colton (1939), and Midwestern Taxonomic (McKern 1939) systems. The Gladwin and Colton schemes are phylogenetic or historico-genetic. Phylogeny involves relationships that are not only formal but also causal (i.e., based on common ancestry) and temporal. A and B are related not only formally but because

150

they derive from C, which is, perforce, earlier in time. The use of the organic evolutionary model is, we believe, specious (see Willey 1953: 369). The Midwest taxonomists, on the other hand, seem to be involved in a hopeless contradiction in attempting to set up a scheme so heavily committed to the same factors of phylogenic causality, and implied evolution and time, while insisting that it must operate independently of the time dimension. To be sure, it was McKern's idea that once the higher cultural units had been delineated by means of the classificatory method, they could be arranged in temporal sequence through dates obtained by some other means. Failure of this hope is becoming apparent now that Carbon 14 is furnishing evidence for the extremely long duration and overlapping of many of these units.

We now turn back to our diagram and the two "systems" it is designed to reveal. If it be granted that the component-phase system deals mainly in relationships of a formal or structural nature, it certainly will be allowed that tradition and horizon style belong to a different system in which the properties of space and time play dominant roles. The difference we are talking about here is only a difference in the proportions of the space-time-form mixture. In tradition and horizon style, form, or content is important—when is it not?—but the temporal and spatial ingredients are dominant. The real point, however, is not whether these two sets are essentially different conceptually, which is arguable, but that in actual operation they are not subject to any necessary logical or systematic relationship. Components and phases enter into traditions and horizon styles, their external relationships may be revealed and expressed by them, but they are not in any manner combined to form them. In fact, the opposite process is more nearly in accord with cultural reality; two or more traditions usually converge in any given phase. In short, the effectiveness of the method, as we see it, depends upon interplay between these two pairs of conceptual tools without systematic limitations of any kind.

To summarize briefly: insofar as this can be formulated as a program for New World archeology, we are advocating: (1) that the primary emphasis continue to be placed on the organization of components and phases (or their equivalents) in local and regional sequences under stratigraphic control; (2) that phases be studied intensively as the effective contexts of archeological culture; (3) that their internal spatial and temporal dimensions be kept within manageable limits of magnitude; and (4) that their external spatial, temporal and formal relationships be studied and expressed in terms of traditions and horizons without recourse to any taxonomic formulations of a higher order than themselves. From this, as a common platform on which it would not seem unreasonable to hope we might stand united, further studies could be carried to meet specific objectives.

PEABODY MUSEUM, HARVARD UNIVERSITY
    CAMBRIDGE, MASSACHUSETTS

## NOTES

[1] Taylor (1948) has referred to this dichotomy as "chronicle" and "historiography." See also Willey's (1953) use of the terms "historical" and "processual."

[2] Phillips, Ford, and Griffin, 1951: 63–64, discuss this problem of the "empirical" versus the "cultural" type. ". . . let us make it clear that, although the empirical typology here described— 'working' typology as Krieger (1944) perhaps would call it—cannot be expected to show any strong relationship to cultural 'reality,' it does not follow that such relationship is precluded now and forever. To a certain extent, the characters we select as criteria for type definition, however dictated by expediency, not to say necessity, are bound to correspond to characters that might have served to distinguish one sort of pottery from another in the minds of the people who made and used it. We should, of course, make every possible effort to increase this correspondence. In course of time, with increased information in respect to vessel shapes and overall patterns of design—let us not forget that we are classifying vessels, though we have for most types only sherds to do it with—our types will be redefined in ever closer approximation to cultural 'realities.' In short, an eventual synthesis is possible between the seemingly antithetical attitudes loosely characterized above as 'empirical' and 'cultural,' in which the product of classification, the pottery type, will finally achieve cultural meaning. The limits of the variability of the type will then no longer be wholly arbitrary decisions of the classifier, as is now the case, but will bear some correspondence to ethnographic distributions in time and space." See also Rouse, 1939.

[3] It should be pointed out that no resemblance to the space-time continuum of the higher metaphysics is implied. It is perhaps unfortunate that archeologists in America, the present writers included, have pounced upon this high-sounding term. When the archeologist talks about space he is referring to simple two-dimensional geographical space.

[4] Also for the same reason given by Beardsley for his preference for "facies," i.e., to avoid the implication that the whole Midwestern system was to be duplicated in California. Beardsley's definition of "facies" as "groups of intimately related settlements or components" corresponds closely to our concept of phase (1948: 3).

[5] For a more detailed statement about "style" in this connection, see Willey 1951: 109–111.

[6] Kroeber's (1939) *culture whole*, for those who prefer the term, means about the same thing. Bennett (1948) indicated that the Southwest might well offer an example of the area co-tradition, a suggestion which was followed up by Martin and Rinaldo's (1951) somewhat controversial "The Southwestern Co-Tradition."

[7] McGregor 1950, paper submitted in 1946.

[8] Many students who do not accept the Midwestern taxonomic scheme as a whole nevertheless feel that up to the level of *aspect* it is a very useful tool. It will be said by them, that, in limiting our terminology to component and phase (the rough equivalent of focus) we are forgoing the use of a means of expressing relationships between phases closer than those implied in the concepts of horizon and tradition. Our reply is that if such a relationship between two or more phases can be demonstrated, and contemporaneity is indicated, they probably should be combined in a single phase anyhow. Our definition of phase is elastic enough to permit this. If, on the other hand, the formal relationship is close, but contemporaneity is *not* indicated, it would seem wiser to continue to regard them as separate and sequent phases of a common cultural tradition. In other words, the concept of phase, though approximately equivalent to focus, can be stretched to accommodate most aspects that have been established, and if it cannot, it is probably because the aspect in question is not a significant cultural "unit."

## BIBLIOGRAPHY

BEARDSLEY, RICHARD K. 1948 Culture Sequences in Central California Archaeology. American Antiquity 14, no. 1: 1–28.

BENNETT, WENDELL C. 1948 The Peruvian Co-Tradition *in* A Reappraisal of Peruvian Archaeology. American Antiquity 13, no. 4, part 2. Memoir no. 4: 1–7.

CHILDE, V. GORDON 1950 Prehistoric Migrations in Europe. Instituttet For Sammenlignende Kulturforskning, Ser. A: Forelesninger XX: V, Oslo.

COLTON, H. S. 1939 Prehistoric Culture Units and their Relationships in Northern Arizona. Museum of Northern Arizona, Bulletin 17.

GLADWIN, W. and H. S. 1934 A Method for the Designation of Cultures and Their Varieties. Medallion Papers No. 15. Globe, Arizona.

GOGGIN, JOHN 1949 Cultural Traditions in Florida Prehistory *in* The Florida Indian and His Neighbors: 13–44. J. W. Griffin, ed. Winter Park.

KIDDER, A. V., JESSE D. JENNINGS and E. M. SHOOK 1946 Kaminaljuyu. Carnegie Institution of Washington, Publication 561.

KROEBER, A. L. 1939 Cultural and Natural Areas of Native North America. University of California Publications in American Archaeology and Ethnology 38. Berkeley.

——— 1944 Peruvian Archaeology in 1942. Viking Fund Publications in Anthropology No. 4. New York.

MARTIN, PAUL S. and JOHN B. RINALDO 1951 The Southwestern Co-Tradition. Southwestern Journal of Anthropology 7, no. 3: 215–229.

McGREGOR, JOHN C. 1950 Weighted Traits and Traditions *in* For the Dean, pp. 291–298. Erik K. Reed and Dale S. King, eds. Santa Fe, New Mexico.

McKERN, WILLIAM C. 1939 The Midwestern Taxonomic Method as an Aid to Archaeological Study. American Antiquity 4, no. 4: 301–313.

MURDOCK, GEORGE PETER 1949 Social Structure. New York.

PHILLIPS, PHILIP, JAMES A. FORD and JAMES B. GRIFFIN 1951 Archaeological Survey in the Lower Mississippi Valley 1940–1947. Peabody Museum Papers, vol. 25. Harvard University, Cambridge.

ROUSE, IRVING 1939 Prehistory in Haiti. Yale University Publications in Anthropology No. 21. New Haven.

SPAULDING, ALBERT C. 1953 Statistical Techniques for the Discovery of Artifact Types. American Antiquity 18, no. 4: 305–313.

TAYLOR, WALTER W. 1948 A Study of Archaeology. American Anthropologist 50, no. 3, pt. 2. Memoir No. 69.

UHLE, MAX 1913 Die Ruinen von Moche. Société de Américanistes de Paris. N.S. 10: 95–117.

WILLEY, GORDON R. 1945 Horizon Styles and Pottery Traditions in Peruvian Archaeology. American Antiquity 11: 49–56.

——— 1951 The Chavin Problem: a Review and Critique. Southwestern Journal of Anthropology 7, no. 2: 103–144.

——— 1953 Archaeological Theories and Interpretation: New World *in* Anthropology Today pp. 361–385. A. L. Kroeber, ed. University of Chicago Press, Chicago.

# Social Anthropology and the Method of Controlled Comparison*

FRED EGGAN
*University of Chicago*

## I

THE contemporary student of anthropology is in a difficult position in attempting to achieve a sound orientation in our rapidly changing and developing discipline. Nowhere is this more true than in the general field of cultural anthropology, where there is an apparent schism between those who call themselves ethnologists and the newer group of social anthropologists. Ethnology, which has had its major development in the United States, has been concerned primarily with culture history and culture process; social anthropology, on the other hand, is primarily a product of British anthropology and has emphasized social structure and function as its major concepts. These differences in emphasis and interest have led to considerable misunderstanding on both sides. As one who has had a foot in both camps for some two decades I may perhaps be permitted some observations on this situation, along with some suggestions as to a common meeting-ground.[1]

Since World War II rapid changes have taken place in all branches of anthropology. Genetics and the experimental method, plus a host of new fossil finds from Africa, are revolutionizing physical anthropology; archeology, with the aid of radiocarbon dating and other new techniques, is beginning to achieve a world-wide chronology and is turning to cultural anthropology for further insight into cultural development; linguistics, with structural methods well established, is returning anew to historical problems and re-examining the relations of language and culture. But ethnology, one of whose tasks it is to synthesize and interpret the conclusions reached by its sister disciplines, is lagging behind.

It is not clear how long anthropology can remain partly a biological science, partly a humanity, and partly a social science. As we shift from the descriptive, data-gathering phases of anthropology to analysis, interpretation and theory, it is inevitable that realignments will come about. My predecessors in the presidency during the postwar period have sketched some of these new developments and realignments as they have seen them.[2] It is highly probable that the forces for fusion will prevail over the tendencies to fission in the near future, so far as the United States is concerned; in England the forces are more nearly balanced, and the outcome is more uncertain.[3] In the long run we may or may not follow the patterns set by other disciplines.

Turning to the field of cultural anthropology, one of the important developments of the last few years has been the series of articles and books defining, denouncing, or defending "social anthropology." Murdock, in the most out-

* Presidential paper, 1953, American Anthropological Association.

743

spoken attack, notes that: "For a decade or more, anthropologists in other countries have privately expressed an increasingly ambivalent attitude toward recent trends in British anthropology—a curious blend of respect and dissatisfaction" (1951:465). His analysis of the strengths and weaknesses of British social anthropology, as revealed in current productions, and his diagnosis of the social anthropologists as primarily "sociologists" have led to replies and counterreplies.

At the International Symposium on Anthropology sponsored by the Wenner-Gren Foundation a special session was devoted to "Cultural/Social Anthropology," in which various scholars presented the usages current in their respective countries. Tax's (Tax and others 1953:225) summary of the consensus is to the effect that we ought to "use the words 'cultural' and 'social' anthropology interchangeably and forget about the question of terminology"; but Kroeber in his "Concluding Review" (1953:357–76) returns to the problem of society and culture and finds distinctions. If these distinctions were merely a question of factional dispute or of alternate terms for similar activities, we could agree, with Lowie (1953:527–28), on some neutral term such as "ethnography"—or allow time to make the decision in terms of relative popularity.

But the distinctions being made are not merely a matter of British and American rivalry or of terminology, and it is essential that we realize that there is a problem and that it is an important one. After accepting contemporary British social anthropologists as "true ethnographers" interested in the realities of culture, Lowie (1953:531) goes on to unequivocally reject Fortes' contention that "social structure is not an aspect of culture but the entire culture of a given people handled in a special frame of theory" (Fortes 1953*a*: 21). However, many British social anthropologists would go even further than Fortes! In general they make a clear distinction between the concepts of *society* and *culture* and think of social anthropology as concerned primarily with the former. Murdock's (1951:471) startling conclusion that the Britishers are sociologists was anticipated by Radcliffe-Brown (1931*a*) and recently reaffirmed by Evans-Pritchard: "I must emphasize that, theoretically at any rate, social anthropology is the study of all human societies. . . . Social anthropology can therefore be regarded as a branch of sociological studies, that branch which chiefly devotes itself to primitive societies" (1951:10–11). In contrast, the current Americanist opinion subsumes social structure as one aspect of culture, following Tylor (Lowie 1953:531), or separates the two but gives primacy to the concept of culture.

Before we read our British brethren out of the anthropological party, however, it might be wise to see whether we may not have taken too narrow a view of cultural anthropology. Lowie, who, along with many American anthropologists, takes his cultural text from Tylor, defines the aim of ethnography as "the *complete* description of all cultural phenomena everywhere and at all periods" (1953:528, italics Lowie's). It may be both possible and useful to view the "capabilities and habits acquired by man *as a member of society*" under the heading of social structure, despite the fact that Lowie finds it inconceivable. We might wait for the remainder of Fortes' materials on the Tallensi before rendering a verdict. And if we look more closely at Tylor's famous definition it seems clear that anthropology should be concerned with *both* society and culture, as they are interrelated and reflected in human behavior. We need a complete description and interpretation of both social and cultural phenomena, not to mention those concerned with the individual, if we are going to think in global terms. I would agree with Hallowell that society, culture, and personality may "be conceptually differentiated for specialized types of analysis and study. On the other hand, it is being more clearly recognized than heretofore that society, culture and personality cannot be postulated as completely independent variables" (1953:600). We can wait until we know more about each of these concepts before we rank them as superior and inferior.

More important, we cannot afford to ignore the contributions of the British social anthropologists to both theory and description. In the last thirty years they have been developing a new approach to the study of man in society, which is currently producing significant results. Is is no accident that many of the best monographs of the postwar period have come out of the small group of British social anthropologists. Reviewing *African Systems of Kinship and Marriage*, Murdock states (1951:465) that "the ethnographic contributions to the volume reveal without exception a very high level of professional competence in field research and in the analysis of social structural data, equalled only by the work of the very best men in other countries." What some of these contributions are has been recently pointed out by Firth (1951*a*, *b*), Evans-Pritchard (1951), and Fortes (1953*a*, *b*), among others. While Fortes recognizes that they lack the wide and adventurous sweep of American anthropology, "the loss in diversity is amply balanced by the gains we have derived from concentration on a limited set of problems" (1953*a*:17). Most American anthropologists are inclined to attribute the relative excellence of these contributions to good field techniques or perhaps to superior literary abilities, considering the British theoretical approach as rather barren and lifeless. But this seems to me to be a mistake. The structural point of view makes possible a superior organization and interpretation of the cultural data, and good monographs may well be related to this point of view. If we are to meet this competition (particularly in view of Firth's [1951*a*] account of their new directions) we need to do more than label our British colleagues as "comparative sociologists" or invoke the magical figures of Tylor and Franz Boas.

If I may venture a prescription based on my own experience, we need to adopt the structural-functional approach of British social anthropology and integrate it with our traditional American interest in culture process and history. For the weaknesses of British social anthropology are in precisely those aspects where we are strong, and if we can develop a way of relating the two approaches we can perhaps save ethnology from the destiny to which Kroeber has assigned it—"to a premature fate or a senescent death as one may see it"

(1953:366). I feel encouraged in this attempt because I have a genuine interest in both culture and social structure and because Murdock believes I have succeeded "in fusing functional analysis with an interest in history and an awareness of process in a highly productive creative synthesis" (1951:469).

In contrast to most of my contemporaries I arrived at this synthesis without too many conflicts. My early anthropological education was in the Boas tradition as interpreted by Cole, Sapir, and Spier—with additions from Redfield. But before the mold had hardened too far I came under the influence also of Radcliffe-Brown. The early thirties was a period of intense excitement among graduate students at Chicago, enhanced by debates between Linton and Radcliffe-Brown and heated arguments about functionalism. Redfield's (1937) account gives something of the flavor of this period, as well as a brief characterization of Radcliffe-Brown's contributions to anthropology. And Linton's *Study of Man* (1936) shows definite evidence of the impact of the structural and functional points of view on his thinking: culture and society are clearly differentiated, though they are mutually dependent, and concepts such as social system, status and role, integration and function are intermixed with the more usual cultural categories. But *The Study of Man*, while widely admired, was little imitated by Linton's colleagues—though it has had important effects on social science as a whole and on some of his students.

Once we were in the field, however, some of us discovered that the alternatives about which we had been arguing were in reality complementary. We found that the structural approach gave a new dimension to the flat perspectives of American ethnography and allowed us to ask new kinds of questions. Functionalism gave us meaningful answers to some questions and enabled us again to see cultures as wholes. But we also maintained an interest in cultural regions and a concern for culture process and cultural development. The resulting data were utilized for a variety of purposes. Some students prepared "descriptive integrations" which approximated to that complex reality which is history. Others were attracted to the formulation of general propositions as to society or culture. I, myself, began by working in limited areas on problems of kinship and social structure, utilizing comparison as a major technique and attempting to see changes over time. When Radcliffe-Brown went to Oxford in 1937 we put together some of these studies under the ambitious title, *Social Anthropology of North American Tribes*.

The distinction between society and culture, far from complicating the procedures of analysis and comparison, has actually facilitated them. Generalization requires repeatable units which can be identified, and social structures, which tend to have a limited number of forms, readily lend themselves to classification and comparison. Cultural data, on the other hand, tend to fall into patterns of varying types which are more easily traced through time and space. Social structures and cultural patterns may vary independently of one another, but both have their locus in the behavior of individuals in social groups. Depending on our problems one or the other may be central in our analysis, and we may utilize one or another of the basic methods of investigation—history or science. I would agree with Kroeber (1935:569) that these latter need differentiation, "precisely because we shall presumably penetrate further in the end by two approaches than by one," but I see no reason why we should not use the two approaches together when possible.

The crucial problem with regard to generalization, whether broad or limited, is the method of comparison which is used. In the United States, for reasons which I will mention later on, the comparative method has long been in disrepute and was supplanted by what Boas called the "historical method." In England, on the other hand, the comparative method has had a more continuous utilization. Nadel (1951:222–55) discusses the techniques and limitations of the comparative method and the nature of the results which may be obtained from its application. As Radcliffe-Brown has stated: "It is only by the use of the comparative method that we can arrive at general explanations. The alternative is to confine ourselves to particularistic explanations similar to those of the historian. The two kinds of explanation are both legitimate and do not conflict; but both are needed for the understanding of societies and their institutions" (1952a:113–14).

The particular adaptation of the comparative method to social anthropology which Radcliffe-Brown has made is well illustrated in The Huxley Memorial Lecture for 1951, where he begins with exogamous moiety divisions in Australia and shows that the Australian phenomena are instances of certain widespread general tendencies in human societies. For him the task of social anthropology is to "formulate and validate statements about the conditions of existence of social systems . . . and the regularities that are observable in social change" (1951:22). This systematic comparison of a world-wide variety of instances, while an ultimate objective of social anthropology, is rather difficult to carry out in terms of our present limited knowledge of social systems. We can make some general observations about institutions such as the family; and the war between the sexes in aboriginal Australia has some interesting parallels with the world of Thurber. But I am not sure, to give one example, that the "Yin-Yang philosophy of ancient China is the systematic elaboration of the principle that can be used to define the social structure of moieties in Australian tribes" (1951:21), though Radcliffe-Brown's analysis and wide experience give it a certain plausibility.

My own preference is for the utilization of the comparative method on a smaller scale and with as much control over the frame of comparison as it is possible to secure. It has seemed natural to utilize regions of relatively homogeneous culture or to work within social or cultural types, and to further control the ecology and the historical factors so far as it is possible to do so. Radcliffe-Brown has done this with great skill in *The Social Organization of Australian Tribes* (1931b). After comparing the Australian moiety structures and finding their common denominators, I would prefer to make a comparison with the results of a similar study of moiety structures and associated practices of the Indians of Southern California, who approximate rather closely the Australian sociocultural situation. The results of this comparison could then be matched against comparable studies of Northwest Coast and other similar moiety systems, and the similarities and differences systematically examined by the method of concomitant variation. I think we would end up, perhaps, with Radcliffe-Brown's relationship of "opposition," or the unity of opposites, but we would have much more, as well, in the form of a clearer understanding of each type or subtype and of the nature of the mechanisms by which they are maintained or changed. While I share Radcliffe-Brown's vision of an ultimate science of society, I think that we first have to cultivate more intensively what Merton (1949:5) has called the middle range of theory. I suggest the method of controlled comparison as a convenient instrument for its exploration, utilizing covariation and correlation, and avoiding too great a degree of abstraction.

Before examining the ramifications and possible results of such exploration it may be useful to glance at selected aspects of the history of anthropology to see how certain of the present differences between American and British anthropologists have come about. We are somewhere in the middle of one of Kroeber's "configurations of culture growth," and it is important to see which patterns are still viable and which are close to exhaustion.

## II

The early developments in American cultural anthropology have been delineated by Lowie (1937) and parallel in many respects those which were occurring in England. In addition to Morgan, Bandelier, Cushing, J. O. Dorsey, Alice Fletcher, and others were among the pioneers whose work is today largely forgotten in the United States. For with the advent of Franz Boas a major break was made with the past, resulting not so much from his program for cultural anthropology as in its selective implementation. Boas in "The Limitations of the Comparative Method" (1896) outlined a program which included two major tasks. The first task involved detailed studies of individual tribes in their cultural and regional context as a means to the reconstruction of the histories of tribal cultures and regions. A second task concerned the comparisons of these tribal histories, with the ultimate objective of formulating general laws of cultural growth, which were psychological in character (1940:278–79). This second task, which Boas thought of as the more important of the two, was never to be fully implemented by his students.

Boas formulated this program in connection with a destructive criticism of the comparative method as then practiced in England and America. After stating as a principle of method that uniformity of processes was essential for comparability, he goes on to say: "If anthropology desires to establish the laws governing the growth of culture it must not confine itself to comparing the results of growth alone, but whenever such is feasible, it must compare the processes of growth, and these can be discovered by means of studies of the cultures of small geographical areas" (1940:280). He then compares this "historical method" with the "comparative method," which he states has been remarkably barren of results, and predicts that it will not become fruitful until we make our comparisons "on the broader and sounder basis which I ventured to outline." The requirement that only those phenomena can be compared which are derived psychologically or historically from common causes, valuable as it may have been at that time, has had the effect of predisposing most of Boas' students against the comparative method—except in linguistics where genetic relationships could be assumed—and hence against any generalizations which require comparison. And the processes which Boas sought in a study of art and mythology on the Northwest Coast proved more difficult to isolate than was anticipated. Kroeber notes that though Boas was "able to show a multiplicity of processes in culture, he was not able—it was impossible in his day and perhaps is still—to formulate these into a systematic theory" (1953:368).

In the "Formative Period"[4] of American ethnology, from 1900 to 1915, these were minor considerations. There were the vanishing Indian cultures to study, and it was natural for the students of Boas to concentrate on the first portion of his program. They wrote theses, for the most part, on specific problems, or to test various theories which had been advanced to explain art, or myth, or ritual, generally with negative results. This clearing of the intellectual air was essential, but it also led to excesses, as in Goldenweiser's famous study of totemism (1910). It also resulted in the ignoring of earlier anthropologists and even contemporaries. Alice Fletcher's *The Hako: A Pawnee Ceremony* (1904) excellently describes and interprets a ritual but was never used as a model.

The major attention of the early Boas students was devoted to the task of ordering their growing data on the American Indian in tribal and regional context. During this and the following periods many important monographs and studies were published, which formed a solid base for future work. The climax of this fact-gathering revolution was reached with the culture-area concept as crystallized by Wissler (1914, 1922), and in the studies by Boas on the art, mythology, and social organization of the Northwest Coast.

The period which followed, from 1915 to 1930, was a "Florescent Period" in American ethnology. The culture area provided a framework for the analysis and interpretation of the cultural data in terms of history and process. Sapir opened the period with his famous *Time Perspective* (1916), which began: "Cultural anthropology is more and more rapidly getting to realize itself as a strictly historical science. Its data cannot be understood, either in themselves or in their relation to one another, except as the end-points of specific sequences of events reaching back into the remote past." Wissler, Lowie, Kroeber, Spier, Benedict, and many others provided a notable series of regional studies utilizing distributional analyses of cultural traits for chronological inferences—and for the study of culture process. Wissler developed the "law of diffusion" and then turned his attention to the dynamic factors underlying the culture area itself. In *The Relation of Nature to Man in Aboriginal America* (1926) he thought that he had found them in the relationship of the culture center to the underlying ecology. The great museums dominated this period, and American anthropology shared in the general prosperity and optimism which followed the first World War.

One result of these distributional studies was that chronology tended to become an end in itself, and some ethnologists became so preoccupied with seeking time sequences that they did not pay much attention to culture as such. The analysis of culture into traits or elements and their subsequent treatment often violated principles of historical method by robbing them of their context. The normal procedure of historians of basing their analysis on chronology was here reversed—the chronology resulted from the analytic study. The generalizations as to process which were formulated were used as short-cuts to further historical research.

Another important result of these studies was the conception of culture which gradually developed. Culture came to be viewed as a mere aggregation of traits brought together by the accidents of diffusion. Here is Benedict's conclusion to her doctoral dissertation: "It is, so far as we can see, an ultimate fact of human nature that man builds up his culture out of disparate elements, combining and recombining them; and until we have abandoned the superstition that the result is an organism functionally interrelated, we shall be unable to see our cultural life objectively, or to control its manifestations" (1923: 84–85).

The revolt against this mechanical and atomistic conception of culture came both from without and from within. Dixon (1928) criticized both Wissler's procedures and his conceptions of the processes of culture growth, as well as his formulation of the dynamics of the culture area. Spier (1929:222) renounced historical reconstruction as misleading and unnecessary for understanding the nature of the processes of culture growth, advocating in its place a consideration of the actual conditions under which cultural growth takes place. Benedict was soon engaged in the study of cultural patterns and configurations, and her *Patterns of Culture* (1934) represents a complete reversal of her earlier position—here superstition has become reality.

During this period there was little interest in social structure as such, even though Kroeber, Lowie, and Parsons all studied Pueblo life at first hand. The shadows of Morgan, McLennan, Spencer, and Maine still loomed over them, and sociological interpretations were generally rejected in favor of psychological or linguistic ones. Lowie, however, began to develop a moderate functional position and sociological orientation with regard to social organization, perhaps best exemplified in his article on "Relationship Terms" (1929).

The "Expansionist Period" which followed, 1930–1940, was a time of troubles and of transition for American ethnology. The old gods were no longer omniscient—and there was an invasion of foreign gods from overseas. The depression brought the great museums to their knees and temporarily ended their activities in ethnological research; the center of gravity shifted more and more to the universities, as the social sciences grappled with the new social problems. This was a period of considerable expansion for cultural anthropology, much of it in terms of joint departments with sociology. Archeology also experienced a remarkable expansion during the decade, partly as a by-product of its ability to utilize large quantities of WPA labor. The chronological framework that resulted, based on stratigraphy and other techniques, further emphasized the inadequacy of the reconstructions made from distributional analyses alone.

In the meantime *Argonauts* and *The Andaman Islanders* had been published but had made relatively little impression on American scholars. Malinowski's field methods were admired, and his functional conception of culture struck some responsive chords; as for Radcliffe-Brown, his "ethnological appendix" was utilized but his interpretations of Andamanese customs and beliefs were largely ignored. Soon afterwards, however, Malinowski began developing social anthropology in England on the basis of the functional method and new techniques of field research. Brief visits by Malinowski to the United States, including a summer session at the University of California, plus the work of his early students in Oceania and Africa, led to a considerable increase in his influence, but during the 1930's he was largely preoccupied with developing a program of research for Africa.

In 1931 Radcliffe-Brown, who had been first in South Africa and then in Australia, brought to this country "a method for the study of society, well defined and different enough from what prevailed here to require American anthropologists to reconsider the whole matter of method, to scrutinize their objectives, and to attend to new problems and new ways of looking at problems. He stirred us up and accelerated intellectual variation among us" (Redfield 1937: vii).

As a result of these and other forces American ethnologists began to shift their interests in a variety of directions. Kroeber re-examined the relationship between cultural and natural areas in a more productive way and formulated the concept of culture climax to replace Wissler's culture center. He also explored the problem of culture elements more thoroughly, in the course of which he organized the Culture Element Survey; at the other end of the cultural spectrum he wrote *Configurations of Culture Growth* (1944). Herskovits, who had earlier applied the culture-area concept to Africa, developed a dynamic approach to the study of culture (1950) which has had important results. Redfield, in the meantime, was beginning the series of studies which resulted in *The Folk Culture of Yucatan* (1941)—a new and important approach to the study of social and cultural change.

During this period, also, Steward was beginning his ecological studies of Great Basin tribes, Warner was applying social anthropological concepts and methods to the study of modern American communities, and Sapir was shifting his interests in the direction of psychiatry. Linton, with his perception of new and important trends, had put them together with the old, but his interests also shifted in the direction of personality and culture. Acculturation became a respectable subject with the Redfield, Linton, and Herskovits' "Memorandum on the Study of Acculturation" (1936), and applied anthropology secured a foothold in the Indian Service and in a few other government agencies.

These developments, which gave variety and color to American ethnology, also tended to leave a vacuum in the center of the field. We will never know for sure what might have developed out of this interesting decade if World War II had not come along.

The "Contemporary Period"—the decade since the war—is difficult to characterize. In part there has been a continuation of prewar trends, in part a carry-over of wartime interests, and in part an interest in new problems resulting from the war and its aftermath. There is a growing interest in complex cultures or civilizations, such as China, Japan, India, and Africa, both at the village level and at the level of national culture and national character, and new methods and techniques are in process for their study and comparison.

One postwar development of particular interest in connection with this paper has been the gradual but definite acceptance in many quarters in this country of social anthropology as a separable but related discipline.[5] Of even greater potential significance, perhaps, is the growing alliance between social psychology, sociology, and social anthropology as the core groups of the so-called "behavioral sciences," a relationship also reflected in the Institute of Human Relations at Yale and in the Department of Social Relations at Harvard, as well as elsewhere.

Perhaps most important of all the postwar developments for the future of anthropology has been the very great increase in the interchange of both students and faculty between English and American institutions, including field stations in Africa. The Fulbright program, the Area Research Fellowships of the Social Science Research Council, the International Symposium on Anthropology of the Wenner-Gren Foundation, and the activities of the Carnegie, Rockefeller, and Ford Foundations have all contributed to this increased exchange. I am convinced that such face-to-face contacts in seminar and field represent the most effective way for amalgamation of techniques and ideas to take place. The testimony of students back from London or Africa is to the general effect that our training is superior in ethnography and in problems of culture history but is inferior in social anthropology : kinship, social structure, political organization, law, and so on. There are exceptions, of course, but we would like the exceptions to be the rule.

## III

For the details of the complementary developments in England we are indebted to Evans-Pritchard's account in *Social Anthropology* (1951) and to Fortes' inaugural lecture entitled *Social Anthropology at Cambridge Since 1900* (1953c). There are differences in emphasis between the Oxford and Cambridge versions, but in general the developments are clear.

In England cultural anthropology got off to a fine start through the efforts of Tylor, Maine, McLennan and other pioneers of the 1860's and 1870's, but their attempts to construct universal stages of development ultimately fell afoul of the facts. The nineteenth-century anthropologists in England were "armchair" anthropologists; it wasn't until Haddon, a zoologist by training, organized the famous Torres Straits expedition of 1898–1900 and converted an assorted group of psychologists and other scientists into ethnologists that field work began. But from this group came the leaders of early twentieth-century British anthropology: Haddon, Rivers, and Seligman. According to Evans-Pritchard, "This expedition marked a turning point in the history of social anthropology in Great Britain. From this time two important and inter-connected developments began to take place: anthropology became more and more a whole-time professional study, and some field experience came to be regarded as an essential part of the training of its students" (1951:73).

During the next decade a gradual separation of ethnology and social anthropology took place, culminating, according to Radcliffe-Brown (1952*b*:276), in an agreement to use "ethnography" for descriptive accounts of nonliterate peoples, "ethnology" for historical reconstructions, and "social anthropology" for the comparative study of the institutions of primitive societies. The institutional division of labor also took a different organization which has led to different views as to how anthropology should be constituted.

Sir James Frazer dominated social anthropology in the early decades of this century, and the conceptions of evolution and progress held sway long after they had given way in American anthropology. But Fortes notes that, while anthropologists had a magnificent field of inquiry, the subject had no intrinsic unity: "At the stage of development it had reached in 1920, anthropology, both in this country and elsewhere, was a bundle-subject, its data gathered, so to speak, from the same forest but otherwise heterogeneous and tied together only by the evolutionary theory" (1953*c*:14).

Ethnology flourished for a period under Haddon, Rivers, and Seligman, but with the advent of Malinowski and Radcliffe-Brown "social anthropology has emerged as the basic discipline concerned with custom and social organization in the simpler societies" (Fortes 1953*c*:16). From their predecessors the latter received their tradition of field research and the principle of the intensive study of limited areas—a principle that Malinowski carried to its logical conclusion.

Beginning in 1924 Malinowski began to train a small but brilliant group of social anthropologists from all parts of the Commonwealth in the field techniques and functional theory that he had developed from his Trobriand experience, but his approach proved inadequate for the complex problems encountered in Africa. This deficiency was remedied in part by the advent of Radcliffe-Brown, who returned to the newly organized Institute of Social Anthropology at Oxford in 1937 and proceeded to give British social anthropology its major current directions. Evans-Pritchard discusses this period with the authority of a participant, and I refer you to his *Social Anthropology* for the details—and for a summary of what a social anthropologist does.

The postwar developments in England have been largely a continuation of prewar developments together with a considerable expansion stimulated by government support of both social anthropological and applied research. Unlike the situation in the United States there is no large established group of sociologists in England, and social anthropology has in part filled the gap. Major theoretical differences as to the nature of social anthropology as a science or as a humanity are developing, but these differences are subordinate to a large area of agreement as to basic problems, methods, and points of view. Just as the American ethnologists of the 1920's had a common language and a common set of problems, so do the British social anthropologists today.

One important key to the understanding of British social anthropology resides in their conception of social structure. The contributions in this field with regard to Africa have been summarized by Fortes in "The Structure of Unilineal Descent Groups" (1953*a*). Here he points out that the guiding ideas in the analysis of African lineage organization have come mainly from Radcliffe-Brown's formulation of the structural principles found in all kinship systems, and goes on to state that he is not alone "in regarding them as among the most important generalizations as yet reached in the study of social structure" (p. 25). For Fortes the social structure is the foundation of the whole social life of any continuing society.

Not only have the British social anthropologists produced an outstanding series of monographs in recent years but they have organized their training programs in the universities and institutes to insure that the flow will continue. In the early stages of training there is a more concentrated program in social anthropology in the major British universities, though the knowledge demanded of other fields is less, and linguistics is generally conspicuous by its absence. Only the top students are given grants for field research. As Evans-Pritchard (1951:76–77) sketches the ideal situation, the student usually spends at least two years in his first field study, including learning to speak the language of the group under observation. Another five years is allotted to publishing the results, or longer if he has teaching duties. A study of a second society is desirable, to avoid the dangers of thinking in terms of a single society, but this can usually be carried out in a shorter period.

Granted that this is the ideal procedure, it still offers a standard against which to compare our American practices. My impression is that our very best graduate students are approximating this standard, but our Ph.D. programs in general require considerably less in terms of field research and specific preparation. We tend to think of the doctorate as an earlier stage in the development of a scholar and not a capstone to an established career.

This proposed program, however, has important implications for social anthropology itself. If each anthropologist follows the Malinowskian tradition of specializing in one, or two, or three societies and spends his lifetime in writing about them, what happens to comparative studies? Evans-Pritchard recognizes this problem: "It is a matter of plain experience that it [the comparative study] is a formidable task which cannot be undertaken by a man who is under the obligation to publish the results of the two or three field studies he has made, since this will take him the rest of his life to complete if he has heavy teaching and administrative duties as well" (1951:89).

In place of the comparative method he proposes the "experimental method," in which preliminary conclusions are formulated and then tested by the same or other social anthropologists on different societies, thus gradually developing broader and more adequate hypotheses. The old comparative method, he says, has been largely abandoned because it seldom gave answers to the questions asked (1951:90).

This concentration on intensive studies of one or two selected societies has its own limitations. The hypotheses advanced on such a basis can often be modified in terms of studies easily available for comparison. Thus Schneider (1953:582–84) points out that some of Evans-Pritchard's generalizations about the Nuer could well have been tested against the Zulu data. The degree to which comparison may sharpen hypotheses is well illustrated by Nadel's study of "Witchcraft in Four African Societies" (1952). There is a further reason for this lack of interest in comparative studies on the part of Evans-Pritchard in that he thinks of social anthropology as "belonging to the humanities rather than to the natural sciences" (1951:60) and conceives of his task as essentially a historical one of "descriptive integration." His colleagues are currently disagreeing with him (Forde 1950; Fortes 1953c).

Schapera (1953) has recently reviewed a number of studies utilizing some variation of the comparative method and finds most of them deficient in one respect or another. The comparative approach he advocates involves making an intensive study of a given region and carefully comparing the forms taken among the people of the area by the particular social phenomena which are under scrutiny, so as to classify them into types. These types can then be compared with those of neighboring regions. "Social anthropology would benefit considerably, and have more right to claim that its methods are adequate, if in the near future far more attention were devoted to intensive regional comparisons" (p. 360).

One difficulty in the way of any systematic and intensive comparison of African data is being remedied by the Ethnographic Survey under the direction of Daryll Forde. The absence of any interest in linguistics is a major criticism of a group who advocate learning a language to carry out researches in social structure but who ignore the structure in the languages which they learn. Lévi-Strauss (1951) has pointed out some of the problems in these two fields, and it is difficult to see why they are neglected.

Ultimately the British anthropologists will discover that time perspective is also important and will encourage archeology and historical research. The potentialities of Greenberg's recent genetic classification of African languages, and the subgrouping of Bantu languages through shared correspondences and lexico-statistical techniques, are just beginning to be appreciated. And for those who demand documents there are the Arab records and historical collections such as the Portuguese records for Delagoa Bay. That the same tribes speaking the same languages are still in this region after four hundred years suggests that there is considerable historical material which needs to be utilized. For our best insights into the nature of society and culture come from seeing social structures and culture patterns over time. Here is where we can distinguish the accidental from the general, evaluate more clearly the factors and forces operating in a given situation, and describe the processes involved in general terms. Not to take advantage of the possibilities of studying social and cultural change under such relatively controlled conditions is to do only half the job that needs to be done.

## IV

These brief and inadequate surveys indicate that cultural anthropology has had quite a different development in the United States and England and suggest some of the reasons for these differences. They also suggest that the differences may be growing less. In the United States ethnology began with a rejection of Morgan and his interest in the development of social systems, and an acceptance of Tylor and his conception of culture. Tylor's views by-and-large still prevail, though since the 1920's there have been many alternative definitions of culture as anthropologists attempted to get a more *rounded* view of their subject. In England, as Kroeber and Kluckhohn (1952) have pointed out, there has been more resistance to the term "culture"; on the other hand, Morgan is hailed as an important forerunner, particularly for his researches on kinship. Prophets are seldom honored in their own country.

Both Kroeber (1953) and Redfield (1953) have recently reviewed the role of anthropology in relation to the social sciences and to the humanities and have emphasized the virtues of a varied attack on the problems that face us all. With Redfield, I believe we should continue to encourage variety among anthropologists. But I am here particularly concerned with cultural anthropology, and I am disturbed by Kroeber's attitude toward ethnology: "Now how about ethnology?" he writes in his Concluding Review of *Anthropology Today*, "I am about ready to abandon this baby to the wolves." He goes on to detail some of the reasons why ethnology appears to be vanishing: the decrease in primitives, the failure to make classifications and comparisons, and the tendencies to leap directly into large-scale speculations (1953:366–67). His solution is to merge ethnology with culture history and, when that is soundly established, to extricate the processes at work and "generalize the story of culture into its causal factors." This is a return to the original Boas program.

My own suggested solution is an alternate one. While there are few "primitives" in our own back yard, there are the new frontiers of Africa, India, Southeast Asia, Indonesia, and Melanesia to exploit. Here is still a complete range in terms of cultural complexity and degree of culture contact. Africa alone is a much more challenging "laboratory" in many respects than is the American Indian. And for those who like their cultures untouched there is interior New Guinea.

The failure to make adequate classifications and comparisons can in part be remedied by borrowing the methods and techniques of the social anthropologists or by going in the directions pioneered by Murdock (1949). Social structure gives us a preliminary basis for classification in the middle range while universals are sought for. Steward's "sociocultural types" are another step in the directions we want to go.

The tendency to leap directly into large-scale speculations is growing less and will be further controlled as we gradually build a foundation of well-supported hypotheses. Speculations are like mutations in some respects—most of them are worthless but every now and then one advances our development tremendously. We need to keep them for this reason, if for no other.

If we can salvage cultural anthropology in the United States, I do not worry too much about the "anthropological bundle" falling apart in the near future. As a result of the closer co-operation among the subdisciplines of anthropology in this country new bridges are continually being built between them, and joint problems, and even new subfields, are constantly being generated. So long as our interaction remains more intensive than our relations with other disciplines, anthropology will hold together.

One thing we can do is to return to the basic problems American ethnologists were tackling in the 1920's and 1930's, with new methods and points of view and a greater range of concepts. I have elsewhere (1952:35–45) discussed the potential contributions that such a combined approach could achieve, and for the Western Pueblos I have tried to give a specific example (1950). But in terms of present possibilities, not one single region in North America has had adequate treatment. Nor are the possibilities of field research in North America exhausted. The Cheyenne, for example, are still performing the Sun Dance pretty much as it was in Dorsey's day. But despite all the studies of the Sun Dance we still do not have an adequate account giving us the meaning and significance of the rituals for the participants and for the tribe. One such account would enable us to revalue the whole literature of the Sun Dance.

The Plains area is now ripe for a new integration which should be more satisfying then the older ones. In addition to Wissler's and Kroeber's formulations, we now have an outline of cultural development firmly anchored in stratigraphy and radiocarbon dates, and a considerable amount of documentary history as well as a series of monographs on special topics. By centering our attention on social structure, we can see the interrelations of subsistence and ecology, on the one hand, and political and ritual activities, on the other. For those interested in process we can ask: Why did tribal groups coming into the Plains from surrounding regions, with radically different social structures, tend to develop a similar type? The answer is not simply diffusion (Eggan 1937a). Once this new formulation of the Plains is made, new problems will arise which will require a more complex apparatus to solve.

Another type of comparative study which has great potentialities is represented by the investigation of the Southern Athabascan-speaking peoples in the Plains and the Southwest. Here the same or similar groups have differentiated in terms of ecology, contacts, and internal development. Preliminary studies by Kluckhohn, Opler, Hoijer, Goodwin, and others suggest the possibilities of a detailed comparative attack on the problems of cultural development in this relatively controlled situation. Bellah's (1952) recent study of Southern Athabascan kinship systems, utilizing Parsons' structural-functional categories, shows some of the possibilities in this region.

In the Southwest I have attempted to work within a single structural type in a highly integrated subcultural area and to utilize the archeological and historical records, which are here reasonably complete, to delimit and interpret the variations which are found (1950). Clyde Kluckhohn looks at the Southwest from a broader standpoint and with a different but related problem: "One of the main rewards of intensive study of a culture area such as the Southwest is that such study eventually frees investigators to raise genuinely scientific questions—problems of process. Once the influence of various cultures upon others in the same area and the effects of a common environment (and its variant forms) have been reasonably well ascertained, one can then operate to a first approximation under an "all other things being equal" hypothesis and intensively examine the question: Why are these cultures and these modal personality types still different—in spite of similar environmental stimuli and pressures and access over long periods to the influence of generalized area culture or cultures? We are ready now, I believe, for such studies—but no one is yet attempting them seriously" (1954:693).

The Ramah Project, directed by Kluckhohn, has been planned so as to furnish a continuous record of a series of Navaho from childhood to maturity and of the changes in their culture as well. This project is in its second decade, and a variety of participants have produced an impressive group of papers. So far Kluckhohn's major monograph has concerned *Navaho Witchcraft* (1944), which he has interpreted in both psychological and structural terms and which breaks much new ground. A newer project in the same region involves the comparison of the value systems of five groups: Navaho, Zuni, Mormon, Spanish-American, and Texan, but the results are not yet available.

Comparative studies can also be done on a very small scale. The few thousand Hopi are divided into nearly a dozen villages, each of which differs in significant ways from its neighbors in terms of origins, conservatism, contacts, independence, degree of acculturation, and specific sociocultural patterns. And on First Mesa the Hano or Hopi Tewa, who came from the Rio Grande around A.D. 1700, still maintain their linguistic and cultural independence despite biological assimilation and minority status—and apparently differ significantly in personality traits as well. Dozier's (1951) preliminary account of this interesting situation suggests how valuable this comparison may eventually be.

How much can be learned about the processes of social and cultural change by comparative field research in a controlled situation is illustrated by Alex Spoehr's researches in the Southeast. Here some preliminary investigations by the writer (1937b) had led to tentative conclusions as to the nature of changes in kinship systems of the Creek, Choctaw, Chickasaw, and other tribes of the region after they were removed to reservations in Oklahoma. Spoehr (1947) not only demonstrated these changes in detail but has analyzed the historical factors responsible and isolated the resulting processes.

Here Redfield's (1941) comparative study of four Yucatecan communities in terms of progressive changes in their organization, individualization, and secularization as one moves from the tribal hinterland through village and town to the city of Merida should also be mentioned. The significance of its contributions to comparative method has been largely overlooked in the controversies over the nature of the "folk society" and the usefulness of ideal types.

We can also begin to study particular social types wherever they occur. Murdock's *Social Structure* (1949) demonstrates that similar social structures and kinship systems are frequently found in various parts of the world. We can compare matrilineal social systems, or Omaha kinship systems, in different regions of the world without restricting ourselves to the specific requirements originally laid down by Boas. Thus Audrey Richards' (1950) comparison of matrilineal organizations in Central Africa will gain in significance when set against the Northwest Coast data. When variant forms of matrilineal or patrilineal social systems are compared from the standpoint of structure and function, we will have a clearer idea of the essential features of such systems and the reasons for special variants. The results for matrilineal systems promise to give quite a different picture than Lowie originally drew of the "Matrilineal Complex" (1919), and they will help us to see more clearly the structural significance of cultural patterns such as avunculocal residence and cross-cousin marriage.

These and other studies will enable us ultimately to present a comprehensive account of the various types of social structure to be found in the regions of the world and to see the nature of their correlates and the factors involved in social and cultural change. It is clear that new methods and techniques will need to be developed for the evaluation of change over time; quantitative data will be essential to establish rates of change which may even be expressed in statistical terms.

I have suggested that there may be some virtues in combining the sound anthropological concepts of structure and function with the ethnological concepts of process and history. If we can do this in a satisfactory manner we can save the "ethnological baby" from the fate to which Kroeber has consigned it—what we call the infant when it has matured is a relatively minor matter. In suggesting some of the ways in which comparative studies can be made more useful I have avoided questions of definition and ultimate objectives. This is only one of the many ways in which our science can advance, and we have the personnel and range of interests to cultivate them all.

After this paper was substantially completed the volume of papers in honor of Wilson D. Wallis entitled *Method and Perspective in Anthropology* (Spencer 1954) became available. Much of what Herskovits says with regard to "Some Problems of Method in Ethnography" is relevant to points made above, particularly his emphasis on the historical approach and the comparative study of documented change (1954:19) as well as on the importance of repeated analyses of the same phenomena. And Ackerknecht's scholarly survey of "The Comparative Method in Anthropology" emphasizes the importance of the comparative method for cultural anthropology: "One of the great advantages of the comparative method will be that in a field where the controlled experiment is impossible it provides at least some kind of control." He sees signs of a renaissance: "In whatever form the comparative method may reappear, it will express the growing desire and need in cultural anthropology to find regularities and common denominators behind the apparent diversity and uniqueness of cultural phenomena" (p. 125).

Kroeber, in commenting on the papers in this volume, subscribes" whole ·

heartedly to Ackerknecht's position. My one criticism is that he doesn't go far enough. He sees the comparative method as something that must and will be revived. I would say that it has never gone out; it has only changed its tactic" (1954:273). He goes on to point out that all science ultimately seeks knowledge of process, but that this must be preceded by "description of the properties of the form and substance of the phenomena, their ordering or classification upon analysis of their structure, and the tracing of their changes or events" (pp. 273–74). These are the essential points that I have tried to make with reference to cultural anthropology.

On both sides of the Atlantic there is an increasing willingness to listen to one another and a growing conviction that the varied approaches are complementary rather than competitive. We can agree, I think, with Radcliffe-Brown: "It will be only in an integrated and organized study in which historical studies and sociological studies are combined that we shall be able to reach a real understanding of the development of human society, and this we do not yet have" (1951:22). It seems to me that it is high time we made a start—and indeed it is well under way.

In time we may be able to simplify and further order our conceptual schemes in terms of direct observations on human behavior. Sapir, in perhaps a moment of insight, once defined culture "as a systematic series of illusions enjoyed by people." But culture, like the "ether" of the nineteenth-century physicists, plays an essential role today and will do so for a considerable time to come. The distant future is more difficult to predict—I think it was Whitehead who remarked that the last thing to be discovered in any science is what the science is really about!

### NOTES

[1] The publication of this paper has been delayed through no fault of the editors. The opportunity to attend the Eighth Pacific Science Congress in Manila in November, 1953, plus the competition afforded by the Apache Crown Dancers at our Tucson meetings made it easy to follow the precedent, begun the year before by President Bennett, of not reading a presidential address. I have written this paper rather informally, however, and have attempted to give a somewhat personal interpretation of social and cultural anthropology as practiced in the United States and in Great Britain. I have addressed myself primarily to my American colleagues, since there are a number of recent addresses directed toward British anthropologists; and I have omitted many important contributions from here and abroad through reasons of space and competence. Several friends have been kind enough to make suggestions for improvement, notably Edward Bruner, David Schneider, and Milton Singer. I would also like to thank the editors for their forbearance.

[2] See, particularly, Benedict (1948), Hallowell (1950), Beals (1951), Howells (1952), and Bennett (1953).

[3] With regard to the general problem of the integration of anthropological studies Daryll Forde, in his recent presidential address (1951) to the Royal Anthropological Institute, emphasized the importance of this integration and suggested the concept of ecology as a possible common point of reference for all the varied fields of anthropology.

[4] For the limited purposes of this paper I have utilized the terms which Bennett applied to the Andean area in his presidential paper of last year, though I am sure better terms can be found.

[5] The term "social anthropology" has been used by American anthropologists in the past: both Wissler and Radin wrote textbooks under that title, but these involved no new points of view. Chapple and Coon's *Principles of Anthropology* (1942) did present a new point of view, even dispensing with the concept of culture, but has not been widely accepted in the United States.

## REFERENCES CITED

ACKERKNECHT, ERWIN H.
    1954    On the comparative method in anthropology. *In:* Method and Perspective in Anthropology, ed. R. F. Spencer. Minneapolis.

BEALS, RALPH
    1951    Urbanism, urbanization, and acculturation. American Anthropologist 53:1–10.

BELLAH, R. N.
    1952    Apache kinship systems. Cambridge, Harvard University Press.

BENEDICT, RUTH
    1923    The concept of the guardian spirit in North America. Memoirs of the American Anthropological Association No. 29.
    1934    Patterns of culture. Boston and New York, Houghton Mifflin Co.
    1948    Anthropology and the humanities. American Anthropologist 50:585–93.

BENNETT, WENDELL C.
    1953    Area archeology. American Anthropologist 55:5–16.

BOAS, FRANZ
    1896    The limitations of the comparative method in anthropology. Science, n.s. 4:901–8.
    1927    Primitive art. Instittutet for Sammenlignende Kulturforskning, Series B, No. VIII. Oslo.
    1940    Race, language and culture. New York, The Macmillan Co.

CHAPPLE, ELIOT and CARLETON COON
    1942    Principles of anthropology. New York, Henry Holt.

DIXON, R. B.
    1928    The building of cultures. New York, Scribners.

DOZIER, EDWARD P.
    1951    Resistance to acculturation and assimilation in an Indian pueblo. American Anthropologist 53:56–66.

EGGAN, FRED
    1937a   The Cheyenne and Arapaho kinship system. *In:* Social Anthropology of North American Tribes, ed. Fred Eggan. Chicago, University of Chicago Press.
    1937b   Historical changes in the Choctaw kinship system. American Anthropologist 39:34–52.
    1950    Social organization of the Western Pueblos. Chicago, University of Chicago Press.
    1952    The ethnological cultures and their archeological backgrounds. *In:* Archeology of the Eastern United States, ed. J. B. Griffin. Chicago, University of Chicago Press.

EGGAN, FRED (ed.)
    1937    Social anthropology of North American tribes. Chicago, University of Chicago Press.

EVANS-PRITCHARD, E. E.
    1951    Social anthropology. London, Cohen & West Ltd.

FIRTH, RAYMOND
    1951a   Contemporary British social anthropology. American Anthropologist 53:474–89.
    1951b   Elements of social organization. London, Watts and Co.

FLETCHER, ALICE
    1904    The Hako: a Pawnee ceremony. 22nd Annual Report, Bureau of American Ethnology. Washington, D. C.

FORDE, DARYLL
    1947    The anthropological approach in social science. Presidential Address, Section H, British Association for the Advancement of Science. London.
    1950    Anthropology, science and history. Man, 254.
    1951    The integration of anthropological studies. Journal of the Royal Anthropological Institute 78:1–10.

FORTES, MEYER
    1953a   The structure of unilineal descent groups. American Anthropologist 55:17–41.

1953*b* Analysis and description in social anthropology. Presidential Address, Section H, British Association for the Advancement of Science. London.

1953*c* Social anthropology at Cambridge since 1900, an inaugural lecture. Cambridge University Press.

GOLDENWEISER, A. A.
1910 Totemism: an analytic study. Journal of American Folklore 23:1–115.

HALLOWELL, A. IRVING
1950 Personality, structure, and the evolution of man. American Anthropologist 52:159–73.

1953 Culture, personality and society. *In:* Anthropology Today, by Alfred L. Kroeber and others, pp. 597–620. Chicago, University of Chicago Press.

HERSKOVITS, MELVILLE J.
1950 Man and his works, the science of cultural anthropology. New York, A. A. Knopf.

1954 Some problems of method in ethnography. *In:* Method and Perspective in Anthropology, ed. R. F. Spencer. Minneapolis.

HOWELLS, W. W.
1952 The study of anthropology. American Anthropologist 54:1–7.

KLUCKHOHN, CLYDE
1944 Navaho witchcraft. Papers of the Peabody Museum of Harvard University XXII, No. 2.

1949 The Ramah project. Papers of the Peabody Museum of Harvard University XL, No. 1.

1954 Southwestern studies of culture and personality. American Anthropologist 56:685–97.

KROEBER, ALFRED L.
1935 History and science in anthropology. American Anthropologist 37:539–69.

1939 Cultural and natural areas of native North America. Berkeley, University of California Press.

1944 Configurations of culture growth. Berkeley and Los Angeles, University of California Press.

1953 Introduction (pp. 1–4) and Concluding Review (pp. 357–76). *In:* An Appraisal of Anthropology Today, ed. Sol Tax and others. Chicago, University of Chicago Press.

1954 Critical summary and commentary. *In:* Method and Perspective in Anthropology, ed. R. F. Spencer. Minneapolis.

KROEBER, ALFRED L. and CLYDE KLUCKHOHN
1952 Culture, a critical review of concepts and definitions. Papers of the Peabody Museum of Harvard University XLVII, No. 1.

KROEBER, ALFRED L. and others
1953 Anthropology today, an encyclopedic inventory. Chicago, University of Chicago Press.

LÉVI-STRAUSS, CLAUDE
1951 Language and the analysis of social laws. American Anthropologist 53:155–63.

LINTON, RALPH
1936 The study of man. New York, D. Appleton-Century Co.

LOWIE, ROBERT H.
1919 The matrilineal complex. University of California Publications in American Archaeology and Ethnology XVI:29–45.

1929 Relationship terms. Encyclopedia Britannica, 14th ed.

1937 The history of ethnological theory. New York, Farrar & Rinehart, Inc.

1953 Ethnography, cultural and social anthropology. American Anthropologist 55:527–34.

MALINOWSKI, B.
1922 Argonauts of the western Pacific. London, Routledge.

MERTON, R. K.
1949 Social theory and social structure. Glencoe, The Free Press.

MURDOCK, GEORGE PETER
1949 Social structure. New York, The Macmillan Co.

1951     British social anthropology. American Anthropologist 53:465–73.

NADEL, S. F.

1951     The foundations of social anthropology. Glencoe, The Free Press.

1952     Witchcraft in four African societies: an essay in comparison. American Anthropologist 54:18–29.

RADCLIFFE-BROWN, A. R.

1931a    The present position of anthropological studies. Presidential Address, Section H, British Association for the Advancement of Science. London.

1931b    The social organization of Australian tribes. Oceania Monographs, No. 1.

1933     The Andaman Islanders. Reprinted with additions. Cambridge. (1st ed., 1922.)

1951     The comparative method in social anthropology. Huxley Memorial Lecture. London.

1952a    Structure and function in primitive society, essays and addresses. London, Cohen and West Ltd.

1952b    Historical note on British social anthropology. American Anthropologist 54:275–77.

RADCLIFFE-BROWN, A. R. and DARYLL FORDE (eds.)

1950     African systems of kinship and marriage. London, Oxford University Press.

REDFIELD, ROBERT

1937     Introduction to: Social Anthropology of North American Tribes, ed. Fred Eggan. Chicago, University of Chicago Press.

1941     The folk culture of Yucatan. Chicago, University of Chicago Press.

1953     Relations of anthropology to the social sciences and to the humanities. *In:* Anthropology Today, by Alfred L. Kroeber and others, pp. 728–38. Chicago, University of Chicago Press.

REDFIELD, ROBERT, RALPH LINTON and MELVILLE J. HERSKOVITS

1936     Memorandum on the study of acculturation. American Anthropologist 38:149–52.

RICHARDS, AUDREY I.

1950     Some types of family structure amongst the Central Bantu. *In:* African Systems of Kinship and Marriage, ed. A. R. Radcliffe-Brown and Daryll Forde. London, Oxford University Press.

SAPIR, EDWARD

1916     Time perspective in aboriginal American culture: a study in method. Canada, Department of Mines, Geological Survey, Memoir 90, Anth. Ser. 13. Ottawa.

SCHAPERA, I.

1953     Some comments on comparative method in social anthropology. American Anthropologist 55:353–62.

SCHNEIDER, D.

1953     Review of: Kinship and Marriage among the Nuer, by E. E. Evans-Pritchard. American Anthropologist 55:582–84.

SPENCER, R. F. (ed.)

1954     Method and perspective in anthropology, papers in honor of Wilson D. Wallis. Minneapolis, University of Minnesota Press.

SPIER, LESLIE

1929     Problems arising from the cultural position of the Havasupai. American Anthropologist 31:213–22.

SPOEHR, ALEXANDER

1947     Changing kinship systems. Anthropological Series, Chicago Natural History Museum, Vol. 33, No. 4.

TAX, SOL and others (ed.)

1953     An appraisal of anthropology today. Chicago, University of Chicago Press.

WISSLER, CLARK

1914     Material cultures of the North American Indian. American Anthropologist 16:501 ff.

1922     The American Indian. 2nd ed. New York, Oxford University Press.

1926     The relation of nature to man in aboriginal America. New York, Oxford University Press.

# A Problem in Malayo-Polynesian Social Organization[1]

WARD H. GOODENOUGH
*University of Pennsylvania*

DESPITE the wide differences in the social systems which now exist among Malayo-Polynesian societies, Murdock (1948; 1949:228–31, 349–50) offers convincing evidence that they are derived from an original "Hawaiian" type of structure. The features characterizing this type include bilocal extended families, bilateral kindreds, the absence of unilinear kin groups, and Generation-Hawaiian kinship terminology.

Not considered by Murdock, because it was beyond the scope of his immediate interests, is another feature characterizing the organization of a great many Malayo-Polynesian societies: the association of individual rights to land with membership in some kind of kin group. It is so widespread as to suggest that it may be an original Malayo-Polynesian pattern.

If Murdock's reconstruction is correct, the only two kin groups with which land ownership could be associated were the bilateral kindred and the bilocal extended family. Now a person's kindred as defined by Murdock (1949:44, 56–62) includes roughly half of the members of his father's and mother's kindreds, respectively, coinciding with the kindreds of neither of them. This means that there is no continuity of kindred membership from one generation to the next. Kindreds, as so defined, cannot, therefore, function as land-owning bodies. Bilocal extended families could so function, but this would require that all out-marrying members of a family lose membership in the land-owning group while all in-marrying spouses acquire such membership. Yet the present-day Malayo-Polynesian land-owning groups stress consanguinity as the basis of membership, not residence alone. Since, moreover, consanguineal ties are the normal basis for the transmission of land rights, consanguineal groups are more effective instruments of collective land ownership than residential ones. I find it difficult, therefore, to accept the idea that the early Malayo-Polynesians associated ownership directly with the bilocal extended family.

But what alternatives are there? The evidence for Murdock's reconstruction is too consistent to allow for any serious questioning of his conclusions. There is, however, the possibility that he has left something out, something which neither his data nor existing social organization concepts could readily have revealed.

A clue to what this something is may be sought in the current confusion as to what is meant by the term "kindred." In the literature it has two distinct definitions. Rivers (1926a:15–16) and Murdock (1949:56–62) both treat the kindred as a group of persons who have a relative in common, regardless of whether kinship is traced through men or women. Such people cannot all be related to one another. As just indicated, the kindred in this sense is ephem-

71

eral and cannot, therefore, function as a land-owning group. And it is in this sense that Murdock attributes kindreds to early Malayo-Polynesian society.

As defined in *Notes and Queries* (1929:55), on the other hand, the term kindred "should be limited to a group of persons who acknowledge their descent, genealogically or by adoption, from one family, whether through their fathers or mothers." Here, a kindred refers to people who have an ancestor in common as distinct from people who have a relative in common. In this sense a kindred has continuity through time and all its members are related to one another. As *Notes and Queries* defines it, a kindred is any nonunilinear descent group; as Murdock and Rivers define it, it is not a true descent group at all. The source of confusion has clearly been the feature common to both types of group: in both cases consanguineal connections are traced through either sex. The difference is that in the kindred of Rivers and Murdock these connections are traced *laterally* to a common relative, while in the kindred of *Notes and Queries* they are traced *lineally* to a common ancestor. I wish to suggest that the kindred in the latter sense must be added to the kindred in Murdock's sense as an element in the social organization of early Malayo-Polynesian society. Hereinafter, I shall reserve the term kindred for the bilateral group which Rivers and Murdock had in mind and shall refer to the group defined by *Notes and Queries* as a nonunilinear descent group.

As we shall see, nonunilinear descent groups may take many forms. We are, therefore, faced with the problem of ascertaining its probable form in the original Malayo-Polynesian group.

Logically, true descent groups, i.e., groups in which all the members trace descent from a common ancestor, may be of two basic types. The first type we may call an "unrestricted descent group," for it includes *all* of the founder's descendants, whether through males or females. Such groups must of necessity overlap in membership, for each individual will belong to as many of them as he has known ancestors. The second type restricts membership to include only some of the descendants of the original ancestor. The unilinear principle, by which only the children of existing members of one sex are added as new members, is but one of several possible ways of restricting membership in descent groups. A second possibility is to include only those descendants who acquire certain land rights as their share of the original inheritance. If both sexes are eligible to inherit these rights, then the line of descent by which a member carries his genealogy back to the founding ancestor is likely to go sometimes through men and sometimes through women. A third way to restrict membership in a descent group is to include only the children of those members who after marriage continue to reside in the locality associated with the group. If residence is bilocal, then the line of descent will go sometimes through men and sometimes through women. Still another device is to make membership in the father's or mother's group optional depending on the individual's own choice of residence between the localities with which they are respectively associated. These are simple ways of maintaining restricted descent groups of a sort analogous to sibs and lineages, but not unilinear in structure. Such groups can readily function as land-holding units. What evidence do we have among Malayo-Polynesian societies for the presence of such nonunilinear descent groups either now or in the past?

Let us turn to the Gilbert Islands first.[2] Here we must distinguish formally and functionally between five types of kin group.

1. The *utuu*, a true bilateral kindred.

2. The *oo*,[3] an unrestricted descent group including all the persons descended from a common ancestor, regardless whether through men or women. This group functions only in relation to property.

3. The *mweenga*, a household. Formerly it was an extended family unit. It was predominantly patrilocal, but matrilocal marriages kept it from being completely so.

4. The *bwoti*, a nonunilinear descent group based on land rights, functioning in connection with community meeting-house organization.

5. The *kainga*, a nonunilinear descent group based on parental residence. Now defunct, it formerly functioned in connection with some aspects of property organization, feuding, and some economic activities. The *oo*, the *bwoti*, and the *kainga* are all of interest for this discussion.

As already indicated, the *oo* functions only in relation to land, individual rights to which may be held by both sexes. When a man (or woman) dies, his land passes to his children. Each daughter who marries receives a small share of the inheritance. The bulk of it is divided among the sons, with a slightly larger share going to the eldest. Division among the sons may be delayed until their death, being subsequently accomplished by their heirs. If there are no sons, the daughters receive the entire inheritance. Since women also pass their shares on to their children, some of the land allotted among brothers and sisters comes from their father and some from their mother. If their mother is without brothers, they may get more land from her than from their father. As this process continues, a tract of land is divided and subdivided within various lines descended from the original owner. All of his descendants form an *oo*. Some of them may not have acquired a share of this land, but are eligible to do so should present shareholders die without heirs. Since land may not be alienated from the *oo* without the consent of its members, the several holdings of a person who dies without children revert for distribution among the nearest of his kinsmen who, like him, are descended from the original owner. Land which came through his mother cannot revert to kinsmen on his father's side; it can go only to those of his mother's kin who are her *oo* mates with respect to that land. Membership in the *oo* is not terminated by settlement in a different community or atoll. It lasts for as long as the genealogical ties are remembered. The Gilbertese *oo* illustrates how an unrestricted descent group can be associated with land ownership. We must, therefore, enter this type of group as a candidate in our search for original Malayo-Polynesian social forms. Let us now turn to the *bwoti*.

Community meeting houses in the Gilbert Islands, as in Samoa,[4] have a highly formalized organization. Every member of the community has the right to sit in one or more of the traditional seating places under the eaves around the meeting house. Each seating place is named and together with the people who occupy it constitutes a *bwoti*. *Bwoti* membership is based on individual rights in certain plots of land. All persons who own a share in such a plot, if no more than one square foot, have the right to a corresponding seat. Since all persons holding a share in the same plot are theoretically lineal descendants of its original holder and thus members of the same *oo*, all persons entitled to the same seat in the meeting house are *ipso facto* consanguineally related and so recognized. But not all members of the same *oo* with respect to such a plot have actually inherited shares in it; they hold lands acquired from other ancestors. Not holding a share, they are barred from the associated seat, but must sit elsewhere as their present holdings permit. While all *bwoti* mates belong to the same *oo*, only a segment of the *oo* belongs to the same *bwoti*.

From his various ancestors a man may acquire shares in several plots, each entitling him to a different seat. He is potentially a member of several *bwoti* at once, but can activate membership in only one. His children are not bound by his choice, however, and he, himself, may change his affiliation, either because he has quarreled with his mates, or because he wishes to help keep up the numerical strength or to assume the leadership of a *bwoti* in which he has the right of active membership. A man entitled to sit in two places may so divide his land holdings that one son acquires the right to sit in one *bwoti* while another son acquires the right to sit in the other. There are instances where brothers belong to different *bwoti*. Everyone has the right of membership in at least one; people divide their land holdings among their heirs in such a way as to insure this. Women pass on these rights to their children in the same way that men do. We have seen, however, that unless they have no brothers they traditionally receive smaller allotments of land, and then only at marriage. As a result men belong more often to their father's than to their mother's *bwoti*. It is understandable that this kin group should have been erroneously labeled "patrilineal" by such outstanding reporters of Gilbertese custom as Grimble (1933:19–20) and the Maudes (1931:232). In the light of existing concepts, this was the best label they could use.[5] The *bwoti*, then, is a common descent group whose membership is restricted, not by reckoning descent exclusively through one sex, but to those descendants of the common ancestor whose share of the original inheritance includes a portion of a particular plot of land.

*Kainga* appear originally to have had the same membership as *bwoti*, for in some instances their names coincide, and they often have the same founding ancestors. In time, however, they diverged, for the principles governing their membership differ. Like the *bwoti*, each *kainga* was a descent group associated with a tract of land. Its founding ancestor, also, was the original holder of the tract. Theoretically, the original ancestor established residence on his land. Those of his descendants who continued to reside there formed together with their spouses an extended family, or *mweenga*. Together with those who were born and raised there, but had moved away after marriage, they formed a *kainga*. Residence was commonly patrilocal but matrilocal residence was considered proper under some circumstances, as when a man's share of *kainga* lands was small while his wife's was large. While residence did not affect one's own *kainga* membership, it did affect that of one's children. It appears to have been the rule that if a person's parents resided patrilocally he belonged to his father's *kainga*, but if they resided matrilocally he belonged to his mother's. Since residence was predominantly patrilocal, most Gilbertese belonged to their father's *kainga*. Succession to leadership in the *kainga*, moreover, could descend only in the male line. Neither of these facts, however, made the *kainga* a true patrilineal lineage, for if membership were patrilineal then the children of men who went in matrilocal residence would still have belonged to their father's *kainga*. Patrilineal succession to its leadership was guaranteed by having the eligible successor reside patrilocally, so that his son would in turn be a member and eligible to succeed him. We seem to have in the *kainga*, then, a kin group resembling a lineage, but whose membership is determined by parental residence rather than parental sex. This membership principle is, of course, tailor-made for societies practicing bilocal residence.

Normally, each member of the *kainga* had a plot in the tract of land associated with it. If this tract had a corresponding *bwoti* in the meeting house, all the *kainga*'s members would be eligible to sit there. The plots of those members of the *kainga* who moved away after marriage, however, went to their children, who belonged to other *kainga*. These children thus became eligible to membership in a *bwoti* other than that to which most of their *kainga* mates belonged. By this process members of the same *kainga* could and did belong to different *bwoti*, and, conversely, members of the same *bwoti* belonged to different *kainga*, even though both types of group were founded by the same ancestors. While each *kainga* tends to be associated with a specific *bwoti*, their respective personnel are not congruent.

To sum up, all three descent groups are somehow connected with land. An ancestor having established ownership of a tract was the founder of all three. All of his descendants form an *oo*. Those in actual possession of a share in the land are eligible to membership in a *bwoti*. Those whose parents resided on it form a *kainga*. None of these groups is unilinear.

Because of its intimate connection with bilocal residence, we must look upon the *kainga*, like the *oo*, as quite possibly an original Malayo-Polynesian form of kin group. The *bwoti*, too, despite its special function in relation to meeting-house organization, commands our interest on structural grounds. What indications are there of the presence of groups like the *oo*, *bwoti*, and *kainga* among other Malayo-Polynesian peoples? Let us turn to the *oo* and *bwoti* first.

Barton's account of the Ifugao indicates clearly that an unrestricted descent group of the *oo* type occurs there. In describing the Ifugao "family," as he calls it, he leaves no doubt about the presence of bilateral kindreds (1919:15). When he talks of family-owned land, however, he is clearly talking about something else (pp. 39–41). He indicates that some holdings have been associated with a particular family for generations. They may descend through daughters as well as sons (pp. 50–55). When a person dies without children his property reverts for division not to his kindred as a unit but to the nearest of his kin who like him are descended from a former owner. Indeed, as far as the reversion of land to collateral heirs is concerned, Ifugao law is almost identical with Gilbertese law. Members of this land-holding family, moreover, have a voice in its alienation even though they possess no shares in the land. Clearly, when Barton talks about the family as a land-holding unit, he is talking about an unrestricted descent group like the *oo*. The Ifugao are one of the societies considered by Murdock (1949:349) to preserve the original Malayo-Polynesian Hawaiian type of organization unchanged. If he is right, we must accept the *oo* as one of its characteristic features.

Ulawa in the Solomon Islands is another society which exemplifies Murdock's (1949:349) original Hawaiian type of social structure. As reported by Ivens (1927:45–46, 60–61), the Ulawans live in hamlets whose members consider themselves kinsmen. Patrilocal residence prevails, but Ivens notes that commoners marrying into a chief's family may live matrilocally. In addition to extended families there is a kindred, called *komu*. Now, Ivens says that garden grounds and coconut trees belong to the *komu*, and adds that daughters as well as sons may acquire rights in them and retain these rights after moving away in marriage. We have already noted that a kindred cannot be a land-owning group. As such, the *komu* can scarcely be a true kindred. I conclude that the term *komu* must refer in fact to two kinds of kin group—one a kindred, the other a nonunilinear descent group associated with land rights. While the published evidence gives no direct clue as to how membership in the latter group is determined, it is enough to restrict the probabilities. I infer that it is an unrestricted descent group like the *oo* or is restricted either on the basis of land shares like the *bwoti* or on the basis of parental residence like the *kainga*, for Ivens is emphatic about the absence of unilinear groups.

When we turn to Polynesia we find abundant evidence of nonunilinear descent groups. All authorities stress the importance of lineal descent, whether through men or women, in connection with social rank and land rights. Some authorities use the term kindred in the *Notes and Queries* sense for these nonunilinear groups.

Macgregor's account (1937:54) of Tokelau, for example, describes a kindred as all persons descended from a common ancestor, whether through men or women, indicating that it is an unrestricted descent group of the *oo* type. He adds that "the land that was given to the heads of families [in the original settlement] became the common property of the kindreds descended from them. Each member of the kindred received the right to use a section of the land." Children thus acquired claims to a share of land in both their father's and mother's groups. Macgregor states that normally only one of these claims was activated, sometimes on the mother's side and sometimes on the father's. But he does not give the criteria for this choice. It could not have been parental residence for residence was regularly matrilocal, while leadership in the group descended patrilineally in the primogeniture line as in the Gilbert

Islands. We can only conclude that in addition to the unrestricted descent group there was a restricted group comprising persons who actually possessed shares in the ancestral land, resembling in this respect the Gilbertese *bwoti*.

In his account of Uvea, Burrows (1937:62–68) likewise uses the term kindred to refer to two nonunilinear descent groups. One appears to be unrestricted like the *oo*, its members having rights in ancestral land regardless of where they or their parents reside, though if membership is confined to those descendants who actually possess shares as distinct from the right to possess them it corresponds to the Gilbertese *bwoti*. Which is the case is not clear. A segment of this group is localized as a bilocal extended family. This more restricted group is analogous to the Gilbertese *kainga*. In fact, the Uveans use the name *kainga* for it, as well as for the larger group.

Burrows (1936:65–78) develops the same picture on Futuna, where the *kutunga* is either an unrestricted group like the *oo* or a restricted group like the *bwoti*. Here the term *kainga* is reserved for that portion of it which is localized on *kutunga* land. Since residence is bilocal, membership in the *kainga* must be based on parental residence, as in the Gilbert Islands. Burrows calls the *kutunga* a kindred and cites *Notes and Queries* as his authority for doing so. Futunan society is another of those which Murdock (1949:349) regards as typifying original Malayo-Polynesian forms of organization.

The demonstrable presence of unrestricted descent groups associated with land in Ifugao and Gilbertese society, and their probable presence in Uvea, Futuna, and Ulawa means that either they developed independently in Indonesia, Micronesia, Polynesia, and Melanesia, or they were a part of original Malayo-Polynesian social structure. Of these five societies, three are represented in Murdock's survey. That each of them should be considered by him, for other reasons, to preserve the original social structure unchanged is not without significance in this regard.

Given the presence of unrestricted descent groups, it is evident that groups structurally similar to the *bwoti* readily tend to develop. All that is required is a distinction between those who as descendants have rights to acquire a share of ancestral land and those among them who actually have received such shares. If the latter are organized as a separate social group for any reason, they necessarily constitute a restricted descent group in which membership follows the *bwoti* principle. The conditions for its presence, therefore, may well have obtained in early Malayo-Polynesian society. The distributional evidence, however, is too limited to warrant any conclusion in this regard.

In the foregoing survey of possible examples of the *oo* type of group, we have noted the simultaneous presence of the *kainga* type on Uvea and Futuna, where, too, it is called a *kainga*. This suggests that there may be linguistic as well as other evidence for considering the *kainga* type of group an early Malayo-Polynesian form.

The term *kainga*, together with its variant *kainanga*, has a wide distribution in Micronesia and Polynesia. This distribution cannot be attributed to borrowing because its various forms show the proper historical sound shifts as loan-words do not. While the meaning of the term is not always clear, it invariably has to do with land and/or some kind of social group. In Mangareva, for example, *kainga* refers to a section of land (Buck 1938). It means a kinsman in Lau and Tonga (Hocart 1929), and a nonunilinear kin group together with its land in Futuna, Uvea, and the Gilbert Islands, while an ill-defined family group is called *'aiga* in Samoa. The variant form occurs as *'ainana* in Hawaii, where it refers to a local population of some kind. The cognates *kainanga* and *hailang* or *jejinag* refer to patrilineal and matrilineal sibs, respectively, in Tikopia (Firth 1946) and the Central Caroline Islands (Lessa 1950; Goodenough 1951). Clearly there was some kind of descent group associated with land in the society from which both Polynesian and Micronesian peoples are jointly descended. But how in the course of history could this ancestral descent group come to be nonunilinear in some places and unilinear in others? And where it is unilinear, how could it become patrilineal here and matrilineal there? If we start with the assumption that this group was originally, as in the Gilbert Islands, one in which continuity of membership derived from parental residence where the residence rule was bilocal, then the answer becomes clear. In those societies shifting to regular patrilocal residence, the group automatically became patrilineal. Where matrilocal residence became the rule, as in the Carolines, the group became equally automatically matrilineal. And in each case no one need even be aware that a change had in fact occurred. Where bilocal residence continued or tendencies to unilocality did not go too far, the kin group remained nonunilinear. If this is so, where else in addition to Uvea, Futuna, and the Gilbert Islands do we encounter nonunilinear descent groups based on parental residence?

The so-called patrilineal clans of the Lau Islands are definitely kin groups in which membership is based on parental residence. The accounts by both Thompson (1940:54) and Hocart (1929:17) make this clear. Hocart, for example, says: "Usually a man 'follows' his father's clan, but many men live with the mother's people, even though both clans may be in the same village, next to one another. If a man lives with his wife's people, the children follow the mother's clan." The importance of parental residence for *hapu* membership among the Maori has been noted by Firth (1929:99–100). For predominantly patrilocal Tongareva we have the suggestive statement by Buck (1932:40) that "through matrilocal residence the children drop active connection with their father's kin and become incorporated and naturally absorbed into their mother's family and the organization to which it belongs." I suspect a similar situation in Tokelau (Macgregor 1937) and Manua (Mead 1930). Certainly it would be compatible with the meager facts reported there.

For patrilineal Tubuai, Aitken (1930:36) reports that in the absence of sons descent was carried through a daughter for one generation. This practice bears an obvious resemblance to *ambil anak*, or adoptive marriage, as reported for some Indonesian societies, where a patrilineal line may be continued for one generation through a daughter instead of through a son (Ter Haar 1948:175–76; Murdock 1949:21, 45). Here matrilocal residence is the social mechanism whereby descent through a woman is legalized. The daughter who will carry on the line stays with her family of orientation, her husband moves in and the bride-price is waived. In short, the children take their lineage affiliation in accordance with the residence of their parents. Looked at this way, Indonesian kin groups, where these matrilocal marriages are practiced, are basically like the Gilbertese *kainga* and the so-called clans of the Lau Islands. Historically, it would appear that a shift toward patrilocal residence made affiliation with the father's group so common that kin groups came to be viewed as properly patrilineal. Jural recognition of patrilineal descent then required a legal device for reconciling it with the less frequent but traditional practice of matrilineal affiliation under matrilocal residence. This was accomplished simply by adoption of the husband. Adoptive marriage, then, points to the former existence in some Indonesian societies of nonunilinear descent groups of the *kainga* type.

From Melanesia I have no clear example of kin groups corresponding to the *kainga*. There is a possibility, however, that they occur in Ulawa, as has already been noted. Rivers' account (1926b:71–94) of Eddystone Island shows bilocal residence. His one reference to gardening rights (p. 93) indicates that a woman retains a share of her parent's land if she and her husband live matrilocally, her children presumably inheriting from her, but she loses these rights if she lives patrilocally for then her children presumably inherit from their father. If the same principle applies to men, rights in land are based on parental residence. If those having such rights in the same section of land are organized as a group, it is very likely of the *kainga* type.

Melanesian possibilities aside, however, the demonstrable antiquity of the *kainga* for Polynesia and Micronesia, when taken together with the indications of its former presence in Indonesia, warrants the inference that this form of group was present in early Malayo-Polynesian society. Murdock's (1949:152, 228, 349) reconstruction of bilocal residence, without which the *kainga* is impossible, makes this inference even more plausible.

If we accept the proposition that descent groups like the *oo* and *kainga* were both represented in original Malayo-Polynesian society, how can it help us to understand the processes by which some of the complex social systems among present Malayo-Polynesian peoples emerged? By way of introduction to answering this question, I wish to call attention to the peculiar form of the nonunilinear descent group in the community of Bwaidoga in the D'Entrecasteaux Islands, where I had the opportunity to collect some information in 1951.[6]

Bwaidoga consists of several hamlets, *kali:va*, strung along the coast. Each hamlet is associated with one or two kin groups called *unuma*, which are localized there in extended families. Several related *unuma* form a larger nonlocalized kin group, called *ga:bu*. Most men inherit a share of their father's *unuma* lands and reside patrilocally after marriage. Under these conditions a man belongs to his father's *unuma* and *ga:bu*. He may, however, choose to reside with his mother's *unuma*, receiving a share of its land from his maternal grandfather or maternal uncle. By doing this he loses rights in his father's land, unless he returns permanently to his father's *unuma* immediately following his father's death. If he remains with his mother's *unuma*, he forfeits these rights for himself and his heirs in perpetuity. By choosing to affiliate with his mother's *unuma*, a man automatically becomes a member of her *ga:bu* as well.[7]

The Bwaidogan *unuma* and *ga:bu* differ from the *kainga* in that residence is never matrilocal. The choice is between patrilocal and avunculocal residence. Men can acquire land from the *unuma* of either parent, and their choice of residence depends on where they can get the best land. As a result of this system, membership in *unuma* and *ga:bu* is traced sometimes through female and sometimes through male ancestors.

The avunculocal alternative to patrilocal residence suggests that the Bwaidogan *ga:bu* and *unuma* were formerly matrilineal, and that the *unuma* used to be localized as an avunculocal extended family. With a shift in favor of patrilocal residence, membership in the *unuma* became optionally patrilineal. The present system may be seen, then, as transitional from a matrilineal to a patrilineal form of organization. As such, it cannot be viewed as indicative of early Malayo-Polynesian forms. I mention Bwaidoga, however, not only to illustrate another kind of nonunilinear descent group, but to help point up a problem which I believe has played a major determining role in the history of Malayo-Polynesian social organization: the problem of land distribution.

In any community where cultivatable land is not over-abundant in relation to population, and all rights to land depend on membership in strictly unilinear kin groups, a serious problem must soon arise. Unilinear groups inevitably fluctuate considerably in size. The matrilineal lineages on Truk, for example, readily double or halve their membership in the space of one or two generations. As a result, one lineage may have twice as much land as its members need while another has not enough to go around. Unless devices are developed to redistribute land rights to persons outside the owning group, intracommunity conflict is inevitable.

As noted at the beginning of this discussion, Malayo-Polynesian societies characteristically vest land ownership in kin groups. Throughout their history, therefore, they have had to meet the problem of land distribution in the face of constant fluctuations in kin-group size. One of the simplest possible devices for achieving this end is to keep the land-owning groups nonunilinear. With the *oo* type of group a person has membership in as many *oo* as there are distinct land-owning ancestors of whom he is a lineal descendant. While he can expect little from those *oo* which have become numerically large, he can expect a lot of land from those which have few surviving members. The overlapping memberships inevitable with unrestricted descent groups make them an excellent vehicle for keeping land holdings equitably distributed throughout the community.

As a restricted descent group without overlapping personnel, the *kainga* is also admirably suited for keeping group membership balanced in relation to its immediate land resources. With bilocal residence, as the size of one *kainga* decreases in relation to that of other *kainga*, more of its members remain at home after marriage; as its population increases, more move away.

How do these functional considerations help us to understand the development of other social forms?

In those societies where conditions came to favor neolocal residence, the *kainga* could not possibly survive. If the same factors promoted individual ownership of land, the *oo* would also have been weakened, leaving only the bilateral kindred—as among the Kalingas of Luzon (Barton 1949), who now have a social structure corresponding to Murdock's "Eskimo" type.

In areas where there was an abundance of land, and slash-and-burn agriculture made the use of any plot a temporary matter, doing away with the need for permanent tenure, bilocal residence was no longer functionally advantageous. Unilocal residence rules could and did develop, and the *kainga* type of group became unilinear as a result. The large islands of Melanesia provided conditions of this sort, which accounts, I believe, for the high incidence of unilinear forms of organization there.

Tendencies toward unilocal residence and unilinear descent developed elsewhere also, as in the Caroline Islands and parts of Indonesia. These tendencies called for reliance on other devices for redistributing land. In the Carolines this was accomplished by separating use rights from membership in the owning group. Where formerly parental residence had been the basis for membership in the owning group, it now became one of several bases for transmitting use rights outside the owning group. I have shown elsewhere how the more complicated tenure system which resulted served to keep land use equitably distributed on matrilineal Truk (Goodenough 1951:44, 166–71).

Adoption of the land-poor by kinsmen in land-rich groups is another device for solving the land distribution problem. It is not mutually exclusive with other devices, and its wide practice is familiar to all students of Malayo-Polynesian societies. It is of special importance where the land-owning groups have become unilinear. We have already mentioned its wedding with the parental residence principle in Indonesia in connection with adoptive marriage there. Its elaborations on Palau in conjunction with financial sponsorship are so complex as to obscure almost beyond recognition the underlying matrilineal system (Barnett 1949).

The Bwaidogans provide an interesting example of a people whose land-owning kin groups became matrilineal, but, under the stress of land distribution problems, could not remain so. They had to become nonunilinear again. With matrilineal descent and avunculocal residence as the immediate antecedents of this return shift, however, the result was the peculiar type of group already described, not the original *kainga*. Pressures of the kind at work in Bwaidoga may well lie behind the series of shifts which culminated in double descent in Yap (Schneider 1953:216–17) and the bilineal groups of the New Hebrides (Layard 1942).

I conclude, then, that in addition to the characteristics reconstructed by

Murdock for early Malayo-Polynesian society, there were two types of kin group associated with land. One was an unrestricted descent group, while membership in the other was determined by parental residence. Because they stressed kin ties through both parents equally, these groups favored the simultaneous presence of bilateral kindreds and Generation-Hawaiian kinship terms as already reconstructed by Murdock.[8] The structure of both groups helped resolve land distribution problems. Where residence became patrilocal or matrilocal, these groups tended automatically to be transformed into patrilineal or matrilineal sibs and lineages. Where this occurred, greater reliance on adoption, adjustments in the land tenure system, or a subsequent return to optional bases of group affiliation led to the complicated and varied social systems now present in parts of Indonesia and Micronesia, as well as to such unusual ones as we find in Bwaidoga.

## NOTES

[1] This paper is a revised and expanded version of one entitled "The Typology of Consanguineal Groups," presented at the annual meeting of the American Anthropological Association, December 1952.

[2] Field work was conducted in the summer of 1951, when I was a member of a team making an ecological study of the Gilbertese atoll Onotoa, under the auspices of the Pacific Science Board of the National Research Council and the Geography Branch of the Office of Naval Research.

[3] I am not certain that *oo* is the correct native term for this group. Literally, the word means "fence." It was only in the last two days of field work that I learned it referred to some type of kin group as well. Answers to last-minute queries suggested that it referred to the unrestricted descent group which I had already isolated but had thought to be unnamed.

[4] The Samoan *fono* and Gilbertese *mwaneaba* (meeting house) probably have a common origin, for *mwaneaba* customs are attributed to Samoan invaders arriving in the Gilbert Islands several hundred years ago.

[5] There remains the possibility, of course, that the *bwoti* are patrilineal on some Gilbertese atolls. On Onotoa, however, they are not.

[6] In November 1951, I spent two days at Bwaidoga, at which time, due to the generous assistance provided by the Reverend Mr. William Coates of the Wailagi Mission, I was able to obtain from a group of native elders the information presented here. The field work of which the survey of Goodenough Island formed a part was sponsored by the Museum of the University of Pennsylvania.

[7] The *ga:bu* seems to correspond to the totemic group described by Jenness and Ballantyne (1920:66–67) as patrilineal; and the representatives of such a group in one hamlet presumably correspond to the *unuma*. Their characterization of these groups as patrilineal apparently follows from the fact that patrilocal residence and consequent patrilineal affiliation predominated statistically.

[8] The reasons given by Murdock (1949:152, 158) for the association of Generation terminology with bilocal residence and bilateral kindreds, for example, apply with equal force to its association with nonunilinear descent groups of the sort herein described.

## REFERENCES CITED

AITKEN, R. T.
    1930   Ethnology of Tubuai. Bishop Museum Bulletin 70. Honolulu.
BARNETT, H. G.
    1949   Palauan society. University of California Publications.

BARTON, R. F.
    1919    Ifugao law. University of California Publications in Archaeology and Ethnology 15, No. 1.
    1949    The Kalingas. University of Chicago.
BUCK, PETER
    1932    Ethnology of Tongareva. Bishop Museum Bulletin 92. Honolulu.
    1938    Ethnology of Mangareva. Bishop Museum Bulletin 157. Honolulu.
BURROWS, E. G.
    1936    Ethnology of Futuna. Bishop Museum Bulletin 138. Honolulu.
    1937    Ethnology of Uvea. Bishop Museum Bulletin 145. Honolulu.
FIRTH, RAYMOND
    1929    Primitive economics of the New Zealand Maori. New York.
    1946    We, the Tikopia. New York.
GOODENOUGH, W. H.
    1951    Property, kin, and community on Truk. Yale University Publications in Anthropology 46. New Haven.
GRIMBLE, C. M. G.
    1933    The migrations of a pandanus people. Polynesian Society Memoir 12.
HOCART, A. M.
    1929    Lau Islands, Fiji. Bishop Museum Bulletin 62. Honolulu.
IVENS, W. G.
    1927    Melanesians of the southeast Solomon Islands. London.
JENNESS, D. AND A. BALLANTYNE
    1920    The northern D'Entrecasteaux. Oxford.
LAYARD, JOHN
    1942    Stone men of Malekula. London.
LESSA, W. A.
    1950    The ethnology of Ulithi. University of California at Los Angeles (mimeographed).
MACGREGOR, GORDON
    1937    Ethnology of Tokelau Islands. Bishop Museum Bulletin 146. Honolulu.
MAUDE, H. C. AND H. E.
    1931    Adoption in the Gilbert Islands. Journal of the Polynesian Society 40:225–35.
MEAD, MARGARET
    1930    Social organization of Manua. Bishop Museum Bulletin 76. Honolulu.
MURDOCK, G. P.
    1948    Anthropology in Micronesia. Transactions of the New York Academy of Sciences (Ser. 2) 2, No. 1:9–16.
    1949    Social structure. New York.
*Notes and Queries*
    1929    5th ed. London.
RIVERS, W. H. R.
    1926a   Social organization. New York.
    1926b   Psychology and ethnology. London.
SCHNEIDER, D. M.
    1953    Yap kinship terminology and kin groups. American Anthropologist 55:215–36.
TER HAAR, B.
    1948    Adat law in Indonesia. New York.
THOMPSON, LAURA
    1940    Southern Lau, Fiji. Bishop Museum Bulletin 162. Honolulu.

# Types of Latin American Peasantry: A Preliminary Discussion*

ERIC R. WOLF
*University of Illinois*

## THE PEASANT TYPE

A S ANTHROPOLOGY has become increasingly concerned with the study of modern communities, anthropologists have paid increasing attention to the social and cultural characteristics of the peasantry. It will be the purpose of this article to draw up a tentative typology of peasant groups for Latin America, as a basis for further field work and discussion. Such a typology will of necessity raise more questions than can be answered easily at the present time. To date, anthropologists working in Latin America have dealt mainly with groups with "Indian" cultures, and available anthropological literature reflects this major interest. Any projected reorientation of inquiry from typologies based mainly on characteristics of culture content to typologies based on similarities or dissimilarities of structure has implications with which no single writer could expect to cope. This article is therefore provisional in character, and its statements wholly open to discussion.

There have been several recent attempts to draw a line between primitives and peasants. Redfield, for example, has discussed the distinction in the following words (1953:31):

There were no peasants before the first cities. And those surviving primitive peoples who do not live in terms of the city are not peasants. . . . The peasant is a rural native whose long established order of life takes important account of the city.

Kroeber has also emphasized the relation between the peasant and the city (1948:284):

Peasants are definitely rural—yet live in relation to market towns; they form a class segment of a larger population which usually contains also urban centers, sometimes metropolitan capitals. They constitute part-societies with part-cultures.

Peasants thus form "horizontal socio-cultural segments," as this term has been defined by Steward (1950:115).

Redfield further states that the city was made "possible" through the labor of its peasants (1953), and both definitions imply—though they do not state outright—that the city consumes a large part of what the peasant produces. Urban life is impossible without production of an agricultural surplus in the countryside.

Since we are interested less in the generic peasant type than in discriminating between different types of peasants, we must go on to draw distinctions between groups of peasants involved in divergent types of urban culture (for

* The writer would like to thank Morton H. Fried, Sidney W. Mintz, Robert F. Murphy, Robert Redfield, Julian H. Steward, and Ben Zimmerman for helpful criticisms and suggestions.

452

a discussion of differences in urban centers, cf. Beals 1951:8–9; Hoselitz 1953). It is especially important to recognize the effects of the industrial revolution and the growing world market on peasant segments the world over. These have changed both the cultural characteristics of such segments and the character of their relations with other segments. Peasants everywhere have become involved in market relations of a vastly different order of magnitude than those which prevailed before the advent of industrial culture. Nor can this expansion be understood as a purely unilineal phenomenon. There have been different types of industry and markets, different types of industrial expansion and market growth. These have affected different parts of the world in very different ways. The peasantries found in the world today are the multiple products of such multilineal growth. At the same time, peasants are no longer the primary producers of wealth. Industry and trade rather than agriculture now produce the bulk of the surpluses needed to support segments not directly involved in the processes of production. Various kinds of large-scale agricultural enterprises have grown up to compete with the peasant for economic resources and opportunities. This has produced a world-wide "crisis of the peasantry" (Firth 1952:12), related to the increasingly marginal role of the peasantry within the prevalent economic system.

In choosing a definition of the peasant which would be adequate for our present purpose, we must remember that definitions are tools of thought, and not eternal verities. Firth, for example, defines the term as widely as possible, including not only agriculturists but also fishermen and rural craftsmen (1952:87). Others might be tempted to add independent rubber gatherers and strip miners. For the sake of initial analysis, this writer has found it convenient to consider each of these various kinds of enterprise separately and thus to define the term "peasant" as strictly as possible. Three distinctions may serve as the basis for such a definition. All three are chosen with a view to Latin American conditions, and all seem flexible enough to include varieties which we may discover in the course of our inquiry.

First, let us deal with the peasant only as an agricultural producer. This means that for the purposes of the present article we shall draw a line between peasants, on the one hand, and fishermen, strip miners, rubber gatherers, and livestock keepers, on the other. The economic and cultural implications of livestock keeping, for example, are sufficiently different from those of agriculture to warrant separate treatment. This is especially true in Latin America, where livestock keeping has been carried on mainly on large estates rather than on small holdings.

Second, we should—for our present purpose—distinguish between the peasant who retains effective control of land and the tenant whose control of land is subject to an outside authority. This distinction has some importance in Latin America. Effective control of land by the peasant is generally insured through direct ownership, through undisputed squatter rights, or through customary arrangements governing the rental and use of land. He does not have to pay dues to an outside landowner. Tenants, on the other hand, tend to seek security primarily through acceptance of outside controls over the arrangements of production and distribution, and thus often accept subordinate roles within hierarchically organized networks of relationships. The peasants generally retain much greater control of their processes of production. Outside controls become manifest primarily when they sell their goods on the market. Consideration of tenant segments belongs properly with a discussion of *haciendas* and plantations rather than with a discussion of the peasantry. This does not mean that in dealing with Latin America we can afford to forget for a moment that large estates overshadowed other forms of landholding for many centuries, or that tenant segments may exert greater ultimate influence on the total sociocultural whole than peasants.

Third, the peasant aims at subsistence, not at reinvestment. The starting point of the peasant is the needs which are defined by his culture. His answer, the production of cash crops for a market, is prompted largely by his inability to meet these needs within the sociocultural segment of which he is a part. He sells cash crops to get money, but this money is used in turn to buy goods and services which he requires to subsist and to maintain his social status, rather than to enlarge his scale of operations. We may thus draw a line between the peasant and another agricultural type whom we call the "farmer." The farmer views agriculture as a business enterprise. He begins his operations with a sum of money which he invests in a farm. The crops produced are sold not only to provide goods and services for the farm operator but to permit amortization and expansion of his business. The aim of the peasant is subsistence. The aim of the farmer is reinvestment (Wolf 1951:60–61).

The term "peasant" indicates a structural relationship, not a particular culture content. By "structural relations" we mean "relatively fixed relations between parts rather than . . . the parts or elements themselves." By "structure," similarly, we mean "the mode in which the parts stand to each other" (Kroeber and Kluckhohn 1952:62, 63). A typology of peasantries should be set up on the basis of regularities in the occurrence of structural relationships rather than on the basis of regularities in the occurrence of similar culture elements. In selecting out certain structural features rather than others to provide a starting point for the formulation of types we may proceed wholly on an empirical basis. The selection of primarily economic criteria would be congruent with the present interest in typologies based on economic and sociopolitical features alone. The functional implications of these features are more clearly understood at present than those of other features of culture, and their dominant role in the development of the organizational framework has been noted empirically in many studies of particular cultures.

In setting up a typology of peasant segments we immediately face the difficulty that peasants are not primitives, that is, the culture of a peasant segment cannot be understood in terms of itself but is a part-culture, related to some larger integral whole. Certain relationships among the features of peasant culture are tied to bodies of relationships outside the peasant culture, yet help determine both its character and continuity. The higher the level of integration of such part-cultures, the greater the weight of such outside determinants. In complex societies certain components of the social superstructure rather than ecology seem increasingly to be determinants of further developments [Steward 1938:262].

This is especially true when we reach the organizational level of the capitalist market, where the relationship of technology and environment is mediated through complicated mechanisms of credit or political control which may originate wholly outside the part-culture under investigation.

We must not only be cognizant of outside factors which affect the culture of the part-culture. We must also account for the manner in which the part-culture is organized into the larger sociocultural whole. Unlike other horizontal sociocultural segments, like traders or businessmen, peasants function primarily within a local setting rather than on an interlocal or nonlocal basis. This produces considerable local variation within a given peasant segment. It means also that the peasantry is integrated into the sociocultural whole primarily through the structure of the community. We must therefore do more than define different kinds of peasants. We must also analyze the manner in which they are integrated with the outside world. In other words, a typology of peasants must include a typology of the kinds of communities in which they live.

The notion of type also implies a notion of history. The functioning of a particular segment depends on the historical interplay of factors which affect it. This point is especially important where we deal with part-cultures which must adapt their internal organization to changes in the total social field of which they are a part. Integration into a larger sociocultural whole is a historical process. We must be able to place part-cultures on the growth curve of the totality of which they form a part. In building a typology, we must take into account the growth curve of our cultural types.

Here we may summarize briefly our several criteria for the construction of a typology of peasant groups. First, it would seem to be advisable to define our subject matter as narrowly as possible. Second, we shall be interested in structure, rather than in culture content. Third, the initial criteria for our types can be primarily economic or sociopolitical, but should of course include as many other features as possible. Fourth, the types should be seen as component parts of larger wholes. The typical phenomena with which we are dealing are probably produced principally by the impact of outside forces on preexisting local cultures. Fifth, some notion of historical trajectory should be included in the formulation of a type.

## TWO TYPES OF PEASANT PART-CULTURES

To make our discussion more concrete, let us turn to an analysis of two types of peasant segments. The first type comprises certain groups in the high highlands of Latin America; the second covers peasant groups found in humid low highlands and tropical lowlands. While these types are based on available field reports, they should be interpreted as provisional models for the construction of a typology, and thus subject to future revision.

Our first type (1) comprises peasants practicing intensive cultivation in the high highlands of Nuclear America. While some production is carried on to cover immediate subsistence needs, these peasants must sell a little cash produce to buy goods produced elsewhere (Pozas 1952:311). Production is largely unsupported by fluid capital. It flows into a system of village markets which is highly congruent with such a marginal economy.

The geographical area in which this type of peasant prevails formed the core area of Spanish colonial America. It supported the bulk of Spanish settlement, furnished the labor force required by Spanish enterprises, and provided the mineral wealth which served as the driving force of Spanish colonization. Integration of this peasantry into the colonial structure was achieved typically through the formation of communities which inhibited direct contact between the individual and the outside world but interposed between them an organized communal structure. This structure we shall call here the "corporate" community. It has shown a high degree of persistence, which has been challenged successfully only in recent years when alternative structures are encroaching upon it. Anthropologists have studied a number of such communities in highland Peru and Mexico.

The reader will be tempted immediately to characterize this type of community as "Indian" and perhaps to ask if we are not dealing here with a survival from pre-Columbian times. Since structure rather than culture content is our main concern here, we shall emphasize the features of organization which may make this type of community like corporate communities elsewhere, rather than characterize it in purely ethnographic terms. Moreover, it is necessary to explain the persistence of any survival over a period of three hundred years. As we hope to show below, persistence of "Indian" culture content seems to have depended primarily on maintenance of this structure. Where the structure collapsed, traditional cultural forms quickly gave way to new alternatives of outside derivation.

The distinctive characteristic of the corporate peasant community is that it represents a bounded social system with clear-cut limits, in relations to both outsiders and insiders. It has structural identity over time. Seen from the outside, the community as a whole carries on a series of activities and upholds certain "collective representations." Seen from within, it defines the rights and duties of its members and prescribes large segments of their behavior.

Fortes recently analyzed groupings of a corporate character based on kinship (1953:25–29). The corporate peasant community resembles these other units in its corporate character but is no longer held together by kinship. It may once have been based on kinship units of a peculiar type (see Kirchhoff 1949:293), and features of kinship organization persist, such as a tendency toward local endogamy (for Mesoamerica, cf. Redfield and Tax 1952:31; for the Quechua, cf. Mishkin 1946:453) or in occasionally differential rights of old and new settlers. Nevertheless, the corporate community in Latin America represents the end product of a long process of reorganization which began in pre-Columbian times and was carried through under Spanish rule. As a result

of the conquest any kinship feature which this type of community may have
had was relegated to secondary importance. Members of the community were
made co-owners of a landholding corporation (García 1948:269), a co-owner-
ship which implied systematic participation in communal political and religious
affairs.

Several considerations may have prompted Crown policy toward such communities. First, the corporate community performing joint labor services for
an overlord was a widespread characteristic of European economic feudalism.
In trying to curtail the political power of a potential new landholding class in
the Spanish colonies the Crown took over management of Indian communities
in order to deny the conquerors direct managerial control over labor. The
Crown attempted to act as a go-between and labor contractor for both
peasant community and landowner. Second, the corporate community fitted
well into the political structure of the Spanish dynastic state, which attempted to incorporate each subcultural group and to define its radius of activity by law (Wolf 1953:100–1). This enabled the Crown to marshal the resources of such a group as an organized unit, and to impose its economic,
social, and religious controls by a type of indirect rule. Third, the corporate
structure of the peasant communities permitted the imposition of communal
as well as of individual burdens of forced labor and taxation. This was especially important in view of the heavy loss of labor power through flight or
disease. The imposition of the burden on a community rather than on individuals favored maintenance of a steady level of production.

Given this general historical background, what is the distinctive set of
relationships characteristic of the corporate peasant community?

The first of these is location on *marginal land*. Needs within the larger
society which might compel the absorption and exploitation of this land are
weak or absent, and the existing level of technology and transportation may
make such absorption difficult. In other words, the amount of energy required to destroy the existing structure of the corporate community and to
reorganize it at present outweighs the capacity of the larger society.

In the corporate peasant community marginal land tends to be exploited
by means of a *traditional technology* involving the members of the community
in the continuous physical effort of manual labor.

Marginal location and traditional technology together limit the production power of the community, and thus its ability to produce cash crops for
the market. This in turn limits the number of goods brought in from the outside which the community can afford to consume. The community is *poor*.

Within this economic setting, the corporate structure of the community is
retained by community *jurisdiction over the free disposal of land*. Needless to
say, community controls tend to be strongest where land is owned in common
and re-allocated among members every year. But even where private property
in land is the rule within the community, as is common today, the communal
taboo on sale of land to outsiders (cf. Aguirre 1952:149; Lewis 1951:124;
Mishkin 1946:443) severely limits the degree to which factors outside the

community can affect the structure of private property and related class differences within the community. Land is thus not a complete commodity. The taboo on sale of land to outsiders may be reinforced by other communal rights, such as gleaning rights or the right to graze cattle on any land within the community after the harvest.

The community possesses a system of power which embraces the male members of the community and makes the achievement of power a matter of community decision rather than a matter of individually achieved status (Redfield and Tax 1952:39; Mishkin 1946:459). This system of power is often tied into a religious system or into a series of interlocking religious systems. The *political-religious system* as a whole tends to define the boundaries of the community and acts as a rallying point and symbol of collective unity. Prestige within the community is largely related to rising from religious office to office along a prescribed ladder of achievement. Conspicuous consumption is geared to this communally approved system of power and religion rather than to private individual show. This makes individual conspicuous consumption incidental to communal expenditure. Thus the community at one and the same time levels differences of wealth which might intensify class divisions within the community to the detriment of the corporate structure and symbolically reasserts the strength and integrity of its structure before the eyes of its members (Aguirre 1952:242; Mishkin 1946:468).

The existence of such leveling mechanisms does not mean that class divisions within the corporate community do not exist. But it does mean that the class structure must find expression within the boundaries set by the community. The corporate structure acts to impede the mobilization of capital and wealth within the community in terms of the outside world which employs wealth capitalistically. It thus blunts the impact of the main opening wedge calculated to set up new tensions within the community and thus to hasten its disintegration (cf. Aguirre 1952; Carrasco 1952:48).

While striving to guarantee its members some basic livelihood within the confines of the community, the lack of resources and the very need to sustain the system of religion and power economically force the community to enter the outside market. Any imposition of taxes, any increase in expenditures relative to the productive capacity of the community, or the internal growth of the population on a limited amount of land, must result in *compensatory economic reactions in the field of production*. These may be wage labor, or the development of some specialization which has competitive advantages within the marginal economy of such communities. These may include specializations in trade, as among the Zapotecs, Tarascans, or Collas, or in witchcraft, as among the Killawallas or Kamilis of Bolivia.

In the field of consumption, increases of expenditures relative to the productive capacity of the economic base are met with attempts to decrease expenditure by decreasing consumption. This leads to the establishment of a culturally recognized standard of consumption which consciously excludes cultural alternative (on cultural alternatives, their rejection or acceptance, cf.

Linton 1936:282–83). By reducing alternative items of consumption, along with the kinds of behavior and ideal norms which make use of these items of consumption, the community reduces the threat to its integrity. Moore and Tumin have called this kind of reaction ignorance with a "structural function" (1949:788).

In other words, we are dealing here not merely with a lack of knowledge, an absence of information, but with a *defensive ignorance*, an active denial of outside alternatives which, if accepted, might threaten the corporate structure (Beals's "rejection pattern" [1952:229]; Mishkin 1946:443). Unwillingness to admit outsiders as competitors for land or as carriers of cultural alternatives may account for the prevalent tendency toward community endogamy (Redfield and Tax 1952:31; Mishkin 1946:453).

Related to the need to maintain a steady state by decreasing expenditures is the conscious effort to eat and consume less by "pulling in one's belt," while working more. This "exploitation of the self" is culturally institutionalized in what might be called a *"cult of poverty."* Hard work and poverty as well as behavior symbolic of these, such as going barefoot or wearing "Indian" clothes (cf. Tumin 1952:85–94), are extolled, and laziness and greed and behavior associated with these vices are denounced (Carrasco 1952:47).

The increase in output and concomitant restriction of consumption is carried out primarily within the *nuclear family*. The family thus acquires special importance in this kind of community, especially in a modern setting (Redfield and Tax 1952:33; Mishkin 1946:449–51). This is primarily because

> on the typical family farm . . . the farmer himself cannot tell you what part of his income comes to him in his capacity as a worker, what in his capacity as a capitalist who has provided tools and implements, or finally what in his capacity as owner of land. In fact, he is not able to tell you how much of his total income stems from his own labors and how much comes from the varied, but important efforts of his wife and children [Samuelson 1948:76].

The family does not carry on cost-accounting. It does not know how much its labor is worth. Labor is not a commodity for it; it does not sell labor within the family. No money changes hands within the family. It acts as a unit of consumption and it can cut its consumption as a unit. The family is thus the ideal unit for the restriction of consumption and the increase of unpaid performance of work.

The economy of the corporate community is congruent, if not structurally linked, with a marketing system of a peculiar sort. Lack of money resources requires that sales and purchases in the market be small. The highland village markets fit groups with low incomes which can buy only a little at a time (for Mexico, cf. Foster 1948:154; for the Quechua, cf. Mishkin 1946:436). Such markets bring together a much larger supply of articles than merchants of any one community could afford to keep continuously in their stores (Whetten 1948:359). Most goods in such markets are homemade or locally grown (Whetten 1948:358; Mishkin 1946:437). Local producers thus acquire the needed supplementary income, while the character of the commodities offered for sale reinforces the traditional pattern of consumption. Specialization on the part of villages is evident throughout (Whetten 1948; Foster 1948; Mishkin 1946:434). Regular market days in regional sequence making for a wider exchange of local produce (Whetten 1948; Mishkin 1946:436; Valcárcel 1946:477–79) may be due to the fact that villages producing similar products must find outlets far away, as well as to exchanges of produce between highlands and lowlands. The fact that the goods carried are produced in order to obtain small amounts of needed cash in order to purchase other needed goods is evident in the very high percentage of dealings between producer and ultimate consumer. The market is in fact a means of bringing the two into contact (Whetten 1948:359; Foster 1948; Mishkin 1946). The role of the nuclear family in production and in the "exploitation of the self" is evident in the high percentage of goods in whose production the individual or the nuclear family completes an entire production cycle (Foster 1948).

Paralleling the mechanisms of control which are primarily economic in origin are psychological mechanisms like *institutionalized envy*, which may find expression in various manifestations such as gossip, attacks of the evil eye, or in the fear and practice of witchcraft. The communal organization of the corporate community has often been romanticized; it is sometimes assumed that a communal structure makes for the absence of divisive tensions. Lewis has demonstrated that there is no necessary correlation between communal structure and pervasive good-will among the members of the community (Lewis 1951:428–29). Quite the contrary, it would seem that some form of institutionalized envy plays an important part in such communities (Gillin 1952:208). Kluckhohn has shown that fear of witchcraft acts as an effective leveler in Navaho society (1944:67–68). A similar relationship obtains in the type of community which we are discussing. Here witchcraft, as well as milder forms of institutionalized envy, have an integrative effect in restraining non-traditional behavior, as long as social relationships suffer no serious disruption. It minimizes disruptive phenomena such as economic mobility, abuse of ascribed power, or individual conspicuous show of wealth. On the individual plane, it thus acts to maintain the individual in equilibrium with his neighbors. On the social plane, it reduces the disruptive influences of outside society.

The need to keep social relationships in equilibrium in order to maintain the steady state of the corporate community is internalized in the individual as strong conscious efforts to adhere to the traditional roles, roles which were successful in maintaining the steady state in the past. Hence there appears a strong tendency on the social psychological level to stress "uninterrupted routine practice of traditional patterns" (Gillin 1952:206). Such a psychological emphasis would tend to act against overt expressions of individual autonomy, and set up in individuals strong fears against being thrown out of equilibrium (Gillin 1952:208).

An individual thus carries the culture of such a community, not merely passively as a social inheritance inherited and accepted automatically, but actively. Adherence to the culture validates membership in an existing society and acts as a passport to participation in the life of the community. The particular traits held help the individual remain within the equilibrium of relationships which maintain the community. Corporate communities produce "distinctive cultural, linguistic, and other social attributes," which Beals has aptly called "plural cultures" (1953:333); tenacious defense of this plurality maintains the integrity of such communities.

It is needless to add that any aspect relates to any other, and that changes in one would vitally affect the rest. Thus the employment of traditional technology keeps the land marginal from the point of view of the larger society, keeps the community poor, forces a search for supplementary sources of income, and requires high expenditures of physical labor within the nuclear family. The technology is in turn maintained by the need to adhere to traditional roles in order to validate one's membership in the community, and this adherence is produced by the conscious denial of alternative forms of behavior, by institutionalized envy, and by the fear of being thrown out of equilibrium with one's neighbor. The various aspects enumerated thus exhibit a very high degree of covariance.

The second type (2) which we shall discuss comprises peasants who regularly sell a cash crop constituting probably between 50 and 75 per cent of their total production. Geographically, this type of peasant is distributed over humid low highlands and tropical lowlands. Present-day use of their environments has been dictated by a shift in demand on the world market for crops from the American tropics during the latter part of the nineteenth century and the early part of the twentieth. On the whole, production for the market by this type of peasant has been in an ascendant phase, though often threatened by intermittent periods of decline and depression.

In seasonally rainy tropical lowlands, these peasants may raise sugar cane. In chronically rainy lowlands, such as northern Colombia or Venezuela or coastal Ecuador, they have tended to grow cocoa or bananas. The development of this peasant segment has been most impressive in humid low highlands, where the standard crop is coffee (Platt 1943:498). This crop is easily grown on both small and large holdings, as is the case in Colombia, Guatemala, Costa Rica, and parts of the West Indies.

Such cash crop production requires outside capitalization. The amount and kind of capitalization will have important ramifications throughout the particular local adaptation made. Peasants of this type receive such capitalization from the outside, but mainly on a traditional, small-scale, intermittent and speculative basis. Investments are not made either to stabilize the market or to reorganize the apparatus of production and distribution of the peasantry. Few peasant groups of this type have been studied fully by anthropologists, and any discussion of them must to some extent remain conjectural until further work adds to our knowledge. For the construction of this type the writer has relied largely on his own field work in Puerto Rico (Wolf 1951) and on insights gained from studies made in southern Brazil (Herrmann 1950; Pierson and others 1951).

The typical structure which serves to integrate this type of peasant segment with other segments and with the larger sociocultural whole we shall here call the "open" community. The open community differs from the corporate peasant community in a number of ways. The corporate peasant community is composed primarily of one subculture, the peasantry. The open community comprises a number of subcultures of which the peasantry is only one, although the most important functional segment. The corporate community emphasizes resistance to influences from without which might threaten its integrity. The open community, on the other hand, emphasizes continuous interaction with the outside world and ties its fortunes to outside demands. The corporate community frowns on individual accumulation and display of wealth and strives to reduce the effects of such accumulation on the communal structure. It resists reshaping of relationships; it defends the traditional equilibrium. The open-ended community permits and expects individual accumulation and display of wealth during periods of rising outside demand and allows this new wealth much influence in the periodic reshaping of social ties.

Historically, the open peasant community arose in response to the rising demand for cash crops which accompanied the development of capitalism in Europe. In a sense, it represents the offshoot of a growing type of society which multiplied its wealth by budding off to form new communities to produce new wealth in their turn. Many peasant communities were established in Latin America by settlers who brought to the New World cultural patterns of consumption and production which from the outset involved them in relations with an outside market. Being a Spaniard or Portuguese meant more than merely speaking Spanish or Portuguese or adhering to certain kinds of traditional behavior and ideal norms. It implied participation in a complex system of hierarchical relationships and prestige which required the consumption of goods that could be produced only by means of a complicated division of labor and had to be acquired in the market. No amount of Indian blankets delivered as tribute could make up for the status gained by the possession of one shirt of Castilian silk, or for a small ruffle of Cambrai lace. Prestige goods as well as necessities like iron could only be bought with money, and the need for money drove people to produce for an outside market. The demand for European goods by Spanish colonists was enormous and in turn caused heavy alterations in the economic structure of the mother country (Sombart 1928, I, Pt. 2:780–81). In the establishment of the open community, therefore, the character of the outside society was a major determinant from the beginning.

It would be a mistake, moreover, to visualize the development of the world market in terms of continuous and even expansion, and to suppose therefore that the line of development of particular peasant communities always leads from lesser involvement in the market to more involvement. This line of reasoning would seem to be especially out of place in the case of Latin America where the isolation and homogeneity of the "folk" are often secondary, that is to say, follow in time after a stage of much contact and heterogeneity. Redfield has recognized aspects of this problem in his recent category of "remade folk" (1953:47). Such a category should cover not only the Yucatecan Indians who fled into the isolation of the bush but also groups of settlers with a culture of basically Iberian derivation which were once in the mainstream of commercial development, only to be left behind on its poverty-stricken margins (cf. e.g., the Spanish settlements at Culiacán, New Galicia, described by Mota [1940:99–102], and Chiapa Real, Chiapas, described by Gage [1929:151–53]).

Latin America has been involved in major shifts and fluctuations of the market since the period of initial European conquest. It would appear, for example, that a rapid expansion of commercial development in New Spain during the sixteenth century was followed by a "century of depression" in the seventeenth (cf. Borah 1951; Chevalier 1952:xii, 54). The slack was taken up again in the eighteenth century, with renewed shrinkage and disintegration of the market in the early part of the nineteenth. During the second part of the nineteenth century and the beginning of the twentieth, many Latin American countries were repeatedly caught up in speculative booms of cash crop production for foreign markets, often with disastrous results in the case of market failure. Entire communities might find their market gone overnight, and revert to the production of subsistence crops for their own use.

Two things seem clear from this discussion. First, in dealing with present-day Latin America it would seem advisable to beware of treating production for subsistence and production for the market as two progressive stages of development. Rather, we must allow for the cyclical alternation of the two kinds of production within the same community and realize that from the point of view of the community both kinds may be alternative responses to changes in conditions of the outside market. This means that a synchronic study of such a community is insufficient, because it cannot reveal how the community can adapt to such seemingly radical changes. Second, we must look for the mechanisms which make such changes possible.

In the corporate peasant community, the relationships of individuals and kin groups within the community are bounded by a common structure. We have seen that the community aims primarily at maintaining an equilibrium of roles within the community in an effort to keep intact its outer boundary. Maintenance of the outer boundary reacts in turn on the stability of the equilibrium within it. The open community lacks such a formalized corporate structure. It neither limits its membership nor insists on a defensive boundary. Quite the contrary, it permits free permeation by outside influences.

In contrast to the corporate peasant community where the community retains the right to review and revise individual decisions, the open community lends itself to rapid shifts in production because it is possible to mobilize the peasant and to orient him rapidly toward the expanding market. Land is usually owned *privately*. Decisions for change can be made by individual families. Property can be mortgaged, or pawned in return for capital. The community *qua* community cannot interfere in such change.

As in the corporate peasant community, land tends to be marginal and technology primitive. Yet functionally both land and technology are elements in a different complex of relationships. The buyers of peasant produce have an interest in the continued "backwardness" of the peasant. Reorganization of his productive apparatus would absorb capital and credit which can be spent better in expanding the market by buying means of transportation, engaging middlemen, etc. Moreover, by keeping the productive apparatus unchanged, the buyer can reduce the risk of having his capital tied up in the means of production of the peasant holding, if and when the bottom drops out of the market. The buyers of peasant produce thus trade increasing pro-ductivity per man-hour for the lessened risks of investment. We may say that the *marginality of land* and the *poor technology* are here a function of the speculative market. In the case of need, the investor merely withdraws credit, while the peasant returns to subsistence production by means of his traditional technology.

The fact that cash crop production can be undertaken on peasant holdings without materially reorganizing the productive apparatus implies furthermore that the amount of cash crop produced by each peasant will tend to be *small*, as will be the income which he receives after paying off all obligations. This does not mean that the aggregate amounts of such production cannot reach respectable sums, nor that the amounts of profit accruing to middlemen from involvement in such production need be low.

In this cycle of subsistence crops and cash crops, subsistence crops guar-antee a stable minimum livelihood, where cash crops promise higher money re-turns but involve the family in the hazards of the fluctuating market. The peasant is always concerned with the problem of striking some sort of balance between subsistence production and cash crop production. Preceding cycles of cash crop production have enabled him to buy goods and services which he cannot afford if he produces only for his own subsistence. Yet an all-out effort to increase his ability to buy more goods and services of this kind may spell his end as an independent agricultural producer. His tendency is thus to rely on a basic minimum of subsistence production and to expand his cash pur-chases only slowly. Usually he can rely on traditional norms of consumption which define a decent standard of living in terms of a fixed number of culturally standardized needs. Such needs are of course not only economic but may in-clude standardized expenditures for religious or recreational purposes, or for hospitality (cf. Wolf 1951:64). Nor are these needs static. Viewing the ex-pansion of the market from the point of view of subsistence, however, permits the peasant to expand his consumption only slowly.

In cutting down on money expenditures, he defers purchases of new goods, and distrib-utes his purchases over a long period of time. The peasant standard of living is under-going change but the rate of that change is slow [Wolf 1951:65].

The cultural yardstick enables him to limit the rate of expansion but also permits him to retrench when he has overextended himself economically. As in the corporate peasant community, the unit within which consumption can best be restricted while output is stepped up is again the *nuclear family*.

This *modus operandi* reacts back on his technology and on his ability to increase his cash income. The buyer of peasant produce knows that the peasant will be slow in expanding his demand for money. He can therefore count on accumulating his largest share of gain during the initial phase of a growing market, a factor which adds to the speculative character of the economy.

Peasants who are forced overnight to reorient their production from the production of subsistence crops for their own use to cash crop production are rarely able to generate the needed capital themselves. It must be pumped into the peasant segment from without, either from another segment within the community, or from outside the community altogether. The result is that when cash crop production grows important, there is a tightening of bonds between town and country. Urban families become concerned with the production and distribution of cash crops and tie their own fate to the fate of the cash crop. In a society subject to frequent fluctuations of the market but possessed of little fluid capital, there are few formal institutional mechanisms for insuring the flow of capital into peasant production. In a more highly capitalized society, the stock market functions as an impersonal governor of relationships between investors. Corporations form, merge, or dissolve according to the dictates of this governor. In a society where capital accumulation is low, the structure of incorporation tends to be weak or lacking. More important are the *informal alliances of families and clients* which polarize wealth and power at any given time. Expansion of the market tends to involve the peasant in one or the other of these blocs of family power in town. These blocs, in turn, permit the rapid diffusion of capital into the countryside, since credit is guaranteed by personal relationships between creditor and debtor. Peasant allegiance then acts further to reinforce the social and political position of a given family bloc within the urban sector.

When the market fails, peasants and urban patrons both tend to be caught in the same downward movement. Open communities of the type we are analyzing here are therefore marked by the repeated "circulation of the elite." Blocs of wealth and power form, only to break up and be replaced by similar blocs coming to the fore. The great *concern with status* is related to this type of mobility. Status on the social plane measures the position in the trajectory of the family on the economic plane. To put it in somewhat oversimplified terms, status in such a society represents the "credit rating" of the family. The economic circulation of the elite thus takes the form of shifts in social status. Such shifts in social and economic position always involve an urban and a rural aspect. If the family cannot find alternate economic supports, it loses prestige within the urban sector, and is sooner or later abandoned by its peasant clientele who must needs seek other urban patrons.

We are thus dealing with a type of community which is continuously faced with alignments, circulation and realignments, both on the socioeconomic and political level. Since social, economic, and political arrangements are based primarily on personal ties, such fluctuations act to redefine personal relationships, and such personal relationships are in turn watched closely for indices of readjustment. Relations between two individuals do not symbolize merely the respective statuses and roles of the two concerned; they involve a whole series of relations which must be evaluated and readjusted if there is any indication of change. This "overloading" of personal relations produces two types of behavior: behavior calculated to retain social status, and a type of behavior which for want of a better term might be called "redefining" behavior, behavior aimed at altering the existing state of personal relationships. Both types will be present in any given social situation, but the dominance of one over the other will be determined by the relative stability or instability of the economic base. Status behavior is loaded with a fierce consciousness of the symbols of status, while "redefining" behavior aims at testing the social limits through such varied mechanisms as humor, invitations to share drinks or meals, visiting, assertions of individual worth, proposals of marriage, and so forth. The most important of these types of behavior, quite absent in the corporate community, consists in the ostentatious exhibition of commodities purchased with money.

This type of redefining behavior ramifies through other aspects of the culture. Wealth is its prerequisite. It is therefore most obvious in the ascendant phases of the economic cycle, rather than when the cycle is leveling off. Such accumulation of goods and the behavior associated with it serves as a challenge to existing relations with kin folk, both real and fictitious, since it is usually associated with a reduction in relations of reciprocal aid and hospitality on which these ties are based.

This disruption of social ties through accumulation is inhibited in the corporate peasant community, but can go on unchecked in the type of community which we are considering. Here forms of envy such as witchcraft are often present, but not institutionalized as in the first type of community. Rather, fear of witchcraft conforms to the hypothesis proposed by Passin (1942:15) that

in any society where there is a widespread evasion of a cultural obligation which results in the diffusion of tension and hostility between people, and further if this hostility is not expressed in overt physical strife, . . . sorcery or related non-physical techniques will be brought into play.

Fear of witchcraft in such a community may be interpreted as a product of guilt on the part of the individual who is himself disrupting ties which are valued, coupled with a vague anxiety about the loss of stable definitions of situations in terms of clear-cut status. At the same time, the new possessions and their conspicuous show serves not only to redefine status and thus to reduce anxiety but also as a means of expressing hostility against those who do not own the same goods (cf. Kluckhohn 1944:67, fn. 96). The "invidious" comparisons produced by this hostility in turn produce an increase in the rate of accumulation.

## SUGGESTIONS FOR FURTHER RESEARCH

The two model types discussed above by no means exhaust the variety of peasant segments to be found in Latin America. They were singled out for consideration because I felt most competent to deal with them in terms of both time and field experience. Pleading greater ignorance and less assurance, I should nevertheless like to take this opportunity to indicate the rough outlines of some other types which may deserve further investigation. These types may seem to resemble the "open" communities just discussed. It is nevertheless important to conceptualize them separately. We may expect them to differ greatly in their basic functional configurations, due to the different manner of their integration with larger sociocultural systems, and to the different histories of their integration.

Thus, it seems that within the same geographical area occupied by the second type, above, there exists a third type of peasant (3) who resembles the second also in that a large percentage of his total production is sold on the market. This percentage is probably higher than that involved in the second case; between 90 and 100 per cent of total production may go directly into the market. This peasant segment seems to differ from the second one in the much greater stability of its market and in much more extensive outside capitalization. Much of the market is represented by the very high aggregate demand of the United States, and United States capital flows into such peasant segments through organizations such as the United Fruit Company. In the absence of foreign investment, capital may be supplied by new-style local groups of investors of the kind found in the coffee industry of Antioquía, Colombia (cf. Parsons 1949:2–9). Anthropologists have paid little attention to this type of peasantry.

(4) A fourth type is perhaps represented by peasants who habitually sell the larger part of their total production in restricted but stable local markets. Such markets are especially apt to occur near former political and religious settlements in the high highlands which play a traditional role in the life of the country but do not show signs of commercial or industrial expansion. Outside capitalization of such production would appear to be local in scale, but a relatively stable market may offer a certain guarantee of small returns. Into this category may fit groups relatively ignored by anthropologists, such as many Mexican *ranchero* communities (cf. Armstrong 1949; Humphrey 1948; Taylor 1933) or the settlers of the Bogotá Basin (cf. Smith and others 1945).

(5) The fifth group is perhaps represented by peasants located in a region which once formed a key area of the developing system of capitalism (Williams 1944:98–107). This region is located in the seasonally rainy tropical lowlands of northeastern Brazil and the West Indies. Here sugar plantations based on slave labor flourished in the sixteenth, seventeenth, and eighteenth centuries. These plantations were weakened by a variety of factors, such as the end of the slave trade and the political independence movement in Latin America, and most of them were unable to compete with other tropical areas. Where the old plantation system was not replaced by modern "factories in the field," as has been the case in northeastern Brazil (Hutchinson 1952:17) and on parts of the south coast of Puerto Rico (Mintz 1953:244–49), we today find peasant holdings as "residual bits" of former large-scale organizations (Platt 1943:501) which have disintegrated, as in Haiti or Jamaica. The economy

of such areas has been contracting since the end of slavery, with the result that this type of peasant seems to lean heavily toward the production of subsistence crops for home use or toward the production and distribution of very small amounts of cash produce.

(6) A sixth group is perhaps represented by the foreign colonists who introduced changes in technology into the forested environment of southern Brazil and southern Chile. These areas seem to show certain similarities. In both areas, the settlers chose the forest rather than the open plain for settlement and colonization. In both areas, colonization was furthered by the respective central governments to create buffers against military pressures from outside and against local movements for autonomy. In both areas, the settlers found themselves located on a cultural ecological frontier. In southern Brazil, they faced cultural pressures from the Pampa (Willems 1944:154–55) and from the surrounding population of casual cash crop producers (Willems 1945:14–15, 26). In southern Chile, they confronted the Araucanians. In both areas, an initial period of deculturation and acculturation would seem to have been followed by increasing integration into the national market through the sale of cash crops.

(7) A seventh type is perhaps made up of peasants who live on the outskirts of the capitalist market, on South America's "pioneer fringe" (Bowman 1931). This would include people who raise crops for the market in order to obtain strategic items of consumption, like clothing, salt, or metal, which they cannot produce themselves. The technological level characterizing this type of peasant seems to be low; his agriculture would appear to be mainly of the slash-and-burn type. His contacts with the market seem to be sporadic rather than persistent, and the regularity with which he produces a cash crop seems to depend both on uncertain outside demand and on his periodic need for an outside product.

Due largely to the requirements of the agricultural system, families live in dispersal, and the family level is probably the chief level of integration. Since there is no steady market, land lacks commercial value, and occupance is relatively unhampered. A family may occupy land for as long as required and abandon it with decreasing yields. Such circulation through the landscape would require large amounts of land and unrestricted operation. Concepts of fixed private property in land would tend to be absent or nonfunctional. The land may belong to somebody who cannot make effective commercial use of it at the moment, and permits temporary squatting (for the *tolerados* of Santa Cruz, Bolivia, cf. Leonard 1952:132–33; for the *intrusos* of southern Brazil, cf. Willems 1942:376; for the squatters in other parts of Brazil, cf. Smith 1946:459–60; for Paraguay, cf. Service Ms.).

Once again I want to express the caution that the above list represents only suggestions. Further work will undoubtedly lead to the formulation of additional or other types, and to the construction of models to deal with transitional phenomena, such as changes from one type of segment to another. Since segments relate with other segments, further inquiry will also have to take account of the ways in which type segments interrelate with each other and of the variety of community structures which such combinations can produce.

In summary, this article has made an attempt to distinguish among several types of peasantry in Latin America. These types are based on cultural structure rather than on culture content. Peasant cultures are seen as part-cultures within larger sociocultural wholes. The character of the larger whole and the mode of integration of the part-culture with it have been given primary weight in constructing the typology. The types suggested remain wholly provisional.

## BIBLIOGRAPHY

AGUIRRE BELTRÁN, GONZALO
    1952    Problemas de la población indígena de la cuenca del Tepalcatepec. Memorias del Instituto Nacional Indigenista 3. México, D. F.

ARMSTRONG, JOHN M.
    1949    A Mexican community: a study of the cultural determinants of migration. Ph.D. dissertation, Yale University, New Haven.

BEALS, RALPH L.
    1951    Urbanism, urbanization and acculturation. American Anthropologist 53:1–10.
    1952    Notes on acculturation. *In* Heritage of Conquest, ed. Sol Tax, pp. 225–31.
    1953    Social stratification in Latin America. American Journal of Sociology 58:327–39.

BORAH, WOODROW
    1951    New Spain's century of depression. Ibero-Americana 35. Berkeley, University of California Press.

BOWMAN, ISAIAH
    1931    The pioneer fringe. American Geographical Society Special Publication 13. New York.

CARRASCO PIZANA, PEDRO
    1952    Tarascan folk religion: an analysis of economic, social and religious interactions. Middle American Research Institute Publication 17:1–64. Tulane University, New Orleans.

CHEVALIER, FRANÇOIS
    1952    La Formation des Grands Domaines au Mexique: Terre et Société aux XVIe-XVIIe Siècles. Travaux et Mémoires de l'Institut d'Ethnologie 56. Paris.

FIRTH, RAYMOND
    1952    Elements of social organization. London, Watts.

FORTES, MEYER
    1953    The structure of unilineal descent groups. American Anthropologist 55:17–41.

FOSTER, GEORGE M.
    1948    The folk economy of rural Mexico with special reference to marketing. Journal of Marketing 12:153–62.

GAGE, THOMAS
    1929    [1648] A new survey of the West Indies, the English American. Argonaut Series. New York, McBride.

GARCÍA, ANTONIO
    1948    Regímenes Indígenas de salariado. America Indígena 8:249–87.

GILLIN, JOHN
    1952    Ethos and cultural aspects of personality. *In* Heritage of Conquest, ed. Sol Tax, pp. 193–212.

HERMANN, LUCILA
    1950    Classe Media em Guarantiguetá. Materiales para el Estudio de la Clase Media en

la America Latina 3:18–59. Publicaciones de la Oficina de Ciencias Sociales, Union Panamericana, Washington, D. C.

HOSELITZ, BERT F.
1953 The role of cities in the economic growth of underdeveloped countries. Journal of Political Economy 61:195–208.

HUMPHREY, NORMAN D.
1948 The cultural background of the Mexican immigrant. Rural Sociology 13:239–55.

HUTCHINSON, HARRY W.
1952 Race relations in a rural community of the Bahian Reconcavo. *In* Race and Class in Rural Brazil, ed. Charles Wagley, pp. 16–46. Paris, UNESCO.

KIRCHHOFF, PAUL
1949 The social and political organization of the Andean peoples. *In* Handbook of South American Indians, ed. Julian Steward, Vol. 5, pp. 293–311.

KLUCKHOHN, CLYDE
1944 Navaho witchcraft. Papers of the Peabody Museum of American Archaeology and Ethnology, Harvard University 22, No. 2. Cambridge, Mass.

KROEBER, ALFRED L.
1948 Anthropology. New York, Harcourt-Brace.

KROEBER, ALFRED L. and CLYDE KLUCKHOHN
1952 Culture. Papers of the Peabody Museum of American Archaeology and Ethnology, Harvard University 47, No. 1. Cambridge, Mass.

LEONARD, OLEN E.
1952 Bolivia. Washington D. C., Scarecrow Press.

LEWIS, OSCAR
1951 Life in a Mexican village: Tepoztlán revisited. Urbana, University of Illinois Press.

LINTON, RALPH
1936 The study of man. New York, Appleton-Century.

MINTZ, SIDNEY W.
1953 The culture history of a Puerto Rican sugar cane plantation, 1876–1949. Hispanic American Historical Review 33:224–51.

MISHKIN, BERNARD
1946 The contemporary Quechua. *In* Handbook of South American Indians, ed. Julian Steward, Vol. 2, pp. 411–76.

MOORE, WILBERT E. and MELVIN M. TUMIN
1949 Some social functions of ignorance. American Sociological Review 14:787–95.

MOTA ESCOBAR, ALONSO DE LA
1940 [1601–3] Descripción Geográfica de los Reinos de Nueva Galicia, Nueva Vizcaya y Nuevo León. México, D. F., Editorial Pedro Robredo.

PARSONS, JAMES J.
1949 Antioquía colonization in western Colombia. Ibero-Americana 32. Berkeley, University of California Press.

PASSIN, HERBERT
1942 Sorcery as a phase of Tarahumara economic relations. Man 42:11–15.

PIERSON, DONALD and others
1951 Cruz das Almas: a Brazilian village. Institute of Social Anthropology Publication 12, Smithsonian Institution, Washington, D. C.

PLATT, ROBERT
1943 Latin America: countrysides and united regions. New York, Whittlesey House.

POZAS, RICARDO
1952 La Situation économique et financière de l'Indien Américain. Civilization 2:309–29.

REDFIELD, ROBERT
1953 The primitive world and its transformations. Ithaca, N. Y., Cornell University Press.

REDFIELD, ROBERT and SOL TAX
1952 General characteristics of present-day Mesoamerican Indian society. *In* Heritage of Conquest, ed. Sol Tax, pp. 31–39.

SAMUELSON, PAUL A.
1948 Economics: an introductory analysis. New York, McGraw-Hill.

SERVICE, ELMAN R.
Ms. Tobati: a Paraguayan community. (To be published.)

SMITH, T. LYNN and others
1945 Tabio: a study in rural social organization. Office of Foreign Agricultural Relations, U. S. Department of Agriculture, Washington, D. C.
1946 Brazil: people and institutions. Baton Rouge, Louisiana State University Press.

SOMBART, WERNER
1928 Der Moderne Kapitalismus. 2 vols. München-Leipzig, Duncker and Humblot.

STEWARD, JULIAN H.
1938 Basin-plateau aboriginal sociopolitical groups. Bureau of American Ethnology Bulletin 120, Smithsonian Institution, Washington, D. C.
1950 Area research: theory and practice. Social Science Research Council Bulletin 63. New York.

STEWARD, JULIAN H. (ed.)
1946–51 Handbook of South American Indians. Bureau of American Ethnology Bulletin 143, Smithsonian Institution, Washington, D. C.

TAX, SOL (ed.)
1952 Heritage of conquest. Glencoe, Ill., Free Press.

TAYLOR, PAUL S.
1933 A Spanish-American peasant community: Arandas in Jalisco, Mexico. Ibero-Americana 4. Berkeley, University of California Press.

TUMIN, MELVIN M.
1952 Caste in a peasant society. Princeton, Princeton University Press.

VALCÁRCEL, LUIS E.
1946 Indian markets and fairs in Peru. *In* Handbook of South American Indians, ed. Julian Steward, Vol. 2, pp. 477–82.

WHETTEN, NATHAN L.
1948 Rural Mexico. Chicago, University of Chicago Press.

WILLEMS, EMILIO
1942 Some aspects of cultural conflict and acculturation in southern rural Brazil. Rural Sociology 7:375–84.
1944 Acculturation and the horse complex among German-Brasilians. American Anthropologist 46:153–61.
1945 El Problema Rural Brasileño desde el punto de vista antropológico. Jornadas 33. México, D. F., Colegio de México, Centro de Estudios Sociales.

WILLIAMS, ERIC
1944 Capitalism and slavery. Chapel Hill, University of North Carolina.

WOLF, ERIC R.
1951 Culture change and culture stability in a Puerto Rican coffee community. Ph.D. dissertation, Columbia University, New York.
1953 La formacion de la nación: un ensayo de formulación. Ciencias Sociales 4:50–62, 98–111, 146–71.

# The Nature of Deference and Demeanor

ERVING GOFFMAN

*National Institute of Mental Health, Bethesda, Maryland*

UNDER the influence of Durkheim and Radcliffe-Brown, some students of modern society have learned to look for the symbolic meaning of any given social practice and for the contribution of the practice to the integrity and solidarity of the group that employs it. However, in directing their attention away from the individual to the group, these students seem to have neglected a theme that is presented in Durkheim's chapter on the soul (1954: 240–272). There he suggests that the individual's personality can be seen as one apportionment of the collective *mana*, and that (as he implies in later chapters) the rites performed to representations of the social collectivity will sometimes be performed to the individual himself.

In this paper I want to explore some of the senses in which the person in our urban secular world is allotted a kind of sacredness that is displayed and confirmed by symbolic acts. An attempt will be made to build a conceptual scaffold by stretching and twisting some common anthropological terms. This will be used to support two concepts which I think are central to this area, deference and demeanor. Through these reformulations I will try to show that a version of Durkheim's social psychology can be effective in modern dress.

Data for the paper are drawn chiefly from a brief observational study of mental patients in a modern research hospital.[1] I use these data on the assumption that a logical place to learn about personal proprieties is among persons who have been locked up for spectacularly failing to maintain them. Their infractions of propriety occur in the confines of a ward, but the rules broken are quite general ones, leading us outward from the ward to a general study of our Anglo-American society.

## INTRODUCTION

A rule of conduct may be defined as a guide for action, recommended not because it is pleasant, cheap, or effective, but because it is suitable or just. Infractions characteristically lead to feelings of uneasiness and to negative social sanctions. Rules of conduct infuse all areas of activity and are upheld in the name and honor of almost everything. Always, however, a grouping of adherents will be involved—if not a corporate social life—providing through this a common sociological theme. Attachment to rules leads to a constancy and patterning of behavior; while this is not the only source of regularity in human affairs it is certainly an important one. Of course, approved guides to conduct tend to be covertly broken, side-stepped, or followed for unapproved reasons, but these alternatives merely add to the occasions in which rules constrain at least the surface of conduct.

Rules of conduct impinge upon the individual in two general ways: directly, as *obligations*, establishing how he is morally constrained to conduct himself;

473

indirectly, as *expectations*, establishing how others are morally bound to act in regard to him. A nurse, for example, has an obligation to follow medical orders in regard to her patients; she has the expectation, on the other hand, that her patients will pliantly co-operate in allowing her to perform these actions upon them. This pliancy, in turn, can be seen as an obligation of the patients in regard to their nurse, and points up the interpersonal, actor-recipient character of many rules: what is one man's obligation will often be another's expectation.

Because obligations involve a constraint to act in a particular way, we sometimes picture them as burdensome or irksome things, to be fulfilled, if at all, by gritting one's teeth in conscious determination. In fact, most actions which are guided by rules of conduct are performed unthinkingly, the questioned actor saying he performs "for no reason" or because he "felt like doing so." Only when his routines are blocked may he discover that his neutral little actions have all along been consonant with the proprieties of his group and that his failure to perform them can become a matter of shame and humiliation. Similarly, he may so take for granted his expectations regarding others that only when things go unexpectedly wrong will he suddenly discover that he has grounds for indignation.

Once it is clear that a person may meet an obligation without feeling it, we can go on to see that an obligation which *is* felt as something that *ought* to be done may strike the obligated person either as a desired thing or as an onerous one, in short, as a pleasant or unpleasant duty. In fact, the same obligation may appear to be a desirable duty at one point and an undesirable one at another, as when a nurse, obliged to administer medication to patients, may be glad of this when attempting to establish social distance from attendants (who in some sense may be considered by nurses to be not "good enough" to engage in such activity), yet burdened by it on occasions when she finds that dosage must be determined on the basis of illegibly written medical orders. Similarly, an expectation may be perceived by the expectant person as a wanted or unwanted thing, as when one person feels he will deservedly be promoted and another feels he will deservedly be fired. In ordinary usage, a rule that strikes the actor or recipient as a personally desirable thing, apart from its propriety, is sometimes called a right or privilege, as it will be here, but these terms have additional implications, suggesting that special class of rules which an individual may invoke but is not required to do so. It should also be noted that an actor's pleasant obligation may constitute a recipient's pleasant expectation, as with the kiss a husband owes his wife when he returns from the office, but that, as the illustration suggests, all kinds of combinations are possible.

When an individual becomes involved in the maintenance of a rule, he tends also to become committed to a particular image of self. In the case of his obligations, he becomes to himself and others the sort of person who follows this particular rule, the sort of person who would naturally be expected to do so. In the case of his expectations, he becomes dependent upon the assumption that others will properly perform such of their obligations as affect him, for their treatment of him will express a conception of him. In establishing himself as the sort of person who treats others in a particular way and is treated by them in a particular way, he must make sure that it will be possible for him to act and be this kind of person. For example, with certain psychiatrists there seems to be a point where the obligation of giving psychotherapy to patients, *their* patients, is transformed into something they must do if they are to retain the image they have come to have of themselves. The effect of this transformation can be seen in the squirming some of them may do in the early phases of their careers when they may find themselves employed to do research, or administer a ward, or give therapy to those who would rather be left alone.

In general then, when a rule of conduct is broken we find that two individuals run the risk of becoming discredited: one with an obligation, who should have governed himself by the rule; the other with an expectation, who should have been treated in a particular way because of this governance. Both actor and recipient are threatened.

An act that is subject to a rule of conduct is, then, a communication, for it represents a way in which selves are confirmed—both the self for which the rule is an obligation and the self for which it is an expectation. An act that is subject to rules of conduct but does not conform to them is also a communication—often even more so—for infractions make news and often in such a way as to disconfirm the selves of the participants. Thus rules of conduct transform both action and inaction into expression, and whether the individual abides by the rules or breaks them, something significant is likely to be communicated. For example, in the wards under study, each research psychiatrist tended to expect his patients to come regularly for their therapeutic hours. When patients fulfilled this obligation, they showed that they appreciated their need for treatment and that their psychiatrist was the sort of person who could establish a "good relation" with patients. When a patient declined to attend his therapeutic hour, others on the ward tended to feel that he was "too sick" to know what was good for him, and that perhaps his psychiatrist was not the sort of person who was good at establishing relationships. Whether patients did or did not attend their hours, something of importance about them and their psychiatrist tended to be communicated to the staff and to other patients on the ward.

In considering the individual's participation in social action, we must understand that in a sense he does not participate as a total person but rather in terms of a special capacity or status; in short, in terms of a special self. For example, patients who happen to be female may be obliged to act shameless before doctors who happen to be male, since the medical relation, not the sexual one, is defined as officially relevant. In the research hospital studied, there were both patients and staff who were Negro, but this minority-group status was not one in which these individuals were officially (or even, in the main, unofficially) active. Of course, during face-to-face encounters individuals may participate officially in more than one capacity. Further, some unofficial weight is almost always given to capacities defined as officially irrelevant, and the reputation earned in one capacity will flow over and to a degree determine the reputation the individual earns in his other capacities. But these are questions for more refined analysis.

In dealing with rules of conduct it is convenient to distinguish two classes, symmetrical and asymmetrical (Thouless 1951:272–273). A symmetrical rule is one which leads an individual to have obligations or expectations regarding others that these others have in regard to him. For example, in the two hospital wards, as in most other places in our society, there was an understanding that each individual was not to steal from any other individual, regardless of their respective statuses, and that each individual could similarly expect not to be stolen from by anyone. What we call common courtesies and rules of public order tend to be symmetrical, as are such biblical admonitions as the rule about not coveting one's neighbor's wife. An asymmetrical rule is one that leads others to treat and be treated by an individual differently from the way he treats and is treated by them. For example, doctors give medical orders to nurses, but nurses do not give medical orders to doctors. Similarly, in some hospitals in America nurses stand up when a doctor enters the room, but doctors do not ordinarily stand up when a nurse enters the room.

Students of society have distinguished in several ways among types of rules, as for example, between formal and informal rules; for this paper, however, the important distinction is that between substance and ceremony.[2] A substantive rule is one which guides conduct in regard to matters felt to have significance in their own right, apart from what the infraction or maintenance of the rule expresses about the selves of the persons involved. Thus, when an individual refrains from stealing from others, he upholds a substantive rule which primarily serves to protect the property of these others and only incidentally functions to protect the image they have of themselves as persons with proprietary rights. The expressive implications of substantive rules are officially considered to be secondary; this appearance must be maintained, even though in some special situations everyone may sense that the participants were primarily concerned with expression.

A ceremonial rule is one which guides conduct in matters felt to have secondary or even no significance in their own right, having their primary importance—officially anyway—as a conventionalized means of communication by which the individual expresses his character or conveys his appreciation of the other participants in the situation.[3] This usage departs from the everyday one, where "ceremony" tends to imply a highly specified, extended sequence of symbolic action performed by august actors on solemn occasions when religious sentiments are likely to be invoked. In wanting to stress the common element in such practices as tipping one's hat and a coronation, I will neglect what many anthropologists would see as overriding differences.

In all societies rules of conduct tend to be organized into codes which guarantee that everyone acts appropriately and receives his due. In our society the code which governs substantive rules and substantive expressions comprises our law, morality, and ethics, while the code which governs ceremonial rules and ceremonial expressions is incorporated in what we call etiquette. All of our institutions have both kinds of codes, but in this paper attention will be restricted to the ceremonial one.

The acts or events, that is, the sign-vehicles or tokens which carry ceremonial messages, are remarkably various in character. They may be linguistic, as when an individual makes a statement of praise or depreciation regarding self or other, and does so in a particular language and intonation (Garvin and Riesenberg 1952); gestural, as when the physical bearing of an individual conveys insolence or obsequiousness; spatial, as when an individual precedes another through the door, or sits on his right instead of his left; task-embedded, as when an individual accepts a task graciously and performs it in the presence of others with aplomb and dexterity; part of the communication structure, as when an individual speaks more frequently than the others, or receives more attentiveness than they do. The important point is that ceremonial activity, like substantive activity, is an analytical element referring to a component or function of action, not to concrete empirical action itself. While some activity that has a ceremonial component does not seem to have an appreciable substantive one, we find that all activity that is primarily substantive in significance will nevertheless carry some ceremonial meaning, provided that its performance is perceived in some way by others. The manner in which the activity is performed, or the momentary interruptions that are allowed so as to exchange minor niceties, will infuse the instrumentally-oriented situation with ceremonial significance.

All of the tokens employed by a given social group for ceremonial purposes may be referred to as its ceremonial idiom. We usually distinguish societies according to the amount of ceremonial that is injected into a given period and kind of interaction, or according to the expansiveness of the forms and the minuteness of their specification; it might be better to distinguish societies according to whether required ceremony is performed as an unpleasant duty or, spontaneously, as an unfelt or pleasant one.

Ceremonial activity seems to contain certain basic components. As suggested, a main object of this paper will be to delineate two of these components, deference and demeanor, and to clarify the distinction between them.

### DEFERENCE

By deference I shall refer to that component of activity which functions as a symbolic means by which appreciation is regularly conveyed *to* a recipient *of* this recipient, or of something of which this recipient is taken as a symbol, extension, or agent.[4] These marks of devotion represent ways in which an actor celebrates and confirms his relation to a recipient. In some cases, both actor and recipient may not really be individuals at all, as when two ships greet each other with four short whistle blasts when passing. In some cases, the actor is an individual but the recipient is some object or idol, as when a sailor salutes the quarterdeck upon boarding ship, or when a Catholic genuflects to the altar. I shall only be concerned, however, with the kind of deference that occurs when both actor and recipient are individuals, whether or not they are acting on behalf of something other than themselves. Such ceremonial activity is perhaps seen most clearly in the little salutations, compliments, and apologies which punctuate social intercourse, and may be referred to as "status rituals" or "interpersonal rituals."[5] I use the term "ritual" because this activity, however informal and secular, represents a way in which the individual must guard and design the symbolic implications of his acts while in the immediate presence of an object that has a special value for him.[6]

There appear to be two main directions in which the study of deference rituals may go. One is to settle on a given ritual and attempt to discover factors common to all of the social situations in which it is performed, for it is through such an analysis that we can get at the "meaning" of the ritual. The other is to collect all of the rituals that are performed to a given recipient, from whomever the ritual comes. Each of these rituals can then be interpreted for the symbolically expressed meaning that is embodied in it. By piecing together these meanings we can arrive at the conception of the recipient that others are obliged to maintain of him to him.

The individual may desire, earn, and deserve deference, but by and large he is not allowed to give it to himself, being forced to seek it from others. In seeking it from others, he finds he has added reason for seeking them out, and in turn society is given added assurance that its members will enter into interaction and relationships with one another. If the individual could give himself the deference he desired there might be a tendency for society to disintegrate into islands inhabited by solitary cultish men, each in continuous worship at his own shrine.

The appreciation carried by an act of deference implies that the actor possesses a sentiment of regard for the recipient, often involving a general evaluation of the recipient. Regard is something the individual constantly has for others, and knows enough about to feign on occasion; yet in having regard for someone, the individual is unable to specify in detail what in fact he has in mind.

Those who render deference to an individual may feel, of course, that they are doing this merely because he is an instance of a category, or a representative of something, and that they are giving him his due not because of what they think of him "personally" but in spite of it. Some organizations, such as the military, explicitly stress this sort of rationale for according deference, leading to an impersonal bestowal of something that is specifically directed toward the person. By easily showing a regard that he does not have, the actor can feel that he is preserving a kind of inner autonomy, holding off the ceremonial order by the very act of upholding it. And of course in scrupulously observing the proper forms he may find that he is free to insinuate all kinds of disregard by carefully modifying intonation, pronunciation, pacing, and so forth.

In thinking about deference it is common to use as a model the rituals of obeisance, submission, and propitiation that someone under authority gives to someone in authority. Deference comes to be conceived as something a sub-ordinate owes to his superordinate. This is an extremely limiting view of defer-ence on two grounds. First, there are a great many forms of symmetrical de-ference which social equals owe to one another; in some societies, Tibetan for example, salutations between high-placed equals can become prolonged dis-plays of ritual conduct, exceeding in duration and expansiveness the kind of obeisance a subject may owe his ruler in less ritualized societies. Similarly, there are deference obligations that superordinates owe their subordinates; high priests all over the world seem obliged to respond to offerings with an equivalent of "Bless you, my son." Secondly, the regard in which the actor holds the recipient need not be one of respectful awe; there are other kinds of regard that are regularly expressed through interpersonal rituals also, such as trust, as when an individual welcomes sudden strangers into his house, or capacity-esteem, as when the individual defers to another's technical advice. A sentiment of regard that plays an important role in deference is that of affec-tion and belongingness. We see this in the extreme in the obligation of a newly married man in our society to treat his bride with affectional deference when-ever it is possible to twist ordinary behavior into a display of this kind. We find it more commonly, for example, as a component in many farewells where, as in our middle-class society, the actor will be obliged to infuse his voice with sadness and regret, paying deference in this way to the recipient's status as someone whom others can hold dearly. In "progressive" psychiatric establish-ments, a deferential show of acceptance, affection, and concern may form a constant and significant aspect of the stance taken by staff members when con-tacting patients. On Ward B, in fact, the two youngest patients seemed to have become so experienced in receiving such offerings, and so doubtful of them, that they would sometimes reply in a mocking way, apparently in an effort to re-establish the interaction on what seemed to these patients to be a mo· e sincere level.

It appears that deference behavior on the whole tends to be honorific and politely toned, conveying appreciation of the recipient that is in many ways more complimentary to the recipient than the actor's true sentiments might warrant. The actor typically gives the recipient the benefit of the doubt, and may even conceal low regard by extra punctiliousness. Thus acts of deference often attest to ideal guide lines to which the actual activity between actor and recipient can now and then be referred. As a last resort, the recipient has a right to make a direct appeal to these honorific definitions of the situation, to press his theoretic claims, but should he be rash enough to do so, it is likely that his relationship to the actor will be modified thereafter. People sense that the recipient ought not to take the actor literally or force his hand, and ought to rest content with the show of appreciation as opposed to a more substantive expression of it. Hence one finds that many automatic acts of deference con-tain a vestigial meaning, having to do with activity in which no one is any longer engaged and implying an appreciation long since not expected—and yet we know these antique tributes cannot be neglected with impunity.

In addition to a sentiment of regard, acts of deference typically contain a kind of promise, expressing in truncated form the actor's avowal and pledge to treat the recipient in a particular way in the on-coming activity. The pledge affirms that the expectations and obligations of the recipient, both substantive and ceremonial, will be allowed and supported by the actor. Actors thus promise to maintain the conception of self that the recipient has built up from the rules he is involved in. (Perhaps the prototype here is the public act of allegiance by which a subject officially acknowledges his subservience in certain matters to his lord.) Deferential pledges are frequently conveyed through spoken terms of address involving status-identifiers, as when a nurse responds to a rebuke in the operating room with the phrase, "yes, Doctor," signifying by term of address and tone of voice that the criticism has been understood and that, however unpalatable, it has not caused her to rebel. When a putative recipient fails to receive anticipated acts of deference, or when an actor makes clear that he is giving homage with bad grace, the recipient may feel that the state of affairs which he has been taking for granted has become unstable, and that an insubordinate effort may be made by the actor to reallocate tasks, relations, and power. To elicit an established act of deference, even if the actor must first be reminded of his obligations and warned about the consequence of discourtesy, is evidence that if rebellion comes it will come slyly; to be pointedly refused an expected act of deference is often a way of being told that open insurrection has begun.

A further complication must be mentioned. A particular act of deference is something an actor, acting in a given capacity, owes a recipient, acting in a given capacity. But these two individuals are likely to be related to one another through more than one pair of capacities, and these additional relationships are likely to receive ceremonial expression too. Hence the same act of deference may show signs of different kinds of regard, as when a doctor by a paternal gesture shows authority over a nurse in her capacity as subordinate technician but affection for her as a young female who is dependent on him in his capacity as a supportive older male. Similarly, an attendant in cheerfully addressing a doctor as "doc" may sometimes show respect for the medical role and yet male-solidarity with the person who fills it. Throughout this paper we must therefore keep in mind that a spate of deferential behavior is not a single note expressing a single relationship between two individuals active in a single pair of capacities, but rather a medley of voices answering to the fact that actor and recipient are in many different relations to one another, no one of which can usually be given exclusive and continuous determinacy of ceremonial conduct. An interesting example of this complexity in regard to master-servant relations may be cited from a nineteenth-century book of etiquette (Anon. 1836:188):

"Issue your commands with gravity and gentleness, and in a reserved manner. Let your voice be composed, but avoid a tone of familiarity or sympathy with them. It is better in addressing them to use a higher key of voice, and not to suffer it to fall at the end of a sentence. The best-bred man whom we ever had the pleasure of meeting always employed, in addressing servants, such forms of speech as these—'I'll thank you for so and so,'—'Such a thing if you please.'—with a gentle tone, but very elevated key.

The perfection of manner, in this particular, is, to indicate by your language, that the performance is a favour, and by your tone that it is a matter of course."

Deference can take many forms, of which I shall consider only two broad groupings, avoidance rituals and presentational rituals.

Avoidance rituals, as a term, may be employed to refer to those forms of deference which lead the actor to keep at a distance from the recipient and not violate what Simmel (1950:321) has called the "ideal sphere" that lies around the recipient:

"Although differing in size in various directions and differing according to the person with whom one entertains relations, this sphere cannot be penetrated, unless the personality value of the individual is thereby destroyed. A sphere of this sort is placed around man by his honor. Language poignantly designates an insult to one's honor as 'coming too close;' the radius of this sphere marks, as it were, the distance whose trespassing by another person insults one's honor."

Any society could be profitably studied as a system of deferential stand-off arrangements, and most studies give us some evidence of this (e.g., Hodge 1907:442). Avoidance of other's personal name is perhaps the most common example from anthropology, and should be as common in sociology.

Here, it should be said, is one of the important differences between social classes in our society: not only are some of the tokens different through which consideration for the privacy of others is expressed, but also, apparently, the higher the class the more extensive and elaborate are the taboos against contact. For example, in a study of a Shetlandic community the writer found that as one moves from middle-class urban centers in Britain to the rural lower-class islands, the distance between chairs at table decreases, so that in the outermost Shetland Islands actual bodily contact during meals and similar social occasions is not considered an invasion of separateness and no effort need be made to excuse it. And yet, whatever the rank of the participants in an action, the actor is likely to feel that the recipient has some warranted expectation of inviolability.

Where an actor need show no concern about penetrating the recipient's usual personal reserve, and need have no fear of contaminating him by any penetration into his privacy, we say that the actor is on terms of familiarity with the recipient. (The mother who feels at liberty to pick her child's nose is an extreme example.) Where the actor must show circumspection in his approach to the recipient, we speak of nonfamiliarity or respect. Rules governing conduct between two individuals may, but need not, be symmetrical in regard to to either familiarity or respect.

There appear to be some typical relations between ceremonial distance and other kinds of sociological distance. Between status equals we may expect to find interaction guided by symmetrical familiarity. Between superordinate and subordinate we may expect to find asymmetrical relations, the superordinate having the right to exercise certain familiarities which the subordinate is not allowed to reciprocate. Thus, in the research hospital, doctors tended to call nurses by their first names, while nurses responded with "polite" or "formal" address. Similarly, in American business organizations the boss may thoughtfully ask the elevator man how his children are, but this entrance into another's life may be blocked to the elevator man, who can appreciate the concern but not return it. Perhaps the clearest form of this is found in the psychiatrist-patient relation, where the psychiatrist has a right to touch on aspects of the patient's life that the patient might not even allow himself to touch upon, while of course this privilege is not reciprocated. (There are some psychoanalysts who believe it desirable to "analyze the countertransference with the patient" but this or any other familiarity on the part of the patient is strongly condemned by official psychoanalytical bodies.) Patients, especially mental ones, may not even have the right to question their doctor about his opinion of their own case; for one thing, this would bring them into too intimate a contact with an area of knowledge in which doctors invest their special apartness from the lay public which they serve.

While these correlations between ceremonial distance and other kinds of distance are typical, we must be quite clear about the fact that other relationships are often found. Thus, status equals who are not well acquainted may be on terms of reciprocal respect, not familiarity. Further, there are many organizations in America where differences in rank are seen as so great a threat to the equilibrium of the system that the ceremonial aspect of behavior functions not as a way of iconically expressing these differences but as a way of carefully counterbalancing them. In the research hospital under study, psychiatrists, psychologists, and sociologists were part of a single ceremonial group as regards first-naming, and this symmetrical familiarity apparently served to allay some feeling on the part of psychologists and sociologists that they were not equal members of the team, as indeed they were not. Similarly, in a study of small business managers, the writer (1952) found that filling-station attendants had the right to interrupt their boss, slap him on the back, rib him, use his phone, and take other liberties, and that this ritual license seemed to provide a way in which the manager could maintain morale and keep his employees honest. We must realize that organizations that are quite similar structurally may have quite different deference styles, and that deference patterns are partly a matter of changing fashion.

In our society, rules regarding the keeping of one's distance are multitudinous and strong. They tend to focus around certain matters, such as physical places and properties defined as the recipient's "own," the body's sexual equipment, etc. An important focus of deferential avoidance consists in the verbal care that actors are obliged to exercise so as not to bring into discussion matters that might be painful, embarrassing, or humiliating to the recipient. In Simmel's words (1950:322):

"The same sort of circle which surrounds man—although it is value-accentuated in a very different sense—is filled out by his affairs and by his characteristics. To penetrate this circle by taking notice, constitutes a violation of his personality. Just as material property is, so to speak, an extension of the ego, and any interference with our property is, for this reason, felt to be a violation of the person, there also is an intellectual private-property, whose violation effects a lesion of the ego in its very center. Discretion is nothing but the feeling that there exists a right in regard to the sphere of the immediate life contents. Discretion, of course, differs in its extension with different personalities just as the positions of honor and of property have different radii with respect to 'close' individuals, and to strangers, and indifferent persons."

Referential avoidance may be illustrated from Ward A, where rules in this regard were well institutionalized.[7] The fact that two of the female patients had had experience in a state-type mental hospital was not raised either in serious conversation or in jest, except when initiated by these women themselves; nor was a question of the age of these patients (who were in their middle thirties) raised. The fact that the two male patients were conscientious objectors was never raised, even by the CO's themselves. The fact that one of the patients was blind and that another was colored was never raised by the others in their presence. When a poor patient declined to participate in an outing on a claim of indifference, her rationalization for not going was accepted at face-value and her fiction respected, even though others knew that she wanted to go but was ashamed to because she did not have a suitable coat. Patients about to be given drugs experimentally, or who had just been given drugs, were not questioned about their feelings, unless they themselves raised the topic. Unmarried women, whether patients or nurses, were not directly questioned about boy friends. Information about religious affiliations was volunteered but rarely requested.

Violation of rules regarding privacy and separateness is a phenomenon that can be closely studied on mental wards because ordinarily there is so much of it done by patients and staff. Sometimes this results because of what are felt to be the substantive or instrumental requirements of the situation. When a mental patient checks into a hospital, an itemized account is usually made of every one of his belongings; this requires his giving himself up to others in a way that he may have learned to define as a humiliation. Periodically his effects may have to be searched in a general effort to clear the ward of "sharps," liquor, narcotics, and other contraband. The presence of a microphone known to be concealed in each patient's room and connected with a speaker in the nurses' station is an additional invasion (but one provided only in the newest hospitals); the censoring of outgoing mail is another. Psychotherapy, especially when the patient appreciates that other staff members will learn about his progress and even receive a detailed report of the case, is another such invasion; so too is the practice of having nurses and attendants "chart" the course of the patient's daily feelings and activity. Efforts of staff to "form relations" with patients, to break down periods of withdrawal in the interest of therapy, is another example. Classic forms of "nonperson treatment" are found, with staff members so little observing referential avoidance that they discuss intimacies about a patient in his presence as if he were not there at all. There will be no door to the toilet, or one that the patient cannot lock; dormitory sleeping, especially in the case of middle-class patients, is a similar encroachment on privacy. The care that is given to "very disturbed" patients in many large public hospitals leads in a similar direction, as with forced medication, cold packs applied to the naked body, or confinement while naked in an empty strongroom into which staff and patients may look. Another instance is forced feeding, whereby a frightened mute patient who may want to keep certain food out of his mouth is matched against an attendant who must see that patients are fed.

Invasions of privacy which have an instrumental technical rationale can be paralleled with others of a more purely ceremonial nature. Thus "acting out" and "psychopathic" patients are ones who can be counted on to overreach polite bounds and ask embarrassing questions of fellow-patients and staff, or proffer compliments which would not ordinarily be in their province to give, or proffer physical gestures of appreciation such as hugging or kissing, which are felt to be inappropriate. Thus, on Ward B, male staff members were plagued by such statements as "Why did you cut yourself shaving like that," "Why do you always wear the same pants, I'm getting sick of them," "Look at all the dandruff you've got." If seated by one of the patients, a male staff member might have to edge continuously away so as to keep a seemly safe distance between himself and the patient.

Some of the ways in which individuals on Ward A kept their distance were made clear in contrast to the failure of Ward B's patients to do so. On Ward A the rule that patients were to remain outside the nurses' station was observed. Patients would wait for an invitation or, as was commonly the case, stay in the doorway so that they could talk with those in the station and yet not presume upon them. It was therefore not necessary for the staff to lock the station door when a nurse was in the station. On Ward B it was not possible to keep three of the patients out of the station by request alone, and so the door had to be kept locked if privacy was to be maintained. Even then, the walls of the station were effectively battered down by continuous banging and shouting. In other words, on Ward A the protective ring that nurses and attendants drew around themselves by retreating into the station was respected by the patients, whereas on Ward B it was not.

A second illustration may be cited. Patients on Ward A had mixed feelings about some of their doctors, but each patient knew of one or two doctors that he or she liked. Thus, while at table, when a favorite doctor passed by, there would be an exchange of greetings but, ceremonially speaking, nothing more. No one would have felt it right to chase after the doctors, pester them, and in general invade their right of separateness. On Ward B, however, the entrance of a doctor was very often a signal for some of the patients to rush up to him, affectionally presume on him by grasping his hand or putting an arm around him, and then to walk with him down the corridor, engaging in a kidding affectionate conversation. And often when a doctor had retired behind a ward office door, a patient would bang on the door and look through its glass window, and in other ways refuse to keep expected distance.

One patient on Ward B, Mrs. Baum, seemed especially talented in divining what would be an invasion of other people's privacy. On a shopping expedition, for example, she had been known to go behind the counter or examine the contents of a stranger's shopping bag. At other times she would enter a stranger's car at an intersection and ask for a lift. In general she could provide the student with a constant reminder of the vast number of different acts and objects that are employed as markers by which the borders of privacy are staked out, suggesting that in the case of some "mental disorders" symptomatology is specifically and not merely incidentally an improper keeping of social distance.

Analysis of deferential avoidance has sometimes been held back because there is another kind of ceremonial avoidance, a self-protective kind, that may resemble deferential restraint but is analytically quite different from it. Just as the individual may avoid an object so as not to pollute or defile it, so he may avoid an object so as not to be polluted or defiled by it. For example, in Ward B, when Mrs. Baum was in a paranoid state she refused to allow her daughter to accept a match from a Negro attendant, appearing to feel that contact with a member of a group against which she was prejudiced would be polluting; so, too, while kissing the doctors and nurses in an expansive birthday mood, she gave the appearance that she was trying but could not bring herself to kiss the attendant. In general, it would seem, one avoids a person of high status out of deference to him and avoids a person of lower status than one's own out of a self-protective concern. Perhaps the social distance sometimes carefully maintained between equals may entail both kinds of avoidance on both their parts. In any case, the similarity in the two kinds of avoidance is not deep. A nurse who keeps away from a patient out of sympathetic appreciation that he wants to be alone wears one expression on her face and body; when she maintains the same physical distance from a patient because he has been incontinent and smells, she is likely to wear a different expression. In addition, the distances an actor keeps out of deference to others decline when he rises in status, but the self-protective ones increase.[8]

Avoidance rituals have been suggested as one main type of deference. A second type, termed *presentational rituals*, encompasses acts through which the individual makes specific attestations to recipients concerning how he regards them and how he will treat them in the on-coming interaction. Rules regarding these ritual practices involve specific prescriptions, not specific proscriptions; while avoidance rituals specify what is not to be done, presentational rituals specify what is to be done. Some illustrations may be taken from social life on Ward A as maintained by the group consisting of patients, attendants, and nurses. These presentational rituals will not, I think, be much different from those found in many other organizations in our society.

When members of the ward passed by each other, salutations would ordinarily be exchanged, the length of the salutation depending on the period that had elapsed since the last salutation and the period that seemed likely before the next. At table, when eyes met a brief smile of recognition would be exchanged; when someone left for the weekend, a farewell involving a pause in on-going activity and a brief exchange of words would be involved. In any case, there was the understanding that when members of the ward were in a physical position to enter into eye-to-eye contact of some kind, this contact would be effected. It seemed that anything less would not have shown proper respect for the state of relatedness that existed among the members of the ward.

Associated with salutations were practices regarding the "noticing" of any change in appearance, status, or repute, as if these changes represented a commitment on the part of the changed individual which had to be underwritten by the group. New clothes, new hairdos, occasions of being "dressed up" would call forth a round of compliments, whatever the group felt about the improvement. Similarly, any effort on the part of a patient to make something in the occupational therapy room or to perform in other ways was likely to be commended by others. Staff members who participated in the hospital amateur theatricals were complimented, and when one of the nurses was to be married, pictures of her fiancé and his family were viewed by all and approved. In these ways a member of the ward tended to be saved from the embarrassment of presenting himself to others as someone who had risen in value, while receiving a response as someone who had declined, or remained the same.

Another form of presentational deference was the practice of staff and patients pointedly requesting each and every patient to participate in outings, occupational therapy, concert-going, meal-time conversation, and other forms of group activity. Refusals were accepted but no patient was not asked.

Another standard form of presentational deference on Ward A was that of extending small services and aid. Nurses would make minor purchases for patients in the local town; patients coming back from home visits would pick up other patients by car to save them having to come back by public transportation; male patients would fix the things that males are good at fixing and female patients would return the service. Food came from the kitchen already allocated to individual trays, but at each meal a brisk business was done in exchanging food, and outright donations occurred whereby those who did not care for certain foods gave them to those who did. Most members of the ward took a turn at conveying the food trays from the kitchen cart to the table, as they did in bringing toast and coffee for the others from the sidetable. These services were not exchanged in terms of a formal schedule worked out to ensure fairness, but rather as an unplanned thing, whereby the actor was able to demonstrate that the private objectives of the recipient were something in which others present sympathetically participated.

I have mentioned four very common forms of presentational deference: salutations, invitations, compliments, and minor services. Through all of these the recipient is told that he is not an island unto himself and that others are, or seek to be, involved with him and with his personal private concerns. Taken together, these rituals provide a continuous symbolic tracing of the extent to which the recipient's ego has not been bounded and barricaded in regard to others.

Two main types of deference have been illustrated; presentational rituals through which the actor concretely depicts his appreciation of the recipient; and avoidance rituals, taking the form of proscriptions, interdictions, and taboos, which imply acts the actor must refrain from doing lest he violate the right of the recipient to keep him at a distance. We are familiar with this distinction from Durkheim's classification of ritual into positive and negative rites (1954: 299).

In suggesting that there are things that must be said and done to a recipient, and things that must not be said and done, it should be plain that there is an inherent opposition and conflict between these two forms of deference. To ask after an individual's health, his family's well-being, or the state of his affairs, is to present him with a sign of sympathetic concern; but in a certain way to make this presentation is to invade the individual's personal reserve, as will be made clear if an actor of wrong status asks him these questions, or if a recent event has made such a question painful to answer. As Durkheim (1953:37) suggested, "The human personality is a sacred thing; one dare not violate it nor infringe its bounds, while at the same time the greatest good is in communion with others."[9] I would like to cite two ward illustrations of this inherent opposition between the two forms of deference.

On Ward A, as in other wards in the hospital, there was a "touch system."[10] Certain categories of personnel had the privilege of expressing their affection and closeness to others by the ritual of bodily contact with them. The actor places his arms around the waist of the recipient, rubs a hand down the back of the recipient's neck, strokes the recipient's hair and forehead, or holds the recipient's hand. Sexual connotation is of course officially excluded. The most frequent form that the ritual took was for a nurse to extend such a touch-confirmation to a patient. Nonetheless, attendants, patients, and nurses formed one group in regard to touch rights, the rights being symmetrical. Any one of these individuals had a right to touch any member of his own category or any member of the other categories. (In fact some forms of touch, as in playful fighting or elbow-strength games, were intrinsically symmetrical.) Of course some members of the ward disliked the system, but this did not alter the rights of others to incorporate them into it. The familiarity implicit in such exchanges was affirmed in other ways, such as symmetrical first-naming. It may be added that in many mental hospitals, patients, attendants, and nurses do not form one group for ceremonial purposes, and the obligation of patients to accept friendly physical contact from staff is not reciprocated.

In addition to these symmetrical touch relations on the ward, there were also asymmetrical ones. The doctors touched other ranks as a means of conveying friendly support and comfort, but other ranks tended to feel that it would be presumptuous for them to reciprocate a doctor's touch, let alone initiate such a contact with a doctor.[11]

Now it should be plain that if a touch system is to be maintained, as it is in many hospitals in America, and if members of the ward are to receive the confirmation and support this ritual system provides, then persons other than doctors coming to live or work on the ward must make themselves intimately available to the others present. Rights of apartness and inviolability which are demanded and accorded in many other establishments in our society must here be forgone, in this particular. The touch system, in short, is only possible to the degree that individuals forego the right to keep others at a physical distance.

A second illustration of the sense in which the two forms of deference act in opposition to each other turns upon the point of social participation. On Ward A there was a strong feeling of in-group solidarity among all nonmedical ranks —nurses, attendants, and patients. One way in which this was expressed was through joint participation in meals, card-games, room-visits, TV parties, occupational therapy, and outings. Ordinarily individuals were ready not only to participate in these activities but also to do so with visible pleasure and enthusiasm. One gave oneself to these occasions and through this giving the group flourished.

In the context of this participation pattern, and in spite of its importance for the group, it was understood that patients had the right of disaffection. Although it was felt to be an affront to group solidarity to come late for breakfast, late-comers were only mildly chided for doing so. Once at table, a patient was obliged to return the greetings offered him, but after this if his mood and manner patently expressed his desire to be left alone, no effort would be made to draw him into the meal-time conversation. If a patient took his food from the table and retired to his room or to the empty TV lounge, no one chased after him. If a patient refused to come on an outing, a little joke was made of it, warning the individual what he would miss, and the matter would be dropped. If a patient refused to play cards at a time when this would deny the others a necessary fourth, joking remonstrances would be made but not continued. And on any occasion, if the patient appeared depressed, moody, or even somewhat disarrayed, an effort was made not to notice this or to attribute it to a need for physical care and rest. These kinds of delicacy and restriction of demands seemed to serve the social function of keeping informal life free from the contamination of being a "treatment" or a prescription, and meant that in certain matters the patient had a right to prevent intrusion when, where, and how he wanted to do so. It is apparent, however, that the right to withdraw into privacy was a right that was accorded at the expense of those kinds of acts through which the individual was expected to display his relatedness to the others on the ward. There is an inescapable opposition between showing a desire to include an individual and showing respect for his privacy.

As an implication of this dilemma, we must see that social intercourse involves a constant dialectic between presentational rituals and avoidance rituals. A peculiar tension must be maintained, for these opposing requirements of conduct must somehow be held apart from one another and yet realized together in the same interaction: the gestures which carry an actor to a recipient must also signify that things will not be carried too far.

## DEMEANOR

It was suggested that the ceremonial component of concrete behavior has at least two basic elements, deference and demeanor. Deference, defined as the appreciation an individual shows of another to that other, whether through avoidance rituals or presentational rituals, has been discussed and demeanor may now be considered.

By demeanor I shall refer to that element of the individual's ceremonial behavior typically conveyed through deportment, dress, and bearing, which serves to express to those in his immediate presence that he is a person of certain desirable or undesirable qualities. In our society, the "well" or "properly" demeaned individual displays such attributes as: discretion and sincerity; modesty in claims regarding self; sportsmanship; command of speech and physical movements; self-control over his emotions, his appetites, and his desires; poise under pressure; and so forth.

When we attempt to analyze the qualities conveyed through demeanor, certain themes become apparent. The well-demeaned individual possesses the attributes popularly associated with "character training" or "socialization," these being implanted when a neophyte of any kind is housebroken. Rightly or wrongly, others tend to use such qualities diagnostically, as evidence of what the actor is generally like at other times and as a performer of other activities. In addition, the properly demeaned individual is someone who has closed off many avenues of perception and penetration that others might take to him, and is therefore unlikely to be contaminated by them. Most importantly, perhaps, good demeanor is what is required of an actor if he is to be transformed into someone who can be relied upon to maintain himself as an interactant, poised for communication, and to act so that others do not endanger themselves by presenting themselves as interactants to him.[13]

It should be noted once again that demeanor involves attributes derived from interpretations others make of the way in which the individual handles himself during social intercourse. The individual cannot establish these attributes for his own by verbally avowing that he possesses them, though sometimes he may rashly try to do this. (He can, however, contrive to conduct himself in such a way that others, through their interpretation of his conduct, will impute the kinds of attributes to him he would like others to see in him.) In general, then, through demeanor the individual creates an image of himself, but properly speaking this is not an image that is meant for his own eyes. Of course this should not prevent us from seeing that the individual who acts with good demeanor may do so because he places an appreciable value upon himself, and that he who fails to demean himself properly may be accused of having "no self-respect" or of holding himself too cheaply in his own eyes.

As in the case of deference, an object in the study of demeanor is to collect all the ceremonially relevant acts that a particular individual performs in the presence of each of the several persons with whom he comes in contact, to interpret these acts for the demeanor that is symbolically expressed through them, and then to piece these meanings together into an image of the individual, an image of him in others' eyes.

Rules of demeanor, like rules of deference can be symmetrical or asymmetrical. Between social equals, symmetrical rules of demeanor seem often to be prescribed. Between unequals many variations can be found. For example, at staff meetings on the psychiatric units of the hospital, medical doctors had the privilege of swearing, changing the topic of conversation, and sitting in undignified positions; attendants, on the other hand, had the right to attend staff meetings and to ask questions during them (in line with the milieu-therapy orientation of these research units) but were implicitly expected to conduct themselves with greater circumspection than was required of doctors. (This was pointed out by a perceptive occupational therapist who claimed she was always reminded that a mild young female psychiatrist was really an M.D. by the fact that this psychiatrist exercised these prerogatives of informal demeanor.) The extreme here perhaps is the master-servant relation as seen in cases where valets and maids are required to perform in a dignified manner services of an undignified kind. Similarly, doctors had the right to saunter into the nurses' station, lounge on the station's dispensing counter, and engage in joking with the nurses; other ranks participated in this informal interaction with doctors, but only after doctors had initiated it.

On Ward A, standards of demeanor were maintained that seem to be typical in American middle-class society. The eating pace maintained at table suggested that no one present was so over-eager to eat, so little in control of impulses, so jealous of his rights, as to wolf down his food or take more than his share. At pinochle, the favorite card game, each player would coax spectators to take his hand and spectators would considerately decline the offer, expressing in this way that a passion for play had in no way overwhelmed them. Occasionally a patient appeared in the day-room or at meals with bathrobe (a practice permitted of patients throughout the hospital) but ordinarily neat street wear was maintained, illustrating that the individual was not making his appearance before others in a lax manner or presenting too much of himself too freely. Little profanity was employed and no open sexual remarks.

On Ward B, bad demeanor (by middle-class standards) was quite common. This may be illustrated from meal-time behavior. A patient would often lunge at an extra piece of food or at least eye an extra piece covetously. Even when each individual at table was allowed to receive an equal share, over-eagerness was shown by the practice of taking all of one's share at once instead of waiting until one serving had been eaten. Occasionally a patient would come to table half-dressed. One patient frequently belched loudly at meals and was occasionally flatulent. Messy manipulation of food sometimes occurred. Swearing and cursing were common. Patients would occasionally push their chairs back from the table precipitously and bolt for another room, coming back to the table in the same violent manner. Loud sounds were sometimes made by sucking on straws in empty pop bottles. Through these activities, patients expressed to the staff and to one another that their selves were not properly demeaned ones.

These forms of misconduct are worth study because they make us aware of some aspects of good demeanor we usually take for granted; for aspects even more usually taken for granted, we must study "back" wards in typical mental hospitals. There patients are denudative, incontinent, and they openly masturbate; they scratch themselves violently; drooling occurs and a nose may run unchecked; sudden hostilities may flare up and "paranoid" immodesties be projected; speech or motor activity may occur at a manic or depressed pace, either too fast or too slow for propriety; males and females may comport themselves as if they were of the other sex or hardly old enough to have any. Such wards are of course the classic settings of bad demeanor.

A final point about demeanor may be mentioned. Whatever his motives for making a well demeaned appearance before others, it is assumed that the individual will exert his own will to do so, or that he will pliantly co-operate should it fall to someone else's lot to help him in this matter. In our society, a man combs his own hair until it gets too long, then he goes to a barber and follows instructions while it is being cut. This voluntary submission is crucial, for personal services of such a kind are done close to the very center of the individual's inviolability and can easily result in transgressions; server and served must co-operate closely if these are not to occur. If, however, an individual fails to maintain what others see as proper personal appearance, and if he refuses to co-operate with those who are charged with maintaining it for him, then the task of making him presentable against his will is likely to cost him at the moment a great deal of dignity and deference, and this in turn may create complex feelings in those who find they must cause him to pay this price. This is one of the occupational dilemmas of those employed to make children and mental patients presentable. It is easy to order attendants to "dress up" and shave male patients on visitors' day, and no doubt when this is done patients make a more favorable appearance, but while this appearance is in the process of being achieved—in the showers or the barbershop, for example—the patients may be subjected to extreme indignities.

## DEFERENCE AND DEMEANOR

Deference and demeanor are analytical terms; empirically there is much overlapping of the activities to which they refer. An act through which the individual gives or withholds deference to others typically provides means by which he expresses the fact that he is a well or badly demeaned individual. Some aspects of this overlapping may be cited. First, in performing a given act of presentational deference, as in offering a guest a chair, the actor finds himself doing something that can be done with smoothness and aplomb, expressing self-control and poise, or with clumsiness and uncertainty, expressing an irresolute character. This is, as it were, an incidental and adventitious connection between deference and demeanor. It may be illustrated from recent material on doctor-patient relationships, where it is suggested that one complaint a doctor may have against some of his patients is that they do not bathe before coming for an examination (Dichter 1950:5–6); while bathing is a way of paying deference to the doctor it is at the same time a way for the patient to present himself as a clean, well demeaned person. A further illustration is found in acts such as loud talking, shouting, or singing, for these acts encroach upon the right of others to be let alone, while at the same time they illustrate a badly demeaned lack of control over one's feelings.

The same connection between deference and demeanor has had a bearing on the ceremonial difficulties associated with intergroup interaction: the gestures of deference expected by members of one society have sometimes been incompatible with the standards of demeanor maintained by members of another. For example, during the nineteenth century, diplomatic relations between Britain and China were embarrassed by the fact that the *Kot'ow* demanded of visiting ambassadors by the Chinese Emperor was felt by some British ambassadors to be incompatible with their self-respect (Douglas 1895:11, 291–296).

A second connection between deference and demeanor turns upon the fact that a willingness to give others their deferential due is one of the qualities which the individual owes it to others to express through his conduct, just as a willingness to conduct oneself with good demeanor is in general a way of showing deference to those present.

In spite of these connections between deference and demeanor, the analytical relation between them is one of "complementarity," not identity. The image the individual owes to others to maintain of himself is not the same type of image these others are obliged to maintain of him. Deference images tend to point to the wider society outside the interaction, to the place the individual has achieved in the hierarchy of this society. Demeanor images tend to point to qualities which any social position gives its incumbents a chance to display during interaction, for these qualities pertain more to the way in which the individual handles his position than to the rank and place of that position relative to those possessed by others.

Further, the image of himself the individual owes it to others to maintain through his conduct is a kind of justification and compensation for the image of him that others are obliged to express through their deference to him. Each of the two images in fact may act as a guarantee and check upon the other. In an interchange that can be found in many cultures, the individual defers to guests to show how welcome they are and how highly he regards them; they in turn decline the offering at least once, showing through their demeanor that they are not presumptuous, immodest, or over-eager to receive favor. Similarly, a man starts to rise for a lady, showing respect for her sex; she interrupts and halts his gesture, showing she is not greedy of her rights in this capacity but is ready to define the situation as one between equals. In general, then, by treating others deferentially one gives them an opportunity to handle the indulgence with good demeanor. Through this differentiation in symbolizing function the world tends to be bathed in better images than anyone deserves, for it is practical to signify great appreciation of others by offering them deferential indulgences, knowing that some of these indulgences will be declined as an expression of good demeanor.

There are still other complementary relations between deference and demeanor. If an individual feels he ought to show proper demeanor in order to warrant deferential treatment, then he must be in a position to do so. He must, for example, be able to conceal from others aspects of himself which would make him unworthy in their eyes, and to conceal himself from them when he is in an undignified state, whether of dress, mind, posture, or action. The avoidance rituals which others perform in regard to him give him room to maneuver, enabling him to present only a self that is worthy of deference; at the same time, this avoidance makes it easier for them to assure themselves that the deference they have to show him is warranted.

To show the difference between deference and demeanor I have pointed out the complementary relation between them, but even this kind of relatedness can be overstressed. The failure of an individual to show proper deference to others does not necessarily free them from the obligation to act with good demeanor in his presence, however disgruntled they may be at having to do this. Similarly, the failure of an individual to conduct himself with proper demeanor does not always relieve those in his presence from treating him with proper deference. It is by separating deference and demeanor that we can appreciate many things about ceremonial life, such as the fact that a group may be noted for excellence in one of these areas while having a bad reputation in the other. Hence we can find a place for arguments such as De Quincey's (1890), that an Englishman shows great self-respect but little respect for others while a Frenchman shows great respect for others but little respect for himself.

We are to see, then, that there are many occasions when it would be improper for an individual to convey about himself what others are ready to convey about him to him, since each of these two images is a warrant and justification for the other, and not a mirror image of it. The Meadian notion that the individual takes toward himself the attitude others take to him seems very much an oversimplification. Rather the individual must rely on others to complete the picture of him of which he himself is allowed to paint only certain parts. Each individual is responsible for the demeanor image of himself and the deference image of others, so that for a complete man to be expressed, individuals must hold hands in a chain of ceremony, each giving deferentially with proper demeanor to the one on the right what will be received deferentially from the one on the left. While it may be true that the individual has a unique self all his own, evidence of this possession is thoroughly a product of joint ceremonial labor, the part expressed through the individual's demeanor being no more significant than the part conveyed by others through their deferential behavior toward him.

## CEREMONIAL PROFANATIONS

There are many situations and many ways in which the justice of ceremony can fail to be maintained. There are occasions when the individual finds that he is accorded deference of a misidentifying kind, whether the misidentification places him in a higher or lower position than he thinks right. There are other occasions when he finds that he is being treated more impersonally and unceremonially than he thinks proper and feels that his treatment ought to be more punctuated with acts of deference, even though these may draw attention to his subordinate status. A frequent occasion for ceremonial difficulty occurs at moments of intergroup contact, since different societies and subcultures have different ways of conveying deference and demeanor, different ceremonial meanings for the same act, and different amounts of concern over such things as poise and privacy. Travel books such as Mrs. Trollope's (1832) are full of autobiographical material on these misunderstandings, and sometimes seem to have been written chiefly to publicize them.

Of the many kinds of ceremonial transgressions there is one which a preliminary paper on ceremony is obliged to consider: it is the kind that appears to have been perpetrated on purpose and to employ consciously the very language of ceremony to say what is forbidden. The idiom through which modes of proper ceremonial conduct are established necessarily creates ideally effective forms of desecration, for it is only in reference to specified proprieties that one can learn to appreciate what will be the worst possible form of behavior. Profanations are to be expected, for every religious ceremony creates the possibility of a black mass.[12]

When we study individuals who are on familiar terms with one another and need stand on little ceremony, we often find occasions when standard ceremonial forms that are inapplicable to the situation are employed in what is felt to be a facetious way, apparently as a means of poking fun at social circles where the ritual is seriously employed. When among themselves, nurses at the research hospital sometimes addressed one another humorously as Miss ; doctors under similar conditions sometimes called one another "Doctor" with the same joking tone of voice. Similarly, elaborate offering of a chair or precedence through a door was sometimes made between an actor and recipient who were actually on terms of symmetrical familiarity. In Britain, where speech and social style are clearly stratified, a great amount of this unserious profanation of rituals can be found, with upper class people mocking lower class ceremonial gestures, and lower class people when among themselves fully returning the compliment. The practice perhaps reaches its highest expression in music hall revues, where lower class performers beautifully mimic upper class ceremonial conduct for an audience whose status falls somewhere in between.

Some playful profanation seems to be directed not so much at outsiders as at the recipient himself, by way of lightly teasing him or testing ritual limits in regard to him. It should be said that in our society this kind of play is directed by adults to those of lesser ceremonial breed—to children, old people, servants, and so forth—as when an attendant affectionately ruffles a patient's hair or indulges in more drastic types of teasing (Taxel 1953:68; Willoughby 1953:90). Anthropologists have described this kind of license in an extreme form in the case of "siblings-in-law who are potential secondary spouses" (Murdock 1949:282). However apparent the aggressive overtones of this form of conduct may be, the recipient is given the opportunity of acting as if no serious affront to his honor has occurred, or at least an affront no more serious than that of being defined as someone with whom it is permissible to joke. On Ward B, when Mrs. Baum was given a sheet too small for her bed she used it to playfully bag one of the staff members. Her daughter occasionally jokingly employed the practice of bursting large bubblegum bubbles as close to the face of a staff person as possible without touching him, or stroking the arm and hand of a male staff member in parody of affectional gestures, gleefully proposing sexual intercourse with him.

A less playful kind of ritual profanation is found in the practice of defiling the recipient but in such a way and from such an angle that he retains the right to act as if he has not received the profaning message. On Ward B, where staff members had the occupational obligation of "relating to" the patients and responding to them with friendliness, nurses would sometimes mutter *sotto voce* vituperations when patients were trying and difficult. Patients, in turn, employed the same device. When a nurse's back was turned, patients would sometimes stick their tongues out, thumb their noses, or grimace at her. These are of course standard forms of ritual contempt in our Anglo-American society, constituting a kind of negative deference. Other instances may be cited. On one occasion Mrs. Baum, to the amusement of others present, turned her back on the station window, bent down, and flipped her skirt up, in an act of ritual contempt which was apparently once more prevalent as a standard insult than it is today. In all these cases we see that although ceremonial liberties are taken with the recipient, he is not held in sufficiently low regard to be insulted "to his face." This line between what can be conveyed about the recipient while in a state of talk with him, and what can only be conveyed about him when not in talk with him, is a basic ceremonial institution in our society, ensuring that face-to-face interaction is likely to be mutually approving. An appreciation of how deep this line is can be obtained on mental wards, where severely disturbed patients can be observed co-operating with staff members to maintain a thin fiction that the line is being kept.

But of course there are situations where an actor conveys ritual profanation of a recipient while officially engaged in talk with him or in such a way that the affront cannot easily be overlooked. Instead of recording and classifying these ritual affronts, students have tended to cover them all with a psychological tent, labelling them as "aggressions" or "hostile outbursts," while passing on to other matters of study.

In some psychiatric wards, face-to-face ritual profanation is a constant phenomenon. Patients may profane a staff member or a fellow-patient by spitting at him, slapping his face, throwing feces at him, tearing off his clothes, pushing him off the chair, taking food from his grasp, screaming into his face, sexually molesting him, etc. On Ward B, on occasion, Betty would slap and punch her mother's face and tramp on her mother's bare feet with heavy shoes; and abuse her, at table, with those four-letter words that middle-class children ordinarily avoid in the presence of their parents, let alone in reference to them. It should be repeated that while from the point of view of the actor these profanations may be a product of blind impulse, or have a special symbolic meaning (Schwartz and Stanton 1950), from the point of view of the society at large and its ceremonial idiom these are not random impulsive infractions. Rather, these acts are exactly those calculated to convey complete disrespect and contempt through symbolic means. Whatever is in the patient's mind, the throwing of feces at an attendant is a use of our ceremonial idiom that is as exquisite in its way as is a bow from the waist done with grace and a flourish. Whether he knows it or not, the patient speaks the same ritual language as his captors; he merely says what they do not wish to hear, for patient behavior which does not carry ritual meaning in terms of the daily ceremonial discourse of the staff will not be perceived by the staff at all.

In addition to profanation of others, individuals for varieties of reasons and in varieties of situations give the appearance of profaning themselves, acting in a way that seems purposely designed to destroy the image others have of them as persons worthy of deference. Ceremonial mortification of the flesh has been a theme in many social movements. What seems to be involved is not merely bad demeanor but rather the concerted efforts of an individual sensitive to high standards of demeanor to act against his own interests and exploit ceremonial arrangements by presenting himself in the worst possible light.

In many psychiatric wards, what appears to staff and other patients as self-profanation is a common occurrence. For example, female patients can be found who have systematically pulled out all the hair from their head, presenting themselves thereafter with a countenance that is guaranteed to be grotesque. Perhaps the extreme for our society is found in patients who smear themselves with and eat their own feces (for descriptions of this behavior see Wittkower and La Tendresse 1955).

Self-profanation also occurs of course at the verbal level. Thus, on Ward A, the high standards of demeanor were broken by the blind patient who at table would sometimes thrust a consideration of her infirmity upon the others present by talking in a self-pitying fashion about how little use she was to anybody and how no matter how you looked at it she was still blind. Similarly, on Ward B, Betty was wont to comment on how ugly she was, how fat, and how no one would want to have someone like her for a girl-friend. In both cases, these self-derogations, carried past the limits of polite self-depreciation, were considered a tax upon the others: they were willing to exert protective referential avoidance regarding the individual's shortcomings and felt it was unfair to be forced into contaminating intimacy with the individual's problems.

## CONCLUSIONS

The rules of conduct which bind the actor and the recipient together are the bindings of society. But many of the acts which are guided by these rules occur infrequently or take a long time for their consummation. Opportunities to affirm the moral order and the society could therefore be rare. It is here that ceremonial rules play their social function, for many of the acts which are guided by these rules last but a brief moment, involve no substantive outlay, and can be performed in every social interaction. Whatever the activity and however profanely instrumental, it can afford many opportunities for minor ceremonies as long as other persons are present. Through these observances, guided by ceremonial obligations and expectations, a constant flow of indulgences is spread through society, with others present constantly reminding the individual that he must keep himself together as a well demeaned person and affirm the sacred quality of these others. The gestures which we sometimes call empty are perhaps in fact the fullest things of all.

It is therefore important to see that the self is in part a ceremonial thing, a sacred object which must be treated with proper ritual care and in turn must be presented in a proper light to others. As a means through which this self is established, the individual acts with proper demeanor while in contact with others and is treated by others with deference. It is just as important to see that if the individual is to play this kind of sacred game, then the field must be suited to it. The environment must ensure that the individual will not pay too high a price for acting with good demeanor and that deference will be accorded him. Deference and demeanor practices must be institutionalized so that the individual will be able to project a viable, sacred self and stay in the game on a proper ritual basis.

An environment, then, in terms of the ceremonial component of activity, is a place where it is easy or difficult to play the ritual game of having a self. Where ceremonial practices are thoroughly institutionalized, as they were on Ward A, it would appear easy to be a person. Where these practices are not established, as to a degree they were not in Ward B, it would appear difficult to be a person. Why one ward comes to be a place in which it is easy to have a self and another ward comes to be a place where this is difficult depends in part on the type of patient that is recruited and the type of regime the staff attempts to maintain.

One of the bases upon which mental hospitals throughout the world segregate their patients is degree of easily apparent "mental illness." By and large this means that patients are graded according to the degree to which they violate ceremonial rules of social intercourse. There are very good practical reasons for sorting patients into different wards in this way, and in fact that institution is backward where no one bothers to do so. This grading very often means, however, that individuals who are desperately uncivil in some areas of behavior are placed in the intimate company of those who are desperately uncivil in others. Thus, individuals who are the least ready to project a sustainable self are lodged in a milieu where it is practically impossible to do so.

It is in this context that we can reconsider some interesting aspects of the effect of coercion and constraint upon the individual. If an individual is to act with proper demeanor and show proper deference, then it will be necessary for him to have areas of self-determination. He must have an expendable supply of the small indulgences which his society employs in its idiom of regard— such as cigarettes to give, chairs to proffer, food to provide, and so forth. He must have freedom of bodily movement so that it will be possible for him to assume a stance that conveys appropriate respect for others and appropriate demeanor on his own part; a patient strapped to a bed may find it impractical not to befoul himself, let alone to stand in the presence of a lady. He must have a supply of appropriate clean clothing if he is to make the sort of appearance that is expected of a well demeaned person. To look seemly may require a tie, a belt, shoe laces, a mirror, and razor blades—all of which the authorities may deem unwise to give him. He must have access to the eating utensils which his society defines as appropriate ones for use, and may find that meat cannot be circumspectly eaten with a cardboard spoon. And finally, without too much cost to himself he must be able to decline certain kinds of work, now sometimes classified as "industrial therapy," which his social group considers *infra dignitatem*.

When the individual is subject to extreme constraint he is automatically forced from the circle of the proper. The sign vehicles or physical tokens through which the customary ceremonies are performed are unavailable to him. Others may show ceremonial regard for him but it becomes impossible for him to reciprocate the show or to act in such a way as to make himself worthy of receiving it. The only ceremonial statements that are possible for him are improper ones.

The history of the care of mental cases is the history of constricting devices: constraining gloves, camisoles, floor and seat chains, handcuffs, "biter's mask," wet-packs, supervised toileting, hosing down, institutional clothing, forkless and knifeless eating, and so forth (Thomas 1953, especially p. 193; Walk 1954). The use of these devices provides significant data on the ways in which the ceremonial grounds of selfhood can be taken away. By implication we can obtain information from this history about the conditions that must be satisfied if individuals are to have selves. Unfortunately, today there are still mental institutions where the past of other hospitals can be empirically studied now. Students of interpersonal ceremony should seek these institutions out almost as urgently as students of kinship have sought out disappearing cultures.

Throughout this paper I have assumed we can learn about ceremony by studying a contemporary secular situation—that of the individual who has declined to employ the ceremonial idiom of his group in an acceptable manner and has been hospitalized. In a crosscultural view it is convenient to see this as a product of our complex division of labor which brings patients together instead of leaving each in his local circle. Further, this division of labor also brings together those who have the task of caring for these patients.

We are thus led to the special dilemma of the hospital worker: as a member of the wider society he ought to take action against mental patients, who have transgressed the rules of ceremonial order; but his occupational role obliges him to care for and protect these very people. When "milieu therapy" is stressed, these obligations further require him to convey warmth in response to hostility; relatedness in response to alienation.

We have seen (1) that hospital workers must witness improper conduct without applying usual negative sanctions, and yet (2) they must exercise disrespectful coercion over patients. A third peculiarity is that staff members may be obliged to render to patients services such as changing socks, tying shoelaces or trimming fingernails, which outside the hospital generally convey elaborate deference. In the hospital setting, such acts are likely to convey something inappropriate since the attendant at the same time exerts certain kinds of power and moral superiority over his charges. A final peculiarity in the ceremonial life of mental hospitals is that individuals collapse as units of minimal ceremonial substance and others learn that what had been taken for granted as ultimate entities are really held together by rules that can be broken with some kind of impunity. Such understanding, like one gained at war or at a kinsman's funeral, is not much talked about but it tends, perhaps, to draw staff and patients together into an unwilling group sharing undesired knowledge.

In summary, then, modern society brings transgressors of the ceremonial order to a single place, along with some ordinary members of society who make their living there. These dwell in a place of unholy acts and unholy understandings, yet some of them retain allegiance to the ceremonial order outside the hospital setting. Somehow ceremonial people must work out mechanisms and techniques for living without certain kinds of ceremony.

In this paper I have suggested that Durkheimian notions about primitive religion can be translated into concepts of deference and demeanor, and that these concepts help us to grasp some aspects of urban secular living. The implication is that in one sense this secular world is not so irreligious as we might think. Many gods have been done away with, but the individual himself stubbornly remains as a deity of considerable importance. He walks with some dignity and is the recipient of many little offerings. He is jealous of the worship due him, yet, approached in the right spirit, he is ready to forgive those who may have offended him. Because of their status relative to his, some persons will find him contaminating while others will find they contaminate him, in either case finding that they must treat him with ritual care. Perhaps the individual is so viable a god because he can actually understand the ceremonial significance of the way he is treated, and quite on his own can respond dramatically to what is proffered him. In contacts between such deities there is no need for middlemen; each of these gods is able to serve as his own priest.

NOTES

[1] Ward A was primarily given over to pharmacological research and contained two normal controls, both nineteen-year-old Mennonite conscientious objectors, two hypertensive women in their fifties, and two women in their thirties diagnosed as schizophrenic and in fair degree of remission. For two months the writer participated in the social life of the ward in the official capacity of a normal control, eating and socializing with patients during the day and sleeping overnight occasionally in a patient's room. Ward B was one given over to the study of schizophrenic girls and their so-called schizophrenogenic mothers: a seventeen-year-old girl, Betty, and her mother, Mrs. Baum; Grace, fifteen years old, and Mary, thirty-one years old, whose mothers visited the ward most days of the week. The writer spent some of the weekday on Ward B in the capacity of staff sociologist. Within limits, it is possible to treat Ward A as an example of an orderly nonmental ward and Ward B as an example of a ward with somewhat disturbed mental patients. It should be made quite clear that only one aspect of the data will be considered, and that for every event cited additional interpretations would be in order, for instance, psychoanalytical ones.

I am grateful to the administrators of these wards, Dr. Seymour Perlin and Dr. Murray Bowen, and to their staffs, for co-operation and assistance, and to Dr. John A. Clausen and Charlotte Greene Schwartz of the National Institute of Mental Health for critical suggestions.

[2] I take this distinction from Durkheim (1953, especially pp. 42–43; see also Radcliffe-Brown 1952:143–144 and Parsons 1937:430–433); sometimes the dichotomy is phrased in terms of "intrinsic" or "instrumental" versus "expressive" or "ritual."

[3] While the substantive value of ceremonial acts is felt to be quite secondary it may yet be quite appreciable. Wedding gifts in American society provide an example. It is even possible to say in some cases that if a sentiment of a given kind is to be conveyed ceremonially it will be necessary to employ a sign-vehicle which has a given amount of substantive value. Thus in the American lower-middle class, it is understood that a small investment in an engagement ring, as such investments go, may mean that the man places a small value on his fiancée as these things go, even though no one may believe that women and rings are commensurate things. In those cases where it becomes too clear that the substantive value of a ceremonial act is the only concern of the participants, as when a girl or an official receives a substantial gift from someone not interested in proper relations, then the community may respond with a feeling that their symbol system has been abused.

An interesting limiting case of the ceremonial component of activity can be found in the phenomenon of "gallantry," as when a man calmly steps aside to let a strange lady precede him into a lifeboat, or when a swordsman, fighting a duel, courteously picks up his opponent's fallen weapon and proffers it to him. Here an act which is usually a ceremonial gesture of insignificant substantive value is performed under conditions where it is known to have unexpectedly great substantive value. Here, as it were, the forms of ceremony are maintained above and beyond the call of duty.

In general, then, we can say that all ceremonial gestures differ in the degree to which they have substantive value, and that this substantive value may be systematically used as part of the communication value of the act, but that still the ceremonial order is different from the substantive one and is so understood.

[4] Some of the conceptual material on deference used in this paper derives from a study supported by a Ford Foundation grant for a propositional inventory of social stratification directed by Professor E. A. Shils of the University of Chicago. I am very grateful to Mr. Shils for orienting me to the study of deference behavior. He is not responsible for any misuse I may have made of his conception.

[5] Techniques for handling these ceremonial obligations are considered in Goffman 1955.

[6] This definition follows Radcliffe-Brown's (1952:123) except that I have widened his term "respect" to include other kinds of regard:

"There exists a ritual relation whenever a society imposes on its members a certain attitude towards an object, which attitude involves some measure of respect expressed in a traditional mode of behaviour with reference to that object."

[7] I am grateful to Dr. Seymour Perlin for bringing my attention to some of these avoidances and for pointing out the significance of them.

[8] Research on social distance scales has often most surprisingly overlooked the fact that an individual may keep his distance from others because they are too sacred for him, as well as because they are not sacred enough. The reason for this persistent error constitutes a problem in the sociology of knowledge. In general, following the students of Radcliffe-Brown, we must distinguish between "good-sacredness," which represents something too pure to make contact with, and "bad-sacredness," which represents something too impure to make contact with, contrasting both these sacred states and objects to ritually neutral matters. (See Srinivas 1952:106–107). Radcliffe-Brown (1952) does introduce the caution that in some societies the distinction between good and bad sacred is much less clearcut than in our own.

[9] Durkheim provides a fuller statement (1953:48):

"The sacred object inspires us, if not with fear, at least with respect that keeps us at a distance; at the same time it is an object of love and aspiration that we are drawn towards. Here then, is a dual sentiment which seems to be self-contradictory but does not for all that cease to be real.

"The human personality presents a notable example of this apparent duality which we have just distinguished. On the one hand, it inspires us with a religious respect that keeps us at some distance. Any encroachment upon the legitimate sphere of action of our fellow beings we regard as a sacrilege. It is, as it were, sacrosanct and thus apart. But at the same time human personality is the outstanding object of our sympathy, and we endeavour to develop it."

[10] The only source I know on touch systems is the very interesting work by Edward Gross (1949) on rights regarding pinching of females of private secretarial rank in a commercial business office.

[11] The then head nurse, a male, initiated arm embraces with the physician acting as ward administrator. This seemed to create a false note and was felt to be forward. The nurse, interestingly enough, has left the service. It should be added that on one ward in the hospital, a ward given over to the close study of a small number of highly delinquent boys, patients and staff of all ranks, including doctors, apparently formed a single ceremonial group. Members of the group were linked by symmetrical rules of familiarity, so that it was permissible for an eight-year-old to call the ward administrator by his first name, joke with him, and swear in his presence.

[12] A kind of ceremonial profanation also seems to exist with respect to substantive rules. In law what are sometimes called "spite actions" provide illustrations, as does the phenomenon of vandalism. But, as previously suggested, these represent ways in which the substantive order is abused for ceremonial purposes.

### REFERENCES CITED

ANONYMOUS
  1836   The Laws of Etiquette. Philadelphia, Carey, Lee and Blanchard.
DE QUINCEY, THOMAS
  1890   French and English Manners. *In* Collected Writings of Thomas De Quincey, ed. David Masson, 14:327–334. 14 vols.; Edinburgh, Adams and Charles Black.
DICHTER, ERNEST
  1950   A Psychological Study of the Doctor-Patient Relationship. California Medical Association, Alameda County Medical Association.
DOUGLAS, R. K.
  1895   Society in China. London, Innes.
DURKHEIM, EMILE
  1953   The Determination of Moral Facts. *In* Sociology and Philosophy, trans. D. F. Pocock, pp. 35–62. Glencoe, Ill., Free Press.
  1954   The Elementary Forms of the Religious Life, trans, J. W. Swain. Glencoe, Ill., Free Press.
GARVIN, P. L. and S. H. RIESENBERG
  1952   Respect Behavior on Ponape: An Ethnolinguistic Study. American Anthropologist 54:201–220.
GOFFMAN, ERVING
  1952   Social Research, Inc., MS.
  1955   On Face-Work. Psychiatry 18:213–231.
  Ms.    Alienation from Interaction. Human Relations.
GROSS, EDWARD
  1949   Informal Relations and the Social Organization of Work. Unpublished Ph.D. dissertation, Department of Sociology, University of Chicago.
HODGE, F. W.
  1907   Etiquette: Handbook of American Indians. Washington, D.C., Government Printing Office.
MURDOCK, GEORGE P.
  1949   Social Structure. New York, Macmillan.
PARSONS, TALCOTT
  1937   The Structure of Social Action. New York, McGraw-Hill.

RADCLIFFE-BROWN, A. R.
  1952 Taboo. *In* Structure and Function in Primitive Society, pp. 133–152. Glencoe, Ill., Free Press.
SCHWARTZ, MORRIS S. and ALFRED H. STANTON
  1950 A Social Psychological Study of Incontinence. Psychiatry 13:399–416.
SIMMEL, GEORG
  1950 The Sociology of Georg Simmel, trans. and ed. Kurt Wolff. Glencoe, Ill., Free Press.
SOCIAL RESEARCH, INC.
  1952 Unpublished study of small business managers. Ms.
SRINIVAS, M. N.
  1952 Religion and Society among the Coorgs of South India. Oxford, Oxford University Press.
TAXEL, HAROLD
  1953 Authority Structure in a Mental Hospital Ward. Unpublished Master's thesis, Department of Sociology, University of Chicago.
THOMAS, W. R.
  1953 The Unwilling Patient. Journal of Mental Science 99: 191–201.
THOULESS, R. H.
  1951 General and Social Psychology. London, University Tutorial Press.
TROLLOPE, MRS.
  1832 Domestic Manners of the Americans. 2 vols.; London, Whittaker, Treacher.
WALK, ALEXANDER
  1954 Some Aspects of the "Moral Treatment" of the Insane up to 1854. Journal of Mental Science 100:807–837.
WILLOUGHBY, ROBERT H
  1953 The Attendant in the State Mental Hospital. Unpublished Master's thesis, Department of Sociology, University of Chicago.
WITTKOWER, E. D. and J. D. LA TENDRESSE
  1955 Rehabilitation of Chronic Schizophrenics by a New Method of Occupational Therapy. British Journal of Medical Psychology 28:42–47.

# Ecologic Relationships of Ethnic Groups in Swat, North Pakistan

FREDRIK BARTH
*Cambridge University*

THE importance of ecologic factors for the form and distribution of cultures has usually been analyzed by means of a culture area concept. This concept has been developed with reference to the aboriginal cultures of North America (Kroeber 1939). Attempts at delimiting culture areas in Asia by similar procedures have proved extremely difficult (Bacon 1946, Kroeber 1947, Miller 1953), since the distribution of cultural types, ethnic groups, and natural areas rarely coincide. Coon (1951) speaks of Middle Eastern society as being built on a mosaic principle—many ethnic groups with radically different cultures co-reside in an area in symbiotic relations of variable intimacy. Referring to a similar structure, Furnivall (1944) describes the Netherlands Indies as a plural society. The common characteristic in these two cases is the combination of ethnic segmentation and economic interdependence. Thus the "environment" of any one ethnic group is not only defined by natural conditions, but also by the presence and activities of the other ethnic groups on which it depends. Each group exploits only a section of the total environment, and leaves large parts of it open for other groups to exploit.

This interdependence is analogous to that of the different animal species in a habitat. As Kroeber (1947:330) emphasizes, culture area classifications are essentially ecologic; thus detailed ecologic considerations, rather than geographical areas of subcontinental size, should offer the point of departure. The present paper attempts to apply a more specific ecologic approach to a case study of distribution by utilizing some of the concepts of animal ecology, particularly the concept of a *niche*—the place of a group in the total environment, its relations to resources and competitors (cf. Allee 1949:516).

*Groups.* The present example is simple, relatively speaking, and is concerned with the three major ethnic groups in Swat State, North-West frontier Province, Pakistan.[1] These are: (1) *Pathans*—Pashto-speaking (Iranian language family) sedentary agriculturalists; (2) *Kohistanis*—speakers of Dardic languages, practicing agriculture and transhumant herding; and (3) *Gujars*—Gujri-speaking (a lowland Indian dialect) nomadic herders. Kohistanis are probably the ancient inhabitants of most of Swat; Pathans entered as conquerors in successive waves between A.D. 1000–1600, and Gujars probably first appeared in the area some 400 years ago. Pathans of Swat State number about 450,000, Kohistanis perhaps 30,000. The number of Gujars in the area is difficult to estimate.

The centralized state organization in Swat was first established in 1917, and the most recent accretion was annexed in 1947, so the central organization has no relevance for the distributional problems discussed here.

*Area.* Swat State contains sections of two main valleys, those of the Swat

1079

and the Indus Rivers. The Swat River rises in the high mountains to the North, among 18,000 foot peaks. As it descends and grows in volume, it enters a deep gorge. This upper section of the valley is thus very narrow and steep. From approximately 5,000 feet, the Swat valley becomes increasingly wider as one proceeds southward, and is flanked by ranges descending from 12,000 to 6,000 feet in altitude. The river here has a more meandering course, and the valley bottom is a flat, extensive alluvial deposit.

The east border of Swat State follows the Indus River; only its west bank and tributaries are included in the area under discussion. The Indus enters the area as a very large river; it flows in a spectacular gorge, 15,000 feet deep and from 12 to 16 miles wide. Even in the north, the valley bottom is less than 3,000 feet above sea level, while the surrounding mountains reach 18,000 feet. The tributary valleys are consequently short and deeply cut, with an extremely steep profile. Further to the south, the surrounding mountain ranges recede from the river banks and lose height, the Indus deposits some sediment, and the tributary streams form wider valleys.

Climatic variations in the area are a function of altitude. Precipitation is low throughout. The southern, low-altitude areas have long, hot summers and largely steppe vegetation. The Indus gorge has been described as "a desert embedded between icy gravels" (Spate 1954:381). The high mountains are partly covered by permanent ice and snow, and at lower levels by natural mountain meadows in the brief summer season. Between these extremes is a broad belt (from 6,000 to 11,000 feet) of forest, mainly of pine and deodar.

*Pathan-Kohistani distribution.* Traditional history, in part relating to place-names of villages and uninhabited ruins, indicates that Kohistani inhabitants were driven progressively northward by Pathan invaders (cf. Stein 1929:33, 83). This northward spread has now been checked, and the border between Kohistani and Pathan territories has been stable for some time. The last Pathan expansion northward in the Swat valley took place under the leadership of the Saint Akhund Sadiq Baba, eight generations ago. To understand the factors responsible for the stability of the present ethnic border, it is necessary to examine the specific ecologic requirements of the present Pathan economy and organization.

Pathans of Swat live in a complex, multi-caste society. The landholding Pakhtun caste is organized in localized, segmentary, unilineal descent groups; other castes and occupational groups are tied to them as political clients and economic serfs. Subsistence is based on diversified and well-developed plow agriculture. The main crops are wheat, maize, and rice; much of the plowed land is watered by artificial irrigation. Manuring is practiced, and several systems of crop rotation and regular fallow-field rhythms are followed, according to the nature of the soil and water supply. All rice is irrigated, with nursery beds and transplantation.

Only part of the Pathan population is actively engaged in agriculture. Various other occupational groups perform specialized services in return for payment in kind, and thus require that the agriculturalists produce a consider-

able surplus. Further, and perhaps more importantly, the political system
depends on a strong hierarchical organization of landowners and much political
activity, centering around the men's houses (*hujra*). This activity diverts
much manpower from productive pursuits. The large and well-organized
Pathan tribes are found in the lower parts of the Swat valley and along the
more southerly tributaries of the Indus, occupying broad and fertile alluvial
plains. A simpler form of political organization is found along the northern
fringes of Pathan territory. It is based on families of saintly descent, and is
characterized by the lack of men's houses. This simplification renders the
economy of the community more efficient (1) by eliminating the wasteful
potlatch-type feasts of the men's houses, and (2) by vesting political office in
saintly persons of inviolate status, thus eliminating the numerous retainers
that protect political leaders in other Pathan areas.

Pathan territory extends to a critical ecologic threshold: the limits within
which two crops can be raised each year. This is largely a function of altitude.
Two small outliers of Pashto-speaking people (Jag, in Duber valley, and a
section of Kalam) are found north of this limit. They are unlike other Pathans,
and similar to their Kohistani neighbors in economy and political organization.

The conclusion that the limits of double cropping constitute the effective
check on further Pathan expansion seems unavoidable. Pathan economy and
political organization requires that agricultural labor produce considerable
surplus. Thus in the marginal, high-altitude areas, the political organization
is modified and "economized" (as also in the neighboring Dir area), while
beyond these limits of double cropping the economic and social system can
not survive at all.

Kohistanis are not restricted by this barrier. The Kohistani ethnic group
apparently once straddled it; and, as they were driven north by invading
Pathans, they freely crossed what to Pathans was a restricting barrier. This
must be related to differences between Kohistani and Pathan political and
economic organization, and consequent differences in their ecologic requirements.

Kohistanis, like Pathans, practice a developed plow agriculture. Due to
the terrain they occupy, their fields are located on narrow artificial terraces,
which require considerable engineering skill for their construction. Parts of
Kohistan receive no summer rains; the streams, fed from the large snow re-
serves in the mountains, supply water to the fields through complex and
extensive systems of irrigation. Some manuring is practiced. Climatic conditions modify the types of food crops. Maize and millet are most important;
wheat and rice can only be raised in a few of the low-lying areas. The summer
season is short, and fields produce only one crop a year.

Agricultural methods are thus not very different from those of Pathans,
but the net production of fields is much less. Kohistanis, however, have a
two-fold economy, for transhumant herding is as important as agriculture.
Sheep, goats, cattle, and water-buffalo are kept for wool, meat, and milk.

The herds depend in summer on mountain pastures, where most of the Kohistanis spend between four and eight months each year, depending on local conditions. In some areas the whole population migrates through as many as five seasonal camps, from winter dwellings in the valley bottom to summer campsites at a 14,000 foot altitude, leaving the fields around the abandoned low-altitude dwellings to remain practically untended. In the upper Swat valley, where the valley floor is covered with snow some months of the year, winter fodder is collected and stored for the animals.

By having two strings to their bow, so to speak, the Kohistanis are able to wrest a living from inhospitable mountain areas which fall short of the minimal requirements for Pathan occupation. In these areas, Kohistanis long retained their autonomy, the main territories being conquered by Swat State in 1926, 1939, and 1947. They were, and still are, organized in politically separate village districts of from 400 to 2000 inhabitants. Each community is subdivided into a number of loosely connected patrilineal lineages. The central political institution is the village council, in which all landholding minimal lineages have their representatives. Each community also includes a family of blacksmith-cum-carpenter specialists, and a few households of tenants or farm laborers.

Neighboring communities speaking the same dialect or language[2] could apparently fuse politically when under external pressure, in which case they were directed by a common council of prominent leaders from all constituent lineages. But even these larger units were unable to withstand the large forces of skilled fighters which Pathans of the Swat area could mobilize. These forces were estimated at 15,000 by the British during the Ambeyla campaign in 1862 (cf. Roberts 1898, vol. 2:7).

*"Natural" subareas.* The present Swat State appears to the Kohistanis as a single natural area, since, as an ethnic group, they once occupied all of it, and since their economy can function anywhere within it. With the advent of invading Pathan tribes, the Kohistanis found themselves unable to defend the land. But the land which constitutes one natural area to Kohistanis is divided by a line which Pathans were unable to cross. From the Pathan point of view, it consists of two natural areas, one containing the ecologic requisites for Pathan occupation, the other uninhabitable.[3] Thus the Kohistanis were permitted to retain a part of their old territory in spite of their military inferiority, while in the remainder they were either assimilated as serfs in the conquering Pathan society or were expelled.

From the purely synchronic point of view, the present Pathan-Kohistani distribution presents a simple and static picture of two ethnic groups representing two discrete culture areas, and with a clear correspondence between these culture areas and natural areas: Pathans in broad valleys with a hot climate and scrub vegetation as against Kohistanis in high mountains with a severe climate and coniferous forest cover. Through the addition of time depth, the possibility arises of breaking down the concept of a "natural area" into specific ecologic components in relation to the requirements of specific economies.

Analysis of the distribution of Gujars in relation to the other ethnic groups requires such a procedure. Gujars are found in both Pathan and Kohistani areas, following two different economic patterns in both areas: transhumant herding, and true nomadism. But while they are distributed throughout all of the Pathan territory, they are found only in the western half of Kohistan, and neither reside nor visit in the eastern half. The division into mountain and valley seems irrelevant to the Gujars, while the mountain area—inhospitable to Pathans and usable to Kohistanis—is divided by a barrier which Gujars do not cross. The economy and other features of Gujar life must be described before this distribution and its underlying factors can be analyzed.

Gujars constitute a floating population of herders, somewhat ill-defined due to a variable degree of assimilation into the host populations. In physical type, as well as in dress and language, the majority of them are easily distinguishable. Their music, dancing, and manner of celebrating rites of passage differ from those of their hosts. Their political status is one of dependence on the host population.

The Gujar population is subdivided into a number of named patrilineal tribes or clans—units claiming descent from a common known or unknown ancestor, but without supporting genealogies. There are sometimes myths relating to the clan origin, and these frequently serve as etymologies for the clan name. The clans vary greatly in size and only the smallest are localized. The effective descent units are patrilineal lineages of limited depth, though there is greater identification between unrelated Gujars bearing the same clan name than between strangers of different clans. These clans are irrelevant to marriage regulations. There is little intermarriage between Gujars and the host group.

The economy of the Gujars depends mainly on the herding of sheep, goats, cattle, and water buffalo. In addition to animal products, Gujars require some grain (maize, wheat, or millet) which they get by their own agriculture in marginal, high-altitude fields or by trade in return for clarified butter, meat, or wool. Their essential requirements may be satisfied by two rather different patterns of life—transhumance and true nomadism. Pathans differentiate persons pursuing these two patterns by the terms Gujar and Ajer, respectively, and consider them to be ethnic subdivisions. In fact, Gujars may change their pattern of life from one to the other.

Transhumance is practiced mainly by Gujars in the Pathan area, but also occasionally in Kohistan (see map). Symbiotic relationships between Gujars and Pathans take various forms, some quite intimate. Pathans form a multi-caste society, into which Gujars are assimilated as a specialized occupational caste of herders. Thus most Pathan villages contain a small number of Gujars— these may speak Gujri as their home language and retain their separate culture, or may be assimilated to the extent of speaking only Pashto. Politically

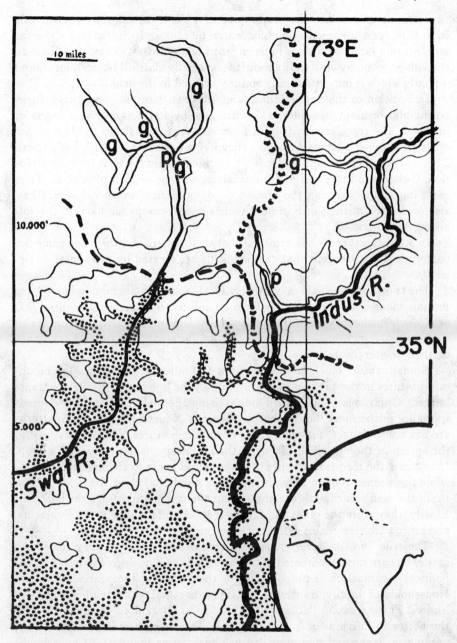

Sketch map of area of Swat State, Pakistan. Stippled area: under cultivation by Pathans. Broken line: border between Pathan and Kohistani areas. Dotted line: border of area utilized by Gujars (the two borders coincide towards the southeast). p: outlying Pathan communities. g: outlying communities of transhumant Gujars. Gujar nomads spend the summer in the mountains central and north on the map, and winter in the southernmost area of the map. Inset: location of sketch map.

they are integrated into the community in a client or serf status. Their role is to care for the animals (mainly water buffalo and draft oxen) either as servants of a landowner or as independent buffalo owners. They contribute to the village economy with milk products (especially clarified butter), meat, and manure, which is important and carefully utilized in the fields.

In addition to their agricultural land, most Pathan villages control neighboring hills or mountain-sides, which are used by Pathans only as a source of firewood. The transhumant Gujars, however, shift their flocks to these higher areas for summer pasture, for which they pay a fixed rate, in kind, per animal. This rent supplies the landholders with clarified butter for their own consumption. Gujars also serve as agricultural laborers in the seasons of peak activity, most importantly during the few hectic days of rice transplantation. They also seed fields of their own around their summer camps for harvest the following summer.

In Kohistan there is less symbiosis between Gujars and their hosts but the pattern is similar, except that the few fields are located by the winter settlements.

The transhumant cycle may be very local. Some Gujars merely move from Pathan villages in the valley bottom to hillside summer settlements 1,000 or 1,500 feet above, visible from the village. Others travel 20 or 30 miles to summer grazing grounds in the territory of a different Pathan tribe from that of their winter hosts.

Nomads travel much farther, perhaps 100 miles, utilizing the high mountain pastures in the summer and wintering in the low plains. While the transhumant Gujars place their main emphasis on the water buffalo, the nomads specialize in the more mobile sheep and goats. Nonetheless, the two patterns are not truly distinct, for some groups combine features of both. They spend the spring in the marginal hills of Pathan territory, where they seed a crop. In summer the men take the herds of sheep and goats to the high mountains, while the women remain behind to care for the buffalo and the fields. In autumn the men return with the herds, reap the crops, and utilize the pastures. Finally, they store the grain and farm out their buffalo with Pathan villagers, and retire to the low plains with their sheep and goats for the winter.

The true nomads never engage in agricultural pursuits; they may keep cattle, but are not encumbered with water buffalo. The degree of autonomous political organization is proportional to the length of the yearly migration. Households of locally transhumant Gujars are tied individually to Pathan leaders. Those crossing Pathan tribal borders are organized in small lineages, the better to bargain for low grazing tax. The true nomads co-ordinate the herding of flocks and migrations of people from as many as 50 households, who may also camp together for brief periods. Such groups generally consist of several small lineages, frequently of different clans, related by affinal or cognatic ties and under the direction of a single leader. Thus, though migrating through areas controlled by other political organizations, they retain a moderately well-defined organization of their own.

*Gujar distribution.* The co-existence of Gujars and Pathans in one area poses no problem, in view of the symbiotic relations sketched above. Pathans have the military strength to control the mountainous flanks of the valleys they occupy, but have no effective means of utilizing these areas. This leaves an unoccupied ecologic niche which the Gujar ethnic group has entered and to which it has accommodated itself in a politically dependent position through a pattern of transhumance. Symbiotic advantages make the relationship satisfactory and enduring. It is tempting to see the expansion of Gujars into the area as resulting from the Pathan expulsion of Kohistanis from the valley. The Kohistanis, through their own pattern of transhumance, formerly filled the niche and it became vacant only when the specialized agricultural Pathans conquered the valley bottom and replaced the Kohistanis.

But the co-existence of Gujars and Kohistanis poses a problem, since the two groups appear to utilize the same natural resources and therefore to occupy the same ecologic niche. One would expect competition, leading to the expulsion of one or the other ethnic group from the area. However, armed conflict between the two groups is rare, and there is no indication that one is increasing at the expense of the other. On the other hand, if a stable symbiotic or noncompetitive relationship may be established between the two groups, why should Gujars be concentrated in West Kohistan, and not inhabit the essentially similar East Kohistan area? The answer must be sought not only in the natural environment and in features of the Gujar economy, but also in the relevant social environment—in features of Kohistani economy and organization which affect the niche suited to utilization by Gujars.

*East vs. West Kohistan.* As indicated, Kohistanis have a two-fold economy combining agriculture and transhumant herding, and live in moderately large village communities. Although most Gujars also practice some agriculture, it remains a subsidiary activity. It is almost invariably of a simple type dependent on water from the melting snow in spring and monsoon rains in summer, rather than on irrigation, and on shifting fields rather than manuring. The Kohistanis have a more equal balance between agriculture and herding. The steep slopes require complex terracing and irrigation, which preclude shifting agriculture and encourage more intensive techniques. The size of herds is limited by the size of fields, which supply most of the winter fodder, since natural fields and mountain meadows are too distant from the winter dwellings to permit haying. Ecologic factors relevant to this balance between the two dominant economic activities become of prime importance for Kohistani distribution and settlement density.

There are significant differences in this respect between East and West Kohistan, i.e. between the areas drained by the Indus and the Swat Rivers respectively. While the Indus and the lowest sections of its tributaries flow at no more than 3,000 feet, the Swat River descends from 8,000 to 5,000 feet in the section of its valley occupied by Kohistanis. The higher altitude in the west has several effects on the economic bases for settlement: (a) Agricultural production is reduced by the shorter season and lower temperatures in the higher western valley. (b) The altitude difference combined with slightly higher precipitation in the west results in a greater accumulation of snow. The Indus bank is rarely covered with snow, but in the upper Swat valley snow tends to accumulate through the winter and remains in the valley bottom until April or May. Thus the sedentary stock-owner in West Kohistan must provide stored fodder for his animals throughout the four months of winter. (c) The shorter season of West Kohistan eliminates rice (most productive per land unit) as a food crop and reduces maize (most advantageous in return per weight of seed) in favor of the hardier millet.

These features serve to restrict the agricultural production of West Kohistan, and therefore the number of animals that can be kept during the winter season. No parallel restrictions limit the possibility for summer grazing. Both East and West Kohistan are noteworthy for their large, lush mountain meadows and other good summer grazing, and are thus rich in the natural resources which animal herders are able to exploit. However, these mountain pastures are only seasonal; no population can rely on them for year-round sustenance. Consequently, patterns of transhumance or nomadism are developed to utilize the mountain area in its productive season, while relying on other areas or techniques the rest of the year. True nomads move to a similar ecologic niche in another area. People practicing transhumance generally utilize a different niche by reliance on alternative techniques, here agriculture and the utilization of stored animal fodder. There appears to be a balance in the productivity of these two niches, as exploited by local transhumance in East Kohistan. Thus, in the Indus drainage, Kohistanis are able to support a human and animal population of sufficient size through the winter by means of agriculture and stored food, so as to utilize fully the summer pastures of the surrounding mountains. In an ecologic sense, the local population fills both niches. There is no such balance in the Swat valley. Restrictions on agricultural production limit the animal and human population, and prevent full exploitation of the mountain pastures. This niche is thus left partly vacant and available to the nomadic Gujars, who winter in the low plains outside the area. Moreover, scattered communities of transhumant Gujars may be found in the western areas, mainly at the very tops of the valleys. With techniques and patterns of consumption different from those of Kohistanis, they are able to survive locally in areas which fall short of the minimal requirements for permanent Kohistani occupation. The present distribution of Gujars in Kohistan, limiting them to the western half of the area, would seem to be a result of these factors.

A simple but rather crucial final point should be made in this analysis: why do Kohistanis have first choice, so to speak, and Gujars only enter niches left vacant by them? Since they are able to exploit the area more fully, one might expect Gujars eventually to replace Kohistanis. Organizational factors enter here. Kohistanis form compact, politically organized villages of considerable size. The Gujar seasonal cycle prevents a similar development among them. In winter they descend into Pathan areas, or even out of tribal territory and into the administered areas of Pakistan. They are thus seasonally subject to organizations more powerful than their own, and are forced to filter through territories controlled by such organizations on their seasonal migrations. They must accommodate themselves to this situation by travelling in small, unobtrusive groups, and wintering in dispersed settlements. Though it is conceivable that Gujars might be able to develop the degree of political organization required to replace Kohistanis in a purely Kohistani environment, their dependence on more highly organized neighboring areas still makes this impossible.

The transhumant Gujar settlements in Kohistan represent groups of former nomads who were given permission by the neighboring Kohistanis to settle, and they are kept politically subservient. The organizational superiority of the already established Kohistanis prevents them, as well as the nomads, from appropriating any rights over productive means or areas. What changes will occur under the present control by the State of Swat is a different matter.

This example may serve to illustrate certain viewpoints applicable to a discussion of the ecologic factors in the distribution of ethnic groups, cultures, or economies, and the problem of "mosaic" co-residence in parts of Asia.

(1) The distribution of ethnic groups is controlled not by objective and fixed "natural areas" but by the distribution of the specific ecologic niches which the group, with its particular economic and political organization, is able to exploit. In the present example, what appears as a single natural area to Kohistanis is subdivided as far as Pathans are concerned, and this division is cross-cut with respect to the specific requirements of Gujars.

(2) Different ethnic groups will establish themselves in stable co-residence in an area if they exploit different ecologic niches, and especially if they can thus establish symbiotic economic relations, as those between Pathans and Gujars in Swat.

(3) If different ethnic groups are able to exploit the same niches fully, the militarily more powerful will normally replace the weaker, as Pathans have replaced Kohistanis.

(4) If different ethnic groups exploit the same ecologic niches but the weaker of them is better able to utilize marginal environments, the groups may co-reside in one area, as Gujars and Kohistanis in West Kohistan.

Where such principles are operative to the extent they are in much of West and South Asia, the concept of "culture areas," as developed for native North America, becomes inapplicable. Different ethnic groups and culture types will have overlapping distributions and disconforming borders, and will be socially related to a variable degree, from the "watchful co-residence" of Kohistanis and Gujars to the intimate economic, political, and ritual symbiosis of the Indian caste system. The type of correspondence between gross ecologic classification and ethnic distribution documented for North America by Kroeber (1939) will rarely if ever be found. Other conceptual tools are needed for the study of culture distribution in Asia. Their development would seem to depend on analysis of specific detailed distributions in an ecologic framework, rather than by speculation on a larger geographical scale.

## NOTES

[1] Based on field work February–November 1954, aided by a grant from the Royal Norwegian Research Council.

[2] There are four main Dardic languages spoken in Swat State: Torwali, Gawri, and Eastern and Western dialect of Kohistəi or Mayän (Barth and Morgenstierne Ms.).

[3] The Pathan attitude toward the Kohistan area might best be illustrated by the warnings I was given when I was planning to visit the area: "Full of terrible mountains covered by many-colored snow and emitting poisonous gases causing head and stomach pains when you cross the high passes; inhabited by robbers, and snakes that coil up and leap ten feet into the air; with no villages, only scattered houses on the mountain tops!"

## BIBLIOGRAPHY

ALLEE, W. C. et al.:
    1949  Principles of animal ecology. Philadelphia, W. B. Saunders Company.
BARTH, FREDRIK
    1956  Indus and Swat Kohistan—an ethnographic survey. Studies honoring the centennial of Universitetets Etnografiske Museum Vol. II, Oslo.
BARTH, FREDRIK and GEORG MORGENSTIERNE
    Ms.  Samples of some Southern Dardic dialects. In press, Norsk Tidsskrift for Sprog-videnskap.
BACON, ELIZABETH
    1946  A preliminary attempt to determine the culture areas of Asia. Southwestern Journal of Anthropology 2:117–132.
COON, CARLETON S.
    1951  Caravan. New York, Henry Holt & Co.
FURNIVALL, J. S.
    1944  Netherlands India—a study of plural economy. Cambridge University Press.
KROEBER, A. L.
    1939  Cultural and natural areas of native North America. Berkeley and Los Angeles, University of California Press.
    1947  Culture groupings in Asia. Southwestern Journal of Anthropology 3:322–330.
MILLER, ROBERT J.
    1953  Areas and institutions in Eastern Asia. Southwestern Journal of Anthropology 9:203–211.
ROBERTS, FIELD MARSHAL LORD
    1898  Forty-one years in India. London, Richard Bentley & Son.
SPATE, O. H. K.
    1954  India and Pakistan. London, Methuen.
STEIN, SIR AUREL
    1929  On Alexander's track to the Indus. London, Macmillan & Co.

# Ritual and Social Change: A Javanese Example

CLIFFORD GEERTZ

*Harvard University*

AS IN so many areas of anthropological concern, functionalism, either of the sociological sort associated with the name of Radcliffe-Brown or of the social-psychological sort associated with Malinowski, has tended to dominate recent theoretical discussions of the role of religion in society. Stemming originally from Durkheim's *The Elementary Forms of the Religious Life* (1947) and Robertson-Smith's *Lectures on the Religion of the Semites* (1894), the sociological approach (or, as the British anthropologists prefer to call it, the social anthropological approach) emphasizes the manner in which belief and particularly ritual reinforce the traditional social ties between individuals; it stresses the way in which the social structure of a group is strengthened and perpetuated through the ritualistic or mythic symbolization of the underlying social values upon which it rests. The social-psychological approach, of which Frazer and Tylor were perhaps the pioneers but which found its clearest statement in Malinowski's classic *Magic, Science and Religion* (1948), emphasizes what religion does for the individual—how it satisfies both his cognitive and affective demands for a stable, comprehensible, and coercible world, and how it enables him to maintain an inner security in the face of natural contingency. Together, the two approaches have given us an increasingly detailed understanding of the social and psychological "functions" of religion in a wide range of societies.

Where the functional approach has been least impressive, however, is in dealing with social change. As has been noted by several writers (Leach 1954; Merton 1949), the emphasis on systems in balance, on social homeostasis, and on timeless structural pictures, leads to a bias in favor of "well-integrated" societies in a stable equilibrium and to a tendency to emphasize the functional aspects of a people's social usages and customs rather than their disfunctional implications. In analyses of religion this static, ahistorical approach has led to a somewhat over-conservative view of the role of ritual and belief in social life. Despite cautionary comments by Kluckhohn (1944) and others on the "gain and cost" of various religious practices such as witchcraft, the tendency has been consistently to stress the harmonizing, integrating, and psychologically supportive aspects of religious patterns rather than the disruptive, disintegrative, and psychologically disturbing aspects; to demonstrate the manner in which religion preserves social and psychological structure rather than the manner in which it destroys or transforms it. Where change has been treated, as in Redfield's work on Yucatan (1941), it has largely been in terms of progressive disintegration: "The changes in culture that in Yucatan appear to 'go along with' lessening isolation and homogeneity are seen to be chiefly three: disorganization of the culture, secularization and individualization"

32

(p. 339). Yet even a passing knowledge of our own religious history makes us hesitate to affirm such a simply "positive" role for religion generally.

It is the thesis of this paper that one of the major reasons for the inability of functional theory to cope with change lies in its failure to treat sociological and cultural processes on equal terms; almost inevitably one of the two is either ignored or is sacrificed to become but a simple reflex, a "mirror image," of the other. Either culture is regarded as wholly derivative from the forms of social organization—the approach characteristic of the British structuralists as well as many American sociologists; or the forms of social organization are regarded as behavioral embodiments of cultural patterns—the approach of Malinowski and many American anthropologists. In either case, the lesser term tends to drop out as a dynamic factor and we are left either with an omnibus concept of culture ("that complex whole . . . ") or else with a completely comprehensive concept of social structure ("social structure is not an aspect of culture, but the entire culture of a given people handled in a special frame of theory" [Fortes 1953]). In such a situation, the dynamic elements in social change which arise from the failure of cultural patterns to be perfectly congruent with the forms of social organization are largely incapable of formulation. "We functionalists," E. R. Leach has recently remarked, "are not really 'anti-historical' by principle; it is simply that we do not know how to fit historical materials into our framework of concepts" (1954:282).

A revision of the concepts of functional theory so as to make them capable of dealing more effectively with "historical materials" might well begin with an attempt to distinguish analytically between the cultural and social aspects of human life, and to treat them as independently variable yet mutually interdependent factors. Though separable only conceptually, culture and social structure will then be seen to be capable of a wide range of modes of integration with one another, of which the simple isomorphic mode is but a limiting case—a case common only in societies which have been stable over such an extended time as to make possible a close adjustment between social and cultural aspects. In most societies, where change is a characteristic rather than an abnormal occurrence, we shall expect to find more or less radical discontinuities between the two. I would argue that it is in these very discontinuities that we shall find some of the primary driving forces in change.

One of the more useful ways—but far from the only one—of distinguishing between culture and social system is to see the former as an ordered system of meaning and of symbols, in terms of which social interaction takes place; and to see the latter as the pattern of social interaction itself (Parsons and Shils 1951). On the one level there is the framework of beliefs, expressive symbols, and values in terms of which individuals define their world, express their feelings, and make their judgments; on the other level there is the ongoing process of interactive behavior, whose persistent form we call social structure. Culture is the fabric of meaning in terms of which human beings interpret their experience and guide their action; social structure is the form that action takes, the actually existing network of social relations. Culture and social structure are then but different abstractions from the same phenomena. The one considers social action in respect to its meaning for those who carry it out, the other considers it in terms of its contribution to the functioning of some social system.

The nature of the distinction between culture and social system is brought out more clearly when one considers the contrasting sorts of integration characteristic of each of them. This contrast is between what Sorokin (1937) has called "logico-meaningful integration" and what he has called "causal-functional integration." By logico-meaningful integration, characteristic of culture, is meant the sort of integration one finds in a Bach fugue, in Catholic dogma, or in the general theory of relativity; it is a unity of style, of logical implication, of meaning and value. By causal-functional integration, characteristic of the social system, is meant the kind of integration one finds in an organism, where all the parts are united in a single causal web; each part is an element in a reverberating causal ring which "keeps the system going." And because these two types of integration are not identical, because the particular form one of them takes does not directly imply the form the other will take, there is an inherent incongruity and tension between the two and between both of them and a third element, the pattern of motivational integration within the individual which we usually call personality structure:

"Thus conceived, a social system is only one of three aspects of the structuring of a completely concrete system of social action. The other two are the personality systems of the individual actors and the cultural system which is built into their action. Each of the three must be considered to be an independent focus of the organization of the elements of the action system in the sense that no one of them is theoretically reducible to terms of one or a combination of the other two. Each is indispensable to the other two in the sense that without personalities and culture there would be no social system and so on around the roster of logical possibilities. But this interdependence and interpenetration is a very different matter from reducibility, which would mean that the important properties and processes of one class of system could be theoretically *derived* from our theoretical knowledge of one or both of the other two. The action frame of reference is common to all three and this fact makes certain "transformations" between them possible. But on the level of theory here attempted they do not constitute a single system, however this might turn out to be on some other theoretical level" (Parsons 1951:6).

I will attempt to demonstrate the utility of this more dynamic functionalist approach by applying it to a particular case of a ritual which failed to function properly. I shall try to show how an approach which does not distinguish the "logico-meaningful" cultural aspects of the ritual pattern from the "causal-functional" social structural aspects is unable to account adequately for this ritual failure, and how an approach which does so distinguish them is able to analyze more explicitly the cause of the trouble. It will further be argued that such an approach is able to avoid the simplistic view of the functional role of religion in society which sees that role merely as structure-conserving, and to substitute for it a more complex conception of the relations between religious belief and practice and secular social life. Historical materials can be fitted into such a conception, and the functional analysis of religion can therefore be widened to deal more adequately with processes of change.

### THE SETTING

The case to be described is that of a funeral held in Modjokuto, a small town in eastern Central Java.[1] A young boy, about ten years of age, who was living with his uncle and aunt, died very suddenly but his death, instead of being followed by the usual hurried, subdued, yet methodically efficient Javanese funeral ceremony and burial routine, brought on an extended period of pronounced social strain and severe psychological tension. The complex of beliefs and rituals which had for generations brought countless Javanese safely through the difficult post-mortem period suddenly failed to work with its accustomed effectiveness. To understand why it failed demands knowledge and understanding of a whole range of social and cultural changes which have taken place in Java since the first decades of this century. This disrupted funeral was in fact but a microcosmic example of the broader conflicts, structural dissolutions, and attempted reintegrations which, in one form or another, are characteristic of contemporary Indonesian society.

The religious tradition of Java, particularly of the peasantry, is a composite of Indian, Islamic, and indigenous Southeast Asian elements (Landon 1949). The rise of large, militaristic kingdoms in the inland rice basins in the early centuries of the Christian era was associated with the diffusion of Hinduist and Buddhist culture patterns to the island; the expansion of international maritime trade in the port cities of the northern coast in the fifteenth and sixteenth centuries was associated with the diffusion of Islamic patterns. Working their way into the peasant mass, these two world religions became fused with the underlying animistic traditions characteristic of the whole Malaysian culture area. The result was a balanced syncretism of myth and ritual in which Hindu gods and goddesses, Moslem prophets and saints, and local place spirits and demons all found a proper place.

The central ritual form in this syncretism is a communal feast, called the *slametan*. Slametans, which are given with only slight variations in form and content on almost all occasions of religious significance—at passage points in the life cycle, on calendrical holidays, at certain stages of the crop cycle, on changing one's residence, etc.—are intended to be both offerings to the spirits and commensal mechanisms of social integration for the living. The meal, which consists of specially prepared dishes, each symbolic of a particular religious concept, is cooked by the female members of one nuclear family household and set out on mats in the middle of the living-room. The male head of the household invites the male heads of the eight or ten contiguous households to attend; no close neighbor is ignored in favor of one further away. After a speech by the host explaining the spiritual purpose of the feast and a short Arabic chant, each man takes a few hurried, almost furtive, gulps of food, wraps the remainder of the meal in a banana-leaf basket, and returns home to share it with his family. It is said that the spirits draw their sustenance from the odor of the food, the incense which is burned, and the Moslem prayer; the human participants draw theirs from the material substance of the food and from their social interaction. The result of this quiet, undramatic little ritual is twofold: the spirits are appeased and neighborhood solidarity is strengthened.[2]

The ordinary canons of functional theory are quite adequate for the analysis of such a pattern. It can rather easily be shown that the slametan is well designed both to "tune up the ultimate value attitudes" necessary to the effective integration of a territorially-based social structure, and to fulfill the psychological needs for intellectual coherence and emotional stability characteristic of a peasant population. The Javanese village (once or twice a year, village-wide slametans are held) is essentially a set of geographically contiguous, but rather self-consciously autonomous, nuclear family households whose economic and political interdependence is of roughly the same circumscribed and explicitly defined sort as that demonstrated in the slametan. The demands of the labor-intensive rice and dry-crop agricultural process require the perpetuation of specific modes of technical co-operation and enforce a sense of community on the otherwise rather self-contained families—a sense of community which the slametan clearly reinforces. And when we consider the manner in which various conceptual and behavioral elements from Hindu-Buddhism, Islam, and "animism" are reinterpreted and balanced to form a distinctive and nearly homogeneous religious style, the close functional adjustment between the communal feast pattern and the conditions of Javanese rural life is even more readily apparent.

But the fact is that in all but the most isolated parts of Java, both the simple territorial basis of village social integration and the syncretic basis of its cultural homogeneity have been progressively undermined over the past fifty years, Population growth, urbanization, monetization, occupational differentiation, and the like, have combined to weaken the traditional ties of peasant social structure; and the winds of doctrine which have accompanied the appearance of these structural changes have disturbed the simple uniformity of religious belief and practice characteristic of an earlier period. The rise of nationalism, Marxism, and Islamic reform as ideologies, which resulted in part from the increasing complexity of Javanese society, has affected not only the large cities where these creeds first appeared and have always had their greatest strength, but has had a heavy impact on the smaller towns and villages as well. In fact, much of recent Javanese social change is perhaps most aptly characterized as a shift from a situation in which the primary integrative ties between individuals (or between families) are phrased in terms of geographical proximity to one in which they are phrased in terms of ideological like-mindedness.

In the villages and small towns these major ideological changes appeared largely in the guise of a widening split between those who emphasized the Islamic aspects of the indigenous religious syncretism and those who emphasized the Hinduist and animistic elements. It is true that some difference between these variant subtraditions has been present since the arrival of Islam; some individuals have always been particularly skilled in Arabic chanting or particularly learned in Moslem law, while others have been adept at more Hinduistic mystical practices or specialists in local curing techniques. But these contrasts were softened by the easy tolerance of the Javanese for a wide range of religious concepts, so long as basic ritual patterns—i.e., slametans— were faithfully supported; whatever social divisiveness they stimulated was largely obscured by the over-riding commonalities of rural and small-town life.

However, the appearance after 1910 of Islamic modernism (as well as vigorous conservative reactions against it) and religious nationalism among the economically and politically sophisticated trading classes of the larger cities strengthened the feeling for Islam as an exclusivist, antisyncretic creed among the more orthodox element of the mass of the population. Similarly, secular nationalism and Marxism, appearing among the civil servants and the ex- panding proletariat of these cities, strengthened the pre-Islamic (i.e., Hinduist- animist) elements of the syncretic pattern, which these groups tended to prize as a counterweight to puristic Islam and which some of them adopted as a general religious framework in which to set their more specifically political ideas. On the one hand, there arose a more self-conscious Moslem, basing his religious beliefs and practices more explicitly on the international and univer- salistic doctrines of Mohammed; on the other hand there arose a more self- conscious "nativist," attempting to evolve a generalized religious system out of the material—muting the more Islamic elements—of his inherited religious tradition. And the contrast between the first kind of man, called a *santri,* and the second, called an *abangan,* grew steadily more acute, until today it forms the major cultural distinction in the whole of the Modjokuto area.[3]

It is especially in the town that this contrast has come to play a crucial role. The absence of pressures toward interfamilial co-operation exerted by the technical requirements of wet-rice growing, as well as lessened effectiveness of the traditional forms of village government in the face of the complexities of urban living, severely weaken the social supports of the syncretic village pat- tern. When each man makes his living—as chauffeur, trader, clerk, or laborer— more or less independently of how his neighbors make theirs, his sense of the importance of the neighborhood community naturally diminishes. A more differentiated class system, more bureaucratic and impersonal forms of govern- ment, greater heterogeneity of social background, all tend to lead to the same result: the de-emphasis of strictly geographical ties in favor of diffusely ideo- logical ones. For the townsman, the distinction between santri and abangan becomes even sharper, for it emerges as his primary point of social reference; it becomes a symbol of his social identity, rather than a mere contrast in belief. The sort of friends he will have, the sort of organizations he will join, the sort of political leadership he will follow, the sort of person he or his son will marry, will all be strongly influenced by the side of this ideological bifurcation which he adopts as his own.

There is thus emerging in the town—though not only in the town—a new pattern of social living organized in terms of an altered framework of cultural classification. Among the elite this new pattern has already become rather highly developed, but among the mass of the townspeople it is still in the process of formation. Particularly in the *kampongs*, the off-the-street neighborhoods in which the common Javanese townsmen live crowded together in a helter-skelter profusion of little bamboo houses, one finds a transitional society in which the traditional forms of rural living are being steadily dissolved and new forms steadily reconstructed. In these enclaves of peasants-come-to-town (or of sons and grandsons of peasants-come-to-town), Redfield's folk culture is being constantly converted into his urban culture, though this latter is not accurately characterized by such negative and residual terms as "secular," "individualized," and "culturally disorganized." What is occurring in the kampongs is not so much a destruction of traditional ways of life, as a construction of a new one; the sharp social conflict characteristic of these lower-class neighborhoods is not simply indicative of a loss of cultural consensus, but rather indicative of a search, not yet entirely successful, for new, more generalized, and flexible patterns of belief and value.

In Modjokuto, as in most of Indonesia, this search is taking place largely within the social context of the mass political parties, as well as in the women's clubs, youth organizations, labor unions, and other sodalities formally or informally linked with them. There are several of these parties (though the recent general election severely reduced their number), each led by educated urban elites—civil servants, teachers, traders, students, and the like—and each competing with the others for the political allegience of both the half rural, half urban kampong dwellers and of the mass of the peasantry. And almost without exception, they appeal to one or another side of the santri-abangan split. Of this complex of political parties and sodalities, only two are of immediate concern to us here: Masjumi, a huge, Islam-based political party; and Permai, a vigorously anti-Moslem politico-religious cult.

Masjumi is the more or less direct descendent of the pre-war Islamic reform movement. Led, at least in Modjokuto, by modernist santri intellectuals, it stands for a socially conscious, antischolastic, and somewhat puritanical version of back-to-the-Koran Islam. In company with the other Moslem parties, it also supports the institution of an "Islamic State" in Indonesia in place of the present secular republic. However, the meaning of this ideal is not entirely clear. Masjumi's enemies accuse it of pressing for an intolerant, medievalist theocracy in which abangans and non-Moslems will be persecuted and forced to follow exactly the prescripts of the Moslem law, while Masjumi's leaders claim that Islam is intrinsically tolerant and that they only desire a government explicitly based on the Moslem creed, one whose laws will be in consonance with the teachings of the Koran and Hadith. In any case, Masjumi, the country's largest Moslem party, is one of the major spokesmen on both the national and the local levels for the values and aspirations of the santri community.

Permai is not so impressive on a national scale. Though it is a nation-wide party, it is a fairly small one, having strength only in a few fairly circumscribed regions. In the Modjokuto area however, it happened to be of some importance, and what it lacked in national scope it made up in local intensity. Essentially, Permai is a fusion of Marxist politics with abangan religious patterns. It combines a fairly explicit anti-Westernism, anti-capitalism, and anti-imperialism with an attempt to formalize and generalize some of the more characteristic diffuse themes of the peasant religious syncretism. Permai meetings follow both the slametan pattern, complete with incense and symbolic food (but without Islamic chants), and modern parliamentary procedure; Permai pamphlets contain calendrical and numerological divinatory systems and mystical teachings as well as analyses of class conflict; and Permai speeches are concerned with elaborating both religious and political concepts. In Modjokuto, Permai is also a curing cult, with its own special medical practices and spells, a secret password, and cabalistic interpretations of passages in the leaders' social and political writings.

But Permai's most notable characteristic is its strong anti-Moslem stand. Charging that Islam is a foreign import, unsuited to the needs and values of the Javanese, the cult urges a return to "pure" and "original" Javanese beliefs, by which they seem to mean to the indigenous syncretism with the more Islamic elements removed. In line with this, the cult-party has initiated a drive, on both national and local levels, for secular (i.e., non-Islamic) marriage and funeral rites. As the situation stands now, all but Christians and Balinese Hindus must have their marriages legitimatized by means of the Moslem ritual.[4] Funeral rites are an individual concern but, because of the long history of syncretism, they are so deeply involved with Islamic customs that a genuinely non-Islamic funeral tends to be a practical impossibility.

Permai's action on the local level in pursuit of non-Islamic marriage and funeral ceremonies took two forms. One was heavy pressure on local government officials to permit such practices, and the other was heavy pressure on its own members to follow, voluntarily, rituals purified of Islamic elements. In the case of marriage, success was more or less precluded because the local officials' hands were tied by Central Government ordinances, and even highly ideologized members of the cult would not dare an openly "illegitimate" marriage. Without a change in the law, Permai had little chance to alter marriage forms, though a few abortive attempts were made to conduct civil ceremonies under the aegis of abangan-minded village chiefs.

The case of funerals was somewhat different, for a matter of custom rather than law was involved. During the year I was in the field, the tension between Permai and Masjumi increased very sharply. This was due in part to the imminence of Indonesia's first general elections, and in part to the effects of the cold war. It was also influenced by various special occurrences—such as a report that the national head of Permai had publically called Mohammed a false prophet; a speech in the nearby regional capital by a Masjumi leader in which he accused Permai of intending to raise a generation of bastards in

Indonesia; and a bitter village-chief election largely fought out on santri vs. abangan grounds. As a result, the local subdistrict officer, a worried bureaucrat trapped in the middle, called a meeting of all the village religious officials, or Modins. Among many other duties, a Modin is traditionally responsible for conducting funerals. He directs the whole ritual, instructs the mourners in the technical details of burial, leads the Koran chanting, and reads a set speech to the deceased at the graveside. The subdistrict officer instructed the Modins— the majority of whom were village Masjumi leaders—that in the case of the death of a member of Permai, they were merely to note the name and age of the deceased and return home; they were not to participate in the ritual. He warned that if they did not do as he advised, they would be responsible if trouble started and he would not come to their support.

This was the situation on July 17, 1954, when Paidjan, nephew of Karman, an active and ardent member of Permai, died suddenly in the Modjokuto kampong in which I was living.

## THE FUNERAL

The mood of a Javanese funeral is not one of hysterical bereavement, unrestrained sobbing, or even of formalized cries of grief for the deceased's departure. Rather, it is a calm, undemonstrative, almost languid letting go, a brief ritualized relinquishment of a relationship no longer possible. Tears are not approved of and certainly not encouraged; the effort is to get the job done, not to linger over the pleasures of grief. The detailed busy-work of the funeral, the politely formal social intercourse with the neighbors pressing in from all sides, the series of commemorative slametans stretched out at intervals for almost three years—the whole momentum of the Javanese ritual system is supposed to carry one through grief without severe emotional disturbance. For the mourner, the funeral and postfuneral ritual is said to produce a feeling of *iklas*, a kind of willed affectlessness, a detached and static state of "not caring"; for the neighborhood group it is said to produce *rukun*, "communal harmony."

The actual service is in essence simply another version of the slametan, adapted to the special requirements of interment. When the news of a death is broadcast through the area, everyone in the neighborhood must drop what he is doing and go immediately to the home of the survivors. The women bring bowls of rice, which is cooked up into a slametan; the men begin to cut wooden grave markers and to dig a grave. Soon the Modin arrives and begins to direct activities. The corpse is washed in ceremonially prepared water by the relatives (who unflinchingly hold the body on their laps to demonstrate their affection for the deceased as well as their self-control); then it is wrapped in muslin. About a dozen santris, under the leadership of the Modin, chant Arabic prayers over the body for five or ten minutes; after this it is carried, amid various ritual acts, in a ceremonial procession to the graveyard, where it is interred in prescribed ways. The Modin reads a graveside speech to the deceased, reminding him of his duties as a believing Moslem; and the funeral is over, usually only two or three hours after death. The funeral proper is followed by commemorative slametans in the home of the survivors at three, seven, forty, and one hundred days after death; on the first and second anniversary of death; and, finally, on the thousandth day, when the corpse is considered to have turned to dust and the gap between the living and the dead to have become absolute.

This was the ritual pattern which was called into play when Paidjan died. As soon as dawn broke (death occurred in the early hours of the morning), Karman, the uncle, dispatched a telegram to the boy's parents in a nearby city, telling them in characteristic Javanese fashion that their son was ill. This evasion was intended to soften the impact of death by allowing them to become aware of it more gradually. Javanese feel that emotional damage results not from the severity of a frustration but from the suddenness with which it comes, the degree to which it "surprises" one unprepared for it. It is "shock," not suffering itself, which is feared. Next, in the expectation that the parents would arrive within a few hours, Karman sent for the Modin to begin the ceremony. This was done on the theory that by the time the parents had come little would be left to do but inter the body, and they would thus once more be spared unnecessary stress. By ten o'clock at the very latest it should all be over; a saddening incident, but a ritually muted one.

But when the Modin, as he later told me, arrived at Karman's house and saw the poster displaying Permai's political symbol, he told Karman that he could not perform the ritual. After all, Karman belonged to "another religion" and he, the Modin, did not know the correct burial rituals for it; all he knew was Islam. "I don't want to insult your religion," he said piously, "on the contrary, I hold it in the utmost regard, for there is no intolerance in Islam. But I don't know your ritual. The Christians have their own ritual and their own specialist (the local preacher), but what does Permai do? Do they burn the corpse or what?" (This is a sly allusion to Hindu burial practices; evidently the Modin emjoyed himself hugely in this interchange.) Karman was, the Modin told me, rather upset at all this and evidently surprised, for although he was an active member of Permai, he was a fairly unsophisticated one. It had evidently never occurred to him that the anti-Molsem-funeral agitation of the party would ever appear as a concrete problem, or that the Modin would actually refuse to officiate. Karman was actually not a bad fellow, the Modin concluded; he was but a dupe of his leaders.

After leaving the now highly agitated Karman, the Modin went directly to the subdistrict officer to ask if he had acted properly. The officer was morally bound to say that he had, and thus fortified the Modin returned home to find Karman and the village policeman, to whom he had gone in desperation, waiting for him. The policeman, a personal friend of Karman's, told the Modin that according to time-honored custom he was supposed to bury everyone with impartiality, never mind whether he happened to agree with their politics. But the Modin, having now been personally supported by the subdistrict officer, insisted that it was no longer his responsibility. However, he suggested, if

Karman wished, he could go to the village chief's office and sign a public statement, sealed with the Government stamp and countersigned by the village chief in the presence of two witnesses, declaring that he, Karman, was a true believing Moslem and that he wished the Modin to bury the boy according to Islamic custom. At this suggestion that he officially abandon his religious beliefs, Karman exploded into a rage and stormed from the house, rather uncharacteristic behavior for a Javanese. By the time he arrived home again, at his wit's end about what to do next, he found to his dismay that the news of the boy's death had been broadcast and the entire neighborhood was already gathering for the ceremony.

Like most of the kampongs in the town of Modjokuto, the one in which I lived consisted both of pious santris and ardent abangans (as well as a number of less intense adherents of either side), mixed together in a more or less random manner. In the town, people are forced to live where they can and take whomever they find for neighbors, in contrast to the rural areas where whole neighborhoods, even whole villages, still tend to be made up almost entirely of either abangans or santris. The majority of the santris in the kampong were members of Masjumi and most of the abangans were followers of Permai, and in daily life, social interaction between the two groups was minimal. The abangans, most of whom were either petty artisans or manual laborers, gathered each late afternoon at Karman's roadside coffee shop for the idle twilight conversations which are typical of small town and village life in Java; the santris—tailors, traders and store-keepers for the most part—usually gathered in one or another of the santri-run shops for the same purpose. But despite this lack of close social ties, the demonstration of territorial unity at a funeral was still felt by both groups to be an unavoidable duty; of all the Javanese rituals, the funeral probably carries the greatest obligation on attendance. Everyone who lives within a certain roughly defined radius of the survivors' home is expected to come to the ceremony; and on this occasion everyone did.

With this as background, it is not surprising that when I arrived at Karman's house about eight o'clock, I found two separate clusters of sullen men squatting disconsolately on either side of the yard, a nervous group of whispering women sitting idly inside the house near the still clothed body, and a general air of doubt and uneasiness in place of the usual quiet busyness of slametan preparing, body washing and guest greeting. The abangans were grouped near the house where Karman was crouched, staring blankly off into space, and where Sudjoko and Sastro, the town Chairman and Secretary of Permai (the only nonresidents of the kampong present) sat on chairs, looking vaguely out of place. The santris were crowded together under the narrow shadow of a coconut palm about thirty yards away, chatting quietly to one another about everything but the problem at hand. The almost motionless scene suggested an unlooked-for intermission in a familar drama, as when a motion picture stops in the mid-action.

After a half hour or so, a few of the abangans began to chip half-heartedly away at pieces of wood to make grave markers and a few women began to construct small flower offerings for want of anything better to do; but it was clear that the ritual was arrested and that no one quite knew what to do next. Tension slowly rose. People nervously watched the sun rise higher and higher in the sky, or glanced at the impassive Karman. Mutterings about the sorry state of affairs began to appear ("everything these days is a political problem," an old, traditionalistic man of about eighty grumbled to me, "you can't even die any more but what it becomes a political problem"). Finally, about 9:30, a young santri tailor named Abu decided to try to do something about the situation before it deteriorated entirely: he stood up and gestured to Karman, the first serious instrumental act which had occured all morning. And Karman, roused from his meditation, crossed the no-man's-land to talk to him.

As a matter of fact, Abu occupied a rather special position in the kampong. Although he was a pious santri and a loyal Masjumi member, he had more contact with the Permai group because his tailor shop was located directly behind Karman's coffee shop. Though Abu, who stuck to his sewing machine night and day, was not properly a member of this group, he would often exchange comments with them from his work bench about twenty feet away. True, a certain amount of tension existed between him and the Permai people over religious issues. Once, when I was inquiring about their eschatological beliefs, they referred me sarcastically to Abu, saying he was an expert, and they teased him quite openly about what they considered the wholly ridiculous Islamic theories of the after life. Nevertheless, he had something of a social bond with them, and it was perhaps reasonable that he should be the one to try to break the deadlock.

"It is already nearly noon," Abu said, "things can't go straight on like this." He suggested that he send Umar, another of the santris, to see if the Modin could now be induced to come; perhaps things were cooler with him now. Meanwhile, he could get the washing and wrapping of the corpse started himself. Karman replied that he would think about it, and returned to the other side of the yard for a discussion with the two Permai leaders. After a few minutes of vigorous gesturing and nodding, Karman returned and said simply, "all right, that way." "I know how you feel," Abu said, "I'll just do what is absolutely necessary and keep the Islam out as much as possible." He gathered the santris together and they entered the house.

The first requisite was stripping the corpse (which was still lying on the floor, because no one could bring himself to move it). But by now the body was rigid, making it necessary to cut the clothes off with a knife, an unusual procedure which deeply disturbed everyone, especially the women clustered around. The santris finally managed to get the body outside and set up the bathing enclosure. Abu asked for volunteers for the washing; he reminded them that God would consider such an act a good work. But the relatives, who normally would be expected to undertake this task, were by now so deeply shaken and confused that they were unable to bring themselves to hold the boy on their laps in the customary fashion. There was another wait while people looked hopelessly at each other. Finally, Pak Sura, a member of Karman's group but no relative, took the boy on his lap, although he was clearly frightened and kept whispering a protective spell. One reason the Javanese give for their custom of rapid burial is that it is dangerous to have the spirit of the deceased hovering around the house.

Before the washing could begin, however, someone raised the question as to whether one person was enough—wasn't it usually three? No one was quite sure, including Abu; some thought that although it was customary to have three people it was not obligatory, and some thought three a necessary number. After about ten minutes of anxious discussion, a male cousin of the boy and a carpenter, unrelated to him, managed to work up the courage to join Pak Sura. Abu, attempting to act the Modin's role as best he could, sprinkled a few drops of water on the corpse and then it was washed, rather haphazardly and in unsacralized water. When this was finished, however, the procedure was again stalled, for no one knew exactly how to arrange the small cotton pads which, under Moslem law, should plug the body orifices. Karman's wife, sister of the deceased's mother, could evidently take no more, for she broke into a loud, unrestrained wailing, the only demonstration of this sort I witnessed among the dozen or so Javanese funerals I attended. Everyone was further upset by this development, and most of the kampong women made a frantic but unavailing effort to comfort her. Most of the men remained seated in the yard, outwardly calm and inexpressive, but the embarrassed uneasiness which had been present since the beginning seemed to be turning toward fearful desperation. "It is not nice for her to cry that way," several men said to me, "it isn't proper." At this point, the Modin arrived.

However, he was still adamant. Further, he warned Abu that he was courting eternal damnation by his actions. "You will have to answer to God on Judgment Day," he said, "if you make mistakes in the ritual. It will be your responsibility. For a Moslem, burial is a serious matter and must be carried out according to the Law by someone who knows what the Law is, not according to the will of the individual." He then suggested to Sudjoko and Sastro, the Permai leaders, that they take charge of the funeral, for as party "intellectuals" they must certainly know what kind of funeral customs Permai followed. The two leaders, who had not moved from their chairs, considered this as everyone watched expectantly, but they finally refused, with some chagrin, saying they really did not know how to go about it. The Modin shrugged and turned away. One of the bystanders, a friend of Karman's, then suggested that they just take the body out and bury it and forget about the whole ritual; it was extremely dangerous to leave things as they were much longer. I don't know whether this remarkable suggestion would have been followed, for at this juncture the mother and father of the dead child entered the kampong.

They seemed quite composed. They were not unaware of the death, for the father later told me he had suspected as much when he got the telegram; he and his wife had prepared themselves for the worst and were more or less resigned by the time they arrived. When they approached the kampong and saw the whole neighborhood gathered, they knew that their fears were well founded. When Karman's wife, whose weeping had subsided slightly, saw the dead boy's mother come into the yard, she burst free of those who were comforting her and with a shriek rushed to embrace her sister. In what seemed a split second, both women had dissolved into wild hysterics and the crowd had rushed in and pulled them apart, dragging them to houses at opposite sides of the kampong. Their wailing continued in undiminished volume, and nervous comments arose to the effect that they ought to get on with the burial in one fashion or another, before the boy's spirit possessed someone.

But the mother now insisted on seeing the body of her child before it was wrapped. The father at first forbade it, angrily ordering her to stop crying— didn't she know that such behavior would darken the boy's pathway to the other world? But she persisted and so they brought her, stumbling, to where he lay in Karman's house. The women tried to keep her from drawing too close, but she broke loose and began to kiss the boy about the genitals. She was snatched away almost immediately by her husband and the women, though she screamed that she had not yet finished; and they pulled her into the back room where she subsided into a daze. After awhile—the body was finally being wrapped, the Modin having unbent enough to point out where the cotton pads went—she seemed to lose her bearings entirely and began to move about the yard shaking hands with everyone, all strangers to her, and saying "forgive me my faults, forgive me my faults." Again she was forcibly restrained; people said, "calm yourself, think of your other children—do you want to follow your son to the grave?"

The corpse was now wrapped and new suggestions were made that it be taken off immediately to the graveyard. At this point, Abu approached the father, who, he evidently felt, had now displaced Karman as the man legally responsible for the proceedings. Abu explained that the Modin, being a Government official, did not feel free to approach the father himself, but he would like to know: how did he wish the boy to be buried—the Islamic way or what? The father, somewhat bewildered, said, "Of course, the Islamic way. I don't have much of any religion, but I'm not a Christian, and when it comes to death the burial should be the Islamic way. Completely Islamic." Abu explained again that the Modin could not approach the father directly, but that he, being "free," could do as he pleased. He said that he had tried to help as best he could but that he had been careful to do nothing Islamic before the father came. It was too bad, he apologized, about all the tension that was in the air, that political differences had to make so much trouble. But after all, everything had to be "clear" and "legal" about the funeral. It was important for the boy's soul. The santris, somewhat gleefully, now chanted their prayers over the corpse, and it was carried to the grave and buried in the usual manner. The Modin gave the usual graveyard speech, as amended for children, and the funeral was finally completed. None of the relatives or the women went to the graveyard; but when we returned to the house—it was now well after noon—the slametan was finally served, and Paidjan's spirit presumably left the kampong to begin its journey to the other world.

Three days later, in the evening, the first of the commemorative slametans was held, but it turned out that not only were no santris present but that it was as much a Permai political and religious cult meeting as a mourning ritual. Karman started off in the traditional fashion by announcing in high Javanese that this was a slametan in remembrance of the death of Paidjan. Sudjoko, the Permai leader, immediately burst in saying, "No, no, that is wrong. At a third day slametan you just eat and give a long Islamic chant for the dead, and we are certainly not going to do that." He then launched into a long, rambling speech. Everyone, he said, must know the philosophical-religious basis of the country. "Suppose this American (he pointed to me; he was not at all pleased by my presence) came up and asked you: what is the spiritual basis of the country? and you didn't know—wouldn't you be ashamed?"

He went on in this vein, building up a whole rationale for the present national political structure on the basis of a mystical interpretation of President Sukarno's "Five Points" (Monotheism, Social Justice, Humanitarianism, Democracy, and Nationalism[5]) which are the official ideological foundation of the new republic. Aided by Karman and others, he worked out a micro-macrocosm correspondence theory in which the individual is seen to be but a small replica of the state, and the state but an enlarged image of the individual. If the state is to be ordered, then the individual must also be ordered; each implies the other. As the President's Five Points are at the basis of the state, so the five senses are at the basis of an individual. The process of harmonizing both are the same, and it is this we must be sure we know. The discussion continued for nearly half an hour, ranging widely through religious, philosophical, and political issues (including, evidently for my benefit, a discussion of the Rosenbergs' execution).

We paused for coffee and as Sudjoko was about to begin again, Paidjan's father, who had been sitting quietly and expressionless, began suddenly to talk, softly and with a curiously mechnical tonelessness, almost as if he were reasoning with himself but without much hope of success. "I am sorry for my rough city accent," he said, "but I very much want to say something." He hoped they would forgive him; they could continue their discussion in a moment. "I have been trying to be iklas ("detached," "resigned") about Paidjan's death. I'm convinced that everything that could have been done for him was done and that his death was just an event which simply happened." He said he was still in Modjokuto because he could not yet face the people where he lived, couldn't face having to tell each one of them what had occurred. His wife, he said, was a little more iklas now too. It was hard, though. He kept telling himself it was just the will of God, but it was so hard, for nowadays people didn't agree on things any more; one person tells you one thing and others tell you another. It's hard to know which is right, to know what to believe. He said he appreciated all the Modjokuto people coming to the funeral, and he was sorry it had been all mixed up. "I'm not very religious myself. I'm not Masjumi and I'm not Permai. But I wanted the boy to be buried in the old way. I hope no one's feelings were hurt." He said again he was trying to be iklas, to tell himself it was just the will of God, but it was hard, for things were so confused these days. It was hard to see why the boy should have died

This sort of public expression of one's feelings is extremely unusual—in my experience unique—among Javanese, and in the formalized traditional slametan pattern there is simply no place for it (nor for philosophical or political discussion). Everyone present was rather shaken by the father's talk, and there was a painful silence. Sudjoko finally began to talk again, but this time he described in detail the boy's death. How Paidjan had first gotten a fever and Karman had called him, Sudjoko, to come and say a Permai spell. But the boy did not respond. They finally took him to a male nurse in the hospital, where he was given an injection. But still he worsened. He vomited blood and went into convulsions, which Sudjoko described rather graphically, and then he died. "I don't know why the Permai spell didn't work," he said "it has worked before. This time it didn't. I don't know why; that sort of thing can't be explained no matter how much you think about it. Sometimes it just works and sometimes it just doesn't." There was another silence and then, after about ten minutes more of political discussion, we disbanded. The father returned the next day to his home and I was not invited to any of the later slametans. When I left the field about four months later, Karman's wife had still not entirely recovered from the experience, the tension between the santris and the abangans in the kampong had increased, and everyone wondered what would happen the next time a death occurred in a Permai family.

## ANALYSIS

"Of all the sources of religion," wrote Malinowski, "the supreme and final crisis of life—death—is of the greatest importance" (1948:29). Death, he argued, provokes in the survivors a dual response of love and loathing, a deep-going emotional ambivalence of fascination and fear which threatens both the psychological and social foundations of human existence. The survivors are drawn toward the deceased by their affection for him, repelled from him by the dreadful transformation wrought by death. Funeral rites, and the mourning practices which follow them, focus around this paradoxical desire both to maintain the tie in the face of death and to break the bond immediately and utterly, and the insure the domination of the will to live over the tendency to despair. Mortuary rituals maintain the continuity of human life by preventing the survivors from yielding either to the impulse to flee panic-stricken from the scene or to the contrary impulse to follow the deceased into the grave:

"And here into this play of emotional forces, into this supreme dilemma of life and final death, religion steps in, selecting the positive creed, the comforting view, the culturally valuable belief in immortality, in the spirit independent of the body, and in the continuance of life after death. In the various ceremonies at death, in commemoration and communion with the departed, and worship of ancestral ghosts, religion gives body and form to the saving beliefs . . . Exactly the same function it fulfills also with regard to the whole group. The ceremonial of death which ties the survivors to the body and rivets them to the place of death, the beliefs in the existence of the spirit, in its beneficent influences or malevolent intentions, in the duties of a series of commemorative or sacrificial ceremonies—in all this religion counteracts the centrifugal forces of fear, dismay, demoralization, and provides the most powerful means of reintegration of the group's shaken solidarity and of the re-establishment of its morale. In short, religion here assures the victory of tradition over the mere negative response of thwarted instinct" (ibid:33–35).

To this sort of theory, a case such as that described above clearly poses some difficult problems. Not only was the victory of tradition and culture over "thwarted instinct" a narrow one at best, but it seemed as if the ritual were tearing the society apart rather than integrating it, were disorganizing personalities rather than healing them. To this the functionalist has a ready answer, which takes one of two forms depending upon whether he follows the Durkheim or the Malinowski tradition: social disintegration or cultural demoralization. Rapid social change has disrupted Javanese society and this is reflected in a disintegrated culture; as the unified state of traditional village society was mirrored in the unified slametan, so the broken society of the kampong is mirrored in the broken slametan of the funeral ritual we have just witnessed. Or, in the alternate phraseology, cultural decay has led to social fragmentation; loss of a vigorous folk tradition has weakened the moral ties between individuals.

It seems to me that there are two things wrong with this argument, no matter in which of the two vocabularies it is stated: it identifies social (or cultural) conflict with social (or cultural) disintegration; it denies independent roles to both culture and social structure, regarding one of the two as a mere epiphenomenon of the other.

In the first place, kampong life is not simply anomic. Though it is marked by vigorous social conflicts, as is our own society, it nevertheless proceeds fairly effectively in most areas. If governmental, economic, familial, stratificatory, and social control institutions functioned as poorly as did Paidjan's funeral, a kampong would indeed be an uncomfortable place in which to live. But though some of the typical symptoms of urban upheaval—such as increased gambling, petty thievery, and prostitution—are to some degree present, kampong social life is clearly not on the verge of collapse; everyday social interaction does not limp along with the suppressed bitterness and deep uncertainty we have seen focused around burial. For most of its members most of the time, a semiurban neighborhood in Modjokuto offers a viable way of life, despite its material disadvantages and its transitional character; and for all the sentimentality which has been lavished on descriptions of rural life in Java, this is probably as much as one could say for the village. As a matter of fact, it is around religious beliefs and practices—slametans, holidays, curing, sorcery, cult groups, etc.—that the most seriously disruptive events seem to cluster. Religion here is somehow the center and source of stress, not merely the reflection of stress elsewhere in the society.[6]

Yet it is not a source of stress because commitment to the inherited patterns of belief and ritual has been weakened. The conflict around Paidjan's death took place simply because all the kampong residents did share a common, highly integrated, cultural tradition concerning funerals. There was no argument over whether the slametan pattern was the correct ritual, whether the neighbors were obligated to attend, or whether the supernatural concepts upon which the ritual is based were valid ones. For both santris and abangans in the kampongs, the slametan maintains its force as a genuine sacred symbol; it still provides a meaningful framework for facing death—for most people the only meaningful framework. We cannot attribute the failure of the ritual to secularization, to a growth in skepticism, or to a disinterest in the traditional "saving beliefs," any more than we can attribute it to anomie.

We must rather, I think, ascribe it to a discontinuity between the form of integration existing in the social structural ("causal-functional") dimension and the form of integration existing in the cultural ("logico-meaningful") dimension—a discontinuity which leads not to social and cultural disintegration, but to social and cultural conflict. In more concrete, if somewhat aphoristic terms, the difficulty lies in the fact that socially kampong people are urbanites, while culturally they are still folk.

I have already pointed out that the Javanese kampong represents a transitional sort of society, that its members stand "in between" the more or less fully urbanized elite and the more or less traditionally organized peasantry. The social structural forms in which they participate are for the most part urban ones. The emergence of a highly differentiated occupational structure in place of the almost entirely agricultural one of the countryside; the virtual disappearance of the semihereditary, traditional village government as a personalistic buffer between the individual and the rationalized central government bureaucracy, and its replacement by the more flexible forms of modern parliamentary democracy; the evolution of a multiclass society in which the kampong, unlike the village, is not even a potentially self-sufficient entity, but is only one dependent subpart—all this means that the kampong man lives in a very urban world. Socially, his is a *Gesellschaft* existence.

But on the cultural level—the level of meaning—there is much less of a contrast between the kampong dweller and the villager; much more between him and a member of the urban elite. The patterns of belief, expression, and value to which the kampong man is committed—his world-view, ethos, ethic, or whatever—differ only slightly from those followed by the villager. Amid a radically more complex social environment, he clings noticeably to the symbols which guided him or his parents through life in rural society. And it is this fact which gave rise to the psychological and social tension surrounding Paidjan's funeral.

The disorganization of the ritual resulted from a basic ambiguity in the meaning of the rite for those who participated in it. Most simply stated, this ambiguity lay in the fact that the symbols which compose the slametan had both religious and political significance, were charged with both sacred and profane import. The people who came into Karman's yard, including Karman himself, were not sure whether they were engaged in a sacralized consideration of first and last things or in a secular struggle for power. This is why the old man (he was a graveyard keeper, as a matter of fact) complained to me that dying was nowadays a political problem; why the village policeman accused the Modin not of religious but of political bias for refusing to bury Paidjan; why the unsophisticated Karman was astonished when his ideological commitments suddenly loomed as obstacles to his religious practices; why Abu was torn between his willingness to submerge political differences in the interest of a harmonious funeral and his unwillingness to trifle with his religious beliefs in the interest of his own salvation; why the commemorative rite oscillated between political diatribe and a poignant search for an adequate explanation of what had happened—why, in sum, the slametan religious pattern stumbled when it attempted to "step in" with the "positive creed" and "the culturally valuable belief."

As emphasized earlier, the present severity of the contrast between santri and abangan is in great part due to the rise of nationalist social movements in twentieth-century Indonesia. In the larger cities where these movements were born, they were originally of various sorts: tradesmen's societies to fight Chinese competition; unions of workers to resist plantation exploitation; religious groups trying to redefine ultimate concepts; philosophical discussion clubs attempting to clarify Indonesian metaphysical and moral notions; school associations striving to revivify Indonesian education; co-operative societies trying to work out new forms of economic organization; cultural groups moving toward a renaissance of Indonesian artistic life; and, of course, political parties working to build up effective opposition to Dutch rule. As time wore on, however, the struggle for independence absorbed more and more the energies of all these essentially elite groups. Whatever the distinctive aim of each of them—economic reconstruction, religious reform, artistic renaissance—it became submerged in a diffuse political ideology; all the groups were increasingly concerned with one end as the prerequisite of all further social and cultural progress—freedom. By the time the revolution began in 1945, reformulation of ideas outside the political sphere had noticeably slackened and most aspects of life had become intensely ideologized, a tendency which has continued into the post-war period.

In the villages and small town kampongs, the early, specific phase of nationalism had only a minor effect. But as the movement unified and moved toward eventual triumph, the masses too began to be affected and, as I have pointed out, mainly through the medium of religious symbols. The highly urbanized elite forged their bonds to the peasantry not in terms of complex political and economic theory, which would have had little meaning in a rural context, but in terms of concepts and values already present there. As the major line of demarcation among the elite was between those who took Islamic doctrine as the overall basis of their mass appeal and those who took a generalized philosophical refinement of the indigenous syncretic tradition as such a basis, so in the countryside santri and abangan soon became not simply religious but political categories, denoting the followers of these two diffuse approaches to the organization of the emerging independent society. When the achievement of political freedom strengthened the importance of factional politics in parliamentary government, the santri-abangan distinction became, on the local level at least, one of the primary ideological axes around which the process of party maneuvering took place.

The effect of this development has been to cause political debate and religious propitiation to be carried out in the same vocabulary. A koranic chant becomes an affirmation of political allegiance as well as a paean to God; a burning of incense expresses one's secular ideology as well as one's sacred beliefs. Slametans now tend to be marked by anxious discussions of the various elements in the ritual, of what their "real" significance is; by arguments as to whether a particular practice is essential or optional; by abangan uneasiness when santris lift their eyes to pray and santri uneasiness when abangans recite a protective spell. At death, as we have seen, the traditional symbols tend both to solidify individuals in the face of social loss and to remind them of their differences; to emphasize the broadly human themes of mortality and undeserved suffering and the narrowly social ones of factional opposition and party struggle; to strengthen the values the participants hold in common and to "tune up" their animosities and suspicions. The rituals themselves become matters of political conflict; forms for the sacralization of marriage and death are transformed into important party issues. In such an equivocal cultural setting, the average kampong Javanese finds it increasingly difficult to determine the proper attitude toward a particular event, to choose the meaning of a given symbol appropriate to a given social context.

The corollary of this interference of political meanings with religious meanings also occurs: the interference of religious meanings with political ones. Because the same symbols are used in both political and religious contexts, people often regard party struggle as involving not merely the usual ebb and flow of parliamentary maneuver, the necessary factional give-and-take of democratic government, but involving as well decisions on basic values and ultimates. Kampong people in particular tend to see the open struggle for power explicitly institutionalized in the new republican forms of government as a struggle for the right to establish different brands of essentially religious principles as official: "if the abangans get in, the koranic teachers will be forbidden to hold classes"; "if the santris get in, we shall all have to pray five times a day." The normal conflict involved in electoral striving for office is heightened by the idea that literally everything is at stake: the "if we win, it is our country" idea that the group which gains power has a right, as one man said, "to put his own foundation under the state." Politics thus takes on a kind of sacralized bitterness; and one village election in a suburban Modjokuto village actually had to be held twice because of the intense pressures generated in this way.

The kampong man is, so to speak, caught between his ultimate and his proximate concepts. Because he is forced to formulate his essentially metaphysical ideas, his response to such basic "problems" as fate, suffering, and evil, in the same terms as he states his claims to secular power, his political rights and aspirations, he experiences difficulty in enacting either a socially and psychologically efficient funeral or a smoothly running election.

But a ritual is not just a pattern of meaning; it is also a form of social interaction. Thus, in addition to creating cultural ambiguity, the attempt to bring a religious pattern from a relatively less differentiated rural background into an urban context also gives rise to social conflict, simply because the kind of social integration demonstrated by the pattern is not congruent with the major patterns of integration in the society generally. The way kampong people go about maintaining solidarity in everyday life is quite different from the way the slametan insists that they should go about maintaining it.

As emphasized earlier, the slametan is essentially a territorially based ritual; it assumes the primary tie between families to be that of residential propinquity. One set of neighbors is considered a significant social unit (politically, religiously, economically) as against another set of neighbors; one village as against another village; one village-cluster as against another village-cluster. In the town, this pattern has in large part changed. Significant social groups are defined by a plurality of factors—class, political commitment, occupation, ethnicity, regional origins, religious preference, age, and sex, as well as residence. The new urban form of organization consists of a careful balance of conflicting forces arising out of diverse contexts: class differences are softened by ideological similarities; ethic conflicts by common economic interests; political opposition, as we have been, by residential intimacy. But in the midst of all this pluralistic checking and balancing, the slametan remains unchanged, blind to the major lines of social and cultural demarcation in urban life. For it, the primary classifying characteristic of an individual is where he lives.

Thus when an occasion arises demanding sacralization—a life-cycle transition, a holiday, a serious illness—the religious form which must be employed acts not with but against the grain of social equilibrium. The slametan ignores those recently devised mechanisms of social insulation which in daily life keep group conflict within fixed bounds, as it also ignores the newly evolved patterns of social integration among opposed groups which balance contradictory tensions in a reasonably effective fashion. People are pressed into an intimacy they would as soon avoid; where the incongruity between the social assumptions of the ritual ("we are all culturally homogeneous peasants together") and what is in fact the case ("we are several different kinds of people who must perforce live together despite our serious value disagreements") leads to a deep uneasiness of which Paidjan's funeral was but an extreme example. In the kampong, the holding of a slametan increasingly serves to remind people that the neighborhood bonds they are strengthening through a dramatic enactment are no longer the bonds which most emphatically hold them together. These latter are ideological, class, occupation, and political bonds, divergent ties which are no longer adequately summed up in territorial relationships.

In sum, the disruption of Paidjan's funeral may be traced to a single source: an incongruity between the cultural framework of meaning and the patterning of social interaction, an incongruity due to the persistence in an urban environment of a religious symbol system adjusted to peasant social structure. Static functionalism, of either the sociological or social psychological sort, is unable to isolate this kind of incongruity because it fails to discriminate between logico-meaningful integration and causal-functional integration; because it fails to realize that cultural structure and social structure are not mere reflexes of one another but independent, yet interdependent, variables. The driving forces in social change can be clearly formulated only by a more dynamic form of functionalist theory, one which takes into account the fact that man's need to live in a world to which he can attribute some significance, whose essential import he feels he can grasp, often diverges from his concurrent need to maintain a functioning social organism. A diffuse concept of culture as "learned behavior," a static view of social structure as an equilibrated pattern of interaction, and a stated or unstated assumption that the two must somehow (save in "disorganized" situations) be simple mirror images of one another, is rather too primitive a conceptual apparatus with which to attack such problems as those raised by Paidjan's unfortunate but instructive funeral.

## NOTES

[1] The names of the town and of all individuals mentioned in this paper are pseudonyms. The field work extended from May 1953 until September 1954, with a two-month gap in July and August of 1953, and was undertaken as part of a co-operative project of six anthropologists and a sociologist under the sponsorship of the Center for International Studies of the Massachusetts Institute of Technology. A full description of the town and of the villages around it, prepared by the entire team, is in the process of publication. I wish to thank Victor Ayoub, Robert Bellah, Hildred Geertz, Arnold Green, Robert Jay, and Elizabeth Tooker for reading and criticizing various drafts of this paper.

[2] A fuller description of the slametan pattern, and of Javanese religion generally, will be found in my contribution to the forthcoming project report on the Modjokuto community study: Geertz, in press.

[3] For a description of the role of the santri-abangan distinction in the rural areas of Modjokuto, see Jay 1956. A third religious variant which I have discriminated elsewhere (Geertz 1956, and in press), the *prijaji*, is mainly confined to upper-class civil servants, teachers, and clerks, and so will not be dealt with here.

[4] Actually, there are two parts to Javanese marriage rites. One, which is part of the general syncretism, is held at the bride's home and involves a slametan and an elaborate ceremonial "meeting" between bride and groom. The other, which is the official ceremony in the eyes of the Government, follows the Moslem law and takes place at the office of the subdistrict religious officer, or Naib. See Geertz, in press.

[5] For a fuller discussion of President Sukarno's *pantjasila* ideology and his attempt to root it in general Indonesian values, see Kahin 1952:122–127.

[6] For a description of a somewhat disrupted celebration of the end of the Fast holiday, Hari Raya (îd al-fitr) in Modjokuto, which shows many formal similarities to Paidjan's funeral, see Geertz, in press.

REFERENCES CITED

DURKHEIM, ÉMILE
  1947  The elementary forms of the religious life. Glencoe, Illinois.
FORTES, MEYER
  1953  The structure of unilineal descent groups. American Anthropologist 55:17-41.
GEERTZ, CLIFFORD
  1956  Religious belief and economic behavior in a central Javanese town: some prelim-
        inary considerations. Economic Development and Cultural Change IV:134-158.
  N.D.  Religion in Modjokuto. (In press, Cambridge, Massachusetts.)
JAY, ROBERT
  1956  Local government in rural central Java. The Far Eastern Quarterly XV:215-227.
KAHIN, GEORGE McTURNAN
  1952  Nationalism and revolution in Indonesia. Ithaca, New York.
KLUCKHOHN, CLYDE
  1944  Navaho witchcraft. Peabody Museum Papers, No. XXII. Cambridge, Massachu-
        setts.
LANDON, K.
  1949  Southeast Asia, crossroad of religions. Chicago.
LEACH, E. R.
  1954  Political systems of highland Burma. Cambridge, Massachusetts.
MALINOWSKI, BRONISLAW
  1948  Magic, science and religion and other essays. Glencoe, Illinois, and Boston, Massa-
        chusetts.
MERTON, ROBERT
  1949  Social theory and social structure. Glencoe, Illinois.
PARSONS, TALCOTT
  1951  The social system. Glencoe, Illinois.
PARSONS, TALCOTT and EDWARD A. SHILS
  1951  Toward a general theory of action. Cambridge, Massachusetts.
REDFIELD, ROBERT
  1941  The folk culture of Yucatan. Chicago, Illinois.
ROBERTSON-SMITH, W.
  1894  Lectures on the religion of the Semites. Edinburgh.
SOROKIN, P.
  1937  Social and cultural dynamics, 3 vols. New York.

# The Meaning of Kinship Terms[1]

ANTHONY F. C. WALLACE AND JOHN ATKINS

*Eastern Pennsylvania Psychiatric Institute and University of Pennsylvania*

## INTRODUCTION

THE meaning of kinship terms in foreign languages (or in English, for that matter) has traditionally been rendered by English-speaking ethnologists by a simple and direct procedure: each term is matched with a primitive English term (e.g., "mother"), with a relative product of two or more primitive English terms (e.g., "mother's brother"), or with a group of such primitive and/or relative product terms. Each primitive English term and each English relative product denotes an English "kin-type." Thus the meaning of the term is given by a list of nonredundant English kin-types, each of which includes one or more individuals in the group of persons to which the foreign term refers, and none of which includes any individual outside the group of persons to which the term refers. The validity of the matching derives, in general, from the prior use of a genealogical method of inquiry and from a general knowledge of the language and culture of the society. Murdock's *Social Structure* (1949) illustrates a convenient notation for such an analysis of meanings, and there is also a variety of other devices available, ranging from plotting terms on genealogical charts (each of whose points is defined by an English primitive or a relative product) to listing descriptive statements in tabular form. In Murdock's notation, the first two letters of eight primitive terms (father, mother, brother, sister, son, daughter, husband, wife) are used as the primitive symbols (Fa, Mo, Br, Si, So, Da, Hu, Wi); other kinship categories are conceived as relative products of these categories (e.g., FaBr for father's brother, SoWi for son's wife). Additional primitives (e.g., younger and older) are added as required. Similar notations are commonly used by other ethnologists and we shall call this traditional kind of notation the "kin-type notation." This process of definition is not to be confused with that of finding a convenient English rubric for a foreign term. For purposes of readable English rendering, the ethnologist may translate a foreign term into a common English one, for example, Pawnee *atías* into "my father" (Lounsbury 1956), but he is careful to indicate that insofar as it represents a native term, the English label applies not only to at least one of its own English kin-types, but also, as the case may be, to other kin-types as well.

Defining a foreign term by listing all the English kin-types to the sum of which it corresponds is, however, sometimes tedious and may yield a veritable thicket of symbols, for one term may extend over a set of individuals which is parcelled out among dozens of English kin-types. In fact, many such lists are

58

admittedly incomplete and conclude with an "etc." because the boundaries are not clearly or concisely definable in terms of English kin-types. Furthermore, this procedure somewhat begs the question of the principle of grouping which is inherent in the foreign concept by tacitly implying that it is the English kin-types which are grouped. And it is in the principle of grouping that, intuitively, one suspects that the meaning of the term *to its users* resides. Types of grouping of the English kin-types may be usefully classified, of course, to yield the various typologies of kinship terminology, such as Crow, Eskimo, or Sudanese. But a term may not mean to its users that collection of kin-types which the English-speaking ethnologist finds it convenient to regard as its meaning.

Recently students of social organization have developed a method called "componential analysis" for the elucidation of the meaning of kinship terms.[2] This method claims to reach a higher level of ethnographic validity than the traditional listing of kin-types. Furthermore, because this method moves much farther toward definition of the meaning of terms according to the conceptual criteria employed by their users than does mere kin-type listing, it awakens, in particular, the interest of psychologically oriented anthropologists. Therefore it is necessary to examine closely the assumptions and operations of componential analysis in order to evaluate both its utility for ethnographic studies of kinship and its adequacy as a model of semantic (and thus cognitive) process. Such an examination may suggest modifications or amplifications which will increase the effectiveness and scope of componential analysis as a tool, not only in kinship studies but in other areas of anthropological investigation as well. Such an examination may suggest also limitations on the applicability of the method. Componential analysis has so far been successfully applied primarily to definitive meaning (e.g., to the criteria by which a kinsman is recognized as belonging to a certain class). It may or may not ultimately prove to be convenient to analyze other kinds of meaning by the componential method; but we do not hope to settle such ultimate questions here. It is the more restricted purpose of this paper to use some of the resources of logical formalism to build, on a foundation of conceptualization and method provided by traditional techniques of kin-type analysis and by more recent procedures of componential analysis, toward more valid ethnographic description and more effective anthropological theories of cognitive processes in cultural behavior.

## THE METHOD OF COMPONENTIAL ANALYSIS AS APPLIED TO KINSHIP

We shall consider as our source material six papers, two of them published in *Language* (Goodenough 1956, and Lounsbury 1956), one published in the AMERICAN ANTHROPOLOGIST (Romney and Epling 1958), and three delivered at the 1957 annual meetings of the American Anthropological Association and distributed there in mimeographed form (Goodenough 1957, Metzger 1957, and Jay Romney 1957). Goodenough's and Lounsbury's original papers explicate the method most fully; the other four papers illustrate and introduce modifications and extensions. We are here interested neither in exploring the historical background and contemporary analogues of the methodology, whether they be in kinship studies per se, in linguistics, Morris's semiotic, biological taxonomics, symbolic logic, or mathematics, nor in the uses and applications of the methodology in other fields of inquiry, such as the theory of typology. Nor are we primarily concerned with inter-author differences in notation and terminology except as they reflect differences in assumption and procedure.

The componential analysis of a kinship lexicon commonly consists of five steps: (1) the recording of a complete set (or a defined sub-set) of the terms of reference or address, using various boundary-setting criteria, such as a constant syntactic context, a type of pragmatic situation, or common inclusion within the extension of a cover term for "kinsmen"; (2) the definition of these terms in the traditional kin-type notation (i.e., as Fa, FaBr, DaHuBr); (3) the identification, in the principles of grouping of kin-types, of two or more conceptual dimensions each of whose values ("components") is signified (not connoted) by one or more of the terms; (4) the definition of each term, by means of a symbolic notation, as a specific combination, or set of combinations, of the components; (5) a statement of the semantic relationship among the terms and of the structural principles of this terminological system. (It should be noted here that the semantic structure of the terminological system is only one aspect of "the kinship system" of a society. The semantic structure to which we refer is a structure of the logical relationships of definitional meanings among terms and does not pretend to describe such phenomena as marital exchange or authority relations. A pair of terms may designate overlapping, mutually exclusive, identical, or inclusive sets of kin-types and the logical relations among the terms will correspondingly be those of logical independence, contrariety, equivalence, and implication. Thus the English term "uncle" designates a set of kin-types which is mutually exclusive with those denoted by "aunt," and the logical relation between the terms is that of contrariety. The structure of the terminological system is the product of these set—or logical—relationships.)

To give a simple example of the method, we shall now take a familiar group of American-English consanguineal terms in their formal and referential sense, and perform a componential analysis of their meaning. (This analysis is not offered as a definitive ethnographic statement; its purpose is to provide a readily apprehended illustration of the procedure.) Stage 1: we select: *grandfather, grandmother, father, mother, brother, sister, son, daughter, grandson, granddaughter, uncle, aunt, cousin, nephew, niece*, a group of common terms in American English, as they are used to refer to consanguineal relatives. Stage 2: we define these terms, employing the primitive kin-types Fa, Mo, Br, Si, So, Da, and the operators (:) ("refers to") and possessive relation (expressed by precedent juxtaposition, as in MoFa, which reads "mother's father"), as follows:

| | | | |
|---|---|---|---|
| grandfather | : FaFa, MoFa | aunt | : FaSi, MoSi, FaFaSi, MoFaSi, |
| grandmother | : FaMo, MoMo | | etc. |
| father | : Fa | cousin | : FaBrSo, FaBrDa, MoBrSo, |
| mother | : Mo | | MoBrDa, FaSiSo, FaSiDa, |
| brother | : Br | | MoSiSo, MoSiDa, FaFaBrSo, |
| sister | : Si | | FaMoBrSo, MoFaSiDa, etc. |
| son | : So | nephew | : BrSo, SiSo, BrSoSo, SiSoSo, |
| daughter | : Da | | etc. |
| grandson | : SoSo, DaSo | niece | : BrDa, SiDa, BrDaDa, SiDaDa, |
| granddaughter | : SoDa, DaDa | | etc. |
| uncle | : FaBr, MoBr, FaFaBr, MoFaBr, | | |
| | etc. | | |

The reader will note that for simplicity of exposition we have elected to bound the generational range of the kin-type universe at two generations above and two generations below ego. A more complete analysis would involve a larger generational range of kin-types. Furthermore, we have taken the last five terms in an extended sense, thus including the kin-types to which cousin in the sense of second-cousin-once-removed, aunt in the sense of great-aunt, and nephew in the sense of grand-nephew, and so on, refer. These five terms are actually homonyms, usable both as cover terms for an indefinitely large group of kin-types, and also as specific terms for more limited sets of kin-types. Stage 3: we observe that all but one of these terms (*cousin*) specifies sex of relative; some specify generation; all specify whether the relative is lineally or nonlineally related to ego; and nonlineal terms specify whether or not all the ancestors of the relative are ancestors of ego, or all the ancestors of ego are ancestors of the relative, or neither. From these observations we hypothesize that three dimensions will be sufficient to define all the terms: sex of relative (A): male ($a_1$), female ($a_2$); generation (B): two generations above ego ($b_1$), one generation above ego ($b_2$), ego's own generation ($b_3$), one generation below ego ($b_4$), two generations below ego ($b_5$); lineality (C): lineal ($c_1$), co-lineal ($c_2$), ablineal ($c_3$). We use Goodenough's definition of the values on this dimension of lineality: lineals are persons who are ancestors or descendants of ego; co-lineals are non-lineals all of whose ancestors include, or are included in, all the ancestors of ego; ablineals are consanguineal relatives who are neither lineals nor co-lineals (Goodenough, private communication). Stage 4: we define the terms now by components, adopting the convention that where a term does not discriminate on a dimension,

| | | | |
|---|---|---|---|
| grandfather | : $a_1b_1c_1$ | grandson | : $a_1b_5c_1$ |
| grandmother | : $a_2b_1c_1$ | granddaughter | : $a_2b_5c_1$ |
| father | : $a_1b_2c_1$ | uncle | : $a_1b_1c_2$ and $a_1b_2c_2$ |
| mother | : $a_2b_2c_1$ | aunt | : $a_2b_1c_2$ and $a_2b_2c_2$ |
| brother | : $a_1b_3c_2$ | cousin | : a b $c_3$ |
| sister | : $a_2b_3c_2$ | nephew | : $a_1b_4c_2$ and $a_1b_5c_2$ |
| son | : $a_1b_4c_1$ | niece | : $a_2b_4c_2$ and $a_2b_5c_2$ |
| daughter | : $a_2b_4c_1$ | | |

the letter for that dimension is given without subscript. The definitions are represented paradigmatically in Fig. 1:

| | c₁ a₁ | c₁ a₂ | c₂ a₁ | c₂ a₂ | c₃ a₁ | c₃ a₂ |
|---|---|---|---|---|---|---|
| b₁ | grandfather | grandmother | uncle | aunt | | |
| b₂ | father | mother | | | | |
| b₃ | [ego] | | brother | sister | cousin | |
| b₄ | son | daughter | nephew | niece | | |
| b₅ | grandson | granddaughter | | | | |

FIG. 1. A componential paradigm of American English consanguineal core terms.

Evidently each term has been so defined, with respect to the components selected, that no term overlaps or includes another; every component is discriminated by at least one term; and all terms can be displayed on the same paradigm. We do not wish to argue that this is the best representation; only that it is adequate to define the set of terms chosen.

These stages of analysis are exhibited in the several papers mentioned above with some variability of notation. Goodenough (1956), who, like us, employs an algebraic notation, drops the letter symbol for a dimension when the term does not specify a particular component on that dimension but ranges over the entire dimension; and he uses juxtaposed capital letters with numerical subscripts (with a standard prefix 'A' for each formula, indicating membership in the set of kinship terms) to indicate a commutative product (or "class product"). Lounsbury (1956) employs the commutative Boolean operators ($\cdot$) and ($+$), a noncommutative relational operator (non-Boolean) signified by ordered juxtaposition, and the Boolean distributive law, to state the relationship of the components in those combinations where a single class product will not suffice to give the meaning of a term; Goodenough simply lists the various combinations. (See Birkhoff and MacLane 1953, for discussions of Boolean algebra, set theory, and logic, and their interrelations. "Boolean algebra" is an algebraic calculus for stating logical relationships among classes. Set theory is a calculus of the relations between groups of "elements." Both can be conceived as mathematizations of the logic of classes; and Boolean algebra is sometimes defined as the "algebra of sets.") Romney (1957) and Metzger (1957) draw matrix diagrams to represent semantic relationships; Goodenough (1956) and Lounsbury (1956) do not, preferring a tabular form of presentation. Although these and similar notational differences, as well as differences in details of procedure, would appear superficially to be merely variations in notation, they depend to some degree on differences in implicit assumptions about the logical structure of componential analysis. And assumptions about logical structure are intimately involved with the unresolved problems of analysis which we shall now consider.

### ANALYTICAL PROBLEMS IN COMPONENTIAL ANALYSIS

In this section we outline five methodological problem areas which require solutions before any method of semantic analysis can become maximally useful as a tool in anthropological conceptualization and investigation. These areas will be discussed in detail in succeeding sections.

(1) *The problem of homonyms and metaphors.* Homonyms and metaphors are words or phrases, phonemically or graphically identical, which have different meanings (e.g., "night" and "knight" are phonemic homonyms; "light" and "light," as illumination and as not-heavy, are graphic homonyms; "to let the cat out of the bag" is both a description of one way of behaving toward felines and a metaphor implying the unintended betrayal of a secret). Goodenough (1956) and Lounsbury (1956) confront the problem of homonyms and metaphors in their analyses of Trukese and Pawnee terms. The issue is important because it concerns both the principles of finding the boundary of the system being described and also the logical nature of semantic systems.

(2) *The problem of definition vs. connotation.* All of our authors explicitly assert an interest in definitive meaning only. When the possibility of synonyms is considered, however, the necessity of making an absolute distinction between definition and connotation may become an encumbrance.

(3) *The problem of complementarity, paradigms, and spaces.* Goodenough and Lounsbury adhere to the principle that all terms should be complementary on at least one of a group of dimensions, and thus should form a paradigm. The paradigm concept can be more powerfully defined and supplemented by the notion of "logical space."

(4) *The problem of noncommutative relational concepts.* Noncommutative relations are relations which cannot be reversed in order without change of meaning (e.g., "father's brother" does not have the same meaning as "brother's father"). Although the traditional English anthropological usage employs noncommutative relational operators in the kin-type notation (e.g., precedent juxtaposition in FaBr for "father's brother"), and although noncommutative relations (such as possession) may be psychologically real and linguistically recognized, none of the authors except Lounsbury (and he sparingly) uses a logic of noncommutative relations in componential analysis.

(5) *The problem of psychological reality, social-structural reality, and the indeterminacy of semantic analysis.* Goodenough (1956) points out that the componential analysis of meaning is, in fact, the analysis of cognitive structure. Romney's analysis (1957), on the other hand, seems to emphasize the structural properties of terminological systems without reference to cognitive models. These issues involve an apparent indeterminacy in analysis which in turn raises a number of basic theoretical problems concerning the purposes of componential analysis, the nature of model-building in anthropology, and the constraints on purpose imposed by the technical demands of a convenient model. Of particular importance is the distinction between "psychological" and "structural" reality.

## HOMONYMS AND METAPHORS

Homonyms and metaphors enter the discussion of the meaning of kinship terms for two reasons: first, because some of the terms which signify kin relationships may, on occasion, also signify nonkin relationships (e.g., "father" may signify priest or male parent); and second, because the same term may have, or may seem to have, two or more kinship uses (e.g., "uncle" may refer both to brothers of parents and to spouses of sisters of parents). The semantic analyst therefore wishes, on the one hand, to exclude from his statement of the meaning of a kinship term those meanings which apply to nonkinship relationships, and also to avoid giving a kinship term two or more definitions when one will suffice.

Both Goodenough (1956) and Lounsbury (1956) exclude extra-kin meanings for terms by defining a universe of possible "denotata" which includes only the traditional English kin-type primitives and their relative products. A denotatum of a term, in this usage, is not a person to whom the term points, but an expression of the form FaBr, Mo, or MoSi, which stands for a class —usually a conceptually familiar class—of persons. Since the classes of denotata of the terms selected are restricted to the kin-types, metaphoric meanings and nonkinship homonyms are excluded automatically. (In a more general model, the extensions of components and terms can be persons rather than kin-types.) The Trukese analysis consequently is not concerned with the fact that some of the Trukese words are used to refer both to kin-types and to classes of individuals distinguished by their membership status in landholding corporations (a status different from, if related to, kinship) (Goodenough 1951); and Lounsbury (1956) can treat as "metaphorical extension" the Pawnee reference to corn as "Our Mother."

The situation is different where possible kin-homonyms are involved. These are homonyms within the universe of kin-type denotata. Here Goodenough and Lounsbury diverge slightly in method. They agree, initially, in refusing to regard a term which has more than one kin-type denotatum as *ipso facto* a homonym. Trukese *neji*, "child," for instance, has twelve listed denotata (others are implied by "etc."); Pawnee *atías*, "father," has fifteen listed denotata. Neither of these terms is treated as a homonym. In Goodenough's notation (which we modify here, and throughout this paper, by eliminating the constant prefix "A" signifying "kinsman"), *neji* is defined as equivalent simply to $b_3$ (junior generation with respect to ego). In Lounsbury's notation, *atïas* is defined as equivalent to $\male \cdot A^1$ (male of agnatic rank one).

But both Goodenough and Lounsbury feel that whenever a term cannot be given a "unitary definition" on the dimensions which yield significata (Lounsbury 1956:175), it is a homonym (Goodenough 1956) or a case of "polysemy" (Lounsbury 1956:175). The crucial question thus becomes: what is a "unitary definition"? For Goodenough, a unitary definition is a definition which, in the logical sense, is either a single value on one dimension, or a simple class product (a combination of *one* value from each of two or more dimensions, sometimes connected by "$\cdot$," "$\wedge$," or "$\times$," but here written by commutative juxtaposition of letters, each with one subscript, as in $a_1b_1c_1$ for male, one generation above ego, lineal—i.e., "father"). For Lounsbury, if the expression can be written as a simple class or relative product (e.g., $\male \cdot A^{-1}$ or $AU$), without the Boolean "$+$" ("and/or," also expressed by $\vee$), it is a unitary definition. Both feel that a unitary definition is preferable, as the product of analysis, to a composite definition, because a composite definition seems to imply homonymity. Composite definitions are, in the logical sense, class sums (the referent may belong to any one of two or more alternative classes, as in $a_1b_1c_1 \vee a_2b_1c_2$, for male, one generation above ego, lineal; or, female, one generation above ego, lineal—i.e., "parent").

But, as a matter of fact, the terms in both Trukese and Pawnee cannot all be given unitary definitions on every definitionally adequate group of dimensions. Lounsbury, indeed, is forced to write extended composite definitions of the following kind (1956:180):

The "grandchild" class, *raktïki*, is the reciprocal of the "grandfather" and "grandmother" classes: $A^{-2}+G^{-2}+A^{-1}U^{-1}$; i.e. persons who are of agnatic rank *minus two*, or persons who are of second descending generation, or persons who are first-descending-generation uterine kinsmen to those of agnatic rank *minus one*.

And Goodenough notes that some groups of dimensions, otherwise perfectly adequate for defining the terms, yield homonymic definitions which he relates to one another by the English word "or." Goodenough and Lounsbury where possible follow an analytical convention which minimizes the apparent number of composite definitions, however: where a term does not discriminate among the values on a dimension which other terms in the set discriminate, that dimension is not regarded as semantically significant. But this invokes the danger of confusing ambiguity with irrelevance. Furthermore, considerations of economy apart, any convention of considering a dimension to be semantically nonsignificant on which no discrimination is made by some, but not all, of the terms in a lexicon invokes other difficulties, both practical and theoretical. As a practical device for reducing the number of composite definitions, the convention is of value only in special cases. It will work only if the term is ambiguous for all values on a dimension; if the ambiguity is with respect to some, but not all, values, then the ambiguity cannot be removed without redefining dimensions or selecting new dimensions. Thus, if a dimension has three values, and a term ranges over two of these values and excludes the third, then (under the convention aforementioned) the term must be treated as a homonym; only if it ranges over either three or one is it not a homonym. This problem occurs in Trukese Paradigm 4 with respect to *pwiij* (Goodenough 1956:212).

Theoretically, one may question whether terms which *can* be given either unitary definitions or composite definitions are necessarily given the unitary definition by the native user of the term, and whether the circumstance of composite definition on an English semantic matrix necessarily implies homonymity in the native cognitive world. Some terms, like *pwiij* in Paradigm 4, signify the extremes of a continuum of ordered values on a dimension and may be regarded as semantically homogeneous with respect to their extremity; their appearance as homonyms is a function of the exigencies of the paradigm. Some terms may well, in the context of a particular lexicon, signify a set of discrete unordered class products and may be used to refer to events which belong to any one of these products. But these terms likewise may not be true homonyms: they may be merely different "senses" of the term. The Trukese kinship lexicon does not happen to contain any terms which demand defining expressions involving the operator "and/or," if one follows the convention of omitting reference to semantically ambiguous dimensions. But the Pawnee terms cannot be defined without the use of the "and/or" operator. This operator must be used in order to construct a composite definition whenever two values on different dimensions cannot simultaneously complete a definition but each can separately, and whenever more than one but less than all of the values on a dimension are signified by a term. Such cases, by virtue of this fact alone, hardly qualify as true homonyms, however, any more than do terms which denote two or more kin-types, unless one wishes to insist on an equivalence between homonymity and the use of class sum ("and/or"). In general, we may observe that some terms will probably have to be componentially analyzed as class sums if a sufficiently large number of terms are taken for analysis on the same large set of dimensions. Thus "unitary definition" is an absolutely inadequate criterion for homonymity.

In order to avoid these dilemmas, we suggest the following alternative definition of homonyms: *two or more words, phonemically or graphically identical, which cannot be economically defined on the same set of dimensions without overlap or inclusion of one by the other.* (The restriction permits recognition of such homonyms as "duck" as species, and "duck" as female of that species.) Furthermore, we suggest that a policy of avoiding "homonyms" in English semantic translations is something of a red herring in analysis, interfering with the development of a consistent and logical notation, influencing the choice of either dimensions and values or the size of lexicon, and interposing an arbitrary preference for one kind of logical operator (the class product) in a situation where, in general, both class sums and class products must be used anyway. And, of course, in the interest of keeping analytical tasks within finite limits, it is always necessary initially to bound the semantic space (the range of possible meanings) by stating some major parameters (such as "kinsman"), as Goodenough and Lounsbury do, in order to exclude metaphors and to preclude reference to biological kinsmen (or kin-types) more remote than the actual native extension of the term. This may, of course, establish a semantic fence where none is intended by the native speaker, but it is justifiable to do so provided the possibility of continuity of meaning across such boundaries is recognized.

## DEFINITION AND CONNOTATION

Both Goodenough and Lounsbury describe their initial purpose in the semantic analysis of kinship terms as the statement of "definitions in terms of distinctive semantic features." The individual kin-types to which a term refers are its *denotata;* the class of these kin-types is its *designatum;* and the "distinctive features of this class" constitute its *significatum* (Lounsbury 1956:168). The significatum of a term is a set of "contextual elements . . . without which it cannot properly occur. Significata are prerequisites while connotata are probabilities and possibilities. Only the former have definitive value" (Goodenough 1956:195).

The key words in the definition of significatum thus are "distinctive," "properly," and "prerequisite." A significatum is a statement of various necessary and sufficient conditions for a kin-type to belong to the class of kin-types denoted by a term. Just which conditions are considered to be necessary and sufficient will depend, in part, on the prior definition of the universe of denotata and in part on the particular set of terms being considered. In general (and synonyms excepted), each term should have a different significatum; but, as we have seen, whether a significatum need be considered as a simple class or relative product is a moot point involved in the problem of homonyms. Nor is it necessary that a significatum, unitary or composite, be unique; as Goodenough has shown, several different significata, based on different groups of dimensions, may be adequate.

A further problem must now be introduced: synonymy. Consider the set of English words *father*, *dad*, *daddy*, *pop*, and *old man*. They are all referential kinship terms which denote kin-types; all, except possibly *dad*, have nonkin homonyms or metaphoric extensions (or are metaphoric extensions of nonkin terms). (In this illustrative discussion we shall not deal with the problem of their usage in kinship address, which is recognized for all but *old man*.) All can be defined straightforwardly on the paradigm shown on page 61 as $a_1b_2c_1$ ("male, one generation above ego, lineal"). In the context of this particular paradigm, obviously, they are synonyms. But equally obviously they do not "mean" quite the same thing in colloquial usage. How then shall we consider them: as same-language synonyms with different connotations, as equivalent terms in different age, sex, and social-class languages, or as nonsynonyms?

If we elect the synonymous-with-different-connotation alternative, we must first observe that the connotata have the force of significata and are not culturally irrelevant idiosyncratic associations. A particular pattern of uses and nonuses of these terms is enjoined by the age, social group, and momentary situation of the speaker, and his usage, to the discriminating listener, conveys important information about his attitudes. We do not intend to formalize the analysis of these terms here, but only to point out that if the distinguishing features of the terms are regarded as connotations, then connotations as a class must be conceived as having two sub-classes: culturally or linguistically enjoined connotations, and idiosyncratic or optional connotations.

To regard the terms as belonging to different English languages eliminates the question of synonyms but replaces it by the problem of translation and leaves the problem of signification untouched. Should a (hypothetical) lower class "pop" be translated into a (again hypothetical) middle class "dad"? Presumably the answer is "yes," since the designata of the terms are identical. But identical designata are no guarantee of identical significata. Thus we now have five componential analyses to do instead of one. And, on the other hand, it is something of a fiction to regard these terms as belonging to different languages; as a matter of fact, most speakers of American English use or recognize these terms.

Finally, we can elect to say that the terms are nonsynonymous in the same language: i.e., their significata are different. This, however, requires that we redefine the universe of denotata from simple kin-types to kin-types with qualifiers, and change the matrix of dimensions from A-B-C to A-B-C-D- · · · -N, adding sufficient dimensions to allow each term a distinctive significatum corresponding to the culturally enjoined "connotations." But, if we do this, we give a new definition of *father:* $a_1b_2c_1 \cdots n_r$ (for, in the context of *dad, daddy, pop,* and *old man, father* does not mean merely "male, one generation above ego, lineal").

We can offer no final solution to this dilemma: evidently, the definition of the universe of denotata and the choice of dimensions must be determined in part by the task of discrimination imposed by the list of terms originally selected. Thus the meaning of a term will be in part dependent on the size and composition of the particular list of terms being defined. This indicates that the meaning of a kinship term as given by a componential analysis is apt to be a minimal meaning, probably not complete in specification of culturally or linguistically relevant dimensions, and certainly devoid of most of the connotations which it will have for individuals and even subgroups in the society. This fact does not diminish the value of componential analysis as a method but suggests that the signification of a kinship term be defined as those semantic features which are in fact used to distinguish the kin-type designatum of the term from the kin-type designata of the other terms *in a given set of terms.* The significatum of a term can, in fact, be conceived to include connotations as well as definitive dimensions; there is no formal limit to the number of dimensions which may be analyzed componentially.

## COMPLEMENTARITY, PARADIGMS, AND SPACES

Central to the conceptions and procedures of componential analysis is the notion of complementarity. A term may be said to complement one or more other terms if it signifies some value which the other terms definitely deny in favor of another value. For instance, English *mother* complements *father* with respect to the two values male and female: *mother* signifies female, *father* signifies male, which is equivalent to not-female, on the dimension of sex. Values which stand in a relation of complementarity thus constitute a single dimension whose two or more values are mutual contraries.

Goodenough's operating procedure, after listing a set of terms and defining the universe of kin-type denotata, is to divide the denotata into two or more groups, and the terms into two or more corresponding groups, on the basis of the complementarity of values on one dimension (for example, sex) which distinguishes the groups of denotata; then to divide each of these groups of terms into subgroups according to the principle of complementarity of their kin-type denotata on another dimension; and so on until each term stands alone as the complement of some other term on a single dimension. Where a term which signifies a particular value on a dimension has no complementary term signifying another logically necessary value on that dimension, the existing term is said to be complemented by "no lexeme." The signification of each term is given by the values which specify its complementarity with respect to other terms.

Now it is evident that the stages of reduction of the set, beyond the first stage, allow a choice to the analyst: he can, on each level of analysis, utilize the same dimensions for the reduction of all the terms on that level, or he can use different dimensions for different groups. Trukese Paradigm 3 illustrates a case where the *same* dimension (L) was used to reduce the groups $e_1$ and $e_2$; Trukese Paradigm 1 (see Fig. 3) illustrates a case where different dimensions were used, after the B-level reduction: no further reduction of $b_3$ (since it contains only one term, reduction would require pairs of mutually complementary "no-lexemes"); $b_2$ reduced by D and E; $b_2d_1e_2$ reduced by F; $b_2d_1e_2f_1$ reduced by C; and $b_1$ reduced by C and J. Lounsbury, although he does not use the word complementarity and does not exhibit the formulas in paradigmatic arrangement, also follows the same general procedure. We are not concerned at the moment to discuss the source of the dimensions utilized: they are developed partly from standard ethnographic concepts (e.g., Kroeber 1909 and Murdock 1949), partly from concepts peculiar to the local culture and social structure; and as we have seen the choice of dimensions is in general not determinate from formal considerations: a number of sets of dimensions will, with more or less elegance, accomplish the partition of the universe of terms.

We draw attention, however, to the implications of a regular or an irregular reduction of terms. In regular reduction, not only must all remaining terms be reduced on each level of analysis, but all terms on each level must be reduced on the same dimension. If the reduction is regular on *at least one* level of analysis, then all the terms can be displayed in the same paradigm.

If the reduction is *not* regular on *any* level of analysis, then the terms cannot be displayed in the same paradigm, for their significata are not logically complementary on any dimension. We refer here to Goodenough's concise definition of paradigm: "any set of linguistic forms . . . which signify complementary sememes [significata] may be said to belong to the same paradigm" (Goodenough 1956:197). Goodenough's Paradigm 1 is a paradigm according to his own and our definition, therefore, even though his dimensions F and J are logically nonindependent. Expressions whose significata do not include reference to one or more of the dimensions may by Goodenough's definition also exist on the same paradigm: *neji* ($b_3$), for instance, is the complement of every other term with respect to generation.

A paradigm, however, is merely a mapping of a particular set of terms on a semantic space. A definite number of different sets of terms can be mapped on any given finite semantic space; and any given set of terms can be mapped on an infinite number of spaces. Thus a paradigm is essentially a logical function, comparable to a mathematical function, each term (value of the function) being equivalent to a specific cell or group of cells in a defined space.

The general properties of semantic spaces are not discussed by any of the authors considered above. We are developing a theory of semantic spaces and a suitable calculus of semantic functions, but detailed presentation here would be tedious. Nevertheless, it is necessary at this point to make some brief exposition in order to clarify the further development of this paper.

A semantic space may be initially characterized as a group of values (logical predicates) related by certain definite logical rules. Each of these values refers to a subset $\alpha_i$ of a set of empirical phenomena $A$ (for example, $A$ might be the set of all members of a community). Any values $d_i$, $d_j$, $\cdots$ $d_n$ which refer to mutually exclusive subsets $\alpha_i$, $\alpha_j$, $\cdots$ $\alpha_n$ of $A$, and are therefore mutual contraries of one another, will be said to belong to a single dimension D. In fact, the group of values will subdivide into several dimensions A, B, C, $\cdots$ N. At least one of these dimensions will be logically independent of at least one other (i.e., no value or group of values on that dimension implies, or denies, a value or group of values on the other); some of the other dimensions, if any, may be logically dependent. A semantic space may now be redefined as the class product, or the relational product, or both, of the dimensions A, B, C, $\cdots$ N.

Now class-product spaces may be of at least three kinds (and all three have been used in componential analysis). Orthogonal spaces are constructed from independent dimensions. An orthogonal space may be defined as the set of class-products formed by all unique combinations of values from the N dimensions, each product including one value from each dimension, and each product not being self-contradictory. These class-products are significata, in Goodenough's and Lounsbury's sense, whose values (components) have the special property of being mutually contrary on every dimension. A set of terms whose reduction has not been regular on every level of analysis evidently cannot be represented on one orthogonal space.

A nonorthogonal class-product space is constructed from a group of dimensions at least one pair of which is nonindependent: that is to say, whenever there is a negative logical entailment of at least one value on any dimension by any value on any other dimension, the space is nonorthogonal. There are two types of nonorthogonal spaces: in the first type, all the dimensions span the same set of referents $A$, but at least two values from different dimensions are mutually contrary $([a_i \rightarrow \sim b_j] \wedge [b_j \rightarrow \sim a_i])$; in the second type, each dimension overlaps at least one other dimension, and all dimensions can be arranged in an interlocking chain, but at least two dimensions span different sets of referents ($A_1$ and $A_2$), and hence at least one value on one dimension is mutually contrary with each of the $n$ values on another dimension

$$[a_i \rightarrow \sim \{b_j \vee b_k \vee \cdots \vee b_n\}] \wedge [\{b_j \vee b_k \vee \cdots \vee b_n\} \rightarrow \sim a_i].$$

The three types of class-product spaces may be represented, for purposes of discussion here, by three simple diagrams constructed in each case from two binary dimensions containing, respectively, the values $a_1$ and $a_2$ and $b_1$ and $b_2$, as in Fig. 2:

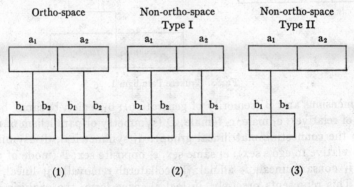

FIG. 2. Types of class-product spaces formed of two binary dimensions.

In diagram (1), the dimensions are independent and both extend over the same set of denotata. In diagram (2), the dimensions are nonindependent but both still extend over the same set of denotata. In diagram (3), the dimensions are nonindependent and the dimension B extends over only a part of the set of denotata spanned by A. (The denotata may be considered to be either persons or kin-types; the identity of the elements of the set of denotata need not be considered here.)

Now, when the space is nonorthogonal, it may be convenient to map a paradigm on it either as if it were a congeries of spaces, related hierarchically, or as a rectangular matrix with "holes" (impossible cells). When the space is orthogonal, the paradigm may most concisely be mapped on a "solid" rectangular matrix (a grid or property-space; see Barton 1955). By the hierarchical method, one representation of Trukese Paradigm 1 (corresponding to the process of reduction as given by Goodenough 1956:206) is given in Fig. 3:

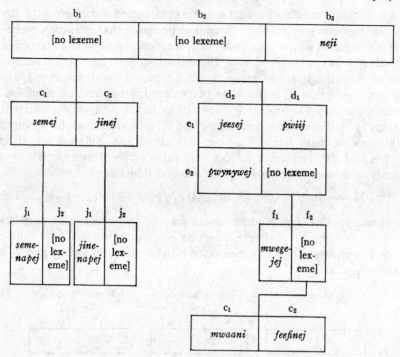

Fig. 3. Trukese Paradigm 1.

The dimensions are: B (seniority of generation): $b_1$ senior, $b_2$ same, $b_3$ junior; C (sex of relative): $c_1$ male, $c_2$ female; D (symmetry or parallelism of relationship to the connecting matrilineal group): $d_1$ symmetrical, $d_2$ asymmetrical; E (sex relative to ego's sex): $e_1$ same sex, $e_2$ opposite sex; F (mode of relationship); $f_1$ consanguineal, $f_2$ affinal; J (collateral removal): $j_1$ lineal, $j_2$ nonlineal. This represents precisely, in logical-space form, the analysis given in Goodenough's list-form Paradigm 1 (1956:206), except that it reveals three additional "no-lexemes" ($b_1$, $b_2$, and $b_2d_1e_2$) which strict application of a complementarity rule requires.

By contrast, the analysis of Paradigm 4 appears as a single space as follows:

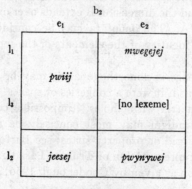

Fig. 4. Trukese Paradigm 4.

The question now arises: can paradigms on nonorthogonal spaces, like some of those presented by Goodenough and Lounsbury and like our representation of American English (Fig. 1), be transformed by an appropriate selection of dimensions into paradigms on orthogonal spaces on which all the terms, or lexemes, in a lexicon can be represented? After considerable experimentation, we are prepared to state that it will rarely be possible to represent all the terms of any full kinship lexicon on a single orthogonal space, but that it is possible in some cases to present all of the kinship lexemes (expressions whose signification cannot be deduced from the signification and arrangement of their parts) and certain groups of "core terms" on one orthogonal space. The Trukese lexemes shown in Fig. 4, together with three others (*semej*, *jinej*, and *neji*), can all be represented on an orthogonal space; all of the Pawnee terms except those for "grandparents" and "grandchildren" can be shown likewise. We have tried assiduously, however, to place the forty-nine Lapp terms on one space without success, nor can all American English terms be convincingly shown on one orthogonal space.

We must also now observe that the practice of omitting reference to dimensions, as performed by Goodenough and Lounsbury, produces still another serious uncertainty. Once a space of N dimensions has been defined, the omission of a letter for a dimension should mean only that the space is nonorthogonal, Type II, and that the dimension omitted in defining a term was omitted because that dimension is irrelevant to the signification of the term. If the term is merely ambiguous as to a dimension on an orthogonal space, it should be entered without subscript; if the space is nonorthogonal, Type I, the implied value with its proper subscript must be specified. Without such a rule, the omission of a dimensional symbol may mean any one of three things: the term refers to a class sum ("and/or") of values on a dimension; the term refers to a definite single value which it shares with other complementary terms; the dimension is irrelevant to the meaning of the term.

The further analysis of the formal properties of logical and semantic spaces would take us too far afield, however, from the limited purposes of this paper, and we defer the development of the theory of semantic spaces to another occasion.

## NONCOMMUTATIVE RELATIONAL CONCEPTS

The Trukese kinship lexicon contains relational linguistic forms in which two or more root morphs are connected by suffixed possessive pronouns (for example, *seme-nape-j*). These expressions are formally comparable to descriptive English expressions like "father's brother"; but some of them act not as descriptive statements but as kinship terms. Thus English "father's brother" is not a kinship term but *semenapej* is. We may also observe that Lounsbury, in analyzing Pawnee, used a noncommutative possessive relation between kintypes, which he symbolized by juxtaposing two or more symbols without writing an intervening relative product operator, with the preceding symbol "possessing" the latter. His usage is identical with traditional usage in the definition of the English kin-type denotata on which both he and Goodenough rely:

FaBr, MoSi, WiBrWi, are possessive relational concepts implying an unwritten relative product operator. Goodenough does not utilize relational concepts of this kind in statements of significata (although he recognizes that the Trukese use relative products of his "lexemes" to construct other expressions in the larger lexicon). Lounsbury does depend on relative products, both to define his dimension of agnatic rank, and to state the significata for "grandparental" and "grandchild" classes. In our analysis of the English terms, furthermore, we used explicity relational concepts to define the values on the dimension of lineality, and other dimensions could have been expressed relationally.

Let us ask the general question: May not the users of many kinship lexicons cognitively define at least some of their terms relationally, even though it may be possible for the ethnographer to analyze them as class products? The answer must be "yes," both for English and Pawnee, and probably also for the Trukese full lexicon. Requests to English-speaking informants to define common English kinship terms yield responses of both class product and relational types: *father* may be defined, for instance, as "male parent," which can be analyzed as the class product "male$\wedge$lineal$\wedge$one generation above ego"; but *nephew* may be defined as "son of sister or brother," and *aunt* and *uncle* respectively as "sister of parent" and "brother of parent." The latter definitions are the relative products "son/sister," "son/brother," "sister/parent," "brother /parent." The adequacy of these definitions (which were provided by English-speaking informants) is beside the point: cognitively, the relation *aunt* may be reckoned by an informant not as a class product but as a relative product.

These observations lead us to ask whether many a kinship lexicon may not profitably be analyzed by a combination of class and relational calculi. There will often be a set of primitive terms, "lexemes" in Goodenough's sense, which may be exemplified by the two English sets: (a) parent, child, sibling, ancestor, and descendant, and (b) mother, father, brother, sister, son, daughter, husband, wife; and which can be defined discursively, or componentially analyzed on a single paradigm or even on a single class product space. And there will be a set of terms, some of which may be "lexemes" (but not primitives), which can be defined either as class products or as relative products of *the primitive terms of that lexicon.* The logical structure of noncommutative relations, involving the operator "/," is somewhat different from that of commutative relations involving operators "$\wedge$" (and) and "$\vee$" (and/or). In consequence, paradigms composed of relative products will have a different structure from those composed of conjunctive and disjunctive products. The details of the appropriate logical calculi, and the relative merits of relational and class-product significata and paradigms, however, are not the point of discussion here. Furthermore, the choice of one mode of analysis or another will depend on the purpose of the investigation. And it is to the matter of purpose that we now turn our attention.

## PSYCHOLOGICAL REALITY, SOCIAL-STRUCTURAL REALITY, AND INDETERMINACY

Goodenough repeatedly states in his paper on Trukese terminology (1956) that the purpose of the componential analysis of kinship terms is to provide psychologically real definitions. He speaks of people having "certain criteria in mind by which they make the judgment that A is or is not B's cousin" (p. 195); he alludes to the method as a means of learning about "human cognitive processes" (p. 198); he discusses "concepts" which exist in "the Trukese cognitive world" (p. 213). In his earlier monograph on Truk he justifies the choice of components by characterizing them as "criteria" or "rules," valid in "Trukese thinking," by which the Trukese "appraise[s] his relationship with another individual." This does not contradict his prefatory caution that "he does not intend to present [the Trukese culture] as the Trukese see it." What Goodenough is avoiding is not description of Trukese practical thinking about kinsmen but Trukese rationalization about their own kinship terminology (cf. Goodenough 1951:11, 100–101.) The intention of componential analysis in Goodenough's sense is to state the meaning of the terms to the native users of the terms.

Now this is a major theoretical commitment. It happens to be one which we share: a part of anthropology's mission which is of particular concern to us is the development of formal theories and methods which will describe the relationship between cultural forms and processes, and their social-structural correlates, whose locus is a society, and psychological (cognitive) forms and processes, whose locus is the individual. This commitment need not, however, be shared by all users of the method of componential analysis, or of any other method of semantic analysis; and these semantic methods do not inevitably yield psychologically real descriptions of meaning. Semantic analysis may, in fact, be profitably used for nonpsychologically oriented social-structural analysis. It is therefore particularly important to clarify the distinction between these equally valid purposes, psychological and structural, because two methodological difficulties inherent in the method itself affect these two purposes differently.

By "psychological reality" we mean what the senior author has discussed under the concept of mazeway (Wallace 1956a). The psychological reality of an individual is the world as he perceives and knows it, in his own terms; it is his world of meanings. A "psychologically real" description of a culture thus is a description which approximately reproduces in an observer the world of meanings of the native users of that culture. "Structural reality," on the other hand, is a world of meanings, as applied to a given society or individual, which is real to the ethnographer, but it is not *necessarily* the world which constitutes the mazeway of any other individual or individuals. The difference is well illustrated in the difference which sometimes obtains between descriptions of a given society by social anthropologists who are interested in predictive models of relations among groups and in related economic and demographic processes, and by ethnographers who are interested in describing the world as the individual sees it. In the province of the semantics of kinship terminology, psychological and structural reality should be related extensionally via the identity of the sets of persons (or kin-types) denoted by pairs of expressions. The statement, *the English term cousin means any nonlineal consanguineal relative who is a descendant of a sibling of an ancestor of ego* is structurally real to an anthropological observer because he can predict the usage of the term accurately from his definition, but is hardly a psychologically real definition for all speakers of the English language; yet it is extensionally equivalent to, or at least implies, many psychologically real definitions of *cousin*.

The first of the methodological difficulties alluded to above is an almost unavoidable ethnocentrism. If the analyst is writing a paper in ethnographers' English (or any language other than the idiom of his informants), he is to a degree constrained by the terminological resources of his own language in his efforts to state the meaning of a foreign expression. Even the simple kin-type denotata of which we have made such heavy use are not, to my knowledge, absolutely universal human concepts. One need not introduce here an idealistic, Whorfian linguistic relativism; the principle more closely approaches that of complementarity, in the mathematical physicist's sense. Just as the physicist cannot measure both the position and momentum of a particle under the same conditions, so the semantic analyst cannot state simultaneously the meaning of an event in his own language and in that of another person, because the two languages impose different conditions of analysis. Statements can be made in one language which will be highly predictive and therefore approximately equivalent in truth value to statements in another language; but they will not be tautologically equivalent statements in the strictest sense. Statements can be made which (in the strictest sense) are tautologically equivalent to one another in *one* language or calculus but not in two.

While preoccupation with this problem of "linguistic complementarity" leads to solipsism, ignoring it inhibits one's ability to develop increasingly proximate solutions to the second problem, that of indeterminacy. This, in semantics, is precisely equivalent to the physicist's relativity. Goodenough, for instance, exhibits three separate paradigms containing the terms *pwiij*, *mwegejej*, *jeesej*, and *pwynywej*. Each paradigm contains a different set of dimensions; one of them is an orthogonal space; one of them contains only unitary definitions, one only composite definitions, and one both unitary and composite definitions. We have produced for our own edification still other paradigms which also define the same terms. All of these analyses are extensionally valid. What then is the source of the multiplicity of solutions?

The discussion up to this point has revealed several major sources of indeterminacy: the fact that the set of all kin-type denotata has no finite boundaries; variation in the universe of denotata chosen; variation in the number and identity of terms selected from a lexicon for analysis on the same semantic space; variation in the identity of the dimensions chosen; variation as to the use of logical operators (class or relative products); variation in type of class-product space; variation as to inclusion or exclusion of "connotative" dimensions. These variations in themselves will not affect the extensional validity of the analysis: the only criteria of extensional validity available are the identity of the sets of kin-types, or of the persons, denoted by the significatum of the term and by the term itself. If a significatum denotes, in any set of denotata, the same subset as the term itself, it is an extensionally valid meaning of the term. There is, in fact, an indeterminate number of equivalent significata, both conjunctive and disjunctive, which will with equal extensional validity define any given term.

Goodenough (1956:213) seems to adopt the working principle that no evaluative discrimination is possible, that all extensionally valid definitions are equally real psychologically: "Since we can reproduce Trukese kinship usage equally well from any one of these three paradigms, we cannot eliminate from the Trukese cognitive world any one of the alternative conceptual variables E, K, D, F, and L." Romney, on the other hand, expresses disturbance over this generic indeterminacy of semantic analysis (which he believes, we think mistakenly, to be the peculiar product of Goodenough's reduction procedure) and offers a technique of analysis by "range-sets" which is said to yield a "determinate solution." Romney's technique is to define certain dimensions (in his terminology, "range-sets") by specifying a set of binary operations (such as changing sex of kin-type, taking reciprocal, etc.) which will transform the designatum of one term into the designatum of another. Since the denotata are the traditional kin-types, together with sex of speaker and age relative to ego, and a criterion of symmetry is imposed, only a limited number of such operations is possible. Dimensions with more than two variables are excluded from range-set analysis. All denotata which can be related by a single operation form a range-set; relations between the dimensions which constitute range-sets are defined by componential analysis on a logical space. This logical space does not state the meanings of terms, however; it only defines range-sets in terms of their position in the space. The result thus is simply a statement about the logical relationships among the dimensions. For instance, in his analysis of Goodenough's Trukese dimensions, Romney finds that three of them are expressible as binary operations on the kin-types; the other two are not so expressible; and not all of the dimensions are logically independent. The determinacy of this analysis by range-sets depends therefore on a special method of defining dimensions; it yields, not a semantic analysis of terms, but a logical analysis of the dimensions chosen; and it reduces only that fraction of the indeterminacy which remains after other sources of indeterminacy are held constant by stating, for a given set of terms, which dimensions can be defined as the result of binary operations on a known grouping of kin-types.

The crux of the difference between a psychologically valid description and one which is only structurally valid lies, of course, in the choice of the dimensions and logical operators (class or relative products) used in defining the space, and in the choice of the logical operators (class products, class sums, and relative products) employed in defining the terms and mapping the paradigm on the space. The ingenuity of the analyst is most severely tested in the identification of the dimensions of kinship in psychologically real spaces. Here the standard and "universal" dimensions, such as those suggested by Kroeber (1909) and Murdock (1949), must often be re-defined and supplemented by dimensions peculiar to the particular informant and his society. Such dimensions may be given by structural features of the kinship system—marriage classes, clans, land-holding lineages, and so forth—which function as principles of classification in the particular society. It cannot be emphasized too strongly that the point of the difference between psychological and structural reality lies in qualitative differences in semantic spaces and not in differences between individual and group characteristics. Psychologically real and structurally real descriptions alike can each apply to both individuals and groups.

The foregoing considerations lead to two major conclusions: first, that by working only on ethnographic data, two or more extensionally valid and perhaps even tautologically equivalent (in one language, either the ethnographer's or the native's) definitions can usually be obtained for any given term; and second, that while more than one definition may be psychologically real, in the sense of representing how users think with and about that term, one or more definitions may be real only in a structural sense, even though such definitions must be extensionally equivalent to psychologically real definitions.

A problem for research, then, must be to develop techniques for stating and identifying those definitions which are most proximate to psychological reality. This is a formidable task. The formal methods of componential analysis, even with refinement and extension of their logico-semantic assumptions, will not yield discriminations between psychologically real and non-psychologically but social-structurally real meanings. It may be noted that the psychologist Osgood, who is also concerned with the meanings of some kinship terms and has developed a formal testing procedure called the "semantic differential" (Osgood 1957) avoids definitive meaning entirely and deals only with the connotative significata of fixed sets of terms (including nonkinship as well as kinship terms) on a fixed set of three dimensions (active-passive, potent-impotent, and evaluative) which define a "universal" connotative space. Ethnographers like Goodenough and Lounsbury obtain clues to psychological reality from observations on the cultural milieu of the terminology such as residence and marriage rules or historical changes. But the only way of achieving definite knowledge of psychological reality will be to study the semantics of individuals both before and after a formal, abstract, cultural-semantic analysis of the terms has been performed. Simple demands for verbal definition, the use of Rivers' genealogical method, and analysis of the system of kinship behaviors may not be sufficient here: additional procedures, by individual representative informants, of matching and sorting, answering hypothetical questions, and description of relationships in order to reveal methods of reckoning will probably all be required. This sort of information is not always obtained, or published if obtained, by ethnographers, although a good deal of it is scattered in field notes or distilled in memory. It is possible to say fairly that not only in kinship, but also in other ethnographic subjects, the degree of psychological reality achieved in ethnographic reporting is not only uneven but on the average probably rather low. Social-structural reality can be achieved; psychological reality can only be approximated. But such approximations are sorely needed. The problem of extending the psychological reality of ethnographic description is not just a "culture-and-personality" problem, it is a general anthropological issue with implications for anyone concerned with the relationship between cultural and cognitive processes. Indeed, it is a general issue for the behavioral sciences, because structurally real descriptions do not predict certain phenomena so well as psychologically real descriptions.

## CONCLUSION

Semantic analysis in anthropology concerns, primarily, neither personality and culture, nor linguistics, nor culture and social structure per se, but cognitive processes in culturally organized behavior. This paper has defined two methods of semantic analysis which have been applied to kinship terms: the traditional kin-type designations and componential analysis. The methods of componential analysis are examined and illustrated in some detail with respect to their various assumptions and procedures. Its difficulties in handling five problem areas are analyzed: homonyms and metaphors; definition, connotation, and synonymy; paradigms and semantic spaces; relational logic; and indeterminacy, psychological reality, and social-structural reality. Some solutions and recommended lines of attack are suggested, based on formal semantic calculi. The distinction between psychologically and structurally real analysis is analyzed at some length. We feel that the application, in ethnographic and psychological research, of formal logico-semantic methods is not an exercise in technical virtuosity but an essential procedure for solving problems in analysis already confronting this generation of social anthropologists. In this paper, however, we are not concerned with presenting a theory of semantic spaces, or a semantic calculus, but in analyzing, evaluating, and making more effective the method of componential analysis for the practical study of cognitive processes in one aspect of cultural behavior: kinship terminology.

### NOTES

[1] We wish to acknowledge our gratitude to Harold Conklin, J. L. Fischer, Walter Goldschmidt, Ward Goodenough, and David Schneider for helpful advice both in matters of analysis and of style.

[2] We realize that componential analysis has a precursor or ally in any method which aims at defining some or all of the concepts which are explicit or implicit in any terminological system (see, e.g., Edmonson 1957 and Fischer 1958). We also realize that the study of the semantics of kinship terminology is only one aspect of the study of kinship behavior. In this paper we are not attempting to trace the history of kinship studies nor to deal with aspects of kinship behavior other than the definitional meaning of kinship terms.

## REFERENCES CITED

BARNETT, H. G.
 1953 Innovation. New York, McGraw-Hill.

BARTON, A. H.
 1955 The concept of property-space in social research. *In* The language of social research, P. F. Lazarsfeld and Morris Rosenberg, eds. Glencoe, The Free Press.

BIRKHOFF, GARRETT and SAUNDERS MACLANE
 1941 A survey of modern algebra. New York, Macmillan.

EDMONSON, M. S.
 1957 Kinship terms and kinship concepts. American Anthropologist 59:393–433.

FISCHER, J. L.
 1958 Genealogical space. Unpublished manuscript read at annual meeting of American Anthropological Association, Washington.

GREENBERG, J. H.
 1949 The logical analysis of kinship. Philosophy of Science 16:58–64.

GOODENOUGH, W. H.
 1951 Property, kin, and community on Truk. New Haven, Yale University Press.
 1956 Componential analysis and the study of meaning. Language 32:195–216.
 1957 Componential analysis of Lapp kinship terminology. Unpublished manuscript read at annual meeting of American Anthropological Association, Chicago.

KROEBER, A. L.
 1909 Classificatory systems of relationship. Journal of the Royal Anthropological Institute 39:77–84.

LOUNSBURY, F. G.
 1956 A semantic analysis of the Pawnee kinship usage. Language 32:158–194.

METZGER, DUANE
 1957 The formal analysis of kinship: II. special problems as exemplified in Zuni. Unpublished manuscript read at annual meeting of American Anthropological Association, Chicago.

MORRIS, C. W.
 1955 Foundations of the theory of signs. *In* International Encyclopedia of Unified Science. Otto Neurath and others, eds. Vol. 1. Chicago, University of Chicago Press.

MURDOCK, G. P.
 1949 Social structure. New York, Macmillan.

OSGOOD, C. E.
 1957 The measurement of meaning. Urbana, University of Illinois Press.

ROMNEY, A. K. and P. J. EPLING
 1958 A simplified model of Kariera kinship. American Anthropologist 60:59–74.

ROMNEY, JAY
 1957 The formal analysis of kinship: I. general analytic frame. Unpublished manuscript read at annual meeting of American Anthropological Association, Chicago.

WALLACE, A. F. C.
 1956a Mazeway resynthesis: a bio-cultural theory of religious inspiration. Transactions of the New York Academy of Sciences 18:626–638.
 1956b Revitalization movements. American Anthropologist 58:264–281.

# The Community as Object and as Sample*

## CONRAD M. ARENSBERG

*Center for Advanced Study in the Behavioral Sciences, Stanford, California*

O NE of the encouraging points of convergence in the various empirically based social sciences is the growing power and sophistication of the community study method (Arensberg 1954; Hollingshead 1948; König 1956; Chiva 1958; Redfield 1956a). The method has come to be much and ably used in ethnography. There it has added much to the emerging possibility of an at-last meaningful comparative sociology of the world's peoples (Steward 1950). The method, of course, has long roots in social surveys, in rural and agricultural sociology and economics, and in human geography (Pauline V. Young 1949; Wilson 1945; Taylor 1945; Utermann 1952; Maget 1953). It has not been confined to small and rural communities alone. It has as well been employed in urban sociology and in the studying and planning of *urbanisme* (Bott 1956; Young and Wilmott 1957; Shevky 1929; Simey 1954; Balandier 1955).

This convergence upon the community study method signals the growing use of the community for many purposes. The community has served as a sample or unit of observation for the study of a culture or society, as a locus or local embodiment of a wider or general social problem or phenomenon, as a testing ground for plans of change, amelioration, or development (Batten 1958; Ruopp 1953; Ware 1952). Convergence upon the community study method thus marks a reentrance of the community, small and large, into the forefront of social science activity. We say reentrance because much of the earliest social science, in the seminal period of the late decades of the last century, was also focused on the community. Such seminal work explored the repeated, often widespread, elementary or simple forms of the local commonwealth; the village, its land-use and settlement pattern, its village constitution; the *polis*, the early city (Maine 1871; Maurer 1854; Peake 1954; Fustel de Coulange 1905; Meitzen 1895). Problems were different then, of course, but the community as field for their study or sample of their universe was even then the workplace.

Despite the long and now renewed history of the community as a center and workplace of social science interest, much confusion about it still persists. The thing-in-itself, the community as object, is imperfectly separated, in concept and in practice, from the use of it, as field or sample, where the community is that within which work is done, observations made, relationships traced out. The separation of the problems is clear enough in the abstract; it is clearly a

---

* This paper has been written at the invitation of Prof. René König, University of Cologne, for his forthcoming *Handbook of Empirical Sociology* (1961).

necessary one. To study a problem in a community, in its natural setting, or in an exemplification in one well chosen community rather than in all its endless local occurrences, one must first recognize and mark off one community among the many. Only later, and after one's field work or local survey or experiment, must one next ask in what way is what I find here representative, in what way is this community, and the place of my problem data in it, capable of standing for, and leading me to explanation of, the universal occurrence of the problem and its place and reasons in the whole culture or society of its occurrence. Identification and definition is the first step; a theory of sampling and of part-whole relationships is the second.

Let us review the obvious separateness of the questions about community. On the one hand, one asks what a community is. One asks as well what kinds there are of them; how and why these kinds developed; what functions they perform. One asks how functions change or shift in their identities, or how they succeed or fail in their execution, as the form, life, or viability and cohesiveness of the community changes, with the emergence and the succession of one variety of community upon another, in response to differing economic, political, religious, or demographic influences. One can ask as well about the pathology of the community, the effect of its falling away, or of its overgrowth, upon human welfare or performance or security; one can ask about its success, even its necessity, in supporting or perfecting these human results, individual or collective. However far one goes, the questions are about the nature of the community as a thing (Brownell 1950; Stein 1959; Sanders 1958).

On the other hand, the questions are different when one asks about the community as a field or a sample in which to study something else than the community itself. How far can one trust what one finds to be general? Or, turning it around, how far can we trust the general to show up in one, or this, community? How is any particular community, so local and unique in place and time, also standard, "average," representative? How does any one stand for all the others, or for the whole of, a society, culture, civilization, or epoch? Can one legitimately see in any one community, even the best chosen one, a microcosm of a whole society, or of a particular, but much wider and more populous, national, religious, or epochal whole? Will what we see in it mirror faithfully what we might see in any and all other unseen parts of that whole? Will what we see in it teach us surely about that whole? Other figures of speech and thought provide us what tentative models of the part-whole connection that seem to justify using the community as field or sample. Are they capable of refinement into justifiable and rigorous scientific method? How far can we use a known community of persons as a portrait, an epitome, a witness of the life, nature, fate, character, and spirit of the unknown others of the people of their age and civilization? Granted we know some things about these others, or about the collectivity, like their works or art products, their social and psychological problems, their common national character or ethos, what is the new light about these things that intimate and detailed knowledge of a community of their fellows in local interaction will throw?

These are the questions about the community as field or sample. They are not addressed to its nature, but to its use by science. Social science is, obviously, only a late-comer to the use of substitute parts of the human and soical scene to stand for the whole welter of experience and to let one think usefully, in manageable compass, about a reality too big to deal with all at once. Artists and humanists have long analyzed and symbolized the large in the small, the human whole in the particular: a biography, a vignette, a genre scene, a pageantry on canvas, or a drama or an epic of event and character. Today, especially, it has been the written novel and the motion picture play which have caught the community. Such mirrorings of life show the crowded, intricate settings of human action.

Naturally it has been incumbent upon the social scientist, though not upon the artist, to systematize, justify, and test out the legitimacy of such selections and close-ups of experience. The scientist in him is forced to turn art into method, to reduce impression to rigorous recording, to develop communicable canons of procedure and inference, to make explicit and economical the models of structure and interconnection he uses to convey his convictions about discovered relationships.

It is unfair, of course, to judge all the users of modern community study method by the completeness with which they have carried out these imperatives of science. It would have been equally unfair to judge all artists by the lucidity of the symbols they used to achieve fidelity to life. Not all the modern users of the community have made explicit in any way either their definition of community or their rationale of inference of connection between local finding and problem illuminated. Scientific procedure does not need to be consciously programmed to be effective. In many studies, the community, used as a field, has been chosen as much for its convenience as for its representativeness. Merely carrying the search for factors in a problem to concrete data in the events of real lives in a real time and place has often been empirical referral enough to cut away misconceptions and assure rewarding discoveries. The community is, as we shall see, not the only field to which modern social science now takes its problems for referral to empirical reality. Nor is the gain from such referral entirely destroyed, with good luck, if it is made blindly or without plan and care.

This referral to empirical reality, part of natural history method in the life sciences, obviously takes a different course than does experimental design or social survey. Community study, as a technique of approach to facts, as a way of selecting and gathering them and of testing their hypothesized interconnections, is one of a number of modern observational methods (Whyte 1951). To come to grips with an *explicandum* in social and cultural science, for example, social disorganization (Whyte 1943), racial bias and discrimination (Wagley 1958), rejection of advanced technology or of western medicine (Dobyns 1951; Spicer 1953; Paul 1955), to use the merest few of the many problems which have been now successfully illuminated by such referral, one recourse of the researcher has been to do close-up observation of his problem matter in a local scene, normally a community, where its connection with other things can be seen, its meaning for persons caught in it within the round of their lives with their fellows can be watched, explored, weighed. In an earlier treatment of the method, I have called this sort of referral study *in vivo*, again on the natural history analogy (Arensberg 1954).

The community is certainly not the only setting for such localization and particularization of a problem of social science. The virtue in using the community has proved to be its massive immersion of the researcher in its interior realities and complexities, where natural history observation, especially in alien, foreign, or otherwise—by class or culture—different ways of life (a fruitful imperative of ethnographic field work *a fortiori*) has been almost inescapable. Natural definition of the field thus acted to catch the curious social science observer up. Limitation and structuring of the community as object or bounded field could wait.

Not so, it seems, with the other localizations in which observational and exploratory methods have been used to refer *explicanda* to raw reality. Chief among these others, in recent decades, have been the workroom, or departmental work place, industrial sociology and industrial relations study (Arensberg 1957; Schneider 1957; Friedmann 1950); the hospital (Lentz and Burling 1956), the medical school (Fox 1959), the psychiatric hospital ward (Caudill 1958); again, also the political machine, caucus room, the lobby, the pressure group (Truman 1951) in political science; the decision-making bodies, committees of various levels of organization in administrative bodies, industrial as well as governmental (Kaufman 1960; Guetzkow 1951); deliberative or "problem solving groups," some of them *ad hoc* or experimental (Bales 1950). Even the American jury has been so studied (Strodtbeck n.d.).

Prominent among such localizations, though using the individual rather than the group, have been similar depth explorations of persons. Studies of culture-and-personality and of "national character" have come in recent years to find in the person the microcosm of the culture or society they explored. Any national, "bearer of the culture," might mirror it, as once, before their refinements of such concepts into scientific method (Metraux 1953; Mead 1953; and Mead 1951), any Slav must carry "l'ame Slave," as Salvador de Madariaga could celebrate Spanish, French, and English national characters in the man of each nation.

The varying and quite differently inspired uses of the community, then, as well as those other localizations of problem materials, are alike in being developments of empirical, observational method. They could yield effective results even before justifying theory, and rigor of method should make their rationale clear. In this they are like many other developments in science, whether natural or social science. Part, at least, of their fruitfulness has been this just cited forced immersion of the researcher, especially in field work, in his field, and the forced referral of his ideas to the facts of it. The other localizations required greater prior definition, perhaps, or presented more difficult access, or left it easier for one to evade, escape, or withdraw. The community as field and sample, especially when a researcher had to travel to it, set up protracted residence in it, often forced an investigator to become participant observer almost in spite of himself in the very act of finding his way about. Thus, community study has perhaps best assured in modern social science research execution of two of the imperatives of all science: that hypothesis be built from empirical perception of interconnections of relevant phenomena and that generalization be checked by a return to it.

Thus, indeed, the uses of the community as mirror or field or sample, which we have instanced, as opposed to the problems about its nature, are all of them interrelated, regardless of the terms, specified or not, in which they are justified. They are alike in being warranted as referrals to reality, essays in controlled empiricism, whatever the part-whole theory they embody and, of course, however diverse the questions, the *explicanda*, brought to the community. The point does not absolve us from a search for better theory, both of the nature of the community and of its role as part to the wholes of cultures, societies, or nations. But it does explain, I think, why we may place fairly strong trust in the findings of the community study method, without too great impatience with as yet unachieved justifications of its variations in design and execution.

Even today the variations continue still to be matters of journeyman experience rather than high plan. The use of the community as mirror is commonest still in problems of ethnographic and ethnological research. There a culture-as-a-whole must still be somehow perceived and demarcated, in comparing people with people, but field work must be executed in a particular and limited community of its "bearers," even though one's problem is a phenomenon common to many peoples and cultures or an institution functionally imbedded in some but not in others. Thus community study is more and more widely employed in such problems of theory of culture and its evolution and nature, as that of the nature of peasantry (Redfield 1956b), the emergence and interaction of high culture ("the great traditions") and low culture ("the little traditions") (Srinivas 1952, 1955), the nature and effect of the plantation and its aftermath (Steward 1955, 1956; Rubin 1958), the "grandmother family" (Smith 1956). It is widespread in studies of cultural and economic change and development, not only in older, extra-European regions (Leighton and Smith 1952; Belshaw 1957), but in the heartland of Atlantic (Western) civilization as well (Taylor 1945; Maget 1955; Wurzbacher 1954; Bancroft 1958; Pitt-Rivers 1954).

Similarly, the use of the community as field is oftener to be found in the disciplines where the researcher's own society and culture can be taken for granted and no comparison with others is required. These disciplines are sociology, social psychology, social psychiatry. For problems as diverse as that of the impact of mass communications on social cohesion and integration (Vidich and Bensman 1958), the success of planned housing (Mogey 1958), the identification of structures of political influence (Hunter 1953; Hunter, Schaffer and Sheps 1956; Kimball 1954), the formation of personality (Oeser

1954; Eaton and Weil 1955), the understanding of classes and class structure (Warner 1952; 1953), to name but a few, a community to be studied has long and often been chosen as the field for deriving, testing, documenting wider theory and explanation.

Recently, social psychiatry has come to take some of its problems to the same field: geriatric question, the etiology of mental illness, the difficulties of case finding, the role of cultural and class factors, have all been linked to inquiry into the structure, customs, stresses of a particular representative community and its people's lives in it (Ruesch 1949; Leighton 1957; Opler 1956). The weaving into older methods of social survey and statistical or ecological inquiry of insights and techniques of community study has certainly brought a new sophistication to research in social and mental hygiene and public health and a fuller attack upon the social and cultural factors of their problems in modern administrative fact finding, planning, and administration in those services (Russell Sage Foundation 1959; Roland 1955; Young 1957).

All in all, then, such gains from community study method and its variants suggest that social science has won for itself a rewarding tool in the method. Better theory of it and of its efficacy will probably, at least to some degree, grow from continued acquaintance with it and from continued experience of its power. Nevertheless, it also seems clear that the tool is so useful that we cannot leave building theory about it solely to cumulative, perhaps wasteful, trial and error. Some hard conceptual work is needed. The reentry of the community into central social science interest which we are witnessing today continues to demand solution of the conceptual and methodological problems corresponding to the two lines of questioning about community as object and community as sample or field which we have distinguished here. The first step toward a better theory of the nature of the community as object cannot be forever left untaken; the second step of a rationale for the community study method, toward a better theory of the part-whole relations of findings in a community and explanations of a problem of a larger universe of many communities, cannot continue to be taken in the dark of vague models of the mirrorings or sampling of reality derived from unspecified and unsystematized canons of art and literature.

What one can do in a single short paper, however summary, cannot be much. Nevertheless, in the space at our disposal here, we would like to take up some of the main difficulties that have been pointed out by critics or practitioners of community studies[1] and suggest answers to these difficulties which derive from a possible, already emergent theory of community as thing and as a sample. Space will not, of course, permit full exposition, let alone full proof, of such a theory; nor am I sure I have it fully complete. But enough of its outline seems already to be arguable to allow us to resolve some, if not all, of the conceptual and methodological difficulties to be cited.

Difficulties raised against the method or about its execution in one study or

[1] What can be said here can only be a small push forward beyond the already excellent recent summaries of König (1956; 1958).

another can be roughly, if badly, summarized under a very few heads. They are four:

1) Representativeness? Which community shall be chosen? The matter is very difficult in countries without seemingly uniform peasant villages, with strong regional differentiation, stratified and segregated classes, ethnically mixed, religiously composite, perhaps racial "plural" societies. It is no easier where economic or administrative or other functional specialization exists among population centers, or where great ranges in size and density separate metropolises from towns and towns from hamlets and dispersed countrysides.

2) Completeness? When is a community a whole one? How is it to be bounded when, usually, one settlement or circle of human interest and contact grades off into and articulates with neighboring or overlapping ones? How, as well, when, often, one community, at one level, seems to be part of another larger one, or subdivides, below, into still smaller ones?

3) Inclusiveness? How far must a community contain in it the institutions, the culture traits, the forces of the whole society or civilization for which it is to serve as a part, sample, or mirror? If it has too few cosmopolitan or external features or influences working locally or extending into it, can it serve as a sample of the world in which they penetrate universally? If it has too many, can it still be counted a viable community?

4) Cohesiveness? And last, when is a community integrated enough, common-minded enough, cooperative or sharing enough, first, to be a community at all? Second, to mirror, but not over- or under-represent, the fissions normal to its society? Communities, especially from close up and within, are as often divided into estranged groups, factions, sects as they are harmonious or concerted. What of limits, balances, unities here?

Now it is plain that these four questions concern the community both as thing and as sample. Distinct as are the steps toward defining the community for itself and for its use and legitimacy as sample, answers to the four questions are necessary in taking either step. Nor can the answers be unrelated among themselves in the end; a community must be identified, and on the identification hangs its usefulness for understanding the whole of which it is a part.

In the other objectification or localization of social science problems, in which the observational method has used other fields and mirrors, identifying and separating out the sample as thing encounters no conceptual difficulty. In national character, or culture and personality studies, any individual not marginal, mixed, overly sophisticated or idiosyncratically fantastic, will do as "bearer" of his culture, we are told (Metraux and Mead 1953), if he is properly placed in his particular role and category within his own society. Certainly no problem of delimiting him arises, as one person separates biologically and ontologically from the next. If general problems are referred to observation in particular workrooms, or factories, or hospitals, or parishes, or bureaus, representativeness is still a question, but certainly formal organizational criteria can be counted upon to identify and separate the personnel within which relationships, behavior, and attitude are to be studied. But it is long recognized that none such can be safely used for the community, where modern administrative or legal boundaries, in most countries, cut at will through and across those of the "natural" community (Koenig 1956c; Loomis and Beagle 1950).

A theory of the community, then, that serves to answer our four questions both for definition and selection of a viable community and for justification of its use as sample and as illuminator of general problems must not only be more explicit than is usual so far in observational and empirical social science, it must also be internally consistent, enough so as to make common sense of both of our next steps in theory building. It must tell us what a community is, that we may use one right, and it must tell us how it mirrors its culture or society, so that we may read back from sample to universe.

I have proposed elsewhere the definition of community which seems empirically and theoretically to serve best for both these purposes (Arensberg 1954; 1955). Let me review the definition, and the reasons for it, and then let me go on to show how the definition provides answers for the questions about the use of the community just posed.

Communities seem to be basic units of organization and transmission within a society and its culture. The definition is suggested both by their repetitive character and by their characteristics of personnel, form, and function. The definition can only be won by modelling and structuring the comparative ethnographic and historical record of human and animal communities, with proper attention to their evolutionary variation in biological and human evolution and to their organizational, sociological, and political constitutions *in addition to* their ecological, economic, and human-geographical aspects.

To date a much too limited understanding of the community and its variations has prevailed. On the one hand ecological factors have been appealed to almost exclusively. The community has been seen—a legitimate and useful view but not a complete one—solely as a land-use pattern, a form of settlement, or a territorial unit or range of environmental exploitation. Or, on the other hand, definitions have taken a psychologistic or collective-sociological turn. They have appealed to the putative need of human beings to belong, or to the survival necessities of cooperation and solidarity, or even to consciousness of kind, or the gregarious spirit. One standard definition combines locality with a sociological criterion, calling the community "the maximal group of persons who normally reside together in face-to-face association" (Murdock 1949: 79). All of these definitions, traditional or learned, are limited, restricted and unspecific. They are quite insufficient to deal with the known varieties of the human community, to cope with its known functions and processes, and to separate it properly from other local, geographical, or associational phenomena of human life. A moment's reflexion will suffice to remind one that none of them except the last ("maximal group of co-residents") addresses itself to the structured and repetitive character of communities in society. The last, while making a start at it, imposes an unnecessary and unrealistic confinement of community life and association to face-to-face contacts. Not all community members need touch one another; a baby's or a slave's contacts are not those of an honored grandfather or a magnate.

Now the undoubted territorial or geographical character of the community as a human grouping, providing a range of land use and a particular ecological resource-base, gives us only our initial comparative datum about communities. Without additional elements of definition, we do not know why such land use is repeated in fairly standard, similar form throughout the occurrence of populations both animal and human, at no matter what level of cultural or biological evolution. No bees have only one hive, nor peasants only one village, nor metropolitans of today only one metropolis. Nor can we distinguish the community from the region, the province, the administrative district, the nomadic band, the farm, the plantation, the *sovkhoz*, the land-use corporation, the parish, the manor, the monastery, etc. All of these may use and bound a tract of land, may even divide the landscape into like tracts, but they may or may not be usefully treated as communities.

Now what distinguishes communities from other human associations based upon territoriality and land use is precisely their repetitive character and their wholeness and inclusiveness. They are like units not so much only as collections of culture traits or social institutions repeated again and again, but first of all as population aggregates. A demographic criterion is part of the definition which allows us to recognize the thing; it is also that part of the definition which makes the thing useful as a sample.

In biology, students of paleontological evolution, as well as geneticists have had to invent the concept of the gene-pool. In nature, the gene-pool may be a territorially delineable breeding unit of the members of the animal species who, in using a terrain, can find one another for mate selection and continuance of the species on a wider than merely familial basis (Bates 1956). Now gene-pools are not communities; the biological point is that some minimal population supports a species.

Anthropologists are more and more rejecting, for human evolution, the notion that human social organization is simply an extension of the family, or that a people is simply a widely expanded common lineage. They see the cultural and physical basis of human sociality instead in the human band.

The human band seems always to have comprised three successive generations of humans beings. It always grouped persons of various ages existing together, foraging together, dividing into constituent marriage pairs, families, and age groups (Count 1958). The personnel basis of the human community is already given in this coexistence of three generations in the human band: that coexistence is required by the biogram of the human animal in which prolonged infancy and late puberty themselves force mate-choice outside of parent-child and sibling relationships (Slater 1959). It is no wonder that the best modern doctrine about primitive social organization continually refers it to the first social invention: the laws of incest requiring extrafamilial mating (Levy-Strauss 1949).

The personnel basis of human living, part of the biogram of the species, thus requires a table of organization, as the military would say. This table of organization of three generations and two sexes is inherent in the community and is thus part of its definition. The human community, like that of any animal, is such a minimal unit of population as must coexist in order to insure the continuance of the species. In the human case, it necessarily counts among minimal personnel some instances of every kind of individual in which the species manifests itself: adult, baby, child, adolescent, and oldster, of each sex.

A definition of community thus enlarged from territorial and resource unit to population unit now begins to make sense of empirical parallels between man and animal that interest both the sociologist and the anthropologist, cultural and physical. These parallels have long tantalized the scientist for their likeness to animal life and excited him for their intricate and elaborate differentiation in human culture and society. Human beings, with culture, and animals, without it, equally well divide into communities, establish boundaries, trend toward exclusive memberships; band together for mutual support, defense, and mate choice; establish rhythms of land use, travel and movement; throw up monuments of one physical sort or another to their coresidential, familial and communal, livings; reuse and rework old settlements and their monuments into new shells for living; or, alternately, bud off new colonial and daughter communities duplicating old ones.

Now a definition of the community, both animal and human, which covers so many observed propensities, properties, and artifacts common over its full range of biological occurrence, and which yet still allows us to deal with the hugely diverse communities, from bands to the villages, cities, and metropolises, of human social history and of modern sociology, must not only contain many elements. It must also structure them in some sort of wholeness.

Another element of the definition, and a prime key to that wholeness, then, is to be found, not so much in the territorial separateness of the community, long explored by the human geographers and the ecologists (Hawley 1950), but rather instead in its temporal dimension. The coexistence of the personnel of our table of organization is a succession of lives. Communities, animal and human both, usually live longer than their members. The characteristic biogram of the species is a progression, for any one individual, from birth to death which others of the species repeat, with luck; but this progression moves through a social field: the neonate is born to adult parents, the youngster deals both with elders and contemporaries, the oldster deals with younger successors.

Thus the unit minimum population aggregate, the community, is a structured social field of interindividual relationships unfolding through time. The community is not only a territorial unit and a unit table of organization; it is also an enduring temporal pattern of coexistences, an ordered time-progress of individuals, from their births to their deaths, through roles and relationships of each kind known to their species or their culture. In short, it is the minimal common cast of characters supporting the drama of the biogram, in biology, or, in social science, its analogue of the way of life. This is its character as thing subsistent in space and time: an enduring natural unit of both process and organization in living phenomena. Where the drama of living is done by and with culture, in a particular ethnographically differentiable human way of life, a community is a natural sample too, because it is a natural unit of the drama of successive repetitions of the life of an enduring culture or society.

It is in dealing with the empirical discoveries of temporal process that perhaps the greatest gain for social science from developing understanding of the community and its sampling of sociological problem materials is to be won from now on. Sociology has been slow in treating process and dynamism rather than structure and stasis, whether in factorial analysis of social variables, where correlation has been looked for in contemporary rather than in successive relationships, or in treatment of change and movement in society. Nevertheless, some theory (MacIver 1942; Arensberg 1951; Bales 1950; Blau 1955) has lately arisen in various branches of sociology to treat processes of causation and succession. Similarly, doctrines of evolution and emergence have, recently, widely reappeared in ethnology (Steward 1955). The early discoveries of "ecological" processes, like ethnic and class successions in residence, of American urban sociology (Park and Burgess 1925) have been little advanced upon. Nevertheless, the empirical evolution of community study method has made standard many treatments of temporal process in community life which are part of ethnographic, social-anthropological field-work method, and which now, properly seen, can be contributed to our understandings of community and culture as progresses through life and as ordered *biogrammata*. Not only has the life history become one of the methods of culture and personality studies (Kluckhohn 1945) in ethnography, where, as we said, the individual rather than the community is chosen as social or cultural sample, but studies of standard progressions from birth to death, through the *passages* of the universal kind first analyzed for all human cultures in the famous *rites de passage* of Van Gennep (1909), have become a required technique within community study method.

Now the nature of the community, just defined above for its temporal dimension, has exacted, both in ecological studies and in community study, quite explicit handling of the rhythms and periodicities of animal and human living. Theory has yet to distinguish well between those rhythms which are inherent, natural concomitants of all social and cultural life in any of its variant expressions in particular societies and cultures, and those which instead mark new social and cultural change and new evolution. Communities, of course, show both new and old events. They show many periodicities, as they occupy their territories in and through time; but not all their events are recurrent. One must learn to distinguish between recurrent rhythms, natural to the successions of role and relationship of biogram or way of life, mirrored in a community for a species and quite new events, themselves instead heralding some sweeping, open-ended change overtaking either a particular community or the society of which it is a part.

For the repeated events observers see, it is consistent with the temporal aspects of our definition that we already connect, implicitly, periodicities of community life with those of the societies or the ways of life social science treats. Communities show dispersals of their persons (to the fields, to the hill pastures, by the season, by day) alternating with assemblage of them (in sleeping quarters, in ceremonies, in communal or marketing efforts, in war). There are climatic and economic rounds, calendars, shorter cycles of euphoria and dysphoria, longer rhythms of generational expansion or colonial budding, monthly, weekly, daily periodicities. All these are standard data to be collected in community study method; all of them are already often cited, without much theorizing, to stand for the temporal processes of larger societies and cultures. We cannot compare societies, or treat their problems, like traffic or criminality or suicide, without confronting these rhythms and their time-rates of record from one community to the next, inside and outside their larger societies.

But the theory that justifies us is little developed so far. It is not enough that we already make implicit comparisons between cultures and societies based on such community rhythms: sedentary versus transhumant societies, tight Apollonian sabatarian ones versus loose Dionysian ones of occasional, irregular celebrations (Benedict 1934; Embree 1948). We must discover explicitly how the rhythm of community life shapes or is shaped by the *Zeitgeist* and the institutions of an age or society; we must see that a way of life, both in a great society and a little community, is also a structure of timing and progressing for human lives and human relationships. Little of this has yet been done. Thus, for example, adolescent ethnic conflict (Child 1943) could be illuminated by a study of Italian-American boys in New Haven, an American city of mixed American and Italian ethnic structure, but no use made of other facts of the same city's life which showed that adult Italian-Americans found roles and a structured adjustment both within and beyond their own minority-placed ethnic group (Warner and Srole 1945). Or juvenile crime and deliquency can only slowly be shown to be, again from urban community studies (Whyte 1943; Tannenbaum 1939), at least in the U.S.A., only a prelude to learned adult life-adjustment, separating, in adult social structure, conflicting middle class and lower class roles and values.

Thus it is that modern community study, whether addressed to social problem or to cultural comparisons, has forced us to the steps in definition we have made. It makes it imperative that the definition of community be expanded to include populational and temporal dimensions in addition to the original spatial and ecological ones.

By the same reasoning, it forces us to see that there is a contentual, a behavior-inventory component, to the definition of community as well. We must include the cultural, the institutional, the learned aspect behavior as well as that genetically determined in the "natural" criterion in our definition of the community as a natural unit of organization in the life and the way of living of man and animal. The community is the natural unit, as well, of cultural transmission, in man, as it is the natural unit, like the gene-pool, of genetic transmission in the animal. It is a "natural" collection of the inventory of behaviors and culture patterns, or institutions, known to the persons of the species—here the culture—too, because it is the natural field and its content which a child learns in becoming a man of his people (Whiting 1941; Kluckhohn 1951).

It is a truism, of course, that the biogram of *homo* involves not only individual learning of inherited capabilities as with the animal, but also the learning, in culture, of the roles and the institutions that mark off the society of one human culture or civilization from another. The community is the minimal unit table of organization of the personnel who can carry and transmit this culture. It is the minimal unit realizing the categories and offices of their social organization. It is the minimal group capable of reenacting in the present and transmitting to the future the cultural and institutional inventory of their distinctive and historic tradition. And *from* it, *in* it, the child learns, from peers and the street as well as from parents and teachers, the lore of his people and what must be learned to become one of them.

It is here, indeed, that we must look to functional reasons for the community's universal existence even in Man, so different from lower animals. Communities collectivize in their territories, among their members, through their lives (which are generations long and thus longer than those of their members) many gains for individual and for social survival or advantage. These are provision of mates, of defense, of cooperative resource exploitation, of sociability, etc. They have been long and often appealed to, both in ecology and in sociology, to account for community, from the beginning of social and political speculation onward, even with Aristotle's initial derivation of community and political life from the nature of man as "politikon zoon," so often quoted. But we can now see that invoking the general functions of social life is as improper and unspecific as is relying on other received definitions.

These functions do not define communities. Any culture has other ways of defense, of mate finding, of socializing, of governing, that extend beyond the community's and may supplant the community's. Likewise, communities, like other things, can develop dysfunctions, pain and thwart members, gain and lose functions without losing identity. The broad functions appealed to neither distinguish the community from other social phenomena nor account for its structure and demography.

Yet some other functional reason, more specific, can well be found for the community. We know already, as we have said, that some local, continuing grouping of men or animals nearly always comes to exist. Bigger than the family or mating pair, smaller than the whole population, it insures continuity of the species. Where the species is human, to wit, one of the cultures of modern comparative ethnography and sociology, a characteristic minimal unit of personnel arises, as surely as among the animals, to subsist in a territory, to endure over its members' lives. It is this minimal unit, the community, which insures continuity of the now culturally-defined species. For it is only in man that differentiation of kind takes not a genetic but a cultural, a taught-and-learned form.

Thus it is that we must recognize that a human community contains within it, specifically—and the content gives us both our definition and our license for sampling—persons and roles and statuses, or the transmitted and learned awarenesses of them, for every kind and office of mankind that the culture knows: husband, artisan, miser, mother, priest, criminal, aristocrat, heretic, etc. The list is different for every human culture. A human community does this as surely as does one of ants, which, too, provides a role for every kind of ant the species has evolved: queen, worker, egg, soldier, larva. The mechanisms, we know, are quite different; the lists are of various lengths; but the structuring of life process in the various species has important parallels.

It is plain, then, that with such a specific and structural definition of the community, many of the complexities of the social and cultural phenomena we must deal with in community study, like many of the questions about the use of the community as field or as sample for the study of other data, take on a new guise. First, of course, we have a justification for the perception of the rich and complex wholeness and separateness of the community, both for itself and as a field for other phenomena, already well won in international social science. We see why other social objects are not and cannot be communities, and why other institutions, however complex, offer a less rounded picture of human life. A monastery, whatever its spirit, cannot be a community. Its population has but one sex. A mining camp, an old age home, a children's village, an army, and so on, cannot serve as one, either in definition or in social science use. When we say a technology, a church, a political party pushes toward engulfing "the whole of the life" of its people, to try to grow from being one institution to dominating a community, we now know what we can mean.

Robert Redfield, among recent writers, has given us the best sense of the experience so won in community study. His celebrated summary (1956a) covered the modern comparative, empirical studies of cultures and civilizations using the "Little Community," as he called his book, to find and explore the data of diverse human social and cultural behavior around the globe. His very chapter headings show us the fullness of experience a community as a living aggregate of the persons following a common way of life provides, as they necessarily act out together their various kinds and roles of the human condition in their successive progresses from cradle to grave. For their coexistence, and the social and cultural system it creates, Redfield entitled his chapters: The Little Community as a Whole, as an Ecological System, as a Social Structure, as a Typical Biography, as a Kind of Person, as an Outlook on Life ("ethos" or "value system"), as a History, as a Community within Communities. This is, of course, in the grand tradition, not only of the arts, but also of both cultural anthropology's recognition of cultures as distinctive ways of life and sociology's definition of classes, from Max Weber, as persons of like life-chances. The structuring of life-times and their activities, *not* of any less durable, less full performances and relationship among human beings, is the burden of the community study method's usefulness in modern social and ethnological science.

With this insight, then, what answers have we for the four questions posed earlier? The four summed up the difficulties of the choice of community to serve as a sample, but they could not be answered until a fuller definition was assured. They were: (1) representativeness: which community of the many to choose? (2) completeness: how should we recognize we have a whole, a viable cummunity before us in the object of our choice and how separate it off from others? (3) inclusiveness, how can we be sure the community as sample samples enough of the phenomena, trends, culture-traits, institutions, problems, of the whole culture or society it is surrogate for? (4) cohesiveness, or how unitary, single-hearted, solidary must it be to save us from choosing a community divisive to the point of uselessness?

The newly-won and many-faceted definition just achieved offers resolutions to all four of the questions. A better and fuller theory of the community, as of anything else, provides a better, fuller methodology of strategy and decision in research.

First, then, a community is representative, and any one so representative can probably be used as sample or field of study for a problem or a comparison, when it offers the personnel, the table of organization we have found to be the demographic component of the definition. If the culture knows two sexes, several ages, several classes, several sects, several ethnic groups including majority and minority ones, several or many professional or full-time specializations, of occupation or technical and economic function, then the community we choose must have some at least of all these people, enough to man at least minimally their roles and statuses.

Second, it must give us these people, this table of organization, in some repetition and continuance. The personnel must be joined, at least in minimal seriation, in a succession of lives. The table of organization must be refilled successively, in some minimal degree, for the continuation of existence of the community to be effected. Only thus is the second, temporal component of our new-won definition satisfied.

Thus we can choose as sample any community minimally "stratified" to offer us some minimal population of each kind of person our culture or society knows as long as that realization of the categories continues to repeat itself through the successive lives of the community's members. Mt. Athos is not a community, though monks have lived there, admitting no female thing, for nearly two thousand years; a dormitory suburb of young marrieds and their babies is not one, however intense neighborhood "togetherness," unless the old people and the bachelors are there too. Many an exogamous Indian village, we are now learning, is a land-use corporation and a residential segregation, in which wives marry in and daughters out and only some of the usual complement of castes may be present, but the Indian community, instead, is the circle of villages from which wives come and around which daughters move and in which all the castes, whether or not they have members in every village, have their councils (*panchayat*) and treat with another. The North American city taken whole, then, not the suburb, the city into which bachelors disappear, or older couples retire after their time in the collective harem of the dormitory suburb is up, is thus itself the community of American modernity. These marrieds', bachelors', and old people's patterns repeat themselves, and individual, progress through such patterns in endless successive moves, as they pass through their age roles in the structuring students of modern urbanism are just beginning to lay clear.

The structure of the community, thus, involves both a full table of organization and a continuity in depth uniting the lives of the people of the table, repeating or reiterating, in the main, their experience from generation to generation. Our sample communities must have both these memberships and these depths.

We can thus spare ourselves the imperative of a fully "stratified" sample in choosing a community. The point distinguishes clearly community study method from social survey methods. Indeed, too strict sampling may be supernumerary, in the former case, though it is of the essence in the latter. Minimal, not ideal, numbers of our personnel identify our sample, not necessarily fully stratified, proportionate ones, as in a nationwide or other random sample survey, where we cannot rely on the natural structuring of the community. The rigor of exactly faithful proportions here is less important than is the fulfillment of the structural and the temporal criteria of our definition. It is less important that some controlled number of each category of personnel of the table of organization be present nicely measured against each other's share of the whole society's population than it is that the categoric subsamples of whatever number be together over time, across their lives, "longitudinally."

The reasons come clearly from our acquired experience with culture and society in research and in the theoretical understanding won from it. Roles, institutions, statuses, we have learned, are filled by *any* competent person. They may be undermanned or overmanned, of course, but some filling there must be if they are to exist. Further, the learning of culture involves also the learning of behavior and attitude of one's culture vis-à-vis *any* filler of such role. It is a prefiguring, a "programming" in the individual for recognition of and reaction to the first such filler-of-role to appear. That some or one appear is enough to evoke prefigured expectation and response.

But the minimal, the even single filler of role and role expectation and evoker of response, whose being is more important than his numbers, *must* both so appear and continue to do so. Roles, culture traits, patterned responses of cultural and social life, are habits of individuals needing at least some repetition if they are not to be extinguished; and they are transmissions to yet other individuals, cultural successors, in whom such repetition must also take place. Perhaps once a generation is enough for some such habits and transmissions of habits. Just as the life of the community is to be found first of all in its continuance from generation to generation of individual lives, so is the test for a cultural or institutional role or other pattern of behavior that it be transmitted, above accidents of personal characteristic and social event, from encumbent-enactor to encumbent-enactor. Succession of individuals through fixity of patterned behavior is of the essence here, not numbers. Structuring is independent of quantity in nature, whether we are dealing with a square, a jet stream, a cell, or a kingship. In *this*, social science does not differ. Numbers can measure and compare such structures once achieved; they do not define them.

The same consideration arises with social and economic stratification other than age-grading. All too many community studies have mistaken one-class or two-class segregations, from dormitory suburbs to peasant villages or proletarian slums, for communities. True, the life of a class, as a subculture, provides a way of life from birth to grave, as we have known from Max Weber down. True, it may provide an inventory of special traits of learned behavior, of value, of institutional and social-relational or associational action. The residential segregation of a slum, a peasant village, a nomad camp, a garden city of the rich, may mirror faithfully such a separated, encapsulated subculture. But the class is only part of a society; its culture only part of a larger order and civilization; its false community only a segregation. When one disputes the representativeness of community study findings about, say, the class structure of the U.S.A., by confronting a rural village of small farmers containing only two classes with a metropolis showing six, as critics have argued against the Warner studies of American life through the six classes and their differences and complementarities in the middle-sized cities of Yankee City, Old South, and Jonesville, U.S.A., such a criticism betrays a naïveté about comparison, about structure, and about society which is close to obscurantism.

Nonetheless, the question of stratified sampling in community study is in point once again. A community chosen for study as a sample or a field of a societal problem need not reflect with complete fidelity the proportion of the classes in the over-all society, even here. Every Middle Eastern villager has experience of bedouin as raiders, harvesters, or beggars; he knows mountaineers as laborers, landlords, or *shitiyyin* (winterers). His village is a complete community, not because cityfolk or nomads or mountaineers are coresident with him, but because he knows of them, has relations with them, and passes his knowledge and his role (even his fear) down to his children. Thus a mining town or a farmers' market village are complete enough, too, however equal the vast majority may be in their common experience as miners or as farmers and in their common disdain or envy of their betters (and their inferiors) and of the other strangers to their local life, as long as they also know and tell their children how to recognize and to deal with these incursors: the squire, the lawyer, the "city-slicker," the tramp, the priest, the teacher, etc., who bring in the outer world. Just as cells can specialize within the body and can change form with function and anatomic position but still take part in the system of metabolism, communication, and excretion which unite them to the other co-inhabitant cells of their body, so can special and differently-functioning communities exist and stand for their over-all societies and their cultures. But one must show the connections and treat the realities.

In the social science case, simply, that community is still representative which knows and deals with persons and things of its culture and society, as long as a minimal number, a minimal contact, and a minimal continuity connects them. Once again, pattern and awareness, structuring and relationships, not numbers, is of the essence.

With this referral of the question of representativeness to the points of our structural definition completed, we are ready now for the other difficulties of the community as sample and as field.

For completeness, the criteria are already foreshadowed. A community is whole when the table of organization and its successive filling is complete. Redfield, as we know, called the Little Community of his book among other things, a Community among Communities. This is, of course, a common figure of speech, and it is inescapable that the circles of relationship and concern of higher placed persons or local representatives strike out wider and higher in the social systems of region, province, nation, and *oikomene* than do those of children or menials. The people of any community, individually taken, may, some of them, range far and wide; they may have overlapping memberships in neighboring communities, communities of relatives, communities of sojourn nearby. *These* villages group round a market center or a seat of administration; *those* round still another. All these circles and placements of human communication and relationship, in and out from any center at which one begins observation, high and low and up and down any reaches of further and further interconnection, structure themselves out for us when we remember our criteria defining a community. The cell-like repeated reiteration of our personnel and their interstructured lives breaks up these continua into systems and their boundaries; the repeated local, generation-long grouping and structuring of minimal fillers of the repeated roles, tells us where the instant community ends, the next one begins, the line between inside and outside and insider and outsider falls.

One already mentioned part of the dynamic of the rhythm of community life in space and time gives us an easiest, most usable criterion. The community, we have learned, always shows an alternation of dispersal and assemblage of its personnel, though different cultures pattern these functions differently. The easiest criterion may well be: who come together and who separate again, characteristically speaking? When we find the people of our table of organization assembled or come together at one time and know the limit of their dispersal at another, only to meet them regathered with one another at a third time, we have found the range, the rhythm, the membership, and the identity of the community we seek.

Our last two questions fall into place quickly enough once such criteria are put to work. Inclusiveness? As we have defined and demarcated a community to serve as sample or as field by structural and systemic criteria, we need not use culture trait inventory or enumeration to guide our choice. Any Maori *hapu* (hamlet) of aboriginal New Zealand had a heraldic bard who might sing the local chief's genealogy and prowess, but Maori culture knew only one College of Heralds. We avoid, certainly, the locus of that College, a pinnacle of specialization, but make sure the hamlet we choose has a herald of its own, or failing him, is looking for an incumbent for the post. A fortiori, we do not choose a capital city, an atomic-laboratory research station, or a Bohême of artists and their hangers-on, to stand for modern life. But we make sure our sample town has felt the lure of the capital, knows the modern skills and the modern awe of powerful physical science in its schools and its press, wonders over and envies a little such bohemians. Specializations in both high culture ("The Great Traditions") and popular or local culture ("The Little Traditions") are not our concern; instead we seek out those persons who in their community stand at the join between them and represent in their community and in their personal experiences the continuous mutual penetration the two sorts of specialization common to all complex societies everywhere display. Here again structure rules. The jointure, the mutual penetration of specialization of the unique sort the whole culture or civilization achieves and that the instant little community has acquired, is the thing we seek in a sample or a field of study. We need not drive ourselves to a rigorous exclusion of anything except the average, the mediocre, and the universally common and indistinguishable cultural possessions of all the citizenry everywhere within our universe. No harm is done if a sample community has local legends, nor if an occasional speciality appears, like a school or a monastery not duplicated exactly in every next town. As long as specialities do not dominate community experience and community culture, and as long as citizens are aware of and prepare their children to recognize, again at least minimally, the outer reaches of such specialization stretching away from their own lores and skills, their community will serve.

And, finally, cohesiveness? Our structural definition spares us deciding between a community of harmony and sweet affection and a bed of hate and fire. The formal sociology of Georg Simmel, or many another, rescues us here. The people of our table of organization, in their lives together, alternate between strife and accommodation, solidarity and antagonism; if they come together again, in their reassemblages, after dispersal, it matters not whether dispersal grew out of hatred, dissension, or flight, or merely out of the need to fan out over a space of sparse and dispersed resources. It matters not whether their coming together again was for massacre or for the headiest unity. The limits of our discrimination of their community, their pattern of alternation between dispersal and assemblage as a social system, are self-enforcing and self-insistent. A collective, assembled internecine fight that ends in full massacre of one part by another, or a dispersal that ends in full flight of one part from another, brings the community to an end and causes it to cease to be. The table of organization is broken; the continuance of lives interlaced has stopped. Here again structural criteria, turned into measures and used for at least minimal recognition, give us our guide. Just as whole societies, whole civilizations (after Toynbee) know civil war, religious schism, flight in emigration, Times of Troubles, so do communities. A sample community must reflect both the unities and the fissions of the parts it samples in its table or organization of the whole society it mirrors. But it need do that again only within the outer limits of its own continuance.

## REFERENCES CITED

ARENSBERG, CONRAD M.
  1951   Behavior and organization: industrial studies. *In* Social psychology at the cross-roads, John Rohrer and Muzafer Sherif, eds. New York, Harper.
  1954   The community study method. American Journal of Sociology 60:109–125.
  1955   American communities. American Anthropologist 57:1143–1162.
ARENSBERG, CONRAD M. and others, eds.
  1957   Research in industrial human relations. New York, Harper.
BALANDIER, G.
  1955   Sociologie des Brazzavilles noires. Paris, Foundation Nationale des Sciences Politiques.
BALES, ROBERT FREED
  1950   Interaction process analysis. Cambridge (Massachusetts), Addison-Wesley Press.
BANCROFT, EDWARD C.
  1958   The moral basis of a backward community. Glencoe, The Free Press.
BATES, MARSTON
  1953   Anthropology and ecology. *In* Anthropology today, Alfred L. Kroeber, ed. Chicago, University of Chicago Press.
BATTEN, T. R.
  1958   Communities and their development. Oxford, Oxford University Press.
BELSHAW, CYRIL S.
  1957   The great village. London, Routledge and Kegan Paul.
BENEDICT, RUTH
  1934   Patterns of culture. Boston, Houghton Mifflin Co.
BLAU, PETER M.
  1955   The dynamics of bureaucracy. Chicago, University of Chicago Press.
BOTT, ELIZABETH
  1956   Urban families: the norms of conjugal roles. Human Relations 9:325–343.
BROWNELL, BAKER
  1950   The human community. New York, Harper.
CAUDILL, WILLIAM
  1958   The psychiatric hospital as a small society. Cambridge, Harvard University Press.
CHILD, IRVIN
  1943   Italian or American? New Haven, Yale University Press.
CHIVA, I.
  1958   Rural communities: problems, methods, types of research. Reports and Papers in the Social Sciences, Bulletin 10, UNESCO.
COUNT, EARL W.
  1958   Eine biologische Entwicklungsgeschichte der menschlichen Sozialität, Sonderdruck. Homo 9:3–83.
DOBYNS, HENRY
  1951   Blunders with bolsas. Human Organization 10:25–33.
EATON, JOSEPH and ROBERT J. WEIL
  1955   Culture and mental disorders. Glencoe, The Free Press.
EMBREE, JOHN
  1948   Southeast Asian culture. *In* The science of man in the world crisis, Ralph Linton, ed. New York, Columbia University Press.

FOX, RENEE
    1959   Experiment perilous. Glencoe, The Free Press.
FRIEDMANN, GEORGES
    1950   Où va le travail humain? Paris, Gallimard.
FUSTEL DE COULANGES
    1905   La cité antique. Paris, Hachette et Cie.
GENNEP, A. VAN
    1909   Les rites de passage. Paris, E. Nourry.
GUETZKOW, H., ed.
    1951   Groups, leadership and men: research in human relations. Pittsburgh, Carnegie
           Press.
HAWLEY, AMOS H.
    1950   Human ecology. New York, Ronald Press Co.
HOLLINGSHEAD, AUGUST B.
    1948   Community research: development and present condition. American Sociological
           Review 13:136–146.
HUNTER, FLOYD
    1953   Community power structure. Chapel Hill, University of North Carolina Press.
HUNTER, FLOYD, RUTH C. SCHAFFER and CECIL B. SHEPS
    1956   Community organization, action and inaction. Chapel Hill, University of North
           Carolina Press.
KAUFMAN, HERBERT
    1960   The forest ranger: a study in administrative behavior. Baltimore, Johns Hopkins
           Press.
KIMBALL, SOLON T. and MARION B. PEARSALL
    1954   The Talladega story: a study in community process. University, University of
           Alabama Press.
KLUCKHOHN, CLYDE
    1945   The personal document in anthropological science. *In* The personal document in
           history, anthropology, and sociology, Clyde Kluckhohn and R. Angell, eds. Social
           Science Research Council Bulletin 53.
    1951   The study of culture. *In* The policy sciences, Daniel Lerner and Harold D. Lass-
           well, eds. Stanford, Stanford University Press.
KÖNIG, RENÉ
    1956a  Die Gemeinde im Blickfeld der Soziologie. *In* Handbuch der kommunalen Wissen-
           schaft und Praxis, Hans Peter, hrsg. Berlin, Westdeutscher Verlag.
    1956b  Die Gemeindeutuntersuchung des deutschen Unesco-institutes. *In* Handbuch der
           kummunalen Wissenschaft und Praxis, Hans Peter, hrsg. Berlin, Westdeutscher
           Verlag.
    1956c  Soziologie der Gemeinde. *In* Sonderheft I, Kölner Zeitschrift für Sociologie und
           Sozialpsychologie 8:1–12.
    1958   Grundformen der Gesellschaft: die Gemeinde. Hamburg, Rowohit.
    1961.  Handbuch der empirischer Sozialforschung, R. König, ed. Stuttgart, Ferdinand
           Enke Verlag.
LEIGHTON, ALEXANDER and ROBERT J. SMITH
    1952   A comparative study of social and economic change. American Philosophical
           Society Proceedings 99.
LEIGHTON, ALEXANDER and others, eds.
    1956   Explorations in social psychiatry. New York, Basic Books.
LENTZ, EDITH and TEMPLE BURLING
    1956   The give and take of hospitals. Ithaca, Cornell University Press.
LEVY-STRAUSS, CLAUDE
    1949   Les structures élémentaires de la parenté. Paris, Presses Universitaires de France.
LOOMIS, CHARLES and ALLAN J. BEAGLE
    1950   Rural social systems. New York, Prentice-Hall.

MacIver, Robert
  1942  Social causation. Boston, Ginn and Co.
Maget, M.
  1953  Ethnographie métropolitaine. Paris, Guide D'étude Directe des Comportements Culturels, Civilisations du Sud.
  1955  Remarques sur le village comme cadre de recherches anthropologiques. Bulletin de Psychologie 8:375–382.
Maine, Sumner
  1871  Village communities in the East and West. London, J. Murray.
Maurer, Georg von
  1854  Einleitung zur Geschichte der Mark-, Hof-, Dorf-, und Stadtverfassung und der öffentlichen Gewalt. Munich, C. Kaiser.
Mead, Margaret
  1951  The study of national character. *In* The policy sciences, Daniel Lerner and Harold D. Laswell, eds. Stanford, Stanford University Press.
  1953  National character. *In* Anthropology today, Alfred L. Kroeber, ed. Chicago, University of Chicago Press.
Meitzen, A.
  1895  Siedlung- und agrarwesen der Westgermanen und Ostgermanen, der Kelten, Römer, Finnen und Slaven. Berlin, W. Hertz.
Metraux, Rhoda and Margaret Mead
  1953  The study of culture at a distance. Chicago, University of Chicago Press.
Mogey, John
  1956  Family and neighbourhood. Oxford, Oxford University Press.
Murdock, George Peter
  1949  Social structure. New York, Macmillan Co.
Oeser, O. A. and F. E. Emery
  1954  Social structure and personality in an Australian community. London, Routledge and Kegan Paul.
Opler, Marvin K.
  1956  Culture, psychiatry and human values. Springfield, Thomas.
Park, Robert E., Ernest W. Burgess and R. D. Mackenzie
  1925  The city. Chicago, University of Chicago Press.
Paul, Benjamin D., ed.
  1955  Health, culture and community. New York, Russell Sage Foundation.
Peake, Harold
  1954  Village community. *In* Encyclopedia of the social sciences. New York, Macmillan Co.
Pitts-Rivers, Julian
  1954  The People of the Sierra. New York, Criterion Press.
Redfield, Robert
  1953  The primitive world and its transformation. Ithaca, Cornell University Press.
  1956a The little community. Chicago, University of Chicago Press.
  1956b Peasant society and culture. Chicago, University of Chicago Press.
Roland, Warren
  1955  Studying your community. New York, Russell Sage Foundation.
Rubin, Vera, ed.
  1958  Caribbean studies. Jamaica, Institute of Social Research.
Ruesch, Jurgen
  1949  Illness and social structure. *In* Personality and culture, nature and society, Clyde Kluckhohn and H. A. Murray, eds. New York, A. A. Knopf.
Ruopp, Phillips, ed.
  1953  Approaches of community development. The Hague, W. Van Hoeve.

RUSSELL SAGE FOUNDATION
　　1959　Annual report. New York, Russell Sage Foundation.
SANDERS, IRWIN T.
　　1958　The community: an introduction to a social system. New York, Ronald Press Co.
SCHNEIDER, EUGENE V.
　　1957　Industrial sociology. New York, McGraw-Hill.
SHEVKY, ESHREF and MARYLIN WILLIAMS
　　1929　Social areas of Los Angeles. Berkeley, University of California Press.
SIMEY, THOMAS S., ed.
　　1954　Neighborhood and community. Liverpool, Liverpool University Press.
SLATER, MARIAM
　　1959　Ecological factors in the origin of incest. American Anthropologist 61:1042–1060.
SMITH, R. T.
　　1956　The Negro family in British Guiana. London, Routledge and Paul.
SPICER, EDWARD, ed.
　　1953　Human problems in technological change. New York, Russell Sage Foundation.
SRINIVAS, M. N.
　　1952　Religion and society among the Coorgs of South India. Oxford, Clarendon Press.
　　1955　Sanskritization. *In* Village India: studies in the little community. The American
　　　　　Anthropological Association Memoir 83.
STEIN, MAURICE
　　1960　The eclipse of community. Princeton, Princeton University Press.
STEWARD, JULIAN H.
　　1950　Area research. New York, New York Social Science Research Bulletin 63.
　　1955　Theory of culture change. Urbana, University of Illinois Press.
STEWARD, JULIAN H. and others
　　1956　The people of Puerto Rico. Urbana, University of Illinois Press.
STRODTBECK, FRED L.
　　n.d.　Social process in the law: a study of the American jury. (forthcoming) Chicago,
　　　　　University of Chicago Press.
TANNENBAUM, FRANK
　　1938　Crime and community. New York, Ginn and Co.
TAYLOR, CARL T.
　　1945　Techniques of community study and analysis as applied to modern civilized socie-
　　　　　ties. *In* The science of man in the world crisis, Ralph Linton, ed. New York, Co-
　　　　　lumbia University Press.
TRUMAN, DAVID B.
　　1951　The governmental process. New York, A. A. Knopf.
UTERMANN, KURT
　　1952　Aufgaben und Methoden der gemeindlichen Sozialforschung. *In* Beiträge zur Socio-
　　　　　logie der industriellen Gesellschaft, Walther G. Hoffmann, hrsg. Dortmund, Ardey.
VIDICH, ARTHUR J. and JOSEPH BENSMAN
　　1958　The small town in mass society. Princeton, Princeton University Press.
WAGLEY, CHARLES and MARVIN HARRIS
　　1958　Minorities in the New World. New York, Columbia University Press.
WARE, CAROLINE
　　1952　Estudio de la comunidad. Washington, Pan-American Union.
WARNER, WILLIAM LLOYD
　　1953　American life: dream and reality. Chicago, University of Chicago Press.
WARNER, WILLIAM LLOYD and others
　　1957　Social class in America. Gloucester (Massachusetts), P. Smith.
WARNER, WILLIAM LLOYD and LEO SROLE
　　1945　The social systems of American ethnic groups. New Haven, Yale University Press.

WHITING, JOHN
    1941    Becoming a Kwoma: teaching and learning in a New Guinea tribe. New Haven, Yale University Press.

WHYTE, WILLIAM FOOTE
    1951    Observational field work methods. *In* Research methods in social relations, two volumes, Marie Jahoda, Morton Deutsch and Steward W. Cook, eds. New York, Dryden Press.
    1958    Street corner society: the social organization of an Italian slum. Chicago, University of Chicago Press.

WILSON, LOGAN
    1945    Sociography of groups. *In* Twentieth century sociology, G. Gurvitch and W. G. Moore, eds. New York, Philosophical Library.

WURZBACHER, GERHARD, hrsg.
    1954    Das Dorf im Spannungsfeld industrieller Entwicklung. Stuttgart, Ferdinand Enke Verlag.

YANG, HSIN-PAO
    1957    Factfinding with rural people. United Nations, FAO.

YOUNG, MICHAEL and PETER WILMOTT
    1957    Family and kinship in East London. London, Routledge and Kegan Paul.

YOUNG, PAULINE V.
    1949    Scientific social surveys and research. New York, Prentice-Hall.

# Cultural Ecology and Ethnography

CHARLES O. FRAKE
*Stanford University*

E COLOGY is the study of the workings of ecosystems, of the behavioral interdependences of different kinds of organisms with respect to one another and to their nonbiotic environment. *Cultural* ecology is the study of the role of culture as a dynamic component of any ecosystem of which man is a part. Unique among organisms, man carves his ecological niches primarily with cultural tools of his own invention rather than with biological specializations. This niche-carving activity of man not only remolds existing biotic communities but also has a shaping effect on the tools—that is on man's cultural knowledge and equipment—themselves. In addition, man constantly devises new tools for carving out more effective places in the ecosystem surrounding him. Because of this progressive cultural adaptation and specialization to environmental conditions, the study of cultural ecology, under one name or another, has been closely linked with theoretical interest in culture history and culture evolution. Steward, who framed the present designation of the subject, construes cultural ecology largely as a methodology for building evolutionary theory (Steward 1955: 30–42).

Although the utility of ecological studies for such pursuits is undeniable, it is not necessary to regard cultural ecology simply as a methodological adjunct to nobler tasks. Cultural ecology, in that it refers to a delimitable system of phenomena, is a legitimate field of anthropological interests in its own right, as legitimate as the study of social systems which has so absorbed the efforts of many of us. If the social system be envisioned as a network of relationships among persons of a *social* community, then the ecological system is a network of relationships between man, the other organisms of his *biotic* community, and the constituents of his physical environment. In both cases the net is woven of cultural threads, and the two networks are, of course, inter-connected at many points.

But before the possibilities for general theory inherent in a study of cultural ecological systems are fully realized, the problem of describing these systems, the ethnographic problem, must, I think, be taken more seriously. As Hymes (1960:343) has remarked of linguistics, "One need not stop with the individual systems, but one must pass through them." The comparative method, whether on the scale of a Murdock (1949), a Steward (1955), or a Gulliver (1955), cannot yield results of greater validity than that of the data being compared. This paper has the purpose of assessing cultural ecology as an ethnographic endeavor. First, I will present some notions of what constitutes an ethnographic description, then I will suggest some ways in which ecological studies might be encompassed within the framework of these notions, giving a brief example from my field work.

Following Goodenough (1957), this paper proposes that a description of cultural behavior is attained by a formulation of what one must know in order to respond in a culturally appropriate manner in a given socio-ecological context. Such a description, like a linguist's grammar, is productive in that it can generate new acts which will be considered appropriate responses by the members of the society being described. A successful strategy for writing productive ethnographies must tap the cognitive world of one's informants. It must discover those features of objects and events which they regard as significant for defining concepts, formulating propositions, and making decisions. This conception of an ethnography requires that the units by which the data of observation are segmented, ordered, and interrelated be delimited and defined according to contrasts inherent in the data themselves and not according to a priori notions of pertinent descriptive categories.

The necessity of coming to terms with one's informants' concepts is well recognized in some ethnographic endeavors, kinship studies providing the most notable example. No ethnographer describes social relations in an alien society by referring to the doings of "uncles," "aunts," and "cousins." Many ethnographers do, however, describe the pots and pans, the trees and shrubs, the soils and rocks of a culture's environment solely in terms of categories projected from the investigator's culture. In comparison with studying religious conceptions or kinship relations, the description of the tangible objects of a culture's ecosystem is usually regarded as one of the ethnographer's simpler tasks. If he does not know a word for a specimen of fauna, flora, or soil, he can always ship it off to a specialist for "identification." However, if one in-

sists that no specimen has been described *ethnographically* until one has stated
the rules for its identification in the culture being studied, then the problem
of describing a tangible object such as a plant may become rather more complex than the relatively simple task of defining contrasts between categories of
kinsmen. Consider, for example, the problem of identifying plants according
to the Hanunóo system of folk botany (Conklin 1954, 1957). The Hanunóo,
tropical-forest agriculturists of the central Philippines, exhaustively partition
their plant world into more than 1,600 categories, whereas systematic bota-
nists classify the same flora into less than 1,200 species. To place correctly, by
Hanunóo standards, a newly encountered plant specimen in the appropriate
one of the 1,600 categories requires rather fine discriminations among plants—
and these discriminations rely on features generally remote from the botanist's
count of stamens and carpels. By discovering what one must know in order to
classify plants and other ecological components in Hanunóo fashion, one
learns what the Hanunóo consider worth attending to when making decisions or how to behave within their ecosystem.

An ethnographer, then, cannot be satisfied with a mere cataloguing of the
components of a cultural ecosystem according to the categories of Western
science. He must also describe the environment as the people themselves
construe it according to the categories of their ethnoscience. From a presentation of the rules by which people decide upon the category membership of
objects in their experience, an ethnographic ecology can proceed to rules for
more complex kinds of behavior: killing game, clearing fields, building houses,
etc. Determining the requisite knowledge for such behavior shows the ethnographer the extent to which ecological considerations, in contrast, say, to
sociological ones, enter into a person's decision of what to do. The ethnographer learns, in a rather meaningful and precise sense, what role the environment in fact plays in the cultural behavior of the members of a particular
society.

A partial description of the settlement pattern of the Eastern Subanun, a
Philippine people, will illustrate the notions of cultural ecological description
advanced here. This analysis would ideally rest upon a presentation of the
pertinent Subanun ethnoscience relating to agriculture and vegetation types.
Limitations of time force a rather inadequate and simplified description, but
one, which if not a contribution to ethnography, may at least point up some
of the desirable features of a legitimate ethnographic contribution to cultural
ecology.

The Subanun have carved a niche for themselves in the tropical rain
forests of Zamboanga Peninsula, on the island of Mindanao, by swidden
agriculture (or "shifting cultivation" Frake 1955, 1960; cf. Conklin 1957).
The tropical forest agriculturist must establish a controlled biotic community
of sun-loving annuals and perennials in a climatic region whose natural climax
community, the tropical rain forest, is radically different in almost every respect from the community agricultural man seeks to foster. The swidden
farmer meets this problem by periodically putting the forest through its suc-

cessional paces. He modifies and operates on an existing ecosystem rather than permanently replacing it with an utterly different kind of biotic and edaphic world, such as that of the wet-rice paddy.

The Subanun settlement pattern is one of clustered new, secondary, and fallow swiddens with individual nuclear family households dispersed within these swidden clusters. This pattern contrasts with that of many other Southeast Asian shifting cultivators who disperse their swiddens around relatively fixed and nucleated settlements.

The Subanun themselves do not have a notion of "settlement pattern" in the sense of an image of spatial relationships among households and settlements to which they must conform. Rather their settlement pattern as seen by an ethnographer is, like their "rule of post-marital residence," the outcome of a large number of individual decisions. These decisions are not made at random, say by flipping a coin, but by evaluation of the immediate circumstances in terms of a set of quite explicit principles about the desirable relations among houses and fields. An ethnographic description of the Subanun settlement pattern as part of their ecological adaptation must consist of more than a map locating house sites and more than a characterization as "neighborhood," "hamlet," or "village." It should comprise a set of rules which state what one must know in order to decide where to live. Ideally the description should be a set of rules which will generate the Subanun settlement pattern appropriate to any given set of conditions.

To simplify the discussion I will take three features of the Subanun ecological adaptation as given, although they too could be derived from further rules of individual decision. The givens are:

1) Swidden agriculture with grain-crop staples, requring an annual shift in locus of primary agricultural effort.

2) Organization of production and consumption is assigned to the nuclear family. Each family has the responsibility for clearing and cultivating its own swidden and enjoys joint and exclusive control over the distribution of its produce. No social group larger than a nuclear family cultivates a single swidden. Any individual who is not currently a member of a nuclear family is responsible for his or her own support by swidden agriculture (see Frake 1960).

3) Division of the population at any one time into discrete social groups, here termed *settlements*. Settlements are local groups emerging from alliances formed by a half-dozen or so related families for cooperation in agriculture and other activities. (One basis for settlement groupings, that of swidden clustering, derives from the rules that follow. But this rule, in itself, is not sufficient to account for the division of the population into settlement groups. Here we take these social groups to be given and concern ourselves only with the spatial arrangement of households within a settlement.)

With these givens in mind any arrangement of households found among the Subanun derives from the application of the following rules to particular ecological and sociological situations:

1) Minimum number of "wild-vegetation boundaries" (*gelunan* "to-be

watches") of a swidden consistent with other swidden-site requirements.

2) Minimum house to swidden distance ("house" means the residence of those persons responsible for cultivating a swidden).

3) Maximum house to house distance consistent with the above rules.

These rules are explicit in that they are based on informants' discussions of actual and potential residence-site choices as well as on observations of settlement and swidden patterns. Many other factors, of course, enter into individual decisions of where to live—house-site auguries, access to water, relations with neighbors, kinship obligations such as bride service, etc.—but these do not affect, in any systematic way, the *spacing* of households with respect to each other.

In most situations, settlement members can feasibly reduce exposed swidden boundaries by clustering all or almost all of their swiddens and by making new swidden clusters adjacent to previous years' clusters. The first rule, then, has the normal consequence of clustering the fields of a settlement.

Since a swidden work group normally consists of a nuclear family (and is never a larger social group) the second rule, by demanding that each group live as close as possible to its own swidden, yields a norm of nuclear family households. It furthermore requires that new houses must be constructed periodically at new locations. A distance from house to swidden such that a separate field-house would be required as a base for agricultural operations is considered beyond the maximum limits. When this point is reached, if not sooner, a new residence is always constructed. When new houses are constructed they are invariably located at the absolute minimum distance from the current grain swidden; that is, they are placed inside it, situated to overlook as much of current and prospective swidden sites as possible. When a prospective swidden site is too far away to be cleared from one's existing household, cultivators must temporarily reside in someone else's house (since all houses are built within swiddens, and a new house cannot be constructed in a swidden before the swidden has been cleared and burned).

Within the restraints imposed by swidden clustering and location of houses with respect to swiddens, the Subanun explicitly endeavor to maximize the distance between households. Two households are never, for example, placed adjacent to one another across a swidden boundary, though such an arrangement would often be consistent with ecological considerations. Temporary compound households are maintained only so long as ecologically necessary to gain access to a new swidden. Once it is feasible to build a new house of its own, a family will always do so. This rule of household dispersal derives from the sociological facts of Subanun life which make it prudent to live sufficiently far from one's nearest neighbor so that family conversations and arguments cannot be overheard (see Frake 1960).

The ecological rules (i.e., Nos. 1 and 2) which determine Subanun swidden and household arrangements are explicitly geared to protection of swiddens from animal pests with a minimum expenditure of time and energy in such tasks as fence building, field-house construction, and travel to fields for daily watching. Yet the practice of clearing large areas adjacent to previously cleared areas increases, under certain conditions, the probabilities of succession to grassland instead of forest, thus removing the land from future swidden cycles. The Subanun emphasize the immediate returns of increased swidden protection and accessibility at the cost of some loss of control over the fallowing stages of the swidden cycle. Other swidden farmers of the same part of the world weigh the advantages and disadvantages of alternative techniques for controlling faunal and floral enemies differently with different consequences for swidden arrangements and settlement patterns (cf. Frake 1954; Freeman 1955; Conklin 1957; Izikowitz 1951). The contrasts among the remarkably different settlement patterns exhibited by Southeast Asian swidden farmers will become ecologically interpretable when one compares the factors which generate these patterns in each case rather than forcing ethnographic observations directly into a priori comparative categories. The full ecological and sociological implications of this analysis of Subanun settlement pattern for both internal and cross-cultural studies cannot be explored here. Hopefully, however, this incomplete account has revealed some of the advantages for the study of cultural ecology derivable from ethnographic description ordered according to the principles by which one's informants interpret their environment and make behavioral decisions. We were able to specify to what extent ecological factors determine settlement pattern, to point out significant general features of the Subanun ecological adaptation, and to discover some meaningful dimensions for cross-cultural comparison. These methodological suggestions are not, of course, intended to replace the analysis of an ecosystem that Western biological science can provide. A scientific knowledge of the climate, soils, plants, and animals of a culture's environment is an essential foundation for ecological ethnography—but it does not, of itself, constitute ethnography.

### REFERENCES CITED

CONKLIN, H. C.
    1954   The relation of Hanunóo culture to the plant world. Doctoral dissertation, Yale University, New Haven.
    1957   Hanunóo agriculture. A report on an integral system of shifting cultivation in the Philippines. Rome, Food and Agricultural Organization of the United Nations.
FRAKE, C. O.
    1955   Social organization and shifting cultivation among the Sindangan Subanun. Doctoral dissertation, Yale University, New Haven.
    1960   Family and kinship among the eastern Subanun. *In* Social Structure in Southeast Asia, G. P. Murdock, ed. New York, Viking Fund Publications in Anthropology No. 29.
FREEMAN, J. D.
    1955   Iban agriculture: a report on the shifting cultivation of hill rice by the Iban of Sarawak. Colonial Research Studies No. 18. London, Her Majesty's Stationery Office.
GOODENOUGH, W. H.
    1957   Cultural anthropology and linguistics. *In* Report of the Seventh Annual Round Table Meeting on Linguistics and Language Study. P. L. Garvin ed. Monograph Series on Languages and Linguistics, No. 9. Washington, D. C., Georgetown University Press.

GULLIVER, P. H.
    1955   The family herds: a study of two pastoral tribes in East Africa, the Jie and the
           Turkana. London, Routledge and Kegan Paul.
HYMES, D. H.
    1960   More on lexicostatistics. Current Anthropology 1:(4):338–45.
IZIKOWITZ, K. G.
    1951   Lamet: hill peasants in French Indochina. Etnologiska Studier 17. Göteburg.
MURDOCK, G. P.
    1949   Social structure. New York, MacMillan.
STEWARD, J. H.
    1955   Theory of culture change: the methodology of multilinear evolution. Urbana, Uni-
           versity of Illinois Press.

# Refocusing on the Neanderthal Problem[1]

C. LORING BRACE

*University of Wisconsin—Milwaukee*

IN A consideration of the known human remains immediately prior to the cultural development known as the Upper Paleolithic, great stress has heretofore been placed upon the classification of the available material into one or more supposedly uniform "types" (Morant 1927, 1930–1931; Howells 1944, 1959; Howell 1951, 1952; Le Gros Clark 1955; Thoma 1957–1958). The insistence upon "type" and the claims of uniformity were chiefly based upon two things. First, there has been an assumption specific in many early writings (Quatrefages 1877; Topinard 1892) and largely tacit in more recent sources (Morant 1927; Howells 1944, 1959; Boule and Vallois 1952; Thoma 1957–1958; Škerlj 1960) that, at an early time level, small population size and geographic isolation would increase inbreeding to the extent where supposedly pure lines would exhibit relatively small ranges of intrapopulation variability. Second, only one fairly complete specimen of pre-Upper Paleolithic man was well known. La Chapelle-aux-Saints is most frequently cited as the one instance where a descriptive and comparative study has been published for a complete adult skeleton (Boule 1911–1913; Hrdlička 1930).

With the expectation of relatively uniform populations, the picture presented by a single fairly complete skeleton has been sufficient to satisfy many authors that the characteristics of the human populations immediately prior to the Upper Paleolithic were well known and that they corresponded to a single, easily recognizable "type" (Boule 1911–1913; Keith 1927; Morant 1927; 1930–1931; Thoma 1957). It has apparently been repugnant to many authors to regard this as the population from which later forms of man have arisen. Since this view is associated with the tradition of paleontological studies in France, one strongly suspects a lingering residue of the influence of Baron Georges Cuvier (Cain 1959:185–87, 216) and a remnant of the 19th century uneasiness when the possibility was contemplated that modern man may have evolved from a form less "refined" than himself (Burkitt 1921:90; Boule 1923:242–43; MacCurdy 1924:209–10; Keith 1927:189; Osborn 1927:79; etc. quoted in Hrdlička 1930:326–27). These same authors have all stressed a relatively sudden change in the character of the Paleolithic population shortly after the climax of the first stage of the final European glaciation. They stress the cultural and anatomical discontinuity which they claim is followed by the abrupt appearance of *Homo sapiens* bearing a suddenly intrusive Upper Paleolithic culture. Lest this appear to be a resurrection of the special creation school of thought identified with pre-Darwinian science, they have sought refuge in an explanation which has a time-honored position in the cultural traditions of Western civilization. *In oriente lux.*

729

The growing appreciation of a number of factors has led to the modification of this view as a general picture of human development. Direct observation of the actual characteristics of naturally occurring groups of higher mammals has shown that there normally exists a considerable range of variation (Schultz 1947, 1951; Erikson 1953; Schuman and Brace 1954). This appreciation of a normal range of variation at one time even led to a rejection of genetics as of importance to morphology, under the assumption that a genetic explanation could only account for the constant transmission of relatively invariant characters (Pearson 1930:4). Increasing sophistication in the field of genetics (Fisher 1930; Huxley 1940; Li 1955) has now made entirely understandable the kind of variation which has long been recognized by such figures as Gauss, Quetelet, Darwin, and Galton (Hogben n. d.). The essential similarity of the results of both genetic and morphological studies has been specifically recognized by Weidenreich (1946:27, 1947:201–2), Dobzhansky (1951:106–7), and Simpson (1953:341).

Coupled with the accumulating finds of fossil men, this agreement of genetics and morphology has had the effect of modifying the view of man evolving in a "pure line." A retreat to a more strategic position is represented by the view that one group of fossil men can still be assigned to an unvarying type, but one which is a relatively isolated and increasingly specialized survival, the so-called classic Neanderthals of Western Europe (Howells 1944, 1959; Howell 1951, 1952, 1960; Le Gros Clark 1955; Thoma 1957–1958; Škerlj 1960). Although these same authors still preserve the attempt to push a form of modern man back to the point where the fossil record dwindles into obscurity, they have nevertheless yielded to the pictures painted by population genetics and morphology to the extent of conceding that these "Presapiens" groups may have presented patterns of morphology no longer present in modern man.

In contrast to the "uniform type" point of view and its derivatives, some authorities have recognized that the pre-Upper Paleolithic inhabitants of the Old World are far from being so invariant as they have often been considered (Hrdlička 1930:319–28; Stewart 1951:105; Washburn 1951:96). In support of this, it should be mentioned that at every pre-Upper Paleolithic site where remains of more than one individual have been found there are undeniable indications that the range of variation was at least as great as that observable in modern primate populations, e.g., Spy (Fraipont and Lohest 1887), Krapina (Gorjanović-Kramberger 1906), La Ferrassie (Capitan and Peyrony 1909; Hrdlička 1930), and Mount Carmel (Keith and McCown 1937; McCown and Keith 1939).

In fact, in the two instances where remains of 10 or more individuals have been found—Krapina and Mount Carmel—the range of variation is embarrassingly great for the proponents of the "uniform type" picture. Since neither of these populations was located in Western Europe, they could not be used directly to challenge the supposed uniformity of the "classic Neanderthals" on morphological grounds. There remains a dating problem for these populations which will not be considered in this paper (Garrod 1958:183; Howell 1958: 189–90; Vuković 1959; Solecki 1960).[2]

To note the variability of those Neanderthals restricted to Western Europe, the information published by Boule himself indicates that there is a 175 mm. difference in the statures of the two adult skeletons found at La Ferrassie (Boule 1912:117). Refiguring the statures using Pearson's formulae (Pearson 1899:196) instead of those of Manouvrier (used by Boule), the difference comes to 170 mm. These compare with the figure of 200 mm. for the difference between the maximum and minimum statures computed for the skeletal remains from Mugharet es-Skhūl, although it is not of the same order as the difference between the maximum Skhūl and the Tabūn skeleton which is 280 mm. (Thoma 1958:40–41). It should be remembered, however, that there are eight individuals (seven at Skhūl) for whom stature has been published at the Mount Carmel sites, while La Ferrassie has but two. A further indication of the variability shown at the La Ferrassie site alone is seen in the difference in the length of the ulna, to take the most extreme instance, which apparently amounts to more than 50 mm. (Boule 1912:135). The length of the La Ferrassie I ulna exceeds the largest racial mean (Schwaben and Allamannen) listed in Martin by 3 mm. and the length of the La Ferrassie II ulna falls 5 mm. short of the smallest racial mean (Negritos) (Martin 1928:1112). Again, of the four cranial capacities listed by Boule, the largest (La Chapelle-aux-Saints) is more than 320 cc. greater than the smallest (Gibraltar) (Boule 1912:189).

These few rather gross figures should indicate that the range of variation of the Mount Carmel material is not out of line with that previously demonstrated, although generally ignored, for Western Europe. In the comparison of unquantifiable features, the contrast between the chin and facial morphology of La Ferrassie I (Boule and Vallois 1952:207) and Le Moustier (Klaatsch and Hauser 1909; Weinert 1925) rivals a similar one between Skhūl IV and Tabūn I at Mount Carmel (McCown and Keith 1939).

La Ferrassie I, the big male skeleton found in 1909 (Capitan and Peyrony 1909:404), has as prominent a chin as many Upper Paleolithic and modern individuals and presents a picture of a markedly orthognathic face beneath a heavy supraorbital torus. This same combination of characters can be seen in Skhūl IV who is rarely pictured in discussions although generally considered to be one of the more "sapiens" appearing specimens at Mount Carmel. In contrast, the mid-facial prognathism of Tabūn I is well known. In this respect Tabūn I resembles Le Moustier and perhaps La Chapelle-aux-Saints, although the latter was practically toothless and a fully correct reconstruction of the alveolar-dental region cannot be made.

The uncovering of the remains of a fossil human population in the rock shelter of Krapina in Croatia between 1899 and 1905 provided the first picture of a pre-Upper Paleolithic group numbering more than a dozen individuals (Gorjanović-Kramberger 1906). The material was exceedingly fragmentary, but it did demonstrate that conformity to rigid type was not one of the characteristics of early man. Although it was counter to the climate of opinion of his time, Professor Gorjanović-Kramberger attempted to view his material as a single normally varying population approaching more recent forms of man in some of its features and showing resemblance to the assumed Neanderthal type in others. Utilizing comparative material from all of the major finds of pre-Upper Paleolithic man published by that time, he produced a remarkably scholarly and balanced analysis of the Krapina remains (Gorjanović-Kramberger 1906).

His interpretation was largely unappreciated and he himself was not entirely sure of it. He later changed his mind and accounted for the observed variation by the presumed occurrence of two different types of fossil men in the Krapina deposits (Gorjanović-Kramberger 1910). A similar but considerably more lurid view was entertained by Klaatsch who viewed the mixture of supposedly sapiens with supposedly Neanderthal features as the result of a battle fought by an Aurignacian and a Mousterian group for the possession of the rock shelter (Klaatsch 1923). Keith (1927:198) could see no reason to view the material as essentially different from the Neanderthal type and it is somewhat ironic that Keith was later to be faced with the same kind of variation which, because of the greater abundance of material and attendant publicity, he could not avoid by claiming that it did not exist. Keith likewise changed his mind about the interpretation of the Mount Carmel remains between 1937 and 1939 (Howells 1944:203) and never did offer a clear-cut conclusion (Keith and McCown 1937; McCown and Keith 1939; Hooton 1946:337–38).

Today we are faced with the unfortunate situation of being no closer to a generally agreed upon interpretation of the only two populations known for the period immediately prior to the Upper Paleolithic. (Shanidar cave may yet produce a population of fossil men which could significantly contribute to our solution of this problem [Stewart 1959; Solecki 1960].) A recent review of the Mount Carmel remains by Thoma (1957–1958) has attempted to achieve such a solution. It is the most extensive recent re-evaluation of the published material, and many European anthropologists feel that it has settled the questions which Keith never solved. Since this is largely unknown to anthropologists familiar with only English language sources, and since it claims to have reached a conclusion which is so clear that it can be "due to no error in method" (Thoma 1958:46), it is now pertinent to examine this conclusion and the methods used to achieve it. This is particularly relevant since much of the writing on fossil man has assumed a similar point of view and it is becoming evident that that a thorough reappraisal needs to be made.

Thoma believes that the diversity of the Mount Carmel material " . . . *can only be explained by a hybridization which had taken place between a neandertal population and another one of some sort of Sapiens form*" (Thoma 1958:43). In the course of arriving at this belief, he makes three sets of assumptions for which he offers no explanation.

First, he assumes that there are only two possible ways of explaining the range of variability present at Mount Carmel. Either it is a case of a population in the throes of rapid evolutionary change or it is the result of a hybridization as indicated above. The possibility that the Mount Carmel fossils may simply be a normal population, neither hybrid nor caught in some specific dramatic act of evolving, never seems to have occurred to him, although there are indications that this explanation requires less in the way of as yet unavailable supporting evidence than either of the other two (Stewart 1951:105; Hunt 1951: 53).

Next he makes the assumption that one of the populations engaged in the possible hybridization experiment must have been made up of individuals all resembling La Chapelle-aux-Saints. This confusion of individual with population has extended to his consideration of known and postulated cases of race mixture in the contemporary and historically known cases which he uses to support his evaluation of fossil man.

For instance, in considering one classic instance of analyzed race mixture, he chooses to ignore the findings of Rodenwaldt (1927) and later Trevor (1953) that the mestizos from the island of Kisar in the East Indies were not more variable than one would expect for a normal human population. Since this does not fit with his assumption of uniformity of racial type, he performs his own analysis upon Rodenwaldt's data and discovers that the Kisar hybrids do exceed the variability of native Kisarese (Thoma 1957:477). However, he fails to note that the Kisarese should be separated into three groupings with diverse social and biological backgrounds, and he completely fails to consider the possibility of variation in the original European element in the cross. In fact he does not consider the nature of the original European element at all.

He makes the same oversight when testing his method on the crania found in an 8th century Eastern European cemetery. In this instance he is on even shakier grounds since he does not demonstrate the characteristic morphology, relative variability (or invariability), or even the existence of the differing racial groups which he assumes were the parents of the population represented in the cemetery. Ten cranial characters for each of the 15 skulls are judged to be either typical mongoloid, intermediate, or atypical which he defines as "Europoïde" (1957:487). Even in cases of known parentage, this technique permits only tentative conclusions to be drawn, since it is based upon essentially subjective appraisal.

When he applies this same procedure to the analysis of the Mount Carmel remains he fails to offer adequate evidence for the morphology, variability, or existence of differing parent populations. Without this having been established, it is difficult to prove hybridity and impossible to evaluate the nature of the supposed parent populations. He is willing to concede that the presumed sapiens population which entered into the mixture conserved some "primitive traits" (1958:43), which means that its nature is even less discernible from the supposed hybrid population.

The only indications he offers for the existence and nature of a sapiens population prior to the Upper Paleolithic are the Swanscombe and Fontéchevade remains (1957:473; 1958:46). Since Stewart (1960:363) has noted that Swanscombe clearly does not represent a modern type of *sapiens* and shows definite affinities for the Neanderthal camp, this must be removed from his argument, leaving only Fontéchevade. This would scarcely be sufficient evidence for the existence of a "sapiens-type" population in Palestine even should the adult status and the third interglacial dating of Fontéchevade be confirmed.

The other element in the postulated mixture, and the only one for which he has attempted to enumerate a list of characteristics, is a Neanderthal group resembling La Chapelle-aux-Saints. Utilizing Boule's own information, it has been shown that no such uniform population can be supposed even in Western Europe, let alone elsewhere. While he is aware of the importance of the work of Simpson (1944) and Huxley (1940), he appears to have ignored Simpson's warning that, although a morphotype is necessary in practice, it is not a population and should be used with caution (Simpson 1953:341).

If these arguments advanced by Thoma are prejudicial to his conclusions, the use he makes of genetics is positively fatal, although many of the genetic facts cited by him are acceptable. His effective acceptance of a "rate of mutation" of between one in 50,000 to one in 100,000 is in accord with the best estimates (Dobzhansky 1955:85; Spuhler 1959:738). Likewise, the figure he accepts for the probability of the survival of a single mutation where no selective advantage is inherent (.01) is acceptable (Fisher 1930), as is his comment that most mutations decrease the vitality of the individual affected. Further, no objection can be raised to his estimate of 1,000 individuals at any given time in the Levalloiso-Mousterian population of Palestine, among whom 200 played an active role in reproduction (cf. Ewing 1951.94–95). He postulates that if a development from a population of fully Neanderthal appearance to one resembling that discovered at Mount Carmal actually occurred in Palestine it must have taken place over a period lasting roughly 10,000 years. During 10,000 years, he would expect approximately 350 generations which, when viewed in terms of the breeding population at any one time, means that some 70,000 individuals could be presumed to have contributed to the line of development. When he enumerates the number of changes that such a transition implies he concludes that far too small a number of individuals is represented in sequence for the required evolution to have been possible.

Among the 27 characters he observed, he noted that 23 do not conform to the assumed form of typical Neanderthal. For purposes of consideration he proposes that " . . . the morphological variation of one given character is the consequence of the mutation of one distinct gene," which he feels would be giving " . . . an almost absurd advantage . . . to the thesis of evolution." His logic then leads him to suppose that "the probability of simultaneous survival of 23 independent single mutations will be: $P = 0.01^{23}$, which borders practically on total improbability." Since, as he has noted, chance mutations are likely to be adaptively detrimental, the "actual probability would be further reduced" (1958:45).

Thus saying, he believes that he has proven the improbability of the development of the Mount Carmel population out of a Neanderthal-type population. If his arithmetic is followed out, he has done much more, although he has not explicitly claimed to do so. He has "proved mathematically" that such an evolutionary development could not have occurred in a period several times as long as that recently postulated for the existence of our universe (Burbridge and Burbridge 1961:51). If his logic were correct, evolution could not be a reality at all and perhaps this is the implicit argument. In this as in many other recent accounts, there seems to be much more effort expended in proving how evolution could not have occurred than in showing how it did.

There are two major flaws in his use of genetics. First, to assume that morphological features correspond directly with single genes ignores the known nature and mode of action of genes. The fact that observable morphology is the end product of a long complex series of interacting processes controlled by a multiplicity of enzymes should make one suspicious of any explanation which assumes a single gene for a single morphological feature.

Recent work has identified deoxyribonucleic acid as the basic genetic material (Watson and Crick 1953:964–67; Pauling 1960:503) and has suggested the mechanism whereby it assembles amino acids into the pre-determined orders which constitute specific proteins (Crick 1958:138–61). Since growth processes are controlled by enzymes (proteins), it should be expected that single genes relate to single enzymes rather than to the aspects of organisms which are perceived as single morphological features. It is not surprising then that the very aspects of man for which a simple genetic base can be demonstrated turn out to be proteins themselves (hemoglobins for instance) or such things as metabolic defects which result from the deficiency of particular enzymes (Harris 1959).

This is far removed from gross observable form, although it is obvious that the modification or elimination of an enzyme can have profound effects upon it. One cannot agree with Thoma that the 23 stated characters whereby the Mount Carmel population differs from a classic Neanderthal type can be accounted for by 23 genes. Furthermore, the demonstrations of studies in balanced polymorphism show that observable changes can occur within a population without the introduction of new genetic material (Allison 1954; Livingstone 1958). All that is needed is a change in the factors effecting the balance.

This suggests the final major flaw in Thoma's set of assumptions relating to genetics. He has completely omitted any consideration of the selective factors involved. This in spite of the fact that he derives some of his information on genetics from Fisher who insisted upon the adaptive significance of genetically controlled features in the very source quoted (Fisher 1930). Since 21 of his 27 characters concern the head, face, and teeth, he feels he has justified this omission by claiming that, "Besides it is evident that the selective value of constitutional properties is far superior to that of the characters of the cranial segment" (1957:499).

As proof he uses Simpson's (1944) observation that variability will be reduced where strict selection is in operation and applies this to an examination of Australian aboriginal measurements (citing Howells 1937). He notes that the body measurements show considerably less variability than those of the face and the head, although a closer examination of the measurements compared reveals that the only cranial measures which do show greater variability are those of the nose and the ear. Since no soft part measurements were considered for the body one can only conclude that the comparison was improperly performed and the conclusion not proven.

In view of the preceding, one cannot share Thoma's confident assertion that the indications of hybridity in Palestine are so clear that "no error in method" can be invoked. Actually, it is more a series of errors in assumptions than in specific method.

A full scale reappraisal of the Mount Carmel population is somewhat premature at this time. It would require final resolution of the dating problem (Howell 1958:183; Garrod 1958:189–90; Solecki 1960:631), the problem of placement within the Middle Eastern archeological sequence (Müller-Beck 1954), and an understanding of the interplay of genetic factors and selective pressures controlling the physical characteristics.

Among the immediately pre-Upper Paleolithic populations for whom we have more than single individuals represented, it can be seen that a normal range of variability was present. This is true for the supposedly classic Neanderthals of Western Europe, although adequate evidence for the range of variation of local breeding populations is still sketchy, and it is true for the inhabitants of the Middle East where the picture of local population is considerably better. It is also true for the available material from the Balkans between Europe and the Middle East.

Although the whole question of the morphology and relationships of pre-Upper Paleolithic and Upper Paleolithic populations is drastically in need of a re-examination based upon original materials, the above discussion should indicate that the currently unquestioned belief that the Western European Neanderthals were isolated, specialized, and peculiar is not based on a consideration of all of even the major pieces of available evidence.

If the relationships of pre-Upper Paleolithic peoples with subsequent, preceding, and contemporary peoples is not to be simply discovered from published morphological evidence, one might expect some help from archeology since archeological material, being less perishable than skeletal remains, is preserved and known in far greater quantity and detail. Recently many physical anthropologists have been clinging to the old view of a sudden migration into Europe of Upper Paleolithic peoples, although they have been unconvinced by the skeletal evidence. According to them the proof is mainly archeological. On the other hand, archeologists have continued paying lip service to the sudden migration view with the feeling that the justification was largely based upon the supposedly clear-cut morphological distinctions made by the physical anthropologists.

This Alphonse and Gaston situation has been notably broken by the French archeologist François Bordes who sees a relatively gradual transition from an essentially Mousterian to an essentially Upper Paleolithic status marked by a gradual change in the number and variety of tools made on blades (Bordes 1958:180). The strong persistence of undeniably local peculiarities associated with the particular geographical areas where Mousterian→Upper Paleolithic continuity is demonstrable should tend to lessen the evidence for any large scale migrations at this time level. In the absence of any large population reservoir, large migrations are unlikely anyway.

The resulting picture of gradual local change with enough intermittent contact between localities to preserve a general similarity in the local changes occurring in the Middle East and Europe is surprisingly like the model of population dynamics in evolution postulated by Weidenreich (1943:253). Perhaps this should not be so surprising, since this model also meets with the approval of geneticists (Dobzhansky 1951:106–107) and ecologists (Bartholomew and Birdsell 1953:485; Birdsell 1958:63–68) when they are thinking in evolutionary terms.

The enduring reluctance to see a development of Upper Paleolithic tool-making traditions from some sort of Mousterian base is compared by Bordes to those who claim that Hamlet was not written by William Shakespeare but by a contemporary of the same name (Bordes 1958:179). It would appear that this analogy is equally applicable to the biological sphere.[3] We find that we have been looking for the ancestors of modern man in populations that are not supposed to be termed Neanderthals, although they look like them.

## NOTES

[1] Much of the material for this paper was gathered in 1959–1960 while the author was the holder of a Frederick Sheldon Travelling Fellowship. Thanks are due to F. Bordes, of the Université de Bordeaux, H. Kelley of the Musée de l'Homme, Paris, H. L. Movius, Jr. of Harvard University, J. Piveteau of the Sorbonne, Paris, J. Poljak of the Narodni Geolosko-Paleontoloski Muzej, Zagreb, and J. S. Weiner of the University at Oxford for access to original materials.

I wish to express my sincere gratitude to James Silverberg and other members of the Department of Anthropology, University of Wisconsin—Milwaukee, for the extensive assistance offered during the writing and re-writing of this paper. Dr. Silverberg was particularly helpful in straightening out many points of basic logic as well as in rephrasing sections where expression was not clear.

[2] Since this paper was written, evidence has been published suggesting that the Skhūl finds may be as much as 10,000 years more recent than the Tabūn material, and may belong in the Göttweiger interstadial somewhere in the neighborhood of 35,000 B.P. instead of back in the Riss-Würm interglacial (Higgs 1961). This would corroborate Stewart's suspicions (Stewart 1951:104; Brothwell 1961) and reinforce the views presented in this paper.

[3] The nature of the relationship between some of the simultaneous biological and cultural changes which occurred during the course of human evolution has been considered by the author in papers presented at the annual meetings of the American Association of Physical Anthropologists in May, 1961, and at the annual meetings of the American Anthropological Association in November, 1961. This is an important and extensive subject and certain facets are scheduled for publication in the fall of 1962 (Brace n.d.).

## REFERENCES CITED

ALLISON, A. C.
　　1954　Notes on sickle-cell polymorphism. Annals of Human Genetics 19:39–57.
BARTHOLOMEW, G. A. and J. B. BIRDSELL
　　1953　Ecology and the protohominids. American Anthropologist 55:481–98.

BIRDSELL, J. B.
   1958   Some population problems involving pleistocene man. Cold Spring Harbor Symposia on Quantitative Biology 22:47–69.

BORDES, F.
   1958   Le passage du Paléolithique moyen au Paléolithique supérieur. *In* Hundert Jahre Neanderthaler, G. H. R. von Koenigswald, ed. Utrecht, Kemink en Zoon N.V.

BOULE, MARCELLIN
   1911–13   L'homme fossile de la Chapelle-aux-Saints. Annales de Paléontologie 6:109–72; 7:21–57, 85–192; 8:1–70.
   1923   Fossil men: elements of human palaeontology. 2nd ed. Jessie Elliot Ritchie and James Ritchie, trans. Edinburgh, Oliver and Boyd.

BOULE, M. and H. V. VALLOIS
   1952   Les hommes fossiles. Paris, Masson et Cie.

BRACE, C. L.
   n.d.   Cultural factors in the evolution of the human dentition. *In* Culture and the evolution of man, M. F. Ashley Montagu, ed. New York, Oxford University Press (in press).

BROTHWELL, D. R.
   1961   The people of Mount Carmel. Proceedings of the Prehistoric Society for 1961 27:155–59.

BURBRIDGE, M. and G. BURBRIDGE
   1961   Peculiar galaxies. Scientific American 204:50–57.

BURKITT, M. C.
   1921   Prehistory. Cambridge, England, The University Press.

CAIN, A. J.
   1959   Deductive and inductive methods in post-Linnaean taxonomy. Proceedings of the Linnean Society of London. 170 Session, 1957–58, Pt. 2, April.

CAPITAN, L. and D. PEYRONY
   1909   Deux squelettes humains au milieu de foyers de l'époque mousterienne. Revue de l'école d'anthropologie de Paris 19:402–9.

CLARK, W. E. LE GROS
   1955   The fossil evidence for human evolution. Chicago, The University of Chicago Press.

CRICK, F. H. C.
   1958   On protein synthesis. Symposia of the Society for Experimental Biology 12:138–63.

DOBZHANSKY, T.
   1951   Comment on the paper by T. D. Stewart. Cold Spring Harbor Symposia on Quantitative Biology 15:106–7.
   1955   Evolution, genetics, and man. New York, John Wiley & Sons, Inc.

ERIKSON, G. E.
   1953   Comparative anatomy of New World primates and its bearing on the phylogeny of anthropoid apes and men. Paper read at Section H of the American Association for the Advancement of Science Meetings, December 27, 1953.

EWING, J. F.
   1951   Comments following paper by T. D. McCown. Cold Spring Harbor Symposia on Quantitative Biology 15:95.

FISHER, R. A.
   1930   The genetical theory of natural selection. Oxford.

FRAIPONT, J. and M. LOHEST
   1887   La race humaine de Néanderthal ou de Canstadt en Belgique. Archives de biologie 7:587–757.

GARROD, D. A. E.
   1958   The ancient shore lines of the Lebanon, and the dating of Mt. Carmel man. *In* Hundert Jahre Neanderthaler, G. H. R. von Koenigswald, ed. Utrecht, Netherlands, Kemink en Zoon N. V.

GORJANOVIĆ-KRAMBERGER, K.
1906 Der diluviale Mensch von Krapina in Kroatien. Wiesbaden, C. W. Kreidel.
1910 Zur Frage der Existenz des *Homo aurignaciensis* in Krapina. Ber. geol. Kommis. Kroat. u. Slavon.: 5–8. Zagreb, Croatia.

HARRIS, H.
1959 Human biochemical genetics. Cambridge (England), at the University Press.

HIGGS, E. S.
1961 Some Pleistocene faunas of the Mediterranean coastal areas. Proceedings of the Prehistoric Society for 1961 27:144–54.

HOGBEN, L.
n.d. Statistical theory. New York, W. W. Norton & Co.

HOOTON, E. A.
1946 Up from the ape. New York, The Macmillan Company.

HOWELL, F. CLARK
1951 The place of Neanderthal in human evolution. American Journal of Physical Anthropology n.s. 9:379–415.
1952 Pleistocene glacial ecology and the evolution of 'classic Neandertal' man. Southwestern Journal of Anthropology 8:377–410.
1958 Upper Pleistocene men of the Southwest Asian Mousterian. *In* Hundert Jahre Neanderthaler, G. H. R. von Koenigswald, ed. Utrecht, Netherlands, Kemink en Zoon N. V.
1960 European and Northwest African Middle Pleistocene hominids. Current Anthropology 1:195–232.

HOWELLS, W. W.
1944 Mankind so far. Garden City, Doubleday & Company.
1959 Mankind in the making. Garden City, Doubleday & Company.

HRDLIČKA, ALEŠ
1930 The skeletal remains of early man. Smithsonian miscellaneous collections 83:1–379.

HUNT, E. E.
1951 Comments following the paper read by A. H. Schultz. Cold Spring Harbor Symposia on Quantitative Biology 15:53.

HUXLEY, J. S., ed.
1940 The new systematics. Oxford, the Clarendon Press.

KEITH, SIR A.
1927 The antiquity of man, vol. I. London, Williams and Norgate.

KEITH, A. and T. D. McCOWN
1937 Mount Carmel man. His bearing on the ancestry of modern races. *In* Early man, G. G. MacCurdy, ed. London, J. B. Lippincott Company.

KLAATSCH, H.
1923 The evolution and progress of mankind. New York.

KLAATSCH, H. and O. HAUSER
1909 Homo mousteriensis Hauseri. Ein altdiluvialer Skelettfund im Departement Dordogne und seine Zugehörigkeit zum Neandertaltypus. Archiv. für Anthropologie. Neue Folge 7:287–97.

LI, C. C.
1955 Population genetics. Chicago, University of Chicago Press.

LIVINGSTONE, F. B.
1958 Anthropological implications of sickle cell gene distribution in West Africa. American Anthropologist 60:533–62.

MACCURDY, G. G.
1924 Human origins, vol. I. New York, D. Appleton & Co.

MARTIN, R.
1928 Lehrbuch der anthropologie. 3 vols. Jena, G. Fischer.

McCown, T. D. and A. Keith
    1939  The stone age of Mount Carmel. The fossil human remains from the Levalloiso-Mousterian, Vol. II. Oxford, at the Clarendon Press.
Morant, G. M.
    1927  Studies of palaeolithic man, II. A biometric study of Neanderthaloid skulls and of their relationships to modern racial types. Annals of Eugenics II(Parts 3 and 4): 318–80.
    1930–31  Studies of palaeolothic man, IV. A biometric study of the upper palaeolithic skulls of Europe and of their relationships to earlier and later types. Annals of Eugenics IV (Parts 1 and 2):109–214.
Müller-Beck, H. J.
    1954  Die Mt. Carmel Materialien im Bernischen Historischen Museum. Jahrbuch des Bernischen Historischen Museum in Bern 34.
Osborn, H. F.
    1927  Man of the cave period. *In* Man rises to Parnassus. Princeton, Princeton University Press.
Pauling, L.
    1960  The nature of the chemical bond and the structure of molecules and crystals: an introduction to modern structural chemistry. 3rd. ed. Ithaca, Cornell University Press.
Pearson, K.
    1899  On the reconstruction of the stature of prehistoric races. Philosophical Trasactions of the Royal Society of London, Series A, Vol. 192, pp. 169–244.
    1930  On a new theory of progressive evolution. Annals of Eugenics IV (Parts I and II).
Quatrefages, A. de
    1877  The human species. *Reprinted in* This is race, E. W. Count, ed. (1950). New York, Henry Schuman, Inc.
Rodenwaldt, E.
    1927  Die Mestizen auf Kisar. Batavia, G. Kolff and Co.
Schultz, A. H.
    1947  Variability in man and other primates. American Journal of Physical Anthropology n.s. 5:1–14.
    1951  The specialization of man and his place among the catarrhine primates. Cold Spring Harbor Symposia on Quantitative Biology 15:37–53.
Schuman, E. L. and C. L. Brace
    1954  Metric and morphologic variations in the dentition of the Liberian chimpanzee: comparisons with anthropoid and human dentitions. Human Biology 26:239–68.
Simpson, G. G.
    1944  Tempo and mode in evolution. New York, Columbia University Press.
    1953  The major features of evolution. New York, Columbia University Press.
Škerlj, B.
    1960  Human evolution and Neanderthal man. Antiquity 34:90–99.
Solecki, R. S.
    1960  Three adult Neanderthal skeletons from Shanidar Cave, Northern Iraq. Smithsonian Report for 1959, 603–35. Washington, Smithsonian Institution.
Spuhler, J. N.
    1959  Physical anthropology and demography. *In* The study of population, an inventory and appraisal, P. M. Hauser and O. D. Duncan, eds. Chicago, The University of Chicago Press.
Stewart, T. D.
    1951  The problem of the earliest claimed representatives of Homo sapiens. Cold Spring Harbor Symposia on Quantitative Biology 15:97–107.
    1959  The restored Shanidar I skull. Smithsonian Report for 1958, 473–80. Washington, Smithsonian Institution.

1960    Indirect evidence of the primitiveness of the Swanscombe skull. American Journal of Physical Anthropology n.s. 18:363.

THOMA, A.
1957, 1958    Métissage ou transformation? Essai sur les hommes fossiles de Palestine. L'Anthropologie 61:470–502; 62:30–52.

TOPINARD, P.
1892    On "race" in anthropology. *Reprinted in* This is race, E. W. Count, ed. (1950). New York, Henry Schuman.

TREVOR, J. C.
1953    Race crossing in man. Eugenics Lab. Memoir 36. Cambridge, at the University Press.

VUKOVIĆ, S.
1959    Verbal information, in Varaždin, Jugoslavija.

WASHBURN, S. L.
1951    Comments following paper by T. D. McCown. Cold Spring Harbor Symposia on Quantitative Biology 15:95–96.

WATSON, J. D. and F. H. C. CRICK
1953    A structure for deoxyribose nucleic acid. Nature 171:964–67.

WEIDENREICH, F.
1943    The skull of *Sinanthropus pekinensis*. Palaeontologica Sinica New Series, D. No. 10. Peking.

1946    Generic, specific, and subspecific characters in human evolution. *Reprinted in* The shorter anthropological papers of Franz Weidenreich published in the period 1939–1948, compiled by S. L. Washburn and Davida Wolffson. The Viking Fund Inc. 1949.

1947    Facts concerning the origin of *Homo sapiens*. American Anthropologist 49:187–203.

WEINERT, H.
1925    Der Schädel des eiszeitlichen Menschen von le Moustier in neuer Zusammensetzung. Berlin, J. Springer.

# The Concept of Race[1]

ASHLEY MONTAGU
*Princeton, New Jersey*

IN THIS paper I desire to examine the concepts of race as they are used with reference to man. I shall first deal with the use of this term by biologists and anthropologists, and then with its use by the man-on-the-street, the so-called layman—so-called, no doubt, from the lines in Sir Philip Sidney's sonnet:

> I never drank of Aganippe well
> Nor ever did in shade of Tempe sit,
> And Muses scorn with vulgar brains to dwell;
> Poor layman I, for sacred rites unfit.

I shall endeavor to show that all those who continue to use the term "race" with reference to man, whether they be laymen or scientists, are "for sacred rites unfit." Once more, I shall, as irritatingly as the sound of a clanging door heard in the distance in a wind that will not be shut out, raise the question as to whether, with reference to man, it would not be better if the term "race" were altogether abandoned.

At the outset it should, perhaps, be made clear that I believe, with most biologists, that evolutionary factors, similar to those that have been operative in producing raciation in other animal species, have also been operative in the human species—but with a significant added difference, namely, the consequences which have resulted from man's entry into that unique zone of adaptation in which he excels beyond all other creatures, namely *culture*, that is to say, the man-made part of the environment.

On the evidence it would seem clear that man's cultural activities have introduced elements into the processes of human raciation which have so substantially modified the end-products that one can no longer equate the processes of raciation in lower animals with those which have occurred in the evolution of man. The factors of mutation, natural selection, drift, isolation, have all been operative in the evolution of man. But so have such factors as ever-increasing degrees of mobility, hybridization, and social selection, and it is the effects of these and similar factors which, at least so it has always seemed to me, makes the employment of the term "race" inapplicable to most human populations as we find them today.

Of course there exist differences, but we want a term by which to describe the existence of these differences. We do not want a prejudiced term which injects meanings which are not there into the differences. We want a term which as nearly mirrors the conditions as a term can, not one which falsifies and obfuscates the issue.

919

Terminology is extremely important, and I think it will be generally agreed that it is rather more desirable to allow the conditions or facts to determine the meaning of the terms by which we shall refer to them, than to have pre-existing terms determine the manner in which they shall be perceived and ordered, for pre-existing terms constitute pre-existing meanings, and such meanings have a way of conditioning the manner in which what we look at shall be perceived. Each time the term "race" is used with reference to man, this is what, I think, is done.

The term "race" has a long and tortured history. We cannot enter upon that here. The present-day usage of the term in biological circles is pretty much the sense in which it was used in similar circles in the 19th century, namely, as a subdivision of a species the members of which resemble each other and differ from other members of the species in certain traits. In our own time valiant attempts have been made to pour new wine into the old bottles. The shape of the bottle, however, remains the same. The man-on-the-street uses the term in much the same way as it was used by his 19th century compeer. Here physical type, heredity, blood, culture, nation, personality, intelligence, and achievement are all stirred together to make the omelet which is the popular conception of "race." This is a particularly virulent term, the epidemiology of which is far better understood by the social scientist than by the biologist—who should therefore exercise a little more caution than he usually does when he delivers himself on the subject.

The difficulty with taking over old terms in working with problems to which they are thought to apply is that when this is done we may also take over some of the old limitations of the term, and this may affect our approach to the solution of those problems. For what the investigator calls "the problem of human races" is immediately circumscribed and delimited the moment he uses the word "races." For "race" implies something very definite to him, something which in itself constitutes a solution, and the point I would like to make is that far from the problem meaning something like a solution to him, it should, on the contrary, constitute itself in his mind as something more closely resembling what it is, namely, a problem requiring investigation.

Instead of saying to himself, as the true believer in "race" does, "Here is a population, let me see how it fits my criteria of 'race,'" I think it would be much more fruitful of results if he said to himself, instead, "Here is a population, let me go ahead and find out what it is like. What its internal likenesses and differences are, and how it resembles and how it differs from other populations. And then let me operationally describe what I have found," that is, in terms of the data themselves, and not with reference to the conditions demanded by any pre-existing term.

The chief objection to the term "race" with reference to man is that it takes for granted as solved problems which are far from being so and tends to close the mind to problems to which it should always remain open. If, with ritual fidelity, one goes on repeating long enough that "the Nordics" are a

race, or that "the Armenoids" are, or that "the Jews" are, or that races may
be determined by their blood group gene frequencies, we have already determined what a "race" is, and it is not going to make the slightest difference
whether one uses the old or the new wine, for we are back at the same old stand
pouring it into the old bottles covered with the same patina of moss-like green.

It is the avoidance of this difficulty that T. H. Huxley had in mind when
in 1865, he wrote, "I speak of 'persistent modifications' or 'stocks' rather than
of 'varieties,' or 'races,' or 'species,' because each of these last well-known terms
implies, on the part of its employer, a preconceived opinion touching one of
those problems, the solution of which is the ultimate object of the science;
and in regard to which, therefore, ethnologists are especially bound to keep
their minds open and their judgements freely balanced "(1865: 209–10).

It is something to reflect upon that, a century later, this point of view has
still to be urged.

In the year 1900, the French anthropologist Joseph Deniker published his
great book, simultaneously in French and in English, *The Races of Man*. But
though the title has the word in it, he objected to the term "race" on much the
same grounds as Huxley. The whole of his introduction is devoted to showing
the difficulties involved in applying to man the terms of zoological nomenclature. He writes, "We have presented to us Arabs, Swiss, Australians, Bushmen,
English, Siouan Indians, Negroes, etc., without knowing if each of these
groups is on an equal footing from the point of view of classification."

"Do these real and palpable groupings represent unions of individuals
which, in spite of some slight dissimilarities, are capable of forming what
zoologists call 'species,' 'subspecies,' 'varieties,' in the case of wild animals, or
'races' in the case of domestic animals? One need not be a professional anthropologist to reply negatively to this question. They are *ethnic groups* formed
by virtue of community of language, religion, social institutions, etc., which
have the power of uniting human beings of one or several species, races, or
varieties, and are by no means zoological species; they may include human
beings of one or of many species, races, or varieties." "They are," he goes on
to say, "theoretic types" (19: 2–3).

When, in 1936, Julian Huxley and A. C. Haddon published their valuable
book on "race," *We Europeans*, they took pains to underscore the fact that
"the existence of . . . human sub-species is purely hypothetical. Nowhere does
a human group now exist which corresponds closely to a systematic sub-
species in animals, since various original sub-species have crossed repeatedly
and constantly. For the existing populations, the non-committal term *ethnic
group* should be used. . . . . All that exists today is a number of arbitrary
ethnic groups, intergrading into each other" (1936:106). And finally, "The
essential reality of the existing situation . . . is not the hypothetical sub-species
or races, but the *mixed ethnic groups*, which can never be genetically purified
into their original components, or purged of the variability which they owe to
past crossing. Most anthropological writings of the past, and many of the

present fail to take account of this fundamental fact" (1936:108). "If *race* is a scientific term," these authors point out, "it must have a genetic meaning" (1936:114).

Haddon, as an anthropologist, was familiar with Deniker's book, and it is possible that the noncommittal term "ethnic group" was remembered by him as one more appropriately meeting the requirements of the situation and thus came to be adopted by both authors in their book. It was from this source, that is from Huxley and Haddon, that I, in turn, adopted the term "ethnic group" in 1936 and have consistently continued to use it since that time. The claim is that the noncommittal general term "ethnic group" meets the realities of the situation head on, whereas the term "race" does not. Furthermore, it is claimed that "ethnic group" is a term of heuristic value. It raises questions, and doubts, leading to clarification and discovery. The term "race," since it takes for granted what requires to be demonstrated within its own limits, closes the mind on all that.

It is of interest to find that quite a number of biologists have, in recent years, independently raised objections to the continuing use of the term "race," even, in some cases, when it is applied to populations of lower animals. Thus, for example, W. T. Calman writes, "Terms such as 'geographical race,' 'form,' 'phase,' and so forth, may be useful in particular instances but are better not used until some measure of agreement is reached as to their precise meaning" (1949:14). Hans Kalmus writes, "A very important term which was originally used in systematics is 'race.' Nowadays, however, its use is avoided as far as possible in genetics" (1948:45). In a later work Kalmus writes, "It is customary to discuss the local varieties of humanity in terms of 'race.' However, it is unnecessary to use this greatly debased word, since it is easy to describe populations without it" (1958:30). G. S. Carter writes that the terms " 'race,' 'variety,' and 'form' are used so loosely and in so many senses that it is advisable to avoid using them as infraspecific categories (1951:163). Ernst Hanhart objects to the use of the term "race" with reference to man since he holds that there are no "true races" among men (1953:545). Abercrombie, Hickman, and Johnson, in their *A Dictionary of Biology* (1951), while defining species and subspecies consistently, decline even a mention of the word "race" anywhere in their book. L. S. Penrose in an otherwise highly favorable review of Dunn and Dobzhansky's excellent *Heredity, Race and Society*, writes that he is unable "to see the necessity for the rather apologetic retention of the obsolete term 'race,' when what is meant is simply a given population differentiated by some social, geographical or genetical character, or . . . merely by a gene frequency peculiarity. The use of the almost mystical concept of race makes the presentation of the facts about the geographical and linguistic groups . . . unnecessarily complicated" (1952:252).

To see what Penrose means, and at the same time to make our criticism of their conception of "race," let us turn to Dunn and Dobzhansky's definition of race. They write, in the aforementioned work, "Races can be defined as populations which differ in the frequencies of some gene or genes" (1952:118). This definition at once leads to the question: Why use the word "race" here when what is being done is precisely what should be done, namely, to describe populations in terms of their gene frequency differences? What, in point of fact, has the antiquated, mystical conception of "race" to do with this? The answer is: Nothing. Indeed, the very notion of "race" is antithetical to the study of population genetics, for the former traditionally deals with fixed clear-cut differences, and the latter with fluid or fluctuating differences. It seems to me an unrealistic procedure to maintain that this late in the day we can re-adapt the term "race" to mean something utterly different from what it has always most obfuscatingly and ambiguously meant.

We may congratulate ourselves, and in fact often do, that the chemists of the late 18th and early 19th centuries had the good sense to throw out the term "phlogiston" when they discovered that it corresponded to nothing in reality, instead of attempting to adapt it to fit the facts which it was not de-signed to describe, and of which, indeed, it impeded the discovery for several centuries. The psychologists of the second decade of this century had the good sense to do likewise with the term "instinct" when they discovered how, like a bunion upon the foot, it impeded the pilgrim's progress toward a sounder understanding of human drives (Bernard 1924).

It is simply not possible to redefine words with so longstanding a history of misuse as "race," and for this, among other cogent reasons, it is ill-advised. As Simpson has said, "There . . . is a sort of Gresham's Law for words; redefine them as we will, their worst or most extreme meaning is almost certain to re-main current and to tend to drive out the meaning we prefer" (1953:268).

For this reason alone it would appear to me unwise to afford scientific sanction to a term which is so embarrassed by false meanings as is the term "race." There is the added objection that it is wholly redundant, and confus-ingly so, to distinguish as a "race" a population which happens to differ from other populations in the frequency of one or more genes. Why call such popula-tions "races" when the operational definition of what they *are* is sharply and clearly stated in the words used to convey what we mean, namely, populations which differ from one another in particular frequencies of certain specified genes? Surely, to continue the use of the word "race" under such circumstances is to exemplify what A. E. Housman so aptly described as "calling in ambiguity of language to promote confusion of thought" (1933:31).

When populations differ from each other in the frequency of the sickle-cell gene or any other gene or genes, all that is necessary is to state the facts with reference to those populations. That is what those populations are in terms of gene frequencies. And those are the operative criteria which we can use as tools or concepts in giving an account of the realities of the situation—the actual operations.

I have thus far said nothing about the anthropological conception of "race" because this is to some extent yielding to genetic pressure, and because the future of what used to be called the study of "race" lies, in my view, largely in the direction of population genetics. The older anthropological conception of "race" still occasionally lingers on, suggesting that it is perhaps beyond the reach both of scientific judgment and mortal malice. Insofar as the genetic approach to the subject is concerned, many anthropologists are, as it were, self-made men and only too obviously represent cases of unskilled labor. However, my feeling is that they should be praised for trying rather than blamed for failing. The new anthropology is on the right track.

Recently Garn and Coon (1955) have attempted to adapt the terms "geographic race," "local race," and "microgeographical race," for use in the human species. They define, for example, "A geographical race" as, "in its simplest terms, a collection of (race) populations having features in common, such as a high gene frequency for blood group B, and extending over a geographically definable area" (1955:997).

In this definition I think we can see, in high relief as it were, what is wrong with the continuing use of the term "race." The term "geographical race" immediately delimits the group of populations embraced by it from others, as if the so-called "geographical race" were a biological entity "racially" distinct from others. Such a group of populations is not "racially" distinct, but differs from others in the frequencies of certain of its genes. It was suggested by the UNESCO group of geneticists and physical anthropologists that such a group of populations be called a "major group" (Montagu 1951:173–82). This suggestion was made precisely in order to avoid such difficulties as are inherent in the term "geographical race." Since Garn and Coon themselves admit that "geographical races are to a large extent collections of convenience, useful more for pedagogic purposes than as units for empirical investigation" (1955:1000), it seems to me difficult to understand why they should have preferred this term to the one more closely fitting the situation, namely, "major groups." It is a real question whether spurious precision, even for pedagogical purposes, or as an "as if" fiction, is to be preferred to a frank acknowledgment, in the terms we use, of the difficulties involved. Garn and Coon are quite alive to the problem, but it may be questioned whether it contributes to the student's clearer understanding of that problem to use terms which not only do not fit the conditions, but which serve to contribute to making the student's mind a dependable instrument of imprecision, especially in view of the fact that a more appropriate term is available.

The principle of "squatter's rights" apparently applies to words as well as to property. When men make a heavy investment in words they are inclined to treat them as property, and even to become enslaved by them, the prisoners of their own vocabularies. High walls may not a prison make, but technical terms sometimes do. This, I would suggest, is another good reason for self-examination with regard to the use of the term "race."

Commenting on Garn's views on race, Dr. J. P. Garlick has remarked, "The use of 'race' as a taxonomic unit for man seems out of date, if not irrational. A hierarchy of geographical, local and micro-races is proposed, with acknowledgements to Rensch and Dobzhansky. But the criteria for their definition are nowhere made clear, and in any case such a scheme could not do justice to the many independent fluctuations and frequency gradients shown by human polymorphic characters. Surely physical anthropology has outgrown such abstractions as 'Large Local Race. . . .Alpine: the rounder-bodied, rounder-headed, predominantly darker peoples of the French mountains, across Switzerland, Austria, and to the shores of the Black Sea' " (1961:169–70).

Garn and Coon do not define "local races" but say of them that they "can be identified, not so much by average differences, but by their nearly complete isolation" (1955:997). In that case, as Dahlberg (1942) long ago suggested, why not call such populations "isolates"?

"Microgeographical races" also fail to receive definition, but are described as differing "only qualitatively from local races." In that case, why not use some term which suggests the difference?

In short, it is our opinion that taxonomies and terms should be designed to fit the facts, and not the facts forced into the procrustean rack of pre-determined categories. If we are to have references, whether terminological or taxonomical, to existing or extinct populations of man, let the conditions as we find them determine the character of our terms or taxonomies, and not the other way round.

Since what we are actually dealing with in human breeding populations are differences in the frequencies of certain genes, why not use a term which states just this, such as *genogroup*, and the various appropriate variants of this?[2] If necessary, we could then speak of "geographic genogroups," "local genogroups," and "microgenogroups." A genogroup being defined as a breeding population which differs from other breeding populations of the species in the frequency of one or more genes. The term "genogroup" gets as near to a statement of the facts as a term can. The term "race" goes far beyond the facts and only serves to obscure them. A *geographic genogroup* would then be defined as a group of breeding populations characterized by a marked similarity of the frequencies of one or more genes.

A *local genogroup* would be one of the member populations of a geographic genogroup, and a *microgenogroup* a partially isolated population with one or more gene frequency differences serving to distinguish it from adjacent or nonadjacent local genogroups.

It is to be noted that nothing is said of a common heredity for similarity in gene frequencies in a geographic genogroup. The common heredity is usually implied, but I do not think it should be taken for granted, except within the local genogroups and the microgenogroups. One or more of the genogroups in a geographic genogroup may have acquired their frequencies for a given gene quite independently of the other local populations comprising the geographic genogroup. This is a possibility which is, perhaps, too often overlooked when comparisons are being made on the basis of gene frequencies between populations, whether geographic or not.

But this must suffice for my criticism of the usage of the term "race" by

biologists and anthropologists. I wish now to discuss, briefly, the disadvantages
of the use of this term in popular usage, and the advantages of the general term
"ethnic group."

The layman's conception of "race" is so confused and emotionally muddled
that any attempt to modify it would seem to be met by the greatest obstacle of
all, the term "race" itself. It is a trigger word. Utter it, and a whole series of
emotionally conditioned responses follow. If we are to succeed in clarifying the
minds of those who think in terms of "race" we must cease using the word,
because by continuing to use it we sanction whatever meaning anyone chooses
to bestow upon it, and because in the layman's mind the term refers to conditions which do not apply. There is no such thing as the kind of "race" in which
the layman believes, namely, that there exists an indissoluble association
between mental and physical characters which make individual members of
certain "races" either inferior or superior to the members of certain other
"races." The layman requires to have his thinking challenged on this subject.
The term "ethnic group" serves as such a challenge to thought and as a stimulus
to rethink the foundations of one's beliefs. The term "race" takes for granted
what should be a matter for inquiry. And this is precisely the point that is
raised when one uses the noncommittal "ethnic group." It encourages the passage from ignorant or confused certainty to thoughtful uncertainty. For the
layman, as for others, the term "race" closes the door on understanding. The
phrase "ethnic group" opens it, or at the very least, leaves it ajar.

In opposition to these views a number of objections have been expressed.
Here are some of them. One does not change anything by changing names. It is
an artful dodge. Why not meet the problem head-on? If the term has been
badly defined in the past, why not redefine it? Re-education should be attempted by establishing the true meaning of "race," not by denying its existence. It suggests a certain blindness to the facts to deny that "races" exist in
man. One cannot combat racism by enclosing the word in quotes. It is not the
word that requires changing but people's ideas about it. It is a common failing
to argue from the abuse of an idea to its total exclusion. It is quite as possible to
feel "ethnic group prejudice" as it is to feel "race prejudice." One is not going
to solve the race problem this way.

Such objections indicate that there has been a failure of communication,
that the main point has been missed. The term "ethnic group" is not offered as
a substitute for "race." On the contrary, the term "ethnic group" implies a
fundamental difference in viewpoint from that which is implied in the term
"race." It is not a question of changing names or of substitution, or an artful
dodge, or the abandonment of a good term which has been abused. It is first
and foremost an attempt to clarify the fact that the old term is unsound when
applied to man, and should therefore not be used with reference to him. At the
same time "ethnic group," being an intentionally vague and general term, is
designed to make it clear that there is a problem to be solved, rather than to
maintain the fiction that the problem has been solved. As a general term it
leaves all question of definition open, referring specifically to human breeding

populations, the members of which are believed to exhibit certain physical or genetic likenesses. For all general purposes, an "ethnic group" may be defined as one of a number of breeding populations, which populations together comprise the species *Homo sapiens*, and which individually maintain their differences, physical or genetic and cultural, by means of isolating mechanisms such as geographic and social barriers.

The re-education of the layman should be taken seriously. For this reason I would suggest that those who advocate the redefinition of the term "race," rather than its replacement by a general term which more properly asks questions before it attempts definitions, would do well to acquaint themselves with the nature of the laymen as well as with the meaning of the phenomena to which they would apply a term which cannot possibly be redefined. If one desires to remove a prevailing erroneous conception and introduce a more correct one, one is more likely to be successful by introducing the new conception with a distinctively new term rather than by attempting redefinition of a term embarrassed by longstanding unsound usage. Professor Henry Sigerist has well said that "it is never sound to continue the use of terminology with which the minds of millions of people have been poisoned even when the old terms are given new meanings" (1951:101).

There is, apparently, a failure on the part of some students to understand that one of the greatest obstacles to the process of re-education would be the retention of the old term "race," a term which enshrines the errors it is designed to remove. The deep implicit meanings this term possesses for the majority of its users are such that they require immediate challenge whenever and by whomsoever the term "race" is used.

Whenever the term "race" is used, most people believe that something like an eternal verity has been uttered when, in fact, nothing more than evidence has been given that there are many echoes, but few voices. "Race" is a word so familiar that in using it the uncritical thinker is likely to take his own private meaning for it completely for granted, never thinking at any time to question so basic an instrument of the language as the word "race." On the other hand, when one uses the term "ethnic group," the question is immediately raised, "What does it mean? What does the user have in mind?" And this at once affords an opportunity to discuss the facts and explore the meaning and the falsities enshrined in the word "race," and to explain the problems involved and the facts of the genetic situation as we know them.

The term "ethnic group" is concerned with questions; the term "race" is concerned with answers, unsound answers, where for the most part there are only problems that require to be solved before any sound answers can be given.

It may be difficult for those who believe in what I. A. Richards has called "The Divine Right of Words" to accept the suggestion that a word such as "race," which has exercised so evil a tyranny over the minds of men, should be permanently dethroned from the vocabulary, but that constitutes all the more reason for trying, remembering that the meaning of a word is the action it produces.

NOTES

[1] Presented at the University Seminar on Genetics and the Evolution of Man, Columbia University, December 6, 1959.

[2] The term "genogroup" was suggested to me by Sir Julian Huxley during a conversation on September 29, 1959.

REFERENCES CITED

ABERCROMBIE, M., C. J. HICKMAN, and M. L. JOHNSON
    1951    A dictionary of biology. Harmondsworth, Penguin Books.
BERNARD, L. L.
    1924    Instinct. New York, Henry Holt and Co.
CALMAN, W. T.
    1949    The classification of animals. New York, John Wiley and Sons.
CARTER, G. S.
    1951    Animal evolution. New York, Macmillan Co.
DAHLBERG, G.
    1942    Race, reason and rubbish. New York, Columbia University Press.
DENIKER, J.
    1900    The races of man. London, The Walter Scott Publishing Co. Ltd.
DUNN, L. C. and TH. DOBZHANSKY
    1952    Heredity, race and society. Rev. ed. New York, The New American Library of World Literature.
GARLICK, J. P.
    1961    *Review of* Human races and Readings on race, by S. M. Garn. Annals of Human Genetics, 25:169–70.
GARN, S. M., and C. S. COON
    1955    On the number of races of mankind. American Anthropologist 57:996–1001.
HANHART, E.
    1953    Infectious diseases. *In* Clinical genetics, Arnold Sorsby, ed. St. Louis, Mosby.
HOUSMAN, A. E.
    1933    The name and nature of poetry. New York, Cambridge University Press.
HUXLEY, J. S. and A. C. HADDON
    1936    We Europeans: a survey of "racial" problems. New York, Harper and Bros.
HUXLEY, T. H.
    1865    On the methods and results of ethnology. Fortnightly Review. *Reprinted in* Man's place in nature and other anthropological essays. London, Macmillan Co., 1894.
KALMUS, H.
    1948    Genetics. Harmondsworth, Pelican Books.
    1958    Heredity and variation. London, Routledge and K. Paul.
MONTAGU, M. F. ASHLEY
    1951    Statement on race. Rev. ed. New York, Henry Schuman.
PENROSE, L. S.
    1952    *Review of* Heredity, race, and society, by Dunn and Dobzhansky. Annals of Human Eugenics 17:252.
SIGERIST, H.
    1951    A history of medicine. Vol. 1. New York, Oxford University Press.
SIMPSON, G. G.
    1953    The major features of evolution. New York, Columbia University Press.

# Earth-Diver: Creation of the Mythopoeic Male

ALAN DUNDES

*University of Kansas*

F EW anthropologists are satisfied with the present state of scholarship with respect to primitive mythology. While not everyone shares Lévi-Strauss's extreme pessimistic opinion that from a theoretical point of view the study of myth is "very much the same as it was fifty years ago, namely a picture of chaos" (1958:50), still there is general agreement that much remains to be done in elucidating the processes of the formation, transmission, and functioning of myth in culture.

One possible explanation for the failure of anthropologists to make any notable advances in myth studies is the rigid adherence to two fundamental principles: a literal reading of myth and a study of myth in monocultural context. The insistence of most anthropologists upon the literal as opposed to the symbolic interpretation, in terms of cultural relativism as opposed to transcultural universalism, is in part a continuation of the reaction against 19th century thought in which universal symbolism in myth was often argued and in part a direct result of the influence of two dominant figures in the history of anthropology, Boas and Malinowski. Both these pioneers favored studying one culture at a time in depth and both contended that myth was essentially nonsymbolic. Boas often spoke of mythology reflecting culture, implying something of a one-to-one relationship. With this view, purely descriptive ethnographic data could be easily culled from the mythological material of a particular culture. Malinowski argued along similar lines: "Studied alive, myth, as we shall see, is not symbolic, but a direct expression of its subject matter" (1954:101). Certainly, there is much validity in the notion of mythology as a cultural reflector, as the well documented researches of Boas and Malinowski demonstrate. However, as in the case of most all-or-nothing approaches, it does not account for all the data. Later students in the Boas tradition, for example, noted that a comparison between the usual descriptive ethnography and the ethnographical picture obtained from mythology revealed numerous discrepancies. Ruth Benedict (1935) in her important Introduction to *Zuni Mythology* spoke of the tendency to idealize and compensate in folklore. More recently, Katherine Spencer has contrasted the correspondences and discrepancies between the ethnographical and mythological accounts. She also suggests that the occurrence of folkloristic material which contradicts the ethnographic data "may be better explained in psychological than in historical terms" (1947:130). However, anthropologists have tended to mistrust psychological terms, and consequently the pendulum has not yet begun to swing away from the literal to the symbolic reading of myth.

1032

Yet it is precisely the insights afforded by advances in human psychology which open up vast vistas for the student of myth. When anthropologists learn that to study the products of the human mind (e.g., myths) one must know something of the mechanics of the human mind, they may well push the pendulum towards not only the symbolic interpretation of myth but also towards the discovery of universals in myth.

Freud himself was very excited at the possibility of applying psychology to mythology. In a letter to D. E. Oppenheim in 1909, he said, "I have long been haunted by the idea that our studies on the content of the neuroses might be destined to solve the riddle of the formation of myths . . ." (Freud and Oppenheim 1958:13). However, though Freud was pleased at the work of his disciples, Karl Abraham and Otto Rank, in this area, he realized that he and his students were amateurs in mythology. In the same letter to Oppenheim he commented: "We are lacking in academic training and familiarity with the material." Unfortunately, those not lacking in these respects had little interest in psychoanalytic theory. To give just one example out of many, Lewis Spence in his preface to *An Introduction to Mythology* stated: "The theories of Freud and his followers as to religion and the origin of myth have not been considered, since, in the writer's opinion, they are scarcely to be taken seriously." What was this theory which was not to be taken seriously? Freud wrote the following: "As a matter of fact, I believe that a large portion of the mythological conception of the world which reaches far into the most modern religions, is *nothing but psychology projected to the outer world*. The dim perception (the endopsychic perception, as it were) of psychic factors and relations of the unconscious was taken as a model in the construction of a *transcendental reality*, which is destined to be changed again by science into *psychology of the unconscious*" (1938:164). It is this insight perhaps more than any other that is of value to the anthropologist interested in primitive myth.

There is, however, an important theoretical difficulty with respect to the psychoanalytic interpretation of myth. This difficulty stems from the fact that there are basically two ways in which psychoanalytic theory may be applied. A myth may be analyzed *with* a knowledge of a particular myth-maker, or a myth may be analyzed *without* such knowledge. There is some doubt as to whether the two methods are equally valid and, more specifically, whether the second is as valid as the first. The question is, to employ an analogy, can a dream be analyzed without a knowledge of the specific dreamer who dreamed it? In an anthropological context, the question is: can a myth be interpreted without a knowledge of the culture which produced it? Of course, it is obvious that any psychoanalyst would prefer to analyze the dreamer or myth-maker in order to interpret more accurately a dream or myth. Similarly, those anthropologists who are inclined to employ psychoanalysis in interpreting myths prefer to relate the manifest and latent content of myths to specific cultural contexts. However, this raises another important question. Do myths reflect the present, the past, or both? There are some anthropologists who conceive of myths almost exclusively in terms of the present. While tacitly recognizing that traditional myths are of considerable antiquity, such anthropologists, nevertheless, proceed to analyze a present-day culture in terms of its myths. Kardiner's theory of folklore, for instance, reveals this bias. Speaking of the myths of women in Marquesan folklore, Kardiner observes, "These myths are the products of the fantasy of some individual, communicated and probably changed many times before we get them. The uniformity of the stories points to some common experience of all individuals in this culture, not remembered from the remote past, but currently experienced." According to Kardiner, then, myths are responses to current realities (1939:417, 214). Roheim summarizes Kardiner's position before taking issue with it. "According to Kardiner, myths and folklore always reflect the unconscious conflicts of the present generation as they are formed by the pressure brought to bear on them by existing social conditions. In sharp contrast to Freud, Reik, and myself, a myth represents not the dim past but the present" (1940:540).

The evidence available from folklore scholarship suggests that there is remarkable stability in oral narratives. Myths and tales re-collected from the same culture show considerable similarity in structural pattern and detail despite the fact that the myths and tales are from different informants who are perhaps separated by many generations. Excluding consideration of modern myths (for the myth-making process is an ongoing one), one can see that cosmogonic myths, to take one example, have not changed materially for hundreds of years. In view of this, it is clearly not necessarily valid to analyze a *present-day* culture in terms of that culture's traditional cosmogonic myths, which in all likelihood date from the prehistoric *past*. An example of the disregard of the time element occurs in an interesting HRAF-inspired cross-cultural attempt to relate child-training practices to folk tale content. Although the tales were gathered at various times between 1890 and 1940, it was assumed that "a folk tale represents a kind of summation of the common thought patterns of a number of individuals. . . " (McClelland and Friedman 1952:245). Apparently common thought patterns are supposed to be quite stable and not subject to cultural change during a 50 year period. Thus just one version of a widely diffused North American Indian tale type like the Eye Juggler is deemed sufficient to "diagnose the modal motivations" of the members of a culture. Nevertheless, Kardiner's theoretical perspective is not entirely without merit. Changes in myth do occur and a careful examination of a number of variants of a particular myth may show that these changes tend to cluster around certain points in time or space. Even if such changes are comparatively minor in contrast to the over-all structural stability of a myth, they may well serve as meaningful signals of definite cultural changes. Thus, Martha Wolfenstein's comparison of English and American versions of Jack and the Beanstalk (1955) showed a number of interesting differences in detail, although the basic plot remained the same. She suggested that the more phallic details in the American versions were in accord with other cultural differences between England and America. Whether or not one agrees with Wolfenstein's conclusions, one can appreciate the soundness of her method. The same myth or folk tale can be profitably compared using versions from two or more separate cultures, and the differences in detail may well illustrate significant differences in culture. One thinks of Nadel's (1937) adaptation of Bartlett's experiment in giving an artificial folk tale to two neighboring tribes in Africa and his discovery that the variations fell along clear-cut cultural lines, rather than along individualistic lines. However, the basic theoretical problem remains unresolved. Can the myth as a whole be analyzed meaningfully? Margaret Mead in commenting briefly on Wolfenstein's study begs the entire question. She states: "What is important here is that Jack and the Beanstalk, when it was first made up, might have had a precise and beautiful correspondence to the theme of a given culture at a given time. It then traveled and took on all sorts of forms, which you study and correlate with the contemporary cultural usage" (Tax 1953:282). The unfortunate truth is that rarely is the anthropologist in a position to know when and where a myth is "first made up." Consequently, the precise and beautiful correspondence is virtually unattainable or rather unreconstructible. The situation is further complicated by the fact that many, indeed, the majority of myths are found widely distributed throughout the world. The historical record, alas, only goes back so far. In other words, it is, practically speaking, impossible to ascertain the place and date of the first appearance(s) of a given myth. For this reason, anthropologists like Mead despair of finding any correspondence between over-all myth structure and culture. Unfortunately, some naive scholars manifest a profound ignorance of the nature of folklore by their insistent attempts to analyze a specific culture by analyzing myths which are found in a great many cultures. For example, the subject of a recent doctoral dissertation was an analysis of 19th century German culture on the basis of an analysis of the content of various Grimm tales (Mann 1958). Although the analyses of the tales were ingenious and psychologically sound, the fact that the Grimm tales are by no means limited to the confines of Germany, and furthermore are undoubtedly much older than the 19th century, completely vitiates the theoretical premise underlying the thesis. Assuming the validity of the analyses of the tales, these analyses would presumably be equally valid wherever the tales appeared in the same form. Barnouw (1955) commits exactly the same error when he analyzes Chippewa personality on the basis of a Chippewa "origin legend" which, in fact, contains many standard North American Indian tale types (Wycoco). It is clearly a fallacy to analyze an international tale or widely diffused myth *as if* it belonged to only one culture. Only if a myth is known to be unique, that is, peculiar to a given culture, is this kind of analysis warranted. It is, however, perfectly good procedure to analyze the differences which occur as a myth enters another culture. Certainly, one can gain considerable insight into the mechanics of acculturation by studying a Zuni version of a European cumulative tale or a native's retelling of the story of Beowulf. Kardiner is at his best when he shows how a cultural element is adapted to fit the basic personality structure of the borrowing culture. His account of the Comanche's alteration of the Sun Dance from a masochistic and self-destructive ritual to a demonstration of feats of strength is very convincing (1945:93).

The question is now raised: if it is theoretically only permissible to analyze the differentiae of widely diffused myths or the entire structure of myths peculiar to a particular culture, does this mean that the entire structure of widely diffused myths (which are often the most interesting) cannot be meaningfully analyzed? This is, in essence, the question of whether a dream can be analyzed without knowledge of the dreamer. One answer may be that to the extent that there are human universals, such myths may be analyzed. From this vantage point, while it may be a fallacy to analyze a world-wide myth as if it belonged to only one culture, it is not a fallacy to analyze the myth as if it belonged to all cultures in which it appears. This does not preclude the possibility that one myth found in many cultures may have as many meanings as there are cultural contexts (Boas 1910b:383). Nevertheless, the hypothesis of a limited number of organic human universals suggests some sort of similar, if not identical, meaning. It should not be necessary to observe that, to the extent that anthropologists are scientists, they need not fear anathematic reductionism and the discovery of empirically observable universals. The formula $e = mc^2$ is nonetheless valid for its being reductionistic.

A prime example of an anthropologist interested in universals is Kluckhohn. In his paper, "Universal Categories of Culture," Kluckhohn contends that "The inescapable fact of cultural relativism does not justify the conclusion that cultures are in all respects utterly disparate monads and hence strictly noncomparable entities" and "Valid cross-cultural comparison could best proceed from the invariant points of reference supplied by the biological, psychological, and socio-situational 'givens' of human life" (1953:520, 521). Of even more interest is Kluckhohn's conviction that these "givens" are manifested in myth. In "Recurrent Themes in Myths and Mythmaking," he discusses "certain features of mythology that are apparently universal or that have such wide distribution in space and time that their generality may be presumed to result from recurrent reactions of the human psyche to situations and stimuli of the same general order" (1959:268). Kluckhohn's recurrent themes appear somewhat similar to Freud's typical dreams. Although Freud specifically warned against codifying symbolic translations of dream content and, although he did clearly state his belief that the same dream content could conceal a different meaning in the case of different persons or contexts, he did consider that there are such things as typical dreams, "dreams which almost every one has dreamed in the same manner, and of which we are accustomed to assume that they have the same significance in the case of every dreamer" (1938:292, 39). While there are not many anthropologists who would support the view that recurrent myths have similar meaning irrespective of specific cultural context, that does not mean that the view is false. For those who deny universal meanings, it might be mentioned that the reasons why a particular myth has widespread distribution have yet to be given. The most ardent diffusionist, as opposed to an advocate of polygenesis or convergence, can do little more than show how a myth spreads. The how rarely includes the why. In order to show the plausibility of a symbolic and universal approach to myth, a concrete example will be analyzed in some detail.

One of the most fascinating myths in North American Indian mythology is that of the earth-diver. Anna Birgitta Rooth in her study of approximately 300 North American Indian creation myths found that, of her eight different types, earth-diver had the widest distribution. Earl W. Count who has studied the myth for a number of years considers the notion of a diver fetching material for making dry land "easily among the most widespread single concepts held by man" (1952:55). Earth-diver has recently been studied quite extensively by the folklorist Elli Kaija Köngäs (1960) who has skillfully surveyed the mass of previous pertinent scholarship. The myth as summarized by Erminie Wheeler-Voegelin is:

In North American Indian myths of the origin of the world, the culture hero has a succession of animals dive into the primeval waters, or flood of waters, to secure bits of mud or sand from which the earth is to be formed. Various animals, birds, and aquatic creatures are sent down into the waters that cover the earth. One after another animal fails; the last one succeeds, however, and floats to the surface half dead, with a little sand or dirt in his claws. Sometimes it is Muskrat, sometimes Beaver, Hell-diver, Crawfish, Mink who succeeds, after various other animals have failed, in bringing up the tiny bit of mud which is then put on the surface of the water and magically expands to become the world of the present time (1949:334).

Among the interesting features of this myth is the creation from mud or dirt. It is especially curious in view of the widespread myth of the creation of man from a similar substance (Frazer 1935:4–15). Another striking characteristic is the magical expansion of the bit of mud. Moreover, how did the idea of creating the earth from a particle of dirt small enough to be contained beneath a claw or fingernail develop, and what is there in this cosmogonic myth that has caused it to thrive so in a variety of cultures, not only in aboriginal North America but in the rest of the world as well?

Freud's suggestion that mythology is psychology projected upon the external world does not at a first glance seem applicable in the case of the earth-diver myth. The Freudian hypothesis is more obvious in other American Indian cosmogonic conceptions, such as the culture hero's Oedipal separation of Father Sky and Mother Earth (Roheim 1921:163) or the emergence myth, which appears to be man's projection of the phenomenon of human birth. This notion of the origin of the emergence myth was clearly stated as early as 1902 by Washington Matthews with apparently no help from psychoanalysis. At that time Matthews proposed the idea that the emergence myth was basically a "myth of gestation and of birth." A more recent study of the emergence myth by Wheeler-Voegelin and Moore makes a similar suggestion en passant, but no supporting details are given (1957:73–74). Roheim, however, had previously extended Matthews' thesis by suggesting that primitive man's conception of the world originated in the pre-natal perception of space in the womb (1921: 163). In any event, no matter how close the emergence of man from a hole in

Mother Earth might appear to be to actual human birth, it does not appear to help in determining the psychological prototype for the earth-diver myth. Is there really any "endo-psychic" perception which could have served as the model for the construction of a cosmogonic creation from mud?

The hypothesis here proposed depends upon two key assumptions. The two assumptions (and they are admittedly only assumptions) are: (1) the existence of a cloacal theory of birth; and (2) the existence of pregnancy envy on the part of males. With regard to the first assumption, it was Freud himself who included the cloacal theory as one of the common sexual theories of children. The theory, in essence, states that since the child is ignorant of the vagina and is rarely permitted to watch childbirth, he assumes that the lump in the pregnant woman's abdomen leaves her body in the only way he can imagine material leaving the body, namely via the anus. In Freud's words: "Children are all united from the outset in the belief that the birth of a child takes place by the bowel; that is to say, that the baby is produced like a piece of faeces" (1953:328). The second assumption concerns man's envy of woman's childbearing role. Whether it is called "parturition envy" (Boehm) or "pregnancy envy" (Fromm), the basic idea is that men would like to be able to produce or create valuable material from within their bodies as women do. Incidentally, it is this second assumption which is the basis of Bruno Bettelheim's explanation of puberty initiation rites and the custom of couvade. His thesis is that puberty rites consist of a rebirth ritual of a special kind to the effect that the initiate is born anew *from males*. The denial of women's part in giving birth is evidenced by the banning of women from the ceremonies. Couvade is similarly explained as the male's desire to imitate female behavior in childbirth. A number of psychoanalysts have suggested that man's desire for mental and artistic creativity stems in part from the wish to conceive or produce on a par with women (Jones 1957:40; Fromm 1951:233; Huckel 1953:44). What is even more significant from the point of view of mythology is the large number of clinical cases in which men seek to have babies in the form of feces, or cases in which men imagine themselves excreting the world. Felix Boehm makes a rather sweeping generalization when he says: "In all analyses of men we meet with phantasies of anal birth, and we know how common it is for men to treat their faeces as a child" (1930:455; see also Silberer 1925:393). However, there is a good deal of clinical evidence supporting the existence of this phantasy. Stekel (1959:45), for example, mentions a child who called the feces "Baby." The possible relevance of this notion to the myth of the origin of man occurred to Abraham (1948:320), Jung (1916:214), and Rank (1922:54). Jung's comment is: "The first people were made from excrement, potter's earth and clay." (Cf. Schwarzbaum 1960:48). In fact, Jung rather ingeniously suggests that the idea of anal birth is the basis of the motif of creating by "throwing behind oneself" as in the case of Deucalion and Pyrrha. Nevertheless, neither Abraham, Jung, nor Rank emphasized the fact that anal birth is especially employed by men. It is true that little girls also have this phantasy, but presumably the need for the phantasy disappears upon the giving of birth to a child. (There may well be some connection between this phantasy and the widespread occurrence of geophagy among pregnant women [Elwin 1949:292, n. 1].)

Both of the assumptions underlying the hypothesis attempting to explain the earth-diver myth are found in Genesis. As Fromm points out (1951:234), the woman's creative role is denied. It is man who creates and, in fact, it is man who gives birth to woman. Eve is created from substance taken from the body of Adam. Moreover, if one were inclined to see the Noah story as a gestation myth, it would be noteworthy that it is the man who builds the womb-ark. It would also be interesting that the flood waters abate only after a period roughly corresponding to the length of human pregnancy. Incidentally, it is quite likely that the Noah story is a modified earth-diver myth. The male figure sends a raven once and a dove twice to brave the primordial waters seeking traces of earth. (Cf. Schwarzbaum 1960:52, n. 15a.) In one apocryphal account, the raven disobeys instructions by stopping to feast on a dead man, and in another he is punished by having his feathers change color from white to black (Ginzberg 1925:39, 164). Both of these incidents are found in American Indian earth-diver myths (Rooth 1957:498). In any case, one can see that there are male myths of creation in Genesis, although Fromm does not describe them all. Just as Abraham, Jung, and Rank had anal birth without pregnancy envy, Fromm has pregnancy envy without anal birth. He neglects to mention that man was created from dust. One is tempted to speculate as to whether male creation myths might be in any way correlated with highly patriarchal social organization.

Of especial pertinence to the present thesis is the clinical data on phantasies of excreting the universe. Lombroso, for example, describes two artists, each of whom had the delusion that they were lords of the world which they had excreted from their bodies. One of them painted a full-length picture of himself, naked, among women, ejecting worlds (1895:201). In this phantasy world, the artist flaunting his anal creativity depicts himself as superior to the women who surround him. Both Freud and Stekel have reported cases in which men fancied defecating upon the world, and Abraham cites a dream of a patient in which the patient dreamed he expelled the universe out of his anus (Freud 1949b:407; Stekel 1959:44; Abraham 1948:320). Of course, the important question for the present study is whether or not such phantasies ever occur in mythical form. Undoubtedly, the majority of anthropologists would be somewhat loath to interpret the earth-diver myth as an anal birth fantasy on the basis of a few clinical examples drawn exclusively from Western civilization. However, the dearth of mythological data results partly from the traditional prudery of some ethnographers and many folklorists. Few myths dealing with excretory processes find their way into print. Nevertheless, there are several examples, primarily of the creation of man from excrement. John G. Bourke (1891:266) cites an Australian myth of such a creation of man. In India, the elephant-headed god Ganesh is derived from the excrement of his mother (Berkeley-Hill 1921: 330). In modern India, the indefatigable Elwin has collected quite a few myths in which the earth is excreted. For instance, a Lanjhia Saora version describes how Bhimo defecates on Rama's head. The feces is thrown into the water which immediately dries up and the earth is formed (1949:44). In a Gadaba myth, Larang the great Dano devoured the world, but Mahaprabhu "caught hold of him and squeezed him so hard that he excreted the earth he had devoured. . . . From the earth that Larang excreted, the world was formed again" (1949:37). In other versions, a worm excretes the earth, or the world is formed from the excreta of ants (1949:47; 1954:9). An example closer to continental North America is reported by Bogoras. In this Chukchee creation myth, Raven's wife tells Raven to go and try to create the earth, but Raven protests that he cannot. Raven's wife then announces that she will try to create a "spleen-companion" and goes to sleep. Raven "looks at his wife. Her abdomen has enlarged. In her sleep she creates without effort. He is frightened, and turns his face away." After Raven's wife gives birth to twins, Raven says, "There, you have created men! Now I shall go and try to create the earth." Then "Raven flies and defecates. Every piece of excrement falls upon water, grows quickly, and becomes land." In this fashion, Raven succeeds in creating the whole earth (Bogoras 1913:152). Here there can be no doubt of the connection between pregnancy envy and anal creation. Unfortunately, there are few examples which are as clear as the Chukchee account. One of the only excremental creation myths reported in North America proper was collected by Boas. He relates (1895:159) a Kwakiutl tale of Mink making a youth from his excrement. However, the paucity of American Indian versions does not necessarily reflect the nonexistence of the myth in North America. The combination of puritanical publishing standards in the United States with similar collecting standards may well explain in part the lack of data. In this connection it is noteworthy that whereas the earlier German translation of Boas' Kwakiutl version refers specifically to excrement, the later English translation speaks of a musk-bag (1910a:159). Most probably ethnographers and editors alike share Andrew Lang's sentiments when he alludes to a myth of the Encounter Bay people, "which might have been attributed by Dean Swift to the Yahoos, so foul an origin does it allot to mankind" (1899:166). Despite the lack of a great number of actual excremental myths, the existence of any at all would appear to lend support to the hypothesis that men do think of creativity in anal terms, and further that this conception is projected into mythical cosmogonic terms.

There is, of course, another possible reason for the lack of overtly excremental creation myths and this is the process of sublimation. Ferenczi in his essay, "The Ontogenesis of the Interest in Money" (1956), has given the most explicit account of this process as he traces the weaning of the child's interest from its feces through a whole graduated series of socially sanctioned substitutes ranging from moist mud, sand, clay, and stones to gold or money. Anthropologists will object that Ferenczi's ontogenetic pattern is at best only applicable to Viennese type culture. But, to the extent that any culture has

357

toilet training (and this includes any culture in which the child is not permitted to play indiscriminately with his feces), there is some degree of sublimation. As a matter of fact, so-called anal personality characteristics have been noted among the Yurok (Posinsky), Mohave (Devereux), and Chippewa (Barnouw, Hallowell). Devereux (1951:412) specifically comments upon the use of mud as a fecal substitute among the Mohave. Moreover, it may well be that the widespread practices of smearing the body with paint or daubing it with clay in preparation for aggressive activities have some anal basis. As for the gold-feces equation, anthropologists have yet to explain the curious linguistic fact that in Nahuatl the word for gold is *teocuitlatl*, which is a compound of *teotl*, "god," and *cuitlatl*, "excrement." Gold is thus "excrement of the gods" or "divine excrement" (Saville 1920:118). This extraordinary confirmation of Freudian symbolism which was pointed out by Reik as early as 1915 has had apparently little impact upon anthropologists blindly committed to cultural relativism. (See also Roheim 1923:387. However, for an example of money/feces symbolism in the dream of a Salteaux Indian, see Hallowell 1938.) While the gold-feces symbolism is hardly likely in cultures where gold was unknown, there is reason for assuming that some sort of sublimation does occur in most cultures. (For American Indian instances of "jewels from excrements" see Thompson 1929:329, n. 190a. In this connection, it might be pointed out that in Oceanic versions of the creation of earth from an object thrown on the primeval waters, as found in Lessa's recent comprehensive study [1961], the items thrown include, in addition to sand, such materials as rice chaff, betel nut husks, and ashes, which would appear to be waste products.) If this is so, then it may be seen that a portion of Ferenczi's account of the evolutionary course of anal sublimation is of no mean importance to the analysis of the earth-diver myth. Ferenczi states: "Even the interest for the specific odour of excrement does not cease at once, but is only displaced on to other odours that in any way resemble this. The children continue to show a liking for the smell of sticky materials with a characteristic odour, especially the strongly smelling degenerated produce of cast off epidermis cells which collects between the toes, nasal secretion, ear-wax, and the dirt of the nails, while many children do not content themselves with the moulding and sniffing of these substances, but also take them into the mouth" (1956:273). Anyone who is familiar with American Indian creation myths will immediately think of examples of the creation of man from the rubbings of skin (Thompson 1955:Motif A 1263.3), birth from mucus from the nose (Motif T 541.8.3), etc. The empirical fact is that these myths do exist! With respect to the earth-diver myth, the common detail of the successful diver's returning with a little dirt under his fingernail is entirely in accord with Ferenczi's analysis. The fecal nature of the particle is also suggested by its magical expansion. One could imagine that as one defecates one is thereby creating an ever-increasing amount of earth. (Incidentally, the notion of creating land masses through defecation has the corollary idea of creating bodies of water such as oceans through micturition [Motif A 923.1].

For example, in the previously mentioned Chukchee myth, Raven, after producing the earth, began to pass water. A drop became a lake, while a jet formed a river.)

The present hypothesis may also serve to elucidate the reasons why Christian dualism is so frequently found in Eurasian earth-diver versions. Earl Count considers the question of the dualistic nature of earth-diver as one of the main problems connected with the study of the myth (1952:56). Count is not willing to commit himself as to whether the earth-diver is older than a possible dualistic overlay, but Köngas agrees with earlier scholars that the dualism is a later development (Count 1952:61; Köngas 1960:168). The dualism usually takes the form of a contest between God and the devil. As might be expected from the tradition of philosophical dualism, the devil is associated with the body, while God is concerned with the spiritual element. Thus it is the devil who dives for the literally lowly dirt and returns with some under his nails. An interesting incident in view of Ferenczi's account of anal sublimation is the devil's attempt to save a bit of earth by putting it in his mouth. However, when God expands the earth, the stolen bit also expands, forcing the devil to spit it out, whereupon mountains or rocks are formed (Köngas 1960:160–61). In this connection, another dualistic creation myth is quite informative. God is unable to stop the earth from growing and sends the bee to spy on the devil to find a way to accomplish this. When the bee buzzes, in leaving the devil to report back to God, the devil exclaims, "Let him eat your excrement, whoever sent you!" God did this and the earth stopped growing (Dragomanov 1961:3). Since the eating of excrement prevented the further growth of the earth, one can see the fecal nature of the substance forming the earth. In still another dualistic creation myth, there is even an attempt made to explain why feces exists at all in man. In this narrative, God creates a pure body for man but has to leave it briefly in order to obtain a soul. In God's absence, the devil defiles the body. God, upon returning, has no alternative but to turn his creation inside out, which is the reason why man has impurities in his intestines (Campbell 1956:294). These few examples should be sufficient to show that the dualism is primarily a matter of separating the dross of matter from the essence of spirit. The devil is clearly identified with matter and in particular with defecation. In a phrase, it is the devil who does the dirty work. Thus Köngas is quite right in seeing a psycho-physical dualism, that is, the concept of the soul as being separable from the body, as the basis for the Christian traditional dualism. However, she errs in assuming that both the creator and his "doppelgänger" are spiritual or concerned with the spiritual (1960:169). Dualism includes one material entity and, specifically in earth-diver dualism, one element deals with dirt while the other creates beauty and valuable substance from the dirt.

It should be noted that earth-diver has been previously studied from a psychoanalytic perspective. Géza Róheim, the first psychoanalytic anthropologist, made a great number of studies of the folklore and mythology of primitive peoples. In his earlier writings, Róheim tended to follow along the lines suggested by Freud, Abraham, and Rank in seeing folk tales as analogous to dreams (1922:182), but later, after he discovered, for example, that the Aranda word *altjira* meant both dream and folk tale (1941:267), he began to speculate as to a more genetic relationship between dream and folk tale or myth. In a posthumously published paper, "Fairy Tale and Dream" (1953a), this new theory of mythology and the folk tale is explained. "To put this theory briefly: It seems that dreams and myths are not merely similar but that a large part of mythology is actually derived from dreams. In other words, we can not only apply the standard technique of dream interpretation in analyzing a fairy tale but can actually think of tales and myths as having arisen from a dream, which a person dreamed and then told to others, who retold it again, perhaps elaborated in accord with their own dreams" (1953a:394; for a sample of Róheim's exegesis of what he terms a dream-derived folk tale, see 1953b). The obvious criticism of this theory has been made by E. K. Schwartz in noting that "one can accept the same psychoanalytic approach and techniques for the understanding of the fairy tale and the dream, without having to accept the hypothesis that the fairy tale is nothing else but an elaboration of a dream" (1956: 747–48). Thus Schwartz, although he lists 12 characteristics of fairy tales which he also finds in dreams, including such features as condensation, displacement, symbolism, etc., does conclude that it is not necessary to assume that fairy tales are dreams. Róheim, in *The Gates of the Dream,* a brilliant if somewhat erratic full-length treatment of primitive myth and dream, had already addressed himself to this very criticism. He phrases the criticism rhetorically: "Then why assume the dream stage, since the unconscious would contain the same elements, even without dreams?" His answer is that the dream theory would explain not only the identity in content but also the striking similarity in structure and plot sequence (1951:348). Actually, the fundamental criticism is not completely explained away. There is no reason why both dream and myth cannot be derived from the human mind without making the myth only indirectly derived via the dream.

Róheim's theory comes to the fore in his analysis of earth-diver. In fact, he even states that the earth-diver myth is "a striking illustration of the dream origin of mythology" (1951:423). Róheim has assumed the existence of what he calls a basic dream in which the dreamer falls into something, such as a lake or a hole. According to Róheim, this dream is characterized by a "double vector" movement consisting both of a regression to the womb and the idea of the body as penis entering the vagina. In interpreting the earth-diver as an example of this basic dream, Róheim considers the diving into the primeval waters of the womb as an erection. Of considerable theoretical interest is Róheim's apparent postulation of a monogenetic origin of earth-diver: "*The core of the myth is a dream actually dreamed once upon a time by one person. Told and retold it became a myth . . .* " (1951:428). Actually, Róheim's over-all theory of the dream origin of myth is not at all necessarily a matter of monogenesis. In fact, he states that it is hardly likely as a general rule that an original dream was dreamed by one person in a definite locality, from which the story spread by migration. Rather, "many have dreamed such dreams, they shaped the narrative form in many centers, became traditional, then merged and influenced each other in the course of history" (1951:348).

The validity of Róheim's interpretation of earth-diver depends a great deal on, first of all, his theory of the dream origin of myth and, secondly, the specific nature of his so-called basic dream. One could say, without going so far as to deny categorically Róheim's theoretical contentions, that neither the dream origin of myth nor the existence of the "basic dream" is necessary for an understanding of the latent content of the earth-diver myth. Curiously enough, Róheim himself anticipates in part the present hypothesis in the course of making some additional comments on earth-diver. In discussing the characteristic trait of the gradual growth of the earth, Róheim cites an Onondaga version in which he points out the parallelism between a pregnant woman and the growing earth. From the point of view of the present hypothesis, the parallelism is quite logically attributable to the male creator's desire to achieve something like female procreativity. Thus the substance produced from his body, his baby so to speak, must gradually increase in size, just as the process of female creativity entails a gradually increasing expansion. (Here again, the observation of the apparently magically expanding belly of a pregnant woman is clearly a human universal.) Róheim goes on to mention what he considers to be a parallel myth, namely that of "the egg-born earth or cloacal creation." As will be shown later, Róheim is quite correct in drawing attention to the egg myth. Then following his discussion of the Eurasian dualistic version in which the devil tries to keep a piece of swelling earth in his mouth, Róheim makes the following analysis: "If we substitute the rectum for the mouth the myth makes sense as an awakening dream conditioned by excremental pressure" (1951: 429). In other words, Róheim does recognize the excremental aspects of earth-diver and in accordance with his theory of the dream origin of myth, he considers the myth as initially a dream caused by the purely organic stimulus of the need to defecate. Róheim also follows Rank (1912, 1922:89) in interpreting deluge myths as transformations of vesical dreams (1951:439–65). Certainly, one could make a good case for the idea that some folk tales and myths are based upon excremental pressures, perhaps originally occurring during sleep. In European folklore, there are numerous examples, as Freud and Oppenheim have amply demonstrated, of folk tales which relate how individuals attempt to mark buried treasure only to awake to find they have defecated on themselves or on their sleeping partners. It is quite possible that there is a similar basis for the Winnebago story reported by Radin (1956:26–27) in which Trickster, after eating a laxative bulb, begins to defecate endlessly. In order to escape the rising level of excrement, Trickster climbs a tree, but he is forced to go higher and higher until he finally falls down right into the rising tide. Another version of this Trickster adventure is found in Barnouw's account of a Chippewa cycle (1955:82). The idea of the movement being impossible to stop once it has started is also suggested in the previously cited Eurasian account of God's inability to stop the earth's growth. That God must eat excrement to stop the movement is thematically similar to another Trickster version in which Trickster's own excrement, rising with flood waters, comes perilously close to his mouth and nose. However, the fact that there may be "excremental pressure myths" with or without a dream origin does not mean that excremental pressure is the sole underlying motivation of such a myth as earth-diver. To call earth-diver simply a dream-like myth resulting from a call of nature without reference to the notions of male pregnancy envy and anal birth theory is vastly to oversimplify the psychological etiology of the myth. Róheim, by the way, never does reconcile the rather phallic interpretation of his basic dream with the excremental awakening dream interpretation of earth-diver. A multi-causal hypothesis is, of course, perfectly possible, but Róheim's two interpretations seem rather to conflict. In any event, Róheim sees creation myths as prime examples of his dream-myth thesis. He says, "It seems very probable that creation myths, wherever they exist, are ultimately based on dreams" (1951:430).

The idea of anal creation myths spurred by male pregnancy envy is not tied to the dream origin of myth theory. That is not to say that the dream theory is not entirely possible but only to affirm the independence of the two hypotheses. In order to document further the psychological explanation of earth-diver, several other creation myths will be very briefly discussed. As already mentioned, Róheim drew attention to the cosmic egg myths. There is clinical evidence suggesting that men who have pregnancy phantasies often evince a special interest in the activities of hens, particularly with regard to their laying of eggs (Eisler 1921:260, 285). The hens appear to defecate the eggs. Freud's famous "Little Hans" in addition to formulating a "lumf" baby theory also imagined that he laid an egg (1949b:227–28). Lombroso (1895:182) mentions a demented pseudo-artist who painted himself as excreting eggs which symbolized worlds. Ferenczi, moreover, specifically comments upon what he calls the "symbolic identity of the egg with faeces and child." He suggests that excessive fondness for eggs "approximates much more closely to primitive coprophilia than does the more abstract love of money" (1950:328). Certainly the egg-creation myth is common enough throughout the world (Lukas 1894), despite its absence in North America. It is noteworthy that there are creations of men from eggs (Motifs T 542 or A 1222) and creation of the world from a cosmic egg (Motif A 641). As in the case of feces (or mud, clay, or dirt), the cloacal creation is capable of producing either men or worlds or both.

Another anal creation myth which does occur in aboriginal North America has the spider as creator. The Spider myth, which is one of Rooth's eight creation myth types found in North America, is reported primarily in California and the Southwest. The spider as creator is also found in Asia and Africa. Empirical observation of spiders would quite easily give rise to the notion of the spider as a self-sufficient creator who appeared to excrete his own world, and a beautiful and artistic world at that. Although psychoanalysts have generally tended to interpret the spider as a mother symbol (Abraham 1948: 326–32; cf. Spider Woman in the Southwest), Freud noted at least one instance in folklore where the thread spun by a spider was a symbol for evacuated feces. In a Prussian-Silesian tale, a peasant wishing to return to earth from heaven is turned into a spider by Peter. As a spider, the peasant spins a long thread by which he descends, but he is horrified to discover as he arrives just over his home that he could spin no more. He squeezes and squeezes to make the thread longer and then suddenly wakes up from his dream to discover that "something very human had happened to him while he slept" (Freud and Oppenheim 1958:45). The spider as the perfect symbol of male artistic creativity is described in a poem by Whitman entitled "The Spider." In the poem, the spider is compared to the soul of the poet as it stands detached and alone in "measureless oceans of space" launching forth filament out of itself (Wilbur and Muensterberger 1951:405). Without going into primitive Spider creation myths in great detail, it should suffice to note that, as in other types of male myths of creation, the creator is able to create without any reference to women. Whether a male creator spins material, molds clay, lays an egg, fabricates from mucus or epidermal tissue, or dives for fecal mud, the psychological motivation is much the same.

Other cosmogonic depictions of anal birth have been barely touched upon. As Ernest Jones has shown in some detail (1951:266–357), some of the other aspects of defecation such as the sound (creation by thunder or the spoken word), or the passage of air (creation by wind or breath), are also of considerable importance in the study of mythology. With respect to the latter characteristic, there is the obvious Vedic example of Pragapati who created mankind by means of "downward breathings" from the "back part" cited by Jones (1951:279). One account of Pragapati's creation of the earth relates the passing of air with the earth-diver story. "Prajapati first becomes a wind and stirs up the primeval ocean; he sees the earth in the depths of the ocean; he turns himself into a boar and draws the earth up" (Dragomanov 1961:28). Another ancient male anal wind myth is found in the Babylonian account of Marduk. Marduk conquers Tiamat by the following means: "The evil wind which followed him, he loosed it in her face. . . . He drove in the evil wind so that she could not close her lips. The terrible winds filled her belly" (Guirand 1959:51). Marduk then pierces Tiamat's belly and kills her. The passage of wind by the male Marduk leads to the destruction of the female Tiamat. Marduk rips open the rival creator, the belly of woman, which had given birth to the world. There is also the Biblical instance of the divine (af)flatus moving on the face of the waters. Köngas (1960:169) made a very astute intuitive observation when she suggested that there was a basic similarity between the spirit of God moving upon the primeval water and the earth-diver myth. The common denominator is the male myth of creation whereby the male creator uses various aspects of the only means available, namely the creative power of the anus.

Undoubtedly anthropologists will be sceptical of any presentation in which evidence is marshalled á la Frazer and where the only criteria for the evidence appears to be the gristworthyness for the mill. Nevertheless, what is important is the possibility of a theory of universal symbolism which can be verified by empirical observation in the field in decades to come. Kluckhohn, despite a deep-seated mistrust of pan-human symbolism, confesses that his own field work as well as that of his collaborators has forced him to the conclusion that "Freud and other psychoanalysts have depicted with astonishing correctness many central themes in motivational life which are universal. The styles of expression of these themes and much of the manifest content are culturally determined but the underlying psychological drama transcends cultural difference" (Wilbur and Muensterberger 1951:120). Kluckhohn bases his assumptions on the notion of a limited number of human "givens," such as human anatomy and physiology. While it is true that thoughts about the "givens" are not "given" in the same sense, it may be that their arising is inevitable. In other words, man is not born with the idea of pregnancy envy. It is acquired through experience, that is, through the mediation of culture. But if certain experiences are universal, such as the observation of female pregnancy, then there may be said to be secondary or derived "givens," using the term in an admittedly idiosyncratic sense. This is very important for the study of myth. It has already been pointed out that from a cultural relativistic perspective, the only portion of mythology which can be profitably studied is limited to those myths which are peculiar to a particular culture or those differences in the details of a widely diffused myth. Similarly, the literal approach can glean only so much ethnographic data from reflector myths. Without the assumption of symbolism and universals in myth, a vast amount of mythology remains of little use to the anthropologist. It should also be noted that there is, in theory, no conflict between accepting the idea of universals and advocating cultural relativism. It is not an "either/or" proposition. Some myths may be universal and others not. It is the all-or-nothing approach which appears to be erroneous. The same is true for the polygenesis-diffusion controversy; they also are by no means mutually exclusive. In the same way, there is no inconsistency in the statement that myths can either reflect or refract culture. (The phrase was suggested by A. K. Ramanujan.) Lévi-Strauss (1958:51) criticizes psychoanalytic interpretations of myth because, as he puts it, if there's an evil grandmother in the myths, "it will be claimed that in such a society grandmothers are actually evil and that mythology reflects the social structure and the social relations; but should the actual data be conflicting, it would be readily claimed that the purpose of mythology is to provide an outlet for repressed feelings. Whatever the situation may be, a clever dialectic will always find a way to pretend that a meaning has been unravelled." Although Lévi-Strauss may be justified insofar as he is attacking the "Have you stopped beating your wife?" antics of some psychoanalysts, there is not necessarily any inconsistency stemming from data showing that in culture A evil grandmothers in fact are also found in myth, while in culture B conscious norms of pleasant grandmothers disguise unconscious hatred for "evil" grandmothers, a situation which may be expressed in myth. In other words, myths can and usually do contain both conscious and unconscious cultural materials. To the extent that conscious and unconscious motivation may vary or be contradictory, so likewise can myth differ from or contradict ethnographic data. There is no safe

monolithic theory of myth except that of judicious eclecticism as championed
by E. B. Tylor. Mythology must be studied in cultural context in order to
determine which individual mythological elements reflect and which refract
the culture. But, more than this, the cultural relative approach must not
preclude the recognition and identification of transcultural similarities and
potential universals. As Kluckhohn said, " . . . the anthropologist for two
generations has been obsessed with the differences between peoples, neglecting
the equally real similarities—upon which the 'universal culture pattern' as well
as the psychological uniformities are clearly built (Wilbur and Muensterberger
1951:121)." The theoretical implications for practical field work of seeking
psychological uniformities are implicit. Ethnographers must remove the
traditional blinders and must be willing to collect *all* pertinent material even
if it borders on what is obscene by the ethnographer's ethnocentric standards.
The ideal ethnographer must not be afraid of diving deep and coming up with
a little dirt; for, as the myth relates, such a particle may prove immensely
valuable and may expand so as to form an entirely new world for the students
of man.

REFERENCES CITED

ABRAHAM, KARL
    1948   Selected papers on psycho-analysis. The International Psycho-Analytical Library
         No. 13. London, Hogarth.
BARNOUW, VICTOR
    1955   A psychological interpretation of a Chippewa origin legend. Journal of American
         Folklore 68:73–85, 211–23, 341–55.
BENEDICT, RUTH
    1935   Zuni mythology. Columbia University Contributions to Anthropology 21.
BETTELHEIM, BRUNO
    1955   Symbolic wounds. London, Thames and Hudson.
BERKELEY-HILL, OWEN
    1921   The anal-erotic factor in the religion, philosophy and character of the Hindus.
         International Journal of Psycho-Analysis 2:306–38.
BOAS, FRANZ
    1895   Indianische sagen von der nord-pacifischen küste Amerikas. Berlin.
    1910a Kwakiutl tales. Columbia University Contributions to Anthropology 2.
    1910b Psychological problems in anthropology. American Journal of Psychology 21:371–
         84.
BOEHM, FELIX
    1930   The femininity-complex in men. International Journal of Psycho-Analysis 11:444–69.
BOGORAS, WALDEMAR
    1913   Chuckchee mythology. Jesup North Pacific Expedition Publications 8.
BOURKE, JOHN G.
    1891   Scatalogic rites of all nations. Washington, W. H. Lowdermilk & Co.
CAMPBELL, JOSEPH
    1956   The hero with a thousand faces. New York, Meridian.
COUNT, EARL W.
    1952   The earth-diver and the rival twins: a clue to time correlation in North-Eurasiatic
         and North American mythology. *In* Indian tribes of aboriginal America, Sol Tax,
         ed. Selected Papers of the 19th International Congress of Americanists. Chicago,
         University of Chicago Press.

DEVEREUX, GEORGE
    1951   Cultural and characterological traits of the Mohave related to the anal stage of psychosexual development. Psychoanalytic Quarterly 20:398–422.
DRAGOMANOV, MIXAILO PETROVIC
    1961   Notes on the Slavic religio-ethical legends: the dualistic creation of the world. Russian and East European Series Vol. 23. Bloomington, Indiana University Publications.
EISLER, MICHAEL JOSEPH
    1921   A man's unconscious phantasy of pregnancy in the guise of traumatic hysteria: a clinical contribution to anal erotism. International Journal of Psycho-Analysis 2:255–86.
ELWIN, VERRIER
    1949   Myths of middle India. Madras, Oxford University Press.
    1954   Tribal myths of Orissa. Bombay, Oxford University Press.
FERENCZI, SANDOR
    1950   Further contributions to the theory and technique of psycho-analysis. International Psycho-Analytical Library No. 11. London, Hogarth.
    1956   Sex in psycho-analysis. New York, Dover.
FRAZER, JAMES GEORGE
    1935   Creation and evolution in primitive cosmogonies. London, Macmillan.
FREUD, SIGMUND
    1938   The basic writings of Sigmund Freud. New York, Modern Library.
    1949a  Collected papers II. London, Hogarth.
    1949b  Collected papers III. London, Hogarth.
    1953   A general introduction to psycho-analysis. New York, Permabooks.
FREUD, SIGMUND and D. E. OPPENHEIM
    1958   Dreams in folklore. New York, International Universities Press.
FROMM, ERICH
    1951   The forgotten language. New York, Grove Press.
GINZBERG, LOUIS
    1925   The legends of the Jews. Vol. I. Philadelphia, Jewish Publication Society of America.
GUIRAND, FELIX
    1959   Assyro-Babylonian mythology. *In* Larousse Encyclopedia of Mythology. New York, Prometheus Press.
HALLOWELL, A. IRVING
    1938   Freudian symbolism in the dream of a Salteaux Indian. Man 38:47–48.
    1947   Myth, culture and personality. American Anthropologist 49:544–56.
HUCKEL, HELEN
    1953   Vicarious creativity. Psychoanalysis 2:(2):44–50.
JONES, ERNEST
    1951   Essays in applied psycho-analysis, II. International Psycho-Analytical Library No. 41. London, Hogarth.
    1957   How to tell your friends from geniuses. Saturday Review 40 (August 10):9–10, 39–40.
JUNG, CARL GUSTAV
    1916   Psychology of the unconscious. New York, Moffat, Yard and Company.
KARDINER, ABRAM
    1939   The individual and his society. New York, Columbia University Press.
    1945   The psychological frontiers of society. New York, Columbia University Press.
KLUCKHOHN, CLYDE
    1953   Universal categories of culture. *In* Anthropology today, A. L. Kroeber, ed. Chicago, University of Chicago Press.
    1959   Recurrent themes in myths and mythmaking. Proceedings of the American Academy of Arts and Sciences 88:268–79.

KÖNGAS, ELLI KAIJA
    1960   The earth-diver (Th. A 812). Ethnohistory 7:151–80.
LANG, ANDREW
    1899   Myth, ritual and religion. Vol. I. London, Longmans, Green, and Co.
LESSA, WILLIAM A.
    1961   Tales from Ulithi Atoll: a comparative study in Oceanic folklore. University of
           California Publications Folklore Studies 13. Berkeley and Los Angeles, University
           of California Press.
LÉVI-STRAUSS, CLAUDE
    1958   The structural study of myth. *In* Myth: a symposium, Thomas A. Sebeok, ed.
           Bloomington, Indiana University Press.
LOMBROSO, CESARE
    1895   The man of genius. London, Walter Scott.
LUKAS, FRANZ
    1894   Das ei als kosmogonische vorstellung. Zeitschrift des Vereins für Volkskunde 4:
           227–43.
MALINOWSKI, BRONISLAW
    1954   Magic, science and religion and other essays. New York, Doubleday Anchor.
MANN, JOHN
    1958   The folktale as a reflector of individual and social structure (Unpublished doctoral
           dissertation, Columbia University.)
MATTHEWS, WASHINGTON
    1902   Myths of gestation and parturition. American Anthropologist 4:737–42.
McCLELLAND, DAVID C. AND G. A. FRIEDMAN
    1952   A cross-cultural study of the relationship between child-training practices and
           achievement motivation appearing in folk tales. *In* Readings in social psychology,
           G. E. Swanson, T. M. Newcomb, and E. L. Hartley, eds. New York, Henry Holt
           and Company.
NADEL, S. F.
    1937   A field experiment in racial psychology. British Journal of Psychology 28:195–211.
POSINSKY, S. H.
    1957   The problem of Yurok anality. American Imago 14:3–31.
RADIN, PAUL
    1956   The trickster. New York, Philosophical Library.
RANK, OTTO
    1912   Die symbolschichtung im wecktraum und ihre wiederkehr im mythischen denken.
           Jarhbuch für psychoanalytische Forschungen 4:51–115.
    1922   Psychoanalytische beiträge zur mythenforschung. Leipzig, Internationaler Psycho-
           analytischer Verlag. (Second edition.)
REIK, THEODOR
    1951   Gold und kot. International Zeitschrift für Psychoanalyse 3:183.
RÓHEIM, GÉZA
    1921   Primitive man and environment. International Journal of Psycho-Analysis 2:157–
           78.
    1922   Psycho-analysis and the folk-tale. International Journal of Psycho-Analysis 3:180–
           86.
    1923   Heiliges geld in Melanesien. Internationale Zeitschrift für Psychoanalyse 9:384–401.
    1940   Society and the individual. Psychoanalytic Quarterly 9:526–45.
    1941   Myth and folk-tale. American Imago 2:266–79.
    1951   The gates of the dream. New York, International Universities Press.
    1953a  Fairy tale and dream. The Psychoanalytic Study of the Child 8:394–403.
    1953b  Dame Holle: dream and folk tale (Grimm No. 24). *In* Explorations in psychoanaly-
           sis, Robert Lindner, ed. New York, Julian Press.

Rooth, Anna Birgitta
    1957   The creation myths of the North American Indians. Anthropos 52:497–508.
Saville, Marshall H.
    1920   The goldsmith's art in ancient Mexico. Indian Notes and Monographs. New York,
           Heye Foundation.
Schwartz, Emanuel K.
    1956   A psychoanalytic study of the fairy tale. American Journal of Psychotherapy 10:
           740–62.
Schwarzbaum, Haim
    1960   Jewish and Moslem sources of a Falasha creation myth. *In* Studies in Biblical and
           Jewish folklore, Raphael Patai, Francis Lee Utley, Dov Noy, eds. American Folk-
           lore Society Memoir 51. Bloomington, Indiana University Press.
Silberer, Herbert
    1925   A pregnancy phantasy in a man. Psychoanalytic Review 12:377–96.
Spence, Lewis
    [1921] An introduction to mythology. New York, Farrar & Rinehart.
Spencer, Katherine
    1947   Reflection of social life in the Navaho origin myth. University of New Mexico
           Publications in Anthropology 3.
Stekel, Wilhelm
    1959   Patterns of psychosexual infantilism. New York, Grove Press.
Tax, Sol et al. (Eds.)
    1953   An appraisal of anthropology today. Chicago, University of Chicago Press.
Thompson, Stith
    1929   Tales of the North American Indians. Cambridge, Harvard University Press.
    1955   Motif-index of folk-literature. Bloomington, Indiana University Press.
Wheeler-Voegelin, Erminie
    1949   Earth diver. *In* Standard Dictionary of Folklore, Mythology and Legend, Vol. I,
           Maria Leach, ed. New York, Funk and Wagnalls.
Wheeler-Voegelin, Erminie and Remedios W. Moore
    1957   The emergence myth in native North America. *In* Studies in folklore, W. Edson
           Richmond, ed. Bloomington, Indiana University Press.
Wilbur, George B. and Warner Muensterberger (Eds.)
    1951   Psychoanalysis and culture. New York, International Universities Press.
Wolfenstein, Martha
    1955   "Jack and the beanstalk": an American version. *In* Childhood in contemporary
           cultures, Margaret Mead and Martha Wolfenstein, eds. Chicago, University of
           Chicago Press.
Wycoco (Moore), Remedios
    1951   The types of North-American Indian tales (Unpublished doctoral dissertation,
           Indiana University.)

# Descent and Symbolic Filiation

SALLY FALK MOORE
*University of Southern California*

KINSHIP networks involve a paradox. On the one hand marriage links exogamic kin groups. On the other hand, it serves to link them only insofar as the ties of each spouse to his (or her) family of birth are maintained. This continuing connection with the natal groups is often represented by the bond between brother and sister, although it also appears in other forms.[1] As male and female of the same generation, their mutual involvement in their kin group makes them in some respects a counter-pair to husband and wife. Since in many systems this sibling relationship serves structural ends, the brother-sister tie is seldom left simply to spontaneous expressions of devotion which might or might not be forthcoming. Instead it is reinforced with ritual, social, and economic obligations.

Some cultures also stress rather than minimize the incestuous overtones of the brother-sister relationship. Sometimes this preoccupation appears in the form of exaggerated prohibitions and avoidances. In other cases, it is woven through the conception of descent, as opposed to parenthood. It is this tying together of incestuous ideas and descent that is the subject of this paper, particularly with regard to brother and sister.

Common to a variety of descent systems are two means of prolonging the relationship between kin groups established by marriage. Both structural devices have the effect of stressing the bond between brother and sister. One method is to repeat the affinal tie through cross-cousin marriage. This binds brother and sister twice over. The other structural device is to make the children of the marriage to some degree descendants of both kin groups, linking the two groups in their persons. (This may, but need not also involve a prohibition on cousin marriage.) Cognatic and double descent systems immediately come to mind. But unilineal systems may also trace descent in some form through both parents. Full membership in the patrilineage of the father and partial membership in the patrilineage of the mother is one way (Nuer). Or there may be a similar near doubling of membership in the matrilineages of mother and father (Hopi, Plateau Tonga). The tracing of descent through both parents in whatever manner extends the affiliations established by marriage at least another generation in the person of the common descendant. This also has the accompanying result that brother and sister have descent links of some kind with each other's children.

Both sorts of ongoing ties not infrequently place brother and sister together in a highly binding relationship to the progeny of one or both. This relationship is often represented in what might be called "the ideology of descent" as if it were a variety of mystical, sexless parenthood, a form of symbolic filiation.

1308

Radcliffe-Brown thought brother-sister ties particularly associated with extreme matrilineality, while he believed that husband-wife bonds were more emphasized in cases of extreme patrilineality. He felt, however, that most systems fell somewhere in between (1952:42). I plan to deal elsewhere with a full structural reappraisal of this Radcliffe-Brown thesis, but the present paper will focus on a single aspect of the problem: the representation of brother and sister as a symbolically parental couple in descent ideology. That this occurs in patrilineal and cognatic systems as well as in matrilineal ones will be plain from the materials examined. These include creation myths, on the theory that people model their mythical first family on their own kinship structure, and also include a few well known beliefs and customs relating to fertility and the procreation and well-being of descendants. Most of the myths collected here show incest explicitly. As would be expected, the kinship beliefs put the matter more delicately and indirectly, but the incestuous symbolism is unmistakable.

Any myth about the creation of man which postulates a single first family is bound to give rise to some incestuous riddles. There is the first man, or woman, or couple. They have children. Who marries the children of the first couple? Adam and Eve had two sons, Cain and Abel. Where did Cain's wife come from?

Many mythological methods exist to supply respectable mates for the original family. Sometimes spouses are simply found when needed. Cain's wife turns up conveniently in the King James version of the Bible, but Saint Augustine seems to have had no doubt that the sons and daughters of Adam and Eve married each other (Saint Augustine 1958:350). In other myths many people emerge from the ground together and there is a kind of simultaneous creation of many ancestors for mankind. However, many peoples cheerfully and explicitly mate the first family to its own members. A number of such myths are listed below. These were collected and examined to discover which members of the family were most often partners in this original incest, and whether there was any observable correlation between the type of kinship system and the type of incest described. A few of the myths cited deal with the primary incest of the gods, a few others with an incest that began a particular lineage,

### SOME PEOPLES HAVING INCESTUOUS CREATION LEGENDS

| People | Descent | Incest in myth | Reference |
|---|---|---|---|
| Greeks | Patrilineal | Brother-sister | Larousse 1960:93 |
| Hebrews | Patrilineal | Brother-sister | Saint Augustine 1958:350<br>Graves 1963:17–18 |
| Murngin | Patrilineal | Father-daughter<br>Brother-sister | Warner 1937:528 |
| Trobriand | Matrilineal | Brother-sister<br>(implied) | Malinowski 1929:497 |
| Berber (Kabyl) | Patrilineal | Brother-sister | Frobenius and Fox 1938:55 |
| Ngona Horn<br>S. Rhodesia | Patrilineal | Father-daughter | Frobenius and Fox 1938:241 |

SOME PEOPLES HAVING INCESTUOUS CREATION LEGENDS

| People | Descent | Incest in myth | Reference |
| --- | --- | --- | --- |
| Maori | Ambilineal | Father-daughter | Best 1924:115–18 |
| Miwok | Patrilineal | Father-daughter<br>Brother-sister | Gifford 1916:143–44 |
| Baiga | Patrilineal | Brother-sister | Verrier 1939:313, 331 |
| Thonga | Patrilineal | Brother-sister | Junod 1913:230 |
| Chibcha | Matrilineal | Mother-son | Kroeber 1947:908 |
| Yaruro | Matrilineal | Brother-sister | Kirchhoff 1948:462 |
| Hawaii | Ambilineal | Mother-son | Dixon 1916:26 |
| Tahiti | Ambilineal | Father-daughter | Dixon 1916–26 |
| Celebes Minahassa | | Mother-son | Dixon 1916:157 |
| Ifugao | Bilateral | Brother-sister | Dixon 1916:170 |
| Katchin | Patrilineal | Brother-sister | Levi-Strauss 1949:307 |
| Mohave | Patrilineal | Brother-sister | Devereaux 1939:512 |
| Pawnee | Matrilineal(?) | Brother-sister | American Folk Lore Society<br>1904:22 |
| Tlingit | Matrilineal | Brother-sister | Krause 1956:175, 185 |
| Aleut | Patrilineal | Brother-sister | HRAF citing Veniaminov and<br>Sarytschew |
| Alor | Bilateral | Brother-sister<br>(implied) | Dubois, 1944:105 |
| Yurok | Bilateral | Father-daughter | Roheim (citing Kroeber) 1950:273 |
| Island Carib Dominica | Matrilineal | Brother-sister | Taylor 1945:310 |
| Veddas | Matrilineal | Brother-sister | Seligmann 1911:74 |
| Lakher | Patrilineal | Brother-sister | Parry 1932:489 |
| Garo | Matrilineal | Brother-sister | Playfair 1909:84 |
| Ba-Kaonde | Matrilineal | Brother-sister | Melland 1923:156, 249–59 |
| Cherokee | Matrilineal | Brother-sister<br>(implied) | Mooney 1902:240 |
| Dogon | Patrilineal | Brother-sister | Griaule and Dieterlen 1954:84–96 |
| Abaluyia | Patrilineal | Brother-sister | Wagner 1954:30, 35 |
| Papuas of Waropen | Patrilineal | Brother-sister | Held 1957:95, 299 |
| Samoa | Ambilineal | Brother-sister | Mead 1930:151 |
| Lovedu | Patrilineal | Father-daughter<br>Brother-sister<br>Cycle of Kings | Krige and Krige 1943:5, 10, 12 |
| Tullishi | Double | Brother-sister | Nadel 1950:351 |
| Lozi | Ambilineal | Brother-sister | Gluckman 1950:177, 178 |
| Andaman Islanders | Bilateral | Brother-sister | Radcliffe-Brown 1933:196 |
| Japanese | Bilateral | Brother-sister | Etter 1949:29 |
| Ainu | Matrilineal | Brother-sister | Etter 1949:20–21 |
| Kei Islands<br>  SE Indonesia | | Brother-sister | Dixon 1916:156 |
| Nambicuara | Bilateral | Brother-sister | Levi-Strauss 1948:369 |
| Egyptians | Patrilineal | Brother-sister<br>King Osiris | Frazer 1960:421 |

Total number of peoples listed 42

Four peoples have more than one type of incest in their origin myth hence the disparity between the total number of peoples and the total instances of incest.

| Descent | bro-sis | fa-da | mo-son |
|---|---|---|---|
| Patrilineal | 16 | 4 | |
| Matrilineal | 10 | | 1 |
| Ambilineal | 2 | 2 | 1 |
| Bilateral | 5 | 1 | |
| Double | 1 | | |
| Unknown | 1 | | 1 |
| | — | — | — |
| Totals | 34 | 7 | 3 |

but most of them tell of an incest from which mankind sprang. All but two are listed with the associated form of descent. The prevalence of brother-sister incest is striking, and the correlation of parent-child incest with descent rules quite suggestive. The examples examined have been culled from ethnographies, from the Human Relations Area Files, from indications in the Stith Thompson Index, from a picking over of the Handbook of South American Indians and other general sources likely to include such information. However, the list is a chance compilation depending upon library accessibility, and is in no sense complete. It is sufficient to suggest the wide appearance of the theme, and, perhaps, some gross correlations.

Some reservations should be made. For one thing, both myths and social organization change. Even assuming that myth is in some symbolic way a rationalization of a kinship system, it may be more or less durable than the social structure from which it sprang. There is also the related question as to what position the origin myth occupies in the total literature of a people. It may be an old story, part of an obscure heritage, seldom retold, but carried along, or it may have a good deal more vitality than that. This is a nuance which is not always discernible from the ethnographic literature (For a penetrating discussion of these and related problems concerning the interpretation of myth, see Fischer 1963.)

It should also be said that though the relation of the form of the incestuous myth to the form of the social organization may be posed as a problem in correlations, it is not really suitable to treat it this way. Many, if not most, peoples do not have such a myth, but they have the same types of kinship structure as the peoples who have the myths. The inference to be drawn from this mythological material is that a fictive and symbolic incest is often a significant symbol of ancestry and descent. It may be found in many forms, of which origin myths are but one example. Hence the origin myths alert one to a kind of symbolism that appears in the ideology of some descent systems even in cultures in which this theme is not expressed in the particular form of a creation legend.

Levi-Strauss has said that " . . . the purpose of myth is to provide a logical model capable of overcoming a contradiction . . . " (1955:443) and that "mythical thought always works from the awareness of oppositions toward their progressive mediation . . . " (1955:440). From this point of view these incestuous origin myths refer to a time when there were no people to explain how there came to be many people. They start with one family to show the source of all families. They tell of an ancient incest that sired the human race, yet plainly the descendants are forbidden to emulate their ancestors. Then and now are contrasted in a systematic way.[2]

Inspecting the table, it is clear that brother-sister incest is the one which most often takes place in the myths. This not only violates the incest prohibition; it also necessarily violates exogamic rules in any descent system. Where mythological parent-child incest occurs in unilineal systems, it, too, seems calculated to violate descent rules. The matrilineal Chibcha are descended from a mother-son incest, the patrilineal Murngin, Miwok, Ngona, and the Lovedu rulers from a father-daughter incest. The numbers involved here are too small to constitute a statistical proof, but they suggest a correlation with structure. It is interesting to note parent-child incest in the myths of three out of five ambilineal peoples and one out of six bilateral peoples. Presumably the structural resemblances of ambilineal systems to unilineal ones accounts for this difference, but the numbers are too small to warrant any firm conclusion.

Why should incest in origin myths be a common theme, and why should it tend so strongly to be sibling incest? And why should mythical parent-child incest tend to correlate with descent group exogamy? If one applies psychoanalytic theory, these myths can be regarded as a reiteration of Oedipal fantasies. The beginning of mankind then stands for the early wishes of the individual, and sibling incest is not more than a lightly veiled version of parent-child incest. This interpretation could account for the commonness of the incestuous theme in mythology. It might even superficially seem to account for the prevalence of the brother-sister over the parent-child type. *But it could in no way account for the correlation of mythological parent-child incest with descent.* Whatever element is unaccounted for in the parent-child cases, is logically unaccounted for in the sibling type, for one explanation must apply to all.

Thus even if one accepts psychoanalytic interpretations, they can only explain the general appeal of the theme of incest, not its particular variations or cultural applications. I agree with Murphy that " . . . the stuff of the unconscious tends to be expressed in cultural symbols where it serves some function in terms of social structure . . . " (1959:97). The explanation of the variations must be sought in the cultural setting in which they are found.

In this matter Levi-Strauss' approach to mythology (1955, 1962) is very useful. His conception of oppositions ties social structure to myth insofar as myths seek to reconcile what life is with what life is not. There is another string to his bow in "Le totemisme aujourd'hui." There he deals not with contrasts and negations, but with the replication of social structure in the classification of animals and plants. Hence mythological symbolism may either repeat or contrast with reality, as the case may be.

The incestuous creation myths do both. In them one finds a literary reconciliation of the incest prohibition and incest itself, both pushed discreetly into the primeval past. Descent postulates common ancestry. Man is of one kind. Thus all mankind has common ancestors. Ancestry is also the basis of the incest prohibition. But if all men are descended from one couple, then every marriage is distantly and vaguely incestuous. In this way the myth metaphorically and economically states both the unity of man, and that marriage is a substitute for incest.

Since the unified descent of mankind is best symbolized in a particular culture not only by incest, but by incest within the descent group, there may be a purely logical reason for the prevalence of the sibling incest theme against the parent-child type. Brother-sister incest conveys concisely for *any* descent system the same triple symbolism that parent-child incest conveys for particular ones, namely the fusion of descent, marriage, and incest. There may be an even simpler explantion. Since primary marriage most often tends to be within the same generation, brother-sister incest may be a closer symbolic replication of marriage than parent-child incest.

Robert Graves, like Frazer before him, interprets mythological sibling incest as an indication of a prior period of matrilineal land inheritance (Frazer 1960:386; Graves 1963:4). This seems a curious inference. As the table shows, sibling incest as an origin myth theme is as clearly associated with patrilineality as matrilineality. To treat legends of this type as accounts of early history is a naively literal approach. It is far more likely that these stories are a fictional validation of the present than an embroidered remnant of the past.

There is no better example than the Dogon of the French Sudan who state explicitly that their kinship system is based on their creation myth. So beautifully does their myth illustrate the sibling constellation and its symbolic content in descent ideology that it is worth making an excursion into Dogon cosmology. A patrilineal people having patrilocal kin groups, the Dogon prefer the marriage of a man with his mother's brother's daughter. Conventionally he also enjoys sexual relations with his mother's brother's wife. All this according to the Dogon has its precedents in the Beginning of Time.

The Dogon creation myth begins with the egg of the world. (I will spare the reader the rather orgasmic seven vibrations of the universe and some other cosmic upheavals.) The egg of the world is divided into twin placenta, each of which contains a "pair of twin Nommo, direct emanations and sons of God. . . . Like all other creatures these twin beings . . . were each equipped with two spiritual principles of opposite sex; each of them, therefore, was in himself a pair . . . " (Griaule and Dieterlen 1954:86).

In Dogon belief every human being is the offspring of two pairs of Nommo like those in the original placenta, the father and the father's sister, the mother and the mother's brother. The ideal, but prohibited marriage, is conceived as that between brother and sister. Mystically, opposite sex siblings are conceived as parents of each other's children.

However, in the creation all did not proceed according to plan, "in one placenta . . . the male person emerged prematurely from the egg. Moreover he tore a fragment from his placenta and with it came down through space outside the egg; this fragment became the earth." Yurugu, for that was the name of this male creature, eventually went back to heaven to get the rest of his placenta and his twin soul. But unfortunately for him, "Amma (God) had handed over this twin soul to the remaining pair in the other part of the egg. . . . Yurugu could not retrieve her; and from that time on . . . (was) . . . engaged in a perpetual and fruitless search for her. He returned to the dry earth where . . . he procreated in his own placenta. . . . "However, this procreation with a symbolic maternal fragment did not produce people, but some sort of incomplete beings. "Seeing this, Amma decided to send to earth the Nommo of the other half of the egg . . . " (Griaule and Dieterlen 1954:86). Mankind was then produced through the coupling of pairs of male and female twins.

The Dogon regard every male child as Yurugu with respect to his mother. He is her brother, her ideal husband. But since the normal incest prohibitions apply, the wife of the maternal uncle is taken as a sexual partner as a substitute for the mother. The boy is allowed to commit whatever thefts he pleases in his mother's brother's household, as these are regarded as a symbolical search for a wife. This comes to an end when the maternal uncle provides a wife, usually one of his daughters. "Clearly there is a correspondence here between the maternal uncle's daughter, his wife, and his sister, who is the mother of the nephew. The marriage is thus in some sense a reenactment of the mythical incest. It is also . . . regarded as a caricature and is thus a kind of defiance hurled at Yurugu . . . " (Griaule and Dieterlen 1954:93).

The Dogon lay out their villages, their fields, their houses, in a pattern that is in keeping with the creation myth. No vestigial tradition, the myth has tremendous vitality and importance. The patriline is thought to follow the original orderly creation of Amma, the uterine group to represent the checkered career of Yurugu. While there is much else that is interesting about Dogon belief, three of its elements are of particular relevance here: first that brother and sister are idealized as a procreative couple; second, the idea that any child is simultaneously produced by two sibling pairs, the father and his sister, the mother and her brother; and third, that structural features, in this case, preferred matrilateral cross-cousin marriage, can have specific symbolically incestuous meanings.

The basic question which elements in the Dogon myth raise is this: Are the Dogon a special case, or does their myth make explicit certain ideas that are symbolically implied in one form or another in many descent systems? If one reflects on the stereotyped kinship roles often prescribed for parent's siblings of opposite sex in primitive cultures, it is difficult to dismiss the Dogon as unique.

## II

Turning from mythology to some beliefs and customs which surround the perpetuation of the descent group: here again examples of the symbolic pairing of brothers and sisters in a quasi-incestuous manner are not far to seek.

Brother and sister may together perpetuate the descent group on a symbolic level, while on a practical level marriage produces the actual descendants.

In Africa the well-known case is that of cattle-linking, in which a man obtains his wife by means of the cattle received for his sister, and she consequently comes to have a special relationship with her brother's children. The striking thing about these African cattle-linked sibling pairs is the extent to which the tie between a particular brother and sister is acknowledged as having a connection with the very existence of the brother's children, giving the father's sister special rights over them. There is a kind of double marriage, the actual one, and the symbolic one of the cattle linking. (See for instance Krige and Krige 1943:142-6 for the Lovedu: Stayt 1931:174, for the BaVenda, Schapera 1950:142 for the Tswana, Holleman 1952:66, 67, 169 for the Shona, and Kuper 1950:102, for the Swazi.)

In Samoa, the male line of the ambilineal Manuans goes on through the good grace of each man's sister. The father's sister has the ability to make her brother or his male line barren, or can cause them to sicken (Mead 1930:137). As the keeper of her brother's fertility, a sister becomes in a mystical sense as responsible for a man's procreation as his wife is in a biological sense.

In the Trobriands, one sees the matrilineal counterpart of the African cattle pairing. Trobriand brothers and sisters are paired off for various purposes. Not only does a particular brother supply a particular sister with food, but "This pairing off extends to other things besides *urigubu* [food]. *A sister may ask her brother to make magic designed to get her impregnated by one of the spirits of their sub-clan.* The brother who is responsible for a sister's food is the one who plays the main role of disciplinarian and tutor of her children. The other brothers are secondary in this respect. . . . " (Fathauer, 1961:250) (Italics mine).

The Trobriand preoccupation with brother-sister incest is clearly threaded throughout the descriptions of Malinowski. The origin of Trobriand love magic is based on brother-sister incest. All clans begin their mythological history with a brother and sister, the sister becoming pregnant without intercourse (Malinowski 1929:35, 180-2). Trobriand brother-sister pairs are clearly associated with descent and figure as symbolic parents of the sister's children much as the African cattle-linking makes siblings figure as symbolic parents of the brother's children.

Among the Murngin, Warner tells us that "No sister may eat a brother's kill of kangaroo, emu, etc. until the brother's wife has had a child" (1930:253). It is as if the sister drained her brother's sexual powers by eating his kill. The sister's actions plainly have an effect on her brother's ability to impregnate his wife.

The African, Samoan, Trobriand and Murngin instances are all cases in which the non-lineal sex has power over the fertility of the lineal sex. But sometimes the position is reversed. The patrilineal Lakher believe that if there is ill-feeling between a woman and her brother or her mother's brother, she will be unable to have children. Patently her relatives retain control over her fertility even after she marries. The ceremony which may be performed to enable her to become pregnant gives her brother or her mother's brother a major role. Either of these men places some fermented rice in the woman's mouth with a hair pin when the moon is waning, and neither of them speaks to her again until a new moon has arisen (Parry 1932:379–80).[3]

All of these are fairly obvious cases in which brother and sister together are involved with the procreativity of one or the other of them. But the sibling link can be expressed in purely spiritual terms as well. The Mende explain the relationship with the mother's brother this way: ". . . since a brother and sister come from the same father they may be considered as one. *Therefore, all that a mother gives her child is given also by her brother, and so her brother's displeasure or pleasure is the same as its mother's.* The physical part of a person, i.e. his bones, flesh, etc. is provided by his father through the semen. . . . The child's spirit—ngafa—, however, is contributed by his mother. This explains why the blessing of the mother's people is so important to the child and why the father asks them to pray for the child when he takes it away from them. The mother is the child's "keeper" in the same sense as a genie may have control over a human being" (Little 1951:111) (Italics mine).

For the patrilineal Mende, then, brother and sister are triply bound. First, they are one as the bodily (i.e. descent) children of one father; second, they are one as the soul keepers of the sister's children; and third, they are descent antecedents of the brother's children. Husband and wife are actual parents, brother and sister symbolic ones. The Mende attitude is a forceful reminder of the Dogon myth.

The pairing of brothers and sisters as a symbolic couple bears on Levi-Strauss' interpretation of totemism. Levi-Strauss (1962) suggests that the reason why animals are suitable symbols of kin groups lies in certain resemblances between the animal world and the human world. The human world and the animal world have in common the subdivisions of their respective kinds. He stresses the fact that totemism involves the use of homologous systems to represent one another. With this general thesis I have no argument.

However, though Levi-Strauss notes that animal species are endogamous, he does not find it logically troublesome that they are used to represent exogamous groups. Instead, he cites Bergson saying that it is not on the animality but on the duality that totemism puts its emphasis (1962:111, 135). The material on symbolic incest and descent reviewed here suggests that this part of the Levi-Strauss argument is superfluous. The endogamy of animal species makes animals not less, but more appropriate as emblems of descent groups. This is obviously not because of any actual endogamy in descent groups, but because descent groups are symbolically self-perpetuating. The descent element in unilineal groups is passed on from generation to generation in a self-propelling stream. To be sure, partners from other lineages are required catalysts or vehicles for the production of biological offspring, but the descent element in the offspring comes from within the lineage only. Kind reproduces kind in the animal and human kingdoms.

The beliefs examined here in which brother and sister have custody of each other's fertility, or are mutually involved in the perpetuation of the descent group, or are together connected with the body or soul of each other's children all state formal social ties in a particular symbolic idiom. Firth has said, "Kinship is fundamentally a reinterpretation in social terms of the facts of procreation and regularized sex union" (1961:577). But if one moves from the realm of structure to the realm of symbolism, the contrary can be true. That is, relationships which are not sexual or filial in reality may be expressed in symbols having a sexual or filial content. Just as fictive kinship may be resorted to, to bind unrelated persons socially, so fictive incest and fictive parenthood can be part of the idiom of descent.

Symbolic filiation is not at all startling when it does not involve any direct mention of the incest. We are entirely accustomed to it in kinship terminology. When the father's sister is called "female father" the term implies that she partakes in her brother's paternity. Where cousins are classified with brothers and sisters they are linked in a fictitious common filiation. The extension of the incest taboo beyond the elementary family is another of the ways in which symbolic filiation may serve structural ends. Clearly descent and symbolic filiation are frequently interlocked concepts. It is not surprising then, that the brother-sister relationship which has such widespread structural importance, not only often appears as a symbol of descent, but does so in the form of a symbolic parenthood. A full recognition of this pervasive *double entendre* and its many variations can deepen our understanding of descent in kin-based societies.

## NOTES

[1] While brother and brother, or sister and sister, may effectively symbolize the descent group, same-sex pairs cannot epitomize the bridge *between* kin groups.

[2] It has been objected that what is involved here and in Levi-Strauss is not the juxtaposition of opposites, but of negatives. This well-taken point of logic undermines the form but not the substance of Levi-Strauss' contention.

[3] The Lakher also believe that if a woman's parents are dead, their spirits may be the cause of her infertility. For this last the cure is a sacrifice on the graves of the parents. Thus brothers and sisters are not by any means the *only* custodians of each other's fertility. Among the matrilineal Pende, for instance, a father is said to enable his daughter to bear children, but sometimes the anger of a mother's brother can make a woman sterile (de Sousberghe 1955:27). Even among the Trobrianders spirit children may be the gift of a woman's mother, mother's brother, or even of her father (Malinowski 1929:173). Among the patrilineal Nuer, a man's mother or his mother's brother can prevent him from having any male children (Evans-Pritchard 1960:138). A Nuer son can, by violating certain taboos, render his mother barren (Evans-Pritchard 1960:165). The curse of the mother or mother's brother among the Nuer would seem to be the counterpart of the father's sister's curse in Polynesia. Relationships of the spirits obviously can have sexual consequences. The power over fertility is often an expression of multiple structural relationships in terms of sexual symbols. Though this paper is confined to this symbolization as it pertains to brother and sister, it should be borne in mind that it can, as indicated, pertain to other relatives.

## REFERENCES CITED

AMERICAN FOLK-LORE SOCIETY
    1904   Memoirs, No. 8

AUGUSTINE
    1958    The city of God. New York, Doubleday and Co.
BEST, ELSDON
    1924    The Maori. Memoirs of the Polynesian Society, Vol. V. Wellington, New Zealand.
DEVEREAUX, GEORGE
    1939    The social and cultural implications of incest among the Mohave Indians. *In* The Psychoanalytic Quarterly 8:510–533.
DIXON, ROLAND B.
    1916    Oceanic mythology. *In* The mythology of all races, Louis H. Gray, ed. Vol. 9, Boston.
DUBOIS, CORA
    1944    The people of Alor. Minneapolis, University of Minnesota Press.
ETTER, CARL
    1949    Ainu folklore. Chicago, Wilcox and Follett.
EVANS-PRITCHARD, E. E.
    1960    Kinship and marriage among the Nuer. London, Oxford University Press.
FATHAUER, GEORGE H.
    1961    Trobriand. *In* Matrilineal kinship, David M. Schneider and Kathleen Gough, eds., Berkeley and Los Angeles, University of California Press.
FISCHER, J. L.
    1963    The sociopsychological analysis of folktales. Current Anthropology 4, No. 3.
FIRTH, RAYMOND
    1961    We, the Tikopia. London, George Allen and Unwin.
FROBENIUS, LEO and DOUGLAS FOX
    1938    African genesis. London.
FRAZER, SIR JAMES GEORGE
    1960    The golden bough. New York, Macmillan.
GIFFORD, E. W.
    1916    Miwok moieties. *In* California kinship systems, University of California Publications in American Archeology and Ethnology 12:139–94.
GLUCKMAN, MAX
    1950    Kinship and marriage among the Lozi. *In* African systems of kinship and marriage, A. R. Radcliffe-Brown ed., London, Oxford University Press.
GRAVES, ROBERT and RAPHAEL PATAI
    1963    Some Hebrew myths and legends. Encounter 114:12–18.
GRIAULE, MARCEL and DIETERLEN, GERMAINE
    1954    The Dogon. *In* African worlds, Daryll Forde, ed., London, Oxford University Press.
HELD, G. J.
    1957    The Papuas of Waropen. The Hague.
HOLLEMAN, J. F.
    1952    Shona customary law. London, Oxford University Press.
HUMAN RELATIONS AREA FILES
    New Haven, Connecticut
JUNOD, HENRI A.
    1913    The life of a south African tribe. Neuchatel, Atlinger Freres.
KIRCHHOFF, PAUL
    1948    Food gathering tribes of the Venezuelan Illanos. *In* Handbook of South American Indians, Julian Steward, ed., Washington, D. C., Government Printing office 4:445–468.
KRAUSE, AUREL
    1956    The Tlingit Indians. Seattle, University of Washington Press.

KRIGE, E. J. and J. D. KRIGE
    1943   The realm of a rain queen. London, Oxford University Press.
KROEBER, ALFRED
    1947   The Chibcha. *In* Handbook of South American Indians, Julian Steward, ed. Washington, D. C., Government Printing Office 2:887–909.
KUPER, HILDA
    1950   Kinship among the Swazi. *In* African systems of kinship and marriage, A. R. Radcliffe-Brown and Daryll Forde, eds. London, Oxford University Press.
LAROUSSE ENCYCLOPEDIA OF MYTHOLOGY
    1960   Batchworth Press, London.
LEVI-STRAUSS, CLAUDE
    1948   The Nambicuara. *In* Handbook of South American Indians, Julian Steward, ed. Washington, D. C., Government Printing Office, 3:361–9.
    1949   Les structures elementaires de la parente. Paris, Presses Universitaires de France.
    1955   The structural study of myth. Journal of American Folk Lore 68:428–44.
    1962   Le totemisme aujourd'hui. Presses Universitaires de France, Paris, 1962.
LITTLE, K. L.
    1951   The Mende of Sierra Leone. London, Routledge and Kegan Paul.
MALINOWSKI, BRONISLAW
    1929   The sexual life of savages in north-western Melanesia. London, Routledge and Sons.
MEAD, MARGARET
    1930   Social organization of Manua. Bernice P. Bishop Museum, Bulletin 76, Honolulu, Hawaii.
MELLAND, FRANK H.
    1923   In witch-bound Africa. London, Seeley, Service.
MOONEY, JAMES
    1902   Myths of the Cherokee. Washington, Government Printing Office.
NADEL, S. F.
    1950   Dual descent in the Nuba hills. *In* African systems of kinship and marriage, A. R. Radcliffe-Brown and Daryll Forde, eds. London, Oxford University Press.
MURPHY, ROBERT F.
    1959   Social structure and sex antagonism. Southwestern Journal of Anthropology 15:89–98.
PARRY, N. E.
    1932   The Lakhers. London, Macmillan and Co.
PLAYFAIR, ALAN
    1909   The Garos. London, D. Nutt.
RADCLIFFE-BROWN, A. R.
    1933   The Andaman islanders. London, Cambridge University Press.
    1952   Structure and function in primitive society.
ROHEIM, GEZA
    1950   Psychoanalysis and anthropology. New York, International Universities Press.
SELIGMANN, C. G. and B. Z.
    1911   The Veddas. London, Cambridge University Press.
SCHAPERA, I.
    1950   Kinship and marriage among the Tswana. *In* African systems of kinship and marriage, A. R. Radcliffe-Brown and Daryll Forde, eds., London, Oxford University Press.
DE SOUSBERGHE, R. P. L.
    1955   Structure de parente et d'alliance d'apres les formules Pende. Brussels, Academie Royale des Sciences Morales et Politiques.
STAYT, HUGH A.
    1931   The Ba Venda. London, Oxford University Press.

TAYLOR, DOUGLAS
    1945   Carib folk-beliefs and customs from Dominica, B. W. I., Southwestern Journal of Anthropology 1:507–530.
THOMPSON, STITH
    1961   Motif-index of folk-literature. Bloomington, Indiana, Indiana University Press.
VERRIER, ELWIN
    1939   The Baiga. London, John Murray.
WAGNER, GUNTER
    1954   The Abaluyia of Kavirondo. *In* African worlds, Daryll Forde, ed., Oxford, Oxford University Press.
WARNER, W. L.
    1930   Morphology and function of the Murngin kinship system. American Anthropologist 32:207–256.
    1937   A black civilization. New York, Harper Bros.

# Peasant Society and the Image of Limited Good*

GEORGE M. FOSTER

*University of California, Berkeley*

"Human behavior is always motivated by certain purposes, and these purposes grow out of sets of assumptions which are not usually recognized by those who hold them. The basic premises of a particular culture are unconsciously accepted by the individual through his constant and exclusive participation in that culture. It is these assumptions—the essence of all the culturally conditioned purposes, motives, and principles—which determine the behavior of a people, underlie all the institutions of a community, and give them unity" (Hsiao-Tung Fei and Chi-I Chang 1945:81–82).

"Human beings in whatever culture are provided with cognitive orientation in a cosmos: there is 'order' and 'reason' rather than chaos. There are basic premises and principles implied, even if these do not happen to be consciously formulated and articulated by the people themselves. We are confronted with the philosophical implications of their thought, the nature of the world of being as they conceive it. If we pursue the problem deeply enough we soon come face to face with a relatively unexplored territory—ethno-metaphysics. Can we penetrate this realm in other cultures? What kind of evidence is at our disposal? . . . The problem is a complex and difficult one, but this should not preclude its exploration" (Hallowell 1960:21).

1. *Cognitive orientation.*
2. *The "Image of Limited Good."*
   2.1. *Economic behavior.*
   2.2. *Friendship.*
   2.3. *Health.*
   2.4. *Manliness and honor.*
3. *Peasant behavior as a function of the "Image of Limited Good."*
   3.1. *Individual and family action.*
   3.2. *Informal, unorganized group action.*
   3.3. *Institutionalized action.*
4. *The "open" aspects of peasant society.*
5. *Peasant cognitive orientation and economic growth.*

1. The members of every society share a common cognitive orientation which is, in effect, an unverbalized, implicit expression of their understanding of the "rules of the game" of living imposed upon them by their social, natural, and supernatural universes. A cognitive orientation provides the members of the society it characterizes with basic premises and sets of assumptions normally neither recognized nor questioned which structure and guide behavior in much the same way grammatical rules unrecognized by most people structure and guide their linguistic forms. All normative behavior of the members

* The Tzintzuntzan field work 1958–1963 which played an important part in the development of the ideas in this paper was supported in part by National Science Foundation Grant No. G7064, and by annual grants from the Research Committee of the University of California (Berkeley). In the preparation of this paper I am indebted for critical comments from Mary L. Foster and Richard Currier. This article appears under the title "El caracter del campesino" in *La Revista Mexicana de Psicoanálisis, Psiquiatría, y Psicologia,* Vol. 1, No. 1, 1965.

293

of a group is a function of their particular way of looking at their total environment, their unconscious acceptance of the "rules of the game" implicit in their cognitive orientation.

A particular cognitive orientation cannot be thought of as world view in a Redfieldian sense, i.e., as something existing largely at a conscious level in the minds of the members of the group.[1] The average man of any society cannot describe the underlying premises of which his behavior is a logical function any more than he can outline a phonemic statement which expresses the patterned regularities in his speech. As Kluckhohn has pointed out, cognitive orientations (he speaks of "configurations") are recognized by most members of a society only in the sense that they make choices "with the configurations as unconscious but determinative backgrounds" (1943:218).

In speaking of a cognitive orientation—the terms "cognitive view," "world view," "world view perspective," "basic assumptions," "implicit premises," and perhaps "ethos" may be used as synonyms—I am as an anthropologist concerned with two levels of problems: (1) the nature of the cognitive orientation itself which I see as something "psychologically real," and the ways in which and the degree to which it can be known; and (2) the economical representation of this cognitive orientation by means of models or integrating principles which account for observed behavior, and which permit prediction of behavior yet unnoted or unperformed. Such a model or principle is, as Kluckhohn has often pointed out, an inferential construct or an analytic abstraction derived from observed behavior.

A model or integrating principle is not the cognitive orientation itself, but for purposes of analysis the two cannot be separated. A well-constructed model is, of course, not really descriptive of behavior at all (as is, for example, the term "ethos" as used by Gillin [1955] to describe contemporary Latin American culture). A good model is heuristic and explanatory, not descriptive, and it has predictive value. It encourages an analyst to search for behavior patterns, and relationships between patterns, which he may not yet have recognized, simply because logically—if the model is sound—it is reasonable to expect to find them. By the same token, a sound model should make it possible to predict how people are going to behave when faced with certain alternatives. A model therefore has at least two important functions: it is conducive to better field work, and it has practical utility as a guide to policy and action in developmental programs.

A perfect model or integrating principle of a particular world view should subsume *all* behavior of the members of a group. In practice it is unreasonable to expect this. But the best model is the one that subsumes the greatest amount of behavior in such fashion that there are no mutually incompatible parts in the model, i.e., forms of behavior cast together in what is obviously a logically inconsistent relationship. Kluckhohn speculated about the possibility of a single model, a dominant "master configuration" characterizing an entire society, for which he suggested the terms "integration" (1941:128) and "ethos" (1943:221), but I believe he never attempted the task of describing a complete ethos. Opler, on the other hand, has described Lipan Apache culture in terms of twenty "themes" which are, however, to a considerable extent descriptive, and which in no way approximate a master model (1946).[2]

How does an anthropologist fathom the cognitive orientation of the group he studies, to find patterns that will permit building a model or stating an integrating principle? Componential analysis and other formal semantic methods have recently been much in vogue, and these techniques unquestionably can tell us a great deal. But the degree of dissention among anthropologists who use these methods suggests that they are not a single royal road to "God's truth" (cf. Burling 1964). I suspect there will always remain a considerable element of ethnological art in the processes whereby we come to have some understanding of a cognitive orientation. However we organize our thought processes, we are engaging in an exercise in structural analysis in which overt behavior (and the simpler patterns into which this behavior is readily seen to fall) is viewed somewhat as a reflection or representation of a wider reality which our sensory apparatus can never directly perceive. Or, we can view the search for a cognitive view as an exercise in triangulation. Of each trait and pattern the question is asked, "Of what implicit assumption might this behavior be a logical function?" When enough questions have been asked, the answers will be found to point in a common direction. The model emerges from the point where the lines of answers intersect. Obviously, an anthropologist well acquainted with a particular culture cannot merely apply simple rules of analysis and automatically produce a model for, or even a description of, a world view. In effect, we are dealing with a pyramidal structure: low-level regularities and coherences relating overt behavior forms are fitted into higher-level patterns which in turn may be found to fall into place at a still higher level of integration. Thus, a model of a social structure, sound in itself, will be found to be simply one expression of a structural regularity which will have analogues in religion and economic activities.

Since all normative behavior of the members of a group is a function of its particular cognitive orientation, both in an abstract philosophical sense and in the view of an individual himself, all behavior is "rational" and sense-making. "Irrational" behavior can be spoken of only in the context of a cognitive view which did not give rise to that behavior. Thus, in a rapidly changing world, in which peasant and primitive peoples are pulled into the social and economic context of whole nations, some of their behavior may appear irrational to others because the social, economic, and natural universe that in fact controls the conditions of their life is other than that revealed to them—however subconsciously—by a traditional world view. That is, a peasant's cognitive view provides moral and other precepts that are guides to—in fact, may be said to produce—behavior that may not be appropriate to the changing conditions of life he has not yet grasped. For this reason when the cognitive orientation of large numbers of a nation's people is out of tune with reality, these people will behave in a way that will appear irrational to those who are more nearly attuned to reality. Such peoples will be seen as constituting a drag (as indeed they may be) on a nation's development, and they will be cutting themselves off from the opportunity to participate in the benefits that economic progress can bring.

In this paper I am concerned with the nature of the cognitive orientation of peasants, and with interpreting and relating peasant behavior as described by anthropologists to this orientation. I am also concerned with the implications of this orientation and related behavior to the problem of the peasant's participation in the economic growth of the country to which he may belong. Specifically, I will outline what I believe to be the dominant theme in the cognitive orientation of classic peasant societies,[3] show how characteristic peasant behavior seems to flow from this orientation, and attempt to show that this behavior—however incompatible with national economic growth—is not only highly rational in the context of the cognition that determines it, but that for the maintenance of peasant society in its classic form, it is indispensable.[4] The kinds of behavior that have been suggested as adversely influencing economic growth are, among many, the "luck" syndrome, a "fatalistic" outlook, inter- and intra-familial quarrels, difficulties in cooperation, extraordinary ritual expenses by poor people and the problems these expenses pose for capital accumulation, and the apparent lack of what the psychologist McClelland (1961) has called "need for Achievement." I will suggest that peasant participation in national development can be hastened not by stimulating a psychological process, the need for achievement, but by creating economic and other opportunities that will encourage the peasant to abandon his traditional and increasingly unrealistic cognitive orientation for a new one that reflects the realities of the modern world.

2. The model of cognitive orientation that seems to me best to account for peasant behavior is the "Image of Limited Good." By "Image of Limited Good" I mean that broad areas of peasant behavior are patterned in such fashion as to suggest that peasants view their social, economic, and natural universes—their total environment—as one in which all of the desired things in life such as land, wealth, health, friendship and love, manliness and honor, respect and status, power and influence, security and safety, *exist in finite quantity* and *are always in short supply*, as far as the peasant is concerned. Not only do these and all other "good things" exist in finite and limited quantities, but in addition *there is no way directly within peasant power to increase the available quantities*. It is as if the obvious fact of land shortage in a densely populated area applied to all other desired things: not enough to go around. "Good," like land, is seen as inherent in nature, there to be divided and redivided, if necessary, but not to be augmented.[5]

For purposes of analysis, and at this stage of the argument, I am considering a peasant community to be a closed system. Except in a special—but extremely important—way, a peasant sees his existence as determined and limited by the natural and social resources of his village and his immediate area. Consequently, there is a primary corollary to The Image of Limited Good: if "Good" exists in limited amounts which cannot be expanded, and if the system is closed, it follows that *an individual or a family can improve a position only at the expense of others.* Hence an apparent relative improvement in someone's position with respect to any "Good" is viewed as a threat to the entire community. Someone is being despoiled, whether he sees it or not. And since there is often uncertainty as to who is losing—obviously it may be ego—*any* significant improvement is perceived, not as a threat to an individual or a family alone, but as a threat to *all* individuals and families.

This model was first worked out on the basis of a wide variety of field data from Tzintzuntzan, Michoacán, Mexico: family behavior, exchange patterns, cooperation, religious activities, court claims, disputes, material culture, folklore, language, and many other bits and pieces. At no point has an informant even remotely suggested that this is his vision of his universe. Yet each Tzintzuntzeno organizes his behavior in a fashion entirely rational when it is viewed as a function of this principle which he cannot enunciate.[6]

The model of Limited Good, when "fed back" to behavior in Tzintzuntzan, proved remarkably productive in revealing hitherto unsuspected structural regularities linking economic behavior with social relations, friendship, love and jealousy patterns, health beliefs, concepts of honor and masculinity, *egoísmo* manifestations—even folklore (Foster 1964a). Not only were structural regularities revealed in Tzintzuntzan, but much peasant behavior known to me from other field work, and reported in the literature, seemed also to be a function of this cognitive orientation. This has led me to offer the kinds of data I have utilized in formulating this model, and to explain the interpretations that seem to me to follow from it, as characterizing in considerable degree classic peasant societies, in the hope that the model will be tested against other extensive bodies of data. I believe, obviously, that if the Image of Limited Good is examined as a high-level integrating principle characterizing peasant communities, we will find within our individual societies unsuspected structural regularities and, on a cross-cultural level, basic patterns that will be most helpful in constructing the typology of peasant society. The data I present in support of this thesis are illustrative, and are not based on an exhaustive survey of peasant literature.

In the following pages I will offer evidence under four headings that seems to me to conform to the model I have suggested. I will then discuss the implications of this evidence.

2.1. When the peasant views his economic world as one in which Limited Good prevails, and he can progress only at the expense of another, he is usually very near the truth. Peasant economies, as pointed out by many authors, are not productive. In the average village there *is* only a finite amount of wealth produced, and no amount of extra hard work will significantly change the figure. In most of the peasant world land has been limited for a long, long time, and only in a few places have young farmers in a growing community been able to hive off from the parent village to start on a level of equality with their parents and grandparents. Customarily land is not only limited, but it has become increasingly limited, by population expansion and

soil deterioration. Peasant productive techniques have remained largely unchanged for hundreds, and even thousands, of years; at best, in farming, this
means the Mediterranean plow drawn by oxen, supplemented by human-
powered hand tools. Handicraft techniques in weaving, pottery-making, wood-
working and building likewise have changed little over the years.[7]

In fact, it seems accurate to say that the average peasant sees little or no
relationship between work and production techniques on the one hand, and
the acquisition of wealth on the other. Rather, wealth is seen by villagers in
the same light as land: present, circumscribed by absolute limits, and having
no relationship to work. One works to eat, but not to create wealth. Wealth,
like land, is someting that is inherent in nature. It can be divided up and
passed around in various ways, but, within the framework of the villagers'
traditional world, it does not grow. Time and tradition have determined the
shares each family and individual hold; these shares are not static, since obviously they do shift. But the reason for the relative position of each villager
is known at any given time, and any significant change calls for explanation.

2.2. The evidence that friendship, love, and affection are seen as strictly
limited in peasant society is strong. Every anthropologist in a peasant village
soon realizes the narrow path he must walk to avoid showing excessive favor
or friendship toward some families, thereby alienating others who will feel
deprived, and hence reluctant to help him in his work. Once I brought a close
friend from Tzintzuntzan, working as a bracero in a nearby town, to my
Berkeley home. When safely away from the camp he told me his brother was
also there. Why did he not tell me, so I could have invited him? My friend
replied, in effect, that he was experiencing a coveted "good" and he did not
want to risk diluting the satisfaction by sharing it with another.

Adams reports how a social worker in a Guatemalan village unwittingly
prejudiced her work by making more friends in one barrio than in the other,
thereby progressively alienating herself from potential friends whose help she
needed (1955:442). In much of Latin America the institutionalized best friend,
particularly among post-adolescents, variously known as the *amigo carnal*, or
the *cuello* or *camaradería* (the latter two described by Reina for Guatemala
[1959]) constitutes both recognition of the fact that true friendship is a scarce
commodity, and serves as insurance against being left without any of it. The
jealousies and feelings of deprivation felt by one partner when the other leaves
or threatens to leave sometimes lead to violence.

Widespread peasant definitions of sibling rivalry suggest that a mother's
ability to love her children is viewed as limited by the amount of love she
possesses. In Mexico when a mother again becomes pregnant and weans her
nursing child, the child often becomes *chípil*. It fusses, cries, clings to her
skirt, and is inconsolable. The child is said to be *celoso*, jealous of its unborn
sibling whose presence it recognizes and whom it perceives as a threat, already
depriving him of maternal love and affection. Chípil is known as *chip* or *chipe*
in Guatemala, where it is described in a classic article by Paul (1950), as
*sipe* in Honduras, and simply as *celos* ("jealousy") in Costa Rica. *Chucaque*

in southern Colombia, described as the jealousy of a child weaned because of its mother's pregnancy, appears to be the same thing (communicated by Dr. Virginia Gutierrez de Pineda).

A similar folk etiology is used among the semi-peasant peoples of Buganda to explain the onset of *kwashiorkor* in a child recently weaned. If the mother is again pregnant, the child is said to have *obwosi*, and shows symptoms of pale hair, sweating of hands and feet, fever, diarrhea, and vomiting. "The importance of pregnancy is such that if a woman takes a sick child to a native doctor the first question he asks is 'Are you pregnant?' " (Burgess and Dean 1962:24). The African logic is the reverse of, but complementary to, that of Latin America: it is the *unborn child* that is jealous of its older sibling, whom it tries to poison through the mother's milk, thereby forcing weaning (Burgess and Dean 1962:25). In both areas, insufficient quantities of love and affection are seen as precipitating the crisis. In Buganda, "In the local culture it is essential that the mother should devote herself to the unborn child or a child recently born, at the expense of any other children; *there does not seem to be an easy acceptance of the idea that there can be enough love for all*" (Burgess and Dean 1962:26. Emphasis added).

Similarly, in an Egyptian village, sibling rivalry is recognized at this period in a child's development. As in Latin America, jealousy is one way; it is always the older who is jealous of the younger. "It is also acknowledged that the youngest child becomes jealous immediately his mother's abdomen becomes enlarged on pregnancy and he is usually told of the forthcoming event." This jealousy, in excess, may have ill effects on the child, causing diarrhea, swellings, lack of appetite, temper tantrums, and sleeplessness (Ammar 1954: 107–109).[8]

In parts of Guatemala chipe is a term used to express a husband's jealousy of his pregnant wife, for temporary loss of sexual services and for the attention to be given to the baby. Tepoztlán husbands also suffer from *chipilez*, becoming sleepy and not wanting to work. Oscar Lewis says a husband can be cured by wearing a strip of his wife's skirt around his neck (1951:378). In Tonalá, Jalisco, Mexico, husbands often are jealous of their adolescent sons and angry with their wives because of the affection the latter show their offspring. A wife's love and affection are seen as limited; to the extent the son receives what appears to be an excessive amount, the husband is deprived (communicated by Dr. May Diaz). In the Egyptian village described by Ammar a new mother-in-law is very affectionate toward her son-in-law, thereby making her own unmarried sons and daughters jealous. By showing affection to the outsider, the woman obviously is seen as depriving her own offspring of something they wish (Ammar 1954:51, 199).

2.3. It is a truism to peasants that health is a "good" that exists in limited quantities. Peasant folk medicine does not provide the protection that scientific medicine gives those who have access to it, and malnutrition frequently aggravates conditions stemming from lack of sanitation, hygiene, and immunization. In peasant societies preoccupation with health and illness is general, and constitutes a major topic of interest, speculation, and discussion. Perhaps the best objective evidence that health is viewed within the framework of Limited Good is the widespread attitude toward blood which is, to use Adams' expression, seen as "non-regenerative" (Adams 1955:446). For obvious reasons, blood is equated with life, and good blood, and lots of it, means health. Loss of blood—if it is seen as something that cannot be renewed—is thus seen as a threat to health, a permanent loss resulting in weakness for as long as an individual lives. Although best described for Guatemala, the belief that blood is non-regenerative is widespread in Latin America. This belief, frequently unverbalized, may be one of the reasons it is so difficult to persuade Latin Americans to give blood transfusions: by giving blood so that someone can have more, the donor will have less.

Similar beliefs are found in Nigeria (communicated by Dr. Adeniyi-Adeniji Jones) and they are well known in Indian peasant villages. Here the psychological problem is further compounded by the equation of blood with semen: one drop of semen to seven (or forty, depending on area) drops of blood. The exercise of masculine vitality is thus seen as a permanently debilitating act. Only so much sexual pleasure is allotted man, and nothing he can do will increase his measure. Sexual moderation and the avoidance of bloodletting are the course of the prudent man.

In parts of Mexico (e.g., the Michoacán villages of Tzintzuntzan and Erongarícuaro) the limits on health are reflected in views about long hair. A woman's long hair is much admired, but the price is high: a woman with long hair is thought always to be thin and wan, and she cannot expect to have vigor and strength. Sources of vitality are insufficient to grow long hair and still leave an individual with energy and a well-fleshed body.

2.4. Oft-noted peasant sensitiveness to real or imagined insults to personal honor, and violent reactions to challenges which cast doubt on a man's masculinity, appear to be a function of the belief that honor and manliness exist in limited quantities, and that consequently not everyone can enjoy a full meas ure. In rural Mexico, among braceros who have worked in the United States, American ethnologists have often been asked, "In the United States it's the wife who commands, no?" Masculinity and domestic control appear to be viewed much like other desirable things: there is only so much, and the person who has it deprives another. Mexican men find it difficult to believe that a husband and wife can share domestic responsibilities and decision making, without the husband being deprived of his *machismo*. Many believe a wife, however good, must be beaten from time to time, simply so she will not lose sight of a God-decreed familial hierarchy. They are astonished and shocked to learn that an American wife-beater can be jailed; this seems an incredibly unwarranted intrusion of the State into God's plans for the family.

The essence of machismo is valor, and *un hombre muy valiente*, i.e., a *macho*, is one who is strong and tough, generally fair, not a bully, but who never dodges a fight, and who always wins. Above all, a *macho* inspires *respeto* ("respect"). One achieves machismo, it is clear, by depriving others of access to it.

In Greece *philotimo*, a "love of honor," equates closely with Mexican machismo. A man who is physically sound, lithe, strong, and agile has philo-timo. If he can converse well, show wit, and act in other ways that facilitate sociability and establish ascendency, he enhances his philotimo. One attacks another male through his philotimo, by shaming or ridiculing him, by showing how he lacks the necessary attributes for a man. Consequently, avoiding ridi-cule becomes a major concern, a primary defense mechanism among rural Greek males. In a culture shot through with envy and competitiveness, there is the ever-present danger of attack, so a man must be prepared to respond to a jeer or insult with a swift retort, an angry challenge, or a knife thrust. "Philotimo can be enhanced at the expense of another. It has a see-saw char-acteristic; one's own goes up as another's declines . . . the Greek, in order to maintain and increase his sense of worth, must be prepared each moment to assert his superiority over friend and foe alike. It is an interpersonal combat fraught with anxiety, uncertainty, and aggressive potentials. As one proverb describes it, 'When one Greek meets another, they immediately despise each other' " (R. Blum and E. Blum 1962:20–22).

3. If, in fact, peasants see their universe as one in which the good things in life are in limited and unexpandable quantities, and hence personal gain must be at the expense of others, we must assume that social institutions, personal behavior, values, and personality will all display patterns that can be viewed as functions of this cognitive orientation. Preferred behavior, it may be argued, will be that which is seen by the peasant as maximizing his security, by preserving his relative position in the traditional order of things. People who see themselves in "threatened" circumstances, which the Image of Limited Good implies, react normally in one of two ways: maximum coopera-tion and sometimes communism, burying individual differences and placing sanctions against individualism; or extreme individualism.

Peasant societies seem always to choose the second alternative. The reasons are not clear, but two factors may bear on the problem. Cooperation requires leadership. This may be delegated democratically by the members of a group itself; it may be assumed by a strong man from within the group; or it may be imposed by forces lying outside the group. Peasant societies—for reasons that should be clear in the following analysis—are unable by their very nature to delegate authority, and assumption of authority by a strong man is, at best, temporary, and not a structural solution to a problem. The truncated political nature of peasant societies, with real power lying outside the com-munity, seems effectively to discourage local assumption and exercise of power, except as an agent of these outside forces. By the very nature of peasant society, seen as a structural part of a larger society, local development of leadership which might make possible cooperation is effectively prevented by the rulers of the political unit of which a particular peasant community is an element, who see such action as a potential threat to themselves.

Again, economic activities in peasant societies require only limited co-operation. Peasant families typically can, as family units, produce most of their food, farm without extra help, build their houses, weave cloth for their clothes, carry their own produce to market and sell it—in short, take care of themselves with a degree of independence impossible in an industrial society, and difficult in hunting-fishing-gathering societies. Peasants, of course, usually do not live with the degree of independence here suggested, but it is more nearly possible than in any other type of society.

Whatever the reasons, peasants are individualistic, and it logically follows from the Image of Limited Good that each minimal social unit (often the nuclear family and, in many situations, a single individual) sees itself in perpetual, unrelenting struggle with its fellows for possession of or control over what it considers to be its share of scarce values. This is a position that calls for extreme caution and reserve, a reluctance to reveal true strength or position. It encourages suspicion and mutual distrust, since things will not necessarily be what they seem to be, and it also encourages a male self image as a valiant person, one who commands respect, since he will be less attractive as a target than a weakling. A great deal of peasant behavior, I believe, is exactly what we would predict from these circumstances. The works of Lewis (1951), Banfield (1958), Simmons (1959), Carstairs (1958), Dube (1958), the Wisers (1963), and Blackman (1927) (summarized by Foster 1960–1961) and many others testify to the "mentality of mutual distrust" (Friedman 1958: 24) that is widespread in peasant societies.

Since an individual or family that makes significant economic progress or acquires a disproportionate amount of some other "good" is seen to do so at the expense of others, such a change is viewed as a threat to the stability of the community. Peasant culture is provided with two principal mechanisms with which to maintain the essential stability:

a) an agreed-upon, socially acceptable, preferred norm of behavior for its people, and

b) a "club" and a "carrot," in the form of sanctions and rewards, to ensure that real behavior approximates this norm.

The agreed-upon norm that promotes maximum community stability is behavior that tends to maintain the status quo in relationships. The individual or family that acquires more than its share of a "good," and particularly an economic "good," is, as we have seen, viewed as a threat to the community at large. Individuals and families which are seen to or are thought to progress violate the preferred norm of behavior, thereby stimulating cultural mechanisms that redress the imbalance. Individuals or families that lose something, that fall behind, are seen as a threat in a different fashion; their envy, jealousy, or anger may result in overt or hidden aggression toward more fortunate people.

The self-correcting mechanisms that guard the community balance operate on three levels, viz:

1) Individual and family behavior. At this level I am concerned with the steps taken by *individuals* to maintain their positions in the system, and the ways in which they try to avoid both sanctions and exploitation by fellow villagers.

2) Informal and usually unorganized group behavior. At this level I am concerned with the steps taken by the *community*, the sanctions that are invoked when it is felt someone is violating the agreed-upon norm of behavior. Negative sanctions are the "club."

3) Institutionalized behavior. At this level I am concerned with the "carrot": major community expressions of cultural forms which neutralize achieved imbalances. Each of these forms will be examined in turn.

3.1) On the individual-family level, two rules give guidance to preferred behavior. These can be stated as:

a) Do not reveal evidence of material or other improvement in your relative position, lest you invite sanctions; should you display improvement, take action necessary to neutralize the consequences.

b) Do not allow yourself to fall behind your rightful place, lest you and your family suffer.

A family deals with the problem of real or suspected improvement in its relative position by a combination of two devices. First, it attempts to conceal evidence that might lead to this conclusion, and it denies the veracity of suggestions to this effect. Second, it meets the charge head on, admits an improvement in relative position, but shows it has no intention of using this position to the detriment of the village by neutralizing it through ritual expenditures, thereby restoring the status quo.

Accounts of peasant communities stress that in traditional villages people do not compete for prestige with material symbols such as dress, housing, or food, nor do they compete for authority by seeking leadership roles. In peasant villages one notes a strong desire to look and act like everyone else, to be inconspicuous in position and behavior. This theme is well summed up in the Wisers' paragraph on the importance of dilapidated walls suggesting poverty as a part of a family's defense (1963:120).

Also much remarked is the peasant's reluctance to accept leadership roles. He feels—for good reason—that his motives will be suspect and that he will be subject to the criticism of neighbors. By seeking, or even accepting, an authority position, the ideal man ceases to be ideal. A "good" man therefore usually shuns community responsibilities (other than of a ritual nature); by so doing he protects his reputation. Needless to say, this aspect of socially-approved behavior heavily penalizes a peasant community in the modern world by depriving it of the leadership which is now essential to its development.

The mechanism invoked to minimize the danger of loss of relative position appears to center in the machismo-philotimo complex. A tough, strong man whose fearlessness in the face of danger, and whose skill in protecting himself and his family is recognized, does not invite exploitation. A "valiant" individual can command the "respect" so much sought after in many peasant societies, and he can strive toward security with the goal in mind (however illusory) of being able to live—as is said in Tzintzuntzan—*sin compromisos* ("without obligations" to, or dependency on, others). A picture of the ideal peasant begins to emerge: a man who works to feed and clothe his family, who fulfills his community and ceremonial obligations, who minds his own business, who does not seek to be outstanding, but who knows how to protect his rights. Since a macho, a strong man, discourages exploitation, it is clear that this personality characteristic has a basic function in peasant society. Not surprisingly, defense of this valuable self-image may, by the standards of other societies, assume pathological proportions, for it is seen as a basic weapon in the struggle for life.

The ideal man must avoid the appearance of presumption, lest this be interpreted as trying to take something that belongs to another. In tracing the diffusion of new pottery-making techniques in Tzintzuntzan I found that no one would admit he had learned the technique from a neighbor. The inevitable reply to my question was *Me puse a pensar* ("I dreamed it up all by myself"), accompanied by a knowing look and a tapping of the temple with the forefinger. Reluctance to give credit to others, common in Mexico, is often described as due to *egoísmo*, an egotistical conceited quality. Yet if egoísmo, as exemplified by unwillingness to admit profiting by a neighbor's new pottery knowledge, is seen as a function of an image of Limited Good, it is clear that a potter *must* deny that the idea is other than his own. To confess that he "borrowed" an idea is to confess that he has taken something not rightfully his, that he is consciously upsetting the community balance and the self image he tries so hard to maintain. Similarly, in trying to determine how compadrazgo (godparenthood) ties are initiated, I found no informant who admitted he had asked a friend to serve; he always was asked by another. Informants appear to fear that admission of asking may be interpreted as presuming or imposing on another, trying to get something to which they may not be entitled.

A complementary pattern is manifest in the general absence of compliments in peasant communities; rarely is a person heard to admire the performance of another, and when admiration is expressed by, say, an anthropologist, the person admired probably will try to deny there is any reason to compliment him. Reluctance of villagers to compliment each other again looks, at first glance, like egoísmo. But in the context of the Limited Good model, it is seen that such behavior is proper. The person who compliments is, in fact, guilty of aggression; he is telling someone to his face that he is rising above the dead level that spells security for all, and he is suggesting that he may be confronted with sanctions.

Consider this interpretation as applied to an incident reported in southern Italy: "My attempt, in private, to praise a peasant friend for his large farm and able system of farming brought a prompt and vigorous denial that he did anything special. He said, 'There is no system, you just plant.' This attitude was expressed by others in forced discussions of farming" (Cancian 1961:8). Dr. Cancian offers this as illustrating the peasant's lack of confidence in his own ability to change his environment. Speaking specifically of agriculture, he writes that "All the examples indicate denial of the hope of progress in agriculture and alienation from the land" (Cancian 1961:8). I believe the peasant viewed Dr. Cancian's praise as threatening, since it reminded him of his vulnerability because of his superior farming methods. His denial is not of hope of progress, but of cause for anyone to envy him.

3.2. The ideal man strives for moderation and equality in his behavior. Should he attempt to better his comparative standing, thereby threatening village stability, the informal and usually unorganized sanctions appear. This is the "club," and it takes the form of gossip, slander, backbiting, character assassination, witchcraft or the threat of witchcraft, and sometimes actual physical aggression. These negative sanctions usually represent no formal community decision, but they are at least as effective as if authorized by law. Concern with public opinion is one of the most striking characteristics of peasant communities.

Negative sanctions, while usually informal, can be institutionalized. In peasant Spain, especially in the north, the charivari (*cencerrada*) represents such an instance. When an older man marries a much younger woman— usually a second marriage for the groom—marriageable youths serenade the couple with cowbells (*cencerros*) and other noisemakers, parade straw-stuffed manikins representing them through the streets, incense the manikins with foul-smelling substances, and shout obscenities. It seems clear that this symbolizes the resentment of youths, who have not yet had even one wife, against the inequalities represented by an older man who has already enjoyed marriage, who takes a young bride from the available pool, thereby further limiting the supply for the youths. By institutionalizing the sanctions the youths are permitted a degree of freedom and abuse not otherwise possible.

3.3. *Attempted* changes in the balance of a peasant village are discouraged by the methods just described; *achieved* imbalance is neutralized, and the balance restored, on an institutional level. A person who improves his position is encouraged—by use of the carrot—to restore the balance through conspicuous consumption in the form of ritual extravagance. In Latin America he is pressured into sponsoring a costly fiesta by serving as *mayordomo*. His reward is prestige, which is viewed as harmless. Prestige cannot be dangerous since it is traded for dangerous wealth; the mayordomo has, in fact, been "disarmed," shorn of his weapons, and reduced to a state of impotence. There is good reason why peasant fiestas consume so much wealth in fireworks, candles, music, and food; and why, in peasant communities the rites of baptism, marriage, and death may involve relatively huge expenditures. These practices are a redistributive mechanism which permits a person or family that potentially threatens community stability gracefully to restore the status quo, thereby returning itself to a state of acceptability. Wolf, speaking specifically of the "closed" Indian peasant community of Mexico as it emerged after the Conquest, puts it this way: "the system takes from those who have, in order to make all men have-nots. By liquidating the surpluses, it makes all men rich in sacred experience but poor in earthly goods. Since it levels differences of wealth, it also inhibits the growth of class distinctions based on wealth. . . . In engineering parlance, it acts as a feedback, returning a system that is beginning to oscillate to its original course" (1959:216).

4. I have said that in a society ruled by the Image of Limited Good there is no way, save at the expense of others, that an individual can get ahead. This is true in a closed system, which peasant communities approximate. But even a traditional peasant village, in another sense, has access to other systems, and an individual can achieve economic success by tapping sources of wealth that are recognized to exist outside the village system. Such success, though envied, is not seen as a direct threat to community stability, for no one within the community has lost anything. Still, such success must be explained. In today's transitional peasant communities, seasonal emigration for wage labor is the most available way in which one can tap outside wealth. Hundreds of thousands of Mexican peasants have come to the United States as braceros in recent years and many, through their earnings, have pumped significant amounts of capital into their communities. Braceros generally are not criticized or attacked for acquisition of this wealth; it is clear that their good fortune is not at the direct expense of others within the village. Fuller finds a similar realistic appraisal of the wealth situation in a Lebanese community: "they [the peasants] realize . . . that the only method of increasing their incomes on a large scale is to absent themselves from the village for an extended period of time and to find work in more lucrative areas" (1961:72).

These examples, however, are but modern variants of a much older pattern in which luck and fate—points of contact with an open systen—are viewed as the only socially acceptable ways in which an individual can acquire more "good" than he previously has had. In traditional (not transitional) peasant communities an otherwise inexplicable increase in wealth is often seen as due to the discovery of treasure which may be the result of fate or of such positive action as making a pact with the Devil. Recently I have analyzed treasure tales in Tzintzuntzan and have found without exception they are attached to named individuals who, within living memory, have suddenly begun to live beyond their means. The usual evidence is that they suddenly opened stores, in spite of their known previous poverty (Foster 1964a). Erasmus has recorded this interpretation among Sonora villagers (1961:251), Wagley finds it in an Amazon small town (1964:128), and Friedmann reports it in southern Italy (1958:21). Clearly, the role of treasure tales in communities like these is to account for wealth that can be explained in no other manner.

The common peasant concern with finding wealthy and powerful patrons who can help them is also pertinent in this context. Since such patrons usually are outside the village, they are not part of the closed system. Their aid, and material help, like bracero earnings or buried treasure, are seen as coming from beyond the village. Hence, although the lucky villager with a helpful patron may be envied, the advantages he receives from his patron are not seen as depriving other villagers of something rightfully theirs. In Tzintzuntzan a villager who obtains a "good" in this fashion makes it a first order of business to advertise his luck and the source thereof, so there can be no doubt as to his basic morality; this behavior is just the opposite of usual behavior, which is to conceal good fortune.

Treasure tales and concern with patrons, in turn, are but one expression of a wider view: that any kind of success and progress is due to fate, the favor of deities, to luck, but not to hard work, energy, and thrift. Banfield notes in a south Italian community, "In the TAT stories, dramatic success came only as a gift of fortune: a rich gentleman gave a poor boy a violin, a rich gentle-woman adopted an abandoned child, and so on" (1958:66). Continuing, "Great success, then, is obtained by the favor of the saints or by luck, certainly not by thrift, work, and enterprise. These may be important if one is already lucky, but not otherwise, and few would invest large amounts of effort—any more than they would invest large amounts of fertilizer—on the rather remote possibility of good fortune" (Banfield 1958:114). Friedmann also finds that the south Italian peasant "firmly believes that the few who have succeeded in making a career were able to do so for some mysterious reason: one hit upon a hidden treasure; another was lucky enough to win in the lottery; another was called to America by a successful uncle" (1958:21).

All such illustrations underlie a fundamental truth not always recognized in comparing value systems: in the traditional peasant society hard work and thrift are moral qualities of only the slightest functional value. Given the limitations on land and technology, additional hard work in village productive enterprises simply does not produce a significant increment in income. It is pointless to talk of thrift in a subsistence economy in which most producers are at the economic margin; there is usually nothing to be thrifty about. As Fei and Chang point out, "In a village where the farms are small and wealth is accumulated slowly, there are very few ways for a landless man to become a landowner, or for a petty owner to become a large landowner. . . . It is not going too far to say that in agriculture there is no way really to get ahead. . . . To become rich one must leave agriculture" (1945:227). And again, "The basic truth is that enrichment through the exploitation of land, using the traditional technology, is not a practical method for accumulating wealth" (Fei and Chang: 1945:302). And, as Ammar says about Egypt, "It would be very difficult with the fellah's simple tools and the sweat involved in his work, to convince him that his lot could be improved by more work" (1954:36).

5. It is apparent that a peasant's cognitive orientation, and the forms of behavior that stem therefrom, are intimately related to the problems of economic growth in developing countries. Heavy ritual expenditures, for example, are essential to the maintenance of the equilibrium that spells safety in the minds of traditional villagers. Capital accumulation, which might be stimulated if costly ritual could be simplified, is just what the villager wants to prevent, since he sees it as a community threat rather than a precondition to economic improvement.

In national developmental programs much community-level action in agriculture, health and education is cast in the form of cooperative under-takings. Yet it is abundantly clear that traditional peasant societies are co-operative only in the sense of honoring reciprocal obligations, rather than in the sense of understanding total community welfare, and that mutual sus-picion seriously limits cooperative approaches to village problems.[9] The image of Limited Good model makes clear the peasant logic underlying reluctance to participate in joint ventures. If the "good" in life is seen as finite and non-expandable, and if apart from luck an individual can progress only at the ex-pense of others, what does one stand to gain from a cooperative project? At best an honorable man lays himself open to the charge—and well-known con-sequences—of utilizing the venture to exploit friends and neighbors; at worst he risks his own defenses, since someone more skillful or less ethical than he may take advantage of the situation.

The Anglo-Saxon virtues of hard work and thrift seen as leading to eco-nomic success are meaningless in peasant society. Horatio Alger not only is not praiseworthy, but he emerges as a positive fool, a clod who not knowing the score labors blindly against hopeless conditions. The gambler, instead, is more properly laudable, worthy of emulation and adulation. If fate is the only way in which success can be obtained, the prudent and thoughtful man is the one who seeks ways in which to maximize his luck-position. He looks for the places in which good fortune is most apt to strike, and tries to be there. This, I think, explains the interest in lotteries in underdeveloped countries. They offer the only way in which the average man can place himself in a luck-posi-tion. The man who goes without lunch, and fails to buy shoes for his children in order to buy a weekly ticket, is not a ne'er-do-well; he is the Horatio Alger of his society who is doing what he feels is most likely to advance his position. He is, in modern parlance, buying a "growth stock." The odds are against him, but it is the *only* way he knows in which to work toward success.

Modern lotteries are very much functional equivalents of buried treasure tales in peasant societies, and at least in Tzintzuntzan the correlation is clearly understood. One elderly informant, when asked why no one had found buried treasure in recent years, remarked that this was indeed true but that "Today we Mexicans have the lottery instead." Hence, the "luck" syndrome in underdeveloped countries is not primarily a deterrent to economic progress, as it is sometimes seen from the vantage point of a developed country, but rather it represents a realistic approach to the near-hopeless problem of mak-ing significant individual progress.

David C. McClelland has argued persuasively that the presence of a human motivation which he calls "the need for Achievement" (*n* Achievement) is a precursor to economic growth, and that it is probably a *causative* factor, that it is "a change in the minds of men which produces economic growth rather than being produced by it" (McClelland 1963:81; 1961). McClelland further finds that in experimental situations children with high *n* Achievement avoid gambling situations because should they win there would be no sense of personal achievement, while children with low *n* Achievement do not perform in a way suggesting they calculate relative risks and behave accordingly. "They [low *n* Achievement children] thus manifest behavior like that of many people in underdeveloped countries who, while they act very traditionally economically, at the same time love to indulge in lotteries—risking a little to make a great deal on a very long shot" (McClelland 1963:86). McClelland sees this as showing an absence of a sense of realistic risk calculation.

If the arguments advanced in this paper are sound, it is clear that *n* Achievement is rare in traditional peasant societies, not because of psychological factors, but because display of *n* Achievement is met by sanctions that a traditional villager does not wish to incur. The villager who feels the need for Achievement, and who does something about it, is violating the basic, unverbalized rules of the society of which he is a member. Parents (or government school programs) that attempt to instill *n* Achievement in children are, in effect, training children to be misfits in their society *as long as it remains a relatively static system.*

As indicated above, I would argue in opposition to McClelland that the villager who buys a lottery ticket *is not* behaving in an inconsistent fashion— that is, rationally in traditional economic matters, irrationally in his pursuit of luck—but in the most consistent fashion possible. He *has* calculated the chances and risks, and in a most realistic manner *in the context of the way in which he sees his traditional environment.* The man who buys a lottery ticket in a peasant society, far from displaying lack of *n* Achievement, is in fact showing a maximum degree of it. It simply happens that this is about the only display of initiative that is permitted him by his society, since it is the only form not viewed as a threat to the community by his colleagues.

Banfield, and Fei and Chang, appear to see the economic factors in the presence or absence of initiative in much the same light. The former writes about the Italian peasant, "The idea that one's welfare depends crucially upon conditions beyond one's control—upon luck or the caprice of a saint—and that one can at best only improve upon good fortune, not create it—this idea must certainly be a check on initiative" (Banfield 1958:114). The latter see, in the Chinese data, evidence that a particular economic attitude is a function of a particular view of life. The traditional economic attitude among Chinese peasants is that of "contentment . . . an acceptance of a low standard of material comfort" (Fei and Chang 1945:82), which is contrasted to "acquisitiveness" characteristic of "modern industry and commerce in an expanding universe" (Fei and Chang 1945:83). "Both attitudes—contentment and acquisitiveness—have their own social context. Contentment is adopted in a closed economy; acquisitiveness in an expanding economy. *Without economic opportunities the striving for material gain is a disturbance to the existing order, since it means plunder of wealth from others.* . . . Therefore, to accept and be satisfied with the social role and material rewards given by the society is essential. But when economic opportunity develops through the development of

technology and when wealth can be acquired through the exploitation of nature instead of through the exploitation of man, the doctrine of contentment
becomes reactionary because it restricts individual initiative" (Fei and Chang
1945:84. Emphasis added). In other words, change the economic rules of the
game and change the cognitive orientation of a peasant society, and a fertile
field for the propagation of *n* Achievement is created.

For the above reasons, I believe most strongly that the primary task in
development is not to attempt to create *n* Achievement at the mother's knee
but to try to change the peasants' view of his social and economic universe,
away from an Image of Limited Good toward that of expanding opportunity
in an open system, *so that he can feel safe* in displaying initiative. The brakes
on change are less psychological than social. Show the peasant that initiative
is profitable, and that it will not be met by negative sanctions, and he acquires
it in short order.

This is, of course, what is happening in the world today. Those who have
known peasant villages over a period of years have seen how the old sanctions
begin to lose their power. Local entrepreneurs arise in response to the increasing opportunities of expanding national economies, and emulative urges, with
the city as the model, appear among these people. The successful small
entrepreneurs begin to see that the ideal of equality is inimical to their personal interests, and presently they neither seek to conceal their well being nor
to distribute their wealth through traditional patterns of ritual extravagance.
*N* Achievement bursts forth in full vitality in a few new leaders, and others
see the rewards and try to follow suit. The problem of the new countries is to
create economic and social conditions in which this latent energy and talent
is not quickly brought up against absolute limits, so that it is nipped in the
bud. This is, of course, the danger of new expectations—released latent *n*
Achievement—outrunning the creation of opportunities.

Viewed in the light of Limited Good peasant societies are not conservative
and backward, brakes on national economic progress, because of economic ir-
rationality nor because of the absence of psychological characteristics in adequate quantities. They are conservative because individual progress is seen
as—and in the context of the traditional society in fact is—the supreme threat
to community stability, and all cultural forms *must* conspire to discourage
changes in the status quo. Only by being conservative can peasant societies
continue to exist as peasant societies. But change cognitive orientation through
changing access to opportunity, and the peasant will do very well indeed; and
his *n* Achievement will take care of itself.

NOTES

¹ Redfield describes world view as "that outlook upon the universe that is characteristic of a
people" (1952:30). Redfield believes that "No man holds all he knows and feels about the world in
his conscious mind at once" (1955:91), but at the same time he feels that a reasonably thoughtful
informant can describe his world view so that an anthropologist can understand it, that if there is
an "emphasized meaning" in the phrase it is "in the suggestion it carries of the structure of things

*as man is aware of them*. It is the way *we see* ourselves in relation to all else" (1953:86. Emphasis added). Hallowell, on the other hand, tends to see world view in terms of a cognitive orientation of which the Ojibwa are not consciously aware and which they do not abstractly articulate (1960).

Kenny recently defined "values" in much the same sense in which I understand "cognitive orientation": "In regard to values, I use the term to denote a series of conceptions from which a preferred type of conduct is evolved and imposed by the social system; which can be abstracted by analysis but which may not be consciously recognized or verbalized by every member of the society" (1962–1963:280).

[2] E.g., Theme 14: "The extended domestic family is the basic social and economic unit and the one to which first allegiance and duties of revenge are due" (1946:152).

[3] By the term "classic" peasant societies I follow Kroeber's statement: "They form a class segment of a larger population which usually contains also urban centers. . . . They constitute part-societies with part cultures" (1948:284). My definition of peasant is structural and relational, only incidentally concerned with how people earn a living. Firth writes, "By a peasant economy one means a system of small-scale producers, with a simple technology and equipment, often relying primarily for their subsistence on what they themselves produce. The primary means of livelihood of the peasants is cultivation of the soil" (1956:87). This, and all other definitions stressing agriculture and purely subsistence economies, seem to me to be deficient. I find "classic" peasant societies rimming the Mediterranean, in the village communities of the Near East, of India, and of China. Emergent peasant communities probably existed in Middle America before the Conquest; today a large proportion of Indian and mestizo villages in Latin America must be thought of as peasant. Parts of Negro Africa, where there are indigenous cities and well-developed markets, are at least semi-peasant, although the lack of a Great Tradition perhaps excludes them from the "classic" label.

As I see it, classic peasant communities have grown up in a symbiotic spatial-temporal relationship to the more complex component of the society of which they are a part, i.e., the preindustrial market and administrative city. Peasant communities "represent the rural expression of large, class-structured, economically complex, pre-industrial civilizations, in which trade and commerce, and craft specialization are well developed, in which money is commonly used, and in which market disposition is the goal for a part of the producer's efforts" (Foster 1960–1961:175).

The reader will realize, I am sure, that the model, drawn up on the basis of an ideal type of rural community in a pre-industrial world, does not in fact fit any contemporary peasant community with exactitude. All modern peasant communities have experienced to a greater or lesser degree inroads from the urban, industrial world, and to that degree they must depart from the model. I freely confess, too, that I tend to see peasant society in the image of Tzintzuntzan, Michoacán, Mexico, and that greater familiarity with other peasant communities might well lead me to different expressions of details in the model.

[4] I don't advocate maintenance of classic peasant society, nor do I think it has a permanent place in the world.

[5] I do not believe the Image of Limited Good is characteristic only of peasant societies. Quite the contrary, it is found, in one degree or another, in most or all socio-economic levels in newly developing countries, and it is, of course, equally characteristic of traditional socialist doctrine. I am not even sure that it is *more* characteristic of peasants than of other groups. I examine the hypothesis in the context of peasant societies simply because they are relatively less complex than many other groups, because good data are readily available, and because my arguments can easily be tested in the field by other anthropologists. I suspect, but will leave the ultimate decision to others, that the Image of Limited Good when applied to peasant society *goes further* in explaining behavior than when applied to any other type of society. That is, and by way of illustration, although the Image of Limited Good certainly is characteristic of many urban Mexicans, including those of the highest social and economic classes, the complexity of that society requires additional themes beyond those needed in peasant society to produce an equally coherent and satisfying explanation.

[6] I have long speculated that the economic world view of classic peasants, and particularly of

people in Tzintzuntzan, the peasant community I know best (Foster 1948, 1960–1961, 1961a, 1961b, 1962, 1963, 1964a, 1964b, 1965) can be described by a principle I have called the Image of the Static Economy. Writing in 1948 I suggested that Tzintzuntzenos see their economic world as one in which "the wealth goal is difficult and almost impossible of achievement; hence, the stimulus of a reasonable chance of success is lacking" (1948:289). Much later I attempted to explain the frequent poor quality of interpersonal relations in peasant society in the same terms, suggesting that the "economic pie" is seen (quite realistically) as constant in size, and unexpandable. Consequently, "If someone is seen to get ahead, logically it can only be at the expense of others in the village" (1960–1961:177). Subsequently I spoke of the Image of the Static Economy as inhibiting village cooperation, particularly in community development programs (1961b). Several sentences by Honigmann about a West Pakistan village stimulated me to think about the wider applicability of the Image of the Static Economy, i.e., that this integrating principle is simply one expression of a total cognitive view with analogues in a great many other areas of life. Honigmann wrote, "One dominant element in the character structure (not only here but elsewhere in West Pakistan) is the implicit belief that good of all kinds is limited. There is only so much respect, influence, power, and love in the world. If another has some, then somebody is certainly deprived of that measure" (1960:287).

Other anthropologists also have recognized the Image of Limited Good, usually indirectly via the corollary that good fortune can be obtained only at the expense of others. Leslie, in describing world view in the Mexican Zapotec Indian peasant village of Mitla, comments that " . . . for the most part they [the Mitleños] assumed that one man's gains were another man's losses" (1960:71). Beals, speaking of a specific incident in an Indian village, writes, "There is only so much land in Gopalpur; what one man farms cannot be farmed by another. Although Danda [a farmer], by developing distant lands, has expanded the economy of Gopalpur, people do not think of his achievement in terms of the creation of wealth. They think rather that Danda's success contributes to their own failure" (1962:64). Mandelbaum, introducing the new edition of the Wisers' *Behind Mud Walls*, notes that the villagers fail to understand "that each may prosper best when all in a community prosper together. There is rather the idea that the good things of the village are forever fixed in amount, and each person must manipulate constantly to garner a large slice for his own" (1963:x).

[7] Cf. Wolf, "Marginal location and traditional technology together limit the production power of the community, and thus its ability to produce cash crops for the market. This in turn limits the number of goods brought in from the outside which the community can afford to consume. The community is *poor*" (1955:457).

[8] In fact, the child who is chípil may have good reason to be fussy: withdrawn from the breast and put on an adult diet, he frequently experiences an acute protein-deficiency condition that stimulates his behavior. And, of course, sibling-rivalry exists, probably, in all societies. The significant thing is not the real physiological or psychological root of the condition, but rather that the condition is explained by a folk etiology which assumes a mother can give only so much love and affection to her children, so that the older ones are deprived in favor of the newest, even before the newest makes its appearance.

[9] Cf. Geertz 1962:244, speaking of Javanese peasants and their need for periodic labor mobilization: "What has developed . . . is not so much a general spirit of cooperativeness— Javanese peasants tend, like many peasants, to be rather suspicious of groups larger than the immediate family—but a set of explicit and concrete practices of exchange of labor, of capital, and of consumption goods which operate in all aspects of life. . . . This sense for the need to support specific, carefully delineated social mechanisms which can mobilize labor, capital, and consumption resources scattered thinly among the very dense population, and concentrate them effectively at one point in space and time, is the central characteristic of the much-remarked, but poorly understood, 'cooperativeness' of the Javanese peasant. Cooperation is founded on a very lively sense of the mutual value to the participants of such cooperation, not on a general ethic of the unity of all men or on an organic view of society which takes the group as primary and the individual as secondary."

REFERENCES CITED

ADAMS, RICHARD N.
1955  A nutritional research program in Guatemala. *In* Health, culture and community (Benjamin D. Paul, ed). New York, Russell Sage Foundation.

AMMAR, HAMED
1954  Growing up in an Egyptian village: Silwa, Province of Aswan. London, Routledge & Kegan Paul, Ltd.

BANFIELD, EDWARD C.
1958  The moral basis of a backward society. Glencoe, The Free Press.

BLACKMAN, WINIFRED S.
1927  The Fellāhīn of Upper Egypt. London, George G. Harrap & Co., Ltd.

BEALS, ALAN R.
1962  Gopalpur: a south Indian village. Case Studies in Cultural Anthropology, G. and L. Spindler, eds. New York, Holt, Rinehart and Winston.

BLUM, RICHARD and EVA
[1962?]  Temperate Achilles: practices and beliefs associated with alcohol use. A supplement to Health and Healing in Rural Greece. Pre-publication draft, Institute for the Study of Human Problems, Stanford University.

BURGESS, ANNE and R. F. A. DEAN (eds.)
1962  Malnutrition and food habits. London, Tavistock Publications.

BURLING, ROBBINS
1964  Cognition and componential analysis: God's truth or hocus-pocus? American Anthropologist 66:20–28.

CANCIAN, FRANK
1961  The southern Italian peasant: world view and political behavior. Anthropological Quarterly 34:1–18.

CARSTAIRS, G. MORRIS
1958  The twice-born: a study of a community of high-caste Hindus. Bloomington, University of Indiana Press.

DUBE, S. C.
1958  India's changing villages: human factors in community development. London, Routledge and Kegan Paul, Ltd.

ERASMUS, CHARLES J.
1961  Man takes control: cultural development and American aid. Minneapolis, University of Minnesota Press.

FEI, HSIAO-TUNG, and CHIH-I CHANG
1945  Earthbound China: a study of rural economy in Yunnan. Chicago, University of Chicago Press.

FIRTH, RAYMOND
1956  Elements of social organization. London, Watts & Co.

FOSTER, GEORGE M.
1948  Empire's children: the people of Tzintzuntzan. Mexico City, Smithsonian Institution, Institute of Social Anthropology, Publ. 6.
1960–61  Interpersonal relations in peasant society. Human Organization 19:174–178.
1961a  The dyadic contract: a model for the social structure of a Mexican peasant village. American Anthropologist 63:1173–1192.
1961b  Community development and the image of the static economy. Community Development Bulletin 12:124–128.
1962  Traditional cultures: and the impact of technological change. New York, Harper & Brothers.
1963  The dyadic contract in Tzintzuntzan, II: Patron-client relationship. American Anthropologist 65:1280–1294.

1964a Treasure tales, and the image of the static economy in a Mexican peasant community. Journal of American Folklore 77:39–44.

1964b Speech forms and perception of social distance in a Spanish-speaking Mexican village. Southwestern Journal of Anthropology 20:107–122.

1965 Cultural responses to expressions of envy in Tzintzuntzan. Southwestern Journal of Anthropology 21:No. 2, Spring.

FRIEDMANN, F. G.
1958 The world of "La Miseria." Community Development Review No. 10:16–28. Washington, D. C., International Cooperation Administration. (Reprinted from Partisan Review, March-April, 1953).

FULLER, ANNE H.
1961 Buarij: portrait of a Lebanese Muslim village. Cambridge, Mass., Distributed for the Center for Middle Eastern Studies of Harvard University.

GEERTZ, CLIFFORD
1962 The rotating credit association: a "middle rung" in development. Economic Development and Cultural Change 10:241–263.

GILLIN, JOHN
1955 Ethos components in modern Latin America. American Anthropologist 57:488–500.

HALLOWELL, A. IRVING
1960 Ojibway ontology, behavior, and world view. *In* Culture in history: essays in honor of Paul Radin (S. Diamond, ed.). New York, Columbia University Press.

HONIGMANN, JOHN J.
1960 A case study of community development in Pakistan. Economic Development and Cultural Change 8:288–303.

KENNY, MICHAEL
1962–1963 Social values and health in Spain: some preliminary considerations. Human Organization 21:280–285.

KLUCKHOHN, CLYDE
1941 Patterning as exemplified in Navaho culture. *In* Language, culture, and personality (Leslie Spier, ed.). Menasha, Wisconsin, Sapir Memorial Publication Fund.

1943 Covert culture and administrative problems. American Anthropologist 45:213–227.

KROEBER, A. L.
1948 Anthropology. New York, Harcourt, Brace and Company.

LESLIE, CHARLES M.
1960 Now we are civilized: a study of the world view of the Zapotec Indians of Mitla, Oaxaca. Detroit, Wayne State University Press.

LEWIS, OSCAR
1951 Life in a Mexican village: Tepoztlán restudied. Urbana, University of Illinois Press.

McCLELLAND, DAVID C.
1961 The achieving society. Princeton, N. J., D. Van Nostrand Co.

1963 The achievement motive in economic growth. *In* Industrialization and society (B. F. Hoselitz and Wilbert E. Moore, eds.) Unesco, Mouton.

MANDELBAUM, DAVID G.
1963 Forward to *Behind Mud Walls 1930–1960*, by William H. Wiser and Charlotte Viall Wiser. Berkeley and Los Angeles, University of California Press.

OPLER, MORRIS EDWARD
1946 An application of the theory of themes in culture. Journal of the Washington Academy of Sciences 36:137–166.

PAUL, BENJAMIN D.
1950 Symbolic sibling rivalry in a Guatemalan Indian village. American Anthropologist 52:205–218.

REDFIELD, ROBERT
1952 The primitive world view. Proceedings of the American Philosophical Society 96:30–36.

1953    The primitive world and its transformations. Ithaca, Cornell University Press.

1955    The little community: viewpoints for the study of a human whole. Chicago, University of Chicago Press.

REINA, RUBEN E.

1959    Two patterns of friendship in a Guatemalan community. American Anthropologist 61:44–50.

SIMMONS, OZZIE G.

1959    Drinking patterns and interpersonal performance in a Peruvian mestizo community. Quarterly Journal of Studies on Alcohol 20:103–111.

WAGLEY, CHARLES

1964    Amazon town: a study of man in the tropics. New York, Alfred A. Knopf, Borzoi Book LA-4.

WISER, WILLIAM H. and CHARLOTTE VIALL WISER

1963    Behind mud walls 1930–1960. Berkeley and Los Angeles, University of California Press.

WOLF, ERIC R.

1955    Types of Latin American peasantry: a preliminary discussion. American Anthropologist 57:452–471.

1959    Sons of the shaking earth. Chicago, University of Chicago Press.

# Anemic and Emetic Analyses in Social Anthropology

GERALD D. BERREMAN
*University of California, Berkeley*

## I

AT THE conclusion of my paper on "Caste in Cross-Cultural Perspective," delivered before the Southwestern Anthropological Association meetings, spring 1965, a gentleman came to me and suggested helpfully that I might use a framework for the comparative study of caste which would be based on *emic, etic* and *allo* concepts. This experience, on brief reflection, inspired me to the title and topic of this essay, which I presented orally before the Kroeber Anthropological Society's ninth annual meeting at Berkeley, on May 8, 1965.

On scarcely more reflection, I thought of the spate of recent and announced journal articles, special issues, and other works by "ethnoscientists" or "componential analysts" who treat culture in a linguistic idiom in the avowed hope of discovering structure and enhancing rigor in ethnology. I especially recalled those in a special edition of this journal entitled *Transcultural Studies of Cognition* (Romney and D'Andrade, 1964).

I then recalled a statement, whose author shall remain anonymous, in which that edition was described as "an attempt to understand the mood and temper of man through empty words. Vacuous, sterile, inconclusive, programmatic, hyper-professionalized, and the product of apolitical, asexual, amoral, asocial anthropology."

A major aim of the ethnoscientists is cogently and readably put by Frake (1962) in an article which should be required reading for all commentators on componential analysis: that by utilizing the linguistic analogy and seeking "contrast sets" of "cultural segregates" we can derive superior ethnography.

Superior ethnography is a concern of mine too. I see the concern of those advocating a linguistic analogy to achieve this end, and my own concern to achieve this end, as deriving from a common source: the problem of how to treat human situations scientifically. It can be phrased, and has often been treated, as a dilemma: how to be scientific and at the same time retain the humanistic insights—the human relevance—without which no account of human beings makes sense.

There are two extreme but common reactions to this dilemma, namely, to ignore one or the other of its two horns. That is, to be scientific at the expense of insight, or to be insightful at the expense of being unscientific. The first is what I would term the "scientistic" refuge. It involves a retreat to, or preoccupation with, such things as quantification, abstract models, simulation, and highly formal methods of data collection and analysis. It rejects intuitive

346

insights. The second refuge I would call "humanist." It rejects any serious attempt at scientific method, relying entirely upon intuitive insights and the qualitative, empathetic ethnographic result thereof. The first approach results most often in descriptions and interpretations which are reliable but whose validity is questionable; the latter results in accounts which may be valid, but whose reliability is undemonstrated.

I believe that the dilemma can be resolved if we take as the relevant question not *whether* to be rigorous or insightful, scientific, or humanistic, but rather, how to be *both*—how to develop a methodology which is at once subject to verification and conducive to perceptive insights in the study of men.

## II

Thomas Gladwin (1964) has written a brilliant article contrasting the method by which the Trukese navigate the open sea, with that by which Europeans navigate. He points out that the European navigator begins with a plan—a course—which he has charted according to certain universal principles, and he carries out his voyage by relating his every move to that plan. His effort throughout his voyage is directed to remaining "on course." If unexpected events occur, he must first alter the plan, then respond accordingly. The Trukese navigator begins with an objective rather than a plan. He sets off toward the objective and responds to conditions as they arise in an *ad hoc* fashion. He utilizes information provided by the wind, the waves, the tides and current, the fauna, the stars, the clouds, the sound of the water on the side of the boat, and he steers accordingly. His effort is directed to doing whatever is necessary to reach the objective. If asked, he can point to his objective at any moment, but he cannot describe his course. The European may not know where his objective is relative to himself at a given moment, but he knows his course and can quickly compute his location on the course.

Gladwin points out that the European can verbalize his navigational techniques whereas the Trukese cannot. The European's system is based on a few general principles applied to any given case. The Trukese' system is based on a great many cues, interpreted as they arise. Presumably, the European can relatively easily teach his navigational techniques to others, whereas the Trukese cannot—it takes apprenticeship to learn them. This does not mean that the Trukese does not *have* techniques; it means, rather, that they are subtle and complex. That they work is evidenced by the fact that Trukese get where they are going just as do the Europeans. Conceivably neither method is superior to the other as a method of getting there. They reflect different styles of thought rather than more or less good ones. For some purposes each is doubtless superior. Also, of course, there are good navigators and bad navigators among both Europeans and Trukese.

I think there is a lesson here for ethnographers. I think scientistic ethnographers are the intellectual brethren of the European navigators. They know how they are going, but often are not sure where. The humanistic ones are spiritual kinsmen of the Trukese. They know where they are going but are not sure how. To extend the parallel, let me quote two paragraphs of Gladwin's analysis:

(1) . . . Once the European navigator has developed his operating plan and has available the appropriate technical resources, the implementation and monitoring of his navigation can be accomplished with a minimum of thought. He has simply to perform almost mechanically the steps dictated by his training and by his initial planning synthesis (Gladwin 1964:175).

(2) This total process [of Trukese navigation] goes forward without reference to any explicit principles and without any planning, unless the intention to proceed to a particular island can be considered a plan. It is nonverbal and does not follow a coherent set of logical steps. As such it does not represent what we tend to value in our culture as "intelligent" behavior. . . . We might refer to this kind of ability as a "knack,". . . . Yet it is undeniable that the process of navigating from one tiny island to another, when this is accomplished entirely through the mental activity of the navigator, must reflect a high order of mental functioning (Gladwin 1964:175).

I hope the parallel is obvious. But there is an important difference between navigation and ethnography. Navigators can prove the validity of their methods by the pragmatic test of whether or not they get where they are going. Ethnographers, when their trip is over, do not know for sure, or cannot agree upon, whether they got where they were going or not. There have been no agreed-upon tests of whether an ethnography is right or not, no standardized measurements of how right it is, though suggestions have been made. Conklin (1964:26), for example, advocates "productivity" (by which he means anticipation of events in a culture), "replicability," and "economy" as criteria of ethnographic adequacy. In his own words, "An adequate ethnography is here considered to include the culturally significant arrangement of productive statements about the relevant relationships obtaining among locally defined categories and contexts [of objects and events] within a given social matrix" (Conklin 1964:25).

The experience of Tepoztlan, of the analyses of Pueblo culture, and several others have made the lack of a standard of ethnographic accuracy and relevance clear. Redfield and Lewis obviously got to different places in their ethnographic voyage through Tepoztlan, as did Benedict and Goldfrank in navigating Pueblo cultures (cf. Bennett 1946). But neither is clearly right or wrong. The scientistic anthropologist offers no help on this matter since the difference between the analyses of Lewis and Redfield, of Goldfrank and Benedict he defines as unscientific questions and hence out of his purview. I believe that they are also the *crucial* questions in the understanding of human behavior. The humanistic anthropologist offers no help on this matter either, because he has no criterion by which to judge two different interpretations of the same data except by how convincing they are.

Under these circumstances, an explicit methodology would be an advantage, for it would enable one to chart a course and to communicate to others the route you intend to follow. Afterwards, you could show how you got where you got to, and even if you didn't know where that was, others could get there too, presumably, if they followed the same course. Since one of our functions as ethnographers and teachers is to train others, this is the most expeditious way it can be done. Since ours is a science, replicability and communicability are obviously essential.

## III

Frake has called for "an explicit methodology" (1964a:236), for "public . . . procedures" (1962:85), for "ethnographic statements that can be demonstrated to be *wrong*, and not simply judged to be unpersuasively written" (1964b:142–43). With this I clearly agree. Humanistic anthropologists tend to ignore the fact that findings are only as good as the theories and methods by which they are derived, and are only convincing if they can be verified. But I think that much of the current effort at providing verifiable statements (and here Frake is among the *least* culpable) has the effect of sacrificing the insight into the nature of human behavior which is the ultimate aim of all ethnography. It results in astoundingly pallid, sterile, and fragmentary ethnography. It is effectively a retreat to methods without sufficient reference to goals. The goals I have in mind are understanding how people relate to one another and to their environment, what is the nature of their social interaction and how it relates to their values, emotions, attitudes, and self-conceptions; their hopes and fears. Without knowing these things we cannot claim to understand a society or the culture its members share. Obviously, a technique *need* not preclude other techniques and need not obscure goals, a fact to which Frake's own work is testimony. But it is empirically demonstrable that those who become enamored of a technique often lose sight of what their technique is for, and the work of many scientistic anthropologists is ample testimony to this. Peter Berger (1963) has compared those who become preoccupied with methods, to the magician who worked so long and hard to find the secret of how to get the mighty jinn out of the bottle that when he finally got him out he couldn't remember what it was he wanted to ask him. He has also stated, in what must become a classic aphorism, that "in science as in love, an overemphasis on technique is quite likely to lead to impotence" (Berger 1963:13).

Frake has called for "non-intuitive" procedures in ethnography. I think in this term, if not in his usage, lies the fundamental fallacy of the scientistic anthropologists. That is, the assumption that intuition is somehow indefinable and therefore invalid, indefensible, and reprehensible. I submit that intuition is nothing more nor less than inference that is unanalyzed because it is based on complex cues, subliminal cues, or subtle reasoning. In the last analysis, intuition is inference and as such it is the basis for all science. By insisting upon "non-intuitive" procedures, naively defined, one reduces insight by focusing on gross facts and interpretations or on a very narrow range of facts and interpretations. Those who insist upon this, confuse verification with discovery and assume that science is comprised of the former, whereas, in fact, the former is only an adjunct of the latter.

What is called for, I think, is a methodology which *combines* rigor and insight, verification and discovery, accuracy and empathy, replicability and human relevance. This, I think, can be achieved through defining—making explicit—the bases for the inferences that lead to insights; that is, by defining the constituents and cultural contexts of intuition. Componential analysis and other linguistic analogies may be one way to do this. But they are by no means the only way nor have they been demonstrated to be a superior or even a particularly effective way. They tend, I think, to oversimplify. This is inevitable, for language, I believe, is far simpler and more rigidly structured than most aspects of culture. Techniques applicable to it, while theoretically applicable elsewhere, may be practically inadequate. One evidence of this is the fact that analyses on the linguistic model have been applied almost entirely to terminological systems—i.e., to linguistic materials. Little effort, and less success, has been manifest in other spheres (see Frake 1964a, describing religious behavior, for a noble effort which he modestly describes as "deficient in detail and rigor" as an ethnographic statement).

I would suggest that extensive, explicit, and perceptive field notes, self-analytical reporting of research procedures and research contexts, documentation of sources, documentation of the bases for inferences, and documentation of the ethnographer's theories of society and his biases, are steps which work toward the same end and with greater promise. What I would call for, in short, if verification is to be enhanced, is a *sociology of ethnographic knowledge;* an *ethnography of ethnography.* Nothing less will achieve the basis for scientific rigor—for verifiability—without sacrificing the significant insights which are equally crucial to science.

My objection to the linguistic analogies is not that they are useless, but that they are too often productive of lifeless descriptions of human life; that they are too often uncritically applied and especially that they characteristically are grimly and unconscionably pretentious. Their advocates often behave like the methodological pixies of whom Everett Hughes has spoken, who have a method and flit about eagerly looking for something to which to apply it, manifesting what C. Wright Mills has described as a kind of "empty ingenuity," and what Berger has termed "humorless scientism." Such efforts are not worthless, but they are unlikely to go far toward contributing to social science unless supplemented by other methods and disciplined by clearly defined goals. Fortunately the most accomplished of their advocates are not totally deficient in this respect, just as their detractors are not totally deficient in rigor. Bur they *are* pretentious. Sturtevant (1964:101) says, for example, that "ethnoscience shows promise as the New Ethnography required to advance the whole of cultural anthropology." He says that it "raises the standards of reliability, validity, and exhaustiveness of ethnography." Whether or not one agrees with that, the next sentence seems unexceptionable: "One result is that the ideal goal of a complete ethnography is farther removed from practical attainment. The full ethnoscientific description of a single culture would require many thousands of pages published after many years of intensive

fieldwork based on ethnographic methods more complete and more advanced
than are now available" (Sturtevant 1964:123). This is exhaustion, if not
exhaustiveness. I doubt that an ethnoscientific ethnography will ever be
written. If it is, I doubt that it will lead to better understanding than extant
ethnographies, or that it will be more valid or more reliable. I doubt that it
will be more convincing or more comprehensive. It will be at best a skeleton
to which only less formal techniques can supply the flesh. Without such techniques, it cannot be expected to accomplish more than accuracy at the expense of relevance. Perhaps a full ethnography is unattainable by any method.
Certainly not all anthropologists need seek it. But it is an ideal worth attempting to approximate, for human behavior occurs in total cultural context, no
part of which is entirely independent of any other.

Frake notes that in ethnoscience the focus has been, of necessity, on particular domains rather than on general accounts of the cultures studied. The
scope of the accomplishments can be indicated by quoting Frake's summary
(1964a:143; cf. Sturtevant 1964:113–122): "Metzger and Williams, for example, emerged from one field session with descriptions of firewood . . . ,
terms of personal reference . . . , curers . . . , and weddings . . . . Conklin
has described ethnobotanical systems, agriculture, betel chewing, pottery,
verbal play, color, kinship and water. . . . None of these descriptions, whatever
the faults, can be called superficial. . . ."

I would say, none of these descriptions, whatever the virtues, can in themselves be called very significant. They sound like ethnoscientific trait lists.
They remind me of Mill's warning that many sociologists have gotten to the
point where they overlook what is important in their search for what is verifiable, and that some of them break down the units of analysis so minutely
that truth and falsity are no longer distinguishable. Many have worked so
hard on what is trivial that it comes to appear important—or at least triviality
and importance become indistinguishable when fitted into the molds of formal
analysis.

I agree with Frake and others that one goal in ethnography, if it is to result in scientific statements, must be verifiability and replicability. I agree
that the way to accomplish this is by utilizing an explicit methodology. I do
not think, however, that the most promising way is to substitute for our present methods a more formal, hence less flexible and creative methodology.
Actually, I would be prepared to argue that componential analysts remain as
intuitive, and obscure in the *crucial* steps of their research, as anyone else,
and that their explicitness is largely illusory. This they share with the quan-
tifiers in sociology—those Mills has called the "abstract empericists." I would
also maintain that their method is actually, except for its jargon and preten-
tion, not nearly as novel as they think or hope. They still base their work on
selective inquiry, selective observation, selective recording, inference, implicit
theories and *ex post facto* analysis, and these are where the research stands or
falls. But I have not space to go into these portentous and perhaps pretentious
assertions. I think the way to scientific ethnography is to explicate our theories

and methodologies, adding to, deleting from, or altering them as this seems useful.

Some ethnoscientists *have* made notable (if to me unconvincing) efforts at explicating their field methods (Frake, 1962; Conklin, 1964). Frake (1962), for example, describes "eliciting frames" or as he calls them synonymously, "situations" or "stimuli" for evoking and defining responses to ethnographic inquiries. This is a step toward replicability. My own innate drive for terminological parsimony leads me to suggest that these three synonymous terms—stimuli, situations, eliciting—be combined, and I would suggest the term "soliciting" as apropos, combining as it does the first phoneme of two of the synonyms with the third synonym. I considered, in fact, subtitling this communication: "Soliciting in Ethnoscience." (One might even define, then, illicit soliciting and licit soliciting in ethnoscience, depending upon the putative validity of the results, or the ethics of the inquiry.) In any event, Frake makes the point that ethnographic inquiries—"discovery procedures"—need to be made problematic. I would carry it further and say that *all* aspects of ethnographic method (including how one selects his informants, how he decides to whom to talk, what to ask, whom to believe, whose information to ignore, what to observe, what to record, etc.) must be made problematic— be made the subject of inquiry, definition, and analysis—if scientific criteria are to be applied to ethnography. Ethnoscience, I think, does this for only limited phases of research, thereby giving the appearance without the fact of rigor.

## IV

Even if the Trukese ethnographers were absolutely correct and could be demonstrated to be so, I doubt that it would be possible to convert the errant Europeans. If the Trukese ethnographers were absolutely wrong and could be demonstrated to be so, I doubt that it would be possible to convert *them*. For an indication of why this is so, I can only refer the reader to an ingenious little study, *When Prophecy Fails*, by Leon Festinger, *et al.* (1956). I will quote a paragraph from the first chapter thereof:

> Suppose an individual believes something with his whole heart; suppose further that he has a commitment to this belief, that he has taken irrevocable actions [such as publication] because of it; finally, suppose that he is presented with evidence, unequivocal and undeniable evidence, that his belief is wrong: what will happen? The individual will frequently emerge, not only unshaken, but even more convinced of the truth of his beliefs than ever before. Indeed, he may even show a new fervor about convincing and converting other people to his view (Festinger *et al.* 1956:3).

The authors go on to show why this is so: "If more and more people can be persuaded that the system of belief is correct, then clearly it must, after all, be correct" (Festinger *et al.* 1956:28). The adherents to one or the other of the extreme positions, the scientistic and the humanistic ethnographers, in fact, often resemble in their commitment and singleness of purpose the cultists studied by Festinger and his associates.

411

I would prefer that we Trukese ethnographers not give up our Trukese methodology, but that instead we define, explicate and thereby improve it. For I think it is possible to demonstrate that it works—that it gets us there—when well and properly done. What we have to do is find out how one goes about doing it well and properly. And there may be many ways of doing it; or a few principles which can be applied in different ways, or many techniques which work in various combinations. Perhaps some new techniques need to be added—Trukese navigators, after all, have by now acquired compasses for use in emergencies. European ethnographers, meanwhile, might unbend a bit—try coming out of the chartroom and observe more of the world around them. Each approach has something to say to the other. Time will tell what is useful and what is not.

Europeans need not become Trukese, but Trukese need not be dazzled by the European technology to the point of hastily and self-consciously giving up their own ways. Europeans may even be, after all, a flash in the pan and the eternal verities just possibly lie with the Trukese. In any case, let us try pluralism in preference to succumbing to colonialism. Reciprocal acculturation and accommodation is more likely to result in a viable synthesis than is precipitous assimilation; selective advantage should be given an opportunity to manifest itself.

Lest the title of this article mislead, let me say that I think linguistics has much to offer the rest of anthropology. I may even *try* using emic, etic, and allo concepts in comparing caste systems cross culturally, for I think some such concepts are essential for comparative studies and I think comparative studies are crucial in anthropology. I just do not see linguistics as the one true science of man, nor its methods as curative for all of the ills of ethnography.

I hasten to add that some of my best friends, after all, are ethnoscientists or componential analysts. I empathize even where I don't sympathize. I too yearn for rigor in my research. I just urge that in my colleagues' search for scientific rigor, they not inadvertently succumb to scientific *rigor mortis.*

### REFERENCES CITED

BENNETT, JOHN W.
  1946  The interpretat on of Pueblo Culture: A question of values. Southwestern Journal of Anthropology 2:361–374.
BERGER, PETER L.
  1963  Invitation to sociology: A humanistic perspective. Garden City, N. Y., Doubleday.
CONKLIN, HAROLD C.
  1964  Ethnogenealogical method. *In* Explorations in cultural anthropology: Essays presented to George Peter Murdock. Ward H. Goodenough, ed. New York, McGraw-Hill.
FESTINGER, LEON, H. W. RIECKEN, and STANLEY SCHACHTER
  1956  When prophecy fails. Minneapolis, The University of Minnesota Press.
FRAKE, CHARLES O.
  1962  The ethnographic study of cognitive systems. *In* Anthropology and human behavior. T. Gladwin and W. D. Sturtevant, eds. Washington, D.C. Anthropological Society of Washington, pp. 72–93.

1964a A structural description of Subanun religious behavior. *In* Explorations in cultural anthropology: Essays presented to George Peter Murdock. Ward H. Goodenough, ed. New York, McGraw-Hill, pp. 111–129.

1964b Notes on queries in ethnography. American Anthropologist 66, No. 3, Part 2, pp. 99–131.

GLADWIN, THOMAS
1964 Culture and logical process. *In* Explorations in cultural anthropology: Essays presented to George Peter Murdock. Ward H. Goodenough, ed. New York, McGraw-Hill.

ROMNEY, A. K. and R. G. D'ANDRADE, eds.
1964 Transcultural studies in cognition, A. K. Romney and R. G. D'Andrade, eds. American Anthropologist 66, No. 3, Part 2.

STURTEVANT, WILLIAM C.
1964 Studies in ethnoscience. American Anthropologist 66, No. 3, Part 2, pp 99–131.

JOHN ADAIR

CONRAD ARENSBERG

JOHN R. ATKINS

FREDRIK BARTH

GERALD D. BERREMAN

C. LORING BRACE

ALAN DUNDES

FRED EGGAN

MEYER FORTES

GEORGE M. FOSTER

CHARLES O. FRAKE

CLIFFORD GEERTZ

WARD H. GOODENOUGH

ASHLEY MONTAGU

SALLY FALK MOORE

S. F. NADEL

PHILIP PHILLIPS

JULIAN H. STEWARD

C. F. VOEGELIN

EVON VOGT

ANTHONY F. C. WALLACE

LESLIE A. WHITE

GORDON R. WILLEY

ERIC R. WOLF

# Index of Authors and Titles